A Good Road from Plymouth Rock to Puget Sound

A Modern Guide to Driving the Historic Yellowstone Trail 1912-1930

John Wm. Ridge
Alice A. Ridge

Yellowstone Trail Publishers
Altoona, Wisconsin, USA
2021

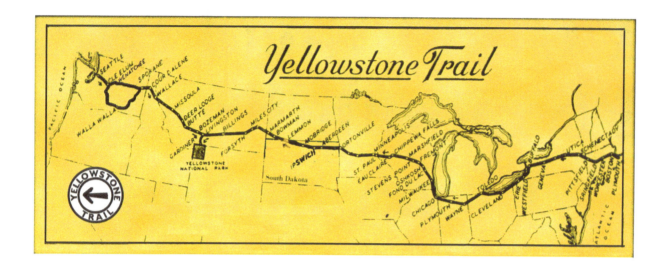

DEDICATION

This book is dedicated to the late Harvey J. Ridge,
teacher, scientist, advisor, traveler,
gardener, entrepreneur and public servant,
without whose memories and photo albums
this journey along the Yellowstone Trail
would never have begun.

Publisher's Cataloging-in-Publication

Title: A Good Road from Plymouth Rock to Puget Sound /
   A Modern Guide to Driving the Historic Yellowstone Trail

Names: Ridge, John Wm., author | Ridge, Alice Ann, author

©2021 by John Wm. Ridge and Alice A. Ridge

All rights reserved. No part of this book may be used or reproduced in any manner whatsoever without written
   permission except in the case of brief quotations embodied in critical articles and reviews.

For information contact the authors through: www.yellowstonetrail.com

Publisher: Yellowstone Trail Publishers, Altoona, Wisconsin 54720 | 2021

LCCN: 2021911595

ISBN 978-0-9702832-5-2

Classifications:
   1. Roads–United States–History–20th Century
   2. Yellowstone Trail Association (U.S.)
   3. Yellowstone Trail –History
   4. Automobile Travel–U.S.–Guidebooks

viii, 428p. : ill., maps ; 22 x 28 cm.

Printer: Documation, LLC. Eau Claire, Wisconsin, USA
   First Printing: July 2021

In the revamping of buffalo paths and pioneer trails around which cluster the names of Lewis and Clark, Coulter, Whitman and border heroes of their time, it is given to us of today to build for those who follow.

... Other lands record the drama of Kings, Ours is the drama of a people.

Parmley Papers, the South Dakota State Historical Society SDSHS-84

The Creed of the Open Road

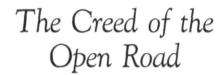

The beauty of the open road is not policed, except by the honor of the traveler.

I, therefore, who love the freedom of the open road, shall not permit that freedom to degenerate into license.

Capable of perceiving the beauty of trees, I shall be incapable of destroying that beauty for those who may follow.

The living radiance of the flowers brightens my journey. I shall not wantonly wrest from them that life and radiance.

It is the very order and cleanliness of a wayside camp that tempts me to halt for rest. I shall not, then, be so boorish a guest as to leave it in disorder and uncleanliness.

I shall respect the lives, the property and the customs of the community through which I pass, and thus endeavor to leave agreeable recollections of the motor and the motorist.

Privilege entails obligation.

I, who ride the open road, value and enjoy its countless privileges.

Equally, therefore, do I assume—with good will and sincerity—its few and legitimate obligations.

—*American Automobile Association*

AAA Tour Book 1926

Chapters followed by indented Trail Tales

⇨

Contents, continued:

How to Get Around

Pages with a **yellow edge** contain an **introduction** to the Yellowstone Trail and its history for that state.

Pages with a **brown edge** contain **Mile-by-Mile** information keyed with mileages from the state's western border (as indicated on the maps) and detailed guide maps for each area.

Pages with a **gravel background** (**History Bits** pages) contain: 1) reproduced newspaper articles with a grey background, 2) notes about the area history with a white background, 3) the authors' Driving Notes with green text, and 4) Waysides containing information about places near the Yellowstone Trail.

Pages with a **green edge**, the **Trail Tales**, interspersed between state chapters, contain stories and information by topic and may be read independently of the state chapters.

While a few places are identified by their GPS coordinates, generally their locations are recorded by mileages to give a quick visual sense of location, allow an easy connection between map locations and mile-by-mile information, and allow the quick calculation of mileages between places.

Map symbols should be familiar or self-explanatory. ☸

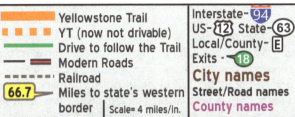

Preface

This book is an invitation to take, by auto or armchair, the Great American Road Trip along the nearly forgotten but historically important Yellowstone Trail. An auto route "from Plymouth Rock to Puget Sound" was started at a time when roads carried wagons, and automobiles were few and still unreliable. The Yellowstone Trail became a major factor in converting from railroads to highways. This book is a guide to finding and exploring that highway's nooks and crannies, scenic features both grand and unusual, and "things" that others have missed. This Preface is a guide to the book and what is in it and how to find your way around.

> **Road vs. Route** -- Two words have caused and still do cause communication problems. Both refer to a path or a way, but there is a difference. A road is something you drive on. A route is a course of travel, perhaps following various roads linked end to end. An auto route follows roads (well, in 1912, sometimes not). While the Yellowstone Trail was definitely a route, its sponsoring Association often promoted good roads for it to follow. Officials of the Yellowstone Trail Association at their headquarters in South Dakota could change the route of the Trail in Ohio, for instance, but they could not make changes in the roads in Ohio. You will find occasions when you need to reflect upon which word was really needed.

Why This Big Book About an Old Auto Route?

Decades ago, an old family friend recalled his childhood riding with his father on many a road trip and especially riding in their new post-war 1949 Nash. He said, "I also remember my parents' references to their memories of a strange, but grand, historic auto route leading to the hugely romantic West. It didn't have a number (no route did); it had yellow-painted rocks along the side of it and sometimes its telephone poles had yellow-stripes." Forgotten were these stories until five decades later when we retired and had time to explore such things. It turned out that that strange auto route was the 1912-1930 Yellowstone Trail, "A Good Road from Plymouth Rock to Puget Sound."

In 1996, we found that old auto route, 3,600 miles of it through 13 northern states. In 2000, after researching it and traveling it, we shared our findings in a little book, *Introducing the Yellowstone Trail*. In 2003 we reproduced the 1914 Yellowstone Trail Association book, *On the Yellowstone Trail, A First Yearbook of the Twin Cities-Aberdeen-Yellowstone Park Trail Association*. It was a quaint combination of records of meetings, boosterism and promotional hype for towns, introductions to the Trail Association and ads that look like old Sears and Roebuck catalogues. But, neither one of those books was an adequate guide to the Trail and its history. Thus, we were inspired to produce this book.

Life in the Slow Lane

To envision what life was like in the Yellowstone Trail's early years, the 19teens, imagine a time when one cranked the Tin Lizzie, when one had to change tires– often. A time when your telephone was on your wall and you answered your particular ring; a time when camping was just coming into vogue, as was indoor plumbing. Telegraph, telephone and the railroad would be your long-distance tools. Trains were a-plenty, but on their schedule, not yours.

A time when auto road maps were few (people tried to use railroad maps). A time when you bought gas by the five-gallon jug from a barrel. A time when some roads had names, not numbers. Cars were selling like hot cakes but roads were atrocious when wet and dusty when dry.

It was a time when governments were recalcitrant about doing anything to better the awful roads so associations of ordinary citizens took action. The Yellowstone Trail was not the product of rich, influential men, nor of a government committee. The Yellowstone Trail Association was the product of ordinary town folk who had a vision of the necessity of good roads and routes that went long distances. Their tool was persuasion. They badgered counties and states to build the road which the Association would mark and advertise its route. You as an individual and small town America were depended upon to support, maintain and participate in the creation of the Trail for trade, tourists, and pleasure. ⇨

Forest Canyon on highway to Kachess Lodge, Snoqualmie Pass, Washington

Continued

Particulars That Need to Be Said (and Should Be Read)

This book has three major types of chapters. The initial sections introduce the Trail and its sponsoring organization. The detailed information about the route and its environs is in the thirteen state sections. And the stories related to the Trail are on the Trail Tale pages, in green, interspersed between the state sections.

Each state section has:

1. **An introduction** to the Trail in that state (on pages with yellow edges).

2. **History Bits** (on the left sides of spreads with a gravel background). History Bits can be:

- Notes. Information of interest at or near that location.

- Newspaper headlines and articles. "Clippings" were taken from original newspapers, reset, severely edited or paraphrased for space, included to capture the flavor and facts of the times. They accurately reflect the original content.

- Waysides. Provide information that might be of interest about places just off the Trail.

- Driving notes. Occasional helpful notes about the route by the authors.

3. **Mile-By-Mile information** (on pages on the right side of the spread with a brown edge).

The states are arranged from west to east, simply because we are accustomed to associate going east with moving to the right on a map. The same holds true within the states. Thus to move across the country to the east the reader goes from a present page to one to the right, the next page of the book. Moving west, the reader moves to the left and thus to the previous page. Very unhandy going west but unavoidable. The authors were very careful to have no mile-by-mile entry require a page turn. Think about it.

Maps. Fairly detailed maps of the Yellowstone Trail are provided on the Mile-By-Mile pages.

The Trail runs well over 3,600 miles. To create maps that cover that distance in the space available in the book, the required scale (four miles per inch) prohibits the detail necessary to quickly and easily find every turn of the Trail. Should you want a bigger scale, you may need to use a county map or your GPS unit to locate a more detailed route than offered here.

The route of the Yellowstone Trail is marked on the maps with a yellow/orange background wide line. If that route can be used today, it is a solid line. If for some reason it cannot be used today the yellow line is "dotted."

Too common
Washington State Archives

The suggested route to use today is marked with a green line on each map. It uses the original route most places but avoids the parts that are now very difficult or impossible. It is the authors' choice that the reader might not accept.

Often the letters N, W, E, S, St., Ave. as abbreviations on maps are omitted to save space on the map when little ambiguity for the driver results.

The yellow "call outs" with black numbers (mileage markers) all along the Trail are based on the mileages along the Trail from each state's western border. While they may be used to determine distances, their primary use is to locate places mentioned in the text. For instance, if a building is recorded in the text as being located at mileage WA-212.4 and there is a mileage marker 200.3 on the map, you can deduce that the building is 12.1 miles east of the marker. You will find the mileages to be generally very accurate.

The authors determined the mileages along the original Trail. In some places there are differences between following the original Trail and following the necessary driving line, but usually the posted mileages are very accurate.

Many sections of the route are not recommended for travel trailers. You can easily find work-arounds along paved roads if needed. Some require judgement by the driver, trailer, or not.

Trail Tales. Between each pair of state sections there are stories related to the Trail or its history called Trail Tales (green pages with green edges.)

Abbreviations.

- ABB or BB: *American Blue Books*, guides written before roads were numbered so contain detailed odometer mileage notations and directions such as "turn left at the red barn."

- MH: *Mohawk-Hobbs Guide* described road surfaces and services along the road.

- WPA: Works Project Administration. This government agency put people to work and paid them during the Great Depression of the 1930s. Some were writers. This agency was similar to the Civilian Conservation Corps (CCC) whose workers built parks, worked in forests and did other outdoor constructive work.

The abbreviation YT for Yellowstone Trail will appear in Driving Notes and picture captions to save space. The whole words Yellowstone Trail and Yellowstone Trail Association will appear in the text for clarity.

Pictures were taken or collected over a period of 25 years. Many were taken by the authors or provided by others, often without attribution. When other sources are known, the attribution is noted.

When specific sources needed to be referenced, we did so *in situ*, rather than with a footnote. It might be noted that academically acceptable primary sources proved to be rare.

⇨

Continued

Finding the History of the YT

Our research of the Yellowstone Trail was begun as a pleasure trip when we retired some twenty five years ago. We had no reason at the time to treat the effort as an academic research project. And, over time, we found that any attempt at a tight, well documented study of a detailed history and location of an early named highway would be a fool's errand. There are no, or few, primary sources.

It must be remembered that decision-making for Trail matters was undertaken by loosely organized citizen groups without government required record-keeping or even a great deal of involvement. Requests of state highway departments for information about alignments of the Trail and bridge construction dates soon taught us that such departments were not founded and/or effective until several years after the Trail was located and bridges had been built by counties.

As a real example of the problem we cite the Mizpah, Montana, bridge over the Powder River. This bridge replaced one built in the late 1800s. It was the scene of a great party at its 1923 opening. It was washed out and replaced in 1926. While consulting with the related state highway department official we were informed the very first bridge was built there in 1927. And he had records to prove it. It appears that the state had no record of that original county bridge and assumed the first state-built bridge was the real first bridge. We learned there and in many other places that trustworthy information about roads and routes during the early years of the Yellowstone Trail is hard to find. One of the best places to find more information was found to be county maps and family stories and records from the period that the reader may pursue!

There was no "mother lode" of information to document the Trail. Only a few county histories had any memory of it. H. O. Cooley and Joe Parmley, important figures in this saga, disparaged of each other and destroyed all records of the Yellowstone Trail Association when they shuttered the organization in 1930. All of our findings came from much digging in small museums and libraries, reading blurry microfilm of dozens of newspapers, purchasing and devouring nearly 50 *Automobile Blue Books**, interviewing nonagenarians, acquiring guides of every stripe, and traveling the whole Trail several times while drawing and correcting maps. When we started there was no Internet help and no cell phone (remember the bag phone in cars?).

---

*Automobile Blue Books are especially interesting and are a required source of information for any investigation of early 1900's long distance auto routes and their context. Annually five or more regional versions were published, each containing 700-1200 pages of small print mile-by-mile descriptions of the routes useful for long-distance auto travel. Small advertisements and local maps provide a helpful context. Just viewing one provides a bit of history and understanding of auto travel before road maps. See **Trail Tale: Guidebooks**, page 362.

Our original naive expectation that the route of the Yellowstone Trail would be found on plentiful maps of the period was quickly dashed. The first map of the route can be found in our reproduction of the 1914 book, *On the Yellowstone Trail*. It is a section-by-section map from St. Paul, Minnesota, to near Three Forks, Montana, the furthest extremes of the route in 1914. The widely available maps and atlases of the early part of the Trail's existence were large scale railroad maps with no reference to auto roads. Some of those rail maps were "revised" to show lines of the major auto routes added by, apparently, drawing a crayon line roughly along the route. It is often hard to even determine the towns on the route. The big name map makers like Rand McNally added the route of the Yellowstone Trail during the late teens, but at a scale not useful for the detail needed. County-produced maps generally used a useful scale but often were uninterested in marking the roads used for long-distance travel.

Our major sources of information turned out to be:

- occasional old letters and documents showing up on eBay
- publications of the original YTA, *Blue Books* and related guides
- AAA and AASC (Automobile Association of Southern California) strip maps
- motor magazines (usually overburdened with superlatives)
- And newspaper articles. Thousands of newspaper articles.

Since we started this project, many old newspapers are now online and Google maps and Google Streetview were invented. One can see far away sites without leaving home.

Acknowledgments

Helping us along during our over-two-decade research ride were so many people that we don't have a count of them nor do we have many of their names. From the National Archives, the Library of Congress, the AAA headquarters in Florida, and state historical societies and Chicago's Newberry Library to very small town libraries, museums, and county court houses we have been received cordially. Contributing to the *American Road* magazine for ten years taught us much about the art of writing. We thank these helpful hundreds.

Along the way we have made many friends who traveled the Trail themselves, including a friendly couple from Japan, and a chap who bicycled the whole of the 3,600 miles. They provided information and pictures. We thank them.

Closer to home, we must thank a few who toiled on our website or on the manuscript itself: geographer Sean Morrison, map-lover Michael Koerner, Ohio professional surveyor Michael Buettner, graphic designer Lori Schmidt, Washington state adventurers Dave Habura and Curt Cunningham, and Minnesotan Lance Sorenson. A special thank you goes to sharp-eyed, multi-talented, hard working Kathy Cooper. ✿

An Invitation to the Yellowstone Trail

Join us as we follow an early auto route across the upper tier of states in the United States. This route was the highway that opened America's Northwest to auto tourism, and that played a prominent role in creating the Great American Road Trip. It allowed the average family to experience the country, its geography, and its culture from coast to coast. And, it visited the Yellowstone National Park, its namesake.

The route was named the Yellowstone Trail.

Interstates and airplanes have replaced its function of "getting you there" but they have lost much of the concept and joy of "the slow lane" provided by the Yellowstone Trail.

Afoot and light hearted I take to the open road;

healthy, free, the world before me;

The brown path before me leading wherever I chose.

… From this hour, freedom!

From this hour I ordain myself loos'd of limits and imaginary lines,

Going where I list, my own master, total and absolute …

Those lines of *Song of the Open Road* by Walt Whitman (1856) communicate a sense of freedom, opportunity, self determination, and absence of obstacles. While Whitman's "road" is, literally, a path in the woods, it is often seen, allegorically, as a personal path through life, or even the attainment of democracy.

During the years around 1912 the concept of an open road took on an extended, more material meaning. The suddenly proliferating automobile was rapidly and fundamentally changing and disrupting American life. Trainloads of autos moved into every area of America. Horses began losing their established roles as providers of transportation and "horsepower," and interestingly, as providers of friendship.

The invading autos reignited a quest for the open road, to go where one wished, to explore "the world before me" in an affordable way. But immediately, the automobile discovered its nemesis: the physical road. The road it was to use was still a "brown path" without culverts to contain the little streams nor bridges to cross the big streams, with ruts and stumps and sand and mud and cattle fences to thwart any experience of pleasure or freedom.

While citizens clamored for better roads through the huge Good Roads Movement begun by bicyclists, state and federal governments were not prepared either in defined purpose nor practical ability to provide those newly desired roads. But the owners of autos and their friends were ready to act. One of those owners, Joe Parmley, a small town land agent from Ipswich, South Dakota, already a Good Roads proponent, did what Americans had learned to do so well to get something done: he formed a group. In this case, he created an organization of local people for concerted action to build a local usable auto road to ease the 26 mile trip from his home to the area business center in Aberdeen, South Dakota. The organization operated like a modern Chamber of Commerce.

With their success, the organization extended its vision with remarkable speed to the creation of a transcontinental auto route using coordinated local efforts under the founders' central leadership. The route was named the Yellowstone Trail. It grew to stretch from coast to coast, from Plymouth Rock to Puget Sound.

Other organizations created "named trails" most with more modest goals of shorter distances and some, probably many, with goals less altruistic. Quick money-making, even thievery, polluted many of the named trails of the time. Upright Parmley never bent.

In short, beginning with the mass arrival of autos, great effort was expended across the country to create open roads, enabling the Great American Road Trip as a way to fulfill Whitman's dream:

Going where I list, my own master, total and absolute …

Since the 1912 beginning of the Yellowstone Trail as a premier provider of a long-distance route, more than a century of constant "improvement" of roads across the country and the spectacular increase of their use has caused, paradoxically, a great loss of the open road. On a freeway of the present era, lost are the freedoms to slow or stop to experience a scene, to change ones immediate destination, to speed up or slow down at will, or to interact with the "locals," whether man or beast. The concept of place or even knowledge of where one is at the moment is lost while following the instructions of the placelessness of a GPS unit. If you seek a different window on the world, following the old Yellowstone Trail gives you a good chance of finding a bit of the concept of place, both in terms of pavement and spirit.

So come ride with us. We will search out the many places where travel is still possible along a less used road. Where there is still a kind of "sense of place" one feels while driving a two-lane road. Motorists seem to be more aware of their surroundings. They can slow down or stop to experience a scene. They can notice cows up close and personal. They might see a Burma Shave sign of yesteryear. They can talk with locals. There may be a calming familiarity in a two-lane road. Memories are allowed to happen there ✿

Once the YT, now MT 2 near Lewis and Clark Caverns

The Yellowstone Trail and the
Yellowstone Trail Association Story

The Yellowstone Trail is a named automobile route across America "from Plymouth Rock to Puget Sound." It was named instead of numbered because route numbering, well, it just wasn't done then. The total lack of usable auto roads and the general incapability of autos for a long-distance trip may explain why!

Roads had been established by the repeated use of horses and wagons. Mostly packed earth. A few miles, a very few miles, of asphalt and concrete showed up but all country roads remained dirt. Or deep sand. Or gumbo.

"Get us out of the mud" was the universal cry of bicyclists and motorists at the beginning of the 20th century. Henry Ford, James Packard, Alexander Winton, Jonathan Maxwell,

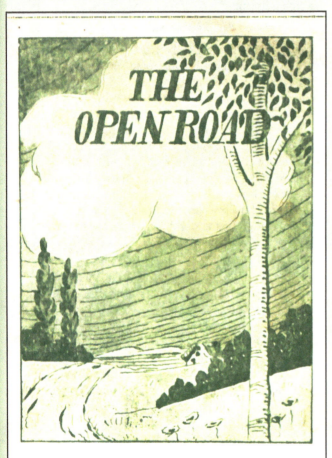

MOTOR TOURIST'S GUIDE

Giving Detailed information
along the
YELLOWSTONE TRAIL

Cleveland to Buffalo and Niagara Falls

Price 10c   1926

George Pierce, and Ransom Olds had been rolling out autos to clambering buyers for several years now, but the roads were atrocious! State and federal governments would not budge in their reticence to build roads. There was no need, they felt. Railroads, built at great expense, often government expense, provided extensive inter-city passenger and freight service. And state constitutions had restrictions on "internal improvements" such as roads.

Bicyclists and the new motorists were vocal and persistent. By 1912 some state legislatures had established state highway departments but with little funding and restricted responsibilities; establishing, building, and funding roads were up to each county or township. Or the local farmer!

Then the world changed. The years around 1912 saw the beginning of a burgeoning of auto manufacturing and the existing Good Roads Movement, started by bicyclists, meant the time had come to be serious about roads and long-distance routes. From the annual American production of hundreds of automobiles at the beginning of the century, it rose to 200,000 in 1912, to around 3,000,000 in 1923. Perfecting the engineering and construction of well designed gravel roads with culverts and bridges and drainage slowly took form. And old Dobbin lost his stable; stables became garages.

The time had come. Route-making became a popular activity. Hundreds of roads across the country sprouted route names, often assigned by auto clubs. Cross-country auto drives and races (often on a build-it-yourself-as-you-go road) were receiving great publicity.

In the South Dakota legislature, Joe Parmley, the hero of our story and Yellowstone Trail founder, had been hooted down and scoffed at in 1907 when he proposed that cash should replace the "labor tax" for county road maintenance. Parmley was so disgusted by the lack of governmental action at any level, and at that wet slough near his home in particular, that he called area men of vision together for a good roads meeting in Ipswich, South Dakota, on April 23, 1912, to do something about the crisis. There had to be a better way.

President Parmley and Treasurer Smith with the "Original Yellowstone Trail Car" decorated with the YT route
Phyllis Herrick

At that April meeting of the founders of the Yellowstone Trail, an exuberant attendee called out a potential motto for the route: "A Good Road from Plymouth Rock to Puget Sound." It hit the newspaper and it stuck. And it pretty well determined the nature of the next eighteen years of the work for the group. The route's end points were fixed and the general route was established. And the ambitiousness of the project was tacitly accepted.

The press called that wet April meeting just another Good Roads Association group. Such groups had been formed in countless towns across America. But mostly they were just preaching to the choir. Actually, this group in Ipswich was more than a Good Roads meeting. It was the beginning of the formation of the Yellowstone Trail Association. This Association became a massive effort to get a "Good Road from Plymouth Rock to Puget Sound" routed, marked, and made into driveable condition, county by county between Boston and Seattle. The creation of this Association would eventually affect a million or more people who would drive at least a few significant parts of those 3,600 miles in those 18 years – 1912-1930.

This fellow (at right) calms his frightened horse as an auto charges by.

The Yellowstone Trail Association was an organization dedicated to giving autoists a better road upon which to travel and a marked route to follow. There never was the intent by the Association to build with pick and shovel, or even improve roads all across the country. The intent was to establish a route across the country on the best roads available and then to promote those improved roads. Usually, the Yellowstone Trail designation of a road motivated improvement. When better or more efficient roads were found by the locals, the Trail was so re-routed.

It was a pioneer of the highway era. Specifically, it initially hoped to establish and map a route along existing roads from the Twin Cities in Minnesota to the Yellowstone National Park [later from coast to coast]. It would advocate for good roads by influencing road construction and by urging financial support from various levels of government. It would attract and motivate tourist traffic to boost economic development in the towns along the route. This last vision of establishing a transcontinental route seems quite forward-thinking when you realize that these founders were from very small towns and seemingly inexperienced in acquiring the resources needed for influencing national issues.

Very shortly after its birth, the Association spread 100 miles west from Ipswich to Mobridge in June with a Sociability

Run of 63 autos and the state engineer, crossing open fields, mapping a route. October found them in Lemmon, South Dakota, 120 miles still further west where they formulated the Twin Cities-Aberdeen-Yellowstone Park Trail Association [later shortened to just Yellowstone Trail Association].

The Yellowstone Trail became one of two of the longest lived, most well known coast-to-coast routes, both beginning life in 1912-1913. One was the Lincoln Highway between New York City and San Francisco begun by major Eastern industrialists with correspondingly major financial backing measured in millions of dollars and corresponding publicity experience. The other was the Yellowstone Trail from Boston to Seattle, begun by businessmen of very small South Dakota towns, with financial backing measured in hundreds of dollars and each accustomed to placing ads in their local newspapers. Both began with an effort to build good roads, moved to establishing a known transcontinental route, incorporated a significant effort to promote travel on their route (with its economic development goals) and ended with the coming of universal route numbering by government agencies and the devastation of the Great Depression.

Each chose their name carefully and with skill. The Lincoln Highway chose to commemorate President Lincoln, thus generating an immediate public sense of familiarity and good will.

The Yellowstone Trail, to arrive at the West Coast following as close to a straight line as possible, would go near Yellowstone National Park, an American feature well known and admired. Thus, the founders chose to "borrow" the Park's name which had immense good will, positive feeling, and excitement in the public mind. The name "Yellowstone" at once paid homage to and gave direction to the park. ⇨

Good Roads Convention...

Lemmon, South Dakota

...Wednesday, October 9th, 1912.

Program

10 A. M.

Address of Welcome —Thomas D. Potwin, President, Lemmon Commercial Club.

Opening Address —J. W. Parmley, Ipswich, Father of "The Parmley Road."

Good Roads in Montana —J. E. Brindle, Ismay.

3 P. M.

"The Parmley Road in Brown County" —F. H. Barnard, Aberdeen.

Engineering Problems in Road Building —S. H. Lea, Pierre, State Engineer.

Effect of Good Roads on Immigration —J. D. Deets, Pierre, Commissioner of Immigration.

How to Arouse Interest in Good Roads —M. P. Beebe, Ipswich.

8 P. M.

Illustrated Lecture on Roads —J. W. Parmley, Ipswich. Smoker and Dutch Lunch to Follow.

F. A. Finch, Promoter of the convention, will preside at all the sessions.

1912 Ipswich to Mobridge Sociability Run on a prairie trail

Agenda for formative meeting of the YTA

Continued

Then They Hired Hal Cooley

The small Land Office of Trail founder Joe Parmley in Ipswich is still there on Main Street. Word has it that the back room served as a morgue for a day or two when a body showed up in the back yard. This office served as the national headquarters of the Yellowstone Trail Association from 1912-1916, the one typewriter and telephone doing double duty for the Association and Parmley's Land Office business. Then they hired Hal Cooley away from the Aberdeen Chamber of Commerce. Ambitious Cooley moved the office from sleepy Ipswich to bustling Aberdeen, 26 miles away. Two years later, 1918, Cooley moved the headquarters to the Big Time - Minneapolis - where it stayed until the Trail's demise 12 years later.

Busy YTA Minneapolis
headquarters, 1918-1930
Hal Meeks

Cooley built the Association, but he was not alone, although he tended to think so. In a 1924 interview for the Stevens Point (WI) *Daily Journal*, Cooley was quoted as saying, rather self-servingly, that when he joined the group, "I found that the Yellowstone Trail existed only as an idea. It had no nucleus of organization or income. It was a picture in the mind of individuals and no machinery to make that picture come true. I changed all that." However, he did see the unique goal of the organization as that of selling automobile travel as a commodity and strove to implement that business plan for 14 successful years.

The organization chart of the Yellowstone Trail Association would show national officers at the top. General Manager (Cooley) and an Executive Committee, made up of one representative from each of the 13 states through which the Trail ran, would be next. The Director of Touring Bureaus was another important officer. There was also a Field Representative who traveled to raise funds to help get bridges built. Lower on the chart would be the state chapters and officers and local Trailmen who kept a responsible eye on local conditions. Lastly, there would be the growing list of members, 8,000 at their peak. The members had a vote in the organization, and state chapters had influence in state Trail affairs, but the *de facto* last word in deciding national issues such as the Trail route would come from the national president and officers. It was quazi-democratic.

Their success, which was remarkable, depended upon the membership and county boards sharing the vision

of long-distance auto travel. People had to realize that a long-distance route was a joint effort among communities. The Trail would bring visitors into your community, but also take visitors to the next. This brings about state and national thought as applied to highways. The Yellowstone Trail Association offered an agency through which this national thought could be expressed. The Association had to take ownership of the idea of "unity" across the miles.

"But regional identity does not develop in a vacuum. ... it existed within other perceptual categories, material realities and time, whether as is part of a nation, economic system or geographical entity," wrote Katherine Morrissey in *Mental Territories: Mapping the Inland Empire* (Cornell University Press, 1997). It was this regional identity problem that the Yellowstone Trail Association had to overcome to sell a transcontinental route.

One hundred years later it was this same regional identity problem that your authors faced from a Convention and Visitors Bureau (CVB) director. Thus, she would not support the idea of a new Yellowstone Trail Association because an advertised Trail "would take people away from her community." She did not see the promotion of the Trail that would bring people to her community. ⇨

Plan Your Vacation Now
PLAN IT BY AUTO

You Pick Your Time and Place

Write us and we'll tell you the best and easiest way to get there.
Our service is free and reliable. Motto: "Our first duty is to the traveling public."

Announces the opening of its system of FREE INFORMATION BUREAUS in

MINNEAPOLIS	MISSOULA
ABERDEEN	SPOKANE
MILES CITY	MILWAUKEE

TOLEDO
On May 10th, 1919.

The seventh successful year of this organization. The third year of its conduct of Information Bureaus—

The Yellowstone Trail Association, Inc.
General Offices, 916 Andrus Bldg., Minneapolis.

A rare find today, an original 1926 sign announcing that the proprietor was an active Association member.

YTA membership card

Pledges were important

The original YTA had a newsletter, *The Arrow*, from which the modern YTA took the title for its newsletter.

To combat this spotty parochial attitude, the original Association ran a long article in the *Aberdeen* (SD) *American* and elsewhere in 1920 explaining, in part:

> Now there are 2,075,000 miles of highway in the United States. If we tried to build all of them at once, the money is scattered so thinly that the result is practically waste. If by reason of a long national highway connecting up state after state, city after town in a continuous line enriches the country, a road might be raised and give special significance to each community, then a national and logical starting place for a road improvement program is provided, and that is the purpose of the Yellowstone Trail Association.

It must be said that the immediate effects of the presence of the Yellowstone Trail and other trails were probably first felt by those in small, rural hamlets. All were subsumed by the larger choices available in bigger, near-by communities and made available to hamlets by better roads. The local gathering sites were disappearing: the one-room school, the rural church, and the chats over the pickle barrel at the village store. By 1924 with the advancement in truck transport it was claimed that good roads for trucks created competition which kept railroad freight rates down, but also kept trains from stopping at small towns.

They Weren't In it For the Money

The Association was a non-profit, grassroots group with none of its earnings going to any member of the organization other than the General Manager, the expenses of the Field Representatives and, we assume, the travel expenses for officers to attend Yellowstone Trail Association meetings and fact-finding missions across the country

The Association recited compelling arguments for counties and states to create sentiment for road improvement along a single road; then the Association created auto travel over that road. Groups such as Commercial Clubs (predecessor to Chambers of Commerce) and fraternal and business organizations, town boards, county boards, and individuals would provide Association membership funds for promotion through the annual dues.

Dues varied over time and size of town. In the early days, individuals paid $1.00 a year, smaller towns $25.00-$50.00. Large towns paid around $1,000. Getting groups to actually cough up their assigned dues fell to Hal Cooley, General Manager. Over the years, as the importance of the Trail became realized, towns sometimes donated more. Billings came up with an extra $4,000 at one time. However, many towns frequently fell in arrears.

The reading public may have thought that the Association was very solvent when it read the Association's repeated reports that they had "raised" money for road projects, declaring sometimes at a year's end that they had raised many thousands of dollars in total for that particular year. By such reporting, it could have appeared to the reader that the Yellowstone Trail Association actually raised and donated those vast funds to road projects. In reality, they had only persuaded towns and counties to spend that much on road construction out of road tax dollars. That ploy may have been misleading the public, although the figures did announce the persuasive strength of the organization. It was a highly moral group. They turned down bribes proffered by cities to be put on the Trail, and were scrupulous with their meager funds.

What They Did With Their Funds

With these dues, the Association created intensive membership drives, publicity campaigns and Tourist Bureaus. On the micro side, yellow paint by the gallon had to be distributed to towns to paint everything in sight along the Trail. Metal signs by the thousands had to be made. See **Trail Tale: Signage**, page 359. A blinding number of pieces of literature was freely handed out from their Bureaus and also sent to boosters for distribution. And there was the newsletter, *The Arrow*.

In 1922 alone, 375,000 maps and *Route Folders* were given away as guidebooks. And, of course, there was postage; even penny post cards add up. No email! In a later year over a million such pieces of literature were given away or mailed. Businesses did their part, too. Spoons, screw drivers, cigar lighters, cigar boxes, and pens were inscribed and used to

Marketing with spoons and garage screw drivers.
Even Cigar makers got in on the act.
Lance Sorenson

keep the name of the Yellowstone Trail at the forefront.

On the macro side, support for relevant national road issues was essential, resulting in their membership in the National Highways Association which spoke with the united voice of many trails. A perceived "strength in numbers" move, perhaps. Allowing autos into the Yellowstone National Park was high on the Yellowstone Trail Association's agenda of support from early on to 1915 when the movement succeeded. The Association was also vocal in supporting the proposed Townsend National Road System Bill of 1919 which favored "a comprehensive national policy that would direct Federal funding to national needs for interstate commerce."

A continuous public relations engine was vital, and visible projects were necessary to keep the Trail in headlines. General Manager Hal Cooley saw to it that articles about the Trail were published regularly in national magazines such as *American Motorist, Motor Age, Midwest Motorist* and *Northwest Motorist*. Their chief efforts were their 1915 and 1916 Relay Races. (See **Trail Tale: 1915 Race**, page 302, and **Trail Tale: 1916 Race**, page 416.) Boosterism was kept paramount. Cooley appeared at all 13 state meetings annually plus many local meetings as a cheerleader (mostly in those towns in arrears of dues payments). Land values along the Trail increased, in some cases by $10/acre, a fact well publicized. Being declared a "military road" in May, 1918, certainly helped lift their profile.

On the local level, annual Trail Days were held wherein hundreds of townsfolk along the Trail pitched in on the same day to patch the Trail. Coverage from an excited press corps

resulted. Dozens of members who owned garages named them Yellowstone Trail Garage, giving free advertising to the Association. Local Trailmen were appointed (a coveted position) to keep an eye on the Trail, and to help lost tourists.

Fifteen major Tourist Bureaus and many minor Bureaus were created. With kiosks in major hotel lobbies or smaller places such as garages, and in their main offices in Minneapolis and Cleveland, they functioned like the AAA today, distributing maps, literature, and weather maps. Bureau personnel would guide long-distance travelers to the next Bureau, and so on to their destination.

All done to get a connected road to member towns and to draw tourists along it.

Routing the Trail

In its 18 year career, a guiding rule of the Association was to route the Trail on the most direct roads from Plymouth Rock to Puget Sound (Boston to Seattle) with prominent access to Yellowstone National Park. After preliminary enthusiasm, they quickly eschewed "splendid laterals," short branches from the major Trail to funnel traffic to the Trail. They were judged to be distractions from the primary goal.

There were many determinants of the route. The dominant long-distance transportation mode available at the time was, of course, the railroad. The railroad close at hand was the Milwaukee Road, at least from Minneapolis to within Montana. Not only had the Milwaukee provided service through Ipswich and Aberdeen, it had in the very recent past actually caused a whole string of towns to be formed from Minneapolis through Baker, Montana. The Yellowstone Trail followed that railroad. Besides, when a motorist broke down miles from a blacksmith or garage he could flag down a train for a ride to the nearest town.

Too often, a usable road was just not available and the Yellowstone Trail Association campaigned for improvements to be made by the locals. Some streams could be forded. Some rivers could be crossed with the help of a ferry. Some hills needed an additional push by the passengers or a friendly driver of a more powerful car that was going your way. Or a horse.

Horses pulling car out of mud.
A familiar site.

The Yellowstone Trail Association could not do all that was needed to create or improve roads; but it did solve the ⇨

problem caused by the lack of direction signs. Following the more used fork in the road often worked, but when you missed a turn you had a big problem. The Association started marking the Trail by painting friendly rocks yellow. Near the North Dakota/South Dakota border those "rocks" were eight feet long, ten inch diameter "hoodoos," naturally formed stone pillars that could be dragged to the highway, erected and painted yellow. Embossed yellow signs with the black circle and arrow of the official logo design were then erected by the hundreds to mark the way.

In the West (that is, west of Ohio) the 1785 Land Survey mandated that land surveys were needed to open the West to homesteading. Space along the section lines was to be reserved for roads. So the Trail followed those mile-long straight roads for a number of miles, made a right angle turn to continue, giving the land a checkerboard appearance. In the established East the idea did not apply nor could it be used in regions with geographic factors like mountains and swamps. West of Ohio many of those right angle turns were abandoned or curved over the years to improve safety and speed. Today, many obviously rounded right-angle turns record the historical use of that local road as a part of a long-distance highway.

Thus the route of the Yellowstone Trail in the center of the country was determined by following established survey lines close to established east-west railroads. Ah, but the two ends to the coasts? The necessary routing there was not too clear.

At the west end of the country, following a line directly as

possible toward Seattle, there were usable roads nearly as far as Missoula. From that area to near the State of Washington there were remnants of the earlier 1859-1862 Mullan Military Road. Parts of it were nearly lost, some with newer rerouted roads, and some in useable shape thanks to the mining boom in the area. All of it was hard going or impossible for autos. But the auto era was arriving and many road improvement efforts were in place.

Within Washington the newly created Washington State Highway Department (1905) had big plans for a network of state highways through the state. In 1915, just as the YT was to enter the state, two potential "highways" were being created, the Inland Empire Highway and the Sunset. (See the Washington chapter, page 10, to see what happened.)

At the east end of the country the destination was mandated by the Association's motto, A Good Road from Plymouth Rock to Puget Sound. Between Illinois and Plymouth, Massachusetts, however, the founders had "no personal knowledge" of the area. An initial choice of routes made in preparation for its 1916 cross country publicity run didn't fill the bill for a permanent route.

Changes to initial routings, however, were undertaken when experience increased, and accessible, improved roads became available. Twice the Association rerouted the Trail in a major way, to shorten the route by many miles.

In the East, their first choice was a well-established route hugging Lake Erie, then through central New York and through Massachusetts to Plymouth. They were rejected a permit because of the many marked trails already there. They were forced to route through Connecticut and southern New York for their 1916 cross-country relay race. Not until 1919, apparently after a permit was issued, did a permanent route get established along a line through the larger cities hugging the Great Lakes which would attract long-distance travelers. For a discussion of the route change, see the Massachusetts chapter, page 396.

The second major change occurred in Washington in May, 1925. The original 1915 route going west used the newly created Inland Empire route. It made a large southern sweep from Spokane through Walla Walla, then northwest to the Sunset Highway over Snoqualmie Pass and into Seattle. The 1925 route change made use of the improved Blewett Pass, now made useful to autos, so nearly the whole of the Yellowstone Trail then used the Sunset Highway. This move cut 150 miles off of the route but made no friends from along the abandoned route. ⇨

The Public Land Survey of 1785

The routing of roads from Ohio west is quite different from the original routing in the East. The Public Land Survey System was mandated since 1785. In order to organize, divide and sell government-owned frontier lands, the U.S. government, such as it was under the Articles of Confederation, divided the land into grids. Each "township" was a square, six miles on each side, further divided into 36 sections of one mile square each. Each square was composed of 640 acres and could be sold that way or broken down into 160 or 80-acre or fewer subsections.

Cross country farm-to-market roads were replaced by right-angled roads wherever permitted by geographic conditions. This system caused the Yellowstone Trail to follow the many square corners because townships created roads along the grid. Roads looking like "stair-steps" can be found from Indiana west into Washington.

Along routes of heavier traffic many of the right angle turns were "rounded" to facilitate travel. Many a picnic area was established within the cut-off areas.

The Trail Association was relieved of this problem east of Ohio when early 20th century routes followed roads established well before 1785 and were outside of the purview of the Land Survey System. The Rocky and Cascade Mountains in the West also defied a grid system, and all road building there was dictated by geography. ✿

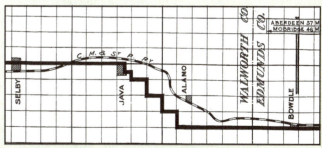

"Stair Step" roads, these on the YT near Java, SD
1914 Year Book

Continued

The End of the Association

The Association and its Trail became very popular in a short time because people saw a possibility of a better road in their area. Towns had fought to be named on the Trail. Visions of tourist dollars had danced in their heads. But the end of the Association loomed ahead both inside and outside of the Association.

The end of the Yellowstone Trail Association in 1930 actually began in 1927. Hal Cooley was hard at work, flogging member towns to pony up their dues and threatening to remove the Trail from recalcitrant towns, a ploy he frequently threatened to marinate the town in dire distress, but apparently never followed through with. Founder J. W. Parmley took exception to Cooley's hard work. Parmley demanded an audit of the books. Cooley said the organization didn't have the $200 for it, etc. Acrimonious letters flew, each defending his management position - Cooley's on practicality, Parmley's on loyalty to promises. Their verbal spats and dirty laundry were aired publicly and printed verbatim in newspapers.

In all this posturing, the real elephant in the room was growing. Routes were beginning to be numbered by governments and trail colors would no longer be needed – or allowed. The American Association of State Highway Officers (AASHO) had met with the Federal Highway Department in Washington D.C. in 1925 to draw up the federal highway numbering system we know today. By 1927 the numbering plan was employed by the states; all colors and names would be driven from US highways, replaced by black numbers with the familiar white US shield as background. The various state and county and townships signs followed.

A howl of frustration went up from trail associations. When the battle became futile, Parmley begged to at least have their route bear one single number across. He failed as did others. Sections of the Yellowstone Trail ultimately were numbered with 25 state, 14 US, two Interstate highways and countless county road numbers.

The Trail's time had come in 1912 and was gone by 1930. People liked the clarity and efficiency of numbers on roads. They also liked the freedom from paying dues, perhaps forgetting that taxes were "dues." People had moved on from personal participation. Technology, taxes, and politics had pushed them from the picture. During 1929 and 1930 the Great Depression administered the final blow. ✿

MAP OF WYOMING SHOWING
4,608 MILES OF STAR AND RURAL FREE DELIVERY POST ROUTES
These are the roads which advocates of "Federal Aid" would have improved. They would appropriate $60.00 or less per mile per year toward this improvement and require 83 years or more to complete the "system"!

MAP OF WYOMING SHOWING
2,455 MILES OF NATIONAL HIGHWAYS
These are the roads which the National Highways Association would have improved and maintained by the Government. This system would require less than ten years to complete.

Throughout the country, roads had been created "by use" to get from one point to another, usually to take farm products from the farm to the railroad. The United States Post Office was an early user of the railroad for long-distance mail movement. The institution of Rural Free Delivery required some augmentation of those farm to market roads. The widespread use of autos resulted in an interest in connected roads to create long-distance routes to give the auto owner wide opportunities. A great deal of ink was used to urge the federal government to fund the multi-use long-distance road.

While the above maps reflect the argument in Wyoming, similar maps and arguments appeared across the country. Proponents of the Yellowstone Trail had no trouble deciding which side of that question to be on. ✿

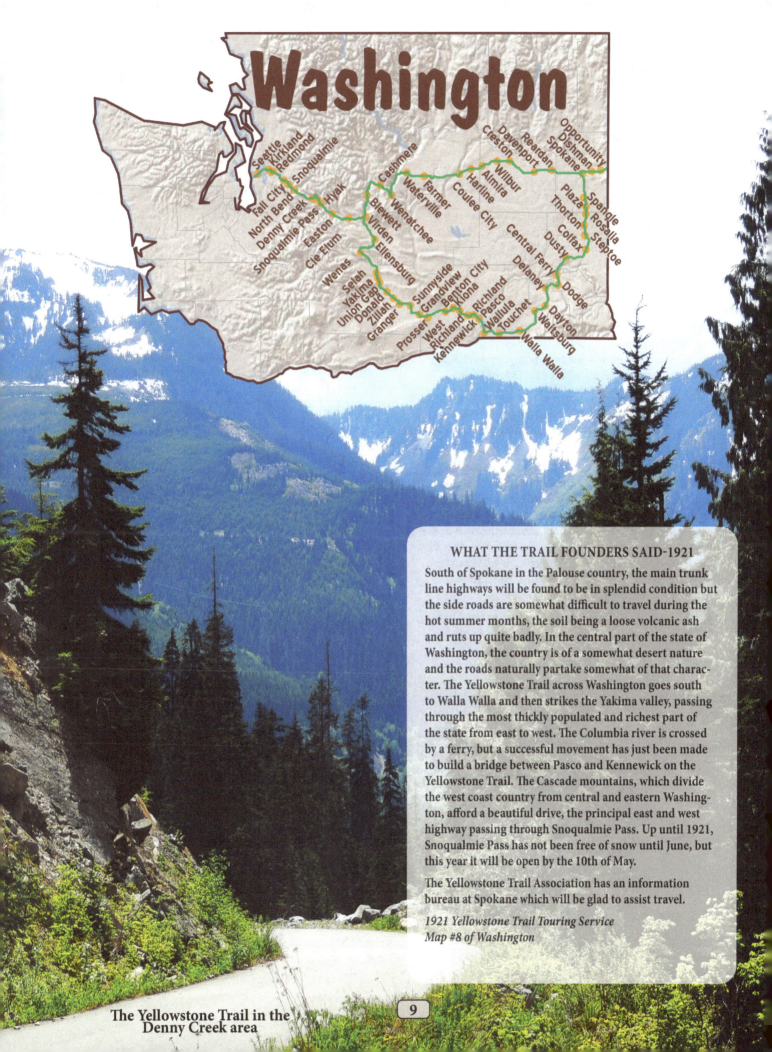

Washington

WHAT THE TRAIL FOUNDERS SAID-1921

South of Spokane in the Palouse country, the main trunk line highways will be found to be in splendid condition but the side roads are somewhat difficult to travel during the hot summer months, the soil being a loose volcanic ash and ruts up quite badly. In the central part of the state of Washington, the country is of a somewhat desert nature and the roads naturally partake somewhat of that character. The Yellowstone Trail across Washington goes south to Walla Walla and then strikes the Yakima valley, passing through the most thickly populated and richest part of the state from east to west. The Columbia river is crossed by a ferry, but a successful movement has just been made to build a bridge between Pasco and Kennewick on the Yellowstone Trail. The Cascade mountains, which divide the west coast country from central and eastern Washington, afford a beautiful drive, the principal east and west highway passing through Snoqualmie Pass. Up until 1921, Snoqualmie Pass has not been free of snow until June, but this year it will be open by the 10th of May.

The Yellowstone Trail Association has an information bureau at Spokane which will be glad to assist travel.

1921 Yellowstone Trail Touring Service
Map #8 of Washington

9

The Yellowstone Trail in the Denny Creek area

INTRODUCING THE YELLOWSTONE TRAIL IN WASHINGTON:
THE EVERGREEN STATE

From its beginnings in South Dakota in 1912, the Yellowstone Trail had progressed west through North Dakota and Montana and by 1914 it was going through the Idaho panhandle and knocking on Washington's door (Spokane) for the 1915 travel season. Good timing. The 1915 state map of Washington's State Highway Commission shows the recently refined routing of two great Washington highways of interest to the Yellowstone Trail: the Sunset Highway, 1915, and the Inland Empire Highway (IEH), 1913. But they were hardly great highways. Major sections were identified as "improved," meaning something between smooth gravel roads and, well, dirt wagon roads that had been dragged, sometimes. But long sections of each are identified as "Other roads open to travel," that is, dirt wagon roads that maybe you can get through. Maybe. Marked so you could find your way? Nah. Nevertheless, no other "highways" connected Spokane with Seattle.

Put three things in mind to avoid being overly ungenerous in your judgment of Washington's lack of long-distance auto roads.

First. If you are not familiar with Washington's geography, take a minute to review the fact that the beautiful Cascade mountains from Canada to Oregon divide the state with a north/south transportation barrier. Note the lack of cross-state highways in the 21st century and note further that in the winter, snow still closes some of those east-west highways for the season. And then there is the meagerly populated eastern half of the state, especially the Palouse area. Not a prime territory for an extensive road system.

Second. Yes, the auto had made its appearance in Washington. By 1912 autos appeared in great numbers. A handful was produced locally but most arrived to Washington's scattered towns and cities by railroad. Except for a few ambitious path finders, drivers didn't drive cross-country because, for the most part, only the roads in or near cities were reasonably passable for autos. Other roads were rough wagon roads created by use; they were not engineered. That is, they were not designed with the necessary drainage, durable surfaces, or

A road the YT drivers faced

acceptable gradients needed for auto travel. And those sharp rocks killed a rubber tire in short order.

Third. Even though Washington was way ahead of many other states in thinking about highways, not all of the necessary political decisions had been made and implemented to establish responsibility for funding, building, and fixing them. State funding for scattered roads first occurred in 1893. However, the Washington State Highway Department was not created by the legislature until 1905. That same year 12 scattered roads were designated as state roads and received funds. The state spent some money on those scattered roads, but improvement was minimal.

That lack of long-distance roads had been noted by Washington's long standing Good Roads Association which was the major "shaker and mover" in road matters. By 1912 it had proposed three long-distance auto roads: the Pacific Highway to run north/south across the state between the ocean and the Cascades, the great curving IEH from Ellensburg to Spokane via Yakima and Walla Walla, and the Sunset Highway from Spokane to Seattle through Wenatchee and Ellensburg. The names stuck and the State Highway Department began implementing the plan.

Vantage Ferry

Why Did the Yellowstone Trail Go Where it Went in Washington?

Today's driver of the Yellowstone Trail has to choose between two routes in Washington, the southern route through Walla Walla or the northern route over Blewett Pass. This is the same choice of routes available to the Yellowstone Trail Association when it first entered the state in 1915. Should the Yellowstone Trail follow the northern Sunset Highway or the southern IEH? That was the only choice to be made. There were no other realistic possibilities.

The difficulties of establishing a Yellowstone Trail route through western Montana, Idaho, and Washington had been brought to the attention of J. W. Parmley (founder of the Yellowstone Trail) so, true to his nature, he took a train from South Dakota to Butte, Montana, and then a car to Washington, in early 1915 to inspect the route alternatives. After considerable consultation, Parmley personally picked the southern IEH.

The more direct Sunset Highway would have been the obvious choice had it not been for worries about the condition of the road through Blewett Pass. If Parmley was shown a copy of the 1915 State Highways map, his worries ⇨

would have been compounded by a weird "reverse curve" that routed the Sunset Highway through Vantage apparently to avoid Blewett Pass (shown as a dotted black and red line on the accompanying map). That routing is strange in many ways: It crosses the Columbia River in three places, only one of which had a bridge, and it follows seeming non-existent roads. Apparently, someone in the State Highway Commission determined that the condition of the Blewett Pass route was just too formidable!

In spite of that perverse map and Parmley's decision to use the IEH, the local managers and drivers in the Yellowstone Trail 1915 Chicago to Seattle Relay Race chose to follow the route over Blewett Pass. Confusing. But that is the way it was. See **Trail Tale: 1915 Race** on page 302.

The southern Yellowstone Trail route on the IEH was made irrevocable by its documentation in the popular *Automobile Blue Book* in the 1916 edition, and the 1916 Plymouth to Seattle Relay Race did follow the IEH route.

The Yellowstone Trail Association 1916 *Route Folder* was almost apologetic in describing the "scenic" route through the southeast Palouse district of Washington. Promises of future connections to the Columbia River Road, Tacoma, and connections to California filled more space than discussion of the actual road in Washington. "You can ship your machine [car] from Seattle to San Francisco for $50" sounds like an invitation to skip Washington entirely.

Automobiles shipped by railroad
arriving in Washington
Curt Cunningham

However, the 1917 *Route Folder*, much more assured, listed 25 Trailmen or supporting organizations from 25 cities on the Trail from Seattle through the southern Pasco and Walla Walla area and north through the Palouse to Spokane. Descriptions of the Palouse praised it as "one of the most famous wheat countries of the world," and, "fruit, nuts, and agriculture abound." To offset the added distance, the *Folder* lamely offered, "the tourist has the advantage of a much better road."

The Association went full throttle in the 1919 *Route Folder*, waxing poetic about the scenery of Idaho and Washington and devoting a whole page to the wonders of 15 towns on the route.

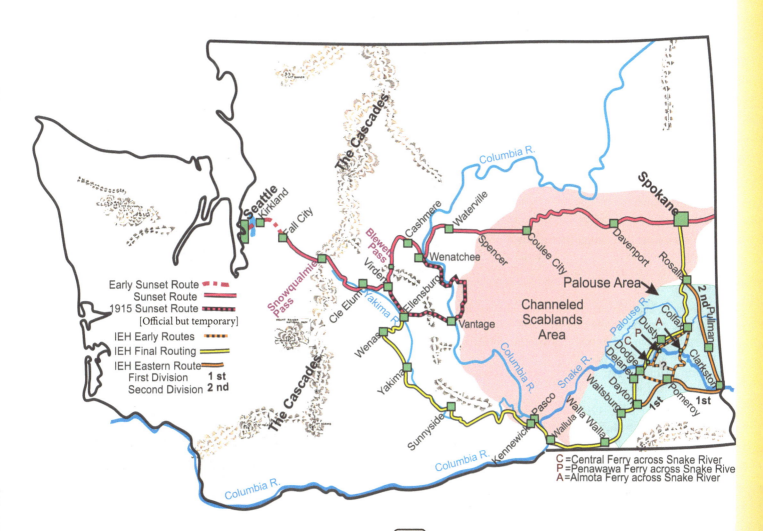

Early Sunset Route
Sunset Route
1915 Sunset Route
[Official but temporary]
IEH Early Routes
IEH Final Routing
IEH Eastern Route
First Division 1 st
Second Division 2 nd

C = Central Ferry across Snake River
P = Penawawa Ferry across Snake Rive
A = Almota Ferry across Snake River

Continued

And Then There Was the Banker in Pomeroy

Well, maybe it was the orchardist at Penawawa. They were both Yellowstone Trail Trailmen listed on one or more of the annual Yellowstone Trail Association *Folders*. One of them was apparently in charge of keeping the home office of the Yellowstone Trail Association informed of the location of the Yellowstone Trail in Southeastern Washington. And, we think, he communicated to keep Pomeroy, his home town, on the Trail a bit longer than was strictly fact. You judge.

Here's the story as we can reconstruct it:

As you might recall, early in 1915 Parmley chose the Inland Empire Highway (IEH) route for the Yellowstone Trail over the shorter Sunset Highway because of the apparent poor condition of Blewett Pass. What Parmley might not have been fully informed of was the condition of the IEH.

First, a bit of background:

1911. The idea for the IEH route as a state highway was proposed by the Washington State Good Roads Association in response to the growing cadre´ of automobilists.

1912. An April 30, 1912 letter from Governor Hay stated that a state highway is being contemplated, the Inland Empire Road, to begin in Aberdeen (on the Pacific coast), and run a great circle through Seattle, Ellensburg, Wenachee, Spokane, Colfax, Pomeroy, Walla Walla, Pasco, and back to Ellensburg. It is, however, "mere talk and its construction is many years in the future," wrote Hay.

1913. The folks in southeastern Washington assumed the IEH was coming "now!" According to the online encyclopedia of Washington state history (www.historylink.org/File/10644),

> The route of the Inland Empire Highway was also a matter of spirited contention in Whitman County. On January 7, 1913, a public meeting of the Good Roads Association of Whitman County in Colfax attracted so many people that the meeting had to be switched from a hotel meeting room to a much larger space at the Whitman County Courthouse.

The Pullman/Clarkston people promoted an eastern route and Colfax area folks promoted a western route. The association eventually agreed on nothing, except to formally endorse no particular route.

1914. The state began improvements (probably graded and added some bridges) on the IEH. The plan for the IEH called for it to go between Colfax and Pomeroy on the "most feasible route, crossing the Snake River on either the Penawawa ferry or the Almota ferry." This certainly had pleased the Banker in Pomeroy.

1915. As reported on the 1915 State Highways map, something less than half that IEH route had been "improved" by state administered funds, and the Seattle/Spokane route (with that "reverse curve" through Vantage) was renamed the Sunset Highway. More important to our story is that after boisterous public meetings, many meetings of the state

highway commission, and grousing on all sides, the IEH was given two routes between Walla Walla and Spokane! One, the western route, ran through Central Ferry between Dayton and Rosalia on the yellow line on the map on the previous page. The other, the eastern route, had two parts: the 1st Division and the 2nd Division, shown in orange.

The Yellowstone Trail by default would follow the more direct Central Ferry route and avoid Pomeroy. That certainly did not please the Banker in Pomeroy.

But, in fact, the Dusty/Central Ferry road was barely a road. The 1915 state map labeled it as an "Other road open to travel." Neither county nor state had touched it.

Apparently, the Trailmen from Pomeroy and Penawawa were slow to communicate the news of the change to the Central Ferry route back to Yellowstone Trail Association headquarters and Pomeroy was shown to be on the Trail maps in 1915 and 1916. Travelers were expected to ask directions locally and cross the Snake River at either Penawawa or Almota and wander south through Pomeroy. See also map on page 55.

However, by 1917 the Central Ferry/Yellowstone Trail route was well established in fact and in the 1917 *Folder*. And all was well. Unless you lived in Pomeroy.

Until 1925.

1925 – The Route Reconsidered

In 1925, Blewett Pass, west of Wenatchee, was improved enough to more easily carry autos, and the Wenatchee city fathers strongly argued for the Trail to move north – through their town. We do not know what Wenatchee offered or if they offered anything besides argument, but whatever it was, it persuaded the Yellowstone Trail Association to abandon the Palouse and move north to the Sunset Highway for the entire distance between Seattle and Spokane

In 1925 the Yellowstone Trail Association picked up its signs from the southern route which it had spent years installing and put them down on the northern route, on the Sunset Highway. We do not possess a 1925 or 1926 *Route Folder* and would really like to have seen their explanation for the move north. The 1927 *Folder* spends time explaining about coulees as it described the sites along the northern route.

Palouse Falls
Dave Habura

Southern Palouse in a fall evening with the Yellowstone Trail in the foreground

Continued

Why Did the Trail Go Where it Went? A Different Perspective

Yes, the Trail was routed by J. W. Parmley and others of the Yellowstone Trail Association but their efforts were built on the work of many men before them. Others developed the mail routes, built some of the necessary bridges, built the towns, and laid the railroad track, all of which determined the location of the road. But the route was ultimately affected by something we seldom name: geology. Traveling from Seattle to Boston the Trail went through Chicago and Cleveland because Lakes Michigan and Erie forced it south of what would have been the shortest possible route. Going west from Montana, the road had to squeeze between hills, around the lakes, and over the rivers of the Bitterroots, part of the great Rocky Mountains. So?

Well, in Washington the "troublesome" geology is spectacularly on display along and near the Yellowstone Trail in Washington. And much of that is compelling because it is new to most of us. We'll consider three "bits" of geology that profoundly affected the route of the Trail in eastern Washington that you can see and enjoy. It is just more of the history of the Trail, but a few thousand or even a million years earlier.

Bit #1: As you follow much of the Trail east of Ellensburg, either the north or south route, you have a whole lot of basaltic rock under (and sometimes around) you. Between six and 17 million years ago, most of it about 15.6 million years ago, lava welled up in many places (not volcanos) in the neighborhood and filled in the entire area of eastern Washington (and into Idaho and Oregon). Actually, it covered up then-existing mountains and valleys, leaving them now, in places, up to 3,000 feet below the new surface. So much lava that the whole area sank so that the surface was at about the same elevation as before the magma came. A lot of that basaltic rock is now seen in layers in erosional cuts in many, many places, such as at Palouse Falls, Dry Falls south of Coulee City and the east shore of Banks Lake in Grand Coulee on your way to Grand Coulee Dam. See pages 32 and 33.

Bit #2: A long time later, in the last ice age, 150,000 to 12,000 years ago, glaciers repeatedly cut across the Clark Fork river valley near Sandpoint, Idaho, and formed a dam backing up drainage to southeast of Missoula, a couple of Great Lakes'

volume of water. Enough water collected to float part of the ice dam, or at least the dam failed, and released the whole lake in a gigantic "Missoula Flood" over eastern Washington, Idaho, and Oregon, creating the Channelled Scablands. The water scoured the land, cut waterfalls bigger than Niagara, eroded out valleys and left some areas undisturbed. After each dam failure, the southward moving ice sheet then created a new lake, and the cycle repeated itself. (See the Mile-by-Mile for WA-N227.2 and related Waysides on pages 32 and 33.)

Bit #3: With the ice age glaciers grinding up rock, lots of fine dust and sand was created and washed over the land to the southwest by the melting glaciers or one of the Missoula Floods. During the periods between the Floods, the dust and sand (now called loess) was blown (actually just dropped from the air) into the Palouse where it formed dune-like hills. Well, that is a current thought; geologists are still trying to figure it all out. Nevertheless, the Palouse is an incredible area visually and agriculturally. See the map of its general area on page 11. Much of the countryside from Spokane to Walla Walla is in the Palouse.

Put all three geology bits together and visit Palouse Falls. See page 54.

Now that you are off the Interstate, look left and right, stop to really explore something, learn and enjoy. Consider the constant, pervasive effect that geology placed on routing the Yellowstone Trail.

If you have the slightest tickle of interest, very understandable and interesting videos and references are easy to find: Search online for 1) Central Washington University's online presentations by Nick Zentner, 2) "Washington's Ice Age Floods" and 3) "Flood Basalts of the Pacific Northwest". ❀

STATE OF WASHINGTON LEADS COUNTRY IN PERCENTAGE GAIN IN USE OF AUTOMOBILES
ONE CAR TO EVERY TEN PERSONS PREDICTED FOR 1921
February 14, 1920 The Evening Record (Ellensburg)

Seattle is the natural gateway to the Orient and Alaska, and to its unrivaled landlocked harbor come vessels from every maritime nation in the world. Lake Washington forms the eastern boundary of the city, and within its limits lie lakes Union and Green. The century old Alaska totem pole at Pioneer place, First Ave. and Yesler Way, is another object of interest. This was the site of Henry Yesler's sawmill in 1854. BB1921-9

Seattle was a ranking city of the Pacific coast. It had a Carnegie Library in 1905, a symphony orchestra concert in 1903, a university, the Milwaukee Road Railroad in 1910, creation of the Port District in 1911, and the digging of the Sound-to-Lake Washington Canal 1911-1916.

Besides the obvious pleasant climate and immediate access to multiple bodies of water, there is the prospect of seeing mountains in their glorious mantles of white, with snow and shadows accentuating their ruggedness: Rainier, Adams, Baker, and Mt. St. Helens.

Yellowstone Trail travelers, having just ended their long trip from the east, would find a plethora of choices of entertainments, water adventures and restaurants to enjoy in Seattle in 1915 when the Trail reached this point. There were a whopping 237,000 people. New arrivals may have been directed to popular sites 100 years ago just as they are today. There are Pioneer Square, Pike Place Market, theaters such as the Moore, Paramount, Neptune, or 5th Ave., or the Athenian Seafood Restaurant. ☼

Historic Theatre District is roughly a triangle of eight city blocks, from the Moore Theatre (1907) at 1932 Second Ave., over to the Paramount Theatre (1928) at 911 Pine St., and up to Town Hall at Eighth and Seneca. A Contemporary Theatre-ACT/Eagles (1925) at 700 Union St. and 5th Avenue Theatre (1926) are included. Not part of the Theatre District, but old and renovated is the Neptune Theatre (1921) at 1303 NE 45th St. ☼

The four block by six block **Pioneer Square** is several things: it is Seattle's First Neighborhood and, thus, an important part of its history; it is a lively, bustling area with unique shops; it is a city transportation center; and it is the center for several charitable groups and social services serving the homeless. The Alaska Totem pole, mentioned above in the 1921 *Automobile Blue Book*, is still there. ☼

Athenian Seafood Restaurant and Bar has been at this Pike Place Market site since it was opened in 1909 by three Greek brothers, hence the name "Athenian." First a candy shop, then a bar, now a full restaurant and bar. But nothing beats its stunning view of Puget Sound. ☼

You could write a television series about the life of the **Merchants Café and Saloon** at 109 Yesler Way. After it was rebuilt in 1890, a liquor store occupied the bottom floor with a brothel in the two floors above in 1892. The building was sold again in 1898 to a gold-rich businessman named Franz Xavier Schreiner. Schreiner, or "FX" as he was known, set up a bank downstairs and exchanged cash for gold dust. He would reportedly cash out as much as $100,000 in gold over a weekend.

Prohibition never stopped FX. He just put the booze and gambling downstairs and bribed the police. Today a boutique hotel occupies the upstairs, a bar and comfortable lounge downstairs and, yes, a restaurant still occupies the ground floor where you'll find the intricately-carved bar that was shipped around Cape Horn in the late 1800s. You'll still find the wooden floors, the pressed tin ceilings, and décor reminiscent of 1898. Look at the picture of the totem pole on the following page. To the right you will see the red brick building on Yesler Way at Pioneer Square. That is the Merchants Cafe. ☼

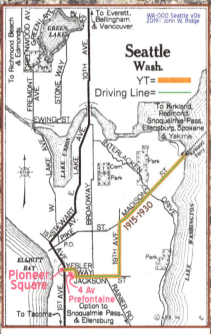

The YT on *Automobile Blue Book* map 1925 Vol. 4 - Annotated

The **Pike Place Market** was already well established when Yellowstone Trail travelers arrived and they would certainly have headed there to view food stalls and artisan wares as they do today. It is now the nation's oldest continuously operating farmers market. And, yes, you must duck as the fishmongers still toss fish about. ☼

WAYSIDE

2702 East D St., Tacoma. **LeMay's America's Car Museum**. Directions: Follow I-5 south to E 26th St in Tacoma. Take Exit 133, turn onto E 26th St. Turn at the 2nd cross street onto East D St. Although this 3.5 acre technologically advanced museum is off the Trail, it is still significant in that it tells the tale, through many, many old autos, of U.S. auto transportation and how the auto shaped our society. We've been there and spent a day enjoying the history of it all.

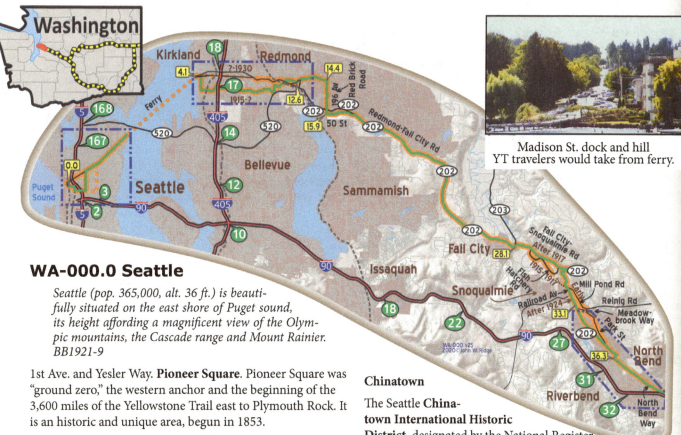

Madison St. dock and hill
YT travelers would take from ferry.

WA-000.0 Seattle

Seattle (pop. 365,000, alt. 36 ft.) is beautifully situated on the east shore of Puget sound, its height affording a magnificent view of the Olympic mountains, the Cascade range and Mount Rainier. BB1921-9

1st Ave. and Yesler Way. **Pioneer Square**. Pioneer Square was "ground zero," the western anchor and the beginning of the 3,600 miles of the Yellowstone Trail east to Plymouth Rock. It is an historic and unique area, begun in 1853.

109 Yesler Way. **Merchants Café and Saloon**. It is the oldest restaurant in Seattle. Built of wood, it was eaten alive by the great 1889 Seattle fire. The building was rebuilt with brick (1890) so that wouldn't happen again. See History Bits on previous page for a more full story.

506 2nd Ave. (Pioneer Square) **Smith Tower**. A designated Seattle Landmark, it was built in 1914, the tallest building in the U.S. outside of New York at the time. An elevator goes to the top 42nd floor restaurant for a fee of $19.14. (Get it?)

1st Ave. and Pike St. Established in 1907, the **Pike Place Market** is an exciting adventure in food (especially fish) and artisan stalls.

1517 Pike Place inside the Pike Place Market. **Athenian Seafood Restaurant and Bar** in business since 1909.

Historic Theatre District. The five Seattle Historic Theatres are within 1.3 miles of each other and every day there is an acclaimed show, lecture, dance, concert or theater performance. The district is roughly a triangle of eight city blocks and include the Moore, Paramount, Town Hall, ACT/Eagles and the 5th Avenue Theatre. All are nearly or over 100 years old.

2700 24th Ave. E. **Museum of History and Industry** at Naval Reserve Armory in South Lake Union Park. The core exhibit provides a chronological history of Seattle and its environs. The 1919 first commercial airplane built by Boeing hangs in the atrium. Be sure to see the SS Virginia V parked behind the building. Built in 1921, she now is available for regular cruises from her dock.

Chinatown

The Seattle **Chinatown International Historic District**, designated by the National Register of Historic Places, is roughly south of Jackson and west of I-5, with Hing Hay Park at its heart.

719 King St. In the East Kong Yick Building (1910) is the **Wing Luke Asian Museum**. The museum's galleries contain re-creations of the Gee How Oak Tin Association's meeting room, kitchens, and apartments that were located inside the hotel. These apartments were occupied by Asian immigrants; the Japanese were removed to internment camps in the 1940s.

The Waterfront

Yellowstone Trail travelers, no doubt, visited a simpler waterfront 100 years ago. Today, the vast Seattle waterfront is not known as just one place, but referred to by several locations.

The one prominent remaining feature is the **1920 Harbor Entrance Pergola**, which is listed on the National Register of Historic Places. Originally it functioned as a landing point for boats bringing passengers from ships.

Then again, just wander the waterfront and see what you will find - great restaurants and shops on historic piers, perhaps.

Totem Pole and Pioneer Square in Seattle

Pioneer Square, western end of the YT

WA

Oregon interests are seeking to have Portland chosen as the terminus of the Yellowstone Trail instead of Seattle. 'The Yellowstone Trail carries twice as many eastern tourists to Seattle as any other highway," said Mr. Douglas Shelor, manager of the Automobile Club of Western Washington. "It is to the interest of every Seattleite to block the effort to have the route diverted to Portland."

November 20, 1920 Western Highways Builder

Note: Oregon newspapers kept up the banter and general badgering for 16 months to get the terminus of the Trail from Seattle to Portland. They ceased only when the Association held a vote among its members about the matter. The vote was 2,751 to 1 to remain in Seattle.

On August 28, 1907, Jim Casey and Claude Ryan established their own downtown delivery service. United Parcel Service grew out of the dispatch office in the basement of a Seattle saloon now marked by Waterfall Park in Pioneer Square. ☙

The famous totem pole, a landmark in Pioneer Square, had a murky beginning in 1899. That year "leading Seattle citizens" went on a tour of southeast Alaska ports aboard a steamship. At Fort Tongass, a Tlingit village, one story says, sailors found the 60 foot totem standing in the Tlingit village, asked permission of the one frightened villager there, then chopped it down, sawed it in half and loaded it on to the steamship with the "leading citizens."

In 1935, another tale is told by James Clise, ringleader of the 1899 escapade. He described it thus:

> … we found a village with about 100 or more totem poles standing. We finally found two decrepit Indians who made no objection to our taking a totem to Seattle. In fact, the Indians were as pleased with our taking it as were the people of Seattle to receive this outstanding example of workmanship of the Northern Indians.

A federal grand jury in Alaska indicted eight of Seattle's most prominent citizens for theft of government property. No papers were ever served. Representatives and Senators from the three Pacific Coast states went to the State Department to ask for dismissal of the suit. They failed. The Tlingit Tribe demanded $20,000 for the theft but settled for $500. Yellowstone Trail travelers would have seen this totem.

In 1938 an arsonist seriously damaged the totem which had been carved about 1790 by the Raven Clan to tell the story of a woman who drowned in the Nass River. The raven was revered in mythology as knowing everything and being everywhere. The one you are now looking at is its 1940 exact replica replacement which was carved by descendants of the carvers of the original totem.

David Wilma, historylink.org/File/2076. ☙

Sam Hill was not related to railroad magnate J. J. Hill, but when he became J. J.'s son-in-law, lawyer Sam joined the Great Northern Railroad management, quitting in 1898 to move to Seattle and advocate for good roads and other civic ventures.

He was well aware of the sad condition of rural roads in Washington at the end of the 19th century. He formed the Washington State Good Roads Association in 1899 in Seattle. An initial hesitation and mistrust of autos by farmers, and of state rather than county road control, was gradually overcome. Wherever men gathered in the U.S. to discuss roads, that meeting was called a good roads meeting, whether or not it was part of the parent organization.

Sam was so enthusiastic about building roads that he raised the ire of Governor M. E. Hay early in the 20th century. Hay wrote,

> … I was not allowing him to run the State Highway Department. I did give him a free hand for about two years, and if he had been allowed to run it longer at the rate we were going we would have busted the state budget and had no roads. Mr. Hill is a great enthusiast, but no more practical than a child. ☙

As was true of the rest of the state, Seattle drivers had a "reasonable and proper" speed limit of 12 miles per hour in town and 30 miles per hour on the open road. BB 1918 Vol. 9.

Seattle's first automatic traffic light began operation on April 21, 1924. The need was apparently due to the burgeoning of autos in the city. It began part-time operation at 4th Avenue S and Jackson Street, having arrived late as other large cities had had them as long as a decade before. Previously, police officers directed traffic with hand signals or with semaphore signals, turning the pole as needed. Problem was that if the officer left his post to address a traffic offender, things descended into chaos. That intersection saw 24,000 cars passing through between 7:00 AM and 10:00 PM. A 30 day testing period was selected. A box was rigged with electric lights behind colored glass - red, amber, green. Words were placed on the glass to educate the driver - "stop, traffic change, go." A gong was sounded before each traffic change, but it was hard to hear. Timing of either light was adjusted to the flow of traffic.

After only a few weeks, the test was judged a great success, traffic accidents dropped and traffic flowed smoothly. A cry went up for more lights in the city running for the morning rush hour as well as at the present evening rush hour. *Phil Dougherty, historylink.org/file/11025.* ☙

WA-004.1 Kirkland

Yellowstone Trail travelers heading east would take a 45-minute ferry ride from Madison St. across Lake Washington and land at Kirkland landing and thence drive along Central Way, then 80th St. and on eastward. The ferry boats MV Kirkland and S.S. Lincoln of Kirkland served Trail customers from 1915 to 1940. Today there are two substantial floating bridges across the lake, but no ferry.

The docks at Kirkland Ave. It was from this area that ferry boats took westbound Yellowstone Trail travelers across Lake Washington to debark at Madison Ave., the route of the Trail, in Seattle on their way to Pioneer Square and the end point of the transcontinental Trail. One can get a tour boat here today to view 17 historic sites including the Madison St. landing and the hill the old Model Ts had to climb immediately after landing.

620 Market St. **Peter Kirk Building**. It was first known as the Kirkland Investment Company Building, 1889, on the corner of Market St. and Seventh Ave., Kirkland's historic commercial core. It is listed on the National Register of Historic Places. Peter Kirk constructed the building as the centerpiece of his planned steel producing city, the "Pittsburgh of the West" he called it. The building was rescued from demolition and restored in the early 1960s as the **Kirkland Arts Center** which it remains to this day. It is the oldest commercial building on the eastside of Lake Washington.

203 Market St. **Kirkland Heritage Society Museum**. To promote public involvement, part of their mission, guest speakers appear here often with Kirkland topics.

WA-012.6 Redmond

A lumbering village in the 1880s, it suffered an economic downturn until World War II brought shipbuilding and upturns. The Evergreen Point Floating Bridge across Lake Washington in 1963 and arrival of technology companies made it the fastest growing city in the state. Among today's major employers in Redmond are Microsoft, Nintendo, and United Parcel.

There are six Landmark-designated buildings on Leary Way, the Yellowstone Trail:

7805 Leary Way NE **Redmond Trading Company**. Built in 1908, the Redmond Trading Company was the anchor store along Redmond's main street for 50 years, and in its first

decades it was the town's largest business in general merchandise. The Trading Company closed in 1955. Some glass windows covering one wall of the original store have been removed, but the front door is still recognizable.

7529 Leary Way NE **Justice White House aka. Redmond Hotel** now houses an architectural firm. Washington state Supreme Court Justice William Henry White built the 14 bedroom house in 1889 next to railroad tracks to attract travelers. As it became more popular, Hotel Redmond entertained more notable visitors such as Presidents Taft and Teddy Roosevelt, William Jennings Bryan the politician and lawyer, James J. Hill, the railroad magnate, and Percy Rockefeller.

7824 Leary Way NE. Bill Brown Saloon, now **Matador Restaurant**, built by Redmond Mayor Bill Brown in 1913 morphed into many purposes since its saloon days, but it still looks like it did a century ago.

7841 Leary Way NE Redmond State Bank is now **Brad Best Realty**. When the first bank in Redmond opened its doors on the corner of Leary and Cleveland in 1911, the handsome brick building looked much the same as it does today. Its dignified façade symbolized stability and security, which bolstered the efforts of early bankers who had to work hard to convince old-timers to deposit their savings, rather than bury money in the ground for safe-keeping.

7875 Leary Way NE Lodge Hall aka. Redmond Hardware 1903, now **Edge and Spoke** shop. Also a many-purposed building over the decades, but for 45 years it held a hardware shop.

7979 Leary Way NE Odd Fellows Hall, now **Redmond Bar & Grill**. Like other old 1903 buildings, this one held many businesses over the years. The symbol of the Independent Order of Odd Fellows, three rings, has been restored and returned to the front façade of the latest inhabitant, Redmond Bar & Grill.

16600 NE 80th St., **Redmond Historical Society**. Guest speakers, activities, and a walking tour are just some of the attractions as the Society collects and explains fascinating facts about this lumbering village that became a booming 21st century town.

WA

Kirkland Ferry dock, part of YT
historylink.org

YELLOWSTONE TRAIL FOLKS TO GATHER

The ninth annual meeting of the Yellowstone Trail Association of Washington will be held Oct. 1 at Kirkland. Among business matters to come up are 18 propositions affecting Washington, Idaho and Montana.

September 23, 1924 Spokane Daily Chronicle

Note: The article noted that, nationwide, members are $9,000 behind in their dues!

Snoqualmie Falls

FALLS CITY TO EVERETT MAY BE PRIMARY ROAD

King County Commissioners of Kirkland, representing the Yellowstone Trail Association, have succeeded in establishing as a state primary highway the county road from Falls City to Redmond to Everett before the joint Senate and House Roads and Bridges Committee. If the legislature affirms this action, $51,000 will be allotted to the highway and ultimately the state will pave the 13 miles between Falls City and Redmond.

February 7, 1925 Seattle Daily Times

Note: It was called Falls City, not Fall City in the 1920s.

WA-033.2: The route entering Snoqualmie from the northwest is not entirely clear and there may have been variations not recorded on the map. Likewise, the Mill Pond Rd. route was probably used but information about it was hard to find. Curt Cunningham reports that the route going southeast from Snoqualmie followed today's 202, turned left onto River St., turned right onto Falls Ave., left onto Newton St., right onto Park St., following it as it turns into Balk Ave. and then merging with Bendigo (or N Bend Blvd.) which it followed into North Bend.

Eric (known only as his online forum name, Sit Properly), using a 1920 *Automobile Blue Book*, found that the route followed a road no longer existing between the intersection of NW 8th St. and Bendigo Blvd. (WA 202 just NW from North Bend) to W North Bend Way at Snoqualmie River.

The YT at WA-014.4, Red Brick Rd., crossed present day WA 202 near the south end of the Red Brick Rd. Today's driver must finagle a way to overcome turn restrictions at that intersection. The YT also ran east/west on 50th from Red Brick Rd. to WA 202, today a pleasant drive past the old Grange Hall. The east end, near WA 202, is probably closed.

Northwest Railway Museum, Snoqualmie

Early use of guard rails, 1914
Washington DOT

Fall City Roadhouse today

HISTORY BITS

WA-014.4 The Red Brick Road

196th Ave. NE between Union Hill Road and Redmond-Fall City Road in the vicinity of Redmond is known as the **Red Brick Road**, an iconic part of the original Yellowstone Trail laid down in 1913. It was an important part of the route to and from Kirkland's ferry landing. It is 18 feet wide and

2.3 miles long and is the only unaltered link of the Yellowstone Trail remaining in King County. It is on both the National and State Register of Historic Places.

Suffice it to say that the neighbors are fighting hard to retain this original road's brick surface and century-old environment against an ever-encroaching culture,

The red brick road

but commuters find the speed limit and uneven brick to be inconsistent with their busy lives. See map on page 15.

WA-016.0 Happy Valley Grange

NE 50th St. at 196th Ave. NE (just south of Yellowstone Trail/Fall City/Redmond Road) is **Happy Valley Grange,** formed here in 1909. Granges were an important political force through much of rural America from 1867 to around 1950 and were responsible for much of progressive agricultural reforms. Granges actively lobbied state legislatures and Congress for political goals such as the lowering of rates charged by railroads, and acquiring rural free mail delivery (RFD). This Grange is still active.

WA-028.1 Fall City

FALL CITY, pop. 300; rooms at Fall City Hotel; Corner Garage leads. Good 50c meals at Riverside Tavern. MH-1928

"When the first transcontinental highway, the Yellowstone Trail, was planned in 1912, the route from Plymouth Rock, Massachusetts, to Seattle went through Fall City. Today's Redmond-Fall City Road follows the original route." (*Jack's History of Fall City* by Jack Kelly, 2006).

4200 Preston-Fall City Rd. SE. At the corner of WA 202 (Yellowstone Trail) and WA 203 is **Fall City Roadhouse Restaurant & Inn**. Built in 1916, exactly 100 years and several owners later, new owners in 2016 made subtle changes and added lots of historical photos to the walls, and the inn rooms were restored with vintage 1920s charm.

33805 SE Redmond. **Model Garage**. Murphy's Garage was opened in 1909, then became the Model Garage about 1920 under new owners at a location a little west of its current site. It moved to its current site in 1926 and by 1980 had expanded to the building we see today. This garage is still in business under the same name. Yellowstone Trail travelers would have seen this at either of its locations.

WA-032.0 Snoqualmie Falls

Snoqualmie Falls, 268 ft. high; an imposing sight. A few rooms and $1.50-$2 dinners at The Lodge. MH-1928

Visit November through March during the rainy and high water time. The falls take on a curtain form, the rushing waters demanding your imagination of why the Native Americans viewed it as a sacred site. The 1899 power generator is unseen, buried deep within the rock beneath the falls. More than 100 years later that equipment is still in use. The thundering falls themselves are on the National Register of Historic Places.

The **Salish Lodge & Spa** is an elegant hotel looking nothing like its 1919 predecessor. Perched above the falls, the views are stunning.

WA-033.2 Snoqualmie

38625 SE King St. **Northwest Railway Museum**. The Northwest Railway Museum is a fairly large railway yard filled with old boxcars, other rail cars, and steam engines with an old Victorian depot. Rail excursions are run from April through October as they were 100 years ago. You can experience early railway travel on a steam train to North Bend and Mt. Si.

WA-036.3 North Bend
(in the shadow of 4160' Mt. Si)

pop. 500; a lumber and logging center. Lies at base of Mt. Si. Cousens Hotel is modern. Camp Mt. Si, many good cottages, $1-$1.50.

HOTEL McGRATH fireproof and best. Sgl.$1.50-$2:dbl.$2,with conn.bath $2.50, bath $3 meals.

SUNSET GARAGE now leads for complete and good service. Labor $1.50; ph. Call for wrecker any time. MH-1928

At the busy corner of North Bend Way and Bendigo Blvd. (Yellowstone Trail) stands the landmark **Sunset Garage**. The first Sunset Garage was built here in 1922. It was replaced by this current concrete garage in 1929, just in time for the Great Depression.

It became a Buick dealership for about three decades, but then stood empty for the past few decades, according to historian Gardiner Vinnedge. In the 1990s, the television show Twin Peaks filmed the jail scenes there. Other businesses then occupied the space. In the fall of 2018 restoration of the building began, "to make it look like its old self" said Craig Glazier, present owner. Present day Trail tourists will rejoice.

320 Bendigo Blvd. S. **Snoqualmie Valley Historical Museum** (serving Snoqualmie, North Bend, Fall City, Snoqualmie Pass). Native American stories, homesteader, logging and farming stories of the Snoqualmie Valley are all told here.

At the tracks see the old **North Bend Depot** for the historic Puget Sound and Snoqualmie Valley Railroad.

902 SE North Bend Way (Yellowstone Trail). **North Bend Ranger Station** houses the local headquarters for the U.S. Forest Service. Don't write this off as a ho-hum stop. These are the folks who frequently repaint the Yellowstone Trail logo near Denny Creek. They also sometimes have hard-to-find information about the historic Snoqualmie Pass.

Partial timeline of the history of the Snoqualmie Pass:

1909 - Alaska-Yukon Exposition with race from New York -Seattle was an incentive for King and Kittitas Counties and the state to improve the road; 150 cars went over the Pass then. Toward the end of the 20th century, 13 million+ went over the Pass.

1910-1915 - Nothing much was done to maintain the road because the Milwaukee Road completed its tracks in 1909 and absorbed much of the traffic. People shipped their autos across the summit by train.

1915 - Gov. Lister, to much fanfare, dedicated Snoqualmie Pass Highway part of the Sunset Highway

1929 - Reconstructed into 4 paved lanes

1971 - One could still see stumps and planks of the old wagon road, and bits of the old narrow gauge railroad used by Arthur Denny in mining gold. ❀

Approaching Snoqualmie Pass summit
on hair pin turns
George Carpenter (above and below)

The old watering trough at WA-57.8

On the YT up Denny Creek
George Carpenter

The YT in Denny Creek campground

Hundred-year-old newspapers announced dates of the spring opening of Snoqualmie Pass to auto traffic as late as July 2 in 1916 and July 3 in 1917. Snow was reported by cabin-dwelling neighbors to be 12 feet deep in winter. Global warming, snowsheds and better snow plows have kept this necessary highway open all winter in modern days. Even today folks speak of two seasons there - winter and July. In 1916 they sprinkled charcoal on the snow, hoping that the dark color would absorb the sun's heat and melt enough snow to open the Pass by May 1. In 1925 they used dynamite in May. ❀

"Descending, the road [Sunset Highway] leads southeast and skirts the eastern banks of beautiful Lake Keechelus where the government is building a huge dam to irrigate the Kittitas and Yakima valleys."
The Beauties of the State of Washington, by Giles, 1915

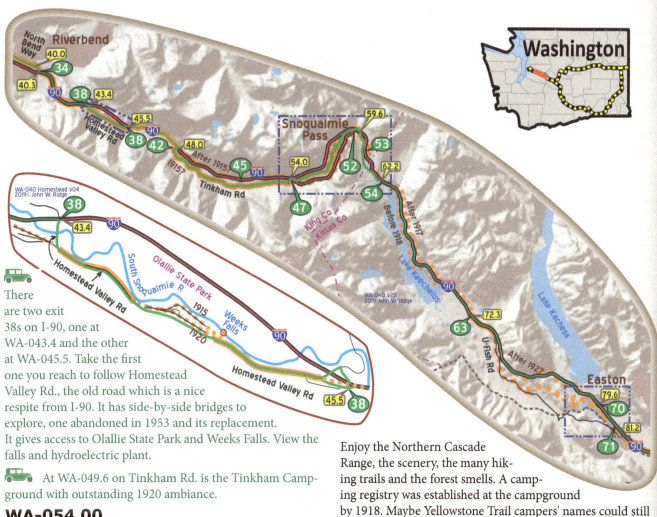

There are two exit 38s on I-90, one at WA-043.4 and the other at WA-045.5. Take the first one you reach to follow Homestead Valley Rd., the old road which is a nice respite from I-90. It has side-by-side bridges to explore, one abandoned in 1953 and its replacement. It gives access to Olallie State Park and Weeks Falls. View the falls and hydroelectric plant.

At WA-049.6 on Tinkham Rd. is the Tinkham Campground with outstanding 1920 ambiance.

WA-054.00

Asahel Curtis Nature Trail (off of Forest Road 55/Tinkham Rd.). The trail departs from the parking lot. Asahel Curtis was one of Washington's most renowned nature photographers and a Vice President of the Yellowstone Trail Association from 1925-1929. The trail is a half mile loop interpreted nature trail. It is an easy walk through one of the last remaining stands of old growth forest in the Snoqualmie Valley.

WA-056.4

On Forest Road 58 drive on the authentically reconstructed

1916 bridge over the south fork of the River at 47.40627, -121.44347. Visible to the south of the bridge is **an original Yellowstone Trail sign** painted on a large rock. Over the years it has been cared for by the Forest Service with fresh paint as needed.

WA-056.7 Denny Creek Campground

Situated near the south fork of the Snoqualmie River in Mt. Baker-Snoqualmie National Forest, **Denny Creek Campground** is a "must see" stop. The original Yellowstone Trail ran on what is now Denny Creek Road through the campground. It was the original Snoqualmie Pass wagon road.

Enjoy the Northern Cascade Range, the scenery, the many hiking trails and the forest smells. A camping registry was established at the campground by 1918. Maybe Yellowstone Trail campers' names could still be found?

Nearby, you might see remnants of an old Snoqualmie Pass wagon road where it intersects the Yellowstone Trail. The old wagon road is a good example of the kinds of roads that existed 100 years ago in these mountainous forests. If you hike this Snoqualmie Pass wagon road, you may see old wagon ruts and remnants.

WA-057.8 (GPS: 47.4192, -121.4352)

Look carefully. There is an **old watering trough** at the side of the road. It is not elevated, but level with the road and possibly shielded by greenery. Yellowstone Trail researchers Curt Cunningham and Dave Habura told us about it and puzzled over its low position, probably too low for horses in harness. Was it placed there for autoists to refill hard-worked Model T radiators?

Between lanes of I-90 near west side
of the summit at mile 59.2

Denny Creek area
Motor Age

The Snoqualmie Pass Summit Inn
George Carpenter

Sunset Lodge at Lake Keechelus opened in 1917.
George Carpenter

Along Lake Keechelus
George Carpenter

Easton dam
Dept. of Interior/Reclamation

YELLOWSTONE
TRAIL ROAD

YT name remains east of the
summit of Snoqualmie Pass

WA-81.8 Using the 1917 and 1927 Snoqualmie National Forest Maps, the route of the Sunset Highway can be mapped fairly well, although the matching with modern roads, especially near Easton, is still ambiguous. The northern route, especially the last 5 miles going east into Cle Elum is guess work, the best fit of old maps, current roads, and terrain because our historic maps just don't "fit" modern maps sufficiently well.

WA-059.2

Stop at the small turnout to see the South Fork of the Snoqualmie River bubbling over a small water falls and rapids. You'd never know that you were in that half mile space between the lanes of I-90! All is serene there.

WA-060.0 Summit of Snoqualmie Pass (elevation 3,022 feet)

Snoqualmie Pass Summit Hotel; rooms, dbl. $1.50, meals 50c, camp and cabins. Good repair shop; wrecker. MH-1928

Snoqualmie Pass, christened Sunset Highway, was finally graveled and opened to auto and wagon traffic and officially dedicated July 1, 1915, six months or so after the Yellowstone Trail Association arrived in Washington. The opening of the Pass enabled the Association to follow the Sunset Highway west to complete its route to Puget Sound, even though it was closed by winter snows regularly.

Because Travelers' Rest Center at the summit of the Pass was built in 1938, early Yellowstone Trail travelers never had the luxury of stopping and resting there. They did, however, have the original Summit Inn, which is no more. Stop and see the great historical pictures and information on the entry walls of Travelers' Rest.

WA-062.2 Hyak and Lake Keechelus

HY AK (Indian for hurry), (2,499 alt., 60 pop.), a commercial resort, overhangs the lake bank, at the eastern end of the Chicago, Milwaukee, St. Paul and Pacific Railroad tunnel through the Cascades. At this point the highway swings away from Lake Keechelus. WPA-WA

The **Snoqualmie Tunnel**, located at the Iron Horse State Park at Hyak, was constructed from 1912–1914 by the Milwaukee Road railroad as part of its line from Chicago to Seattle, and was electrified in 1917. Today the tunnel is part of the Iron Horse State Park rails-to-trails project for hikers and bikers. It is 2.3 miles long and was renovated in 2011. We mention it here because the Trail went through Hyak, following the route of the Milwaukee Road as it usually did, and the tunnel is a relic of the era, the Trail itself having been swallowed by Interstate 90.

LAKE KEECHELUS INN, modern; sgl. $2-$3; dbl. $2.50; bath $3.50; dinner $1.50. WPA-WA

KEECHELUS LAKE (2,475 alt.), is in a basin, whose timbered sides rise abruptly 1,000 feet.

US 10 follows a steep and winding, but safe, grade. During the fishing season anglers line the banks of the Snoqualmie River, which flows close to it for a distance. WPA-WA

Lake Keechelus. Although a natural lake, its discharge is controlled by a 1917 dam at the southern end of the lake, giving rise to the

Yakima River. Observe I-90 here, clinging to the east edge of Lake Keechelus. That modern road probably lies on top of the Yellowstone Trail, Sunset Highway and the National Parks Highway.

Stop just a bit west of Easton to view the eastern, drier side of the Cascades with some picturesque mountain peaks.

WA-081.2 Easton

pop. 300; two small hotels; the Easton leads. Fine meals at Green Tree Inn. Cottages at Egbert Camp. MH-1928

The **Easton Diversion Dam** across the Yakima River was completed in 1929, and thus was possibly visited by late Yellowstone Trail travelers. It received restorative improvements in the 1980s. The water that it backs up is called Lake Easton and provides the recreation for Easton and Iron Horse State Parks, the latter once a part of the path of the Milwaukee Road railroad. A drawdown of the lake once revealed the old Yellowstone Trail.

WA-062.2 to WA-070.2 Hyak Lake Keechelus: Keechelus Dam (WA-070.2) was constructed at the lower end of a natural lake and on the Yakima River 10 miles northwest of Easton. This earthfill dam that enlarged the lake was completed in 1917, is 128 feet high and contains 684,000 cubic yards of material. Local researchers might attempt to determine the relationship of U-Fish Rd. and the old YT.

The roadway on the eastern side appears to have been cut into the hillside not far above the waterline. When the dam at the lower end was built in 1917, the new highway would, of necessity (in places), have been built higher up the hillside. At the northern end, the lake extended considerably north so that the Keechelus Inn, once at the top of the lake, would be at least a mile and a quarter south of the top.

The 1917 National Forest Map is a wildly approximate representation of the route from Easton west to I-90. Curt Cunningham and other maps offered better info. Curt Cunningham and Dave Habura agree this is the best true representation of the old YT. [Note: Pictures of the YT (Sunset) show the old highway hugging a steep shore line, so at most, the alignment moved up but probably not far east; it didn't go through a flat now flooded area.]

WA-064.5: In 1921 this is the location of Keechelus Inn, and Rocky Run Auto Camp, at what was, before 1917, the top of the lake,

Lake Easton and the still existing concrete highway bridge just NW of Easton, were created in 1929. A short section of the replaced pre-1929 YT (and US 10) now lie under the Lake. The YT had traveled Sparks Rd. with its switchback, still visible in Google Maps, going west but after 1929 it followed an alignment which, for the most part, is now under the east-bound lanes of I-90. Much of Sparks road still exists but is essentially unused and is substantially "grown-over", reported Curt Cunningham.

An old Cle Elum Echo newspaper [undated], as reported by Yvonne Prater in *Columbia, the Magazine of Northwest History*, 1996 said,

> The Yellow Trail has been painted through Cle Elum. A yellow splotch with a black arrow marks it for straight ahead, a black R within the yellow for right turn, L for left, X for railway crossing, S for slow and D for danger. These marks, having been completed to Seattle, the Yellow Trail is blazed from coast to coast. Mr. Warwick has been in the trail-marking business for many years. He relies on local businessmen and contributions in each city to pay for paint and expenses as he goes. ❂

STIRRED OVER EFFORTS TO DISCREDIT BLEWETT PASS HIGHWAY AND FORCE TRAVEL OVER OLD COLOCKUM ROUTE, PROTECTIVE ACTION WILL BE TAKEN

July 21, 1916 Cle Elum Echo

Note: Apparently men were stationed at Wenatchee, Ellensburg, and elsewhere warning autoists not to use Blewett Pass, which southern end lead to Cle Elum. They were advised to use a road well east of Cle Elum, missing the town and its businesses entirely. The ruckus even drove a Wenatchee chap to "call up by long-distance telephone" a Cle Elum Good Roads chap to complain. That call must have taken quite a while to place!

THE CIRCUS IS IN TOWN!! BUFFALO BILL'S ORIGINAL WILD WEST - 2 PERFORMANCES!

June 4, 1915 Cle Elum Echo

Cle Elum's tourist park or camp grounds are just hitting their gait. People are in comfort and safety. The grounds have [all the amenities] and a caretaker on the job all the time. During the first three weeks in June 1,844 people have registered.

June 27, 1924 Cle Elum Echo

WA

WHOLE CAR LOAD OF MISSOURI CANARIES ARRIVE FOR SUNSET HIGHWAY WORK

April 28, 1916 Cle Elum Echo

Note: Does anybody know what a "canary" is for road building? Tell us.

Sunset Garage
Day and Night Service
NORTH BEND, WASH.
L. HEIBERG, Prop. Phone 111

LADIES' REST ROOM
Storage—Supplies—Repairs!
Special Equipment for Wrecks
Batteries Charged Over Night

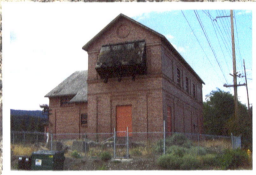

Milwauke Rd. railroad electric substation powered electric trains used in the mountains.

South Cle Elum 1909 depot

WAYSIDE

About 3 miles NW of Cle Elum on WA 903 is Roslyn, an old 1884 coal mining town and filming site of the popular 1990s television show, Northern Exposure. Readers of a certain age may remember that Roslyn was called Cicely, Alaska, in the comfortable comedy. Look for the famous camel mural outside the Roslyn Café and The Brick bar and restaurant in the series and Roslyn Museum, all on Pennsylvania Ave. The Brick claims to be the oldest continuing bar in the state. The last time we were in Roslyn one could still buy tv series memorabilia such as mugs, tee shirts, etc. at the Memory Makers store. Also on that street is the Miners' Memorial statue, dedicated to the miners who lost their lives while mining coal.

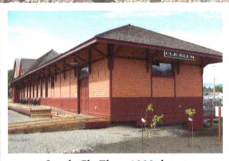

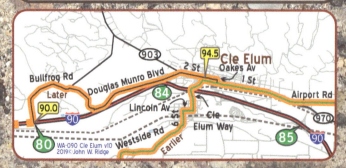

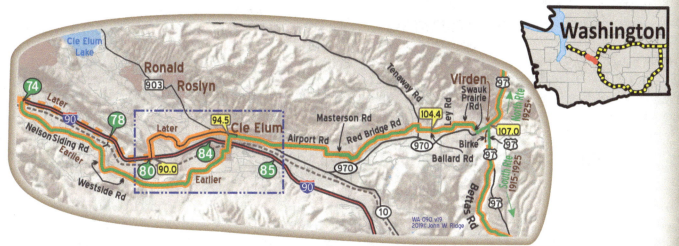

WA-094.5 Cle Elum (it means "swift water")

Park. City Camp, 50c. Cabins.

HOTEL TRAVELERS modern; outside rooms are best. Rates: sgl. $1.50-$2.50; dbl. $2; bath $3.

RELIABLE AUTO CO., finely equipped and has good name. Labor $1.50; towing $4 hr. Ph. 91. Rest room. COX MOTORS, Ford, is open until 9 p. m. MH1928

The market for Cle Elum coal has been reduced, partly because of the development of water power, but mining is still important to the town. Cle Elum also ships lumber and farm and dairy products. HOTHOUSES (visitors welcome), at the end of St. E., grow and ship 100,000 blooms of roses and carnations a year. WPA-WA

CLE ELUM RANGER STATION, headquarters of the Cle Elum Ranger District of the Wenatchee National Forest. This district embraces the headwaters of the Yakima, Cle Elum, and Teanaway Rivers and, because of its high mountains and dense forests, conserves an important part of the water supply for irrigation projects in the Kittitas and Yakima valleys. WPA-WA

221 E 1st St. (the later Yellowstone Trail) **Telephone Museum**. Displays cover the history of telephone technology from 1901 to 1970. See the 15-foot long switchboard and the crank-style phone. This was the site of the last operator-assisted switchboard in the Northwest Bell system.

501 E 1st St. **Cle Elum Bakery**. The Cle Elum Bakery has been in operation since 1906. "We still bake our French Bread in the original brick oven which has never cooled in over 100 years," they say. Time for a bun break on the Yellowstone Trail just like travelers did back in the day? Get the lemon tart. It was delicious.

302 W 3rd St. **Carpenter House Museum & Art Gallery**. The 1914 mansion was donated to the Cle Elum Historical Society to "preserve this bit of Cle Elum heritage." Visitors will see Tiffany lamps, etched light bulbs and original furnishings of the elegant life style of a bank president and his pianist wife.

801 Milwaukee Road Depot. **South Cle Elum Rail Yard National Historic District**. There are about 23 sites on view including the 1909 depot, a turntable and a 1919

electric substation to generate the voltage for the Milwaukee Road electric engines used in the mountains. Smokey's Bar B Que in the Depot has replaced the famous "Beanery" restaurant, long the choice of railroad personnel since 1909. The Depot was the site of the train operations, crew changes and all telegraphic communication. Guides through the rail yards provide a narrative of Cle Elum's history and the coming of the railroad. The rail line is part of Iron Horse State Park. Today the old depot is a joy, saved from decay for its second century of life.

WA-103.3

Red Bridge Road and **red brick house**. Between Cle Elum and Ellensburg, the 1915 Yellowstone Trail followed along what is now the Red Bridge Road, and on it still stands the red brick house which was noted in the 1915 *Automobile Blue Book*. Not far beyond, the old road turns south toward Ellensburg, says Washington explorer Dave Habura.

WA-104.4: Swauk Teanaway Grange Hall might be the restored school shown on the 1924 Automobile Club of Washington map. This road gives a sense of "authenticity." Nice drive.

WA-107.0 & WA-N107.0 Decision Point

If you are traveling east, at this point the Trail offers a choice of ways to Spokane. Turn south and you will be on the 1915 "South" route of the Yellowstone Trail through Ellensburg, Yakima, Tri-Cities, Walla Walla and then north through the small towns of the Polouse area.

Turn north at this point and you will be on the "North" route through historic Blewett Pass, Wenatchee, Waterville and Davenport, the 1925-1930 route of the Yellowstone Trail made possible by the improvement of Blewett Pass.

WA-107.0 & WA-N107.0 Decision Pt
To follow the YT North Route,
go to page 27 and read down.
To go west on the YT
stay on this page and read up.
To follow the YT South Route,
go to page 37 and read down.

BLEWETT PASS ROAD HEARING

Commissioners to take up the engineers' report and adopting plans for six to nine per cent grade.

July 9, 1915 Cle Elum Echo

Two months later the headline in the *Echo* read:

BLEWETT GRADE IS FIVE PER CENT
~~~~~~~~~~~~~~~~~~~~~

WORK NEARLY FINISHED ON BLEWETT ROAD

November 15 will see the completion of the Kittitas end of the Blewett Pass highway, seven months early because of favorable weather and available crews.

October 22, 1915 Cle Elum Echo
~~~~~~~~~~~~~~~~~~~~~

GOVERNMENT TO WORK ON BLEWETT

The anticipated cooperation of the U.S. Forest Service in the building of the Blewett Pass highway will be seen this summer.

April 21, 1916 Cle Elum Echo
~~~~~~~~~~~~~~~~~~~~~

BLEWETT PASS TO BE OPEN IN TEN DAYS
CLEAR THREE MILES FROM SUMMIT ON CHELAN SIDE - THIS SIDE ALREADY CLEAR

June 2, 1916 Cle Elum Echo

Note: A friendly rivalry existed between Kittitas and Chelan Counties, who shared the Blewett Pass, as evidenced in this gratuitous sub-headline in the *Echo*, a Kittitas County newspaper, about cleaning snow.

June 9, 1916 *Cle Elum Echo* sub-heading "Farmer Negotiates Mountain Trip Without Difficulty." In 1918 a writer for *Northwestern Motorist* waxed poetic about the beauty and safety of the Blewett Pass (forgiving Chelan County for its troubles there) and encouraged readers to come. Other newspaper headlines of 1915, 1916 and 1918 rejoiced at the ease of driving the Blewett Pass as reported by travelers, albeit a hair-raising trip of tight turns and a yawning canyon next to the narrow road. Not until 1925 did the official YT route move to the north, through the Blewett Pass. Apparently, it took almost 10 years to build the road up to the standards of the Yellowstone Trail Association. ✿

Lodge at Blewett Pass summit

Blewett Pass

Ingalls Creek Rd. original bridge on YT
George Carpenter

In contrast to Snoqualmie Pass, Blewett Pass has been free of snow for one month, and this pass, 1,000 feet higher than Snoqualmie, has been used by automobile tourists between Wenatchee and Ellensburg since the latter part of May.

July 1917, Northwestern Motorist

This route between Cle Elum and Wenatchee [**Blewett Pass route**] will be open from now on for cars that are in good condition to climb grades 12 to 25%. Several fords exist that will probably cause trouble until bridged.

May 19, 1915 Automobile Club of Seattle newsletter

🚗 WA-N129.8 (GPS: 47.46309, -120.67327): Location of landslide that cut old YT (Ingalls Crk. Rd.)

🚗 The route of the YT between WA-N139 (Peshastin) and Wenatchee is difficult to document, probably because of many small alignment changes and major bridge constructions over the years. The marked route is an approximation.

WA-N107.0 & WA-107.0 Decision Pt
To follow the YT North Route,
stay on this page and read down.
To go west on the YT,
go to page 25 and read up.
To follow the YT South Route,
go to page 37 and read down.

WA-N107.0 Virden

(also known as Lauderdale Junction)

WA-N110.1 Liberty

Along with Virden, Liberty is an old gold mining camp with aged and decaying structures and some occupied homes. A replica of an arrastra is displayed. An arrastra is a primitive tool for grinding down rock to get gold out of it, a rude drag-stone mill for pulverizing ores.

WA-N116.5 (Old) Blewett Pass

Between mile 116.5 (Forest Road 9715) and 126.3 is the Old Blewett Pass. US 97 circumvents this great pass which was the route of the old Yellowstone Trail 1925-1930. Finally, in 1925 the road was passable and the Yellowstone Trail Association moved its signs to this north route from the southern, longer route. You really want to drive this old road over Blewett Pass to appreciate the problems of routing a road in the mountains 100 years ago. This Old Blewett Pass (1915) is wiggly with switchbacks, but with wonderful scenery and is not nearly as scary as it once was. The Pass road today is smooth, winding, and very pretty if you're not in a hurry.

Blewett Pass Summit, at (4.071 alt.), is reached after a twisting climb. A rustic lodge overlooks the upper reaches of the Yakima Valley (winding descent; drive carefully). The next few miles southwest are dense forest. The highway passes through the canyon of Swauk Creek, where tunnels and tailing dumps of old mines are still in evidence along the steep sides. This Swauk formation occupies an area of 1,000 square miles, extending from Lake Wenatchee.

Store, gas, phone, two cabins and very fair repair shop. MH-1928

TOP-O'-THE-HILL TAVERN is good. Modern rooms; good beds. Sgl. $1.50; dbl. $2-$2.50; meals 75c. MH-1928

WA-N127.8 Blewett

(2,325 alt., 54 pop.), now only a handful of cabins, Blewett once had a population of more than 250 miners. Prospectors returning from the Caribou and Fraser districts in 1860 wandered into the foothills of the Cascade Mountains and began placer mining on the creeks. Prior to 1879 Blewett was reached only by trail. WPA-WA

Instead of wagons, saddle horses, and pack mules, today shiny new cars and rattling older models are parked under the pines. Numerous perforations visible in the mountain sides around Blewett are test holes sunk by early prospectors to tap quartz veins. Despite the large-scale development of gold mining, a few prospectors continue their lone search for the scarce yellow metal. WPA-WA

WA-N119.3 to WA-N120.1: It is probable that the YT followed Clark Rd. and a spur of Green Canyon Loop to the east in this area but it is not now possible.

The YT apparently ran just north of the present highway from about WA-N115.5 to WA-N116.5 and curved north on to FS 9715. Some of this alignment appears on aerial views.

This mining town, now a ghost town, at the foothills of the Wenatchee Mountains is marked with plaques indicating the spot of gold mines and the old "stamp mill" where several hundred men worked during the 1880s processing gold ore. The mill ceased operations in 1905. The 1878 arrastra (gold or silver grinder) is on the National Register of Historic Places. Today only ruins of the stamp mill, arrastra, tramway, and mines remain from 1800s Blewett.

WA-N140.8 Dryden

(938 alt., 250 pop.), a fruit-packing and shipping center, it was named by the Great Northern Railroad in honor of a noted Canadian horticulturist. WPA-WA

The Dryden Fruit Growers Union was begun in 1909 and it sent out 18 railroad cars of apples. Currently, Dryden is still a supply and shipping point for local farms and orchards.

Hairpin turns on Blewett Rd. 100 years ago
George Carpenter

Same spot today with authors' car in distance

Old Wenatchee Bridge 1908, still extant

The Yellowstone Trail Association to open office here and organize good roads men to secure road improvements of trail.

December 28, 1917 The Leavenworth Echo

Note: Leavenworth? 1917? Leavenworth attracted tourists then and now, but it is four miles northwest of Peshashstin, the closest point on the Trail **after** it was re-routed in 1925. I'll bet there was a Trail supporter in Leavenworth who really wanted the Trail to follow the Sunset highway!

Old Blewett Pass winding, beautiful and paved today

Blewett Pass
Lee Whiteley

Wenatchee's Yellowstone Trail
Auto Camp Office & Gas Station, 1936

 Aerial views and older maps suggest that for a mile south of Douglas the alignment of the YT was probably quite different than today's US 2. As curvatures were reduced, right-angle turns modified to curves and railroad crossings eliminated, clues were often left for the observant traveler. They might provide the basis for a "travel game" for observant youngsters of most any age.

Cashmere

WA

WA-N145.9 Cashmere

(pop. 700, alt. 630 ft.), situated as it is, in the heart of the Wenatchee valley, Cashmere is in the most famous apple district in the world. It has established free camping sites for the use of automobile tourists. The site is situated along the banks of the Wenatchee river. BB1921-9

Pop-1,200. This vicinity is said to produce the greatest quantity of apples per acre in the world. Blewett Garage for towing. American Cafe is best. MH-1928

HOTEL BLEWETT clean and well furnished; some rooms with bath. Sgl. $1.25-$2; dbl. $1.75, with bath $3. MH-1928

WILSON BROS. GARAGE is far best equipped; owners are master mechanics. Labor $1.50; closed at 6 pm. MH-1928

Shaded by locust and maple trees, Cashmere is known as the home of Aplets, the confection of the fairies, sugar flavored with apple juice and enriched by walnuts and Spices. Cashmere is known for the shipment of apples, pears, and cherries. Orchards claim every available foot of valley land. WPA-WA

117 Mission Ave. **Aplets and Cotlets Liberty Orchards Country Store**. You will be delighted with a stop here, munching on apple and apricot juice candies. Since 1920 they have made fruit candies the same way. You can watch them do it and read their history. Free samples! No doubt Yellowstone Trail travelers were aware of this famous Turkish Delight confection.

600 Cotlets Way. **Cashmere Museum & Pioneer Village**. The museum has a fine collection of Pioneer and Native American artifacts. The Village has 20 pioneer structures, some original, and a Great Northern Railroad caboose. The waterwheel behind the museum is on the Mission Creek bed and is on the National Register of Historic Places.

WA-N150.7 Sunnyslope

WA-N158.4 Wenatchee "The Apple Capital of the World"

(pop. 4,500, alt. 639 ft.), is situated at the confluence of the Columbia and Wenatchee rivers in a sea of apple orchards with the foothills of the Cascades a few miles away. Mounts Rainier, Hood and Baker are seen from Saddle Rock. The Wenatchee district produced 9,000,000 boxes of apples in the fall of 1919, a larger production than any other apple district - in the world. BB1921-9

If you are lucky enough to arrive in late summer you may see oceans of yellow wheat fields undulating in the breeze. In the spring the apple blossom colors and smell are delightful.

Downtown Wenatchee Historic District is roughly bounded by Columbia, N Mission, 1st, and Kittitas Sts., a stretch of two blocks wide and four blocks long. Most buildings are listed on the National Register of Historic Places.

3 N Worthen St. and Orondo. **Pybus Market** is in a restored warehouse near Riverfront Park in the Grandview Historic District. The district, encompassing 34 acres, is a collection of commercial, mixed-use, and warehouse buildings located in the central business district of Wenatchee downtown. We mention this site because of the historicity of it. Look at this particular 100-year-old warehouse with its high ceiling. Although Trail travelers probably did not visit warehouses, repurposing old buildings is preserving history.

127 S Mission St. **Wenatchee Valley Museum & Cultural Center** showcases local and regional history, natural sciences and the arts on four floors. Features offered are field trips, Ice Age Floods information, apple production processes, a miniature railroad and a theater pipe organ.

In 1931 Clyde Pangborn and Hugh Herndon made the first transpacific airplane flight from Japan to the U.S., landing in Wenatchee. Look at a globe. Trace the route from Japan to Alaska to Canada to Wenachee. The pilots belly-landed, having jettisoned landing gear to conserve fuel. The propeller of the plane is displayed here.

1005 N Wenatchee Ave. (Yellowstone Trail). Note the **Gesa Credit Union building**. It is standing on the site of the 1928 Yellowstone Trail Auto Camp. The beloved Chieftain Restaurant and Motel grew out of the Yellowstone Trail Auto Camp, then was auctioned off in1997.

YELLOWSTONE TRAIL CHANGES ITS ROUTE

The change of the route of the Yellowstone Trail to go through Wenatchee instead of Yakima was officially announced, shortening the distance between Seattle and Spokane by 143 miles.

May 8, 1925 Cle Elum Echo

WAYSIDE

Twenty-two miles north of Orondo on US 97 is the turn-off to Chelan, the small town at the foot of spectacular **Lake Chelan**. The lake is worth the boat day trip on this third deepest lake in the U.S. "Chelan" is the Wapato word for deep water. They knew. You hardly know that you are on 1,486 feet of water which extends nearly 400 feet below sea level. You do notice that there is a lot of water, 52 square miles in area, and that there are no roads on either side of your watery highway. Mountains on all sides preclude such construction. The cottages at the few picturesque stops en route are reached only by boat or air. The Chelan dam across the Stehekin River was built in 1927, creating the lake, but latter-day Yellowstone Trail travelers could have detoured to the river or detoured to this larger lake.

Your boat arrives at the north end of the lake at a little, primitive village, Stehekin. Valhalla it is. Enjoy the shore line under the many trees in complete quiet. Or, take a short tour from the visitors' center to learn of the area's protected status in the Lake Chelan National Recreation Area. There are a few buildings scattered among the trees. A National Park Service bus is available to Rainbow Falls. There was a forest fire there in 2016. We don't know the extent of the damage.

Old YT seen below Hwy 2
Jim Marx who bicycled the entire YT

Pine Canyon
1918 Automobile Blue Book

The Waterville Hotel in the early days

Douglas County Historical Museum
with statue of settler dousing
Jim Marx

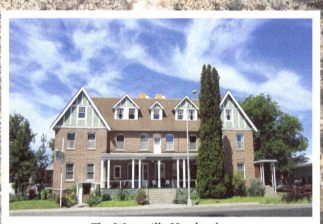

The Waterville Hotel today
Mark Mowbray

WA-N159.7 Columbia River Bridge (1908)

The Columbia River Bridge, also known as the Old Wenatchee Bridge, was built by the Washington Bridge Company in 1908, primarily as a means to carry irrigation water pipelines across the Columbia River. It was the first road bridge over the Columbia south of Canada. As originally built, the bridge carried a 20.5-foot (6.2 m) wide timber roadway, with additional ability to carry a street railway. Today it is pedestrian only and on the National Register of Historic Places. It is fun to walk in the wake of the Yellowstone Trail.

WA-N176.1 Orondo

The village, on the Columbia River, is at the mouth of Pine Canyon.

WA-N180 Pine Canyon

Pine Canyon Road carried Yellowstone Trail travelers from the Columbia River to Waterville, a difference of 2,000 feet in altitude. Today Pine Canyon Road is closed to vehicle traffic, but you can still explore on foot from US 2 to appreciate the spectacular scenery of the yellow pines and hairpin turns surrounding the difficult road that climbed that 2,000 foot difference between the upper plateau and the Columbia River from 1915-1950. The map on page 63 shows the complex route of the old road. See **Trail Tale: Pine Canyon**, page 63.

WA-N186.4 Waterville

pop. 1,000; a county seat and a grain center.

HOTEL WATERVILLE, thirty rooms, all outside; five with bath and one-half with running water. Sgl. $l-$2.25; dbl. $1.50, with run. water $2.25, with bath $3.25; meals 50c.

WILSON MOTOR CO. is best equipped; Buick and Chevy dealer. Good mechanics. Labor $1.25, ph. 862 for wrecker until 10 p. m. Ladies' rest room.

WATERVILLE MOTOR CO., Ford is open until 10 p. m. MH-1928

Waterville is a gateway between western Washington and the agricultural areas of the Columbia Plateau to the east. The economy is supported mainly by agriculture and forest products. "Waterville maintains its historical feeling as if caught in a wrinkle in time. The patchwork quilt of colorful wheat fields and hidden coulees make memorable subjects for photos," says a Waterville Historic Hotel brochure. Much of its main street is on the National Register of Historical Places.

102 E Park St. (Yellowstone Trail). **Waterville Hotel** is a great hotel, representative of good hotels of the past. Built in 1903. What can one say about a 118 year old gracious lady and Waterville landmark that hasn't already been said? Its exterior is little changed, still retaining the Jacobean style architecture. The interior keeps the historic charm of yesteryear while offering a comfortable library, WIFI, and central heating. The proprietors are knowledgeable about the Yellowstone Trail.

124 W Walnut St. (kitty corner across S Central/E Park St. from the Waterville Hotel). **Douglas County Historical Museum**. This museum and historic Waterville Hotel have something in common: they are both on the Yellowstone Trail and share an interest in it. As you enter the museum, note the Yellowstone Trail interpretive sign just outside the door. This museum rocks! With real rocks, that is. It has over 4,500 rock and mineral specimens, some glowing under UV light in a dark room. It also has an iron meteorite, the largest in Washington. Unique is the mural and story of moving goods up from and down to the Columbia River by bucket, a 2,000 foot drop!

WA-N200.0 Farmer

Going west, the tops of the Cascades can be seen.

WA-N207.8 Spencer (Ghost town)

You won't find Spencer on any current Washington map or atlas. The local historical society folks did not know of its existence. Heck, even the ghosts have left this ghost town. But it did exist in Yellowstone Trail days. Perhaps it was even a stage coach stop before that. Sunset-hwy.com declares that "Spencer was barely ever a town. There was an early telephone line and a wagon road and perhaps early automobile traffic used it to cross the coulee." Well, traffic did indeed use it - those following the Yellowstone Trail. They probably navigated the Trail up out of the coulee on the west side of the cliff face along a narrow cut.

Evidence that people did live there and perhaps served Trail travelers lies in the fact that several years ago curious history buffs found bits of a town there: a piece of china from an old hotel and an old Washington license plate. Perhaps there was a gas station of sorts to aid Trail travelers as they rested at the hotel. We include Spencer as a bit of the Trail's lost history.

Between WA-N202.9 and 207.0 is an excellent example of the early alignment. Fun, but it has been reported closed on occasion.

Sun Lakes - Dry Falls State Park

Just about four miles southwest of US 2 (the Yellowstone Trail) on WA 17 is **Sun Lakes - Dry Falls State Park**. Dry Falls is one of the great geological wonders of North America. Carved by Ice Age floods, the former world's largest waterfall is now a stark cliff, 400 feet high and 3.5 miles wide. In its heyday, the waterfall was five times the width of Niagara Falls. Now it is just a vestige of the humungus, prehistoric (Glacial Lake Missoula) floods that scoured the land several times from western Montana through Idaho, Washington, and Oregon at the end of the last ice age. It carved and moved whole swaths of land and rivers, and formed immense cuts, called coulees. We're talking about water the size of Lake Ontario rushing over the land, carving the sights in the Channeled Scablands. See map on page 11. The falls began 20 miles to the south but receded upstream through erosion. The retreat of the falls gave birth to the canyon below, the lower Grand Coulee. The flood spewed several cubic miles of rock over vast areas downstream. Today the falls overlook a desert oasis filled with lakes and abundant wildlife. See page 13 for more about the geology.

Sun Lakes - Dry Falls State Park

The Dry Falls Dam (in Coulee City) flooded the YT alignment just west of Coulee City in the mid-1940s and the highway was rerouted on the dam. The dam created Banks Lake which plays a substantial role in the production of electricity at Grand Coulee Dam and in agricultural irrigation. It also provides a spectacular drive along its east side. Follow it to or from Grand Coulee Dam.

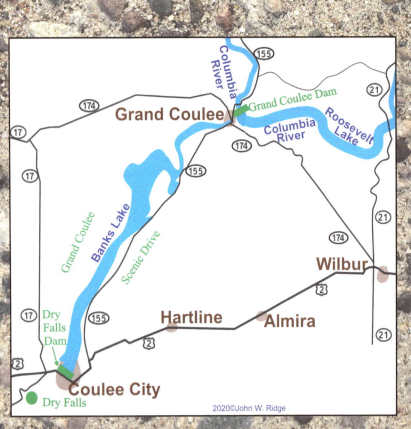

2020©John W. Ridge

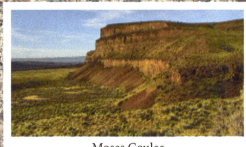

Moses Coulee
Dave Habura

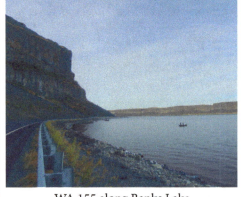

WA 155 along Banks Lake
created by Coulee City's Dry Falls Dam

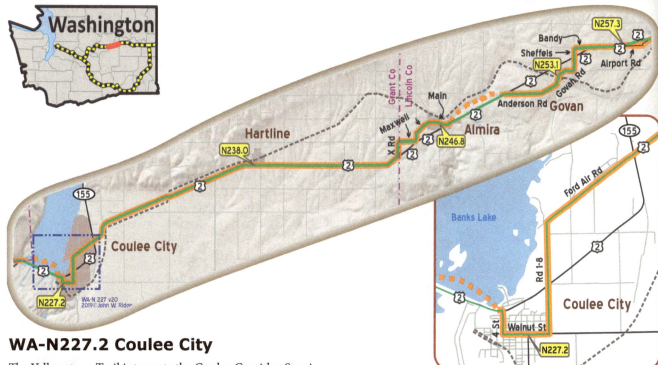

WA-N227.2 Coulee City

The Yellowstone Trail intersects the Coulee Corridor Scenic Byway in Coulee City, Washington.

pop. 500, is sustained by wheat, apples and stock. Gateway to the Grand Coulee region, one of the six leading geological wonders. Two country hotels, the Coulee leads. Aldrich Motors, Ford, is open late. Young's Camp, 50c, seven plain, clean cabins, $1 run. water in some. CITY GARAGE is most modern and leads. Labor $1.50. Tire service. Ph. 26 for wrecker until 9 p. m. MH-1928

DRY FALLS STATE PARK, [Just south] A rustic stone VISTA HOUSE (Visitors register) overlooks the scarred walls of the extinct falls, where a cataract many times greater than Niagara once plunged, a gigantic waterfall with a sheer drop of 417 feet and a width of nearly 3 miles. The dry falls were caused by the erosive glacial waters, the ice cap having changed the course of the Columbia River. Various geologic periods are illustrated in the strata of the walls, and leaves and trees are fossilized in the strata. A trail winds from Vista House down the face of the cliff to the bottom of the falls. At the base of the cliff are Perch and Deep lakes. WPA-WA

The Coulee Corridor Scenic Byway in Coulee City, goes to Grand Coulee Dam and Dry Falls.

WA-N238.0 Hartline

Hartline has rows of towering wheat elevators along the railroad tracks. West of Hartline is evidence of a large lake that once flooded the area. Dry Alkali Lake has deposits of silt, sand and gravel several hundred feet deep and scablands appear again. WPA

WA-N246.8 Almira

Nearly 750,000 bushels of wheat are handled each year through its warehouses. WPA

The landscape alternates between wheat fields and barren rock, called "channeled scablands."

Map in tourist brochure, about 1930.
No Grand Coulee Dam and no Banks Lake

In Wilbur, the YT may have followed Portand St. and Cole St. on the west side of town.

WAYSIDE

Traveling the Yellowstone Trail today you will probably want to take a wayside north to the **Grand Coulee Dam**. Traveling from the Trail/US 2 to the Dam you must take WA155 north from Coulee City, a lovely ride along Banks Lake. Man-made Banks Lake, created by the Coulee City Dam begun in1933, flooded and sank the road once used by the Yellowstone Trail, so the closest to the Trail that we can now route you is to follow present US 2. Of course, the old Trail traveler would not have stopped to see the non-existent Grand Coulee Dam. Travelers then were encouraged to visit the Grand Coulee River, thought to be the old bed of the Columbia River. All is forgiven for flooding out the original Trail with this man-made, beautiful irrigation reservoir.

You all know about the massive Grand Coulee Dam itself, but seeing it in action is something else! It is the largest hydroelectric power producer in the U.S., providing electricity to 11 western states, one of the top 10 largest producers in the world. And know that it has many related jobs: flood control, power generation, irrigation, fish migration flows, recreation. Stay for the evening laser show at the visitors' center … with sound. We loved it! ✿

1920s concrete west of Spokane near Reardon

The YT west of Davenport

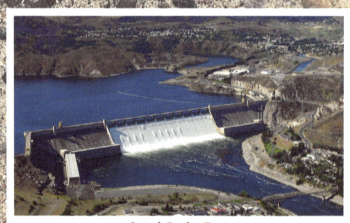
Grand Coulee Dam
Dept. of Interior/Reclamation

A rack of 20th Century road maps in an abandoned gas station in Hartline, early 21st century
Dave Habura

Lava bed at Fictenburg west of Davenport

WA

WA-N260.1 Wilbur

Completion of the Grand Coulee Dam will increase Wilbur's importance as a trading center. A 125-foot municipal swimming pool offers the only facilities for swimming within many miles. WPA-WA

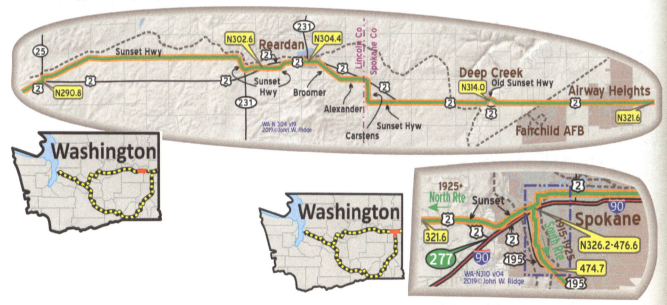

WA-N269.0 Creston

The aforementioned Missoula Floods of the last ice age produced "rushing waters as deep as 200 feet around here, scoured the land across multiple channels miles wide and shaped river valleys and coulees with vertical cliffs on all sides," wrote Yellowstone Trail researcher Dave Habura. What is left is red soil and flat valley floors.

WA-N290.8 Davenport

pop. 1,350; county seat of dairy, stock raising and wheat farming country. The LINCOLN HOTEL is partly modern. Public swimming pool. Sans Souci Camp, 50c, small but good; 4 small cabins, $1. PIONEER MOTOR CO. Ford is a good agency. MH1928

Davenport is surrounded by rolling wheat fields and basaltic coulees on the Columbia Plateau.

It still serves as a central collection point for wheat, with most of it shipped out by truck or railcar.

600 Seventh St. **Lincoln County History Museum**. Through a complete set of programs, the Society collects, preserves, and makes available to all citizens, the heritage of Lincoln County. Visits by school children include a demonstration of pioneer skills and hands-on programs with artifacts from Lincoln County. The Society makes available video presentations on a variety of historical subjects.

WA-N304.4 Reardan

Red soil, desert, scablands, and rolling, treeless terrain describes the landscape west of Reardan, the result of the great Missoula Ice Age Floods.

Three miles west of the center of Reardan on Sunset Highway/Old State Highway (Yellowstone Trail) at 27300 Sprinkle Rd. N is the **Inland Northwest Rail Museum**. Their website describes 13 of their 30 different cars and engines in their collection, including a "diner" car that looks just like a real diner with about 14 swivel seats lined up to a long counter. A box car from 1898 is the oldest piece of rolling stock in their collection.

WA

WA-N326.2 & WA-476.8 Decision Pt

To follow the YT North Route, stay on this page and read up.

To go east on the YT, go to page 61 and read down.

To follow the YT South Route, go to page 59 and read up..

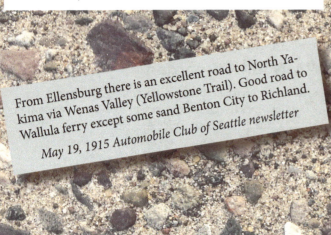

Newspapers reported excitedly for three days the meeting of the Washington state chapter of the Yellowstone Trail Association at Ellensburg in January, 1920. The Yellowstone Trail Association national office made suggestions for topics that should be discussed, but state groups made democratic decisions about Trail marking, location, assessments, improving the Trail locally and Trail information bureaus. The group went on record endorsing the federal Townsend bill for a national highway system, and opposed charging fees for automobiles in national parks. ✿

COOLEY TO TALK AT LOCAL CHAMBER
YELLOWSTONE TRAIL GENIUS TO BE HERE

Mr. Cooley is not pleased with the Roads Committee of the Chamber and has asked to present his proposition to the entire Chamber. Officers of the Chamber told the trail man that this organization could not, under its constitution, pledge any money other than for the current year and that they would recommend that its policy be continued.

February 20, 1923 Evening Record (Ellensburg)

Note: Apparently the idea of two or three year memberships in the Yellowstone Trail Association had been floated to this group by Hal Cooley, General Manager of the Yellowstone Trail Association, and had been rejected by the local Roads Committee. Cooley traveled from South Dakota only to be rejected. That didn't happen often to him, a dynamic speaker and an impassioned leader who traveled to all Trail towns; he was a very early PR man.

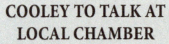 WA-107.0: Bettes Rd. is a good "authentic" drive. Although a 1916 BB suggests that WA 97 might have been used. Needs research! The 1924 Automobile Club of Washington called it Horse Canyon Rd. – with a 10% grade.

The original route apparently used Notcho Ln. between WA-114.1 and WA-115.0. It is now private.

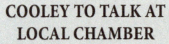 WA-119.3 to WA 120.1: It is probable that the YT followed Clarke Rd. and a spur of Green Canyon loop to the east in this area but it is not now possible.

Woldale School

The Twenty-Third *Psalm*
The Ford is my auto; I shall not want another.
It maketh me to lie down beneath it;
    it soureth my soul.
It leadeth me into the paths of ridicule
    for its namesake.
Yea, though I ride through the valleys
    I am towed up the hill.
For I fear much evil. Thy rods and
    thy engines discomfort me;
I annoint my tires with patches;
    my radiator runneth over.
I repair blow-outs in the presence of mine enemies
Surely, if this thing followeth me all the days of my life,
I shall dwell in the bug-house forever.
From *Funny Stories about the Ford*
Vol. I, Presto Publishing Co., Hamilton, Ohio. 1915 ✿

WA-107.0 = WA-N107.0 Decision Pt
To follow the YT North Route,
   go to page 27 and read down.
To go west,
   go to page 25 and read up.
To follow the YT South Route,
   stay on this page and read down.

WA-121.8

Woldale School, 1907, at the intersection of Faust and Dry Creek Rds, (GPS: 47.02510, -120.59300) is still there complete with flagpole. This would definitely have been seen by Yellowstone Trail travelers in 1915.

Note the scenery. If you are traveling east you will ask: Where are the forests of the Cascades? Now the scenery is drier, rolling, small trees only, sagebrush. The wetter weather does not make it over the Cascades. From here east and through the Palouse area be prepared for a different Washington. Ellensburg experiences only about nine inches of precipitation a year and much sunshine. If you are traveling west you will welcome the cool forests of the Cascades.

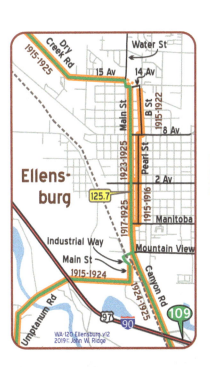

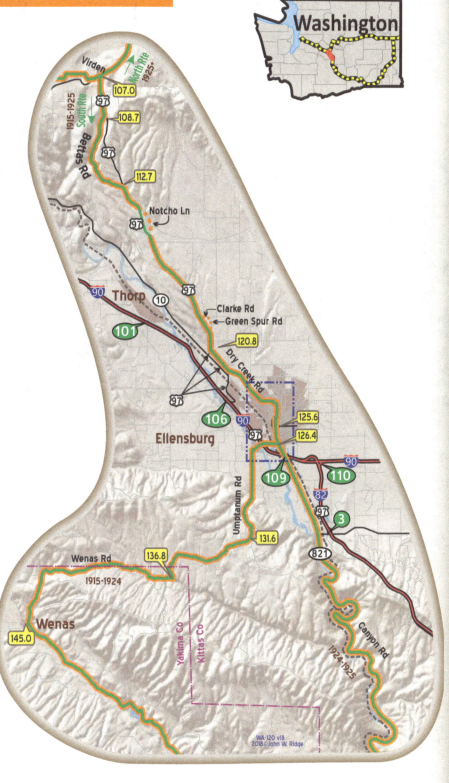

WA

The Davidson Building with its landmark turret, Ellensburg

Kittatas County Historical Museum, Ellensburg

Enough said

The YT on Wenas Rd. from Ellensburg to Yakima

WA-126.4: 1924 Automobile Club of Washington describes the Wenas Rd. (west and south from this point) as "the Old Road to Yakima" and the Canyon Rd. to the south as "the New Road to Yakima."

Wenas Rd. was the YT until about 1924, then Canyon Rd. was completed and became the YT. The Wenas Rd. is a more "authentic" driving experience, but the Canyon Rd. is a very scenic route. It also has the old tunnels from the original 1924 alignmen.

Basalt walls and disused tunnel on YT/Yakima Canyon Rd.

WA-165.6: "The Old Yakima Road" (Wenas Rd.) meets "the New Yakima Road", the Canyon Rd. (821/823). The abandoned Twin Tunnels are about five miles north of this point on 823/821. There is a real possibility that coming from the north, the Canyon Rd. route, rather than turning west onto 823, roughly followed 821 into Yakima. Some of the route would then be under I-82. There is a local research opportunity here!

WA

WA-125.7 Ellensburg

(pop. 6,000, alt. 1,510 ft.), is the metropolis of Kittitas valley, of which 60,000 acres are irrigated. Splendid highways lead to and from this city. One of the state normal schools is located here. BB1921-9

There are at least 31 historic buildings downtown that are still standing and that Yellowstone Trail travelers would probably have seen. The downtown historic district runs from Main St. east to Pine, and 3rd Ave. north to 5th. Seventeen buildings were built in 1889 after the big fire. We cannot feature all of them. Local "Walking Tours" guides by the Chamber of Commerce will lead you to them.

Pearl St. was the route of the Yellowstone Trail 1915-1916. Today, fourteen historic buildings still stand, housing a variety of businesses. When Main St. was improved, the Association moved its signs there 1917-1925. Some of the eight historic buildings on Main St. sport cast iron decorations. In the late 1800s the fashion in architecture was to upgrade your building with cast iron faces and flourishes such as found on the iconic Davidson Block at Pearl St. and 4th Ave.

111 S Pearl St. **The Yellow Church Café**. Here is something eye-catching and bright yellow. The church was built in 1923 and could have been visited by early Yellowstone Trail travelers of German Lutheran persuasion.

323 N Main St. **The Palace Café** has been serving Ellensburg for over 125 years. It was first opened in 1892, moved once, then settled in its present Pearson Building (built 1908) location in the late1940s.

At 4th Ave. and Pearl St., you'll have to laugh. A large cast-aluminum sculpture of a bull is seen lounging on a park bench. We couldn't resist joining him and neither will you. Although he appeared years after the Trail went down Pearl St., current travelers will remember this artwork and Ellensburg.

NE corner of 4th Ave. and Pearl is the **Davidson Building**. This 1889 building is one of the most recognizable landmarks in Ellensburg with its steeple-like turret. A three-foot high Phoenix graces the south facade, a symbol of the rise of the building which was being constructed when the big 1889 fire took 10 city blocks and 200 homes. Also notice the cast iron decorations on the whole building, a popular style with late Victorian architects.

114 W 4th Ave. (just off the Yellowstone Trail). **Fetterer's Furniture Store** has been there for over 120 years! It might be fun to drop in to see their 120-year-old cash register.

114 E 3rd Ave. **Kittitas County Historical Museum**. It collects, preserves and disseminates materials about the history of Kittitas County. The museum is in the old (1889) Caldwell Block, distinguished by horseshoe-shaped windows.

West end of 3rd Ave. **Northern Pacific Historic Train Depot** (1910). Friends of the Northern Pacific Depot have been working for years to restore the old station using period replacements which are hard to find. As of this writing, we do not know the status of the project.

A large swatch of south central Ellensburg is occupied by **Central Washington University**, begun in 1891 as a Normal School. Today, this place presents most of the facilities and programs associated with much larger universities, including, uniquely, the Chimpanzee and Human Communication Institute at the north end of the campus. There you can observe chimpanzees who speak in sign language. Lab open to the public weekends March to November.

WA-145.0 Wenas

Notice that your map shows two green driving lines. This rare instance indicates that either the Wenas or the Yakima Canyon road, both Yellowstone Trail routes at different years, would be driveable today.

The Wenas Rd. was the original Yellowstone Trail southern route from Ellensburg to Yakima which the Trail followed 1915-1924. Out of Ellensburg, the road goes east through a forest of pine trees and crosses lush creeks and ridges. A view of Wenas Lake is possible. The summit of the Wenas is 3,128 feet, about 100 feet higher than Snoqualmie Pass, then the road dips down to farm country. Recently, mammoth bones were discovered on the Wenas. They are now looking for human bones.

On Sept. 22, 1924, the state engineers completed "the new Yakima Canyon Road that will shorten the distance between Ellensburg and Yakima by approximately 13 miles and will follow practically the water grade" but will also require two tunnels. The road today is very wiggly because it hugs the Yakima River as it wanders through the Yakima Canyon. The two tunnels have long since fallen into disuse. This Canyon route has a landscape of soaring basalt canyon walls at the southern end.

WA-167.1 Selah

The name, Selah, means "calm and peaceful" in the Yakima nation language. From fishing to sheep to pressing apple juice and packing fruit, this town has survived. It affords a great view of Mt. Rainier.

The Yakima Valley, along with other areas of southern Washington, have produced more than half of the apples grown in the U.S. for fresh eating. Before the 1980s, vineyards began replacing apple orchards. Thirty years later there were at least 50 wineries in the Valley. Although they were not there and available to Yellowstone Trail travelers, a trip through wine country today would not be complete without a bit of tasting. The Yakima Valley is approximately 200 miles in length and of great scenic and historic interest throughout.

The YT from the north (now along Wenas Ave. and WA 823) apparently turned west at Naches Ave. for one block and then south on 1st St. for two blocks meeting modern WA 823 again to continue south.

Going south on Wenas Ave. (WA 823) at the intersection with I-82 (Exit 30) stay on WA 823 following the middle of I-82 but not on I-82 and continue on 1st through Yakima. Going north just follow WA 823.

Just north of Yakima, the Wenas Rd. intersects Dusty Puddle Rd. Hmm.

The Yakima River fromYakima Canyon Rd./YT

STATE MEETING OF YELLOWSTONE ROAD ENTHUSIASTS HERE
COUNTY TO ASSIST, WILL BUILD BETTER ROADS
February 12, 1919 Yakima Republic

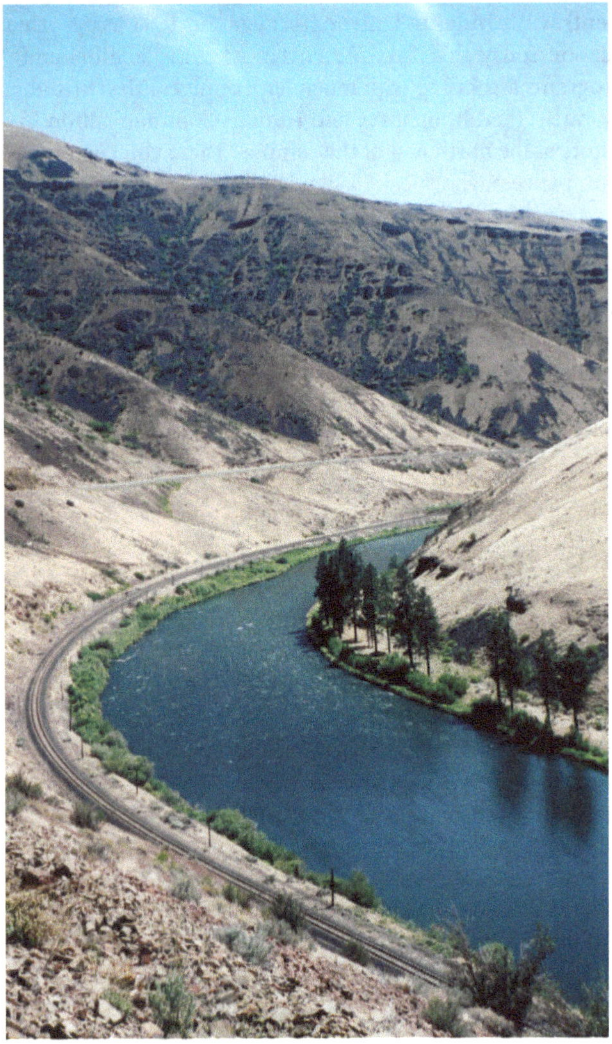

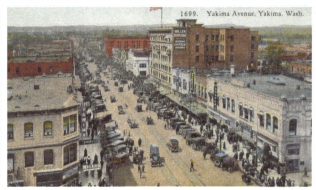

Yakima Ave. c.1913-1919

By 1924 the only Washington roads paved with concrete east of the Cascades were those around Spokane and the Yellowstone Trail from Yakima to Prosser. ❂

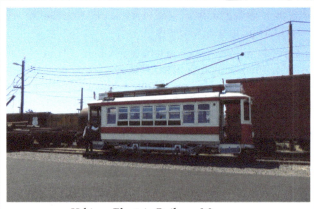

Yakima Electric Railway Museum

Yakima Canyon Basalt

CHANGE IN ROAD OPPOSED
YAKIMA WANTS YELLOW-STONE TRAIL ROUTED AS AT PRESENT
October 31, 1921 Oregonian (Portland, OR)

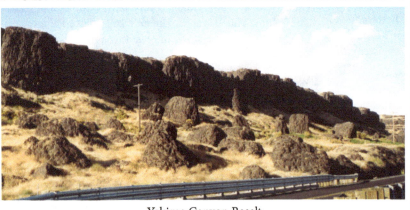

WA-171.2
Yakima

(pop. 25,000, alt. 1,057 ft.), is the chief city and trade center of the famous Yakima valley. From an area under cultivation of little less than 300,000 acres, the agricultural and horticultural products last year were $35,000,000. The city has wide, well-shaded streets connecting with hard surfaced roads. It is on the Yellowstone trail and Evergreen highway. The Yakima valley is irrigated practically its entire length. BB1921-9

As the center of the Yakima Valley apple region, the city gives much publicity to the local apple. Hotels make lobby displays of the fruit, and guests are urged to send boxes of apples to friends. Apple juice cocktails are featured on dinner menus. WA-WPA

Historic Front St. District hosts a collection of nine buildings constructed between 1889 and 1914.

At 32 N Front St. is a 1912 **Northern Pacific Depot**. There is also the old Opera House in the District; defunct as an opera house, it now houses gift shops. Wineries, restaurants and a coffeehouse now enliven the District - much better than dereliction.

2105 Tieton Dr. **Yakima Valley Museum.** A modern, large building houses on two floors the history of the Yakima Valley. It provides new takes on old items. Also, native son Supreme Court Justice William O. Douglas is described as "controversial." Old and musty it certainly is not. Of course, the orchard industry gets space.

306 W Pine St. **Yakima Electric Railway Museum** is listed on the National Register of Historic Places because it is the last authentic, all-original, turn-of-the-century interurban electric railroad in the United States. The Yakima Trolley is the remnant of a once-expansive interurban railway. Presently, approximately five miles of track remain of the original 44, connecting the cities of Yakima and Selah. Electric trains have operated every year since 1907.

19 S 3rd St. **Capitol Theatre.** In 1920 the new theatre featured Vaudeville acts. The City of Yakima purchased the theatre in 1975, but a fire burned most of it. By 1978 donated funds restored the building to its original glory. Today the Capitol hosts an average of 175 events annually as a performing arts facility, including the Yakima Symphony Orchestra, Broadway musicals and a Town Hall series. You might meet "Sparky," the resident ghost.

2008 S 16th Ave. at the airport. **McAllister Museum of Aviation.** This site is included because it was a school for pilots in the Yellowstone Trail days beginning in 1926, although it was just a pasture then. A woman pilot demonstrated flight there in 1913. Stroll about among the old planes.

308 E Yakima Ave. **The Grand Hotel Apartments.** Before it was The Grand it was the Commercial Hotel which had advertised widely by 1915. Well preserved today, it may have been a stop for Yellowstone Trail travelers 100 years ago.

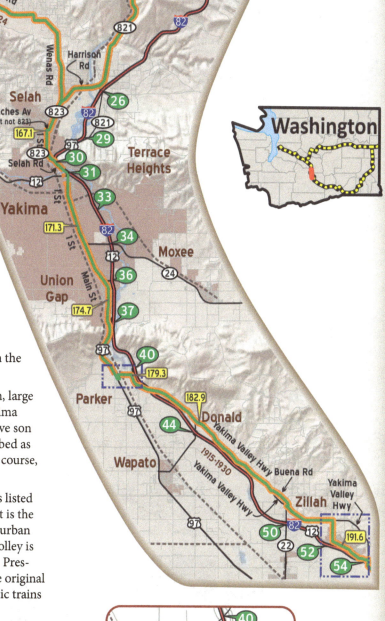

WA

Yakima Nation Museum and Cultural Center. See Wayside to the right.

WA

The Teapot Dome on the YT in early days

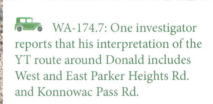 WA-174.7: One investigator reports that his interpretation of the YT route around Donald includes West and East Parker Heights Rd. and Konnowac Pass Rd.

Teapot Dome in the sad days

Teapot Dome saved as a tourist information center, relocated, but still on YT in Zillah

The YT may have entered Zillah using a stair step Cutler Way.

WA-174.7 Union Gap

4508 Main St. (Yellowstone Trail). **Central Washington Agriculture Museum**. This is not just a building but is also 18 acres of outdoor space to wander among 140 tractors dating from the early 1900s and other old farm pieces. There is also a working windmill, a blacksmith shop and two log cabins. Its goal is to show visitors "what it used to take to feed America." Go on a nice day. You might see a bit of Mount Adams and the tip of Mount Reinier.

WA-182.9 Donald

WAYSIDE

At WA-191, turn south on WA 22 for 3 1/2 miles to **Toppenish**.

100 Spiel-yay Loop & Buster Rd. **Yakima Nation Museum and Cultural Center**. The unique building is shaped like a giant Native American winter lodge teepee. It towers and is visible from a long distance. The professionally done displays are very absorbing and sobering. They tell the visitors how they understand their history with focus on their culture and traditions.

22 S B St. **Great American Hop Museum** (as in the ingredient in beer). This is a small museum but very interesting. It's all about hops, the history of the industry, and hop memorabilia. It even includes a short informative movie. Did you know that 75% of the hops used in making beer in the U.S. come from this area? We didn't. We also didn't know that this was the only hop museum in the U.S.

City of Murals. There are around 76 murals painted on businesses' walls so far. Plaques tell what the murals represent, all within a time frame of 1850 to 1950. All mural ideas are vetted by a committee for accuracy. Known artists are invited to guarantee quality. They are a combination of cultural expression and history of the area. Be careful! Flat painted surfaces have three-dimensional detail so don't try walking into them. You can stroll the town or take a horse-drawn carriage ride to see them.

10 Asotin Ave. **Yakima Valley Rail & Steam Northern Pacific Railway Museum.** This unique museum in a restored 1911 depot has a restored telegraph office and numerous displays about Pacific Northwest railroads and the Yakima Valley. Outside the depot are many pieces of Northern Pacific railroad rolling stock from cabooses to boxcars and a 1902 steam locomotive undergoing restoration.

1 S Elm. **Toppenish Museum**. Gold panning, wild horses and early day ranch life top the list of exhibits here.

211 S Toppenish Ave. **Liberty Theatre**. Built in 1915 as the Lois Theatre, it became the Liberty in 1927. Yellowstone Trail travelers would have seen Vaudeville, Chatauqua, and early "talkies" (movies). Note the nice paintings on the exterior. The horses were running freely then. From 1927 to 1984 movies were shown there. At this writing it was undergoing renovation.

WA-191.6 Zillah

Check for Yellowstone Trail signs throughout the valley: Zillah has four.

1st Ave. GPS: 46.40467, -120.26955. Home of the **Teapot Dome Filling Station**, named after the historic oil-for-bribes scandal that brought down President Harding in the 1920s. In 1922 the filling station rested on the Yellowstone Trail (Yakima Valley Highway) at the edge of town, was moved once, then rescued from a near death experience and moved into Zillah to its present, pleasant site in 2012 and used as a travel information station. Learn all about it there.

204 Cheyne Rd. There is a **Christian Worship Center** here. They have a large, humorous sign. It reads "Church of GodZillah."

🚗 WA-191.6: The YT probably followed Railroad St. in the south part of Zillah rather than 1st all the way (with two more RR crossings!). Follow Yakima Valley Highway out of town to get through the area of Exit 54 of I-82.

WA-198.1 Granger

Granger benefited from the Sunnyside Canal which diverted water from the Yakima River for irrigation to this arid land, turning it into lush agricultural and dairy land.

Granger picked the dinosaur as its "mascot" since mastodon tusks and teeth were found nearby in 1958. There are about 30 of the various fiberglass and cement critters here. This has nothing to do with the history of the Yellowstone Trail except it explains the appearance of the many signs of creatures along the highway as you entered the town along the Trail.

Also note the six Yellowstone Trail signs in the community celebrating the short distance the Trail occupied in the town due to I-82 cutting it off. The small community had a great unveiling of the signs in 2015.

"All the lumber you need to build a drag and plans for $1.30 modeled after a U.S. government design." 1915 ad in unnamed newspaper from a Sunnyside lumber company. [Note: Drags were just wooden planks pulled by horses used to smooth out dirt roads.] ☼

In 1925 the Yellowstone Trail picked up its signs from its southern route and placed them on a northern route on "Sunset Highway" through improved Blewett Pass, shortening the route by 133 miles and leaving Grandview, the Zillah Teapot Dome gas station, and all of the southern and eastern towns. Disappointed were many, including famed photographer Asahel Curtis, Grandview resident. The irony was that he was vice-president of the Yellowstone Trail Association at the time they voted on the move! ☼

Grandview pavement
Dianne Hunt

🚗 WA-218.2: In Grandview, the route of the YT is somewhat ambiguous, and the exact way the YT crossed the railroad tracks (Division/4th/Birch) is open to question.

~~~~~~~~~~~~~~~~~~~~~~~~

🚗 WA-227.4: 1916 BB lists the non-Prosser route as an alternative to going through town. In a 1912 map, this northern route was listed as a wagon road, meaning non-auto.

~~~~~~~~~~~~~~~~~~~~~~~~

🚗 WA-252.3 (With the new YT park at WA-253.0): A bridge in West Richland crosses the Yakima River at WA-253.8. *HistoryLink.org Essay 10441* says a bridge was built because school kids need to cross the river. "The bridge, built north of present-day Van Giesen Street, was christened and was used by the YT." So the YT probably followed Fallon Dr. from the west, and crossed the river. On the east side, Google Earth shows probable remains of a road south of the loop now made by MT-224. That is just east of the modern bridge.

GRANDVIEW MAN PATENTS TIRE TOOL

… resembles a large pair of scissors, 24 inches long, which moves the work of removing a clincher tire almost to a pleasure.

December 5, 1924 Grandview Herald

TO GRAVEL EAST SIDE

The property owners were asked to kick in $30/lot, paid over a 5 year period.

March 19, 1926 Grandview Herald

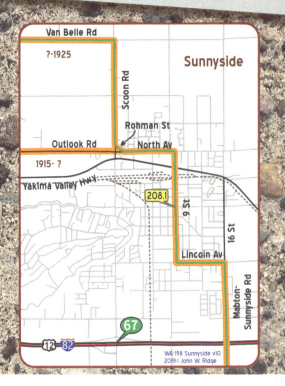

🚗 WA-244.0: There are indications (like the 1924 Automobile Club of Washington strip map #19) that the route through Benton City was more zig-zag. This needs local research.

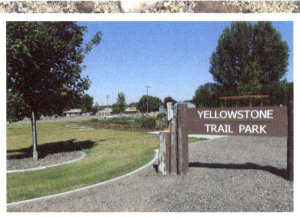

Yellowstone Trail Park with raised planters in the distance, West Richland

WA

WA-208.1 Sunnyside

704 S 4th St. **Sunnyside Historical Museum**. The museum houses a permanent display of Native American artifacts and pioneer life, including an early cattleman's cabin.

At the junction of Scoon Rd. and North Ave. is small, curved Rohman Dr. All are on the Yellowstone Trail and are marked with Trail signs.

In 1892 Walter Granger dug 25 miles of the Sunnyside Canal that brought water to the north slope and immigrant farmers to the valley and the towns of Sunnyside and Zillah sprang up.

WA-218.2 Grandview

Named for its views of Mts. Rainier and Adams, especially from the Grandview Pavement.

Of most interest to us is the **Grandview Pavement Rd./ Yellowstone Trail** on the west side of town between Mabton-Sunnyside Rd. and Apple Way. This three mile stretch was, until 1997, the original pavement of the Yellowstone Trail with the 1921 stamp of the contractor. The road was narrow and bumpy, but it was on the National Register of Historic Places, the Washington Historical Register, the Washington Trust for Historic Preservation and beloved by the 49 families who lived on it and fought for years to retain the original. The road passes very near the home of famed photographer Asahel Curtis, whose home is also a declared National Historic Site. In spite of all of its history and adjudged historic value by many groups, the road was not only not repaved, it was obliterated.

One of the original 1921 contractor's stamps is at the Ray E. Powell Museum in Grandview. An "interpretive center" consisting of two wooden signs was placed along the Grandview Pavement Road. At this writing, a group is improving the marker site.

Pleasant Rd. and Old Prosser Rd. (Old Inland Empire Rd.). **Cornell Farmstead round barn**, 1916. Watch for signs of hops and apricots growing.

WA-227.4 Prosser

7th St. in Prosser City Park. **Benton County Historical Museum**. See an old general store, 1867 piano, homesteader's shack, pictures of wild horses roaming in the pioneer era and other bits of history of the area.

The firmly established apple industry was joined by, and now surpassed by, grape-growing and the wine industry. Around Prosser alone there are upwards of 30 wineries. One hundred years ago Yellowstone Trail travelers would have seen agricultural advances due to irrigation, but no wineries. Prosser is also a cherry-growing district as evidenced by the Chukar Cherries shop.

WA-244 Benton City

Benton City became a green spot in this arid area with the arrival of irrigation in the middle of the 20th century. This, too, is definitely a part of the wine industry that includes other cities in the Yakima Valley, also the Tri-Cities of Pasco, Kennewich and Richland.

WA-245.3 Kiona

Kiona was an early Northern Pacific railway maintenance station which allowed farmers to ship their many dry farming products. In 1917 the Yellowstone Trail was routed through Kiona. Benton City grew up across the Yakima River and Kiona remains unincorporated.

WA-253.8 West Richland

Austin Rd. & Bombing Range Rd. **Yellowstone Trail Park**. You'd never know that this lovely community park is really a storm-drainage facility with five underground drainage tanks. It is now a community garden with donated, raised planters available for rent. Who knew that the Trail would one day see a useful, new life as host to colorful flowers and veggies.

In 1922, after nine years of cogitation, the "Green Bridge" across the Columbia River between Kennewick and Pasco was finally opened. To the Yellowstone Trail Association it meant completion of their auto route in Washington. It was the first bridge of that size to be entirely financed through stock sales. It was dedicated and opened with great hoopla: "speeches, dancing on the bridge, picnics, visitors from the whole state, car caravans and carnivals," said the Kennewick *Courier-Reporter*. Likening it to the "Golden Spike" ceremony linking railroads, this celebration was called "The Golden Rivet" by some. This bridge obviated the use of the slow, small ferry and was considered a great step toward the future of transportation. For nine years a toll was charged until construction costs had been repaid. The bridge was sold to the towns of Pasco and Kennewick for $1 in 1968 and plans for its replacement began which resulted in the "Cable Bridge" which opened in 1978. ✿

The bridge that carried the Yellowstone Trail across the Columbia River from 1922 to1978 was appreciated by many for its role in the history of south central Washington. A new, vibrant bridge was built just a few feet from the old. So the question arose: what to do with the old one? Still hopeful to retain the historic bridge as a walking/bicycling/pedestrian asset, some citizens formed a strong, vocal group. The group persevered in spite of losing a vote in 1980 of both the State Historic Preservation Office and the Federal Highway Administration. They lost a law suit and also their appeal to the Ninth District U.S. Court of Appeals. They went to "the people's court," publishing their own newspaper, and mailing postcards. Eight years after the 1990 "Green Bridge" demolition and 18 years after the court losses, activist Virginia Devine still got angry during our interview. ✿

The beloved "Green Bridge" between Kennewick and Pasco carried the YT

Graceful cable bridge replaced the old "Green Bridge" (with railroad bridge in front)

🚗 The route through Richland is not well established and needs work; probably the route followed Barth Ave. in the south part of town.

From Richland and into Kennewick the route of the YT is obscured by the construction of modern highways, especially the 240 freeway. While the Columba Park Trail along the Columbia River is a reasonable candidate for the original YT and seems consistent with several maps and BB listings, why is there a West Yellowstone Ave. just north of the railroad tracks a few blocks south of Columbia Park Trail? (Needs local research!)

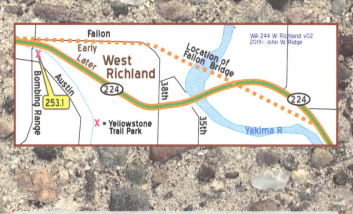

YELLOWSTONE TRAIL MEETING SET
The seventh annual state meeting of the Yellowstone Trail Association will be held at Kennewick October 20. It will coincide with the Kennewick-Pasco Columbia River bridge dedication which will be held the following day.
September 22, 1922 Seattle Star

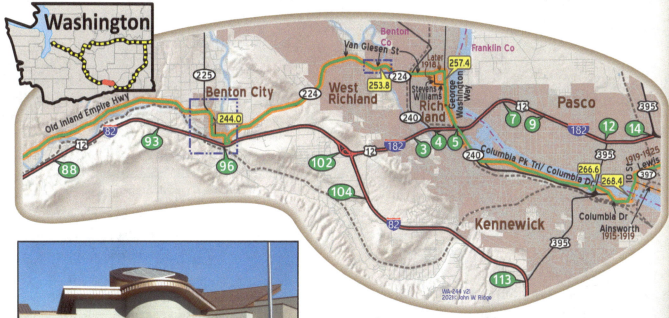

Hanford Reach Interpretive Center, Richland

WA-257.4 Richland

1943 Columbia Park Trl. **Hanford Reach Interpretive Center, above,** tells a wide ranging story of the Hanford nuclear center and the historical and cultural essence of the region. It explores the atomic era and the effort behind the massive secret weapons project. The Manhattan Project (1942-1947), Gallery 2, shows the timeline of the atomic bomb's development here and the $40 billion environmental cleanup.

The museum also features rotating displays of the Grand Coulee River and dam, irrigation projects, and the great Missoula Floods that shaped eastern Washington.

Gold Coast Historic District. Roughly bounded by Willis St., Davison Ave., Hunt Ave., and George Washington Way, this was the area in which scientists lived in government housing while they worked on the Manhattan Project Hanford unit nuclear site.

WA-266.6 Kennewick

pop. 2,700, alt. 365 ft.), the largest town in Benton county, is situated on the Columbia river, and a camp site for tourists is maintained on the banks of this river within the city limits. In the valleys around Kennewick were the winter camps of the Yakima, Snake and Walla Walla Indians. BB1921-9

Columbia Park Trail/Columbia Drive (Yellowstone Trail) is a lovely drive along the Columbia River. The Historic Downtown area is between Kennewick Ave. and Canal Dr. and between Washington and Fruitland Sts. Historic buildings have been renovated and restored.

The 1978 **Ed Hendler Bridge**, a beautiful cable bridge across the Columbia River between Kennewick and Pasco, now stands very near the site of the 1922 Yellowstone Trail bridge, or "Green Bridge" as it was affectionately called. It was finally taken down in 1990, much to the despair of the many who had waged a ferocious battle to preserve it for a walking bridge. The bridge you are on, the cable bridge, is lovely, but memories of the Yellowstone Trail Green Bridge near this very spot live on. There is a small display area near the Kennewick approach to the bridge which features an interpretive sign about the old Green Bridge. For more about the bridge see Kennewick History Bits on preceding page.

205 W Keewaydin Dr. **East Benton County Historical Society Museum**. Built in 1982 through local contributions, the museum features a remarkable, beautiful petrified wood floor. Notice the intricate and varied patterns in this astonishing gift. See also "the forces and movements that shaped the eastern part of Benton County: Indians, the Columbia River, transportation and agriculture," says their exhibit.

WA-269.5 Pasco

The Historic Downtown District follows Lewis St. and Clark St. between Fourth and Tenth Aves. Pasco was long a transportation hub for railroads, river steamers and auto roads.

2503 Sacajawea Park Rd. **Sacajawea State Park & Interpretive Center** is just a little south of the US 12 bridge across the Snake River. The Yellowstone Trail was routed across the bridge's predecessor. Sacajawea Park was not there in Trail days, but you should see it at the confluence of the Snake and Columbia Rivers and refresh your knowledge of Lewis and Clark who camped there.

305 N 4th Ave. **Franklin County Historical Society and Museum** tells the story of transportation and agriculture in the area and the loss of the famous "Green Bridge" in the 1970s.

Before the bridge over the Snake at Burbank was built in 1919 to replace the ferry, the YT apparently followed Ainsworth St. through Pasco.

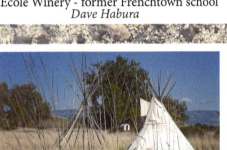
L'Ecole Winery - former Frenchtown school
Dave Habura

The Whitman Monument
Dave Habura

Teepee at Frenchtown Monument site
Dave Habura

When speaking of the Yellowstone Trail the article said, "Thriving towns line the automobile trail and ample accommodations are provided for tourists with garages at frequent intervals with oil stands and other conveniences."
August 1917 Northwestern Motorist

Frenchtown

Below is a very brief summary of a detailed history of Frenchtown delivered by Sam Pambrun in 2005 as part of the 150th Anniversary Observances of the Battle of Frenchtown. The full story may be found at www.frenchtownwa.org/frenchtown. We include this story because it paints a picture of past events in the territory through which the Yellowstone Trail traveler would go, perhaps unknowing of its history. It also makes the Whitman monument at mile 310 more understandable.

About 20 French Canadian Metís (people of mixed blood, Native American and non-Native American) and 20 Objiways, formed the nucleus of the Frenchtown settlement in the Walla Walla Valley about 1813. Frenchtown was not a "town" in the usual sense. It was an area, perhaps 50 miles square, from about present Wallula to near Walla Walla. It was called Frenchtown because French Canadians settled there and married Native American women.

The Canadian Metís who began settling in the Walla Walla Valley, recognizing they were guests of the Waiilatpu and Wallulapam (Cayuse and Walla Walla) Native Americans, sought permission to settle there, and some married into the local tribes. The community essentially became a French and Indian village scattered over 50 square miles with no main street, no saloons, no schools or city council, and land claims were casual. Frenchtown residents considered the Native Americans the governing body of the valley, not the missionaries.

White settlers did not get along well with their neighbors. The Northwest Company began building a post a few miles upriver from the mouth of the Walla Walla River in 1816. As a result of indiscretions by a white man, the Northwest post was attacked. Armed guards appeared and uneasiness prevailed.

When missionaries Dr. and Mrs. Whitman arrived in 1836, there were over a dozen Metís log cabins surrounding their mission. Although they wrote over 100,000 words in articles to their Bishop during their 11-year stay at Waiilatpu, they never once mentioned their Metis neighbors in writing. This raises a question about their relationship with their neighbors. By 1847, the year that the Whitmans and others were massacred, there were well over 50 Metís families living in the Frenchtown area.

Washington Governor Stevens wanted to open more land for white settlement and so drew up the Walla Walla Treaty of 1855. He called into conference the Walla Walla, Umatilla, and Cayuse and granted these sovereign nations a reservation of 510,000 acres in northwestern Oregon. Those tribal nations had not met in conference with Stevens to be put into a reservation. Author Pambrun writes of the emotional arguments posed by the tribal nations at the conference. There clearly was a great difference over the concept of "land ownership." Shortly thereafter, Capt. George McClellan came riding through the Walla Walla Valley announcing that everyone but military must leave immediately, causing the ensuing December Battle of Walla Walla, the last battle between whites and natives in the Walla Walla Valley. The Treaty also triggered a major war between many Oregon and Washington tribes and the government. See the Frenchtown monument at WA-308.0. ⚙

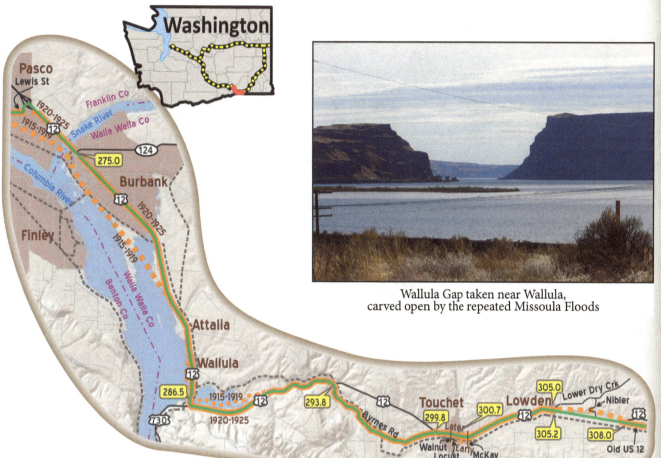

Wallula Gap taken near Wallula,
carved open by the repeated Missoula Floods

WA-275.0 Burbank

The route of the Yellowstone Trail through Burbank is obscured by the changes made with the building of the 1919 Snake River bridge and the later flooding of the Columbia River because of the building of dams. The route between Burback and Wallula is substantially lost due to that flooding. The replacment route is assumed to be similar to today's US 12 alignment.

WA-286.5 Wallula

The first railroad to connect Walla Walla with the Columbia River at Wallula was begun in 1871 and it remained a "railroad town" until mid-20th century. The McNarey Dam and resulting Lake Wallula on the Columbia River drowned the town which packed up and moved two miles to higher ground as the dam was completed in 1954.

 A later (1931) abandoned partial bridge can be seen, and driven to, about 350 feet east of the present US 12 bridge crossing the Walla Walla River just south of Wallula.

WA-300.7 Touchet

The land between Pasco and WallaWalla is so much different from western, forested, mountainous Washington. Here we see dry sagebrush, treeless tracts reminiscent of the Palouse area further east. Vineyards and crops do well only because of heavy irrigation. Now one sees huge windmills powering the area, which looks like a 21st century forest.

In Touchet [TouChee] apparently the YT crossed the tracks twice, at least in 1918, but many maps seem contradictory and inadequate here.

Dams on the Snake River built in 1960s flooded old YT.

WA-305.0 Lowden

WA-308.6 Frenchtown Historic Site and Monument

8364 Old US 12. If you want to learn more about Washington early history, keep your eyes open on Old Hwy 12 (Yellowstone Trail) for a series of markers documenting events. The monument is at St. Rose Cemetery and signs tell the story of the Battle of Frenchtown, 1855.

See History Bit "Frenchtown' (opposite page).

WA-310.7

328 Whitman Mission Rd. Turn south on Swegel Rd. **Whitman Mission National Historic Site and Interpretive Center**. Site of Dr. Marcus Whitman's 1836 Methodist Mission and 1847 massacre, with his wife and others, by Cayuse Indians. The massacre was a poignant example of a clash of cultures and mistrust after 11 years of uneasy coexistence. Traces of the Oregon Trail, which Whitman helped to establish, appear on the property. The massacre shocked Congress into making Oregon a U.S. territory, an unintended consequence of the tragedy. A monument marks the massacre site.

Two sources announced at length the activities of the February 5th meeting of the Washington chapter of the Yellowstone Trail Association in Walla Walla. Reporters wrote enthusiastically about Association members as they wrestled with questions from the group's national headquarters and the establishing of a tourist bureau in the Davenport Hotel at Spokane. January 20 and February 5, 1918 *Walla Walla Bulletin* and February, 1918 *Northwestern Motorist.* ☼

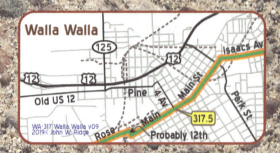

🚗 Entering Walla Walla from the west, the IEH, and thus the YT, followed Wallula Ave. and Rose St. The date of Old US 12 in this area is unknown to the writer but probably after 1925 so the YT never followed it.

WA-311.5 The Oregon Trail and the Whitman Mission off Old US 12 at Sweagle Rd. to Whitman Mission Rd.

The Oregon Trail is a famous 2,170 mile path that emigrant settlers took to the Great West from Independence, Missouri, to Oregon City, Oregon. What may be less well known is that the Oregon Trail also had a spider web of alternative routes. As the trail developed, it became marked by numerous cutoffs and shortcuts. The basic route follows river valleys as grass and water were absolutely necessary. Later, several feeder trails led across Kansas. Many settlers branched off or stopped short of the Oregon goal with their Prairie Schooners and settled at convenient or promising locations along the trail.

One of these alternate routes led through Dr. Marcus Whitman's Methodist mission at Waiilatpu two miles east of Frenchtown amid the Cayuse. From Frenchtown-wa.org we learn that "emigrants starting in the spring from Independence were able to reach the Whitmans' mission by fall. After acquiring provisions at the mission, they followed the Walla Walla River to its mouth, then down the south bank of the Columbia River to the Willamette Valley. Many more emigrants followed in succeeding years through the Frenchtown Historic Site in the traditional homeland of the Cayuse Nation."

The mission was an important stop for settlers, drawing large numbers of them. The Cayuse were suspicious of whites and especially so of their ever-increasing numbers. Dr. Whitman had tried to lessen that suspicion by learning their language, by teaching them to farm and by aiding them during a measles epidemic, fatal to half the local tribe. Sadly, the Whitmans and others were massacred in 1847.

The alternate Oregon Trail runs parallel with and right next to Whitman Mission Rd. as you approach the visitors center. Other remnants of the trail are visible on the property. ☼

Oregon Trail ruts at Whitman Mission
Dave Habura

🚗 WA-317.5: East from Walla Walla, the YT appears to have followed Issacs Ave., to modern US 12 after about 1922. Before that it used the Wellington/Rainier route extended through the area of the modern airport to WA-322.7 at US 12.

Banks at 2nd and Main are listed in 1918 BB.

🚗 WA-335.5: About here the old alignment (1919 USGS) can be seen just west of the modern highway on aerial views.

South of **WA-315.8** 755 NE Myra Rd. is Fort Walla Walla, now a fine museum. It is a terminus of the Mullan Military Road, an important factor in Yellowstone Trail history. See **Trail Tale: Mullan Road**, page 84. ☼

Old Theater, now Macy's, Walla Walla
Dave Habura

WA-317.5 Walla Walla

(pop.15,000) county seat of Walla Walla county, is surrounded by one of the richest agricultural and horticultural sections of the northwest. The old military post, Fort Walla Walla is located here. Six miles west of town, erected on a spot where Marcus Whitman and his associates were massacred by the Indians in 1847, stands the Whitman monument. Wildwood park, a camp ground, is located in the heart of the residence district. It offers accommodations for about 100 machines and is equipped with all amenities. BB1921-9

Walla Walla served as the regional economic center for several decades. Today it sports more than 60 wineries, has restored the charming historic buildings on Main St., sports greenery everywhere and hosts a very sophisticated and alive place. Walla Walla also has 24 historic houses of late 1800s and early 1900s.

SW corner of 4th and Main Sts. **Dacres Hotel**. Opened in 1899, James Dacres erected a "first-

class" hotel which was advertized as "one of the most up-to-date and finest hotels in the country." The Dacres Hotel remained in business until 1963. Currently, the building houses Main Street Studios which features lively musical events. It was added to the National Register of Historic Places.

6 W Rose St. (Yellowstone Trail). **Marcus Whitman Hotel & Conference Center**. This 1928 hotel has been the pride of Walla Walla since it was built, causing a city ordinance to declare that no building could be built higher than the hotel. The ordinance is still in force today. From the 1970s to 1990s the hotel was used for subsistence housing, thereafter receiving restoration to its former glory. Some pieces of the original hotel are still displayed such as fine wood paneling and trim and the old boxes for room keys, a clock and phone booths (remember those?). The original lobby terrazzo floor has been restored. Just walk in and look around to see what later Yellowstone Trail travelers enjoyed.

755 NE Myra Rd. (intersects with Rose St., the Yellowstone Trail) then turn north on Poplar St. to **Fort Walla Walla Museum**. The first Fort Walla Walla was operated from 1856 to 1910, comprising 1,280 acres of fort, farm and forest. In 1917, the fort trained men for World War I. In 1921, the fort and property were deeded to the Veterans Administration where 15 original buildings from the military era remain. Today, the complex contains a park, a museum, and a VA Medical Center. The museum offers living history performances each season.

54 E. Main St. (Yellowstone Trail). **American Theater** 1917-1926 then changed ownership and was called the Liberty. Now it is part of Macy's store with the inclined theater floor leveled. The theater once boasted a gigantic Wurlitzer organ to accompany the silent films or serve visiting performers with its thunderous power. The decorative Dutch exterior seems somehow out of place.

111 N 6th Ave. The historic **Gesa Power House Theatre**. The 120-year-old building was once the Walla Walla Gas Plant, built to produce coal gas and pipe it underground to light Walla Walla. The building was converted to generate electricity around 1905. In 2011, the interior of the building was transformed into a state-of-the-art performing arts theater. The interior design was inspired by the intimacy of Shakespear's Blackfriars Theatre. Plays and musical entertainments are featured now.

416 N 2nd Ave. **Northern Pacific Railway Passenger Depot** (1914) on the northern edge of the business district. The red brick structure offered the usual services - ticket office, separate men's and women's waiting rooms, freight office. The building also featured a dramatic square tower that served as a visual landmark and an observation deck for the rail yards. Remodeled in 1931, the square tower was retained. Passenger service ended in 1956 and freight service was discontinued in the mid-1980s. In 1988, the building was rehabilitated and became The Depot with restaurant and shops. It is on the National Register of Historic Places.

214 N Colville St. **Kirkman House Museum**. One of Walla Walla's grandest mansions-turned-museum was saved from further deterioration and destruction in 1974 and was restored to its original 1880 Victorian glory. It reflects the life of a self-made wealthy man who was also civic-minded. The home shares stories of the early days of Walla Walla through exhibits, programs and events. The home, furnished with family and period pieces, illustrates daily Victorian life.

55 W Cherry St. **Whitehouse-Crawford Restaurant**. Somewhat pricey, but it is housed in a remodeled 1904 sawmill and the food gets rave reviews. Why not go and enjoy the architecture that Yellowstone Trail travelers may have seen?

Dayton Historic Depot
Dave Habura

Columbia County Courthouse in Dayton, 1887
Dave Habura

Waitsburg Hardware and Mercantile at left.
Cast iron trim on Morgan Bldg. at right edge.
Dave Habura

WAYSIDE

2.5 miles northeast of Dayton on Patit Rd. is a most amazing display. There you will find 80 life-sized steel silhouette sculptures depicting a typical Lewis & Clark encampment. The citizens of Dayton created this tableau as part of the Lewis and Clark Bicentennial. In May of 1806 Lewis and Clark passed through what became Dayton. The layout is a re-creation of the camp based partially upon Lewis and Clark journals.

Lewis and Clark encampment statues. Envisioned by Dayton resident George Touchette, approved by the Washington Lewis and Clark Bicentennial Commission, supported by the Washington State Historical Society, and cast by the Northwest Art Casting in Umapine, OR.

HISTORY BITS

WA-338.2 Waitsburg

(pop. 1,400, alt. 1,268 ft.), is one of the oldest towns in the state of Washington, being founded in 1862. Eighteen miles southeast is the site of old Fort Walla Walla, which was manned by regular troops in the early days and was a source of refuge from the Indians for the pioneers. BB1921-9

Territorial Charter required an annual Fall Festival to relive historic demonstrations of churning butter, making candles, sewing sacks for wheat. The area is characterized by loess covering lava, low rolling hills and wheat fields.

132-134 Main St. (Yellowstone Trail). **J. W. Morgan Bldg. and Waitsburg Hardware and Mercantile** seem to be all of a piece, pressed together. However, only the Morgan building is dated - 1892. The adjacent hardware store is going strong. The historic J. W. Morgan building is a primary structure in the Historic District. The trim is cast iron and pressed metal. Yellowstone Trail writer David Habura says that that cast iron store front trim by Mesker Brothers was popular in the late 1800s and early 1900s. There are four such decorated store fronts in Waitsburg.

330 Main St. **Bruce Memorial Museum**. Built in1883 in the Victorian style, the home was saved in 1971 and completely restored and furnished by the Waitsburg Historical Society.

208 Main St. **Plaza Theatre**. Although it has been closed for several years, one can drive by this historic 1928 movie theater in the Historic District and appreciate its Moorish style, a two-story structure with gray and red brick trim. By 1928 "talkies" were the thing, but there still was the big Wurlitzer organ there.

WA-348.0 Dayton

Main street in Dayton runs along the line of the old Indian trails leading from the Mexican border to British Columbia. In1806 Lewis and Clark on their return trip passed thru what is now the town of Dayton followed by Capt. Bonneville in 1834, and in 1836 the missionaries, Dr.Whitman and Mr. and Mrs. Spaulding. BB1921-9

There are many excellent fishing streams and camping sites in this vicinity. The town maintains a tourist park, in which is built a large concrete swimming tank. The widely advertised "Skookum" brand of apples are raised here in abundance. BB1921-9

The Palouse is a huge area of fertile countryside and ancient silt dunes, one result of the massive, ancient Missoula Floods. It is mainly wheat-growing today.

Downtown Dayton's **Historic District** is roughly along Main St. (Yellowstone Trail) from Front to Third St. In all, there are 117 Dayton buildings on the National Register of Historic Places. Self-guided tour brochures are available at the Depot and the Dayton Chamber of Commerce.

341 E Main St. The **Columbia County Courthouse** (1887) is the oldest working courthouse in the state. It is a unique building with a large, ornate cupola.

426 E Main St. **Palus Artifact Museum**. The Palus Artifact Museum offers a collection of locally found artifacts from the Palouse tribe which tells their story. There is also a beautiful collection of native plants.

222 E Commercial. **Dayton Historic Depot**. Built in1882 and used until 1971, it is the oldest Union Pacific Railroad station in Washington. Now an education and interpretation center and museum of local history, it is on the National Register of Historic Places.

235 E Main St. **Weinhard Hotel**. Jacob Weinhard arrived in Dayton in 1880 and began building his local empire of brewery, malt house, beer garden and his Weinhard Hotel building to house the Weinhard Lodge Hall & Saloon. Then, in 1904 came his opera house/movie theater and his large Victorian home.

When the Weinhard Hotel was re-created in 1994, the elements of the lodge hall were used throughout, such as wainscoting, doors, moldings and hardware, thus retaining the architectural heritage of the building. Their website says that "Each guest has the comforts of the twenty-first century while at the same time experiencing the flavors of the past."

344 E Main St. **The Liberty Theater**. The Dreamland Theater first opened in 1910 and changed its name to the Liberty in 1917. Fire burned the building in 1919, but the theater re-opened in 1921. Later, the Liberty brought "talkies" to Dayton where films were shown until the 1970s. For almost 30 years the building was unused, then in 2001 it was renovated and reopened to show first run movies, and host live performances and community events.

410 N 1st St. **Boldman House Museum**. The house was built in 1883, enlarged in 1891 and again c.1909. It was continuously lived in by its various owners, the last family for 87 years. In 1999 Miss Gladys Boldman's will directed the Dayton Historical Society to restore her family home to its original (1912) condition, and that it become a community resource and educational "showplace". The website says that, "Because everything in the house belonged to this one family of savers, these artifacts give us a unique and detailed history of a family and how they lived and interacted with the community and changing times."

Boldman House Museum,
Dayton, WA

WA-338.2: Just east of Waitsburg WA-339.7 to 340.5, roughly, the original YT (Sunset Highway) alignment was apparently converted to an irrigation ditch. Throughout this area, for which good USGS maps exist, it is apparent that over the years the original alignment was straightened and the curves smoothed, leaving little evidence of the past.

Pomeroy has a valid claim to have been on the Yellowstone Trail; the 1917 Yellowstone Trail Association *Folder* clearly so states. Yet the "official" words, in 1915, from Parmley put the Yellowstone Trail on the IEH which "officially" went through Central Ferry. However, in practice that road through Central Ferry was not usable till later and both practice and Yellowstone Trail Association maps had it using the Penawawa Ferry or the Almota Ferry. A modern denizen of Pomeroy believes the Yellowstone Trail followed the Lower Deadman Rd. to Penawawa Ferry. See the Introduction to this Washington Chapter for more information.

So, explore downtown Pomeroy's Historic District which is listed on the National Register of Historic Places. Look up and notice the plethora of antique neon signs sprinkled about on buildings, the collection of Dave Webb. The Sacramento (CA) *Union-Bulletin* reports:

Webb, one of the world's greatest collectors of chemically-induced commercial lighting, is adding the Fun Center sign to his Pomeroy City Walk in Pomeroy, Washington, a grand concourse of neon signs from around the globe. Webb's goal is simple, to hang a restored neon sign on every building in town that wants one.

See Webb's incredible sign museum (if he is home when you visit). Try the Garfield County Museum to find Dave.

708 Columbia St. **Garfield County Museum**. It was a long time acomin' from the first idea of 1901 to the 1972 building completion. Historic county and local items are displayed. Ask to see their glass collection.

67 7th St. **Seeley Theatre**. As is true with many restoration and rejuvenation projects of century-old buildings, finding funds is difficult. That seems to be so with this theatre. However, they are soldiering on, at this writing showing popular films on weekends. The website called her "a lady of distinction." If you pass through on a weekend, stop and see what's showing.

 There existed a road along the Snake River on the south side which carried the traffic from south of Central Ferry to the Penawawa Ferry landing across from Penawawa. It is now under water.

 1916 BB v5, Western Edition, has a highway avoiding Penawawa and going to Central Ferry via Dusty. This is the route not listed by the YTA as the YT until 1917.

 Between about WA-377 and the Snake River, (WA-381.2) there are many changes in the alignment of the road in order to smooth curves and to accommodate the higher water level of the now dammed river. Aerial views of the area clearly show some of the old alignments.

In 1921, teenager Wilmer Siegert traveled from Spokane to Hillsboro, Oregon, and described the ferry which crossed the Snake River:

The ferry was a plank-covered barge with a light wooden fence on the sides and a slim sapling pole laid across the ends as a barrier. It could carry three or four autos.

 To add to the confusion, the Almota Ferry route is shown in 1919 BB Western, including Mayview, as the route of the YT. Other indications suggest the Penawawa ferry route and the Almota ferry route were equally useful during the years 1915 through 1918. The Dusty/Central Ferry/Dodge route was designated to be the IHE from 1915, but was not as drivable as either the Penawawa ferry or the Almota ferry routes until probably 1918.

 1918 BB Vol 9: Via Rosalia, Colfax, Penawawa Ferry and Dayton. Gravel highway to Colfax; dirt and gravel to Snake River; poor road to Dayton; balance of the way gravel. The Central Ferry route [through Dusty] will ultimately become the improved highway, but until completion of same the Penawawa Ferry offers a better way, being about five miles shorter and with equal road conditions. This is a section of the YT which leads through the immense wheat belt of eastern Washington. This section of the Palouse Highway offers a good option between Spokane and Rosalia.

WAYSIDE

Palouse Falls (GPS: 46.6638, -118.2274) is an incredible sight worth the short side-trip. See picture on page 12.

Water emerges from the channeled scablands (see map on page 11) left by the Missoula Floods at the end of the Ice Age and cascades 198 feet onto a solid basaltic rock canyon.

From Delany (WA-362.8) follow WA 261 west and north for less than 21 miles to the entrance to Palouse Falls State Park and about two miles into the park.

The scablands themselves were created by an unimaginable force. As Cassandra Tate describes the events in *Ice Age Floods in Washington* (HistoryLink.org, Essay 8449), "The sound of the great Ice Age Floods would have been terrifying: some 530 cubic miles of water bursting through a wall of ice more than 2,000 feet high; roaring over Eastern Washington with speeds of up to 80 miles an hour; drilling deep crevices into ancient basalt; stripping away topsoil in some areas, piling it up in others; flinging boulders around like ping pong balls. The flood waters pounded down the Columbia Gorge and into the Pacific with enough force to dig channels into the ocean floor." Gives one a whole new perspective of these windy, almost-lonely scablands.

For further discussion of the geology, see page 13.

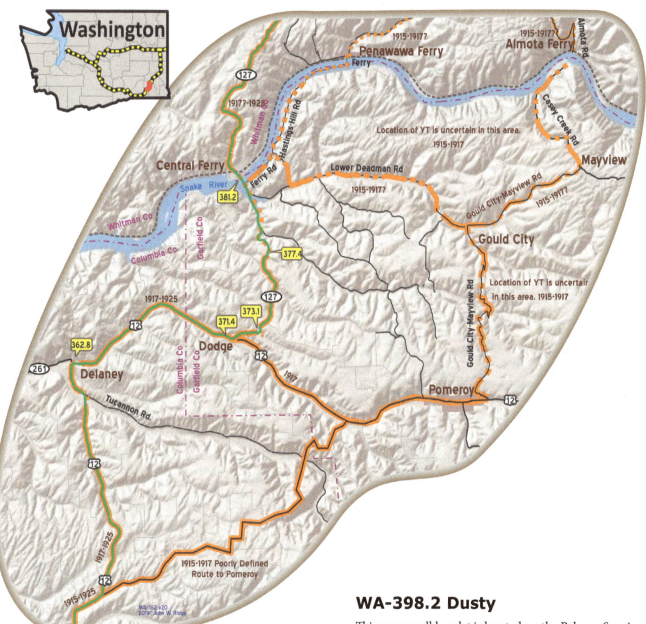

WA-362.8 Delany

 East of Delany, the YT was just north of an abandoned railroad just north of modern US 12.

Just south of Delany, an abandoned bridge over Tucannon River can be seen to the east. A new existing one was built in 1967.

WA-371.4 Dodge
WA-381.2 Central Ferry

The SNAKE RIVER BRIDGE, a steel span, straddles the river, which is very wide at this point. For many years prior to the completion of the bridge, a ferry operated by Robert L. Young, connected Whitman and Garfield Counties. WPA-WA

WA-398.2 Dusty

This very small hamlet is located on the Palouse Scenic Byway. Although the Palouse Scenic Byway runs circuitously from near Lewiston in the south to Rockford near Spokane Valley in the north, it also comprises an east-west and parallel leg which includes the Yellowstone Trail towns of Colfax, Steptoe, and Rosalia. "This is a geologically rich area which includes touches of history, tales that have withstood time, and the absolute beauty and bounty of the Palouse" says their website. Undulating hills and sculptured landscapes are scenes for 208 miles of this meandering Byway.

WA-371.4: The modern road is considerably "smoothed" compared to the YT between WA-372-374. At WA-373.1, the original loop south of the modern highway can be seen from several perspectives.

WA-381.2: There was a bridge built here in 1924 to replace the ferry. Present bridge (longer because of dams) was built in 1969.

COLFAX MEN BOOST YELLOWSTONE TRAIL
NEW ROAD MAP FOLDERS SHOW IMPROVED HIGHWAY IN WHITMAN COUNTY
September 26, 1919 Pullman Herald

HIGHWAY SIGNS BAN IN ERROR
COLFAX MEN SAY YELLOWSTONE TRAIL SIGNS HAVE NOT BEEN ORDERED DOWN
While the state will probably mark the highways soon, it would not necessitate removal of trail signs.

January 4, 1924 Spokesman-Review (Spokane)

Note: This may have referred to the state numbering roads for public maps and road signs - six years after Wisconsin inaugurated the practice.

COLFAX PLANS ROAD MEETING
STATE CONVENTION OF YELLOWSTONE TRAIL MEN
December 4, 1923 Spokesman-Review (Spokane)

Between Colfax and Rosalia, at GPS: 46.85855, -117.42550, try to find an old road and an old road grader.

Colfax resident's ode to
early travel along YT in his yard

The YT near Steptoe

The YT near the wheat fields of the Palouse south of Dayton.

WA-416.5 Colfax

(pop. 3,000, alt. 1,974 ft.), county seat of Whitman county, is a thriving little city situated in one of the richest wheat districts of the U. S. Near Colfax is the historical Steptoe butte named for Col. Steptoe, who battled with the Indians about 1855. While the battle was not fought just at this point, this treeless butte was named in memory of the hero. It can be seen by the auto tourist for many miles. BB1921-9

(1,966 alt., 2,853 pop.), seat of Whitman County, spreads along both sides of the Palouse River. Hemming in the town are rounded hills, now largely given over to wheat growing. Main Street, nearly a mile in length, parallels the river, which occasionally goes on a rampage, and floods the lower levels of the town. WPA-WA

You are in the heart of Palouse country here. The steep, fertile, rolling hills define the unique region known as the Palouse. Steady winds blew sand here eons ago, and still do, leaving the mounds of earth you see around you. The agencies for land formation were wind and waves of the Missoula Floods. Colfax is a nice looking town, hilly, with a "concrete river" for flood control.

Perkins Ave. north end of town. **Perkins House**, a restored 1884 Victorian house, is named for the town's founder, James Perkins. His log cabin is on the grounds along with the comical "codger pole" dedicated to old football players in a contested game, but you have to look hard - so much greenery around. It is on the National Register of Historic Places. Other historic buildings line Main St.

WA-427.1 Steptoe

Steptoe Butte is named to honor Colonel Edward Steptoe who led the U.S. Army in the last U.S. Army/Indian conflict in eastern Washington. The Butte served as Steptoe's reconnaissance point. [See Wayside on next page.]

Steptoe Butte once held a hotel and an observation point built by James S. "Cashup" Davis. The Cashup Hotel closed after Davis' death in 1896 and burned down in 1911. That history and the fantastic views of the Palouse warrant a visit but the greatest reason for a visit is to allow your imagination to visualize the impressive geology of eastern Washington from the top of a geological wonder.

Steptoe Butte is the very top of an ancient mountain composed of billion year old rock which formed part of the western coast of the continent with the view to the west consisting of ocean. Land to the west rose, mountains and valleys were formed and, in time, about 15 million years ago, basaltic lava filled the area covering the huge area of eastern Washington with an uneven layer of basalt, in some areas thousands of feet deep. Predecessors of the Columbia River carved channels through the area and the Missoula Floods raced to Oregon creating the Channeled Scablands of Washington, creating the sights, for instance, near Coulee City (WA-N227.2) and Dry Falls State Park. The glaciers that were instrumental in creating the Missoula Floods also ground down unimaginable amounts of rock to form the dust that then blew out of the Columbia Basin and settled as a thick blanket of silt over the Palouse. That vast loess deposit created the rich farmland of the Palouse, seen today as smooth, round, wheat covered hills.

So the view from 1,100 foot tall Steptoe Butte is of the Palouse, the loess hills, which cover the basaltic rock which in turn covers the ancient mountainous hills and valleys of the land that emerged from the sea. The Butte stood there through the eons, a pink quartzite "island" in a sea of loess-covered Columbia River basalt. Its geology is even more intriguing than Cashup's remote hotel.

WA-431.2 Cashup

Named after James "Cashup" Davis. He paid only with cash. He built an observatory at Steptoe Butte.

WA-435.8 Thornton

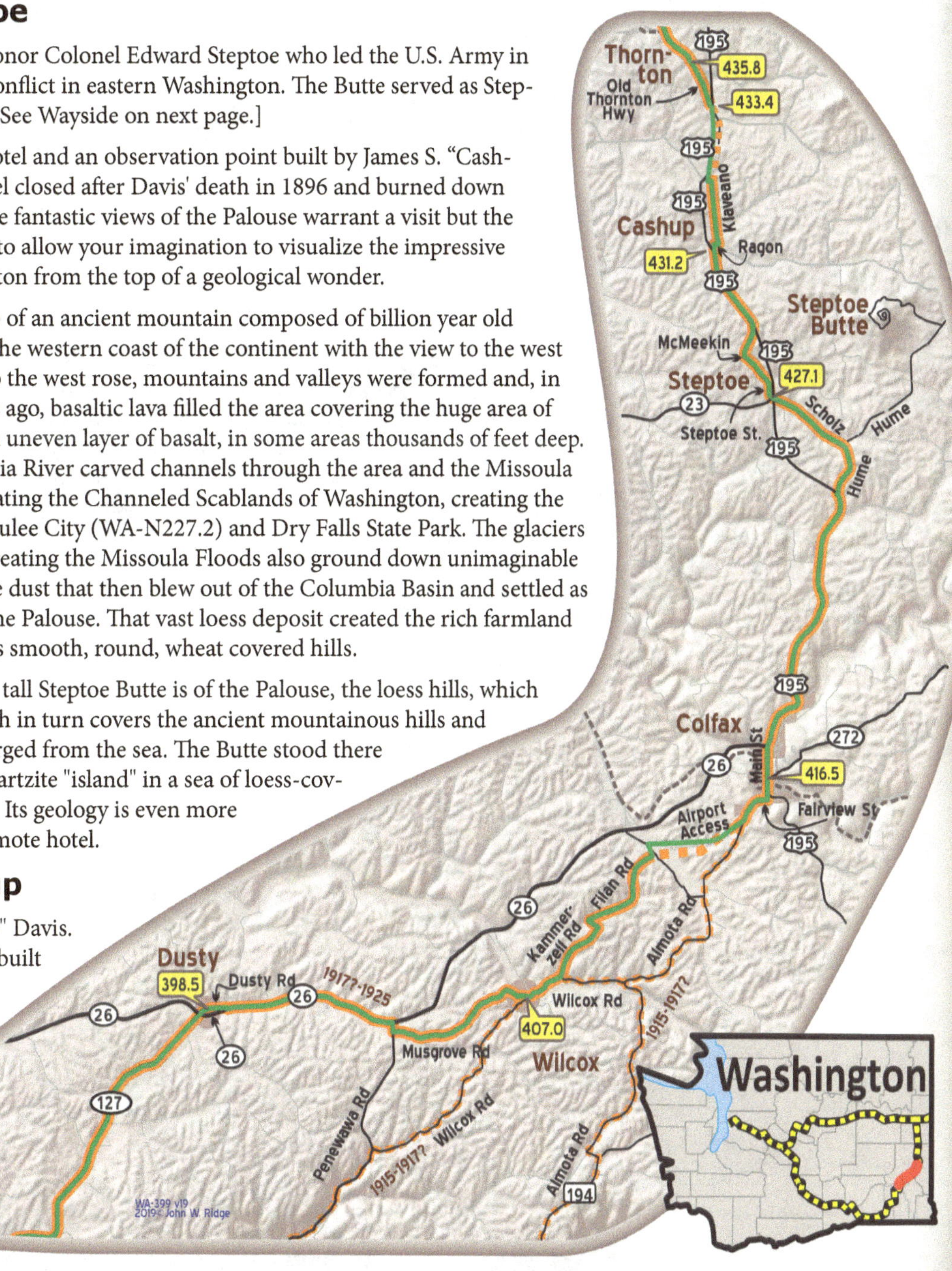

Rules for maintaining a road: 1.) When your road gets too high in the middle, use your split-log drag. 2.) When you grade roads, remove sod or vegetable matter before the road becomes packed. 3.) When your grade is completed, a level line across and touching the center of the road should be the same height above either edge of your road. 4.) If your road is graded 24 feet wide, the center crown should be 12 inches higher than edges of your road.

May 13, 1913 Spokane County Good Roads Assn

Old Milwaukee Road overpass, Rosalia

Texaco Visitors' Center, Rosalia

The YT black arrow on inside of west arch of the old Milwaukee Road overpass at Rosalia

Electric plug-ins for future cars at historic Texaco station

ANNUAL MEET OF YELLOWSTONE TRAIL AT SPOKANE

Delegates from all cities on the Yellowstone Trail in Washington and Idaho were called to meet in the sixth annual state meeting of the Trail Association.

October 29, 1921 The Spokesman-Review (Spokane)

WAYSIDE

South edge of Rosalia. The Steptoe Battlefield site is a four acre day-use park. A Memorial marks the 1858 site of the last Native American victory over Col. Steptoe. Being outnumbered (158 soldiers vs 600-1200 from four tribes), the only thing the soldiers could do was to slip away to win two battles elsewhere later on.

Look carefully. There are three teams of many horses threshing in the Palouse.
1918 Automobile Blue Book Vol. 9

WA-443.6

 Milwaukee Road Bridge (GPS: 47.22227, -117.36322). The YT followed a Trolley line through the whole area. From the 1916 BB v5.

WA-444.7 Rosalia

Here you can see great Palouse wheatfields of eastern Washington. Miles of rolling hills with scattered barns. Between Colfax and Rosalia you can easily spot the old road and follow it, if you like, through Thornton and other small settlements.

"Rosalia is a good Yellowstone Trail stop. It is a nice old town with vintage buildings and visible reminders of old Trail days. Trail travelers of 100 years ago would feel comfortable here," says Washington native and history buff, Dave Habura.

Just at the south edge of town on the Yellowstone Trail you will see a large **Milwaukee Road Railroad overpass**, begun in 1913. Painted on the inside of the west arch at a low level is a black arrow on yellow background. That remnant of the Yellowstone Trail, although maintained, may have faded so you will have to get out of your car and look sharp to see it.

534 Whitman Ave (Yellowstone Trail). Restored 1923 vintage **Texaco Visitor's Center**. You'll get no gas there, but you will hear lots of history of the area and about this gas station from the friendly volunteer. They even have a 24-hour public rest room. And how's this for a time warp: outside of the 1923 gas station is an electric car "refueling pump," a battery charger with four charging stations! Rosalia is certainly looking toward the next 100 years!

Main St. **The Model Garage** was advertised in the 1919 *Automobile Blue Book*. Today it is hard to determine what it is used for. It seems maintained. Readers, any thoughts?

110 W 5th St. **Battle Days Museum** is housed in the city hall and features Rosalia and eastern Washington history.

WA-451.7 Plaza

(2,353 alt., 250 pop.), a score of frame buildings, straggles along the highway and railroad track. Dominating the village are several wheat warehouses and a large grain elevator. WPA-WA

WA-453.7 Powers Rd

The original route of the Mullan Military Road crossed the Yellowstone Trail here. See **Trail Tale: Mullan Road**, page 84.

WA-459.9 Spangle

(2,432 alt., 203 pop.), a village of weather stained houses clustered about a few brick buildings, is one of the oldest settlements in the Inland Empire. The first house built in the vicinity was erected in 1862 and for years served as a stopping place on the Mullan Road. WPA-WA

WA-468.5

Mullan Military Road Marker, at intersection of Excelsior Rd. See **Trail Tale: Mullan Road**, page 84.

WA-476.8=WA-N326.2 N. & S. YT Routes Join

WA-476.8=WA-N326.2 Decision Pt
To follow the YT North Route,
go to page 35 and read up.
To go east on the YT,
go to page 61 and read down.
To follow the YT South Route,
stay on this page and read up..

Building concrete on the YT
near the state line

A Yellowstone Trail Garage in Spokane, 13th Ave.
and Chestnut St., both streets on the YT

IEH entering Spokane along Hangman Creek, 1918

WA

Beautiful Spokane River

WAYSIDE

Just 2.5 miles north of WA-486.9 on Sprague Ave. is the location of **Plante's Ferry**, used on the Spokane River by the Mullan Road. See **Trail Tale: Mullan Road**, page 84.

High bridge over Latah Creek,
site of old campground, Spokane
(called Hangman Creek in YT days)

20th Ave. and Chestnut St.
Old concrete trough for horse and
Model Ts?

Car on gravel YT
near Spokane
1918 Automobile Blue Book

WA-476.8 or WA-N326.2 Decision Pt

To follow the YT North Route,
go to page 35 and read up.

To go east on the YT,
stay on this page and read down.

To follow the YT South Route,
go to page 59 and read up.

WA-476.6 Spokane

(pop. 104,437, alt. 1,891 ft.), situated on the Spokane river, is the commercial and financial center of a large agricultural area. Spokane stands unique where downtown the river plunges over rocky leaps in a cascade of foam. Spokane has a well-equipped motor tourists' camp located on the banks of Hangman creek. BB1921-9

J. R. RICHARDS TIRE CO., East 313 Sprague Ave. on Yellowstone Trail, is convenient for tourists; expert repair work. MH-1928. [Note: Today it is a Karate Center.]

DAVENPORT HOTEL is one of the finest in the West. World famed for its appointments, service and luxurious lobby. Single $2.25-$3.25; dbl. $4, with bath $5-$8; Formal dining to coffee shop; exceptional food and service. MH-1928

Riverside Park in north central Spokane is a "must see." It is along the Spokane River as it winds through some of the town with four beautiful waterfalls.

10 S Post St. (corner of Post and Sprague Ave., the Yellowstone Trail). The elegant **Davenport Hotel** really taxes expression. Called a "beacon of culture and refinement." Go in and stroll about. See historic pictures in the mezzanine and look down upon the glittering lobby. See **Trail Tale: The Davenport Hotel**, page 62.

W 1005 First Ave. Historic **Montvale Hotel**. Opened in 1899, with street-level commercial space (first in Spokane) and two upper-level floors with 60 residential rooms. All for $1 or $2 per week. In 1914 each room had wash basins! After a period of neglect, a full renovation was completed in 2015, restoring the hotel to its original luster, now a true historic boutique hotel.

901 W Sprague. **Bing Crosby Theater**, so named because he attended local Gonzaga University and supposedly got his start at this theater and at local radio station KHQ, which signed on the air in 1922 from its tower on the roof of the Davenport Hotel. KHQ featured many local bands, including The Musicaladers. That group's drummer, Bing Crosby, dropped out of Gonzaga University and became world-famous for his singing voice. The theater features live music and film festivals.

159 S Lincoln. **Steam Plant**. On March 5, 1916, operations started, beginning the important role the Steam Plant played in downtown Spokane. The over 100 year old property now hosts a brewery, restaurant, and retail shops under catwalks open to 80 foot high ceiling skylights. Or look straight up the inside of one of the 225 foot smokestacks.

507 N Howard. **Riverfront Park Clocktower** is all that remains of the 1902 Great Northern Depot.

By 1921 a 200-acre site was up and running at Riverside Ave. and A Street. **High Bridge Park**. Latah Creek had been called Hangman Creek after the hanging of Native Americans there in retaliation of Col. Steptoe's defeat by four Native American tribes in the Indian War of 1858. Today it is a large green space for frisbee golf, but no camping.

2316 W 1st Ave. **The Campbell House** (c.1910) and **Northwest Museum of Arts and Culture**. The Campbells moved from Coeur d'Alene's raucus mining community to refined Spokane and the Tudor home reveals what life was like for the Western wealthy in the early 1900s.

20th Ave.& Chestnut St. Seven blocks further from 13th Ave. we happened on to a great old concrete **spring/watering trough** we had not seen before. There were pipes but no water. Was it for man or beast or a radiator fill-up? Do you know? Tell us.

This area from 13th to 20th Avenues and beyond is called "**Vinegar Flats**," apparently named in memory of the nearby Keller-Lorenze 1890 vinegar company. Vinegar was used as a food preservative, or pickling. The Yellowstone Trail went through the Flats on Chestnut St.

WA-484.9 or N334.3 Dishman. Crossed by the Mullan Miliary Road. See **Trail Tale: Mullan Road**, page 84.

WA-486.9 or N336.3 Opportunity

WA-497.0 Washington/Idaho Line

Spokane's Davenport Hotel

Louis Davenport saw opportunity in the ashes of the 1889 Spokane fire. He leased a brick building on the corner of Sprague Ave. and Post St., then expanded his restaurant to an adjoining building. He hired Kirtland Cutter to make the two buildings appear as one in 1904. The result was the Spanish Mission Revival style in white stucco and red tile which you see today. Architecturally, it certainly did not look like any of the granite buildings downtown.

In 1912 movers and shakers of the business community wanted to erect a fine hotel. They enlisted Davenport and Cutter, even naming it in Davenport's honor. The body of the hotel went up in eight months in 1913 which is startling, considering the building tools available.

Cutter designed spaces inspired by the great European architects. Davenport filled them with fine art and fine Irish linens for his tables and 15,000 pieces of silver flatware. Ever since opening day in 1914, the hotel has promoted itself as "one of America's exceptional hotels." It functioned as a hotel for luxury rail travelers.

Fifteen Yellowstone Trail travel bureaus gave out Yellowstone Trail maps and Trail information to autoists, much as the AAA does today. The Davenport Hotel was one of them. About 1921 the Davenport began to cater to the motoring crowd, saying in advertisements, "Come as you are." Other lodgings also started to adjust to the auto tourist. The "auto court" evolved from cabins to small cottages in a row divided by covered spaces for an auto. These later became the motels we know.

Sadly, apparently, each successive owner through the second half of the 20th century disrespected the Davenport property. The hotel closed in 1985 and stood empty for 15 years, demolition and dismantling having been rejected. We peeked in the windows in 1997 and viewed disrepair and despair. What a joy to lunch there a decade or so later and see the glory returned to this historic site through a massive and excruciatingly careful renovation carried on by Walt and Karen Worthy. ✿

The Davenport Hotel front entrance, 1915

Lobby of the Davenport Hotel

The glorious ballroom of The Davenport Hotel

The 1904 Spanish Mission style building (front) and the 1914 highrise which constitute the Davenport Hotel

An auto court with covered "garages" for auto tourists on Hwy. 10/Yellowstone Trail, seven miles east of Spokane. Such "Motels" grew to serve those tourists not willing or able to stay at hotels such as the Davenport.

The Pine Canyon Road

The Pine Canyon Road is a most interesting part of the 1925-1930 Yellowstone Trail, in addition to being a part of the National Parks Highway and Washington's Sunset Highway. Lori Ludeman, Director of the Douglas County Historical Museum, contributed much to this essay, but questions still remain; we hope some reader can find answers to them.

During 1925, the Yellowstone Trail between Spokane and Cle Elum in Washington was rerouted from the southern Walla Walla through Yakima route to the northern Waterville, Wenatchee, Blewett Pass route after the Blewett Pass had been sufficiently upgraded.

The northern route includes Pine Canyon, between Waterville and the Columbia River. There the road drops 2,000 feet and includes some dramatic scenery. The road was a challenge to build and is a delightful area to explore in the 21st century.

That area is marked by several canyons formed as the Columbia cut 2,000 feet down below the altitude of Waterville. In

YT in Pine Canyon

addition to the major Columbia River canyon there are two tributary canyons of interest. The larger, Corbaley Canyon, is marked on the map (below) in orange. The other, Pine Canyon, is marked in purple. Pine Canyon meets Corbaley Canyon at the point marked B. There appears to be continuing ambiguity about those names; some commentators include the canyon marked in orange as part of Pine Canyon. The USGS does not help the ambiguity by recording the name Pine Canyon only at the coordinates of the canyons' intersection at B.

Transportation around Waterville developed from the immigrant routes from the east and the extension of railroads from the midwest. The 2,000 foot drop to the Columbia River had to be faced to develop transportation to the west toward the Pacific Ocean. One of the early attempts resulted in a tramway described in an article in www.historylink.org (June 8, 2010) by Laura Arksey, late of the Northwest Museum of Arts and Culture in Spokane. ⇨

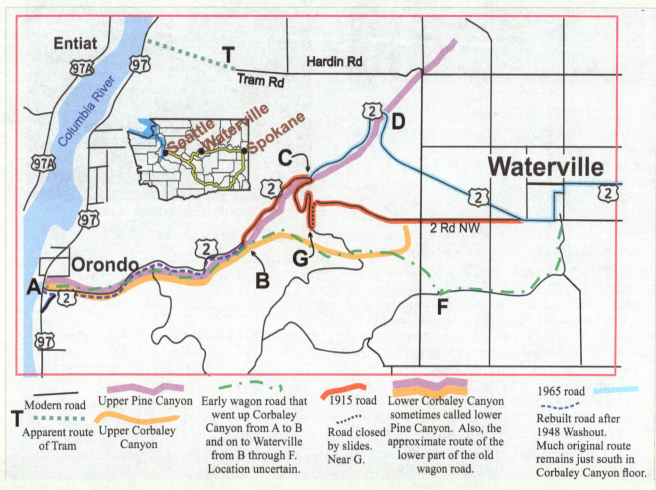

Legend:
- Modern road
- T Apparent route of Tram
- Upper Pine Canyon
- Upper Corbaley Canyon
- Early wagon road that went up Corbaley Canyon from A to B and on to Waterville from B through F. Location uncertain.
- 1915 road
- Road closed by slides. Near G.
- Lower Corbaley Canyon sometimes called lower Pine Canyon. Also, the approximate route of the lower part of the old wagon road.
- 1965 road
- Rebuilt road after 1948 Washout. Much original route remains just south in Corbaley Canyon floor.

Arksey wrote:

Wheat farming was not without some continuing problems, transportation being a major one. Waterville's position high on the plateau above the Columbia made access to the river ports barely possible for heavily-loaded wagons. A solution was found in 1902 when the Columbia River Tramway Company began operating trams from the edge of the bluff down the breaks to a steamboat landing three miles north of Orondo. Large steel buckets on cables supported by wooden towers carried wheat sacks the two miles down and returned laden with freight and merchandise for Waterville stores. At first gravity operated, it soon became obvious that the tram needed a steam engine as well. There are local tales of a few intrepid souls riding the giant buckets, on one occasion being stranded for many hours because of a mechanical malfunction. The tram operated until 1910. One of the buckets salvaged by helicopter in 1973 is on display outside the Douglas County Historical Museum at Waterville next to murals depicting the tramway era.

Pine Canyon

The probable route of the tram is marked with a T and a dotted line on the map. The "Tram Road" name appears on some maps instead of the modern Hardin Road, indicating that was the location of the road from the tram to Waterville. The tramway was near the area GPS: 47.67663,-120.19404.

Arksey also reports that beginning around 1885 a wagon road was created running from Waterville through Corbaley Canyon to the Columbia River. (The dot-dash green line.)

On a difficult old Indian trail George W. Blair and C. C. Rickman established a stage and mail service in 1886, linking Waterville with Ellensburg. It was 'a nightmare for men and horses alike, going and coming, steep and treacherous, and winters turned the route into an icy bobsled run. They had to wrap chains around the runners of the loaded sled to prevent it from shooting downhill out of control.' During the 1890s another company operated a road from the east, roughly following present US 2, which was only marginally better, involving steep grades at Moses Coulee and Douglas Creek Canyon.

Although a few intrepid early motorists did traverse

Corbaley Canyon, and as early as 1914 an automobile "stage line" was transporting passengers and parcels in a Maxwell and a Buick, it was obvious that a new route was needed.

And the new route (pink shaded line on the map) was created. As reported by Lori Ludeman:

A major improvement came in 1915-16 from a road gang of state prison convicts from the penitentiary at Walla Walla who were used as a cost-cutting means; $59,036 had been appropriated from the legislature for construction of five miles of road from a point two miles west of Waterville down Pine Canyon to a point where it runs into Corbaley Canyon.

The road was 30 feet wide, with a maximum grade of five percent. Hillside material was the base. Work began in June 1915. The convicts worked both summer and winter months and were, with the exception of some blasting powder, equipped with only hand tools.

Completion of the road was greeted enthusiastically both by travelers and commercial interests. The route was said to not have a "single turn around which cars cannot be seen."

The original wagon road was in the canyon bottom and two years later spring runoff water from Pine Canyon Creek wiped out two miles of the road's lower section. Repair work was completed soon after. In 1930, the first "bituminous coating" was laid on the road.

No doubt along the bottom of
Lower Corbaley (Pine) Canyon
1918 Automobile Blue Book

Apparently, the 1915 five-mile road together with the existing lower Corbaley Canyon road became known as the Pine Canyon Rd.

Ludeman continued:

The early route had a roadside attraction in Beaver Den Springs. Developed in the early 1920s, there was a tent area, ice cream and fresh fruits. A telephone was also available.

In 1948, a flash flood hit the canyon, destroying the original Pine Canyon highway. State highway officials surveyed and rebuilt the road on a higher level. The new highway is 10 to 150 feet above the old flood washed road.

⇨

Much of the earlier lower road can still be seen from the existing road, now known a US 2. Turn offs along US 2 are available to provide a view of that earlier road. Some of those early sections can be seen from the parking area at GPS: 47.63166, -120.18614 and from others nearby.

Zoom in along US 2 in Satellite view and inspect just south of the road. See the Corbaley Canyon picture, page 64.

Ludeman concluded:

> Later, a new upper portion of the canyon road and a new approach to Waterville were made. The first section of the new road was completed during the summer of 1950, the second section 1965.

That modern alignment of the road, US 2, runs from C on the map to Waterville.

Because of washouts and debris on the road, the upper horse-shoe of the 1915 road (dotted black line on map, near G) was closed at a fairly recent, but unknown, date. It can be seen at: GPS: 47.64371, -120.14724.

The reader is invited to provide clarifications, corrections, additional information, travel diaries, and stories to help document this section of the Yellowstone Trail.

Also see **WA-N180 Pine Canyon**, page 31. ⚙

The old highway (YT) climbing from **WA-N180.7** going to Waterville. The top stretch on the right is now closed by slides but the foreground curve can still be reached.

Frank Guilbert, Washington's Good Roads Man

About a decade after Sam Hill's 1899 Good Roads Association work in Seattle, Frank Guilbert, 400 miles to the east in Spokane, seemed equally obsessed with good roads. He was involved in road issues large and small - from forming the National Parks Highway Association to the minutia of standardizing Spokane drivers' hand signals.

Frank Guilbert

The many-talented Guilbert arrived in Spokane in 1904 from Racine, Wisconsin, to explore opportunities in mining, home building and real estate sales. In 1910 Frank stumbled into the Spokane County Good Roads Association by accident. He was asked to fill in briefly for the vacationing secretary; he stayed for 27 years! Guilbert observed that roads were mostly dirt and scattered; funds were small and viciously fought over. Principles of road building were necessary: roads should be built from main trade centers out; county seats should be connected; a system of spending was needed. The Spokane County Good Roads Association spurred the county on to build and by 1921, 236 miles of county roads, including some of the Sunset Highway and the Inland Empire Highway had been built or improved.

In 1912 Guilbert, an imposing fellow with rounded features and a "can-do" attitude, was elected president of the newly formed Inland Empire Automobile Association. Putting sign-posts along the roads of the Inland Empire was the first order of business. This organization, like the AAA, offered member benefits such as emergency road service, a travel bureau and a publication. Mainly, the Inland Empire Automobile Association supported laws governing traffic control for safety as well as assisted in building better roads.

Guilbert was, apparently, an expedient leader and organizer. Leading the Eastern Washington Highway Association and chairing the executive committee of the Washington State Good Roads Association (in addition to the Spokane County and Inland Empire work) broadened his sphere of influence. The secret of his success seemed to be his actual travel on his associations' roads of interest. He took his camera along for proof of the sad road conditions and lobbied legislators with the pictures.

Collier's magazine cited Guilbert and others for their good roads efforts in 1914.

One of Guilbert's favorite vehicles for examining highways was the "Great Big Baked Potato" named for the car's size and light color. This name was not unique, however. Yakima Valley farmers were growing very large potatoes, too large for general consumption due to the tough skins. The Northern Pacific Railway had a chef, Hazen Titus, who offered them, baked, to travelers on the North Coast Limited. News spread about this new offering, and soon the railroad was advertising that slogan to advertise the railroad's passenger service. A comic postcard was printed and Hollywood stars were hired to promote the railroad's new slogan from 1910 to 1920. No doubt heads turned when they saw Guilbert and his "Great Big Baked Potato."

⇨

Frank Guilbert

Guilbert and the National Parks Highway

The forming of the National Parks Highway Association in February, 1915, was an outgrowth of his widened horizon of road travel. He envisioned a long-distance road from Chicago to Seattle, drawing tourists through national parks Yellowstone, Glacier, Rainier and Crater Lake. Also drawing them through Spokane, of course. Their first general meeting in April featured the planning of a 1916 tour from Chicago to Seattle along their chosen route, taking colored slides and speaking to civic groups as they went. Five men did it, taking them 33 muddy days.

By early 1915, the Yellowstone Trail had spread from Chicago to Coeur d'Alene, Idaho, and was knocking on the door of Washington. O. T. Peterson, Secretary-Treasurer of the Yellowstone Trail Association was dispatched to a meeting of road officials in Spokane in January.

Peterson sought to obtain support for the formal extension of the Yellowstone Trail through Washington to Seattle. Frank Guilbert had his own idea. He was planning his own organization to promote a route from Chicago to Seattle following the route blazed by A. L. Westgard for the AAA in 1912. Westgard had named it the Northwest Trail but it had not become a sponsored or marked route. The Yellowstone Trail followed much of it. Guilbert's proposal to Peterson was that they join forces to establish a named road generally along the Northwest Trail. As an apparent concession to gain Yellowstone Trail Association's support, Guilbert proposed that the established Yellowstone Trail route be used between Terry, in eastern Montana, and the Twin Cities. The rest of this new trail would be called National Parks Highway because it would pass near four national parks.

The Yellowstone Trail Association Resists

Peterson returned home to test the Yellowstone Trail Association membership's feelings about the matter. The response was overwhelmingly negative and the idea was summarily quashed.

"I will never give up the name Yellowstone Trail; you might as well suggest to change the name of your city or state or the members of your family," growled one member. Another wired, "I will fight to the last ditch for the name Yellowstone Trail." Others reasoned that there was "no benefit to be derived from losing its identity." Some said that the Yellowstone Trail had been widely advertised and products now bore the Yellowstone Trail name and logo.

Guilbert was under the impression that Peterson had favored the idea, claiming a preliminary vote had passed unanimously in January. He expressed his "astonishment at being informed by the Yellowstone Trail Association that they could not and would not accept the name National Parks Highway for that portion of the route which they had been boosting." Negotiations were terminated.

Note the chronology here. Peterson was presented with the proposal to join the National Parks Highway in

Guilbert's "Great Big Baked Potato"

January before the National Parks Highway was even formed in February. Perhaps Guilbert had predicted a positive response and could then form his association's route on the usurped Yellowstone Trail and present it thus at his February formation meeting.

The two groups went their separate ways. Instead of absorbing the Yellowstone Trail, the National Parks Highway Association placed their colors upon the Northwest Trail to Chicago.

The Yellowstone Trail followed a route through Washington separate from the central Sunset Highway route of the National Parks Highway. Yellowstone Trail Association *Folders* for 1916 through 1924 defensively said that their southern route was "more scenic and was only made after a thorough investigation of all routes leading west. It is 100 miles longer than the Sunset Highway, but the tourist has advantage of a much better road."

The bad road was the horrendous Blewett Pass near Wenachee. By 1925 Blewett Pass was improved and the Yellowstone Trail switched to the shorter Sunset Highway.

These turf wars were not uncommon in an age of about 250 trail associations nationally vying for the tourist. This failed attempt to steal the Yellowstone Trail should not besmirch Guilbert's reputation as the "Good Roads Man of Washington" and his great influence upon the success of both the Sunset and Inland Empire highways. ❁

Even Guilbert needed a push in 1916.
But are they pushing the car forward or backward?

Idaho

WHAT THE TRAIL FOUNDERS SAID-1921

Automobile travel in the northern or Panhandle district of Idaho and eastern Washington is one of the most delightful features of automobile travel anywhere in the country. In Idaho, the roads are mountain roads through the passes of the Bitter Roots and the Coeur D Alenes. All of it is very scenic. Road conditions are generally good.

1921 Yellowstone Trail Touring Service
Map #8 of WA and ID

The 1919 *Route Folder* adds that from Couer d'Alene to the 4th of July Canyon there is a splendid road. Going east from the Canyon, a wonderful piece of road work is traveled here by cooperation of the state of Idaho, U.S. Forest Service and Kootenai and Shoshone Counties. Going east the Cataldo Mission, Wallace, and Mullan are reached on the road east where one is in the mining district. Mills are here in abundance, both ore and lumber.

The 1921 *Route Folder* adds: In this section are some of the most beautiful places of the continent, and the climate is delightful at all times. It never gets really cold nor does it have extreme heat. Nature has been kind to this section in all respects, and the people have responded.

Kellogg Peak, Kellogg, ID
Period Postcard

INTRODUCING THE YELLOWSTONE TRAIL IN IDAHO:
THE GEM STATE

"There is music in the mountains - the clicking of ore cars and whispers of the pines. The tourist over the Yellowstone Trail reaches the romance of the mines and lure of the beautiful scenery."

Grace Fitzpatrick, *in National Motorist, 1932*

Extending the Yellowstone Trail through the Gem State

By the time of the 1914 Yellowstone Trail Association meeting in Hunter's Hot Springs, Montana, the route of the Trail was inexorably headed through Missoula, Montana, "to the Idaho border" and thence to Seattle. But at that Idaho border most of the route for the Yellowstone Trail was blocked by the Bitterroot Range of the Rocky Mountains, the same mountains that caused Lewis and Clark such difficulty just over 100 years before and made establishing rail routes difficult and expensive 30 years before.

The most direct route across the mountains would be through Superior, Wallace, and Coeur d'Alene to Spokane but in 1914 it was not adequately developed for auto traffic. There was an auto route being developed from Missoula more northward through Paradise, Thompson Falls, Sandpoint, and Spokane, but it would have added well over 100 miles to the trip and missed the Idaho mining area.

The Northern Pacific on the famous S-curve

The general principle of "follow the railroad" didn't work here. Rails were limited to wide curves and low grades, requiring huge trestles, and indirect routes. Roads and rails often could not share the narrow valleys. A prime example of the problems of laying out a railroad is the famous S-curve of the Northern Pacific just south of Mullan. Seeking a useful grade, the railroad had to build a huge curved wooden trestle. In addition to the initial cost it was (and is) in very wild country and subject to Nature's worst. In 1903, a snow avalanche wiped out a major portion of the trestle, leaving a passenger car dangling above the fallen caboose. In 1910 the trestle was lost in the Big Burn. The costs of rebuilding in each case had to be supported by the commercial income

created by the railroad. Auto highways had no such back up and their alignments had to reflect very modest building approaches.

One other precedent to auto roads played a big role here in Idaho. See **Trail Tale: Mullan Road**, page 84. The Mullan Military Road was built by army personnel in the early 1860s. After a couple of years' use, parts of it were maintained by its users, but much of it was left to decay as streams washed out its crude (and plentiful) bridges, avalanches sealed off sections, and lack of use allowed vegetation to take over. Sections of the Mullan Road were used by mining interests and redeveloped; some sections became town streets. In short, as the Yellowstone Trail was developed, parts of the Mullan Road were integrated if those parts were in use by locals in 1914. Today, you will find many references to the Mullan Road across the panhandle of Idaho, including the name of the town of Mullan.

Fortunately, the residents along the direct route were awakening to the need for good auto roads and were attempting to create usable roads through the Bitterroots, a huge task given the terrain and the weather. The engaging story of the development of the Yellowstone Trail, first over the Mullan Pass and then over Lookout Pass, is told in **Trail Tale: Bitterroots**, page 80.

Coincident with the Trail, autos made their impact in the panhandle – motivating an internal interest in auto roads. Residents then began the long, political process of deciding who is responsible for roads.

From Mullan to Cataldo, the Mullan Road had followed the Coeur d'Alene River closely in the narrow valleys, and more generally in the more open flats. Settlements and the mines followed the same path so that there was an obvious path for the Trail.

From Cataldo to Coeur d' Alene, Mullan had chosen his northern route well and alternatives had not been developed, so the Yellowstone Trail followed it very closely, much of it now over laid by the modern I-90. Mullan's first routing attempt, south of Coeur d 'Alene, proved unsustainable because of its natural wetness. From the 4th of July Pass into the city of Coeur d'Alene the modern driver can easily envision the Yellowstone Trail of 1920, and, with a bit more imagination, maybe even the Mullan Road.

From Coeur d' Alene into Washington the roads in 1915 were better developed because of the closeness of bigger cities, but that development had closely followed the Mullan Road.

Gorgeous scenery and difficult road routing

Nature was not kind to road builders in Idaho, but it has afforded the traveler gorgeous views of valleys from hilltops, of miles of impenetrable green forest, of pristine rivers, numerous lakes, and forested shorelines. The whole of the Clearwater drainage system is a magnificently forested mountain paradise. Warm sun has always helped the recreational offerings of the Coeur d'Alene area; the snow gives Kellogg its fame as a winter skiing hub. Mining gave the state its great economic beginning in the Silver Valley and its nickname, the gem state. Mining also caused major pollution which the EPA is cleaning up.

Get off the Interstate. Follow the Yellowstone Trail and explore the little side roads for an up close and personal view of the historic mining industry and scenery that beggars description today as it did 100 years ago. ✿

Mining communities built roads and railroads to get the ore to markets, sometimes, as in Burke, above, one on top of the other to use the only space left.

I-90 and Lake Coeur d'Alene as seen from the YT high above

The Yellowstone Trail from Spokane to Missoula is now open, traffic being routed by way of Sandpoint and Thompson Falls, reports the touring department of the National Automobile Club. The direct route, by way of Wallace, is open, but poor conditions will be encountered. Chains are advisable, as weather conditions are unsettled and heavy rains will leave the road muddy and slippery.
May 25, 1929 Berkeley (ID) Daily Gazette

The Idaho meeting of the Yellowstone Trail Association was in session today. Idaho's portion of the national association's $20,000 program is $550: Coeur d'Alene $175, Wallace $175, Kellogg $100, Mullan $100. Mullan raised it from $50 at its own suggestion. The suggestion was made for towns on the Trail from Missoula, Montana, to Coeur d'Alene to produce a map and descriptive booklet of the route.
January 23, 1920 Coeur d'Alene Press

WORK ON YELLOWSTONE TRAIL THROUGH ST. REGIS PASS TO COEUR D'ALENE HELD UP

It had been expected that the oiling project from Kellogg to the 4th of July Canyon, a stretch of 26 miles, would be completed this year, but early fall rains put a sudden stop to the work after completion of 12 miles.

The Yellowstone Trail has the reputation of being one of the heaviest traveled roads in the state. Traffic counts show an average of 1,200 to 1,500 vehicles during the daylight hours and one 24-hour check showed 2,761 vehicles in that period. 'Tin can tourists' seem to be dying out in favor of those using hotels and bungalows, while free camps are not as popular as they were.
September 22, 1927 Idaho Statesman

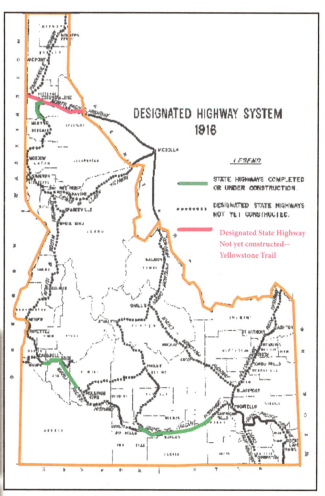

1916 Idaho State Highways map
The black lines within Idaho have been designated state highways. Only the green sections have been constructed or are under construction! The red line is the Yellowstone Trail, only designated - no construction by the state. Any existing roads had been built by mining companies or counties.

START WORK ON THE GREAT APPLE WAY

Work has started on the great Apple Way between Coeur d'Alene and Spokane, through the Spokane Valley 30 miles. The Spokane County Good Roads Association is doing the building in conjunction with the Commercial Club of Coeur d'Alene. The new speedway will be completed early in September. The road will be lined on both sides with apple and other fruit trees.

May 23, 1910 Spokane Press

Note: The road was finally opened in 1912. It became the Yellowstone Trail in 1915.

The Trail near Lake Coeur d'Alene
Museum of North Idaho

🚗 From ID-0.0 to ID-5.6, the 1919 Idaho Dept. of Agriculture/Univ. of Idaho Soil Map suggests the YT followed the old Mullan Road which is now Seltice Way. The 1915 Westgard map shows, from the west, the YT following the Seltice Way, Spokane St., 4th Ave. then joining Seltice Way going east.

🚗 Within northern Coeur d'Alene, the route shown on the city map between Seltice Way and 4th St. is, at best, an approximation, although some travel on Government Way can be assumed.

🚗 Interestingly, Westgard's 1915 map puts the YT on the east side of Coeur d'Alene along the present inland Sunnyside Road from Bennett Bay to Blue Creek Bay and improbably continues east directly to Alder Creek Road. Further research found that that route was the original Mullan Military Road route. Either it was travelable by auto when Westgard visited or, more likely, Westgard simply reported that route without driving it.

James V. Hawkins, postmaster, has received notice of his appointment as representative in this district of the Yellowstone Trail association [Trailman]. He will keep the association informed of the conditions of this part of the highway.

August 30, 1915 The Spokesman-Review (Spokane)

PAVE NEW SECTION OF YELLOWSTONE TRAIL

The Bennett's Bay section of the Yellowstone Trail carries heavy traffic. The topography of the country is very rough and rocky, with vertical cliffs to make location and construction difficult. The section along the shore of Lake Coeur d'Alene became so rough in the spring of 1925 that it was decided to pave the road. ... On December 4, 1925, bids were received for the paving with portland cement concrete.

August 1927 Concrete Highways and Public Improvement

Note: "Paving" now means concrete in populated places; it still meant gravel on rural roads, however.

OIL YELLOWSTONE TRAIL

Gravel resurfacing work is under way on the Yellowstone Trail between Bennett and Wolf Lodge Bays in preparation for oiling.

September 8, 1929 The Spokesman-Review (Spokane)

Early Touring
Museum of North Idaho

Blue Creek Bay, taken at mile ID-014 along the YT, with YT winding below. GPS: 47.6398, -116.6610

🚗 At ID-19.3, in modern times, when traveling from the west on Coeur d'Alene Lake Rd., the intersection with the YT is poorly marked and easy to miss.

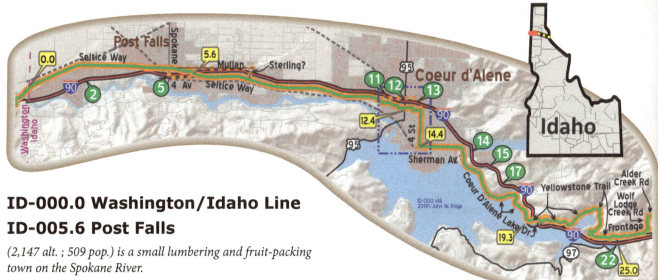

ID-000.0 Washington/Idaho Line

ID-005.6 Post Falls

(2,147 alt. ; 509 pop.) is a small lumbering and fruit-packing town on the Spokane River.

> *A half mile south of it is the Post Falls Dam, which impounds the river and delivers power to the eastern part of the Inland Empire. WPA-ID*

> *A farm and saw mill town. Reynolds Garage leads. Free and pay camp. Kamp Komfort, 9 clean cottages, $1; camp 50c. MH-1928*

101 E 4th Ave. (Yellowstone Trail). **Post Falls Historical Society**. Located in a small 1923 building. Local artifacts and special displays are featured.

316 E 5th Ave. **Vintage Guitars**. We mention this only because there is a 1917 Gibson "harp" guitar there along with other antique guitars, some possibly recognized by Yellowstone Trail travelers 100 years ago. With luck, some current famous guitarist may be there when you stop.

705 N Compton St. near Seltice Way. **Treaty Rock Park.** Treaty Rock Park is the site of the legendary treaty between Chief Seltice of the Coeur d' Alene and Fredrick Post, the town's founder. It features a section of the rock with the words "June 1, 1871, Frederick Post," along with Native American pictographs. The historic petroglyphs and pictographs (by tradition, created 1871), located in the city park, are listed in the National Register of Historic Places.

ID-014.4 Coeur d'Alene

> *On account of its beautiful location at the base of the Coeur d'Alene mountain range, a part of the great Rocky divide, the adjoining lake and its picturesque setting, its steamboat lines and railroad facilities, the city has become known as a summer resort, and is visited by thousands yearly. The great transcontinental highway, adopted by the Yellowstone trail and the National Parks highway, passes through the city, and automobile tourists stop over to enjoy the commodious camping grounds and other recreations, as they speed across the country. BB-1921*

> *COEUR D'ALENE at Powell's Store. Pop. 11,000. Is a noted lumber center. A pleasant trip is to Hayden Lake, about seven miles, where boating, fishing and golf may be enjoyed. Silver Grill is best; lunch 40c. City Camp 50¢, is in town in a fine grove, but not very level. MH-1928*

> *DESSERT HOTEL is best. Nearly all outside rooms.*

> *Well kept. Sgl. $1.50-$2.50; dbl. $2, bath $3-$3.50.*

> *KOOTENAI MOTOR CO. leads; has machine shop, open at all times. Labor $1.50. Ph. 400, for service car.*

> *SIMPSON MOTORS, Ford, a modern agency. Ph. 532.*

> *COEUR D'ALENE TIRE SHOP, 4th St. on Trail, is finely fitted for service. Ph. 479J. MH-1928*

115 Northwest Blvd. **Museum of North Idaho**. Exhibit topics include the Mullan Road, Fort Sherman, early transportation, logging and mining. The remains of "The Mullan Tree" are there. July 4th, 1861, found Captain John Mullan and his military detachment in what is now called 4th of July Canyon between Coeur d'Alene and the Cataldo Mission. Mullan was constructing a military road from Walla Walla, Washington, to Fort Benton, Montana. On that day Mullan carved M. R. into a tree to mark it as being on the military road. That carving remained on the tree until 1962 when the tree blew down. The carving is now here. See **Trail Tale: Mullan Road**, page 84.

See also at the museum the story of the Flyer, a steam boat that provided freight service on the lake and up the St. Joe and St. Maries Rivers. On weekends it doubled as a pleasure boat, popular with the college students. It was important to the growth of Coeur d'Alene from 1909-1939, when the Yellowstone Trail coursed through town.

In 1885 silver was discovered in the area and soon other precious metals were found. From here to the eastern border of Idaho, "mining" and "smelting" were the only operable words for 100 years. Over $5 billion in metals would be mined, and, as Don Root says in the *Idaho Handbook* (Moon Publications, 1997) "... making The Silver Valley one of the most lucrative mining districts in the history of the world, while at the same time turning it into a lifeless toxic waste dump." Today, even Kellogg, which suffered the biggest hit from smelters, looks to be recovering with forests regrown and recreational opportunities abundant. As one travels on the Trail, one sees little, if any, signs of the past, only the beauty of the forested mountains and streams. ✿

Speed limits were set through the 4th of July Canyon: 20 miles per hour. Trucks hauling logs needed special permits. Jitneys had to pay $1.00. [May 1922] ✿

Story has it that the top of the 4th of July Pass once had a rest stop with a store and a dancing bear. ✿

Old Cataldo Mission

For years the treacherous mud, steep hills and dangerous turns on the transcontinental highway (Yellowstone Trail), through the famed Fourth of July Canyon in Idaho have been the despair of automobilists ... arrangements were finally completed for a permanent highway through the canyon to connect with Shoshone County on the east and on to the Apple Way into Spokane.
August 1916 Northwestern Motorist

This highway, to the east of the city for a distance of 18 miles thru the famous Fourth of July canyon, is being constructed into a first-class thorofare winding its way around the shores of Lake Coeur d'Alene, thru mountains, valleys, and canyon. Travelers will find it most delightful and scenic. *Automobile Blue Book*, 1921. ✿.

... according to Mr. A. Leonard who drove to Spokane Saturday, the worst stretches on the road were in the Fourth of July Canyon between Cataldo and Burns summit. The road there was badly worn resulting in numerous washboard stretches and rough spots. Travel has been extremely heavy this season and road maintenance had to be postponed until traffic became lighter.
September 8, 1929 The Spokesman-Review (Spokane)

Four proposed highway routes have been surveyed by air ... a survey by the present Fourth of July Canyon sector of the Yellowstone Trail from Wolf Lodge Bay through Wolf Creek Canyon to eliminate curves.
October 19, 1930 Idaho Statesman

Remnant of YT near Mullan Tree site

On east side of 4th of July Pass
Museum of Northern Idaho

WAYSIDE

1480 Coeur d'Alene River Rd. **Enaville Resort** (AKA Snake Pit) at Enaville a mile or two north of Kingston. If you are on the Yellowstone Trail (Riverview Drive), turn north onto Coeur d'Alene River Road for one mile. If on I-90, take Exit 43 toward Kingston. Turn left onto Coeur d'Alene River Road and travel one mile. The Snake Pit is on your right. Who knows why it is called the Snake Pit, but, in spite of its wildly eclectic interior, there is good food there. Ever had Rocky Mountain oysters? We were last there several years ago so things may have changed, but we include it here because it has been a staple of the area since 1880 and is near the Trail. Chances are Trail travelers stopped there.

ID-028.0 to ID-033.3: The frustrations of research: The 1919 map issued by the Idaho Dept. of Ag. Soil Map is a detailed but poor map for this stretch. Either the surveying was poor, or the map drawing was crude. Close, but not a good match for the terrain. But, the label "Yellowstone Trail" demonstrated the acceptance and common use of that name.

ID-033.3 at Exit 28, Summit of 4th of July Pass

Fourth of July Summit, el. 3,163 ft.; good rooms at Hawley's Tavern; lunch, phone and supplies; cabins, $1.

Uncle Sam's spring; pure water. WPA-ID

The FOURTH OF JULY SUMMIT (3,290 alt.) is marked by a tunnel 394 feet in length. WPA-ID [Built after the YTA ended in 1930.]

Northeast from the summit on a dirt road is the MULLAN TREE . 1 m. Standing in the center of a fifty-acre park, this tree still bears the date, 1861, and the initials M. R. (Mullan Road) [Actually, "Military Road"] It was here on July 4, 1861, that Captain Mullan and his men were encamped while building the Mullan Road. They raised an American flag to the top of the tallest white pine, and from this circumstance the canyon has taken its name. WPA-ID

One mile east of I-90 Exit 28 at the Summit is the most pleasant Mullan Tree Monument rest stop where the tree once stood. Today the Mullan tree carving is preserved at the North Idaho Museum, Coeur d' Alene, but there is a little piece of old US 10/ Yellowstone Trail to contemplate. The sign at the monument says "The first road built over this pass in 1861 followed the creek bed. In 1916 this first "road" was replaced by US Highway 10 [sic] on which you are now standing. A goal for old-timers nursing their early cars up this steep grade was a rest stop at the top containing a store with a dancing bear to attract tourists. A 473 foot long tunnel was built under the pass in 1932 to reduce the steep grade. In 1958, Interstate 90 replaced US 10 and bypassed the tunnel. Reconstruction of I-90 in 1988-89 resulted in the removal of the old tunnel."

ID-037.1 to ID-039.0 Canyon Rd. is probably the YT but it is closed at the west end at the road maintenance shop.

ID-039.0 4th of July Canyon

CANYON GARAGE, small but good; has wrecker. MH-1928

Huckleberries can be found from Coeur d'Alene forests through the Silver Valley to Wallace and into western Montana from June through September. They look just like blueberries to us Easterners. Buy a huckleberry shake or sundae or pancakes or martini or anything huckleberry in the area. The shakes are absolutely yummy.

YT in the 4th of July Canyon
Northwestern Motorist, July 1917

WAYSIDE

ID-44.5 Old Mission State Park

This is an interesting historical short sidetrip.

I-90 was built on top of the Yellowstone Trail in much of this area. If you are on I-90 take Exit 39 to see the Old Mission. If you are on the driveable Yellowstone Trail turn south on Dredge Rd., and continue on Mission Rd.

This beautiful white building, standing on a low mound, was built in 1848 by Father Antonio Ravalli. Also known as the **Mission of the Sacred Heart or Cataldo Mission**, this National Historic Landmark has a fascinating history. It is the oldest standing building in Idaho, constructed with no nails by Fr. Ravalli and members of the Coeur d'Alene tribe. For more about the Old Mission, see **Trail Tale: Cataldo**, page 83.

ID

According to the 2001 *Insiders' Guide to the Idaho Panhandle* by Ellie Emmanuel,

> Silver Valley was somewhat isolated, with a frontier mentality that was more tolerant of drinking, gambling, and prostitution than more sedate, farming areas ... the businesses that followed catered to those interests. There were 28 saloons, one teacher, one preacher, and Molly b'Damm brothel in Wallace. ✿

FOREST FIRES WIPE OUT TWO MINING TOWNS, BLAZE UNCHECKED
FEAR IS FELT FOR TOURISTS ON YELLOWSTONE TRAIL HIGHWAY

The mining towns of Mace and Burke, east of Kellogg, Idaho, are reported destroyed by forest fires sweeping up the western slope of the Bitterroot Mountains. Wire communication is down. Fear is felt for the lives of tourists on the Yellowstone Trail Highway which is understood to be in the path of the flames.

July 14, 1923 The Gloversville Morning Herald (New York)

BIDS CALLED FOR BRIDGES AND CULVERTS NEAR KELLOGG

... A second [proposal] was for construction of five small bridges and additional culverts in the vicinity of Kellogg and the Coeur d'Alene - Yellowstone Trail.

March 24, 1933 The Spokesman-Review

Note: The date of this item is three years almost to the day of the demise of the Yellowstone Trail Association, yet the name of the famous highway remained current. In fact, the name still appeared in newspapers into the 1940s.

🚗 It is believed that the YT ran on today's Yellowstone Ave. near Osburn and crossed the Coeur d'Alene River just west of Terror Gulch road (ID-61.9), following Silver Valley Road to the west and Yellowstone Ave. to the east.

Original YT bridge in Elk Creek, ID-59.8 near Moon Gulch Road

🚗 Near ID-043.0, the YT may have followed Canyon Road and may have used Hayden Loop for some years. The route of the Trail in Cataldo and for several miles west is not clear because of repeated realignments and improvements.

Early motel. Note the garages which, probably, were built between original cabins.

Kellogg 's Yellowstone Trail Garage. Picture believed to be from 1940
Janet Laket

Staff House Museum, Kellogg

🚗 Between ID-059.1 and ID-060.4, the driving line follows Silver Valley Rd. ("Feeder" or "Frontage" often appended to the name), but the original YT followed Elk Creek Rd., now only partially driveable parallel on the north of Silver Valley Rd. Access can be had at ID-59.7 at Moon Gulch Rd.

Just several feet to the east of Moon Gulch Rd. on Elk Creek Rd. is an old Yellowstone Trail bridge of interest, GPS: 47.53347, -116.05906. It might not be driveable, but the YT followed Elk Creek Rd. to the east to ID-060.4 near the Miners' Memorial. Apparently, Elk Creek Rd. went further east behind the location of the Miners' Memorial along a road, now lost, that emerges on to Elk Creek Rd. at ID-061.0. Google maps will be of considerable help here.

ID-045.6 Cataldo

The town was originally named Old Mission. A steel bridge over the Coeur d'Alene River was built in 1919.
April 12, 1919 Western Highways Builder

The road used by the Yellowstone Trail between Cataldo and Kingston was originally built in 1924/1925 and rebuilt by 1938 because it was "narrow, crooked, and unable to withstand present traffic and heavy loads."
1938 Annual Report of the Idaho Transportation Dept, Jeff Stratten
Note: What was used before 1924?

ID-048.6 Kingston

At ID-49.3 the Yellowstone Trail apparently followed Doolittle Rd. running north of Riverview for 7-800 feet. The construction of I-90 relocated the original run just to the east of here, requiring using the overpass today.

ID-050.8 Pinehurst

The Coeur d'Alene Mountains flanks, late in every summer, are blue with ripe huckleberries. WPA-ID

ID-053.8 Smelterville

The name was chosen by the citizens because of the large smelter of the Bunker Hill mine established there.

West of Kellogg with its miracles of machinery, there is still to be seen a poisoned and dead or dying landscape. Trees slain by the invisible giant still stand with lifeless limbs and with roots still sucking the poisoned earth. WPA-ID

At Smelterville, between, roughly, ID-54 and ID-56, the YT followed a twisty road south of McKinley (Old US 10) through the Bunker Hill Superfund site.

ID-056.7 Kellogg

(2,305 alt. ; 4,124 pop.) Kellogg is a famous mining spot, with the Bunker Hill and Sullivan, the largest lead mine in the United States, located here. Above it the denuded mountains declare the potency of lead. The Sullivan Mine here has a development of sixty-four and a half miles and (with 560 men) the largest payroll of any mine in the State. WPA-ID

Home to a major smelter, Kellogg was battered in the early 1980s when the smelter shut down and became an EPA Superfund site. Before that, the citizens had turned to Silver Mountain and tourism as a saving grace. To move skiers from Kellogg to the mountain top, they built the world's longest single-stage gondola. The mountain offers 50 runs, 1,500 acres, and a 2,200 vertical foot drop. **Silver Mountain Gondola** ride ticket office is at 610 Bunker Ave. We mention this obviously post-Yellowstone Trail entertainment because as you drive through town you cannot help but note the gondola as it whisks right over McKinley Ave. (Yellowstone Trail) on its way up the mountain. The gondola also symbolizes the "new" Kellogg, like a phoenix rising from the dregs of poisoned soil to affluent condos.

300 E Cameron Ave. (Yellowstone Trail). **Miners Hat Realty Building**, a doff of the "hat" to the history of the town.

Corner of W Cameron Ave. and S Division St. The former site of the **Yellowstone Trail Garage** in the 1920s. Today this spot is home to the ubiquitous Dave Smith Motors, a multi-state retail auto sales company. Albert Wellman owned The Yellowstone Trail Garage, selling Dodge and Plymouth products. The gas pumps faced Cameron Ave., "which was the highway," according to *Roads Less Traveled* by Dorothy Dahlgren and Simone Kincaid of North Idaho Museum (North Idaho Museum Press, 2007).

820 McKinley Ave. The **Staff House Museum**. Otherwise known as Shoshone County Mining and Smelting Museum. The name comes from the former purpose of the house: to house resident and visiting managers of the Bunker Hill & Sullivan Mining Company. Displays are mainly about mining, and the Bunker Hill Mine in particular, plus an art gallery.

210 Main St. **McConnell Hotel** had an early radio broadcast antenna on the roof for radio station KWAL. If you had one of the early auto radios you might have heard out of the ether "WKAL broadcasting to you from the roof of the McConnell Hotel," wrote Dave Habura in the Yellowstone Trail Association newsletter, the *Arrow*, August 2011. The building now is vacant.

ID-060.4

On Silver Valley Rd. on the Yellowstone Trail at I-90 Exit 54 is the **Sunshine Miners Memorial**, a statue which honors 91 fallen miners killed in a 1972 mine fire. The strong miner is clutching a pneumatic rock drill and his head lamp stays lit all the time. This is an important part of the history and culture of the area.

Sunshine Miners Memorial, 4 miles east of Kellogg

ID-063.4 Osburn

Through this canyon area are numerous streams, majestic forest scenery, and tall hills. To this day it is a beautiful area.

ID-066.1 Silverton

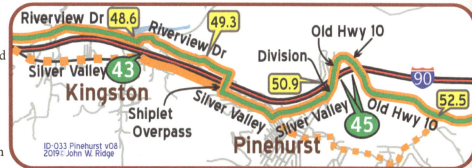

IDAHO PLAYS HOST TO "TRAILERS"

The annual state meeting of the Yellowstone Trail Association was held here (Wallace) February 18. National President M. J. Dowling and General Manager H. O. Cooley came from Minnesota. Current annual dues are: Coeur d'Alene $175; Kellogg $100; Wallace $175, Mullan $50.

The national Association took an active part in forming the National Association of Highways whose goal is for legislation for a national system of federal highways under the supervision of a commission. The group recommended that the Association work for standard laws regulating traffic throughout the nation, especially as to signs, lights, signals and similar matters.

A Mineral County (Montana) Commissioner said that if expected state aid were given, the Mineral County highway would be extended to the state line to Lookout Pass. Plans to meet that road on the Idaho side have been made.
March 22, 1919 Western Highways Builder
Note: Those "plans" took about five years to come to fruition.

On April 12 the representatives of the Yellowstone Trail Association will give a dance in Mullan, the proceeds to be applied to the highway fund and a camping ground for tourists in the city park. The Yellowstone Trail people plan to make it a spot that tourists will make an effort to reach.
April 12, 1919 Western Highways Builder

Bank St. is YT in Wallace

Wallace District Mining Museum

YT Garage in Wallace then (above)
and now (below)

A tortured I-90 skirts Wallace with YT underneath.

Camping near Wallace *Mark Mowbray*

ID-068.1 Wallace

(2,728 alt.; 3,634 pop.), standing in a triangular valley in which many streams enter the main fork of the Coeur d'Alene River, is the seat of Shoshone County and the distributing center of this large mining and lumbering area. The great fire of 1910 partly destroyed this town, since rebuilt and quite picturesque, with its better homes terraced on the mountainside, row on row. In its lovely little park at the western end is another monument to Mullan. WPA-ID

Since Wallace is jammed into a very narrow canyon, there isn't much choice for a road. The Yellowstone Trail went right through town: Front St., 5th, Pine, 6th, Bank. There wasn't much choice for I-90, either. The citizens nixed the idea of splitting the historic town in two, so you will see that the super highway went up and over the northeast side of town, with the Yellowstone Trail running beneath part of it. They used to advertise this town as "the last stop light," referring to the last portion of I-90 which was built there in 1991, eliminating stop lights on that highway across the entire country. The site of that "last stoplight" was the corner of Bank and Seventh St.

The entire town is listed on the National Register of Historic Places and whole blocks in the business district have remained virtually intact for 100 years or more. Note the sign at Bank and 6th St., noting "The Center of the Universe."

509 Bank St. The **Wallace District Mining Museum** is a treasure trove of information about mining and miners' lives with historic photos and artifacts. It also has pictures of two Hollywood movies filmed in Wallace, "Dante's Peak" in 1997 and "Heaven's Gate" in 1979. The "last stoplight" itself, "Old Blinky," referred to above, is there.

6th and Pine Sts. **Northern Pacific Railroad Museum**. This was the hub of the community with freight and passenger trains to Missoula running regularly. Robert Dunsmore, in *Historic Wallace Idaho* booklet says that, additionally, the mining community had three passenger runs daily until 1926.

There is a ton of data about the Northern Pacific Railroad in the West and its role in the Coeur d'Alene mining district in this recreated 1900 station. Spend time looking at the outside of this chateau-style beautiful building. Don Root, in *Idaho Handbook* (Moon Pubs. 1997) says that "this depot was carefully moved 200 feet to this location in 1986 after the new interstate threatened to run right over it."

610 Bank St. White Bender Building, home to the **Silver Capital Arts and Mineral Museum**; it showcases displays of minerals from the Silver Valley and other mining regions of Idaho and the West.

605 Cedar St. **Oasis Rooms Bordello Museum**. It was opened in 1895 and run as an active bordello until 1988, in spite of being outlawed 15 years previously. The rooms are preserved as they were when last used. We include it here because it is part of the history of the Yellowstone Trail era, is the only one we know of along the Trail, and may even have been visited by Trail travelers.

Pretty much all of the downtown of Wallace burned in the "Big Burn" forest fire of 1910. Ed Pulaski led 45 miners to a **mining tunnel** and saved the lives of 40 of them.

Tourists may visit that tunnel and a memorial sign one mile south of Wallace on King (Moon Pass Rd.). Park and see the sign commemorating the 1910 fire and Pulaski. Then hike 2 miles to the tunnel. Two newer monuments were unveiled in August, 2010, the 100th anniversary of the fire. One is on the west side of town at the **Visitor Center** at 10 River St., and another is in the **Nine Mile Cemetery**, 413 Cedar St. Pulaski later invented a fire-fighting axe with a pick on one end of the head and an axe on the other. It is called the "Pulaski Axe" and is still widely used today in firefighting.

Street sign in Wallace

Northern Pacific Railroad Museum in 1900 Depot, Wallace

The YT between Wallace and Mullan
Butch Jacobson

Captain John Mullan Museum at Mullan

Bitteroot Spring on the YT near Mullan

National Mill in Mullan on Friday Rd., the YT.
Many mine and processing mills dotted Silver Valley.

YT (US 10) at summit of Lookout Pass

YT near Montana border

Statue of Captain John Mullan, one of many along his military road. Note I-90 aloft in background. Read **Trail Tale: Mullan**, page 84.

ID-074.8 Mullan

Founded in 1884 between two silver-lead mines and shaken by strikes, it has managed to avoid homelessness of miners that usually falls in towns in such regions. The Morning Mine, still operating here, is the third largest lead producer in the U.S. and sustains most of the population of the town. On the right is the monument to Captain Mullan. WPA-ID

MULLAN, IDA. pop 2,600; an active mining town. Bilberg Hotel has some modern rooms. Mullan Garage is best, has wrecker. Camp 50c, on level land at ball grounds. Fine water at the Bitter Root Spring. MH-1928

229 Earle St. **Captain John Mullan Museum**. Established in the old Liberty Theater, this museum illustrates the history of Mullan with exhibits of historical furnishings, photographs, newspapers, and mining relics. The museum features information on the building of the Mullan Road from 1859-1862 from Fort Benton, Montana, to Fort Walla Walla, Washington.

104 Hunter Ave. **St. Andrew's Episcopal Church**. Built out of wood in 1888.

WAYSIDE

You might be interested in driving to a former mining camp-turned-town-turned-ghost town.

Burke is about 6 1/2 miles northeast of Wallace on ID 4 at the east entrance of Wallace. On the way you can see relics of the past: the Canyon Silver mine, Blackbear mine, and the Standard-Mammouth mines. In Burke was the Hecla-Star mine. The amazing thing about Burke is that the narrow main street is actually a covered flume for a creek and is also the route of a railroad. It is said that when a train went by, merchants had to pull in their awnings. There is even the story of a single hotel built on both sides of the narrow street. It literally had a road, two railroad tracks, and a covered creek running through it. We walked it and can attest to the narrowness of it all. Unfortunately, now there is very little of the town left to see besides the narrow street. There are, however, large mine structures left and the visitor can see the signs of the engines of the economy that drove the Silver Valley. See picture on page 69.

In the early years of the Yellowstone Trail, Lookout Pass did not exist and travelers circumvented the mountain via rustic Yellowstone Trail/Randolph Creek road. If you go out of Mullan to the east on Larson Rd. (not the Interstate) and past Shoshone Park, you will be on the Yellowstone Trail of 1915-1924 which circumvents Lookout Pass. Keep on this road. At the Idaho-Montana state line your road is then called Randolph Creek Rd. and comes out at Taft, Montana, an old mining town which is no more. There you will join I-90 at Exit 5.

This Yellowstone Trail/Randolph Creek Road was inappropriately named Mullan Pass. This was not the route of the Mullan Military Roads, but was officially so recorded and no one has taken the initiative to correct it. You may see that error on present maps. John Mullan experts say that Mullan used what is today called Sohon Pass, south of this area.

After the more direct Lookout Pass opened in 1922, or possibly 1924, the Trail was routed there. For the contentious story of Lookout Pass, see **Trail Tale: Bitterroots**, page 80.

Apparently the route of the YT in downtown Mullan came from the west on Earle St. and from the east on Friday Ave. crossing from one to the other across from the football field (GPS: 47.47013, -115.78923).

ID-083.6 Idaho/Montana Line

Mullan Pass

Original Yellowstone Trail/Randolph Creek Road over mis-named Mullan Pass.

Just to the west of the divide the early YT across Mullan Pass followed a switchback to the north. Sometime in the 1980s that switchback was replaced by the current less-demanding switchback. The old switchback is closed with a Kelly Hump, a pile of rock and soil to deter traffic. The 1917 Forest Atlas confuses the route of the switchback, seeming to have it cross the "river" to the NW side. Strange.

Lookout Pass

Lookout Pass Summit of the Bitter Root Mts.; the Idaho-Montana Line. Telegraph and water only. MH-1928

US 10 crosses the Idaho-Montana Line over Lookout Pass (4,738 alt.). From the summit is afforded a view of a large part of two National Forests, the St. Joe and the Coeur d'Alene. One can still see the scars which remain from one of the worst forest fires in history. This epic of devastation wrote its record in a flood of flame that lighted the sky for a hundred miles and in mountains of smoke that obscured the sun. WPA-ID

In 1938, the newer YT over the Lookout Pass was "oiled 40 feet wide in Mullan and 20 feet wide to the Pass. This eliminated the last unpaved section on the Yellowstone Trail" (referencing only the Idaho part of the YT, no doubt). *1938 Annual Report of the Idaho Transportation Dept.,* Jeff Stratten.

Come Ride with Us:
The Yellowstone Trail in the Bitterroots

We are headed west on I-90 from Missoula, gracefully winding, climbing, and descending as we approach the mountains of the Bitterroots. It is a glorious ride, our Jeep never pulling hard, our eyes Velcroed to the scenery. The area from Saltese, Montana, to Mullan, Idaho, near Lookout Pass is one of breathtaking forest beauty. We are on our way to again visit an original piece of the Yellowstone Trail. We turn off the Interstate at Exit 5 at a place called Taft, five miles east of the Montana/Idaho border. Taft, a busy, rough-and-tumble mining camp in 1911, is now reduced to nothing but that exit sign. We must go east for 3/4 mile to find Lolo National Forest Rd. #286, Randolph Creek Road, which was the Yellowstone Trail. We have begun our adventure into the past on the Trail which is still gravel, still pleasantly driveable.

On the YT Randolph Creek Road

Tall pine trees lean against steep mountain sides. The surrounding quiet is broken by streams gossiping loudly, moving from 6,000 feet down into "gulches" whose names reveal a landscape of colorful history. Logging and old mining roads branch off, cut into blue hillsides to cling to the contours of the land. Six miles and 100 years from I-90 we reach the summit. Almost immediately we see that a cutoff was built in the 1980s to avoid the old wicked switchback just west of the summit. Going down the west side we leave Montana's Randolph Creek Road and continue on Idaho's Yellowstone Trail Rd. Another nine scenic miles later we arrive at the mining town of Mullan. That distance can take hours, though, with stops to walk the old switchback, stare at the mountain views and imagine a 1914 touring car coming over the hill.

The summit bears the misnomer of Mullan Pass. Captain John Mullan, who carved a military wagon road from Fort Walla Walla, Washington, to Fort Benton, Montana, from 1858 to 1862, never saw this pass. His road dropped directly south from Mullan through what is now called Sohon Pass and followed the St. Regis River. The 1956 USGS map only confounds the problem by mistakenly naming the Yellowstone Trail route the Mullan Rd. The short lived military wagon road carried many pioneers but it was soon reduced to a pack horse trail, almost indistinguishable from forest floor. The Northern Pacific Railroad came winding around Lookout Pass in 1883 and made long-distance wagon roads obsolete.

First Attempt: Randolph Creek Road

Good roads had not reached the Northwest, but the auto had. By train. And the only way the autoist could travel through the Bitterroots was to put his car on the Northern Pacific. As always, it was the autoist who pushed hardest for roads. In 1911, reportedly at the insistence of the Wallace (Idaho) Automobile Club, Montana's Missoula County and Idaho's Shoshone County officials met to discuss the feasibility of each building a road, meeting at the state line. The Randolph Creek road project would rest on county shoulders because state aid was unlikely.

For two and one half years they argued. Montana people argued that Wallace could draw all of the mine business if a road were built their way, and Wallace chastised Montana for foot-dragging. Then some cooperation was achieved and the Randolph Road/Yellowstone Trail Road was completed in late fall of 1913. Newspapers on both sides of the border lauded the work as an economic boon, allowing travel from Missoula to Coeur d'Alene and thus connecting the Northwest to the Midwest with an auto road.

On summit of Mullan Pass on
YT/Randolph Creek Road
Cathy Hendryx

The Yellowstone Trail Association had watched the progress of the Randolph Creek road with keen interest. With this road through the Bitterroots, the Yellowstone Trail Association could now boast a route complete from Chicago to Seattle. During 1914 the road was a *de facto* part of the route and by 1915 it was marked and included on Association maps.

Almost immediately, a major problem emerged with the route. Both the Association and the locals knew that it snowed a lot in the mountains, but 10 to 15 feet of it still on the road in May? In 1916, it was eight feet deep on June 10! The inhabitants developed the habit of forming shoveling brigades to open the road, even inviting tourists to help shovel. But to the Yellowstone Trail Association this was a weak link in the chain that threatened the whole of it. Admitting to the driving public that they had to put their cars on the Northern Pacific to cross the Bitterroots nine months out of the year was inconceivable in light of their advertising. A better route had to be found. ⇨

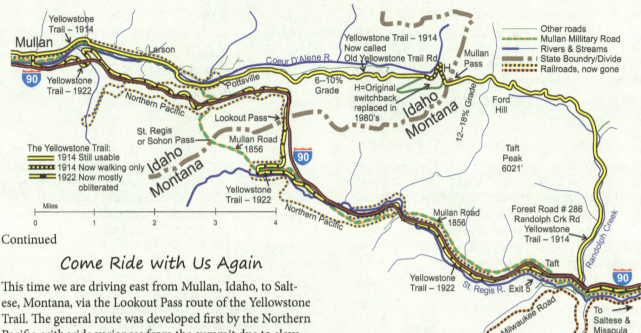

Continued

Come Ride with Us Again

This time we are driving east from Mullan, Idaho, to Salt-ese, Montana, via the Lookout Pass route of the Yellowstone Trail. The general route was developed first by the Northern Pacific, with wide variances from the summit due to elevation challenges, then developed by Shoshone and Mineral Counties, then US 10 after 1926, and now used by I-90. We begin on River Street in Mullan and head over to I-90 east. The original Trail "crossed the flats and Willow Creek" and followed a serpentine path up to Lookout Pass. I-90 follows a gently curving route right in the same place, obscuring the old Yellowstone Trail totally.

In the comfort of our air-conditioned Jeep, we cruise the five miles to the summit of Lookout Pass. Not a good place to find traces of the old highway. We can explore the route of the Trail south for a short bit to the St. Regis River, but we must return to I-90 because there is no through section of the old road.

The Permanent Route: Lookout Pass

The presence of the Interstate, while destroying most of the this route of the Yellowstone Trail, also serves to confirm the selection of the Lookout Pass as a better route for a cross-country highway. Actually, that was probably the conclusion of many locals as well, not long after the Yellowstone Trail/Randolph Creek route was opened. Wesley Everett, manager of the Amazon-Dixie Mining Company, summed up the problems with the Randolph Creek route in a letter to the Superior, Montana, *Mineral Independent* in June 1915. He vigorously protested against the distribution of county tax money on the Randolph Creek road when the real traffic of the mining and lumbering industries and the traveler should go over Lookout Pass. He asked, "Why was the present road turned from the main valley to the summit at 12% grade, where the snow lies two months longer at an elevation of 400 feet higher, where there is a dangerous switchback, and where the road serves one mine only?" Why, indeed?

This salvo apparently found an audience, for it triggered talks between the two counties once again, with agreement to build over Lookout Pass. Thus began a seven year struggle, political and financial. Funds from two counties, two states, and the U.S. government (via the U.S. Forest Service) had to be found.

Idaho's Shoshone County Board became a stumbling block. Three years of appeals by businessmen, Montana's new Mineral County, good roads boosters and Yellowstone Trail representatives were not acknowledged. The threat of losing the Trail and its transcontinental traffic did not budge them. The thought of 400 feet lower elevation with less snow did not impress them. Mineral County jumped to its own defense, attacking its neighbor with headlines:

- MINERAL COUNTY BATTLES FOR THE BEST ROADS. Looking to the Interest of Tourist Traveler in Summer Time

- SHOSHONE COMMISSIONERS BLOCK IMPROVEMENT

- SHOSHONE COUNTY BOARD BLAMED FOR INDIFERENCE SHOWN TOWARD HIGHWAY

Mineral County insisted that it could not move forward unilaterally until the Shoshone County Board "got behind" the idea. Finally, the election of late 1918 created a more accepting Shoshone County Board.

By 1919 each side of the summit had been surveyed and engineers had tramped repeatedly through the forest to suggest a route. Idaho would build eight miles to the summit and Montana three miles, so most of the decisions rested with the Idaho delegation.

Wesley Everett suggested one route, others were suggested. A definite route had not been confirmed until the summer of 1920. From the summit, the road would travel west down to the "flats and Willow Creek" and enter Mullan on Friday Rd. and River St. Going east, the new road would descend down to join the Yellowstone Trail at Taft. W. J. Hall, Commissioner of Public Works for the state of Idaho, suggested that the road be less wide than the standard 18 feet near the top, which would have required deep digging from the hillside, and then widen the road later. The idea was adopted for it would save money and time and would meet state standards later. ⇨

A fracas arose in September of 1921 when Mineral County announced a proposal from the federal government to join the county on a 50-50 basis, which, unfortunately, would delay progress on the road for nine months. Shoshone County objected with a headline.

- BOARD OF TRADE TO INVESTIGATE MINERAL COUNTY ROAD

Financing Lookout Pass Road

The reporting of the finances of the project became comical. Figures varied daily. Shoshone County estimated in 1919 the cost to be $33,000 from the state, $66,000 from Shoshone County, $100,000 federal aid and $200,000 from bond issue. In 1921 a five mill special levy was passed in Mineral County; $20,000 was the estimate needed. In November of 1921 Mineral County was quoted as saying "Contrary to public understanding, this road is being constructed by the Federal Bureau of Public Highways of the Department of Agriculture. The forestry bureau has nothing to do with the work, nor has the state of Montana nor Mineral County." The reader is left to assume that the five mill levy was insufficient and that federal aid was granted.

In Idaho, there was divided opinion about the funding of the Lookout Pass road at the expense of the Fourth of July Pass road, an equally necessary road if the Yellowstone Trail was to succeed as transcontinental.

The *Mineral Independent* reminded readers of the financial problems of Mineral County on January 17, 1924, a topic that should have been addressed seven years earlier to garner more patience from Shoshone County:

"The land in Mineral County is principally owned by the federal government, in a forest reserve, and the road burden is thus placed upon a few who are actual taxpayers. It is claimed that about 92% of the land in Mineral County is in reserve by the government, and thus exempt from taxation. In Mineral County there is [sic.] over 80 miles of main traveled road through this forestry-owned territory which has been built and maintained by the taxpayer."

Headlines, richly textured with promises of imminent action, kept the issue on the front pages. The Wallace Board of Trade was forever conferring with the two county boards, inspecting the progress of the road and issuing false hopes of immediate completion. For instance:

- LOOKOUT PASS ROAD TO BE FINISHED BY NOVEMBER 1 (1921)

There was great interest in opening Mullan Pass each spring, well, summer, anyway. While this is a poor picture, you can see a couple of men sitting on the railing of the short bridge (culvert?) across from the other railing on the lower left. Three fellows are standing by the auto, probably deciding whether it was worth it. All are equipped with shovels. And the auto does have chains on. The bleak landscape is undoubtedly due to the great 1910 fire and resembled much of the area.
Butch Jacobson Collection, Mullan Museum

"Jack Knife turn" near the Mullan Pass
Northwestern Motorist, July 1917

- LOOKOUT PASS ROAD TO OPEN THIS JULY (1921)
- NO SNOW SHOVELING NEEDED [Note: Wrong! Volunteers were sought in April, 1925]

The Yellowstone Trail Association Role

The Yellowstone Trail Association's role in this drama was two-fold. First, five influential men in the Lookout Pass project were representatives and officers of the Association. They spoke frequently in support of the project. The intense interest of the Yellowstone Trail Association in this project was shown by the on-site presence in 1920 of founder Joe Parmley and President H. B. Wiley. Second, the Trail was extremely important to the several communities affected by this new road. They not only valued it for in-state travel but they saw the Trail Association as a means of bringing the most popular transcontinental highway and its tourists to the county. Many news articles over the years included supportive statements such as "we appreciate the importance of the Yellowstone Trail to our county," and "the success of the Yellowstone Trail depends upon the construction of a road across the summit," and "the Yellowstone Trail would at once become the most popular of the northern transcontinental routes."

At Last! Or Was It?

There was no grand opening, no ribbon-cutting ceremony in July, 1922 when the road was declared more or less finished. But, then again, November newspapers said that it "will be ready to open July 1, 1923." In 1924 part of the road was still dirt, not even graveled. It had been declared "open" many times since 1921 and always with caveats. Cars had apparently been sneaking over Lookout Pass, perhaps around construction, for at least a year and reporting their opinions. Construction which started with a bang seemed to end with a relieved sigh.

Thanks for Riding with Us

Well, our round trip is over. Everybody out. But study the map. See where we've been. Notice how the trail and I-90 are entwined. The landscape dictated the route but it also provided the texture of past times. We can see how America's transportation changed: wagon roads for the military and pioneers skirted the Pass; then came railroads which killed all interest in long-distance roads; then automobiles, which brought back the need for highways and opened the Northwest to the automobile tourist and made the Yellowstone Trail a "Good Road from Plymouth Rock to Puget Sound." ✿

Bitterroots

Cataldo Mission

The luminescent Cataldo Mission
David Habura

When the light is right, the **Old Mission** almost looks luminescent standing there serenely on that little knoll in northern Idaho. The Yellowstone Trail ran very near it. You can see it from Exit 39 on I-90. It wasn't always painted white and its name was different when it was completed in 1853. Dedicated to the Sacred Heart of Jesus, it was called the Mission of the Sacred Heart. Later it was called the Cataldo Mission in honor of Father Joseph M. Cataldo. Today it is referred to simply as the Old Mission.

Edmund R. Cody in *History of the Coeur d'Alene Mission of the Sacred Heart* (1930) records the many trials, travels and tribulations that the French Canadian Catholic fur traders, the Iroquois and the Coeur d'Alene and other Native Americans had had for about 20 years to get the "Black Robes" (priests) in their midst. Finally, Father Peter DeSmet arrived in 1839, followed by other enthusiastic Black Robes, all ministering among the Indians throughout the Northwest.

A mission had been built on the southeastern end of Lake Coeur d'Alene along the St. Joe River but its waters frequently flooded, so a site for a permanent mission and church was sought. The knoll upon which it has stood for about 167 years was a fortunate choice. Today, the church can be seen for some distance around, its white exterior framed by the dark of the evergreen woods.

It was DeSmet who designed the beautiful edifice in 1848, but the job of building it fell to Father Anthony Ravalli, a long-experienced missionary. Cody wrote,

> A heart less courageous than that of Ravalli must have quaked at such a prospect. For tools he possessed a broad axe, an augur, some ropes and pulleys and a pen knife. For workmen he had two Brothers and a band of untutored Indians.

Fortunately, Ravalli had some experience in mechanics and had an understanding of mathematics and Native Americans. Some "exemplary Christian Indians" were permitted to help in the building. It was they who felled trees and carried rocks from the hills.

Cody describes the building process of 1848-1853 thus:

> Plans for a church 90 feet long, 40 feet wide and 30 feet high were drawn by Ravalli and were faithfully followed. Uprights about 18 inches square and rafters about 10 inches square were cut from the mighty pines which grew in abundance on the hillsides nearby. The sawing was done in an improvised saw-pit with an improvised whipsaw, and the planing and shaping were done by hand

with a broad axe. Nails were not available so holes were bored in the uprights and rafters and they were joined with wooden pegs.

> The roof and walls were made by boring holes in the uprights and rafters and interlacing willow saplings and closely woven grasses between them. Over the whole was spread adobe mud from the river bank. Timbers were cut and planed for the floor, and columns made from perfect pine trees laboriously planed, were placed to support the roof of the porch.

The interior walls were covered with heavy cloth. And those cast iron chandeliers? They were made of tin! Two paintings, brought from Europe by the priests and now restored, hang there today. There were some pews, but the Indians preferred to squat on the floor to hear the Black Robes' messages.

The hand-sewn fabrics in the interior

Upon its opening in 1853, the Mission became a center of activity in the Northwest. It was a hospice for immigrants, and a rendezvous for hunters, and trappers. Even Governor Stevens appeared. It was a self-sustaining village, all built with ingenuity and faith.

During the mid-1800s, the tribes grew to mistrust governments, emigrants and white men in general. Attacks such as the one on Rev. Whitman's mission in Washington were growing. The Black Robes had been preaching peace for decades, but fear that the white man was usurping their native lands prevailed.

When Father Cataldo arrived in 1877 he would have seen the Coeur d'Alene planting potatoes and wheat and doing farm chores around the mission as they had been doing for three decades. That same year the U.S. Government set the bounds of the Indian Reservation and the Mission did not lie within the set limits. The Native Americans were removed from the very site they helped build and on to the Reservation. In truth, they had more right to the Mission than did the European settlers. The Mission was closed.

In 1928 the Diocese of Boise, through the supporting efforts of multiple groups, restored the Mission to become again what it once was. The foundation, floors, 18-inch walls, pillars, steps all were repaired. And they painted it white.

Today, the Coeur d'Alene still attend the annual August 15th Feast of the Assumption on the lawn of the Old Mission, now a state park. When we last saw it, there was not yet a visitors' center with a video. There was a volunteer who guided his party of two unhurriedly for an afternoon through this monumental yet simple oldest building in Idaho. ✿

Over the Mountains Following the Mullan Military Road

with Don Popejoy

That hot August 5th, 1914, found the Yellowstone Trail Association leaders and interested representatives at a convention at Montana's Hunter's Hot Springs resort, debating the next extension of the Trail (see **Trail Tale: Hunter's Hot Springs**, page 152). It had recently been established as far west as the headwaters of the Missouri River near Three Forks, Montana, with a spur south from Livingston to the Yellowstone National Park, its namesake. The conventioneers now eyed the formidable Rocky Mountains blocking the path to Puget Sound. There existed no suitable auto road between Three Forks, Montana, and Spokane, Washington. Nevertheless, the motion to extend the Yellowstone Trail to the Pacific Coast carried. The route was unspecified.

A contingency from Great Falls, Montana, was adamant that the proposed extension of the Yellowstone Trail be routed north from Livingston and the Yellowstone National Park to Great Falls, then west to Idaho and south to Spokane. While the founders of the Trail were opposed to that radical idea designed only to benefit Great Falls, they deferred the question "for study."

In reality, the decision was made indirectly by the State of Montana. In the previous year, Montana had created the Highway Commission with little funding and one Commissioner with one secretary. But the Commissioner immediately began to designate selected roads as State Roads in an effort for the State to improve long-distance auto travel. He announced to the conference that the existing Yellowstone Trail was designated as one of the first State Roads. And further, that a State Road entering from North Dakota was to continue through Butte and Missoula and St. Regis to the Idaho border near Mullan, Idaho. Without discussion the Great Falls proposal ended even though the State route designation west of Missoula was mountain terrain with very few sections of road ready for auto traffic.

But fifty years previously there had been a wagon road there. The Mullan Military Road had been built between Walla Walla, Washington, and Fort Benton, Montana, including the section over the Bitterroot range of the Rockies to be followed by the Yellowstone Trail. No one mentioned this old road during the 1914 Yellowstone Trail deliberations, no doubt because much of the road was overgrown and many of its bridges over tumultuous rivers were washed out. Only parts of the Mullan Road were usable, those maintained by mining interests and local residents. Bringing together two historic roads separated in time by half a century would be a major task.

Genesis of the Mullan Military Road

An enthusiastic Lieutenant John Mullan, fresh out of West Point, was attached to the 1853 railroad surveying party directed by Washington Governor Isaac Stevens. The survey was part of the great railroad push to open the West. A topographical engineer and surveyor, Mullan was charged with finding a possible railroad route for the Northern Pacific railroad between Missoula and Coeur dAlene. At the same time, Stevens also realized the need for a wagon road and ordered Mullan to observe for a possible wagon route while surveying for a railroad. From this came a series of exploring expeditions throughout the Bitterroot and other Rocky ranges for Mullan.

Coincidentally, Mullan heard of a potentially feasible wagon route from Fort Benton, Montana, on the Missouri River, proceeding southwest to Garrison, Montana, then west over the Bitterroots to near Spokane, then south to Walla Walla. Almost a decade later he would lead a crew of 100 soldiers and 100 laborers in hacking their way through 624 grueling miles to create that very wagon route.

At that time, in the mid-1800s, immigrants and miners demanded more protection from the Army as they moved west because Native Americans repeatedly hassled and attacked them for invading their land and disrupting their lives. Immigrants arrived at the Rockies from both the east and west. From the east of the Rockies they came by horse and wagon on the Oregon Trail or by boat on the Mississippi-Missouri River. From the west of the Rockies they came via the Pacific Ocean, the Columbia River from the Willamette Valley in Oregon, and then by horse and wagon on crude wagon trails. But Governor Stevens wanted a road available for the floods of new settlers from the east. The Mullan Military Road became that other usable route … however, briefly.

The U. S. Military was told to create the needed road (and pay for it!) so that troops and supplies could conduct the "Indian Wars." Lieutenant (later Captain) John Mullan proved to be the obvious choice to lead the effort. Although only five feet five inches in height, he was a dynamo. He was described as having a "natural bent for diplomacy and human compassion" and skill as an arbiter, necessary characteristics as he plowed through Native American-occupied country.

On the Road and Over the Rockies

Mullan's daily records of the 15 month building trek from Walla Walla to Fort Benton (1859-1860) were meticulously kept. Like Merriweather Lewis before him, he noted flora, fauna, latitude and longitude, soil and water conditions, etc. Indeed, today much is known and written about this heroic effort of 160 years ago because of Mullan's complete ⇨

Mullan Road ascending from Alder Creek
R. H. Dunsmore

notes. For instance, Marilyn Wyse and John Robinson in *Roads to Romance* (Montana DOT 1992) say that, "… of the 624 miles, 120 were cut through dense forest with an additional 150 miles through open pine forest, and over 100 bridges and river crossings were built. Crossing the Rockies required 30 miles of earth and rock excavation." It was done with limited equipment and huge human effort.

Mullan and his crew set out in July of 1859 and from Walla Walla to near Coeur d'Alene on the plains the construction was pretty easy going. However, approaching Lake Coeur d'Alene was something different. Maj. Ryan F. Shaw writes that it, " … required heavy rock work. Descending 700 feet from the plains to the St. Joseph River required felling trees, digging rocks, and blasting boulders. At the bottom the crew was obliged to build a 60 foot bridge … and a 400-yard corduroy across the marshy Coeur d'Alene Valley." *The Mullan Road: Carving a Passage through the Frontier Northwest, 1859-62* edited by Paul McDermott, Ronald Grim, and Philip Mobley. (Mountain Press, 2015).

Mullan Road Memorial
south of Spokane

Reaching Lake Coeur d'Alene,they built flatboats to reach their supply point at the Cataldo Mission. See **Trail Tale: Cataldo**, page 83. From there east they followed the Coeur d'Alene River which wandered up the winding, steep-sided valley requiring many miles of excavation. Lacking the time to cut a road through all the steep banks, Mullan chose to build many bridges across the river, leaving a "less-than-optimal" road with 41 bridges across the Coeur d'Alene River, and an additional 46 bridges across the St. Regis River in Montana, reported Shaw.

Because progress was unexpectedly slow, when winter of 1859 came Mullan was still west of the Bitterroot Valley. November 8th brought an "outright blizzard," but they slogged on to about 1.5 miles east of present DeBorgia, Montana, where they wintered in their Cantonment (camp) Jordan. A low rock wall still remains at the site.

Mullan's letters to Capt. A. A. Humphreys of the War Department from Cantonment Jordan in January of 1860 detailed the severity of the winter to man and animals. Also, Lieutenant James White, the officer in charge of 140 "escorts," both civilian and military, reported that "October brought four weeks of incessant rain which rendered our road very … muddy and very nearly impassable." On November 3 he wrote, "The snow again visited us, falling to the depth of fifteen or eighteen inches." After seven consecutive days of snow, a cold front hit. The temperature fell below zero and they were without warm clothing, their supply pack train having been cut off by the snow. John Strachan, expedition civilian member, wrote, "Cattle, horses and mules lay dead in every direction. Hundreds of carcasses dotted the banks of the

stream where they had gathered for water and dropped from fatigue or starvation." These revealing details were reported in *John Mullan: Tumultuous Life of a Western Road Builder* by Keith C. Petersen (WSU Press, 2014). At the end of February Mullan ventured out to Fort Owen, 60 miles southeast and 30 miles from Missoula. The "civilized" Fort and the Flathead Indians provided Mullan with emergency supplies.

The last 55 miles of construction, from Sun River to Fort Benton, was a welcome level prairie with few streams to cross. On August 1,1860, the Mullan Road reached Fort Benton. Soon after, Mullan returned to Walla Walla escorting 300 soldiers along his road.

May of 1861 found Mullan and party once again headed to Fort Benton on his road to repair, widen, and generally to make it more wagon-friendly. In the previous year Mullan had built the road south of Lake Coeur d'Alene. That proved to be a mistake; it crossed many bogs and streams. This year he corrected the route to pass north of Lake Coeur d'Alene, through the present city of Coeur d'Alene. See Mullan Road map on the next page.

Fourth of July
tree carving defaced by
tourists and time
Ruth Johnson

That 1861 route through Idaho gave a section of the road a name: "4th of July canyon." Mullan and his crew took the day off from felling trees, grading, and re-bridging in order to honor the holiday. They fired their guns, raised the flag and got double rations. Mullan carved "MR July 4, 1861" (for Military Road, not Mullan Road) into a pine tree which remained there for 101 years before the tree top blew off in 1962. It was repeatedly repaired but was finally taken down in 1988, the blazed note preserved in the Museum of North Idaho in Coeur d'Alene. That mountain pass and adjoining canyon are still called 4th of July. A plaque marks the location of the tree. (In Mullan Road Hisorical Park , near ID-30.3)

Randall A. Johnson, in HistoryLink.org (Essay 9202) wrote,

> For all its drawbacks and its comparatively short life, the road was a resounding success.
>
> Travelers couldn't wait to start using it. Estimates made at the time indicate that parts of the road were used by 20,000 people, including Indians, during its first year. Six thousand horses and mules, most of them pulling freight wagons, used the road, as did 5,000 head of cattle. Also listed were 52 light wagons and 31 heavy immigrant wagons.

Gold seekers, mule trains, and immigrants did use the road, stimulating some road maintenance, but after three years the Army gave up maintaining it, turning it over to local residents who maintained it to a degree around towns and for the many mines in Idaho. ⇨

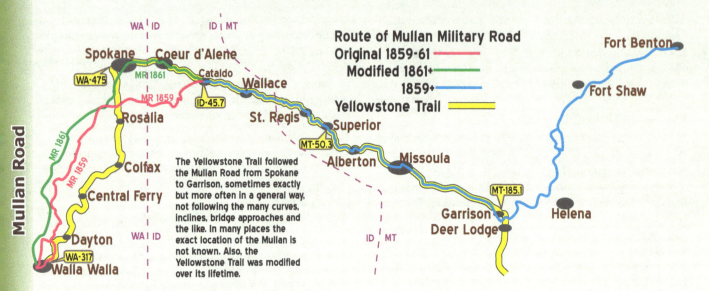

Route of Mullan Military Road
Original 1859-61 ——
Modified 1861+ ——
1859+ ——
Yellowstone Trail ——

The Yellowstone Trail followed the Mullan Road from Spokane to Garrison, sometimes exactly but more often in a general way, not following the many curves, inclines, bridge approaches and the like. In many places the exact location of the Mullan is not known. Also, the Yellowstone Trail was modified over its lifetime.

Enter the era of the railroad. The joining of the Union Pacific and Central Pacific railroads in 1869 and the building of the Northern Pacific railroad soon outpaced wagon traffic. Even a slick road surpassing Mullan's wildest dreams would not eclipse the roar of the iron and the Mullan Road declined in many places to obscurity.

The Yellowstone Trail and the Mullan Military Road

Mullan had found a good route for a road over the northen Rockies and had set the route followed, generally, by much of the Yellowstone Trail, US 10, and I-90. But in 1914 when the Yellowstone Trail arrived, it was in no condition to carry automobile traffic. Remaining tree stumps that had once been satisfactory for higher wagon wheels were impossible for the auto to straddle. Not even Fords. Autos had to ride the rails in 1913. A driver from Wisconsin found they had to build bridges, cut through windfalls, drive up creek beds.

Much of the alignment of the Mullan Military Road is hard to find today. Many of the wooden bridges in the mountainous areas were washed out repeatedly by spring floods, and time allowed forests to reclaim land. Some modern roads are on top of the original alignment. By 1900 some railroad track had been laid directly on the Mullan Road, making it hard to identify. Today, between Garrison, Montana, and Spokane, documenting the alignments of both the Yellowstone Trail and the Mullan Road and determining where they are the same is an exciting challenge, with many unanswered questions.

They danced together, those two historic routes, sometimes moving to their own separate rhythm, sometimes clinging closely for survival. See map above.

Exact alignments of many sections of both the Mullan Military Road and the Yellowstone Trail are not well documented. And there are many places where the Yellowstone Trail diverged from the Mullan both for small and long distances. An Internet search can yield reports of current research progress for the Mullan Road.

MT-079.4: A significant section of the Mullan Road is preserved as the The Point of Rocks trail, just north of I-90 west of Alberton, but it takes some navigating to get there. Traveling east or west, from I-90 Exit 75, the west Alberton exit, follow the North Frontage Road 1.7 miles to the west and turn up Mountain Creek. Almost immediately, the West Mountain Creek Rd. passes between old Milwaukee Road bridge piers, turns left into a former gravel pit and follows the railroad bed another mile to the trailhead at a small parking loop. This is a great place to explore the Mullan Road and the old railroad.

The Legacy of the Mullan Road

"So what" you ask? Why care about something that is no longer? Actually, Mullan's road did matter and now is an important part of the history of the Northwest. It was seen as an alternative to the Oregon Trail, as a trade route, and as a path for gold seekers, many of whom stayed to man the mineral mines which built Idaho. People no longer had to go west to catch a boat to San Francisco in order to catch a stage coach to go east. It also established the route to be followed by the Yellowstone Trail. Crude as it was, the Mullan Military Road personified an open door to the larger West. In parts it ultimately became the Yellowstone Trail, then a four lane highway in the 1940s, then I-90 in the 1960s. It must be a good routing. ✿

MT-017.7: The YT and probably the Mullan Road through the Savenac nursery

Montana

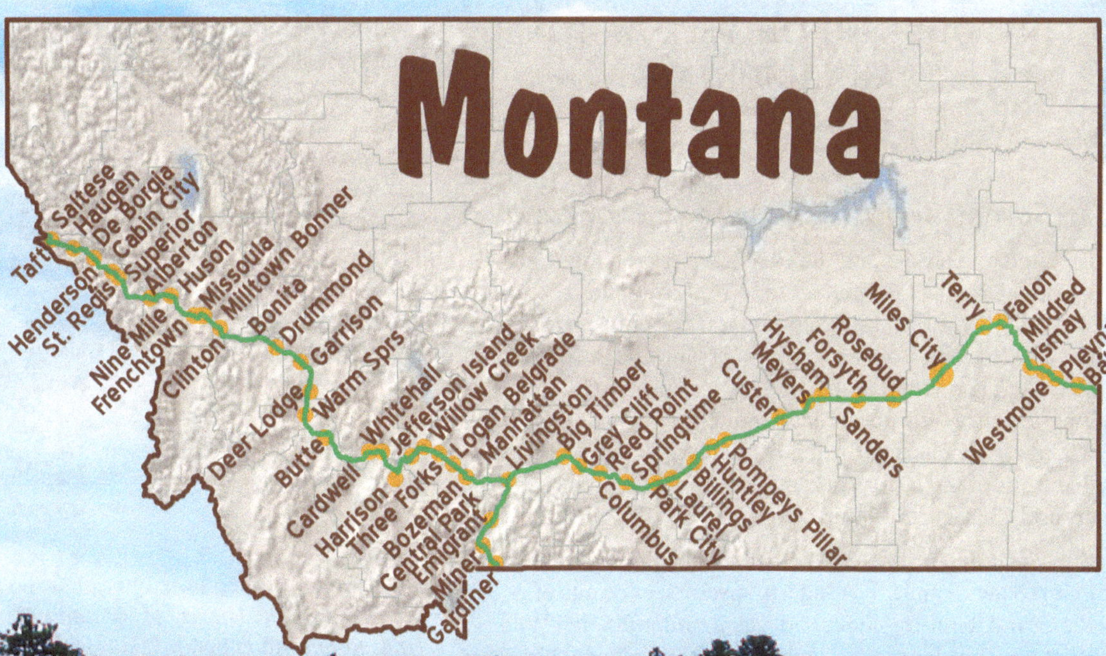

WHAT THE TRAIL FOUNDERS SAID-1921

Montana is a state of magnificent distances. In the agricultural parts of the state, roads follow section lines but in the broken range country and the mountain sections there are comparatively few roads, these being well defined routes reaching between population centers. There is a groundless fear on the part of the public that mountain sections are hard to travel by automobile. This is a mistake. While there are fewer roads through the mountains, the roads as a whole are much better than the roads in the agricultural districts after July 1st of any year. Persons wishing to travel in Montana by automobile are practically certain to find dry roads. Bad roads from rain storms will be of short duration.

The Yellowstone Trail extends across Montana from east to west for over 800 miles, entering the state in the agricultural and grazing or range district and going through the hills until the Yellowstone River is reached at Fallon. For the next 350 miles the Yellowstone River is closely followed through a rich agricultural valley to Livingston. West of Livingston it is a series of mountain passes and valleys, but in the whole distance, there is not really a dangerous place from an automobile touring standpoint. Montana offers the largest selection of scenic wonders of any state in the Union and there is no place in Montana but that is reached by a reasonably good road. A plentiful supply of good water is found in every part of the state. Much of the roads of Montana are natural decomposed granite, making splendid road beds. There is very little paved road in Montana, distances being so great, but at no time is there a serious trouble on account of road conditions. Information bureaus are maintained at Miles City, Butte, and Missoula in the eastern, central, and western part of the state and any of these bureaus will be glad to give local information for reaching any points in Montana.

1921 Yellowstone Trail Touring Service Map # 7 of Montana

The Yellowstone Trail
on Pease Bottom Road
northeast of Custer

87

INTRODUCING THE YELLOWSTONE TRAIL IN MONTANA: *TREASURE STATE*

Something is Different in Montana

Both today's traveler and the 1915 traveler crossing America on the route of the Yellowstone Trail could stay at the Wayside Inn in Massachusetts and learn about American Colonial history. Both travelers could view the Erie Canal in New York and visualize one of America's first major efforts at long-distance transportation. Around the Great Lakes both would see products of the industrial revolution. The incredible fruits of the history of railroads are apparent to both around Chicago and Minneapolis.

But something is different further west beginning in the Plains States. While the modern traveler sees results of the efforts to settle, "civilize," develop, and utilize the Wild West, the traveler of 1915 saw just the beginning of that development and was a direct observer and participant in those efforts. In 1915 it was "now," not history. Farming was replacing ranching, trucks challenged the railroads, and autos arrived to challenge the isolation.

A recent article by Tempe Johnson Javitz in *Montana, The Magazine of Western History*, Winter 2019, paints a good picture of transitions happening in Montana when the Yellowstone Trail arrived. The article, "The Photographic Legacy of Jessamine Spear Johnson," spoke of transitions in the changing West. Jessamine's parents had owned, operated, and benefitted monetarily from open-range cattle operations in northern Wyoming and southeastern Montana. Jessamine married Will Johnson in 1906 and, while they continued cattle operations, the open range, in effect, "closed," and they purchased large tracts of land for their ranching. That cattle business quickly turned to farming. Meadows were fenced for hay, and the plow made its appearance. During 1917, a Maxwell Town Car was added. In 1919 an added Dodge pickup truck was making calls to the city, moving materials and ranch hands, and facilitating social calls to "neighbors" and area Native American villages. A three-story "city-type" home was built.

Not eighty miles away, autoists from the East observed similar developments along the Yellowstone Trail. They experienced the Old West becoming the modern West. They experienced the first efforts to make the roads useful to the automobile. The Yellowstone Trail Association itself was created to be part of that effort to develop the frontier, and then, over the years, it increased its travel promotion efforts as highway development became a governmental responsibility.

The Trail Founding Fathers were inviting Easterners to the great West along the Trail to support member towns. Their 1921 *Route Folder* assured Easterners that, "In general–don't be afraid to tour Montana. Montana is thoroughly civilized, and in America. Carry just as little equipment as you wish, for excellent towns will supply your wants and needs. Chains should always be carried and to have brakes in good condition is only common sense."

An average day touring

For the context of the Yellowstone Trail in Montana, we recommend that those interested should read *Taming Big Sky Country: The History of Montana Transportation From Trails to Interstates* by Jon Axline (The History Press, 2015). Suffice it to say that from 1913 to the present, the many transformations in transportation did not happen easily, including the Yellowstone Trail. Axline explains the issues involved in detail in a readable and interesting fashion. Our purpose is to look at the development of the Trail as it motivated and then followed road improvement in Montana.

In the 1913-1914 record of the new State Highway Commission we find, "In Montana, with its rapid growth and settlement of new country, the demand for roads is coming faster than the money with which to pay for them." Thus, counties were the providers of roads and bridges and the local point of contact for the Yellowstone Trail Association to lobby for a road.

The State Highway Commission was created in 1913 to "give advice, assistance and supervision in regard to road construction and maintenance. Each county is to prepare road maps of primary and secondary roads. The unit of road work is the county to pay 50% of its road improvement; the state paying 50% for state aid." Federal Aid was not available yet. In 1921, the Federal Aid Highway Act limited the supported routes to 7% of each state's roads, while about 40% of the supported roads had to be "interstate in character." Roads for the nearly 800 mile long Yellowstone Trail from North Dakota to Idaho through Montana, therefore, formed the state backbone of auto transportation.

Outside of South Dakota, "big sky country" Montana had the longest and strongest relationship with the Yellowstone Trail of all the 11 other states through which the Trail ran. Miles City hosted the first national Yellowstone Trail convention in March,1913, when the ⇨

> **What the Founders said about Montana**
> **(in their own language):**
> It is a matter of regret, that by some invention or magic, pens are not made—that might bring to the mind of the person who never saw it, a correct impression of Montana. If by some agency one might be made to feel the eternal bigness of things here. But it is only by contact with the quiet grandeur of her mountains, the enormous length of her rivers, the potentialities of her soil, that one may be made to feel the soul of Montana. If on paper this might be made clear, no man would rest content until his feet had trod, and his eyes had seen, and his heart had beat in accord with the mammoth plan of Montana. (Yellowstone Trail *Route Folder*, 1921)

five-months-old Association elected J. E. Prindle of Ismay as the first full term president. In August of 1914 an important second national convention was held at Hunter's Hot Springs which set the route through Montana. Having named the organization after the first national park, the Association then, with others, successfully lobbied to allow automobiles into the park in 1915. The Treasure State hung on as a member of the Yellowstone Trail Association almost until the Association dissolved in 1930.

Why Did the Yellowstone Trail Go Where It Went in Montana?

Well, after the Founders from South Dakota got Parmley's Road started, business people from towns in Minnesota and the Dakotas who were connected by the tracks and services of the Milwaukee Road Railroad clamored to join in. By 1912, auto ownership was growing with the railroad delivering autos in ever growing numbers, into even the smallest burg, and the idea of a long-distance usable road became irresistible. Where should it go? At the beginning of the Trail Association in 1912 there certainly was no plan for locating the entire route. But very early the Founders approved the motto "From Plymouth Rock to Puget Sound." That at least set Seattle as the western terminus; that required a route "straight" through Montana. While the process of working out the details was remarkably democratic within the Association, the decisions were tightly constrained by five major factors:

First Factor: There Was a Lack of Roads

The Yellowstone Trail could not go where there were no usable auto roads. Sometimes routing the Trail had to await the building of those roads.

On the western end of the state the terrain in the Rockies had not allowed the creation of usable wagon roads by simple use as they were in the prairies. The Mullan Military Road had been built in the 1860s but its wagon bridges were often washed out and autos could not straddle the stumps. But the location between Missoula and Spokane was attractive for the Trail and essentially without alternative. See **Trail Tale: Bitterroots**, page 80.

On the eastern end of the state, wagon roads of a sort had developed through use, but they often were not suitable for autos. The *Terry Tribune* of September 27, 1912, reported that one such road, this one along the Powder River, had "... for some time been a great annoyance owing to the numerous gates that the traveler has to open and [the county commissioners] took this trip for the purpose of laying out that part officially so the residents would remove the obstructions to the right-of-way." Ranch or farm fences existed everywhere. Michael Dowling's daughter commented in her 1913 diary of their pathfinding trip: "There were obstacles like bridges collapsed or fence gates to be opened and no clear trail ahead." For more about the area, see **Trail Tale: Knowlton**, page 158.

Second Factor: Yellowstone Nat. Park

That great mecca of rail travelers was on the line between the Dakotas to Seattle, and knowing that, the Founders gave their

route its name: the Yellowstone Trail. So, the Trail just had to include the Park, even though the route would have to have a spur from Livingston to do so. The Northern Pacific did have a spur, because of the geographic reality of a north/south mountain valley which did not allow east/west access. It was the Association's only "splendid lateral," a divergence from the Trail's westward mission.

Third Factor: Following Railroad Routes

Railroad routes were to be followed whenever possible, the Milwaukee Road in particular. The advantages of such a route are obvious: tracks follow flat land, help to a stranded motorist could be found in a passing train, simple railroad watering stations and townlets might be found about every few miles. After all, railroads had created corridors of development to be used for goods and travelers. They created new towns for emigrants, new ways to reach hot springs "health centers," and transport for farm goods and cattle to markets. The Trail Founders' intent of following the Milwaukee Road tracks was foiled at Forsyth, Montana, where the Milwaukee crossed the Yellowstone River and headed northwest rather than directly to the Yellowstone Park. But at Forsyth, both the river and the Northern Pacific railroad then provided guidance for a route into Livingston and to the Park spur. No real alternative presented itself. From Livingston west the Northern Pacific could be followed and it was until near Three Forks where the Milwaukee Road was joined again.

But at the time of the publication of the Association's 1914 *First Year Book*, plans had not jelled for moving the route westward from Three Forks, so the end of the Trail was shown to be at a bridge over a branch of the Jefferson River just upstream from the forming of the Missouri River. That bridge is close to the Northern Pacific tracks heading over Homestake Pass to Butte, but that difficult ⇨

KEEP BLACK ARROWS POINTING TO WHITEHALL

The article speaks of a rumor that the Trail would be re-routed to avoid Butte, Deer Lodge, and Whitehall. It was a false rumor, but it produced a long, booster-high defense of the present route with thick accolades and hyperbole. The next year a real attempt to shift the Trail to Boulder, north of Whitehall, was made at the Western Montana Yellowstone Trail Association meeting. It failed.
January 27, 1920 Jefferson Valley News

PARTY HAS BEEN ON THE ROAD COVERING 7,000 MILES

Mr. Fosberg ... declared that the condition of the Yellowstone Trail from Spokane east through Montana was much better than the other roads. There are signs which mark the way. The Lincoln Highway, the southern route to the Pacific coast, was not marked in any way and people seemed to be in ignorance as to its route.
October 5, 1915
Mineral County Independent (Superior, MT)

terrain to the west motivated the choice to follow the Milwaukee Road through Three Forks and over Pipestone Pass to Butte. The bridge is still used in the 21st century by local traffic but it did not continue as part of the Trail.

The Trail continued along the Milwaukee Road between Butte and Missoula. It followed the only reasonable route available, the river that is now known as the Clark Fork. I-90 followed the same route years later.

Fourth Factor: Geography

Geography plays a prominent role in the selection of any transportation route, but in Montana it leapt forward as a dominant determinant in many areas. As noted, for instance, to route the Trail to the Yellowstone National Park, a spur was needed. "Montana's topographic extremes and the subsequent settlement patterns precluded extensive straight line road building," wrote Marilyn Wyss in *Roads to Romance: The Origins and Development of the Road and Trail System in Montana* (Montana Dept. of Transportation, 1992). Extending the Trail was often slowed by the lack of usable roadways. For instance, the development of the Trail was held up at the Bitterroot Range at the Idaho border until a pathway was completed at Randolph Creek from Taft and across the summit to Mullan, Idaho.

That summit crossing looked so forbidding that the local Yellowstone Trail locating committee called in Association President, Joe Parmley, to come and personally approve their choice. He did, but the route was still a problem; snow drifts lasted to early summers. In the early 1920s, a new road had to be built over Lookout Pass, leading to the route of present day I-90.

And Nature insisted on placing rivers across potential routes. A prominent example of problems created by rivers is seen just into Montana from North Dakota where the lack of a bridge over the Powder River created long lasting confusion and conflict for the Trail. See **Trail Tale: Knowlton**, page 158.

By the time the Trail was established in Montana, useable bridges existed in one shape or another between Miles City and Missoula, but as the Rockies were penetrated, bridges became a major concern, and by 1914 their condition or absence was a major constraint to routing the Trail. The road could not go up and down the mountain sides so it had to follow river valleys, where each bend of the river had a nearly vertical rise on one side and a bench on the other. To stay on the often flat benches required frequent river crossings from one side to the other. Ferries and fording were impossible on the narrow but fast flowing Clark Fork and the St. Regis, so bridges were needed.

Bridges, or lack of them, became a grave problem for routing the Yellowstone Trail. Fording and ferries were unreliable escorts for a transcontinental route. Bridges cost money which most counties didn't have due to sparse population. Even with state aid or the Federal Aid Road Act of 1916 which provided aid for all "post roads," the amount of aid available was minimal.

Even if money became available, building a bridge was not easy. Power equipment, usually steam driven, could not be moved to the building site, so power was provided by horses and manpower. While the iron or steel parts for bridges were brought to near the site by rail, horses brought the material the "last mile."

The bridges between Missoula and Idaho along the route chosen for the Yellowstone Trail are especially interesting to today's traveler and well worth special attention. They are in rugged and beautiful locations. The challenges the builders faced are easily apparent in the mountains. Also they are off of high traffic modern roads, so each offers great scenery and space for a quiet picnic. You might find, as we did, that one of them was manufactured in the Midwest, Wausau, Wisconsin. That made real the incredible role of railroads in "taming the West." We mention three bridges in western Montana:

Cyr Bridge. March, 1916. Two bond issues were put forward in Mineral County: one to replace the old, condemned Cyr Bridge and one to build a bridge at St. Regis. A fierce battle was put up by two competing newspapers, one supporting the bonds and one opposing. The bond issues failed and the losing newspaper, with sarcasm dripping, summed up the loss thus: "No Roads. No Bridges. No Yellowstone Trail. No Free County Library. No Free County High School. No Court House. No Public Improvements. The sovereign people have spoken."

The March 30, 1916 issue of the supportive newspaper, the *Mineral Independent*, raised the question about the anti-bridge supporters. It asked "Who? Who bought the drinks and cigars while proselytizing with falsehoods? Inquiry brings forth the most indignant denials from anti-bridge leaders." Apparently a later bond issue was passed because the bridge bore the date of 1916. It was replaced in 1932 and is now a walking bridge only.

⇨

Original wooden Cyr Bridge replaced in 1932
Jim Cyr

Scenic Bridge. This 1928 bridge replaced an early wooden bridge whose abrupt, narrow approaches had a history of causing many fatal accidents. In 1926, an election was held to determine if the citizens of Mineral County wished to accept federal aid and the indebtedness to match that aid. An overwhelming approval vote resulted in the riveted steel Pratt deck truss you see today. It is startling to see a railroad bridge above it. The Scenic bridge was adapted for this specific, unique site. Completion of this bridge was celebrated royally with bands, picnic dinners, and invited speakers for the 1,000 who attended May 13, 1928. It is a walking bridge only (GPS: 47.02020, -114.65700).

Natural Pier Bridge. This 1918 bridge is the only one in Montana to use a natural feature as part of its construction. A large rock/small island in the middle of the river holds up the middle of this Warren through truss bridge. Work began in spring 1917. Then a financial crisis and a delayed bond election occurred before the bridge was finally completed in 1918. In 1999 the bridge was rehabilitated and is still in use today (GPS: 47.01361, -114.50778). See pictures of bridges, page 96.

Trailblazer A.L. Westgard's vivid 1912 tale of being marooned in a flooded Yellowstone River near Zero, Montana, brought home the consequences of lack of bridges. See **Trail Tale: Westgard**, page 345.

Fifth Factor: Political Machinations

Politics would be expected to play a prominent role in a project of routing a highway from coast-to-coast. After all, roads cost money. Bonds had to be sold in thinly populated areas. "Where people aren't, mountains are," wrote Robert L. Taylor, *et al.*, in *Montana in Maps* (Big Sky Books 1974). West of Ohio, however, politics seems to have played a role only in very local decisions, if at all, and east of Ohio the Yellowstone Trail Association was not as much a Good Roads Movement (that located and built roads) as a tourist promotion agency. The overall route from Plymouth, Massachusetts, to Fort Wayne, Indiana, was complicated by the fact that the Yellowstone Trail Association had to compete with many other named highways for sign permits. The Association played a very limited role in the politics of the East when routing the Trail. This is taken up in the Indiana chapter Introduction, page 310.

The Association faced a political argument of substantial proportions but with a very favorable outcome at the Association's August 1914 Montana meeting at Hunter's Hot Springs resort near Livingston.

It was at Hunter's that the route through the western half of Montana and entry into Idaho was thrashed out. Folks from Great Falls put up a mighty argument for the Trail to run north to Great Falls. The problem was that there was no road west from there and the Trail would have to run a contorted route northwest to Glacier Park, scramble either to Thompson Falls or go way north to Libby to enter Idaho. But then what? There was no auto road into Idaho there. The problem was solved when Highway Commissioner George Metlen stood up and declared that a route was designated by the State Highway Commission to become a state road. The Commis-

sion confirmed the route that the Yellowstone Trail Association had favored, following the Yellowstone and Clark Fork Rivers. Thus began the path to state dominance over highway matters.

In the interest of avoiding a floor fight, the routing matter was referred to a special committee. A "special committee" was immediately created by Yellowstone Trail Association founder and president, Joe Parmley. That committee rejected the Great Falls route. Thirteen years later the chosen route became US 10, and then I-90. For more about the hot springs resort, see **Trail Tale: Hunter's Hot Springs**, page 152.

This routing decision tale reveals the interplay among politics, funding concerns, hometown boosterism, and dreamers of transcontinental auto travel. But most of all, this decision was about finding an existing road, any road, that an auto could use. When there weren't any auto roads for the route to use, they looked for usable wagon paths When there weren't any of those they lobbied local businessmen and governments to do something about it. The roads would, ideally, be the most direct route and connect to an adjoining county's most direct east-west road. Taken together, they would form an uninterrupted auto route "from Plymouth Rock to Puget Sound."

Across Montana from near the North Dakota border to the Idaho border the route of the Yellowstone Trail morphed into the I-94 / I-90 corridor existing today. Enough of the original Yellowstone Trail is available today for a fascinating adventure. ✿

FIRST HARD-SURFACE ROAD EXPERIMENT IN MONTANA

County commissioners and state officials are watching with interest the results of the experiment being made with the first unit of hard-surfaced highway ever constructed in the state, outside of city pavements. The experimental asphaltum road with surface of stone chips is located near Butte, from the city limits to the Five Mile House, a distance of two miles. The first mile of this road had just been finished at the time of the transcontinental speed trip staged in September by the Yellowstone Trail Association, used by the relay car from Bozeman to Butte.
October 1916 Northwestern Motorist

An attempt to direct the route of the Yellowstone Trail so as to include Helena and exclude Butte was defeated at the Western Montana division of the Yellowstone Trail Association convention held at Deer Lodge a few days ago.
February 5, 1920 Three Forks News

Butte county enthusiasts are sending a delegation to petition Congress in behalf of the Yellowstone Trail in the event the federal government decides to improve two east-to-west routes from the Atlantic to the Pacific. They believe their route preferable to the Lincoln Highway and to bring the advantages to the attention of Congress.
August 2, 1919 Western Highway Builders

ROADS TIED UP BY SNOW
RAILROAD OFFICIALS ON
JOB DAY AND NIGHT

Since last Sunday the Chicago, Milwaukee & St. Paul railroad has been badly crippled at the hand of snow. Innumerable tons of snow, carrying rock, trees, logs and other debris have rolled down the steep mountain sides covering railroad tracks in depths varying to 80 feet. The section where slides are prevalent is through the historic fire region of 1910, where no timber is alive to hold the snow.

April 6, 1922 Mineral Independent

Slow progress has been made on clearing the Foraker snow slide on account of not being able to use power machinery owing to the body of Fred Munger not having been recovered. ⚙

Tourist cabins in Saltese

Lookout Pass summit, supposedly in 1934. but probably older, much "touched up", and colorized.
That pavement was really a decent, less trim gravel!

Milwaukee Road trestle with gallow near Saltese. Gallows carried electric wires to provide the power for engines

Camping near DeBorgia

Roger's Red Crown Gas Station, Saltese

Abstracted from the Saltese delegates to the annual Montana state meeting of the Yellowstone Trail Association: The three delegates pushed through a by-law that stated "no road changes can be made by a state association unless submitted to the national association."

March 22,1917 Mineral Independent

Note: This was done to protect the Trail in Mineral County from being moved by groups favoring a northern, Thompson Falls route.

A former Forest Service officer described travel there thus:

Going east over Camel's Hump [MT-023] or west over Ford Hill [MT-001] were big hurdles for a Model T. The Fords overheated on the long pulls, and unless the gas tank was near full, a Ford would stall on steep pitches because the gas feed to the carburetor depended upon gravity flow. When one car stalled it usually held up a line of cars from both directions because there were few turnouts on mountainous roads. ⚙

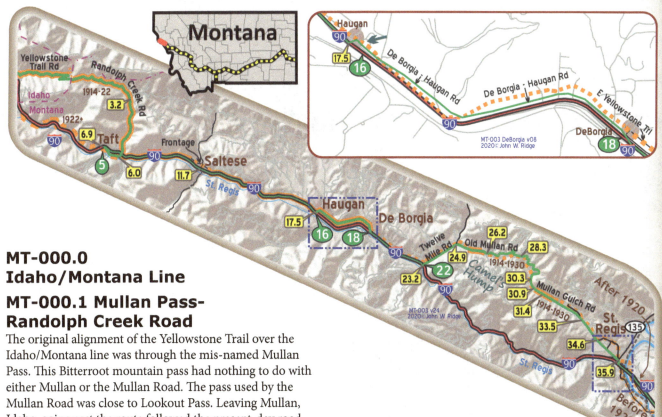

MT-000.0
Idaho/Montana Line

MT-000.1 Mullan Pass-Randolph Creek Road

The original alignment of the Yellowstone Trail over the Idaho/Montana line was through the mis-named Mullan Pass. This Bitterroot mountain pass had nothing to do with either Mullan or the Mullan Road. The pass used by the Mullan Road was close to Lookout Pass. Leaving Mullan, Idaho, going east the route followed the present-day road, Yellowstone Trail, to the pass, then Randolph Creek Road. This was the original route of the Yellowstone Trail from 1915 until Lookout Pass Road was opened around 1924. This historic Yellowstone Trail/Randolph Creek route is a great drive today, scenery is great and it is quite useable, yet looks old. Going west, use I-90 Exit 5, turn immediately right to Co. 286, the Randolph Creek Road. For the story of Lookout Pass, see **Trail Tale: Bitterroots**, page 80.

MT-006.0 Taft

TAFT, MONT., gas, lunch and phone only. Is a nearly abandoned Milwaukee R. R. construction camp. MH-1928

TAFT (3,625 alt.), is a ghost camp of 3 or 4 unoccupied frame buildings. In 1908, when the Milwaukee Road was driving its St. Paul Pass Tunnel through the Bitterroot Mountains, it was a town of 2,000 inhabitants whose many saloons, gambling houses, dance halls, and flimsy buildings crowded the narrow valley. When Idaho and Washington were dry (no alcohol sold) and Montana wet, Taft was one of the supply points for bootleggers operating in the dry States. WPA-MT

"The wickedest city in America ... plague spot of vice," said the September 28, 1909, *Chicago Tribune*. The little town served the Milwaukee Road railroad as a supply and operations center. Two thousand railroad workers blasted an 8,750 foot-long tunnel through mountainous country. Brave "Coyote men" were the blasters whose pay came and went quickly on the town's 500 prostitutes and 27 saloons. The fire of 1910 flattened the town. Today the tunnel is part of a miles-long, popular bicycle path and Main St. is directly under I-90. The former town is noted by a sign at Exit 5 of I-90. It reads simply "Taft area."

MT-011.7 Saltese

pop. 100; kept up by mining and lumber. Good bear and deer hunting; also fishing. Rooms and country hotel; no regular garage. Best meals at the restaurant. Blue Slide Camp, 25¢, good site among pines. Lunch and supplies. Fine fishing in St. Regis River. Riverside Camp, 50c, dining hall; a good site. 3 cabins $1. Good lunch. MH-1928

(3,476 alt., 200 pop.), strung out along the highway and railroad tracks in a narrow canyon, is a supply point for small silver and gold mines in the nearby mountains. During the World War, copper mines to the southwest were very active. High above the town the electrified Milwaukee Road clings to a narrow, winding shelf carved from the rocky mountainside. With old-fashioned western hospitality, Saltese keeps the door of its small jail always open, a gesture of welcome to weary hoboes. WPA-MT

I-90 seems to have bisected the town. The Milwaukee Road electric train tressle and "gallows" can still be seen. Main St. and the railroad tracks run along a narrow canyon. It was a supply point for the surrounding mines 100 years ago. Yellowstone Trail travelers may have stopped at the good campground.

174 W Saltese Frontage Rd. (Yellowstone Trail). **Old Montana Bar & Grill.** An early 1900s building, as seen in moving pictures. Serves bar food and has received rave reviews. Was it always a bar? Would Yellowstone Trail travelers have stopped here for respite while on treacherous mountain roads? We don't know.

Black Diamond Guest Camp & Ranch, with the Mullan Road and the YT running behind it near DeBorgia.

Hotel Albert, DeBorgia. Note "Yellowstone Trail" street sign in foreground.

Between St. Regis and Superior the surrounding mountains restricted the YT to closely following either the north or south side of the Missoula River or, as it is now called, the Clark Fork. Its alignment has scant documentation, and reports and maps often conflict.

Apparently, going east, after coming down the Camel's Hump, the YT crossed the St. Regis River in St. Regis and proceeded east on the south shore of the Clark Fork and then crossed the river into Superior on a wooden bridge built in 1895, replaced in 1932. The south route was apparently used for a number of years before being switched to the north route. The 1918 and 1919 USGS maps suggest that switch occurred after 1919. Local sources give 1923 as the date it switched.

Seemingly conflicting with these dates is the report that until 1917 traffic along the north route crossed the Clark Fork in St. Regis on a ferry which was replaced by a bridge in 1928. The popular magazine *Northwest Motorist* (p12, July 1917) claims the YT going east followed the north/Mullan route in 1917.

Care to work that out?

Top of Camel's Hump on YT. Elevation 3,951 ft.

Hunters with deer antlers on car, Camel's Hump
Mineral County Historical Society

Memoirs of the "Hump" trips from 1916 to 1924 all speak of the "dangerous" route and trouble getting Model Ts over it due to the gas gravity feed engineering. Drivers had to back up the steep hill. Diarists describe the necessity of attaching tree trunks to the back of their cars to serve as additional brakes going down the other side. It was a dreaded route despite Yellowstone Trail Association assurances of a "pleasant journey." ✿

The YT in and around Savenac was relocated, in part, in 1931. The relocation involved, in places, relocating the St. Regis River. No change was made within Savenac.

... the Camel's Hump is in perfect condition, [the road] having been made wide and roomy ...
May 30, 1929 The Mineral Independent

Road crew

To Camel's Hump
34.6
Main St
St Regis Rd
Main St
Mullan Gulch Rd
St. Regis
Main St
135
90
After 1923
35.9
33
Before 1923
90
MT-003 St Regis v06
2020© John W. Ridge

DeBorgia Cantonment Jordan (1859-1860). This was the winter camp for Capt. John Mullan and his building crew as they were building the Mullan Road from Walla Walla, Washington, to Fort Benton, Montana. The Cantonment wall remnants are on the Yellowstone Trail, the present Frontage Rd. near GPS: 47.361889, -115.320556. ✿

MT

MT-017.5 Haugan

Haugan was one of several area towns to be destroyed during the Great Fire of 1910. MH-1928

Haugan was established and maintained as a "pusher station" for the Milwaukee Road railroad trains ascending the Bitterroot Range of the Rocky Mountains.

MT-017.6 Savenac National Forest Nursery

Savenac National Forest nursery; 30 men employed. MT-WPA

From 1907-1969 Savenac was once the largest forest service tree nursery in the U.S. Seedlings, mainly pine and spruce, were used in reforestation projects throughout the U.S. Buildings built by the CCC in the 1930s remain and can be used for group events, volunteer maintenance projects and meetings. Today a traveler can walk the grounds at will, as we have done several times. Note the small bridge. It carried the Yellowstone Trail as the present sign on it says; you can see its route through the property. See **Trail Tale: Savenac**, page 155.

MT-020.1 DeBorgia

pop. 30; best rooms and meals at Albert Hotel. Gas, phone and open camp space. No garage. MH-1928

Buried in the mountains and forests, DeBorgia was almost completely destroyed in the 1910 fire. Only the school and the bar remained. The school, built in 1908, still stands today, repurposed as a community center.

On a gravel road (The street sign says Yellowstone Trail) just east of central DeBorgia is small **Hotel Albert**, built in 1911, right after the big 1910 fire. It has been a hotel and bed and breakfast place on and off for decades, and may not be in business now, but you should see its outsides, at least. The false front shows its 1911 western vintage along with the annex, built to be a restaurant which the *1926 Mohawk-Hobbs Guide* said served good food. Writer Dave Habura says it served passengers from the Milwaukee Road and Northern Pacific railroads as well as Yellowstone Trail travelers.

1281 E DeBorgia-Haugan Frontage Rd. **Black Diamond Guest Ranch**. About 15 years ago the then-owners, JoAnn and the late Richard Hopewell, kindly showed us the Yellowstone Trail which traversed the rear of their guest ranch and their 1926 era cabins. The Trail ran from DeBorgia to Haugan past the Albert Hotel. With the Yellowstone Trail at their back door and the Mullan Cantonment near their front, they certainly qualify as an historic site. When you stop in there, ask the present owners about the exact location of Mullan's Cantonment and the Trail.

MT-023.2 Henderson

MT-023.2 - MT-035.9 Camel's Hump

Camel's Hump, a noted grade, the steepest on the Yellowstone Trail. West side is a 9% grade for a short ways. East side is steep for .8 of a mile and is a 11% grade. Very few cars have trouble. Descend east side in second gear. MH-1928

Camel's Hump was the name given to a 12 mile section of road which, on a map, looks like a "hump" or a half circle road appended to the east side of I-90. The Camel's Hump route, between the sites of St. Regis and DeBorgia, was created by the Mullan Military Road up and over the mountain to avoid the twisting Clark Fork river canyon that would have demanded numerous bridges. The Yellowstone Trail had no choice but to follow that old route, but plans were soon laid to build the valley road. Those plans were thwarted by construction problems and cost to build in the narrow canyon until 1951. I-90 now follows that river route.

The Interstate was laid down on top of the Yellowstone Trail just east of DeBorgia so today's Trail traveler must use I-90 between Exit 18 and Exit 22

Although usually full of snow until May or June, the "Hump" served well, but the 2,200 foot rise of the "Camel's Hump" gave early drivers the shivers. Today, the trip over Camel's Hump is on a nice, smooth road with views of hills, valleys, streams, and shady woods of virgin white pine, feathery tamarack, and fir. Here is the Trail at its best. Glenn Koepke, historian, has said that the hump is "still a living museum to the travel history of western Montana."

MT-024.9 Cabin City

After you have turned onto "Camel's Hump" via Twelve Mile Road, continue on about 1 1/2 miles to a spot once called Cabin City. Today there is no city there and no cabin. There is, however, a **Cabin City Campground** on Twelve Mile Road run by the Forest Service.

Cabin City was once known from coast to coast as a popular tourist camp and lodge. It enjoyed more patronage than any other camp on the Yellowstone Trail in this section. The place was conducted as a hunting lodge.

MT-035.8 St. Regis

pop. 250; country hotel and meals. SEARS GARAGE has a good name; 24-hr. service. MH-1928

2,678 alt., 300 pop.; is composed of straggling clumps of buildings amid convergent railroad tracks. Its center is a bridge across the Clark Fork. Once an important sawmill town, it dwindled to a supply point for small logging operators after the great forest fire that swept western Montana in August 1910. WPA-MT

St. Regis has a long, significant history in transportation. Old US 10 (Yellowstone Trail) follows part of the historic Mullan Road. The Mullan monument marks that route in St. Regis. The town lies at the confluence of the Clark Fork and St. Regis Rivers. There was an "auto court" near the Trail in St. Regis.

1037 Old Highway 10. **Nugget RV Park and Cabins**. We don't know for sure, but it is likely that the site of this present campground is the same or near the campground advertised in Yellowstone Trail era literature. A 1927 Trail *Route Folder* described the St. Regis campground as right on the Yellowstone Trail and as providing electricity, laundry, and bathing facilities, and it was policed.

$186,000 FOR
MINERAL COUNTY HIGHWAY

Superior got $98,000 for the Yellowstone Trail and Saltese got $98,000 for the Yellowstone Trail.

January 31, 1929 Mineral Independent

Note: That doesn't add up right.

The contract for rebuilding the road on the Yellowstone Trail west of Superior was let Friday ... This improvement will eliminate three railroad crossings ...

June 26, 1928 Mineral Independent

Natural Pier Bridge. The island is its middle pier.

Crowd at Scenic Bridge opening 1928

Between the Cyr bridge and the Natural Pier bridge the original YT followed the Mullan Road north of the river, but was moved to the south side of the river to avoid the difficult "Nigger Hill." US 10 was then moved back to a new road on the north side in 1931.

To drive to the west end of Scenic Bridge which is over the Clark Fork and under the Milwaukee Road bridge, take I-90 Exit 65 and follow Old US 10 east. To drive to the east end follow Old US 10 west from near Exit 66.

Original YT metal sign found in Brickner barn

Present Scenic Bridge

Superior from above YT facing west, 1911

During 1928 the road west of Superior was rerouted and rebuilt to eliminate three rail crossings. One will be left between Superior and St. Regis.

June 26, 1928 Mineral Independent

COMMERCIAL CLUB NOW ORGANIZED

The object of the club is to further all interests of the community and especially to promote the Yellowstone Trail ...

March 23, 1922 Mineral Independent

A. P. Johnston, county trailman, put out the call for delegates from all county Yellowstone Trail clubs to meet at Superior January 6 to select representatives to the district meeting at Deer Lodge January 27. Based upon the amount of money raised by each club, Superior will get seven votes at Deer Lodge.

January 1, 1920 Mineral Independent

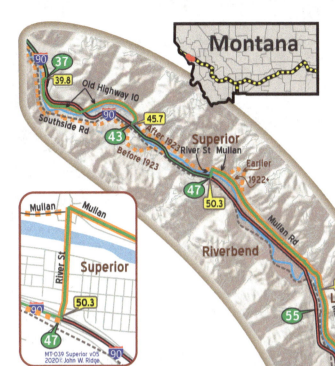

MT-065.8 Tarkio

A Milwaukee Road town and a substation when the Milwaukee Road electrified (which ended in 1973). Lumbering and farming "the Flats" kept the town going. Today the remaining asset is the scenery.

MT-070.3 Scenic Bridge

Scenic Bridge is 10 miles west of Alberton or 4 miles east of Tarkio. Built in 1927-28. Getting to see the Scenic Bridge is tricky. Today, going east, one must leave the Yellowstone Trail and join the Interstate at Exit 61 because the Interstate system has gobbled up the Yellowstone Trail here. Leave the Interstate at Exit 65 and join old US 10 to the bridge which has recently been closed to vehicular traffic. Walk on it and view the Clark Fork river from the bridge and the old Milwaukee Road railroad bridge above it. You must return to the Interstate back to Exit 65 to continue your journey east. If you were westbound, you would leave the Interstate at Exit 66 and follow old US 10, a circuitous route, to the bridge, returning to the Interstate the way you came.

MT-050.3 Superior

pop. 400; a county seat town; sustained by gold mines and the R. R. Mineral Garage for road service. Good Eats Cafe is liked. MH-1928

CHARETTE HOTEL, good, well kept rooms; hot water and bath in hall. Dbl. $1.50-$2.25. Cafe adjoins. EDWARDS GARAGE, across river, has best mechanics. MH-1928

Mineral County became an independent county from Missoula County in 1914, the year that the Yellowstone Trail arrived. Superior is the county seat. Through gold rushes, floods, forest fires, the rise and fall of two major railroads, and the great Yellowstone Trail, Superior has survived.

301 2nd Ave. E. **Mineral County Museum and Historical Society**. These folks are the originators of the important Mullan Society and the annual Mullan Road conference. Displays of mining and other western Montana history adorn walls. Intimate and rewarding.

MT-063.7

Now here is an anomaly. The Trail ran through this farm, called Happy Hollow House. When last we visited, this was the Brickner farm. The Trail ran through the property and exited through their back yard on a small, low bridge over a stream. A larger bridge, carrying the more modern, presently named Mullan Road, is right next to the little Yellowstone Trail bridge. The two historic roads ran parallel for a distance. The Brickners knew of their farm's historic location on the two roads and fished out an original, rusty Yellowstone Trail sign that was once on their property. Since the Trail disappears into the woods, your driving line on these maps does not route you on to their private property (GPS: 47.05357, -114.75839).

MT-074.4 (I-90 Exit 70) Cyr Bridge

About 9 1/2 miles east of Tarkio or 5 1/2 miles west of Alberton is the 1916 Cyr Bridge at Mead Lane (GPS: 47.00657, -114.57835). Kayakers and river rafters enjoy the Clark Fork River for the Alberton Gorge and its rapids. They put in at the historic Cyr Bridge. See picture on page 90.

From the Cyr Bridge part of the old Yellowstone Trail can be explored. From Exit 70, sawmill Gulch Road can be driven south and east along the 1919 Yellowstone Trail as far as an active rail tunnel. Exciting! No road now connects with Plateau Road to the east which carried the Trail to the Natural Pier Bridge. That 1919 route of the Trail south of the river was billed as the first National Forest Road.

Between I-90 Exit 70 to 75 one is forced to drive on the Interstate. Note the closeness of the Clark Fork River on one side of the Interstate and the mountains on the other. Not much room for train, road, and river.

MT-079.0 Natural Pier Bridge

About one mile west of Alberton is an oddity that you must see. A bridge crosses the Clark Fork River with the help of a large rocky outcrop in the river which serves as the "natural pier" holding up the middle of the bridge. This 1918 bridge is the only natural pier bridge in Montana still extant. In 1999 the structure was rehabilitated and is still in use today.

MT

May 21, 1915 Mineral County Board of Commissioners minutes: Due to the accidental shooting of A. F. Klugman, the Board neglected to call in the Clerk to take minutes. ⚙

1919 Mineral County Board of Commissioners minutes. They put up phone poles along the Yellowstone Trail. ⚙

MONTANA'S LONE LEPER ISOLATED

O. C. Willett, state senator, was diagnosed in 1917 with leprosy, apparently contracted in the Philippines during the Spanish-American war. In 1919 he was isolated to a house and garden in rural Alberton with his wife.

June 5, 1919 Mineral Independent

Note: Leprosy was considered highly contagious, so asylum care was eliminated. He received a pension from Congress and died January 12, 1928.

VALUABLE ROAD CHANGE COMING

A novel idea was suggested by the Bureau of Public Roads: build a road over the 9-Mile Creek and under the Milwaukee overpass between Alberton and Nine Mile. Three dangerous crossings of the Milwaukee Road and one dangerous curve would be eliminated.

November 26, 1925 Mineral Independent

James Jennison, of Pillsbury Flouring Mills Co., Minneapolis, and party drove into Superior Friday with one of the hind tires of their large touring car stripped. The party had been stalled for two hours on a grade near Tarkio.

August 24, 1915 Mineral Independent

FORESTRY MAKES $60,000 APPROPRIATION

Mineral County will draw $60,000 for the Tarkio Flats road. The County have guaranteed to also place the Camel's Hump in first class condition, and with the Tarkio Flats and the Hump made good, Mineral County will favorably stand with other sections of the Yellowstone Trail.

January 24, 1924 Mineral Independent

Remnants of Milwaukee Road railroad over YT over Ninemile Creek

Ninemile Ranger Station east of Alberton

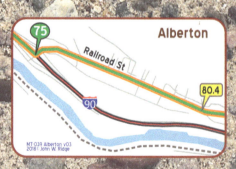

MT-079.4

The Point of Rocks trail is just north of I-90 just west of Alberton. This well-preserved trace of the Mullan Road winds its way around a rocky point. You can still walk through the narrow gaps in the large rocks blasted by Mullan's crews and still see abutments created from hand-lain rock. At I-90 Exit 75 (the west Alberton exit), follow the North Frontage Road to the west for two miles and look for trail-head signs. This route became the Yellowstone Trail.

MT-080.4 Alberton

pop. 300; a Milwaukee R. R. division point. Clean rooms at Montana Hotel. Billy's Cafe is liked.

BEAR CAT GARAGE; good mechanics. Labor $1.50; tow car. MH-1928

147 Railroad Ave. (Yellowstone Trail). **Antique Depot and Railroad Museum**. The Antique Depot is an antiques and collectibles small business located in the original 1890 Northern Pacific railroad station which was moved here from Frenchtown.

701 Railroad Ave. **The Milwaukee Road Depot**. The railroad was very important to Alberton in Yellowstone Trail days where four passenger trains made 30-minute stops daily. It was a major division point 1908 until 1917 when electrification of the line made division points obsolete; the village had virtually no other industry. Today, the station depot also serves as the Community Center and Library. An authentic boxcar contains the Railroad Museum and "the sweet Caboose inside looks just as it did when it last rode the rails."

512 Railroad Ave. **Montana Valley Bookstore**. You've got to stop in here. There are over 100,000 books of all stripes stuffed into a small space located in the middle of this quiet, forested, mountainous area. We stop here whenever we pass through.

The building that the book store is in was formerly Bestwick's Market, a false-fronted commercial building. It is listed on the National Register of Historic Places. Constructed in 1910 with additions in 1915 and 1925, the building housed Bestwick's Market from 1912 to the late 1950s. The building has housed the Montana Valley Book Store since the 1970s.

818 Rosehill Ln. **Alberton School**. Built in 1918 symbolized the transition from a railroad boom town to a permanent town. The school survives today virtually unchanged from its original design.

MT-084.2 Ninemile Tunnel of the Milwaukee Road Railroad

Look west. It is a short tunnel just a few yards from the Yellowstone Trail and hard to see, but you can imagine a time when the two historic transportation modes existed side by side.

MT-085.9

Between Alberton and Ninemile, a very nice drive, is another one-of-a-kind transportation phenomenon. In autumn of 1924 the Yellowstone Trail was built over 9-Mile Creek and underneath the Milwaukee Road railroad overpass. Con-sidered novel when proposed, three railroad crossings and a dangerous curve would be eliminated. Mislead by the mild weather, the contractor poured a 30-foot section of the Yellowstone Trail on December 14. "At noon when the job was finished, the temperature was 65 degrees above zero. By midnight it was 28 degrees below zero, a fall of 93 degrees in 12 hours. The contractor believed that it would have to be replaced. An examination in the spring, however showed it to be entirely unharmed."

An examination by the state in September of 2013 rated that old Yellowstone Trail bridge as 82.0, "equal to present desirable criteria and open with no restrictions." Today, the Yellowstone Trail and bridge are clearly driveable, but the middle section of the railroad overpass is missing.

MT-085.9
(Or I-90 Exit 82 at Ninemile Road)

Ninemile Ranger Station and Remount Depot. Besides being the same turnoff for the Yellowstone Trail and the remains of the collapsed Milwaukee Road viaduct over the creek and the Yellowstone Trail, this is also the turnoff to the U.S. Forest Service Remount Depot, north 2.6 miles on Remount Road. A big fire in 1929 gave impetus to the creation of this centralized fire-fighting depot. Ninemile Remount Depot provided experienced packers and their animals for fighting fires and for backcountry work projects since the 1930s.

In 1962 it rose again as the Ninemile Ranger Station with training in backcountry skills and for firefighting.

MT-090.2 Huson

Between Huson and Frenchtown US 10 climbs over sharp curves to a bench, from which is a view of the Clark Fork Valley. An observation point provides an equally good view westward to the rugged slopes of the Bitterroot Mountains. The highway descends into a narrow canyon lined with outcroppings of rock—rusty red, yellow, and brown. Above, the receding green hills and gulches are topped with pine, larch, and Douglas fir. WPA-MT

There is some indication that during 1929 the YT ran north of the route shown between Frenchtown and Huson, probably much of it now under I-90.

MT-095.0 Frenchtown

A small village. Rooms and small free camp. Frenchtown Garage is fair. MH-1928

An old established valley, its settlement dating from 1860 when Jesuit priests set up a mission there. It is not a lumbering town as are its neighbors, possibly because it is located upon an ancient lake bottom. The Frenchtown pulp mill is now an EPA Superfund cleanup site.

Important advice from the authors: Don't confuse huckleberries for blueberries. Right then you give yourself away as a tourist. But do order anything huckleberry any chance you get. Yum.

BLUE BOOK MAN GOES THROUGH

R. A. Woodall Collects Statistics along Yellowstone Trail and Will Publish Book of Information.

July 30, 1915
Mineral Independent

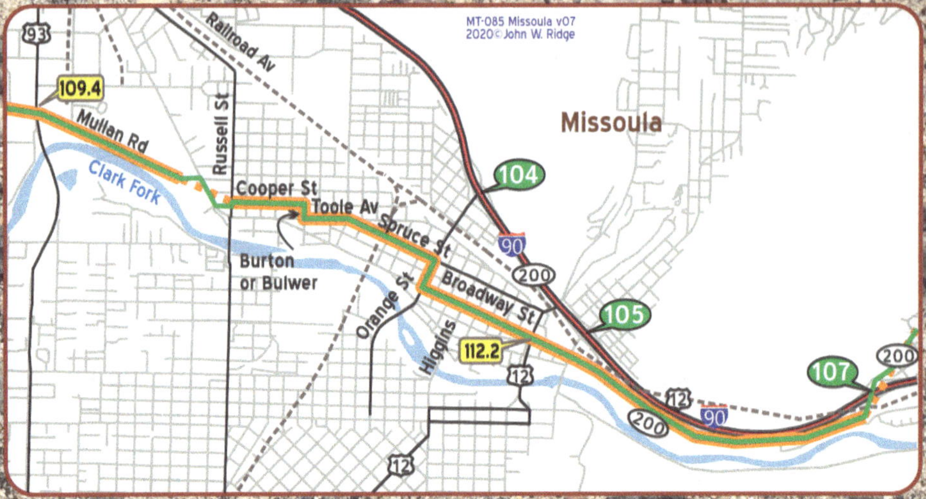

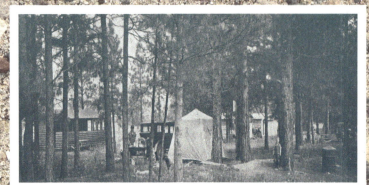

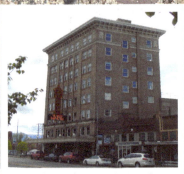

Wilma Theatre, Missoula

Missoula's first street car began operating in 1910 and continued until 1932. ❂

Missoula Auto Park

MT

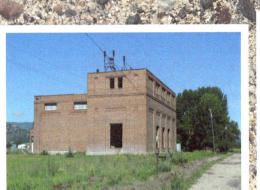

At about MT-102.3 is one of the Milwaukee Road railroad's electrical substations about six miles southeast of Frenchtown and nine miles northwest of Missoula. It supplied electricity to their electrified lines through the mountains (GPS: 46.92809, -114.16771).

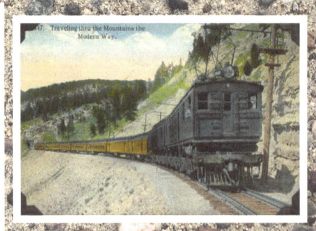

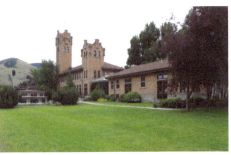

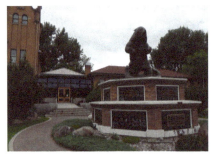

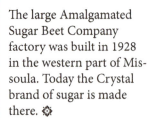

Milwaukee Road Depot, Missoula,
with its Millenium Circle with bronze plaques naming famous conservationists

The large Amalgamated Sugar Beet Company factory was built in 1928 in the western part of Missoula. Today the Crystal brand of sugar is made there. ❂

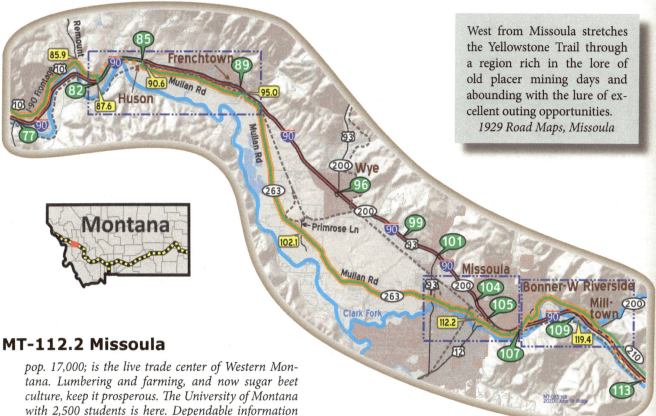

West from Missoula stretches the Yellowstone Trail through a region rich in the lore of old placer mining days and abounding with the lure of excellent outing opportunities.
1929 Road Maps, Missoula

MT-112.2 Missoula

pop. 17,000; is the live trade center of Western Montana. Lumbering and farming, and now sugar beet culture, keep it prosperous. The University of Montana with 2,500 students is here. Dependable information at the Auto Club. Coffee Parlor Cafe is good. MH-1928

PALACE HOTEL is quiet and popular with tourists. Outside rooms are good values. Sgl. $l-$2.50; dbl. $1.50; outside $2.50; with bath $3.50.

STAR GARAGE has best reputation for all-around service and is open 24 hours. Storage 50c; labor $1.50. Ph. 4740 for efficient wrecker or towing.

Missoula Auto Park, 1.5 miles north; Mercer's Cottages also north; new and large cottages with good beds $1.25, camp space 50c. MH-1928

In 1861 two fellows started a store four miles west of present Missoula. That little log cabin store saw plenty of action from the outlaw Plummer gang in the five years of its existence. Then, in 1866 they moved four miles east, started a flour mill and Missoula was born.

Seven historical districts and 27 buildings are on the National Register of Historical Places in this "Garden City" in the valley of the confluence of three rivers. We have selected only a few sites here.

131 S Higgins. **Wilma Theatre** Bldg. Built in 1921, the elegant, restored Wilma now shows a diverse range of entertainment, including movies, spoken word events, music, and plays.

211 W Front. **Jeannette Rankin Peace Resource Center**. Named for the first woman elected to the House of Representatives in 1916, four years before women could vote. She voted against World War I (with 49 others), and again voted against war in 1941 (alone). The Center continues her peace and justice work through educational programs.

147 W Broadway (Yellowstone Trail). **Palace Apartments**. The former Palace Hotel was built in 1909 as the Savoy.

The original structure and a 1941 annex formed Missoula's largest single hotel. A 1995 rehabilitation project created 60 upper-floor housing units. Today the Palace low income apartments beautifully illustrate how preservation can help rejuvenate a city center.

250 Station Dr., west of the Higgins Ave. bridge. **Milwaukee Road Depot**. An impressive double-towered brick structure built in 1910 is now the headquarters of the Boone and Crockett Club, a group formed by Teddy Roosevelt in 1887 to preserve the West. It is on the National Register of Historic Places. You can't miss its two tall towers. The main floor contains a replica waiting room for passengers and the second floor contains offices and a library of conservation materials. The visitors' gallery features a time-line history of wildlife conservation. Don't miss the **"Millennium Circle"** monument outside. It features names of more great, influential conservationist members than we ever thought existed, including John Muir, Aldo Leopold and others.

120 Hickory St. **Montana Natural History Center**. There is much more to say about this center than we can here. The Center is an environmental education organization offering kids' activities, field trips for every age, evening programs, and Montana Public radio programs all focusing on flora, fauna and geology. We picked the Glacial Lake Missoula portion of the Center because it covers a broad area over the Yellowstone Trail. It was marvelous!

You will also want to visit **Fort Missoula** with its many outdoor displays. Go west on South Ave. The **University of Montana**, South 6th St., **Smokejumper Visitor Center** on West Broadway and the **Carousel** in Caras Park all tell the story of Missoula through the ages.

There is some indication (but little evidence) that the original YT left Missoula going east and followed a higher route, perhaps along the Old Marshall Grade Rd and, perhaps, down the Eaglenest Lane (BB 1919 V7).

1.3 mi east of Exit 138 near Bonita. Mullan Road and YT are the same.

At Milltown and Bonner, on both the motor highway and the street-car line, are the lumber mills of the Anaconda Copper Mining Company, where visitors are shown how the logs are pulled dripping from the river and in a few moments are piled as lumber in the drying yards.
1929 Road Maps, Missoula
Note: Logs jammed the Clark Fork River for a distance of two miles as they floated toward Milltown from upstream lumberjack camps.

WAYSIDE

Garnet Ghost town. Remarkably preserved in its original 1898 gold mining camp condition, it is augmented by a new visitor center. In Yellowstone Trail days the town boasted of three livery stables, four hotels and 13 saloons and a population of nearly 5,000. More than 30 buildings have been preserved. See Carol Bernhardt's fun book, *History Galore: Ghost Towns and More* (Outskirts Press, Denver 2013) for more information on this and many more Montana ghost towns.

Garnet Ghost town is about 10 miles northwest of Drummond.

1920s YT east of Missoula near Bearmouth
Missoula Chamber of Commerce Book

For 100 years, Milltown Dam blocked the confluence of the Clark Fork and Blackfoot rivers near Missoula, trapping toxic sediments that washed down from mines in Butte and contaminating local drinking water wells. Just months after the dam was completed in 1908, a massive flood washed tons of mining waste from the smelters at Butte and Anaconda down the Clark Fork. Most of it flowed to Bonner and settled beneath the placid waters of the Milltown Reservoir. In 1981 very high levels of arsenic were found in the drinking water of Milltown. Copper and other heavy metals had swept over the dam killing 75% of fish downstream. In 2008 a massive 10-year-long EPA Superfund project began to remove seven million cubic yards of contaminated sediment. It removed the dam, restored the floodplain, sculpted a new Clark Fork River channel, and re-established wetlands. Now the confluence of the Clark Fork and Blackfoot is open for fish to migrate and for people to enjoy [This information came from the Clark Fork Coalition, the group responsible for the EPA's arrival]. ⚙

Older picture of YT on Milltown Bridge

Near Garnet

Between Milltown and Turah the YT crossed the tracks a number of times, with reduced frequency as time went by. The exact alignment is correspondingly difficult to document.

The route through Bonner-West Riverside is a bit speculative and needs local research, especially to explain the *Anaconda Standard*'s Feb. 4, 1920 article which reported that the State Hwy Commission bid out the reconstruction (project 29) of the Marshall grade "on the Yellowstone Trail between Missoula and Bonner" to eliminate that grade. Modern maps do not provide a satisfactory answer to the locations of the YT. The 1903 USGS Topographic map shows the then existing road meandering up and around Marshall Creek Canyon, but modern aerial pictures show nothing comparable.

MT-163.8 Drummond: Just to the east of Exit 166, MT-176.3, and north of I-90, there is a road named Old Highway (YT?) that winds around and intersects I-90 at about MT-178.1.

Garnet near Bearmouth

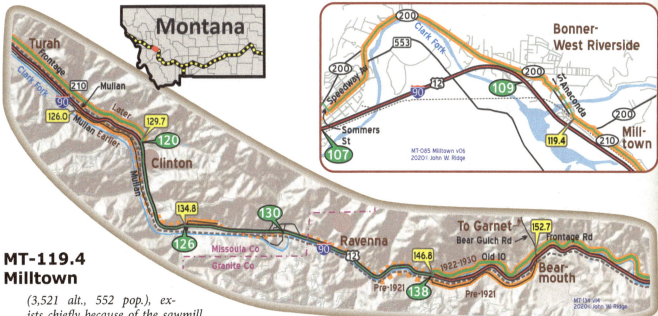

MT-119.4 Milltown

(3,521 alt., 552 pop.), exists chiefly because of the sawmill whose yards stretch along the highway and give the town its character. When the mill is in operation, a clean smell of freshly sawed timber re-enforces the visual impression. WPA-MT

The **Milltown Dam** (GPS: 46.87176, -113.89256) was an earth-fill gravity-type hydroelectric dam on the Clark Fork River at the confluence of the Blackfoot River with the Clark Fork. Built in 1908 by copper mining tycoon William A. Clark, it was meant to supply hydroelectricity to his sawmills in nearby Bonner. It is no more, courtesy of the EPA.

A new state park, **Milltown State Park**, has been completed overlooking the confluence of the Clark Fork and Blackfoot Rivers (GPS: Overlook: 46.870491, -113.896589; Confluence area: 46.874408, -113.894014). Hiking trails and interpretive signs aid the outdoors-inclined.

Today, just northeast of the MT 200 Mill town bridge over the Blackfoot River, you will see a through truss bridge that carried the Yellowstone Trail beginning in 1921. It was open to vehicular traffic until just recently, but now is for foot-traffic only. Go on over. Walk on that historic, narrow bridge; look down at the Blackfoot River. Relive a bit of history.

As you drive toward Clinton, notice the steep hills near the edge of the road to the northeast. It is hard to believe, but the Mullan Road and Yellowstone Trail were carved out of these hills near Turah. Today, you see a slightly re-routed Clark Fork River, made to provide more land to accommodate I-90. A dim route along the side of the hill is visible on Google Earth. This picture gives an idea of the road-building problems of 100 or more years ago in the West.

MT-129.7 Clinton

A scattered village. Good meals and rooms at Clinton Hotel; very fair garage. MH-1928

MT-134.8 Bonita

Gas and oil at small store. MH-1928

The name is Spanish for "beautiful" named by Mexican Northern Pacific Railroad workers.

MT-146.8 Bearmouth Chalet

At mile 152.7 (no Interstate exit at Bearmouth) turn north on Bear Gulch Road to ghost town Garnet. As you turn north you will see the historic Bearmouth Chalet and campground. This area has been the site of rest and supply camps for gold prospectors for over 100 years.

MT-146.8: East of here is a very nice drive. As is true for much of the YT, it is hard to tell exactly where YT was before the new cuts and realignments.

MT-163.8 Drummond

Notice the fantastic grey cliffs along the road. They are Madison Limestone, a rock made up of fossilized remains of countless marine creatures deposited in a shallow sea about 350 million years ago. The tree line across the sides of majestic mountains is quite clear here.

"The town looks much the same today as it did in the 1920s. Some structures remain from the 1880s," says the *Philipsburg Territory*, "steeped in the tradition of the ranch."

The town has been a shipping point for dry goods, mine ores, and cattle from Granite County for well over 100 years and still ships cattle and hay today. As you travel down Front St., the Yellowstone Trail, notice the south side of the road at the east end of the town the cattle-holding pens and the great sign, "**Used cow lot.**" Drummond is also known as the home of the "World Famous Bullshippers." This should tell you that you are in an authentic western community, famous as a cattle shipping point and with a sense of humor!

New Chicago School House Museum (GPS: 46.67148, -113.15049). Built in 1874, the school building was moved from its first location at New Chicago, seven miles south of Drummond into the west side of Drummand next to I-90. The museum offers a number of exhibits giving the visitor a glimpse of the history of Drummond and this area.

MT

Gold Creek is about 11 miles south of Drummond and 8 miles north of Garrison.

(4,201 alt., 35 pop.); The settlement is at the confluence of Clark Fork and Gold Creek. Near the source of the latter, gold was first discovered in Montana in 1852. Gold Creek village was the scene of the ceremony celebrating completion of the Northern Pacific Railway in 1883 and of the Milwaukee Road in 1909 connecting Chicago to Seattle. WPA- MT

The village has built a bright yellow, fake spike to commemorate the Milwaukee Road and Northern Pacific Railway "golden spike" event.

Used cow lot, Drummond

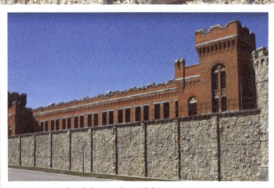
Main building, the Old Montana Prison in Deer Lodge

An original right turn sign for the YT on a building across the river behind the Powell County Museum in Deer Lodge

MT-185.1 Garrison

(4,344 alt., 100 pop.), named for William Lloyd Garrison, abolitionist, is a railroad town on the Clark Fork, sheltered on the north by a high bluff. WPA-MT

A Phosphate Mill of 100 tons capacity grinds rock of high phosphate content brought by truck from several small mines in the nearby mountains. The product is used for fertilizer. WPA-MT

There once was a lovely Pratt truss bridge spanning the Clark Fork River which carried the Yellowstone Trail since 1914. Today that condemned bridge rests in the Deer Lodge Old Montana Prison Museum back yard, saved from demolition by the Powell County Museum and Arts Foundation. It will be used as a pedestrian bridge connecting walking trails.

Garrison Bridge bought by and moved to Powell County Prison Museum

MT-196.6 Deer Lodge

(4,530 alt., 3,510 pop.), seat of Powell County, is bisected by Clark Fork of the Columbia, here called the Deer Lodge River. On the west side of the town are the somber stone walls and guard towers of the State penitentiary, and the yards and shops of the CM. St. P & P R.R., the town's leading industrial unit, which employs 250 men. On the east side, which has broad streets, are many sturdy square houses popular in the West during the 1870s and 1880s. Castles built with the wealth of mines and ranches and log cabin homes survive almost side by side. An important stop on the Mullan Wagon Road, it was one of the few places along the route where immigrants could obtain fresh beef and vegetables, and the services of a blacksmith. WPA-MT

HOTEL DEER LODGE well furnished and modern; elevator service. Sgl. $1.50-$2.50; dbl. $2.50, with bath, $3.25-$3.50. MH-1928

There are at least five museums in the Deer Lodge Old Montana Prison Museum complex:

1106 Main St. (Yellowstone Trail). **Old Montana Prison Museum** (yes, a real historic prison with guard turrets). The castellated red brick cell block was built in 1912. Under Warden Frank Conley (1893-1921) prison laborers built most of the buildings that visitors see today.

1106 Main St. Within the walls of the old museum. **Montana Auto Museum**. Over 160 cars are on display from classic cars to muscle cars.

1107 Main St. **Frontier Montana Museum** features tools, rifles, Conestoga wagons and necessities of frontier life.

1017 Main St. **Yesterday's Playthings** gives visitors the feeling of stepping back into another time where the Railroad ruled, and of mining, outlaws, and toys of "yesterday."

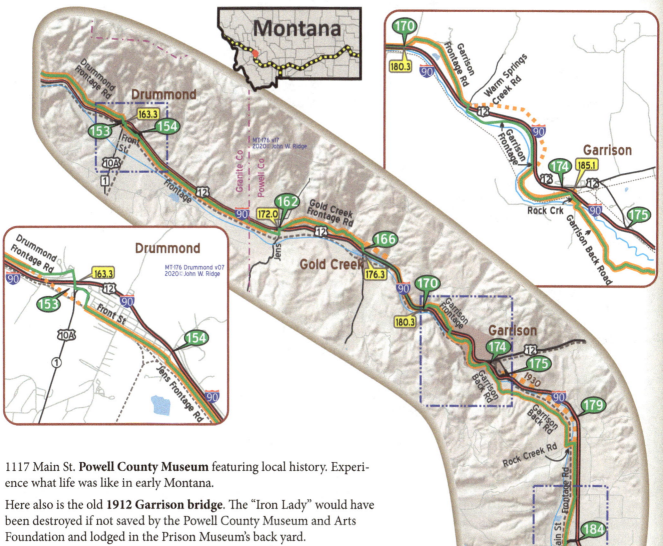

1117 Main St. **Powell County Museum** featuring local history. Experience what life was like in early Montana.

Here also is the old **1912 Garrison bridge**. The "Iron Lady" would have been destroyed if not saved by the Powell County Museum and Arts Foundation and lodged in the Prison Museum's back yard.

The 1912 **Conley Street Bridge** across the Clark Fork River once carried the Yellowstone Trail past the prison and along the Milwaukee Road tracks. At this writing the bridge is being reconstructed and we do not know how much of the original will be left, if any.

At the end of the bridge toward the railroad tracks is a small building with original Yellowstone Trail yellow signs "L" and "R" painted on the building indicating to Trail travelers which way to go to remain on the Trail. The two signs were preserved in plastic the last we knew, but they may be disintegrating.

As of this writing, the 1911 **Deer Lodge Hotel** had been taken over by Deer Lodge Preservation, Inc., a non-profit corporation, which is attempting to restore it to its 120-year-old glamour as being "one of the finest in Montana with hot and cold water in every room." Fund-raising and volunteer work has been going on since 2014 and they were still looking for investors.

418 Main St. **Rialto Theatre**. The Rialto was constructed in 1921 in the Beaux-Arts "Movie Palace" architectural style, with 720 seats. A disastrous fire struck in 2006 burning the building substantially. The whole community immediately joined together to rebuild this city landmark and in 2012 it reopened, looking virtually the same, including its sparkling white exterior. It is home to the active non-profit Rialto Community Theatre, Inc.

266 Warren Ln. off Main St. At the northern edge of Deer Lodge is **Grant-Kohrs Ranch National Historic Site**, operated today as an 1880s working ranch by the National Park Service. Original home, furnishings, and horse-drawn equipment can be seen. This large 19th century range ranch illustrates the development of the Northern Plains cattle industry. It provides a glimpse into the real life of cowboys and ranchers.

PRESENT TRAIL IS MOST FAVORED
DEER LODGE DESIROUS NOT TO HAVE IT CHANGED
January 27, 1920 Anaconda Standard

Note: This headline was the city's response to a proposed diversion of the Yellowstone Trail by way of Helena and possibly abandoning the present route through Superior, Saltese, etc. to Idaho. Two days later at the western state Yellowstone Trail Association meeting in Deer Lodge, General Secretary Hal Cooley appeared and quashed the rumor of moving the Trail to Helena.

View of the Pintlers from Racetrack

The YT near Deer Lodge

Just south of Warm Springs the green YT Driving Line is on I-90 because the original YT is, for the most part, lost to new highways and settling ponds that are part of a Superfund site. (See notes at MT-119.4 Milltown.)

The Chamber will order automobile name plates with Deer Lodge and Yellowstone Trail Association on them and sell them, the profits going to Deer Lodge's dues to the association.
February 9, 1922 Anaconda Standard

The 1912 Conley Street Bridge (now being reconstructed), at the south end of the Prison Museum complex, has much to tell about the history of the area. The bridge, and the route itself, told the story of early modern transportation in the West. The Old Stage Road from Gold Creek comes into Deer Lodge via an early version of that very bridge. In 1912 the concrete bridge was built by convicts from the nearby prison overseen by a progressive-minded Frank Conley. Conley wanted the bridge to more conveniently move supplies from the railroad to the prison. It carried the Yellowstone Trail.

It was the first continuous T-beam bridge built in Montana, meaning that the beams were placed on the floor of the bridge flush with the side concrete walls which would carry the new fangled automobiles and trucks. ☸

Did you know that there was a successful game bird farm at Warm Springs? Travelers on the later Yellowstone Trail would have seen its first of 54 years, 1929-1983. "Unchecked hunting and trapping had severely diminished wildlife populations by the 1890s," said Cole Wandler in "On the Wing" in *Montana the Magazine of Western History*, Autumn 2020. It is a long story of efforts by many to successfully raise game birds and find ideal habitat. By the early 1920s the Montana Fish and Game Department noted that the Deer Lodge Valley successfully produced more than 2,500 pheasants and partridges so it established a game bird farm at Warm Springs, eventually producing hundreds of thousands of birds. Today, "the bird populations, by and large, are self sustaining," wrote Wandler. ☸

The **Marsh Rainbow Arch Bridge** (see picture next page) seems to be drowning in the old Anaconda Mining Company settling pond #2. The bridge, named for designer J. B. Marsh, was built to make passable a county road from nearby Morel, a Milwaukee Road Substation, to Anaconda. It was built in 1914 by convict labor. It was described as "a concrete bridge with reinforced concrete arches tied to piers." The arches rise above the bridge deck, thus the name "rainbow arch." The Marsh Rainbow was a very popular style of bridge in the midwest at a time when rural highways and infrastructure were demanded by the Good Roads Movement. This bridge is the only one of its kind in Montana. The old pond is managed by the State of Montana as a wildlife and recreational site.

Information from *Conveniences Sorely Needed: Montana's Historic Highway Bridges 1860-1956*, Montana Historical Society Press, (2005) by Jon Axline.

Bridgehunter.com/mt/deer-lodge/morel says it well: "Everything about this bridge seems wrong! 1. The bridge does not cross anything. 2. The bridge sits on land. And not just that … 3. The bridge is on an island, or buried in the island. And to add insult to injury … 4. While most bridges cross water, this bridge is on land surrounded by water! Go figure."

See Chippewa Falls, WI, page 256, and Ortonville, MN, page 218, for two more Rainbow Arch bridges. ☸

Marsh Rainbow Arch Bridge

Warm Springs Bridge carried the YT

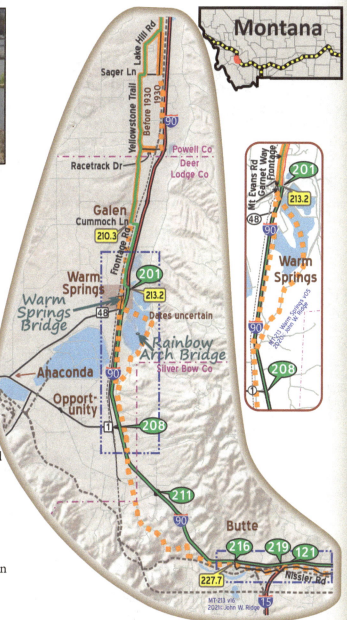

MT-206.7 Racetrack

About 10 miles south of Deer Lodge near the Powell County/Deer Lodge County line on the Yellowstone Trail is a place called Racetrack. Racetrack, Montana, was so named because the flat land lent itself to horse racing, popular in Montana's history. Copper King Marcus Daley housed and trained his horses in Hamilton, Montana, but participated in races throughout Montana and the nation. "While horse racing in Montana became big business, the industry's roots were planted first in communities like Virginia City, Deer Lodge, and Helena during the 1860s," wrote Ellen Baumler in the *Helena Independent Record*.

As you travel south on the Yellowstone Trail at Racetrack area, look west at the junction of Racetrack Dr. At 931 Racetrack Dr. was the Log Cabin Bar. For 116 years it stood, a cool place of refreshment for the area ranchers, prison personnel, and Yellowstone Trail travelers. When we were last there, the dark interior was a pleasant respite from the glaring summer sun. Owner Mary Harrington wanted to retire so it closed in 2006. Today it is called the **Gem Bar and Store**. We have no details to offer.

MT-210.0 Galen

At Galen, a TB sanitarium was built in 1913. That site is now used for mental health patients.

MT-213.2 Warm Springs

Named for the hot water springs on the campus of the State Hospital for the insane built there in 1895. The springs have built up a tower of limestone 40 feet or more. The original buildings have been razed, and new buildings on the site house civil court commitment clients.

There is a **1912 concrete bridge** used by the Yellowstone Trail straddling Warm Springs Creek. From the south exit

I-90 at Exit 201, follow Garnet St. west, then Mt. Evans Way to the south. From the north keep on the frontage road at Warm Springs and turn west at Garnet St. A short distance later, turn south at Mt. Evans Way. A short distance later you will be on a small bridge. Satellite views show a faint path of the old Yellowstone Trail which ran over this bridge. You will not be able to see the bridge from the Frontage Road because of the many trees. That bridge was built by convicts from the state penitentiary at Deer Lodge during a period of great use of convicts as an economical move. It is rather a plain bridge with no markings except for the date "1912" at the end of one guardrail.

About mile #203 on the Interstate (which you must drive on to get to Butte) look to the east. It is hard to see, but a **bridge is visible** looking like it is on an island in the middle of Settling Pond #2 of the old Anaconda Mining Company. The bridge was built to join the Milwaukee Road Morel Substation with Anaconda. See History Bits for more information.

The historic
M&M Cigar Store, Butte

CITY [BUTTE] RANKS FIFTH IN YELLOWSTONE TRAIL TOWNS FOR NUMBER OF TOURISTS
June 20, 1922
Anaconda Standard

The tourist camping grounds of Butte have made a hit with the hundreds of travelers who have stopped there according to the compliments given to Arthur Mattson, manager of the Yellowstone Trail bureau and also to Dave Hudloff, head of the Yellowstone Trail bureau at the Nine Mile.
June 21, 1922
Anaconda Standard

Butte's Tourist Camp

YT Garage, Butte

Butte, the home of many immigrant miners, was the site of much labor unrest. The IWW (Industrial Workers of the World), a basically Communist organization, caused much of it, but Copper Kings worked the men hard, lowered wages, ignored labor unions, and caused much labor unrest as well. In 1914 the Union Hall fire killed 168 men at a meeting, effectively destroying unions until 1934. ✿

ONE KILLED AND THREE INJURED AT BUTTE
The mine owners did not find the gold, they did not mine the gold, they did not mill the gold, but by some weird alchemy all the gold belonged to them!
June 26, 1914 The Terry Tribune

In 1915 W. A. Clark had finished the beautiful Columbia Gardens as a playground for Butte's children, featuring a roller coaster, zoo, dance hall and carousel. One had to take the trolley to reach the Gardens and Thursdays children could ride the trolley for free. The expansion of open pit mining eliminated the beloved Gardens as well as hundreds of homes and businesses in 1973. People remember it fondly to this day and, for a time, planned to rebuild it elsewhere. (See YouTube for Butte video.) ✿

🚗 The roads just west of Butte have been obscured by new streets and highways., including realignments of US 12. Travelers will lose a little "feel" of the historic road by following I-90/Bus. I-15. Those with an explorer's bent can follow the route of the YT along (beginning around I-90, exit 216) Nessler, Grizzly Trail, Excelsior, Rocker, Santa Claus and Excelsior (into Butte) as is found to be possible!

Harding Way, the YT from Butte to Pipestone Pass, apparently was rebuilt and, to some extent, relocated, early in the 1920s. At some later time it was relocated around the Butte airport.

An innovation in handling the travelers added this year to the Butte bureau was the use of the radio. Each evening KFAP has informed tourists within a radius of 1500 miles just what roads they may find in Montana. This information was furnished daily by Mr. Mattson, Yellowstone Trail Association bureau manager.
Late 1922 Yellowstone Trail Association Route Folder

Clark Mansion, Butte

The Finlen Hotel then, Butte

MT-236.4 Butte

(pop. 40,000 alt. 5,484 ft.), is the foremost mining center of the world. In 1864 an outcropping or ledge of mineral was discovered, which has since developed the world's greatest deposit of silver, cooper, and zinc and made the Anaconda mine famous the world over. Since the time of its location, twelve hundred million dollars in minerals have been taken from this hill, and from the lowly little western mining camp, Butte has grown until today it stands the largest city between Minneapolis and Spokane and the leading business and railroad center of the Rocky mountain northwest. BB1921-9

HOTEL FINLEN finest by far and fireproof. All rooms outside and with toilet. Sgl. $2-$4; dbl. with toilet $3-$3.50, bath $4.50-$6; lunch 75e; dinner $1.25; coffee shop.

ARIZONA HOTEL location detracts but second best account being fireproof; nearly new, well furn.; good values. Sgl. $1.25-$2.50; dbl. $1.50-$2.50, bath $2.50-$3.50.

ACOMA HOTEL small but well kept; outside rooms best; good beds. Sgl. $1.50-$2.50; dbl. $2.50, bath $3.50.

PATTERSON MOTOR CO. 209 S. Mont. St., is well equipped; does fine mechanical work. Labor $1.65. Ph. 477.

CRAWLEY MOTOR SUPPLY CO., 220 E. Broadway. Outstanding for tires and accessories. Drive-in shop; highly efficient tire service; complete stock. Ph. 661 until 6. Mohawk Sealer. MH-1928

Butte was not so much a "melting pot" of nationalities; it was a "tossed salad." Each nationality was distinct from others in separate neighborhoods and customs. But they all had an interest in surviving as miners.

This mining city of immigrants sat on top of a Boulder Batholith, a vast block of granite, rich in copper, gold, silver and zinc. No wonder the place was called "the richest hill on earth." We do not call attention to today's obvious tourist attraction, the huge toxic, water-filled Berkeley Pit, because it was not there 100 years ago for Yellowstone Trail travelers to see. The open pit mine began operations in 1955. It was the 200 mines that made Butte and gave it the heritage celebrated today. Many "headframes" can be seen today marking the remnants of mines that honeycombed the Butte hill.

219 W Granite St. **Copper King Mansion**. William Clark, one of the three Copper Kings of Butte, became a U.S. Senator and "one of the 100 men who owned America." At a cost of $240,000, it is a massive and opulent home in every way. Although it is a B&B now, it is still open to the public for tours.

17 W Mercury St. **Mai Wah Society Museum**. This Chinese museum might be overlooked by the tourist because of the building's unprepossessing appearance. Housed in the historic Wah Chong Tai Co. and Mai Wah Noodle Parlor buildings, the museum explains the Chinese experience in Butte. Original furnishings and Asian merchandise are present.

20 W Broadway. (Yellowstone Trail). **Piccadilly Museum of Transportation**. From the quirky name of the establishment to the eclectic interior, this is a one-of-a-kind transportation site with advertising art and memorabilia from around the world. Even old cars.

50 W Broadway. Legatt Apts. Started as **Legatt Hotel** in 1914. It has been fully fireproofed, as the large sign on its exterior wall says, and is still going, for over 100 years, as a residence.

155 Museum Way (next to Montana Tech campus) **World Museum of Mining**. Twelve acres of outdoor and indoor displays built on a 100-year-old silver and zinc mine site. The underground mine tours should not be missed. The museum also depicts the historical legacy of mining and the culture of Butte.

316 W Park St. **The Mother Lode Theatre**. It was built in Butte's cultural heyday, 1923, as the Temple Theatre by the Masonic Order adjacent to their six-story building. It was restored in the 1980s as the beauty it is today.

100 E Broadway St. (Yellowstone Trail). **Finlen Hotel**. Opened in 1924 and updated in 2016, it still is a fine boutique hotel with elegant architecture and decor. It's right in historic downtown Butte "where Copper Kings have slept," says their ad. The January 24, 2018 *Missoulian* reported that "The Finlen Hotel, opened as one of the most elegant hotels between Minneapolis and Seattle."

220-236 E Broadway. **Broadway Garage**. In Yellowstone Trail days this garage served drivers well, repairing what damage the poor roads inflicted upon the family buggy. Looking today just as it did almost 100 years ago, it now serves as a popular vehicle storage building.

117 S Main St. **Pekin Noodle Parlor**. A 108-year-old Chinese restaurant, currently owned by the Tam family, is still serving food in the heart of Butte's Chinatown. The game of Keno was said to have been invented in the lower level of the upstairs restaurant. Each table is secluded from others by walls and a curtain. After we were served, the curtain was closed in our cubicle to afford privacy (whether you want it or not). The rumor that the cubicles were once occupied by prostitutes is false.

9 N Main St. The **M&M Cigar Store** was opened in 1890 by Sam Martin and Wm. Mosby. "This is Butte's one remaining cigar store from Butte's days as a 'wide open town' when drinking parlors sold cigars to cater to working miners off shift," says the *Copperway Walking Tours*. Actually it was a 24-hour-a-day drinking and gambling bar. The "cigar" title was in deference to Prohibition. It has had a rocky time with several changes of ownership. We have been surprised lately that the place that advertised "it never closed" was closed. Presently, it is open but, as expected, is updated from the character of the "old days" in looks, menu, and hours. Some old codgers are sad; some folks are just happy that this historic icon was not razed.

This just in. Late at night May 6, 2021, and into May 7 fire gutted the famous icon - The M&M. Donations are flowing in to rebuild this beloved Butte fixture. The neon sign was saved.

Following I-90 to the east takes one through exfoliated rocks and the "singing rocks" in Town of Pipestone.

Harding Way (west of Pipestone Pass)
Lance Sorensen

Point of Rocks then
Pipestone Pass
US 2 MT-250

Point of Rocks now
GPS: 45.86210,
-112.44596

Original Butte
Taxi sign at YT
Mile 257

FORMIDABLE GRADE ON YELLOWSTONE TRAIL HAS BEEN ELIMINATED

One of the most formidable grades on the Yellowstone Trail has been eliminated by the completion of a new stretch of highway westward from the Pipestone Pass where the transcontinental highway crosses the continental divide southeast of Butte. It has been named Harding Way.

May 29, 1922 Albuquerque Journal (New Mexico)

At a special meeting last Thursday of the Whitehall Commercial Club it was decided to put Whitehall on the Yellowstone Trail map soon to be published by the Yellowstone Trail Association. The cost was $30 which was raised by popular subscription among Whitehall business people the following day.

March 23, 1916 Jefferson Valley News

HUNTERS KILL HALF AN ELK
Fall 1915 Jefferson Valley News

Yellowstone markers are up in Whitehall, 9 x 9 inches, heavy enameled tin, yellow with black circles around a black arrow with the words "Yellowstone Trail" thereon. Whitehall Businessmen's club helped put up the signs. It is hoped that they will take moving pictures along the Trail.

July 12, 1917 Jefferson Valley News

USING A FORD DELIVERY TRUCK

Greene & Sons will do double quick time with their new Ford delivery truck.

November 18, 1915 Jefferson Valley News

Note: In 1915 this was really news on page 2 in small town newspapers. Turns out the truck was a used touring car. No mention of what product Greene & Sons delivered.

In 1929 James Wyne built the "Green and White Tourist Camp" at the corner of N Division St. and W 2nd St. with six cabins, then 11, a gas station, and convenience store. Prices were 50¢ to camp, upwards from $1.00 for a cabin. In 1934 he moved his camp to East Legion Ave. because Legion (Yellowstone Trail) was part of the recently numbered US 10. This morphed into the first motel in Whitehall. ⚙

1922 the radio club at the high school was experimenting with the outside world. Two members had radios. ⚙

WHITEHALL ROAD BOOSTERS CAPTURE '22 CONVENTION

The Western Montana Yellowstone Trail Association will host the 1922 convention, as just announced at the 1921 convention at Butte.

November 3, 1921 Jefferson Valley News

Whitehall's YT, 1923
Jefferson Valley Museum

Watering trough still on Pipestone Pass

Hwy 2 (YT) near Whitehall

Old Ford garage today, in Whitehall, little changed over nine decades

MT

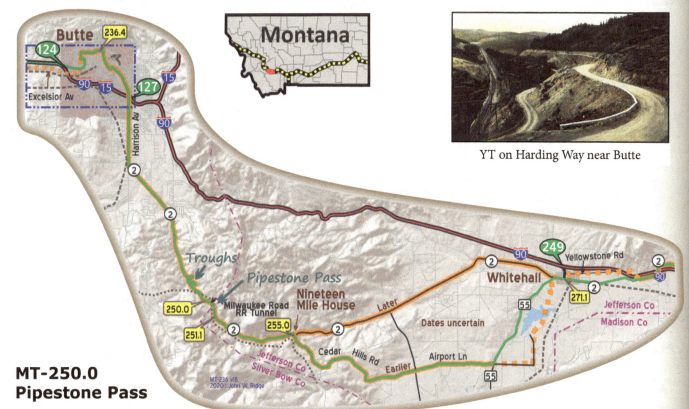

YT on Harding Way near Butte

MT-250.0
Pipestone Pass

This mountainous pass crosses the Continental Divide. This was the Yellowstone Trail's route, then it was US 10 in 1926. Today, I-90 is routed through nearby Homestake Pass with its easier curves, leaving this fine route for slower autos with views of the Beaverhead-Deerlodge National Forest from its 6,347 foot elevation. You may still see an ancient ad for a Butte taxi company painted on a rock near the road. This road was known locally as Harding Way in honor of visiting President Harding (1921-1923). This road marks the juncture of the Yellowstone Trail and the Vigilante Trail.

The Milwaukee Road used the pass for its crossing of the Continental Divide, cutting under the Pass in a tunnel. The line was electrified in 1915 and was abandoned in 1980.

Keep your eyes open on the north side of the Pass for **old watering troughs** along US 2. The fountains provided drinking water for travelers and water for overheated auto radiators. They were recently maintained by the Heinze family of Butte; there is no water available now.

Western Tourism Magazine, Fall 1923 describes "The Continental Divide Through Montana" and says: "The Yellowstone Trail … is making the Continental Divide area of Montana a new summer playground. Harding Way, the much-traveled crossing of the Great Divide at the front door of Butte marks the juncture of the Yellowstone and Vigilante Trails."

MT-271.1 Whitehall

pop. 600; a farm and stock center. Three modern hotels. Modern Hotel [Borden's] is good. Free camp.

PALM HOTEL well kept; fine meals. Dbl. $1.50-$2.

TAIT'S GARAGE is far best. Almost every service. Labor $1.50; ph. 35; 24-hr. towing. Mohawk Dealer. MH-1928

(4,371 alt., 553 pop.), is a long, narrow, quiet town, the trading center for the southern part of Jefferson County, one of the original Territorial counties. It is apparently merely a line of stores and houses strung out along US 10, but actually, most of it sits back among shade trees and shrubbery. The number of settlers in the region increased slowly but Whitehall did not have much importance until 1889 when the Northern Pacific branch between Logan and Garrison was built. WPA-MT

Twelve murals depicting Lewis and Clark's travels through the area adorn downtown buildings.

The main drag of Whitehall, Legion St., was close to the railroad tracks, as was usual in western small towns. However, a small space was left between the tracks and the street. This space was grassed and turned into a "tourist camping grounds." Today that long narrow space (the length of the downtown) serves as a beautiful boulevard park and picnic area with many trees, enhancing the town immeasurably.

303 S Division St. **Jefferson Valley Museum** is housed in a renovated 1914 red barn of the old Sanitary Dairy located three blocks south from the middle of Whitehall. Look for a sign at corner of Legion and Division. The museum features artifacts depicting the history of the Jefferson Valley area. Retired Director, Roy Millegan, brought forth an excellent and enduring picture of Jefferson Valley and personally guided us along the Yellowstone Trail in the area some years ago.

101-105 W Legion St. (Yellowstone Trail). **Borden's Hotel.** Borden's pool hall, café and dance hall were expanded in 1916 into a hotel. Today, after a $1.5 million renovation in 2015, there are nine apartments and two rentals, a conference center and businesses on the lower floor. Of course, there is the persistent rumor of the ghost of Mrs. Hilda Borden ambling about. It is on the National Register of Historic Places.

Keystone Cops in Big Sky Country: The Harrison Bank Robbery of 1930 by Dave Walter in *Speaking Ill of the Dead: Jerks* (2000) Falcon Press. The Harrison Bank was the target. Ralph Harrington was the "jerk" who would foil the planned robbery for his own notoriety. Things went awry, killing the sheriff, who planned to capture the crooks for his own notoriety. Mistaken identities, a high speed car chase and a gun fight gave enough excitement to Harrison to last almost a century. ✿

MADISON COUNTY PROPERTY OWNERS WANT BETTER ROADS

... It was urged by the chief spokesman for the petitioners that the Yellowstone Trail be improved the entire distance from Jefferson Island to Harrison. Madison County should get in line with neighboring counties in the good roads movement.

June 7, 1917 Jefferson Valley News

VIOLENT QUAKE HITS MONTANA

...Bridges in and around Three Forks on the Yellowstone Trail and those over the Jefferson River are declared to have been sprung out of line and are dangerous. Three Forks has sustained $200,000 property loss. Willow Creek is on fire and is in danger of total destruction.

June 28, 1925 Illinois State Journal (Springfield)

BIG ATTENDANCE SURE FOR WEST-END TRAIL CONFERENCE
BOOSTERS WILL GATHER JEFFERSON ISLE

Western Montana Yellowstone Trail Association ... will convene on Monday in the commodious tourist park building of Shadan LaHood, good roads booster and nationally known advocate of the Yellowstone Trail.

October 8, 1925 The Anaconda Standard

The stretch of road from Willow Creek to Harrison was known from coast to coast as one of the worst highways in the country. People in Willow Creek called it the Harrison Hill. People in Harrison called it the Willow Creek Hill. That hill in the wintertime is as slick as glass and in summer when it rained, it was a mud hole with gumbo.

undated Three Forks Herald

Note: One hundred years later, while researching the Trail, we took one look at that hill and gumbo after a rain and declined the climb. The next visit it was dry and passible. Near **MT-300.0**.

Near **MT-300.0**.

WAYSIDE

Norris Hot Springs is 11 miles south of Harrison on MT 84 and MT 387. Geothermal hot springs feed the pools here. Casual and family-oriented, open all year, soak your bones in a wooden pool.

TRAIL ROAD NOW OPEN

Roy Robinson, who lives seven miles east of Jefferson Island on the Yellowstone Trail, says that Wednesday for the first time people were traveling over the Trail without chains. Up to Wednesday it was an everyday occurrence to pull from one to a half-dozen cars out of mud holes.

April 20, 1922 Jefferson Valley News

WAYSIDE

Shadan LaHood of Syria opened a mercantile business in Jefferson Island. He was a model citizen and, for some years after 1909, ran a general store. He was a booster of the Yellowstone Trail and provided services for tourists. Then in 1929 the new highway, now MT 2, was opened between Three Forks and Whitehall. It bypassed Jefferson Island.

LaHood bought land along the new route and built a hotel, cafe, and service station to serve the tourists coming through the Jefferson River Canyon to the Lewis and Clark Caverns. The area became known as **LaHood Park**. It prospered through the 1930s and in 1936 Frank Bliss painted a unique depiction on the four wood panels under the canopy which protected the fuel pumps. He drew a map of the entire Yellowstone Trail from coast to coast, giving it the U.S. highway numbers current in 1936. The site closed after LaHood died in 1957. Unfortunately, the site burned down in 2001.

LaHood's Service Station with entire Trail drawn under its canopy

LaHood after the fire of 2001

YT today near Willow Creek

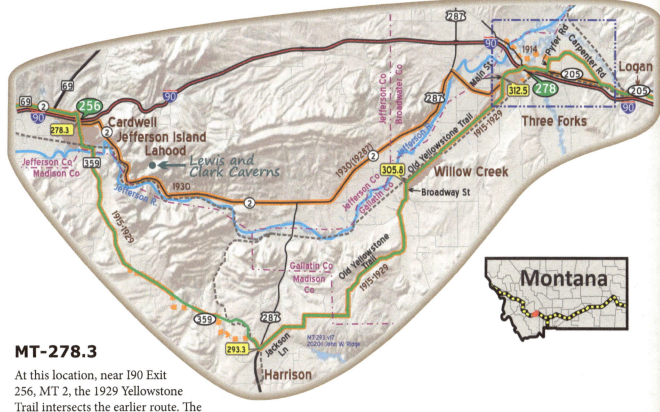

MT-278.3

At this location, near I90 Exit 256, MT 2, the 1929 Yellowstone Trail intersects the earlier route. The green "driving line" is marked on the older route because of its more historical experience but MT 2 goes through LaHood and the Jefferson River gorge and past the **Lewis and Clark Caverns**. The gorge runs through fossil-ridden limestone with an occasional hillside cave on the north side and meandering railroad tracks and the Jefferson River on the south side. Beautiful, actually, with National Forests all around.

WAYSIDE

Lewis and Clark Caverns State Park. 25 Lewis and Clark Caverns Road, about 14 beautiful miles east of Whitehall on MT 2, the 1930 route of the Yellowstone Trail. Lewis and Clark Caverns overlooks the trail of Lewis and Clark along the Jefferson River.

Having been discovered in 1882, the cave was first developed for tours around 1900 and officially named by Teddy Roosevelt. It is Montana's first state park. It features one of the largest known limestone caverns in the Northwest which is lined with stalactites, stalagmites, columns, and helictites. Although Lewis and Clark never saw the limestone cavern, they did pass through portions of the modern day 160 acre monument park and the nearby Jefferson River.

The cavern equals the well-known Luray caves of Virginia. The entrance to the cave is locked and the keys are in the custody of the chief of the field division of the general land office in Helena, Mont. BB1921-9

The full journey requires vigor, sure-footedness, and a readiness to cling and sometimes to crawl by the light of a miner's lantern. The air is good. WPA-MT

MT-279.1 Cardwell

MT-280.1 Jefferson Island

pop. 50; a shipping point; mechanic at store. Lahood's camp, 50c, is popular. Fine community house; dining hall. 4 clean cabins, $1.25-$1.50. MH 1928

MT-293.2 Harrison

MT-305.8 Willow Creek

All we have to say is watch out for the gumbo on the old Yellowstone Trail on the "Harrison Hill!" After 100 years, it is still sticky and rolls up around tires and gets so thick that it will stop cars.

The initial 1867 survey point for the state of Montana is located on Old Yellowstone Trail, a few miles south of town. A historic marker signifies the spot. Gumbo was just as bad on this side of "Harrison Hill."

WAYSIDE

Parker Homestead State Park. Eight miles west of Three Forks is a frustration. On this one-acre space is a preserved sod-roofed cabin built in the early 1900s. It was similar to many of the first homes built by early Montana settlers and was the smallest park in the state. We visited it every time we passed by. We walked right up to it and peered into the interior. Unfortunately, the state park commission let the lease expire, and in 2010 the homestead reverted to private ownership. It was still standing when we last visited it, but you must view it from the road.

Sacajawea Hotel then,
Three Forks

The late 1800s Maguire Opera House (in Butte) is no more, but Mark Twain found it surprising that the citizenry who packed the house for his presentation in 1895 seemed to be as cosmopolitan and sophisticated as any New York audience. ❖

Muddy Harrison grade
A Look Back at Yesterday's Montana
by Betty Martin

MANHATTAN ANTICIPATING BIG AUTO TRAIL BUSINESS

Within the next week work will be started on the large cement garage by I. U. Dunley on Main St. The main part of the building ... is to have a floor space 50 by 75 feet and to be without any supporting posts on the floor ... Manhattan being on the main route of the Yellowstone Trail, this addition will mean much, not only to the town, but should also be a station of no little importance for all tourists.
April 11, 1915 Anaconda Standard

Manhattan Auto Inn

A traveler reported that

...the Yellowstone Trail is going to be the most beautiful highway in the country. From Butte to Miles City the old sheep herders' log huts along the way have been fixed up with stoves and coffee pots for the accommodation of tourists who wish to camp on the way.
December 5, 1915 Omaha Daily Bee

The end of the YT in 1914.
An old town road one mile
NW of I-90 Exit 278
(GPS: 45.91410, -111.54250).

Gumbo! Beatrice Larned Massey in her 1919 memoir, *It Might Have Been Worse: A Motor Trip From Coast to Coast,* describes her experience with gumbo in Montana:

"One man advised us to put chains on, but with a superior 'don't-believe-we-will-need-them' air, we left. In ten minutes we had met gumbo, and were sliding, swirling, floundering about in a sea of mud. A perfectly solid (apparently) clay road can become as soft as melted butter in an hour. Try to picture a narrow road with deep ditches and just one track of ruts covered with fly paper, Vaseline, wet soap, molasses, mire, and any other soft, sticky, slippery, hellish mess that could be mixed. If you once got out of the ruts your car acted as if it were drunk. It slid, zigzagged, slithered and headed for the ditch. Your feet stuck in the gumbo so that when you pulled up one foot a mass of mire as large as a market basket stuck to it."

What Massey did not describe was the condition of tires. The gumbo sticks to them and just rolls with the tire, "fattening" them up until the tire cannot rotate any more and becomes immobile. ❖

Mountains in distance, Three Forks

PLANS COMPLETED FOR YELLOWSTONE TRAIL CONVENTION

The convention of the Western Division of the Montana state Yellowstone Trail Association will be held in Three Forks February 20 and is going to be one of the most important good roads meetings to be held in this state.
February 13, 1919 Three Forks News

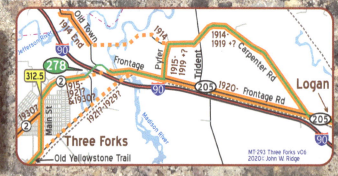

HISTORY BITS

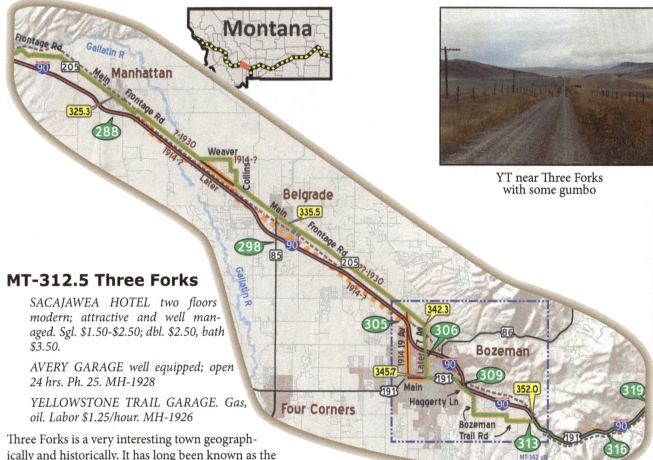

YT near Three Forks
with some gumbo

MT-312.5 Three Forks

SACAJAWEA HOTEL two floors modern; attractive and well managed. Sgl. $1.50-$2.50; dbl. $2.50, bath $3.50.

AVERY GARAGE well equipped; open 24 hrs. Ph. 25. MH-1928

YELLOWSTONE TRAIL GARAGE. Gas, oil. Labor $1.25/hour. MH-1926

Three Forks is a very interesting town geographically and historically. It has long been known as the "headwaters" of the Missouri River and as the home area of Sacajawea and it is here where many Native American battles were fought and colorful legends were born.

Go to **Headwaters Park** to view the three rivers (Jefferson, Madison, Gallatin) become one (Missouri).

202 S Main St. (Yellowstone Trail). **Headwaters Heritage Museum**. Thousands of artifacts are housed in this former 1910 bank building relating to important moments in Western history.

302 S Main St. **Masonic Temple**. The building still stands, first as a bank with the Lodge upstairs in 1909. Various banks occupied the lower floor over the years and the 1925 earthquake destroyed the stonework around the eaves of the building, but the Masons are still there. Don't let the boarded-up windows fool you.

5 N Main St. **Sacajawea Hotel**. It was built by the Milwaukee Road as a hotel for railroad men in 1882 and moved to its present site and expanded in 1910 to serve as a jumping off point for tours to Yellowstone Park. The Hotel has risen from a low point closure in 2001 to today's premier status. A member of Historic Hotels of America and recipient of the 2011 Historic Preservation Award of Excellence, the elegant Sacajawea Hotel was, no doubt, used by Yellowstone Trail travelers.

Across the road from the Sacajawea Hotel is a recently moved railroad station. Interesting history and project. Ask locally.

The route in and near Logan is uncertain due to I-90 construction, railroad disappearing, and changing rivers.

MT-320.0 Logan

LOGAN, a N. P. R. R. freight division point. Good country hotel; very fair garage; open camp space. MH-1928

MT-325.5 Manhattan

pop. 700; a farm, stock and sugar beet center. Auto Inn Garage leads. Camp, 50¢.

METROPOLITAN HOTEL good rooms and meals. MH-1928

(4,258 alt., 501 pop.), is a one-street town with a few business buildings facing a tree-enclosed park. It was named by a group of New Yorkers who operated under the name of the Manhattan Co. and owned land here. The George Sinton ranches, one of the largest cattle spreads north of Texas, has headquarters here. WPA-MT

105 S Broadway. **Manhattan Area Museum and Historical Society**. "The Manhattan Area Museum serves to preserve and make available for study and research the history and culture of the area," says their website. We stopped in; it is small but interesting.

114 E Main St. (Yellowstone Trail). **Manhattan Auto Inn**. A 1915 auto garage used as an auto storage and repair garage in Yellowstone Trail days. Today it is a mixed-use space with a bar in front and event space in the rear. The building was noted because it was made of concrete and "had no supporting posts on the floor." A similar garage with "no supporting posts" was built in 1914 in nearby Belgrade, Montana.

The Western Montana State Yellowstone Trail Association meeting will be on January 15th in Bozeman.

January 7, 1915 Three Forks News

Note: Apparently attendees of the above mentioned meeting were not as insular as might be thought. The Yuma, Arizona, *Weekly Examiner* and the Maysville, Kentucky, *Public Ledger* each carried stories of the meeting, written by attendees.

Hotel Bozeman

TRAIL DAY FOR ALL ROADS OF COUNTRY
THOUSANDS OF PEOPLE SHOULD LEND A HAND MAY 22

May 5, 1914 Livingston Enterprise

Note: This was a notice sent out from Yellowstone Trail Association for all towns along the Trail to lend a hand and improve the Trail in their area. And people turned out by the hundreds all along the Trail in 1914. Today, Trail Day is still celebrated by some towns on the Trail, some with parades, some with "fests" but no actual road work.

YT near Bozeman, 1926

YELLOWSTONE TRAIL PUSHING WESTWARD
MEETING AT BOZEMAN ON THE FIFTEENTH

The entrance into Eastern Montana has been marked with the yellow circle and black arrow pointing westward. ... Enthusiasm is working westward. So the next object to be attained will be the marking of the western entrance with the yellow circle and the arrow pointing eastward.

January 4, 1915 Anaconda Standard

Note: The iconic black arrow always pointed in the direction of the Yellowstone National Park, thus Trail signs placed west of the Park featured black arrows pointing east.

The Bob Evans family of Bozeman at a familiar task
Bob Evans

WHILE IN BOZEMAN
EAT AT

Kramer's Cafe

D. E. Kramer, Prop.

Ask for Flying D Steaks
and B-K Peas

Official Yellowstone Trailsman

Watch for the Trail Sign In Center of Business District

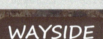

Information Bureau

Bozeman Trailman card
Bob Evans

THIRTEEN AUTOS IN UNIQUE TRAIN
FIRST MILITARY CONVOY OFF FOR BOZEMAN - PRACTICE FOR DRAFTEES

Thirteen "junker" cars were being driven from Butte to Bozeman to be used to train draftees in the art of vehicle maintenance before the soldiers were to be sent to the front in Europe during World War I. "While the train will leave Butte on time, no hour or date is fixed for their arrival in Bozeman ... some wagered that they might get there before the war was over. They would learn how to make a self-propelled vehicle out of a bundle of junk.

June 16, 1918 Anaconda Standard

WAYSIDE

4050 Bridger Canyon Rd., **Bozeman Fish Technology Center**, 4.8 miles northeast of Bozeman (via S Rouse Ave. and MT 86). Formerly Bozeman National Fish Hatchery. Bozeman National Fish Hatchery was established in1892, for production and stocking of trout in Montana and surrounding states. Trout production ceased in 1966 when the hatchery was designated as a Fish Cultural Development Center to conduct research on developing methods for improving salmonid culture. In 1983, the facility was designated as a Fish Technology Center to conduct research and provide technical assistance on a variety of aquatic resource issues.

On a tour of the center, you can see people working on research of fish cultural techniques, diseases, etc. Technical assistance in these areas is provided to federal and state fisheries agencies and the private sector throughout the United States. This hatchery was mentioned in the 1914 *First Year Book*.

MT-345.7 Bozeman: Betweeen I-90 Exits 319 and 330, Bozeman Hill Rd. runs just south of I-90 and it is likely that it is in the location of one alignment of the YT, but it retains none of the old characteristics. and, frustratingly, just west of Livingston the USGS map and the 1914 maps are impossible to reconcile.

MT

MT-329.3 Central Park
MT-335.6 Belgrade

(pop. 800, alt. 4,437 ft.), is centrally located in the great Gallatin valley, made world famous by its many prize winning products as well as by its scenic grandeur. The Belgrade Chamber of Commerce has provided camping facilities at Athletic park for the free use of tourists. BB1921-9

ELECTRIC HOTEL modern and good. Dbl. $2, bath $2.50.

FOERSCHLER GARAGE leads. Progressive and well equipped. Labor $1.25. Ph. 54W.

HESPEN TIRE AND BATTERY SHOP gives a skilled service and is unexcelled. Ph.11-J. MH-1928

27 E Main St. (Yellowstone Trail). **Mint Bar and Cafe** opened in 1904; claims to be one of the oldest continuously run establishments in Montana. Its neon sign looks 1930s. It has had multiple incarnations, but now blends modern with classic western. Live music of every modern stripe. Yellowstone Trail travelers may well have frequented the place 100 years ago.

MT-345.7 Bozeman

pop.10,000, alt. 4,754 ft. is commonly termed "the Egypt of America." It is one of the great flour and cereal milling centers of the state. The Montana state agricultural college is located there. There are 13 beautiful canyons within a short drive of Bozeman. At the mouth of the Bridger canyon is located the government fish hatchery where millions of fish are hatched and transferred to the local streams. Bozeman has a splendidly equipped camp for auto tourists. BB1921-9

BOZEMAN, (6,855 Pop) is, for Montana, an old and decorous town. Local ordinances prohibit dancing anywhere after midnight and in beer halls at any time, it is illegal to drink beer while standing, so all Bozeman bars have stools. WPA-MT

BYRON'S CAFE is best; lunch 40c. Gilkerson Cafeteria is liked. Bozeman Camp, 50c, good.

BOZEMAN HOTEL is largest; 100 outside rooms. Sgl.$1.50-$2.50; dbl. $2.50, bath $3-$3.50.

BOZEMAN AUTO CO., Buick; best general garage and finely equipped. Very large stock replacement parts. Labor $1.50. Ph. 168, after 9 ph. 775-W.

MAIN ST. GARAGE, 24-hr. mechanical work; storage. MH-1928

Bozeman is located on a beautiful site in the Gallatin Valley with the Gallatin and Madison Ranges to the south, the Bridger Range to the northwest, and the Absarokato Range to the southeast.

105 W Main St. (Yellowstone Trail). **Baxter Hotel**. "Built in 1929, the Baxter is a renovated, historic hotel in the historic district of downtown Bozeman. As you enter the lobby, you're welcomed by marble floors, vaulted ceilings, warm lighting, and historic elegance. The Baxter no longer offers lodging accommodations, but "is home to fine and pub

style dining, and residential and commercial rental spaces," says their website. Latter-day Yellowstone Trail travelers may well have visited the place when it was a hotel.

17 W Main St. **The Ellen Theatre**. According to *Montana's Cultural Treasures*, The Ellen Theatre "First opened in 1919 and was a favored stop on the vaudeville circuit featuring variety shows with stars such as Edgar Bergen. The Ellen also hosted symphony concerts, traveling operas, and starting in 1926, 'talking pictures.' Shuttered and abandoned for years, the Ellen was purchased and restored in 2008 ... and now hosts a wide variety of programming from Broadway musicals to classic films ..."

317 W Main St. **Gallatin History Museum of Bozeman**. Formerly called Pioneer Museum, it is in a 1911 former jail! In addition to jail cells and a hanging gallows, the museum maintains displays of local history, Native American history in the Gallatin Valley, relics of old Fort Ellis, 25,000 historic photos, and a Lewis and Clark research library.

600 W Kagy Blvd. **Museum of the Rockies**, located at the Montana State University (called the State Agricultural College in Yellowstone Trail days), is an affiliate of the Smithsonian. It houses a spectacular paleontology collection of dinosaurs and dinosaur eggs and exhibits of geology and Montana history. There are also a planetarium and a living history farm.

415 N Bozeman Ave. **Beall City Park** is a 2.2 acre park with an ice rink, grill and picnic tables, and Art Center available. We mention this park because it has been there from before the 1930s and would have been visited by Yellowstone Trail travelers.

Bozeman's Main Street Historic District is located on either side of Main St., between Rouse Ave. and just west of Willson Ave., a four block area. As the traditional heart of commerce and culture in southwest Montana, the Main Street Historic District has a period of historic significance from 1867-1940.

811 S Willson. The 1910 **Story Mansion** is one of only three living examples of city-block mansions in Montana. Situated in Bozeman's well-preserved BonTon Historic District, the Story Mansion is recognized as a Montana treasure and national landmark. T. Byron Story inherited a successful milling business from his father, Nelson Story. He expanded it, founded a canning company to can the 17,000 acres of sweet peas being grown in the area, and was a philanthropist, founding the Ellen Theatre, named for his mother. The mansion is on the National Register of Historic Places.

BIG LIVINGSTON DELEGATION IS AFTER YELLOWSTONE TRAIL
CITY'S BOOSTERS NOW ON SCENE FOR ACTION

… The Cody route would make an eastern entrance that is not near as attractive as the Gardiner entrance …

May 26, 1913 Livingston Daily Post

Note: Next year's Western Montana Yellowstone Trail Association would meet in Livingston.

ONE HUNDRED CARS TO MAKE A SOCIABILITY RUN TO HUNTERS HOT SPRINGS

June 24, 1914 Livingston Enterprise

Note: A planned major run to a national meeting of the Association at Hunter's Hot Springs was postponed until August due to big rains and washouts of the Yellowstone Trail. Elaborate plans for a major parade of autos from Minneapolis were also washed out.

WAYSIDE

North 1.25 miles of the YT on US 89 east of Livingston and then east on Horse Thief Trail is a neat old bridge over the Shields River. Just to explore.

YELLOWSTONE TRAIL IS HIT OF 1914 SEASON

A live theater performance of the play, Yellowstone Trail, was performed at Hefferlin's Opera House with "vim and vigor and catchy songs."

February 21, 1914 Livingston Enterprise

COMPLETE PLANS FOR YELLOW TRAIL MEETING

The Montana state meeting featured a trip over the Trail to Bozeman and "over the convict road up the Yellowstone" to inspect the Trail.

March 21, 1914 Livingston Enterprise

Note: They divided the state into two sections of the state Association, Eastern Montana and Western Montana in 1919 because the vast distance limited attendance and issues were disparate.

BOYS AND GIRLS TO OBSERVE YELLOWSTONE TRAIL DAY BY PICKING STONES OFF THE ROAD

April 18, 1914 Livingston Enterprise

HISTORY BITS

(pop. 7,200, alt. 4,487 ft.) is the gateway to the Yellowstone National park and is visited annually by thousands of tourists. It is just a pleasant auto drive of fifty miles from this city up the beautiful Yellowstone River valley. The town is picturesquely located on the banks of the Yellowstone river, which stream partly encircles the city. A free auto camping ground is maintained by the Chamber of Commerce a few blocks from the center of town. BB1921-9

pop. 7,000; is the widely known and busy northern gateway to Yellowstone Park. Prospers also from the N. P. R. R. shops and trade from the territory north. Headquarters for elk, deer and bear hunting. Information at the live C. of C. The Grill is the best cafe. Park Hotel is popular. Yellowstone Camp, 50c, in fine grove on Yellowstone River; good kitchen; all conveniences; Many cabins, some very fine, with run. water, toilet and bath, $1.50-$2.

MURRAY HOTEL leads because most modern and only one fireproof. Sgl-. $1.50-$2.50; dbl. $2.50, bath $3.50-$5. Cafe.

GRABOW HOTEL is quietest; clean and well kept. Dbl. $2.25, with bath $3-$4. Café.

HOME AUTOMOBILE CO. is largest, most modern and best equipped. Open 24 hrs. Labor $1.50 or flat rate. Ph. 706 for wrecker. Mohawk Dealer. Telephone at ranch house. MH 1928

A town with a history of western legends and cattle drives became gentrified but still maintains a Western atmosphere. Magnificent sights of four mountain ranges surround the city, and, bordered by the Yellowstone River, it became a tourist destination and locomotive repair and division site. The whole downtown and many homes are on the National Register of Historic Places, with buildings of the 1880s and '90s still standing, well preserved, as a testimony to the Old West.

Names from the past such as William Clark (of Lewis and Clark), John Bozeman, Jim Bridger, Calamity Jane, and Soapy Smith come as easily to the minds of residents as present-day movie stars who live in the area.

Corner of Park and Main. **Livingston Bar and Grille**, is a local restaurant, housed in an 1800s building which once housed the Bucket of Blood Saloon, a wild and raucous place back then.

118 W Chinook St. **Yellowstone Gateway Museum of Park County**. These folks know about the Yellowstone Trail.

They told us about the rock slide on the Trail, blocking it for the foreseeable future. The museum features collections of Native American history, early transportation, mining, and Yellowstone National Park history. A gem is the only surviving ⇨

An original YTA tourist information tent at the Yellowstone Gateway Museum, Livingston

MILE-BY-MILE

The SPUR of the Yellowstone Trail to the YELLOWSTONE NATIONAL PARK goes south from Livingston. See pages 144 to 149

Montana

YT spur to YNP →

An original Yellowstone Trail rock at Yellowstone Gateway Museum

tent of the many used by the Yellowstone Trail as portable travel bureaus to hand out literature in the 1920s. See the "Tally Ho" stage coach which transported Yellowstone Park visitors before autos were admitted to the Park in 1915.

200 W Park St. (Yellowstone Trail). **Livingston Depot Center** is in a restored 1902 Northern Pacific Railway station, turned into an historical museum after the Northern Pacific abandoned it in the 1980s. The beautiful Italianate building must have impressed passengers who arrived on their way to Yellowstone Park. The museum houses displays which examine the broader railroad history and the role the Northern Pacific played in the west. The museum also features an exhibit about the many films made in Montana. Listed on the National Register of Historic Places.

201 W Park St. The 116-year-old **Murray Hotel** still stands gracefully, offering 30 rooms or suites. Since its grand opening as an elegant railroad hotel in 1904, conveniently across the street from the Northern Pacific Railway station, the Murray has drawn a plethora of famous guests from Buffalo Bill and Calamity Jane to movie director Sam Peckinpah (in a suite for 7 years). Its antique furniture, marble lobby and staircase, animal heads on walls, oak doors, and watering hole bar are all redolent of 10 decades ago.

"Humorist Will Rogers and his buddy Walter Hill, must have been satisfied. They liked the place well enough that they tried to bring a favorite saddle horse to a third floor suite via the hand-cranked, 1905 Otis elevator. Celebrities have been stopping here for 90 years, rubbing elbows with the cowpokes, railroaders, and other travelers that provide a hotel's life blood," says their website.

Murray Hotel, Livingston

109 W Callender St. **Sax & Fryer**. Known in Livingston since 1883, it has occupied this location since 1914. This purveyor of books and stationery carried our first book, *Introducing the Yellowstone Trail*. The place feels warm and inviting. Early Yellowstone Trail travelers may well have stopped here for picture postcards of the West.

229 River Drive E. **Sakajawea Park**. Although this park is fairly recent and not related to the Yellowstone Trail, we recommend a visit. The park features a lovely statue of Sakajawea on a horse with little Pomp. The park area honors the Lewis and Clark expedition because they camped at the Livingston site. The statue, created in 2006, marks the 200th anniversary of that famous trek.

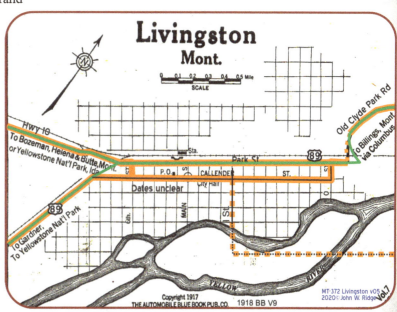

MT

Grand Hotel in Big Timber, 1914

Grand Hotel now, Big Timber

Crazy Mts to the north

🚗 Springdale, MT-392, was the train stop for visitors going to Hunter's Hot Springs. The resort had horse carriage service from the station to the hotel. The nearby bridge over the Yellowstone River was built in 1908 and served until 1981. The extent and dates that the bridge served YT autoists is unclear, but the Yellowstone Trail Road from the 1914 Voges Bridge (MT-401) is a more logical route.

1908 Springdale Bridge transferred train passengers by carriage over the Yellowstone River to nearby Hunter's Hot Springs. Piers still visible today just to the west of new bridge.

On the main route of the Trail east of Livingston is The Old Clyde Park Road (Yellowstone Trail). Also called the Convict Grade Road, it took travelers from Livingston east to Hunter's Hot Springs. When driving east, this convict-built road has its back to spectacular mountain scenery as you cross the Shields River and move through pleasant, rolling hills with just a glance over its shoulder at the Crazy Mountains to the north. ☼

Crazy Mountain Museum, Big Timber, has an original YT sign telling drivers to turn left.

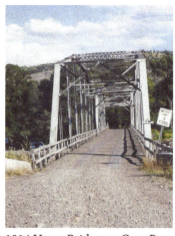
1914 Voges Bridge on Grey Bear Road (I-90 Exit 362). Used by autoists from the east going to Hunter's Hot Springs. Replaced in 2000

Four autos passed through Big Timber over the Yellowstone Trail this week, enroute west - one from Altoona, Penn., two from Texas and the fourth from Missouri.
August 21, 1913 Big Timber Pioneer

In a paean to the Yellowstone Trail, the Editor wrote of the great economic value the Trail was to Big Timber. "The advent of autos into the Yellowstone Park means doing away with railway travel. So far there has [sic.] been many auto parties through Big Timber. One party will stop for lunch, another for dinner, another for the night and the town receives the benefit of what would otherwise go to a railway diner and sleeping car."
[Specific date unknown] 1913 Big Timber Pioneer

The remains of the famous Hunter's Hot Springs

🚗 In Big Timber, the YT apparently used the now missing bridge over Boulder River on McCleod St. The old Pony Truss bridge on Old Boulder Rd., built in 1940, is still in use.

MT

MT-390.0 Hunter's Hot Springs

HUNTERS HOT SPRINGS HOTEL 150 rooms; many modern and good. A. P. $3.50-$5.50; E. P. Sgl. $1.50-03.00; dbl. $2.50-$4; with bath $5. Lunch 75c; dinner $1. MH-1928

As you drive into the hot springs, it is hard to believe that a low wall of rubble and hard-to-find foundations are all that remain of a once major hotel complex. Here were excellent accommodations, food, glassed-in sun porches, a greenhouse and a hot water swimming pool fed by many springs. All for folks seeking Dr. Hunter's mineral cures, and for recreation-seekers, beginning c.1870. The Yellowstone Trail Association met there in a pivotal session in August, 1914. The property has gone through several owners and purposes over the years, but one may still wander about and see a spring near the low wall of rubble. See **Trail Tale: Hunter's Hot Springs**, page 152.

MT-392.0 Springdale

This was a railroad station stop for people on their way to Hunter's Hot Springs, two miles away. The Yellowstone Trail Association had a meeting at Hunter's and it was a stop well-known to Trail travelers.

Just upriver of the Yellowstone River bridge at Springdale can be seen the footings of the old bridge used by the YT.

MT-407.2 Big Timber

pop. 1,000; located in sheep and cattle country; fine water. Best meals at Big Timber Bakery. Camp, 50c, east side of river in nice cotton-wood grove. GRAND HOTEL largest and best. Most rooms modern; good beds. Sgl. $1-$2; dbl. $1.50-$2; with bath $2.50.

MOTOR INN [garage] far best equipped; skilled and dependable. Labor $1.25; ph. 206K for wrecker any time. MH-1928

Big Timber was an important wool exporting city in the late 1800s. Tourism is now a major contributor to their economy with tourists driving through to Yellowstone Park. The old US 10 (Yellowstone Trail) from Reed Point to Big Timber is very pleasant. If you are here in the autumn, note the heavy snow on the Crazy Mountains. Picturesque.

Many a Montana town lays claim to Calamity Jane. Restless Calamity apparently had a cabin on the east bank of the Yellowstone River here.

2 Cemetery Rd. (at I-90 Exit 367) **Crazy Mountain Museum** is located in a beautiful little glen with cottonwood trees, the Crazy Mountains to the north, and the Beartooths to the south. The museum displays western items such as chaps, sheep and wool industry items, and western archeology, but also a unique "Stabbur," a Norwegian style cache to keep food from wild predators.

139 McLeod St. (Yellowstone Trail). Grand Hotel, now the **Grand Bed & Breakfast**. It serves lunch and dinner to the general public. Built in 1890, it's still in business 130 years later. It got an overhaul in 2015 and the meal reviews are extraordinary, including ours. It is listed on the National Register of Historic Places "as an important center for social and commercial activity." A fire in 1908 destroyed most businesses along McLeod St. but not the Grand Hotel which still maintains its frontier theme.

Adjacent to the north edge of Big Timber is the **Yellowstone River Trout Hatchery** (GPS: 45.83598, -109.96058). In 1919, the Big Timber Rod and Gun Club raised money for purchase of land and donated it to the State of Montana to be used for the Big Timber Fish Hatchery. The State Fish and Game Commission had offered to initiate a small hatchery. Now called the Yellowstone River Trout Hatchery, it is the home of the Yellowstone cutthroat broodstock. Visitors are welcome.

1st Ave East is the **Yellowstone Trail Garage**. Now it serves as a substantial storage building. An ad for this garage appeared in the 1914 Yellowstone Trail Association publication, *First Year Book.*

October 6, 1916 in Genevieve Robinson's *Golden Days of Reed Point: 1915-1922* (pub. unknown), "T. W. Marshall of Reed Point State Bank has made a rubber stamp which reads: 'Reed Point, population 300, hotels, garages, supplies' which officials of the Yellowstone Trail Association will stamp over the place in their guide book which had formerly read: 'Reed Point, population 0. No accommodations.'" ✿

August 5,1914 Minutes of the Annual Meeting of the Montana Division of the Yellowstone Trail Association. George Metlen, Secretary of the State Highway Commission said, "[The Springtime Rd.] is part of the Yellowstone Trail and it is quite a stretch of bad road. We will have a crew of prisoners available … I intend to put 125 men there and we can improve that road in 60 to 90 days." ✿

Notes from the Reed Point Community Club:

- Oct. 9, 1917. Moved, carried that this Club subscribe for 50 feet of the Yellowstone Trail Association proposed film of the Trail at 55¢ per foot.

- April 12, 1920. Moved, passed that the Club would pay the $50 Yellowstone Trail Association dues and that businessmen of Reed Point should pay it.

- August 6 and 10, 1920. It was reported that Billings was actively advising tourists to get to the Yellowstone Park via Cody, saying the Trail west was bad. A committee was selected to go to Billings and investigate. They found that the report was true. Club Secretary was ordered to write to their neighboring towns along the Trail to share the news. All towns will write to the Billings Chamber to object.

- April 12, 1928. Voted not to pay Yellowstone Trail Association dues as a Club, but those who wish to contribute as individuals may do so. ✿

A young man was granted a patent for a motor he invented that runs on air only, no fuel. The government has taken his idea to try it out on an aeroplane.
January, 1918 Northwestern Motorist

Unusual iron YT sign found at Hotel Montana, Reed Point. May have been attached to a bridge.

🚗 MT-445.2 Springtime: The 1928 route (The YT and US 10) was roughly along modern Old US 10. The pre 1928 route here is unclear but was on or north of the 1928 route. On the east part the original route is south of I-90 and the west is under or north of I-90 and is abandoned.

🚗 MT-430.8 Reed Point: The 1914 route of the YT in this area as shown in the 1914 *First Year Book* is, at best, an approximation. The terrain fully suggests that the route varied in a number of places, especially near and just north of Springtime. An oral interview with a resident of Springtime Road reported that there were several previous more curving alignments north of Springtime Road known because a family member was responsible for the grading of that road. Modern aerial photos show several possible such variations. [Can they be found?].

American Garage, Columbus. Note very early auto, gas pump, and long dresses.

Annual Reed Point Sheep Run - Old tradition, Modern attraction
Country Discoveries

The YT near Columbus
Billings Western Heritage Center

🚗 MT-453.9 Columbus: The map in the 1914 *First Year Book* has a significant apparent error about 4 miles west of Columbus. Sure complicates research.

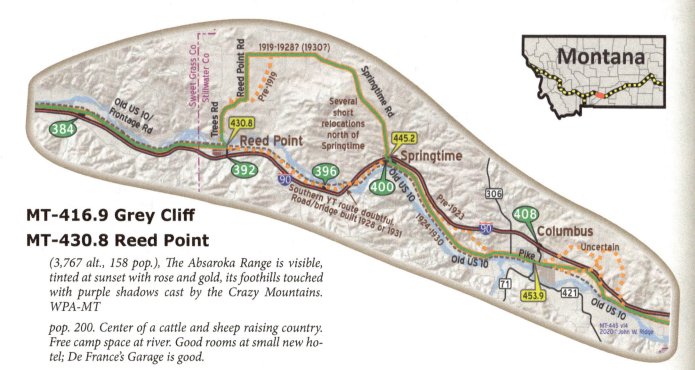

MT-416.9 Grey Cliff

MT-430.8 Reed Point

(3,767 alt., 158 pop.), The Absaroka Range is visible, tinted at sunset with rose and gold, its foothills touched with purple shadows cast by the Crazy Mountains. WPA-MT

pop. 200. Center of a cattle and sheep raising country. Free camp space at river. Good rooms at small new hotel; De France's Garage is good.

A splendid view of the high and wild Absaroka Mountain range over south. MH-1928

After the bridge was built across the Yellowstone River to the north in 1911 at Reed Point, many people rushed to the area to acquire a homestead and begin sheep ranches. In a short time the town practically burst its seams. However, by 1920 the drought had caused the town to diminish measurably.

Last time we were there, the Hotel Montana and Wild Horse Saloon on Division St. was an abandoned shell. Too bad. That was an ageless, great piece of "real western" culture. On 209 Division St. the **Waterhole Saloon** - "Ain't no city bar"- is still there, though. If the saloon wasn't there 100 years ago, the building sure looks like it was. Featured on PBS and advertised as an authentic old wild west saloon, the horse trough and hitching posts certainly bear that out. Order a beer called "Moose Drool." You'll like it.

Sunday of Labor Day Weekend. "Great Montana Sheep Drive," also called the "Running of the Sheep" recalls the old days. Hundreds of Montana-bred sheep charge down the four blocks of the main street. It also includes a parade, sheep-shearing contest and various sheep-beauty contests. First run as a spoof to the Montana Centennial Cattle Drive in 1989, it continues to draw big crowds.

MT-445.2 Springtime

MT-453.9 Columbus

pop. 1,000; grain, sheep and cattle raising are chief industries.

Camping at Columbus Park 50c. hot shower; no shade; 7 very fair cabins $1.25-$1.50.

COMMERCIAL HOTEL modern; light and well-kept rooms. Sgl. $1.50; dbl. $2; with bath $2.50. Good meals 50c.

SCOVILL GARAGE leads. Modern and well equipped; labor $1. Phone 119W until 11 p.m. MH-1928

(3,624 alt, 835 pop.) At the foothills of the Beartooth range, seat of Stillwater County. Lying between the large sheep and cattle ranches to the south, and the wheat farms to the north, it developed as a trade center and shipping point. WPA-MT

440 E 5th Ave. (5 blocks north of Pike Ave.,Yellowstone Trail) **Museum of the Beartooths**. These folks know about the Yellowstone Trail, having hosted Trail speakers in the past. See their area history and artifacts of the Crow Nation.

528 E Pike Ave. (Yellowstone Trail). **The New Atlas Bar**. (Formerly just the Atlas Bar.) Opened in 1916, this old saloon doesn't advertise. It doesn't have to because the word of locals has kept it going for over 100 years. It "unquestionably possesses one of the most intact historic bar interiors in Montana," said Jon Axline, State Preservation officer. It is called "the dead animal zoo" by some because of the many mounted animal heads. Visitors Lucky Lindy, Ernest Hemmingway, Mel Gibson, real cowboys, and real oldtimers "bend their elbows the same way."

523 E Pike Ave. **The Atlas Block**. The east section was completed first and was initially used by the Columbus Mercantile Company. By December 1915, fraternal, civic and religious organizations held meetings on the second floor.

MT-467.1 Youngs Point

MT-472.6 Park City

pop. 200; free camp. The Trail garage is good. Rooms and meals obtained at Trewin Hotel. The sugar beet industry is outstanding in this vicinity. Best mechanic at Ebel's Garage. MH-1928

Named by settlers who planted trees there, the settlers rejected the Northern Pacific Railroad Company's desire to place a station there, so Laurel was established as a major railroad hub instead.

John Gibson came from Fromberg, 20 miles south of Trail town, Laurel. He was an energetic manufacturer of flexible concrete blocks for culverts and bridges. He was a booster of the Yellowstone Trail Association and apparently had influence over the organization in its early days because in the Association's 1914 *First Year Book* a map showed the Trail going south from Laurel through Fromberg to the east entrance of the Yellowstone Park. That was, of course, erroneous. The Trail had only one "splendid lateral" veering from the "most direct route possible." That lateral went to the north entrance of the Yellowstone Park from Livingston.

He also caused to have his concrete company identified on three maps in tiny print, whereas no other of the many companies advertising in that book were named right on the face of maps. ✿

The Yellowstone County Roads Association was formed to further the federal aid improvements of the Yellowstone Trail from the Dakota line to Bozeman.
May 20, 1919 The Spokesman Review

EAST MONTANA TRAIL MEN REFUSE PROPOSED CHANGES IN ROUTE

At the annual meeting of the Eastern Montana section of the Yellowstone Trail Association attendees opposed any change in the routing of the Trail or branch roads, voluntarily raised yearly assessment to $2,840, favored marking the Trail to Seattle, and favored the state road bond issue.
January 30, 1920 Anaconda Standard

Laurel's vast railroad yard busy today as it was 100 years ago

Greg Childs poses with a YT interpretative sign in Laurel.

The outrageous conduct of the watchmen of the tourist park at Billings toward tourists traveling the Yellowstone Trail and the misinformation regarding roads given out by these men to secure visitors for the Cody entrance is meeting with general condemnation. Three citizens went to Billings and 'got the goods'.
August 27, 1920 Livingston Enterprise
Note: It seems that Reed Point Trail boosters heard reports from tourists that Billings was sending tourists to the Yellowstone Park via Cody and the east park entrance rather than along the Yellowstone Trail towns to Livingston and, thus, to the north entrance of the park. Newspapers along the Trail westward raised a fuss, and, presumably, the problem was solved in Billings but we have no record of their effect.

Laurel took its place among the many towns along the Yellowstone Trail Friday when about 30 of the businessmen of the town took their picks and shovels and started to improve the condition of the local highway.
May 27, 1914 The Laurel Outlook

TRAIL MEET AT BILLINGS MARCH 6-7

The upshot of this meeting was to encourage every town along the Trail to pay its dues to the Yellowstone Trail Association to support its good work for those very towns and across the nation.
March 2, 1917 Baker Sentinel

WAYSIDE

Seven miles north of Laurel on Co 532 is a wayside featuring a sandstone monument and panels explaining the Canyon Creek Battle of 1877 between Chief Joseph of the Nez Perce and the cavalry. Joseph and his band were trying to reach Canada. This is a quiet place, and here is a piece of important Montana history often missed by tourists.

MT-480.8 Laurel

YELLOWSTONE GARAGE is best. Good mechanics. Open 24 hours; labor $1.50; storage 50c; tel. 6, for wrecker.

MOBSMAN. Gas at store. Camp space.

Campo Camp 50c gas plates in kitchen. 15 single cabins with gas plates and garage $1-$1.25. MH-1928

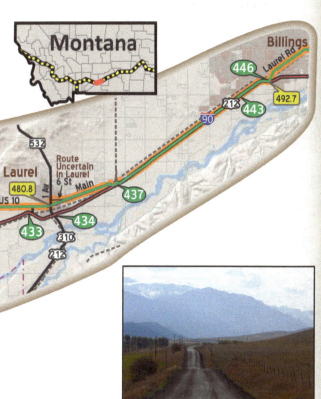

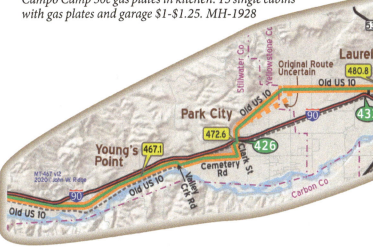

pop 3,000. Terminal of the Burlington, Great Northern and Northern Pacific Rlwys. N. P. shops employ 220; also a sugar beet center. Merchant Hotel has running water; dbl. $2.' The Owl Cafe is good. Laurel Park Camp, pay shower; gas plates. MH-1928

If you are going east, look about you at the last view you will have of the Beartooth Mountains. If you are going west, here will be the first view you will have of the Rocky Mountains.

Roberta Cheney, in *Names on the Face of Montana* (Mountain Press 1984) said that "Laurel struggles on both sides of an intricate pattern of railroad tracks." Three major railways, a large oil refinery, a large railroad roundhouse and I-90 now determine the profile of this historic town.

The southside of Laurel was once called "German Town" once settled by Volga River German immigrants. Their "Russian" homes are still standing and many have been restored.

Historic Main Street (Yellowstone Trail) has been renewed. There are 11 historic buildings on Main St. including the 1923 Block. Thirteen of the 16 historic sites on the walking tour of Laurel are on Main St., all of them are on the National Register of Historic Places. Take a walking tour offered by the Chamber of Commerce.

301 E Main. Site of the former **New Yellowstone Hotel**, now a bowling alley.

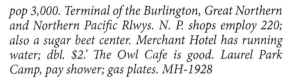

East Rosebud Road

East Rosebud Lake

WAYSIDE

East Rosebud Lake. This Wayside is further away (41 miles) than others, but the scenery and exploration possibilities are worth the drive. Go south from Columbus on MT 78 to Roscoe, then take E Rosebud Rd. west to the lake. Approaching the lake is a bit problematical in that E Rosebud Rd. seems to end at a gated community. So explore a bit westward to find an unnamed road that leads you toward the lake. To say the least, it is a beautiful setting. The lake is about one mile long and one-half mile wide, 100 feet deep and at a 7,000 foot elevation. The road follows the E Rosebud Creek through a narrow valley among mountains in the Absorka-Beartooth Wilderness of the Beartooth Range.

A Mr. Wittam, Superintendent of the Beartooth Forest Reserve, wrote about the lake with lyrical language in the 1914 *First Year Book*. He opined that soon this beautiful area will be opened to all conveniences of civilization. "Chief among these is Rosebud Lake, which is a rival in beauty and grandeur to the far-famed Lake Louise of the Canadian Rockies. In 1911 an automobile road was built to this lake at enormous expense, making it possible to reach by a half-day's trip from Billings. Cabins and a resort are being built now. Many trails will lead to the most beautiful places ..."

Fortunately, Mr. Wittam's optimism about "civilization" arriving was not borne out. Only a hard-to-find, unnamed road leads to the lake. The gated community is hardly a "resort," but beauty, quiet, and solitude reign in this wilderness.

Pictograph State Park. Seven miles southeast of Lockwood Exit 452 of I-90, follow signs on Coburn Rd. to see Pictograph Cave. Prehistoric hunters left about 30,000 artifacts and over 100 pictographs, the oldest being over 2,000 years. Paved trails lead to caves. Take binoculars.

Chief Plenty Coups State Park is southwest of Billings just off MT 416, then MT 418.

Surviving sign on a downtown building in Billings for another named highway, the Glacier To Gulf highway

Hotel Lincoln, Billings

Charles Lindbergh worked briefly in the Westover Garage, 1st Ave. N (the YT), Billings
Joyce Jenson

Westover Garage today, Billings

HISTORY BITS

MT-496.5 Billings

It is the center of an irrigated and dry farming district, and its chief industries are the manufacture of beet sugar, packing house products, dairy produce, flour and building materials. Large oil, gas and coal deposits are located near by. BB1921-9

NORTHERN HOTEL is best; All rooms light. Sgl. $1.50-$3.50; dbl. $2.50-$3; with bath $4-$5. Cafe in connection.

GRAND HOTEL is newest and fireproof; competes for first place. Sgl. $1.50-$3; dbl. $2.50;. with bath $3.50-$4.

LINCOLN HOTEL; modern, central, but quiet location. Has fine beds. Sgl. $1.25-$2.50; dbl. $2-$2.50,; with bath $3-$3.50.

WESTOVER GARAGE; best for wrecker serv. Ph. 6262. MH-1928

Billings, named after a president of the Northern Pacific Railroad Company, still maintains its early history of cattle ranching and shipping. Boothill Cemetery, the Rimrocks and a huge oil refinery describe the rugged history of Billings.

Montana Ave. (Yellowstone Trail) from north 26th St. to north 22nd St. and north to 1st Ave. N is the **Billings Historic District**, the heart of old Billings. Since the sad condition of the area in the mid 1980s, Montana Ave. has risen like a phoenix from the dust through the efforts of many businessmen and preservationists.

2310 Montana Ave. **The Northern Pacific Depot**. From 1909 to 1979 trains rumbled and hissed to a stop here; at one time 26 per day from three railway companies rattled through. By 1914 almost 10,000 homesteaders alighted here and claimed land. The Depot building, one of four in the original complex, featured a spacious waiting area for 200 passengers, a gentlemen's smoking room, and a ladies' waiting room. The baggage area and waiting area are preserved. It was placed on the National Register of Historic Places in 1978.

2401 Montana Ave. Here is the beautifully restored buff sandstone and red brick turn-of-the-twentieth-century, small, **Rex Hotel**. After a close shave near a wrecking ball, the building was saved in the 1970s, upgraded several times, and expanded. The building was purchased in 2018; the owner planned to reopen the popular restaurant on the ground floor and to continue to rent the upper floors as offices.

2419 Montana Ave. the 1910 **McCormick Hotel** contains businesses at street level, but the hotel does not house travelers anymore. There may still be a "ghost sign" on the upper story of the building advertising McCormick Seeds. In Yellowstone Trail days W. H. McCormick took over his uncle's seed company that became, probably, the largest seed house in Montana and is still a major seed/spice company today. W.H was a vice president of the Yellowstone Trail Association 1914-1915.

2501 Montana Ave. The **Carlin Hotel**, built in the 1910s and completely renovated recently, now offers extended stay lodgings.

MILE-BY-MILE

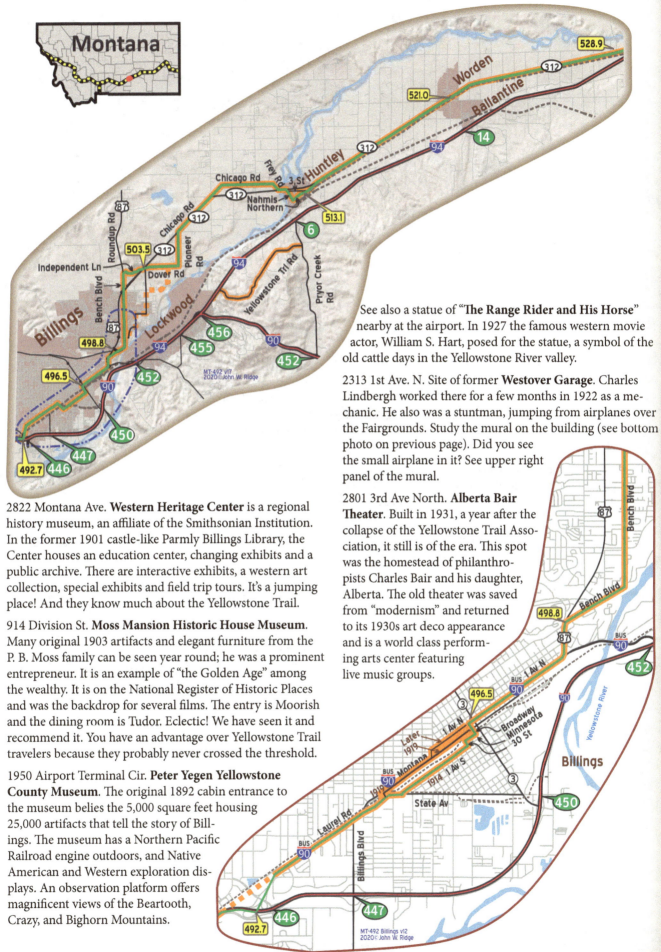

2822 Montana Ave. **Western Heritage Center** is a regional history museum, an affiliate of the Smithsonian Institution. In the former 1901 castle-like Parmly Billings Library, the Center houses an education center, changing exhibits and a public archive. There are interactive exhibits, a western art collection, special exhibits and field trip tours. It's a jumping place! And they know much about the Yellowstone Trail.

914 Division St. **Moss Mansion Historic House Museum**. Many original 1903 artifacts and elegant furniture from the P. B. Moss family can be seen year round; he was a prominent entrepreneur. It is an example of "the Golden Age" among the wealthy. It is on the National Register of Historic Places and was the backdrop for several films. The entry is Moorish and the dining room is Tudor. Eclectic! We have seen it and recommend it. You have an advantage over Yellowstone Trail travelers because they probably never crossed the threshold.

1950 Airport Terminal Cir. **Peter Yegen Yellowstone County Museum**. The original 1892 cabin entrance to the museum belies the 5,000 square feet housing 25,000 artifacts that tell the story of Billings. The museum has a Northern Pacific Railroad engine outdoors, and Native American and Western exploration displays. An observation platform offers magnificent views of the Beartooth, Crazy, and Bighorn Mountains.

See also a statue of "**The Range Rider and His Horse**" nearby at the airport. In 1927 the famous western movie actor, William S. Hart, posed for the statue, a symbol of the old cattle days in the Yellowstone River valley.

2313 1st Ave. N. Site of former **Westover Garage**. Charles Lindbergh worked there for a few months in 1922 as a mechanic. He also was a stuntman, jumping from airplanes over the Fairgrounds. Study the mural on the building (see bottom photo on previous page). Did you see the small airplane in it? See upper right panel of the mural.

2801 3rd Ave North. **Alberta Bair Theater**. Built in 1931, a year after the collapse of the Yellowstone Trail Association, it still is of the era. This spot was the homestead of philanthropists Charles Bair and his daughter, Alberta. The old theater was saved from "modernism" and returned to its 1930s art deco appearance and is a world class performing arts center featuring live music groups.

The improved roads brought by the YT (marked with the black arrow) opened up pleasure travel for the locals, too.

MARTIN'S MONTANA PICKLES

Martin's Montana Pickles are put up in the following varieties:
Sun Cured German Dills (Very Fine), Sour, Sweets, Sour Mixed, Sweet Mixed, Sour Kraut, Pickling Onions, Chow Chow, Distributors of Vinegar

Write today for prices and get acquainted with a live Montana Industry

Martin Pickling Company, Huntley, Montana

1914 First Year Book

MT

Helen Clark wrote to us of her life as a child on "the [Huntley] Project" beginning in 1915. Clark reported that

> The plots were only 40 acres, but were increased as it was seen that such a small farm was not practical. We eventually got 360 acres. Some of this land was irrigatable, some suited for dry land crops and the rest pasture land or hills with cedar and pine trees.

She went on to say that there were roads, communities, irrigation and schools; a better place to farm than in drought-ridden east Montana.

"Since the Trail at that time was not much more than two ruts cut through my dad's homestead on the Project when we moved there in 1915, I've always been interested in it."

Letter from Helen Clark to the authors, 1997 ✿

The Martin Pickle Factory of Huntley will increase capacity of the plant by purchase of new machinery and erection of new buildings.

October 30, 1930 The Iron Trade Review

The Huntley Irrigation Project irrigation headgates opened in 1907 after the Reclamation Act of 1902. The Project blossomed in the "Dirty '30s" when many farmers lost their farms in western Dakotas and eastern Montana to drought and the Depression and turned to these rent-to-own acres from the government. Those who accepted the deal found irrigation, schools, communities of farmers, and sustainability. The Project is made up of four small communities: Huntley, Worden, Ballentine and Pompey's Pillar. The second U.S. Bureau of Reclamation project irrigated 33,000 acres stretching 27 miles long by four miles wide. About 30,000 acres are farmed today. ✿

🚗 MT-553.3 Custer: The YT, from the north, followed 5th St. into town. and then directly west from the business area on 2nd. Ave., then at the edge of town following a road roughly the same alignment as the Custer Frontage Rd. running north of I-90.

Just north of Custer, remnants of the old bridge used by the YT can be seen just west of the modern bridge. Northeast of Custer the 1914 *First Year Book* shows a long stretch of seemingly "impossible" route. Frustrating!

Huntley Project Museum

WAYSIDE

29 miles south of Custer on MT 47, then 15 miles further south on I-90 to Exit 510 is **Little Bighorn Battlefield National Monument**. This battle is much studied and written about but is included here because it is an important part of our history and we think that Yellowstone Trail travelers of 100 years ago, no doubt, stopped here to view this historic site.

Continue on south to Garryowen to visit **Custer Battlefield Museum**.

ARTHUR MATTSON NAMED HEAD OF BILLINGS INFORMATION BUREAU

This Yellowstone Trail Association bureau is the largest of the three in the state, the others being located at Miles City and Missoula.

May 18, 1921 Anaconda Standard

MT-505.1 Pioneer Elementary School

Corner of Dover and Pioneer Rds. (both the Yellowstone Trail). The 1905 school is still in use as a school today, accompanied by a 1960s addition and its placement on the National Register of Historic Places. Things have changed since the kids caught water snakes and frogs in the dirt floor coal room. Today grades 1-6 enjoy computers, a student-to-teacher ratio of 1 to 6, standardized tests and field trips.

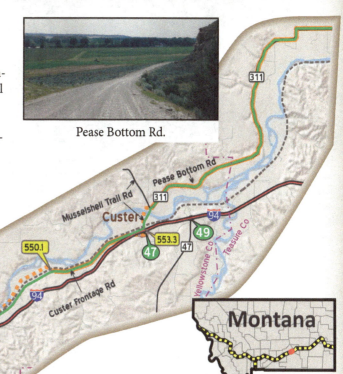

Pease Bottom Rd.

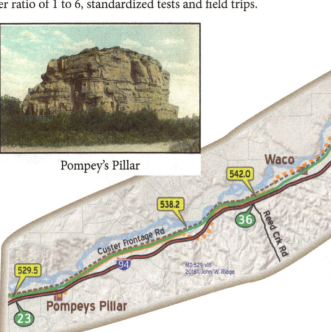

Pompey's Pillar

MT-513.1 Huntley

770 Old Hwy 312 (Yellowstone Trail) 3 mi. E of Huntley. **Huntley Project Museum of Irrigated Agriculture.** On 10 acres, 18 buildings feature hundreds of turn-of-the-20th-century farm equipment pieces, a history of the 1907 Project, and artifacts that portray life on the Project to the late 20th century. It also displays the 1916 First National Bank of Pompey's Pillar which closed in 1928 after grasshoppers and Mormon crickets decimated the crops at the start of the Great Depression. Joseph Cox tells the story in *Project Overflight: One Family Looks Back at the Early Times on the Huntley Project* (self published 1986).

Today, **The Southern Agricultural Research Center**, under the aegis of the Montana State University, maintains a research farm in 100-year-old barns near Huntley. See History Bits for more of the story of the Huntley Project.

MT-528.8 Pompey's Pillar National Monument

Yes, we know that much has been written about this 1806 signature carved in this butte by Capt. William Clark of the Lewis and Clark expedition. We include it here because the Yellowstone Trail ran right past it well before I-94 did and Yellowstone Trail travelers, no doubt, stopped to view Capt. Clark's signature 100 years ago. You'll have to do a little stair climbing, though, to see it. Do stop at the stunning, visitor center.

MT-531.5 Community of Pompey's Pillar

At MT-538.1 (GPS: 46.03103, -107.82426), the 1914 route followed "Old Hwy" to the east (leaving today's Custer Frontage Road now on private land), running south of a lake and crossing I-94 several times, rejoining Frontage Rd at MT-540.5 (GPS: 46.03879, -107.80491).

MT-544.9 Waco

I-94 Milepost 41 between Exits 36 and 41 there is a wayside rest area which contains an interpretive sign about the Yellowstone Trail written by Jon Axline, Historian for the Montana Department of Transportation. It is a useful and pretty complete explanation of the Trail in Montana. Axline's historic work has been displayed on many such helpful outdoor signs throughout the state.

MT-553.3 Custer

CUSTER, pop. 175; good home-cooked meals 50c at Park Hotel; also clean rooms. Sgl. $1; dbl. $1.50. Not modern.

YELLOWSTONE GARAGE does good work on all cars; open until 10 p. m. Road service. MH-1928

The **Great Northern Railway depot** was being restored, the last we heard. The depot is located in the park.

MT-564.2 Fort Pease

As you leave Custer going east, you will be on MT secondary highway 311, the Yellowstone Trail. The road is also called Pease Bottom Rd., further east called Myers Rd. The little that is left of Fort Pease is on private property and is inaccessible. Just notice this nice drive to Myers.

Ranchers School is on Myers Rd. This white 1910 school still looks usable. It even has a bell tower.

YT Garage in Custer c.1930
Billings Gazette

BODY MEETS WITH REMARKABLE SUCCESS IN GETTING RESULTS AT FORSYTH – LOCAL MEMBERS ON IMPORTANT COMMITTEES
May 27, 1913 Livingston Daily Post
Note: The meeting was in Forsyth, but this Livingston paper spent half of the article commenting on the Livingston delegation's successes and only a few paragraphs on the point of the meeting. This was typical of the pride towns took in participating with the Yellowstone Trail Association.

The Jennison party from Minnesota thought they were to encounter a real, wild-and-woolly holdup when a young man in full cowboy regalia dismounted from his cayuse and took his stand at the roadside with a huge rock in his hand, eyeing threateningly the eastern tourists as they shot past at full speed. They will visit the Pan American Exposition.
August 24, 1915 Mineral Independent, Superior MT

Custer Bridge on YT

THE YELLOWSTONE TRAIL ASS'N WILL MEET IN THIS CITY
10TH ANNUAL MEETING OF GOOD ROAD ENTHUSIASTS OF EASTERN MONTANA TO BE HELD IN FORSYTH NOV. 29
November 11, 1920 Forsyth Times-Journal
Note: It couldn't be the 10th annual because the Yellowstone Trail Association only met in Montana for the first time in 1913. False news is not the purview only of the 21st century.

Pease Bottom Road

Historic Yucca Theater, Hysham

MT-605.3 Forsyth: The BB1919-7 gives somewhat detailed instructions to "follow the RR and river" but the mileages do not work out well, although the entrance to Forsyth makes sense. Must have been along the railroad work area near the tracks!

Reported by YTA member: the YT followed a route through town from east that went straight west then south to main. Needs some local research.

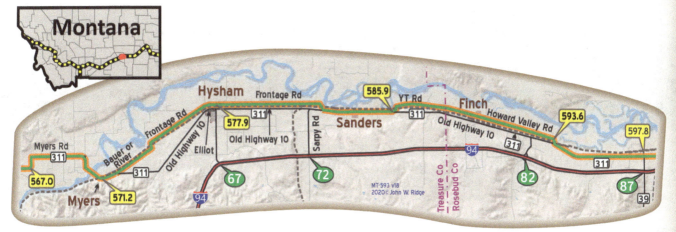

MT-571.3 Myers

About 2/10 of a mile west of the present Yellowstone River bridge near Myers can be seen the foundation of the 1914 Yellowstone River bridge.

MT-577.2 Hysham

Hysham pop. 350; a county seat town situated in a wheat, sugar beet and alfalfa section. Best rooms at Eureka Hotel. Hysham Garage has wrecker and is well equipped; labor $1.25. Free camp space. MH-1928

US 10 now winds through lonely badlands. Under an uncompromising sun the sides of the buttes are mottled with brown, buff, and gray. After sundown, as twilight shades into dusk, the masses of guttered rock take on eerie tones of purple and black. Only the bark and scurry of prairie dogs by day, and the dismal howl of coyotes by night, indicate the presence of living things. WPA-MT

Hysham has had a colorful history of cattle ranges, the Crow Indian Reservation, and 19th century forts and trading posts.

325 Elliot Ave. (Frontage Rd/Yellowstone Trail). **Treasure County 89ers Museum**. Pioneer history, and a display of Apollo 8 astronaut Frank Borman's mementos of his trip around the moon and back are featured. The museum and the Yucca Theater across the street comprise an historical complex. .

324 Elliot Ave. The historic **Yucca Theater**, built in 1931, is Mission Style architecture, reflecting the grandiose style and flamboyant design of movie theaters during the 1930s. It has a white buffalo statue and statues of Lewis and Clark and Sakajawea and infant Pomp all in front of the theater. The last we knew, classic movies were shown on Sunday evenings in summer via a DVD player. Go look at the outside, anyway. The museum folks have the keys to the theater and if you ask nicely, they might let you see the inside

MT-584.0 Sanders

MT-593.6 Howard School

This 1904 clapboard school was expanded in 1916 when they expected more families from the 1909 Homestead Act and Mexican beet workers' children. The fairly large school, for rural standards, served elementary through high school grades and even featured a chemistry lab. Later, an upstairs "teacherage" apartment was added. It appears to be in great shape and is used presently as a community center.

Howard School

Howard School, 1904-1947, replaced a log one built in 1882. You will not find this school on tourist literature, but it is an important site on the Yellowstone Trail. It reminds us of the value placed on education in an era of great difficulty in acquiring education in rural areas. Students walked or rode horses up to nine miles to this school. A barn was built to house four or five horses during the day. A "teacherage" was included on the second floor, which was unique. Usually, a teacher was housed with the nearest farmer, as was the case with one of your author's family. High school classes were also held on the second floor until a better road to Forsyth was built. "The community of Howard solidified around the school," said the application for acceptance on the National Register of Historic Places. "… it showed the community's confidence and investment in its future." It serves as a community center today. ✿

Chief engineer of the state highway commission conferred with an engineer of the Northern Pacific Railway company relative to the elimination of two dangerous railroad crossings on the Yellowstone Trail west of Forsyth.

May 12, 1920 Anaconda Standard

Now a professional and commeri-
cal building, Forsyth (Note
added floor in bank building!)

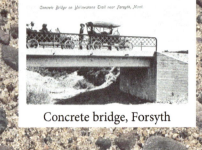
Concrete bridge, Forsyth

1912 "Blue Front" rooming house
used by railroad men. Today,
Clark Hardware (next door) is interesting.

Then a 1905 bank and
mercantile building, Forsyth

Spectacular road for YT near Forsyth

Good road on YT leading to Forsyth

The alignment of the original YT route running
north of the Yellowstone River between Rosebud and
Miles City is well specified in the 1914 *First Year Book* .
However, careful comparison with modern USGS maps
shows: 1) the map creators left out a mile section, 2) the
shown route of the YT is often impossible or at least very
improbable, and 3) the RR is apparently wrong in several
areas. We must assume that the lack of location identification marks on the ground with the need to "do the
best we can" resulted in the many errors. We made the
reasonably safe assumption for our maps that the original YT followed quite closely to the modern highway 446
and Sheffield Rd from Cartersville to a point near the old
Fort Keogh bridge over the Yellowstone, where the YT
crossed that bridge going into Miles City. BridgeHunter.
com reported that the bridge, built in 1902 was damaged
by flooding in 2011 and removed in spring 2012.

Frontage road (Old US 10) between Rosebud and Forsyth is probably the old YT.

The later YT route south of the Yellowstone River
between Miles City and near Rosebud, became US 10
and US 12 and underwent several relocations, after
which I-94 obscured parts of the route. A fair amount of
the old highway remains, but it is not suitable/passable
for today's travel.

The difficulty in tracing the early route of the YT is
illustrated by a quotation from the 1919 BB vol. 7 relating
to a place about 2.7 miles east of Hathaway (apparently at
GPS: 46.29872, -106.15402): "Caution — enter creek bed
and curve right under RR, following up creek for a short
distance. Curve left out of same, ascending grade. Avoid
road to the left at sign." [Note: Maybe they should have
taken the old north route?]

The development of **Fort Keogh** as a military installation
soon stimulated traders to supply the liquor and other
service businesses.

"When Colonel Miles got tired of having his guard house
filled to overflowing, whiskey causing him more trouble
than the Indians, he ordered the purveyors of liquor to
leave the military reservation. John Carter rode east on
his big bay horse until he was the required two miles
away, beyond the edge of the reservation. He found a flat
spot along the Yellowstone, built a crude log hut out of
driftwood and started selling whiskey. The soldiers soon
found the place, other merchants followed, and Miles
City was born." *Wikipedia*

"Fort Keogh's Commissary" by Ryan Booth in *Montana,
A Magazine of Western History* (Spring 2020) writes of
army life as revealed by the commissary and posits that
the shop "proved a common ground through necessity
and convenience" for officers, enlisted men, and civilian
contractors and their families. Demands of officers for
exotic foods such as oysters and specialty tobacco revealed a "broadened, globalized consumer culture" which
may have spread to the population of "Milestown." ✿

MT-605.3 Forsyth

pop. 2,000; a prosperous little railroad town in the center of a wheat and sugar beet area. Goodman Cafe is good. Tourist Camp 25c. MH-1928

NEW ALEXANDER Hotel is best; nearly all rooms with running water. Sgl. $l-$2.50; dbl. $1.50-$2; with bath $3.50. MH-1928

SICKLER MOTOR SALES CO. is best for work on all cars. Open from 5:30 a. m. to 11 p. m.; labor $1.25 (lathe work $1.50); ph. 159 for tow car.

TEPEE MOTOR CO. is the Ford agency. MH-1928

The Northern Pacific and Milwaukee Road railways created this commercial center, shipping its farm products and many head of cattle. Being along the famed Lewis and Clark Trail and the site of General Custer's camp on his way to Little Bighorn Battlefield has given Forsyth a legitimate place in the history of Montana. Agate hunting is still a popular sport.

Main Street Historic District. Main St. (Yellowstone Trail) is a one-sided street, facing the railroad tracks. The town planners hoped to make a statement of progress for business travelers to see, back in the day.

1335 Main St. **Rosebud County Pioneer Museum** has a restored steam engine, early family collections, and western items. The museum is next to the historic (1913) courthouse with its stained glass, murals, and copper dome. It is on the National Register of Historic Places.

1195 Main St. **Clark Hardware Co**. This is a special place. Cal MacConnel, proprietor, has been a member of the modern Yellowstone Trail Association since its beginning and knows about the Trail in Forsyth. Stop in and talk with him. Better yet, examine his hardware store which features some vintage hardware items.

981 Main St. **Roxy Theatre**. "It's a one screen theater in a small, quaint town. It's like stepping back in time," said a reviewer. From the Roxy's website: "The Roxy Theatre (1930) has retained its old-fashioned charm, with the lobby, marquee and facade remaining mostly unchanged from when it was new. The auditorium has been modernized, and the booth contains modern equipment including digital sound." We include it here because it was on the Yellowstone Trail during its last throes of life and could have attracted travelers on the Trail into the '30s.

807 Main St. **Howdy Hotel**, formerly the Commercial Hotel. Built between 1903 and 1906, it is a landmark on Main St. It sports huge "HOWDY" and "HOTEL" in block letters on the roof. And, for the century it's been open, it's stayed in the same family. *Montana Historical Landscape* calls it "a rare surviving small-town 'booster' hotel, built to impress traveling businessmen that Forsyth was a place of promise." Obviously, the hotel has been upgraded over the years to meet modern expectations. There is still a barber shop off the lobby, just as in olden days. And their restaurant draws praise.

MT-616.2 Rosebud

pop. 200; sheep, wheat and sugar beets are the principal sources of revenue. Two garages. Riverside Hotel has clean rooms. Fair Cabin Camp east. MH-1928

The area has been described as a windblown grassy range, with piney slopes and treeless plateaus. Cattle and sheep grazed around yellowish buttes.

St. Philip's Epicopal Church (Rosebud Community Chapel) is the oldest continuously operating log church in the state. Built in 1906, it has a long history of interfaith/community development.

Fort Keogh

The site of the United States remount station is just outside of Miles City to the west. Thousands of horses are trained here for the cavalry and are sent to all the principal forts in the U. S. BB1921-92

43 Fort Keogh Road. On the western edge of Miles City lies the site of Fort Keogh, built 1876-1877 and named for a captain killed in "Custer's last stand." It was commanded by Col. Nelson A. Miles, for whom the adjacent town was named.

There isn't much, if any, left of the 60 buildings of the fort, later a remount station. On the grounds the US Department of Agriculture established an animal husbandry research station in 1924, today called the USDA Agricultural Research Service. You have to obtain a severely limiting permit to proceed onto the grounds. Cattle genetics, nutrition and growth are apt research topics for this "cow town."

The early Yellowstone Trail went through the grounds of the fort and over the Yellowstone River on a 1902 through truss bridge, demolished in 2012.

Fort Keough 1902 Bridge carried YT

The historic Montana Bar,
Miles City

Miles City, 1915

Amorette Allison reported on the Yellowstone Trail of 100 years ago and the Ingham Hotel in the *August 5, 2015 Miles City News Online*,

The Ingham Hotel and Restaurant set up a register for travelers, and the *Miles City Star* began to report daily tallies of those who passed through. The paper reported on July 24, 1915, that one observer remarked last night that he regarded the talk about the large number of tourists that would come over the Yellowstone Trail this year as "hot air." After seeing the number of auto touring parties camping out, he was convinced.

The Ingham Hotel register reported the names and number of each party; where they were from and where they were going; what "machine" they were driving and how many miles they averaged a day. That last number was around 150 a day. One party that registered reported that they had previously traveled the Lincoln Highway and found the Yellowstone Trail "far superior." In fact, that party averaged 200 miles a day. ⚙

Modern Miles City with historic Olive Hotel at left

Olive Hotel's classy antique lobby
Carl Roehl

A carload of King split log drags was loaded at McKenna, Wash. recently for Miles City, Montana where they will be presented by O. T. Peterson of the Yellowstone Trail Association to 140 different communities in Montana. Mr. J. W. Parmley of Ipswich, S.D. who represents the Yellowstone Trail Association and who has accepted the drags, said "… In the first place, the logs for these drags, while common enough in this country, are almost impossible to obtain in Montana …"

September 1, 1915 New Seattle Chamber of Commerce Record

Note: Drags, which are log frames pulled by horses, were used to smooth out dirt roads. Remarkable gift if they were a gift from Washington! Notice the date. The Trail had entered Washington only a few months prior to this gift. Did Seattle folks see the value of supporting a transcontinental highway even though it was only in its infancy? Or did the Yellowstone Trail Association pay for them?

In the old rough days, the south side of Main St. was a solid block of saloons, gambling dens, and brothels, while the "decent" element (composed of buffalo buyers, bankers, and pawnshop keepers) lived on the north side. On one occasion, it is said, a member of the respectable group hit a gambler on the head and killed him. To save the good man embarrassment, his friends hastily hanged the dead man as a dangerous character. WPA-MT ⚙

MT-653.3 Miles City

During the season, wool buyers from New England states and elsewhere come to Miles City and the annual sales of wool frequently exceed 10,000,000 pounds. BB1921-9

Miles City is located in the center of the Tongue river canal and irrigation system, comprising 10,000 acres producing enormous crops of sugar beets, corn, alfalfa, wheat and oats. Surrounding the city are cattle ranches, on which 10,000 to 20,000 head of cattle graze.

An annual event, attracting thousands from all parts of the U. S., is the wild west show known as the "Round-up," lasting for three days, always including July 4th. BB1921-9

Metropolitan Cafe is Amer., and best; lunch 45c; dinner 75c-90c. City Camp, near center of city is level and well kept, dining hall; 4 tents with floors 50c.

HOTEL INGHAM; most modern and is now best; fine new beds being installed. Sgl. $1.25-$3; dbl. $1.75-$3; with bath, $3-$4.

HOTEL OLIVE is largest. Sgl. $1.50-$2.50; dbl. $2.50;with bath, $3.50-$4.

CALVIN-LOVE MOTOR CO., Ford and Lincoln; a fine agency; best road service; good storage 50c. Expert elec. work. Ph. 461 for wrecker any time. MH-1928

The city became a major livestock shipping point in the late 19th century and this "Cow Capital of the West" is still proud of and carrying on the traditions of "cowboy towns" with rodeos and an annual Bucking Horse Sale. Cowboys "buck out" horses (ride wild, bucking horses) as buyers scoop the horses up for rodeos nationwide. The most legendary horse sale in the world.

There are several buildings on historic Main St. and in the historic residential district on the Register of Historic Places. Some date to 1877 when Col. Nelson Miles established Fort Keogh. A 2010 fire on Main St. destroyed some historic buildings.

On Main St. just west of Tongue River is **Range Riders Museum and Bert Clark Gun Collection**. The museum includes rare firearms from the Revolutionary War era and others. The museum is composed of 11 outbuildings with thousands of artifacts that portray authentic Great Plains pioneer life, Native American and military life.

85 Waterplant Rd. **Waterworks Art Museum**. It is not the art for which we include this site, wonderful as it is with the L. A. Huffman photographs. It is the 1911 old water works building itself that produced drinking water for Miles City for over 60 years. Although greatly adapted, the art museum has retained the brick exterior, oak cabinets, tanks, and workshop spaces of the 1911 building. It is on the National Register of Historic Places. The surrounding park, located near the Tongue and Yellowstone Rivers and having long been a popular picnic site, could well have been visited by Trail travelers.

501 Main St. The Olive Hotel is now called the **Olive Motor Inn**. Built in 1898-99 after the "hard winter" of 1886-87 and subsequent great loss of cattle, the hotel was a beacon of hope for the economic future of the city. When the Milwaukee Road came in 1908, the hotel saw a major expansion and updating in 1909, reflecting an invigorated economy. The hotel was extensively remodeled in the 1970s but still has the look of an historic building and is still in business.

612 Main St. **Montana Bar.** Since its opening in 1893, the Montana Bar was expanded in 1914, but looks much the same as it did during those glory days. It has been called "the most authentic western bar in the state." There is the three-arch back bar and matching liquor hutch made of oak. The original pressed-tin ceiling, and the Italian terrazzo tile floor is watched over by six mounted longhorn steer heads. Big, dark booths and cherry-wood tables lend atmosphere. You can tell that we've been there several times and have enjoyed its eclectic clientele. It is on the National Register of Historic Places.

The later Yellowstone Trail, after 1918, entered Miles City over the Powder River Bridge on Pacific St. That route was later swallowed first by US 12 and then by I-94. Jon Axline, in *Conveniences Sorely Needed: Montana's Historic Highway Bridges 1860-1956* Montana Historical Society Press (2005) said that bridge "... provided the first reliable non-railroad crossing between Miles City and Fort Keogh. It was among the first steel truss bridges built in southeastern Montana."

The first annual convention of the new Yellowstone Trail Association was held in Miles City on February 17, 1913 to many, many newspaper huzzas. Newspapers from South Dakota to central Montana were all agog with the prospect of a national road organization actively taking shape. Eleven newspaper items heralded the coming of the convention and seven reported the results of the meeting, the *Aberdeen American* spending 36 inches on the event results alone. ✿

Just northeast of Tusler, MT-663, was the Brink ranch. Francie Brink Berg and her sisters have written a very lively narrative of growing up herding, riding in blizzards, dealing with gumbo, getting to school, and other facets of pioneer life on the Trail. *Montana Stirrups, Sage, and Shenanigans* (Flying Diamond Books, 2013).

February 13, 1914. Outlying Custer County towns were so excited about a transcontinental road coming through their area that they formed a county area Yellowstone Trail Association. This group would later be subsumed by the Eastern Montana Yellowstone Trail Association. This group named J. E. Prindle of Ismay its President. They then sent four members to the second annual national Yellowstone Trail Association meeting in Mobridge the very next week armed with a long list of their accomplishments. Prindle had been President of the national Yellowstone Trail Association the past year and was well equipped to form a small county boosting group. Elmer Holt, later Governor of Montana, was also an early leader in the county organization. ✿

I wish to say that the good roads committee of the Miles City Chamber of Commerce contributed 150 memberships at $3.00 each, one life membership at $50.00 and 10 five-year memberships at $10 to the Yellowstone Trail Association.

May 1917 Northwestern Motorist

Note: We include this information for the reader to see how maps, tourist bureaus, annual informational *Folders*, conventions, and general publicity of the Association got paid for.

YELLOWSTONE TRAIL ASSOCIATION MET IN MILES CITY

The gist of the report is that some members needed to be reminded that their dues were used for the organization's expenses, not "to build somebody else's road." Some were under that false impression, even at this late date of seven years as an organization.

February 28, 1919 The Ismay Journal

Glendive, a town northeast of Miles City near the North Dakota border, was anxious to get on the Yellowstone Trail and expressed sour grapes when it became clear that it would not be on the proposed route. The city fathers wrote the following to the *Miles City Independent* in 1913: "These Miles City business men would better quit flirting with the Yellowstone Trail Association, which is vainly seeking to bring the transcontinental automobile trail into Montana along the Milwaukee Road right of way, and get in line with Glendive on this proposition. If Miles is ever on that route, it will only be through Glendive … The road will assuredly never enter Montana via Ismay and Baker." But the Trail did assuredly enter via Ismay and Baker. ✿

EASTERN MONTANA MEETING
YELLOWSTONE TRAIL IS HELD
VISITORS BANQUETED
AT THE OLIVE FRIDAY NIGHT

Mention was made of the very dusty road, due to the long dry weather and constant dragging of the Trail. The "long dry weather" began about 1918 and kept on until 1921. This major drought drove farmers off their farms to head west in hopes of finding a better life.

November 11, 1921 Miles City Independent

Today's YT near Tusler

MILES CITY-TERRY ROAD IS MARKED

Dr. Brown and Lee Scheffius put the Yellowstone Trail mark on many natural objects along the unmarked Trail between the towns.

May 8, 1914 Terry Tribune

YT Secretary Peterson and County Commissioner Furnish inspect a gravel section of the YT between Terry and Miles City, 1914.w.

The Powder River Bridge 6 miles southwest of Terry. Replaced in 1946.

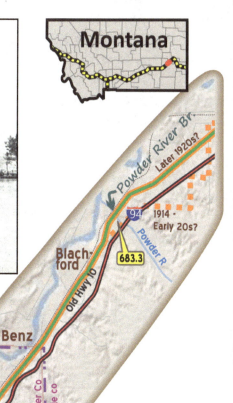

MT-661 to MT-681

Tusler, Shirley, Benz, Zero, and Blatchford were not towns. They were names of railroad maintenance stations that were used to identify locations.

MT-683.3 Powder River Bridge

This bridge, or rather the lack of this bridge, played a central role in the machinations of determining the route of the Yellowstone Trail between North Dakota and Miles City, Montana. With the urging and support of the Yellowstone Trail Association, the Powder River Bridge was completed in time to offer a useful route for autoists entering Montana from the east while staying close to the Milwaukee Road tracks, the defining goal of the siting of the Trail. See **Trail Tale: Knowlton**, page 158.

For a road that has been in operation only a few months, the road between Miles City and Terry shows a vast amount of work done. The completion of the bridge at the Powder River enabled the Yellowstone Trail tourist to save the long detour by way of Knowlton.

1914 Terry (Montana) Tribune

The Yellowstone Trail brought tourism to the Powder River Bridge.

NEW AUTOMOBILE GARAGE FOR TERRY
May 17, 1912 Terry Tribune

Towns along the Red Trail (National Parks Highway) investigate the cause of lack of tourists and find that the Yellowstone Trail is getting them.

August 10, 1928 Marmarth Mail

MAYOR WRIGHT SAYS "USE MY GRADER"
Mayor Alfred Wright has informed the town council that they can have use of his grader free of charge for use in grading the streets of Terry.

July 12, 1912 Terry Tribune

South of Terry, near Powder River *"A horse abattoir was established to make profitable use of the thousands of horses that cluttered the range after farm mechanization and other causes had reduced the market for horses. It was fully equipped with modern slaughterhouse machinery. Horses were driven in from large corrals, shot, skinned, boned and converted into a kind of inspired beef, much of which was shipped to Belgium."* MT-WPA ✿

The steam-heated, 4-hole 1905 outhouse behind Prairie County Museum with protective fence, Terry

An original YT sign on the back of the Prairie County Museum, Terry, telling drivers to turn right at the corner. It was recently touched up with yellow paint.

WANT THEIR TRAIL GRADED IN FALLON
The petitioners set forth that they are not asking for a mecademized or paved road, but asked that the road be graded.

June 8, 1916 Fallon County Times

DR. KENISTON GREETED BY LARGE CROWD
The Ways and Means Committee of the Commercial Club invited Keniston, special representative of the Yellowstone Trail Association to speak about the Trail. He showed pictures of the Trail "on the curtain" and encouraged Terry to raise its share to support the Trail - $250. They raised $350 in a few hours. Keniston also explained the gnawing problem of a need for a bridge over the Little Missouri River at Marmarth, North Dakota, and road work on the Standing Rock Indian Reservation in South Dakota.

April 10, 1914 Terry Tribune

Coming out of Terry going west, the original YT route was Yellowstone St., jogging onto Cemetery Loop Rd. Later it left Terry on Spring St., south on Hoagland St. (or one of its parallel streets) then onto Cemetery Loop. Both followed Cemetery Loop South which becomes Conns Coulee Rd. until just south of I-94, then jogging southwest on primitive roads now lost.

The 1914 Kempton Hotel then, Terry

The Kempton Hotel now, Terry

Prairie County Museum, Terry

Preparing for a sociability run? Terry

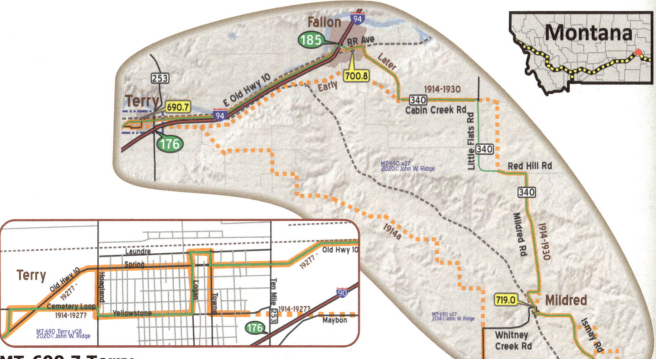

MT-690.7 Terry

KEMPTON HOTEL attractive, clean rooms; nearly all with run. water. Sgl. $1.25-$2.50; dbl. $1.50-$1.75; with bath, $3. Meals 50c. Kempton Hotel Cafe is liked. Kempton camp, has 7 good new cabins with gas plates; $1-$1.50

PATTERSON AND TURNBULL GARAGE is largest and leads by far; splendidly equipped. Ladies' rest room. Labor $1.25; ph. 73 for wrecker until 12 p. m. MH-1928

For a dozen miles the highway crosses a dry upland, parched by repeated years of drought. Only the scavenger magpie is at home in this waste. WPA-MT

Terry was a sheep and cattle shipping station. The Northern Pacific railroad had its own wool house.

101 S Logan St. (Yellowstone Trail). **Prairie County Museum** is in an historic 1915 bank building which is an antique by itself with beautiful marble floors and rich wood paneling. It probably is the only museum with a steam-heated outhouse out back. Pioneer items of eastern Montana ranching and photos by turn-of-the-century photographer Evelyn Cameron are among its treasures.

There are two sites dedicated to Evelyn Cameron, a famous local photographer: the Gallery and the Heritage Center:

Next to the museum is the **Evelyn Cameron Gallery** featuring a large photo collection of early eastern Montana, and the interesting story of late 1800s English photographer, Evelyn Cameron. Her candid pictures, taken with a glass plate 5X7 Graflex camera, show a story of rugged range life and beautiful scenery of Montana. Many are on display.

212 Laundre Ave. **Evelyn Cameron Heritage, Inc**. West of the museum is the Evelyn Cameron Heritage center. Established in 2009, Evelyn Cameron Heritage, Inc. is a non-profit Corporation that actively pursues improving tourism and economic growth by promoting the photographic works and life of Evelyn Cameron. The organization owns over 900 original Evelyn Cameron vintage photographs of the old west; the people, the landscape, the events and more.

See **Trail Tale: Cameron**, page 156.

204 Spring St. **Kempton Hotel**. Built in 1914 and still going today. The historic 1926 neon sign is not easy to miss. The hotel has undergone many remodeling projects in recent years and has earned good reviews. However, apparently there is no central air conditioning. For those inclined for adventure, you might want to stay overnight and chat with the ghosts.

MT-700.8 Fallon

Cattle and sheep cut grass so low that top soil blew away in Dust Bowl years.

Lazy Jo's Bar and Café on Railway Ave. (Yellowstone Trail) in a 100-year-old building, is across the street from an historic icon, an old water trough. Was it for horses or thirsty Model T radiators?

The authors found that the Fallon-Ismay-Plevna route of the YT gives the best way in the U.S. to get the original YT experience. But gas up first.

In Fallon, the newer route of the YT followed Railway Ave. and Co. 340 going south.

Between Terry and Ismay, it may be found that the names of roads differ and conflict from map to map and may be at odds with the few signs on the ground.

Between Terry and Fallon: If old US 10 is open, it is the better route here, rather than I-94. The YT had several routes as the main highway developed in this area and then some fell under I-94. The original route just east of Terry followed Yellowstone St. in town and then Maybon Rd. At some unknown date it moved to Spring St. and Old US 10.

MILDRED WANTS TRAIL

Good roads boosters hosted J. E. Prindle of near-by Ismay and a founder of the Yellowstone Trail Association as speaker to the Commercial Club who persuaded Mildredites to join the Yellowstone Trail Association.

January 31, 1913 Ismay Journal

The YT near Mildred. Probably at GPS: 46.67175, -104.95539 looking south along O'Fallon Creek.

TERRY TRAIL BOOSTERS MAKE TRIP TO MILDRED

About 60 men in 19 autos loaded with shovels, picks and equipment to repair the Yellowstone Trail, worked their way to Mildred, 24 miles away. In addition to filling pot holes and grading as they went, they spent a full hour or more at a coulee crossing where they changed the road, graded it and plowed furrows for drainage. They finished their tasks by 2:00 PM.

April 17, 1914 Terry Tribune

J. E. Prindle office: real estate, live stock sales, notary public, and ice cream parlor
1914 First Year Book
Note: Ismay had electric lighting!

Wilson Brothers Garage, Ismay
1914 First Year Book

Ismay retirees sit below YT sign possibly in 1950s

The Ismay delegates to the Yellowstone Trail convention held in Miles City Monday were: R. L. Anderson, J. E. Prindle, H. L. Bruskmeyer, and H. W. Wilson.

February 14, 1913 Ismay Journal
Note: Joe Prindle had just been elected President of the national Yellowstone Trail Association at that convention. He also founded Ismay's Commercial Club, predecessor to today's Chamber of Commerce.

The town received condemning letters in 1912 from people who believed the town was named after J. Bruce Ismay, Managing Director of the White Star Line, owner of the Titanic. When the Titanic went down, Mr. Ismay survived, but lived in disgrace ever after. The town was actually named after sisters Isabelle and May Peck, daughters of a Milwaukee Road official. ✿

ISMAY EXTENDS WELCOME

A splendid crowd on Wednesday greeted the 75 members of the Minneapolis Civic and Commerce Association who are touring the northwest as far as Miles City. The Association recently invited J. E. Prindle to speak in Minneapolis about the Yellowstone Trail.

May 23, 1913 Ismay Journal

From two to six automobiles are passing through Ismay daily, east or west over the Yellowstone Trail. And, incidentally, these parties are leaving quite a bit of money behind them.

July 25, 1913 Ismay Journal
Note: Later, in 1920 the report was 8,000 cars and 25,000 tourists through Ismay that summer, as counted by the Yellowstone Trail Association.

ISMAY'S FIRST RADIO SET

Ismay's first radio set was installed last Monday at the Rexall Drug Store and Monday evening the first broadcasted program was heard in Ismay. The drug store has been crowded with people eager and curious to know just how the radio works …

December 22, 1922 Ismay Journal

They came west from Ismay via Knowlton cut off, and the Powder River bridge near the Mizpah, and expected to go back via Terry and possibly might try fording Powder River in order to save a long trip around Knowlton. Mr. Brainerd said he had not encountered any difficulty in Custer County.

July 25, 1913 Miles City Independent
Note: This was four months before the bridge at Terry opened.

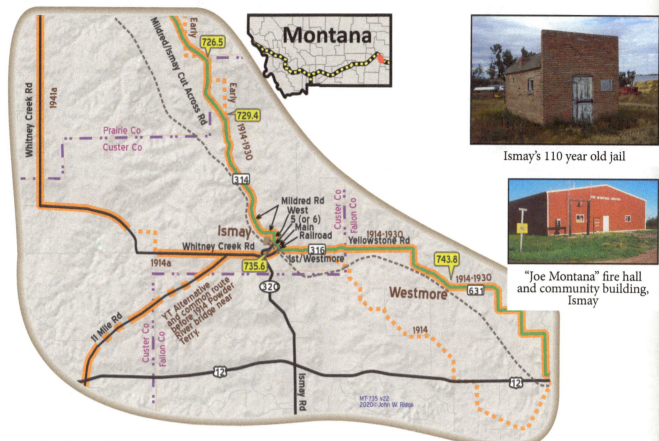

Ismay's 110 year old jail

"Joe Montana" fire hall
and community building,
Ismay

MT-719.0 Mildred

Mildred was once a thriving place with many civic events and tourists passing through. First a cyclone then the railroad moving, then a drought. There are few signs of life there, just a memory of the Yellowstone Trail.

MT-735.6 Ismay

Today one sees a modern fire station, a church, a working grain elevator, and empty lots where once stood a busy, proud town and cattle shipping station. The empty lots bear little signs that named the building that once stood there. Sort of like a cemetery. The Milwaukee Road railroad brought in immigrant farmers and took out herds of cattle to market. Electric street lights came. Autos came. The first radio came in 1922. Then came falling prices, over-extension at the bank and over-dependence on thin, arid topsoil. People moved out. Jonathan Raban in *Bad Land* (Random House 1996) describes the present Ismay in colorful, almost poetic language the sagging buildings and bleak environment of the little doomed town.

When last we were there, Gene Nemitz was mayor of all 22 citizens (plus or minus). He had an upbeat attitude, mentioning the 20 or so trains rumbling through town from the Bakken oil fields and the possibility of housing oil workers. He runs a successful "cleaning" mill which cleans chaff from wheat seeds which he ships to farmers, seemingly the only business in town. As a publicity lark in the 1990s the town was officially (briefly) named "Joe" after the football player Joe Montana.

As you stand on Main St., 100 feet north of the railroad tracks, look north and you may see the remnants of Judge

J. E. Prindle's fading white frame land office with Mrs. Prindle's café attached. Prindle was president of the Yellowstone Trail Association in 1913-1914, and a major figure of the town.

Ismay Jail. Walk a bit to the southwest to see the still standing 1910 brick jail, complete with the National Register of Historic Places plaque. It held the "railroad rowdies," drunks, and those awaiting extradition to Miles City county jail.

MT-743.8 Westmore

You are now in "a silent, empty terrain interacting with the attendant clouds and sky, where austerity gives a clear definition to this arid land." *Maynard Dixon and a Changing West, 1917-1935* by Donald J. Hagerty

Ice cream parlor for sale. Best little railroad town on the Milwaukee and on the Yellowstone Trail. $1800 and all.
March 8, 1922 Bismarck Tribune
Note: Did Mrs. Prindle sell out? Got to be a story there.

The map of the YT between Marmarth and Ismay recorded in the 1914 *First Year Book*, has many "approximations" and outright fibs or, at least errors, due to poor information. The railroad is straight east of Baker on the map but curves on the ground. Towns are often ½ section off. The alternative line Plevna to Ismay is but a figment of imagination. Hump 3 miles east of Ismay is grossly exaggerated. North of Ismay seems always "off."

Well, modern maps, digitized or not, have some errors! Many maps do not show the road NE of the tracks at Westmore, when it has been there a long time.

November 26, 1920. Letter from Baker's Trailman to Yellowstone Trail Association General Manager H. O. Cooley responding to Cooley's reminder about the upcoming Eastern Montana Trail meeting at Forsyth. Trailman responded, "Will take it up with the boys and try and see that Baker is well represented."

Note: This shows the degree to which Cooley micromanaged a national organization with perhaps 16 state and regional meetings. He also attended and spoke at all of those meetings, perhaps relying on the Trailmen to produce a large audience. ✿

Two months before the Yellowstone Trail Association collapsed, we see a Baker movie ad January, 1930 for coming "all talkies," apparently still a rarity in small towns, three years after their invention. Although the Association collapsed, people in small towns still referred to the Trail's newly numbered replacement as the Yellowstone Trail in printed town business ads, on maps and in the vernacular into the 1940s. ✿

September 1952. A large celebration was held spanning the miles from Marmarth, North Dakota, west to Baker on US 12 upon the occasion of that span of highway being oiled. Three thousand people showed up for the traveling celebration from Marmarth to the free food in Baker. Bands played, speakers spoke. Here it is 1952 and they are only oiling gravel on a reasonably major U.S. highway!! ✿

Notes from the authors:

Between Plevna and Fallon, the original Trail can be followed quite closely. While today's gravel surface is much superior to the original packed (and supposedly graded) dirt surface, it still is one of the longest sections on which the modern traveler, with a small bit of imagination, can recreate early Yellowstone Trail travel.

Trip Diary from unknown author: "The Morning of June 30 We left Marmarth (North Dakota) at 7:30 this morning, earlier than usual, upon being awakened at an ungodly hour by the flapping of the tent in a fresh wind racing across our unprotected camp site. The scenery is still bleak but increasingly fascinating as we enter an area of "badlands." At Baker we found a progressive little city. ✿

Baker tourist camp
O'Fallon Historical Museum

Badlands from the YT

The Knowlton Cutoff today.
Co. 403 near US 12

YELLOWSTONE TRAIL BETWEEN BAKER AND PLEVNA IS COMPLETED
October 21, 1921 The Producers News, (Plentywood, MT)
Note: Just what does "completed" mean? Gravel? Oiled gravel? Dragged dirt?

The route of the original Yellowstone Trail entering Montana from Marmarth, North Dakota, and going through Baker to Plevna followed primitive trails which are, for the most part, lost to the modern traveler. Much of the road was disused after a new route (now US 12) was built. Much has reverted to private ownership. At one point an oil well has disrupted the route. Isolated stretches, one to several miles long, have been improved and are in local use. The area is interesting to explore but the cross-country traveler can make no use of the original Trail. ✿

Baker Garage today

MT-753.5 Plevna

The *Custer Country Guide* says, "Small towns on the prairie have long been one of Montana's greatest crops." That could describe the easternmost 80 miles of Montana - from Fallon to Broadus to the North Dakota line. The plains here in eastern Montana provide a little topographical relief to the eye in the form of cottonwood trees. When you see them you know where the stream is. The grasses move to the wind and you see an immenseness around you.

MT-767.2 Baker

HOTEL BAKER 41 modern rooms; good beds; well maintained. Sgl. $1.50-$2.50; dbl. $2.25; with bath $3.50.

KEIRLE MOTOR CO., Ford; in fine modern bldg.; work on all cars. Labor $1.25; ph. 48.

Note: New road open soon will be much better and shorter. MH-1928

Natural gas was discovered in eastern Montana in 1915. One still sees many working oil well-head pumps today throughout the area. Eastern Montana is underlain by sedimentary rocks. Sand and silt were carried by rivers from the mountainous west to the east and embedded with swampland vegetation to form vast coal and gas seams.

Begun as a watering station for Milwaukee Road steam trains, Baker was once called the "first Montana city on the Yellowstone Trail" referencing its proximity to the Trail coming out of North Dakota. The town still preserves its history of cattle ranches by printing 88 area ranch brand symbols on restaurant napkins for tourists to see.

723 S Main St. **O'Fallon Historical Museum**. Displayed in the six-building complex are a 1907 cabin, a claim shack, a 1916 one room school and homestead items. They even have an original metal Yellowstone Trail sign! Part of the museum is housed in the former jail and sheriff's living quarters, used as such from 1916 to 1974. Star attraction here is Steer Montana, the 1923 skeleton of the largest steer in Montana. Across the street is the Historical Society's newish building housing farm machinery, cars, tractors and buggies from the 100-year-old time of the Yellowstone Trail. Parts are on the National Register of Historic Places.

MT-779.6 Montana/N. Dakota Line

Touring near Ismay

This 1914 Model T Ford, model 41 Inter-State, was snapped in 1919 near Ismay. The picture was posted on the Model T Ford Forum recently. Friend of the Trail, Stan Howe, was asked if he recognized the site of this old picture taken near Ismay. He answered, "Yup, about 15 miles west of my place. I know exactly the place and the road hasn't improved too much since then. That's on the Yellowstone Trail which passes right through the middle of my place running close along the Milwaukee Road line, which was pretty new when that photo was taken."

The fun of doing historical research is that it brings back memories. ❁

An elderly modern citizen from the Baker area reported that the YT followed Willow Rd. just east of Baker. From there, maps begin showing the route to North Dakota to be the modern US 12 route, although some maps seem to significantly miss the actual route. The original stair step route into North Dakota apparently had alternative "steps." Today some of those roads are used and obscured by the modern oil industry.

Historic Old Saloon in Emigrant

Early traveling on the Trail to Yellowstone National Park   *Paul Shea*

MT

The SPUR -- The Yellowstone Trail, Livingston to the Park

"There at the foot of the grade stretches out a wide, gently curving remnant of the original road. The route and the modern highway merge in the distance, reminding you that you've been traveling the same route used by early travelers." taken from *Travelin' Magazine* p. 10 Jan/Feb 1998 by James Soe Nyun

The Yellowstone Trail Association named itself after the great National Park, so the Trail would have to run there, the only "splendid lateral" they allowed to veer from the direct east-west route. The Yellowstone Trail entered Paradise Valley in 1914 when the road to the park gate was improved by convict labor. Over the years, both the Yellowstone Trail and US 89 were routed here, like braided strands of hair, on alternate sides or the same side of the Yellowstone River.

This 1913 route became known as Yellowstone Trail Road and remains so named today. The main highway moved about over the years, including various routes on the east side of Yellowstone River, and it is presumed that the route of the Trail moved accordingly at the time, but this western route was first, was primary, and still retains the name.

The aptly named **Paradise Valley**, carved by the Yellowstone River, lies between Livingston and 55 miles south to Gardiner, protected in the east by the volcanic lava Absaroka Mountains and the folded sedimentary Gallatin Range in the west. Eagles, deer, Canada geese and fly fishermen haunt the clear Yellowstone River valley with its 10 kinds of flowering flora. Many movies have hung a story on Paradise Valley; residents have lived storied lives here for well over 100 years.

In 1915 the Yellowstone Trail Association joined with many other groups to pressure the Army to admit autos into the park which happened in August, 1915. ✿

Fridley Creek. Private picnic grounds with two historic bridges: the original Yellowstone Trail bridge (above) and the Northern Pacific bridge with a badly faded YT arrow (below)..

Rail tracks through Yankee Jim Canyon in 1914. The parallel, original Yankee Jim wagon road was higher up the hill to the right. The Yellowstone Trail ran between them. Later, after 1930, this track bed was used for a new auto road, which, in time, was named (confusingly) Old Yellowstone Trail Road.

MT-W25.0 Fridley Creek

Just south of Fridley Creek is a driveway to the west. About 400 feet into the driveway is the hard-to-discern Yellowstone Trail and then the railroad grade. Park here. Walk about 400 feet north to find an original small concrete YT bridge and a bigger railroad bridge with a faded YT marker on it - yellow swatch with a hand-drawn arrow. This is private land. We sought and received permission to walk about. Ask permission.

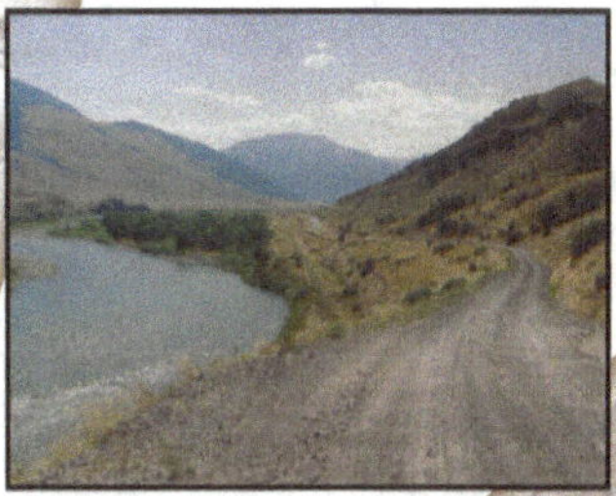

The YT near the
Point of Rocks

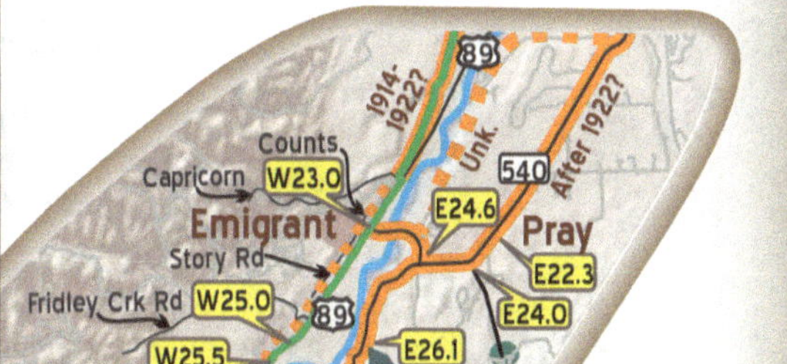

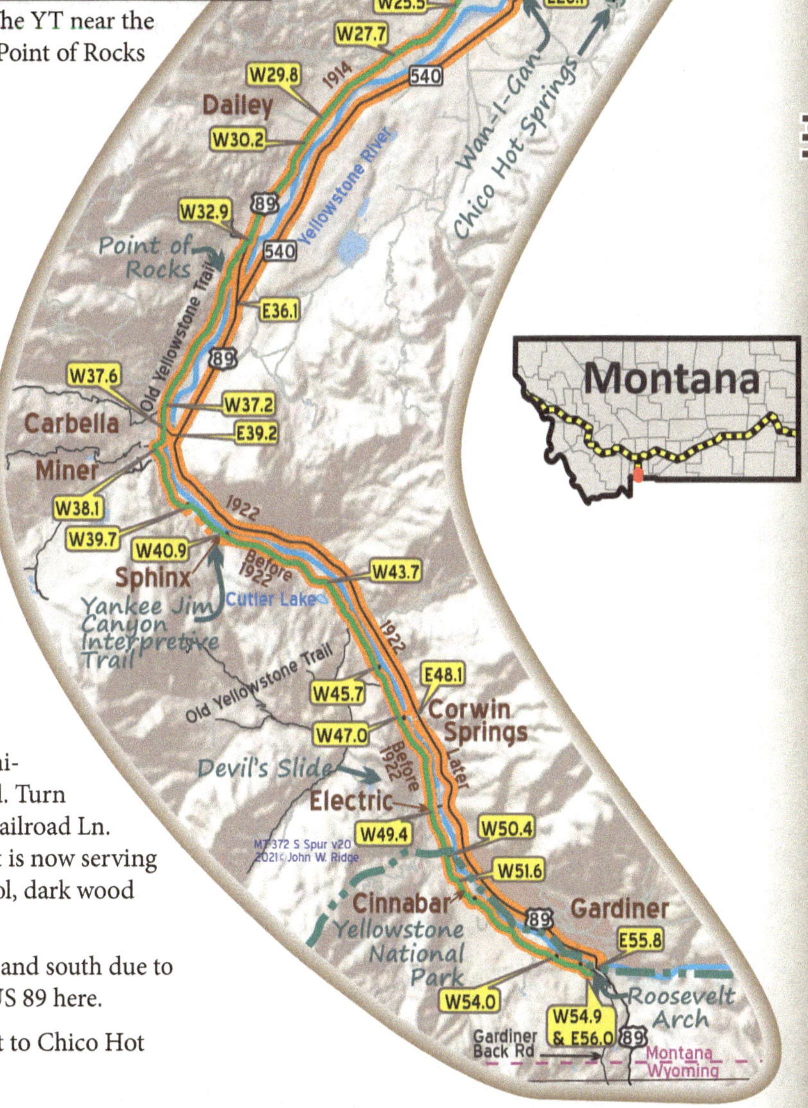

Montana

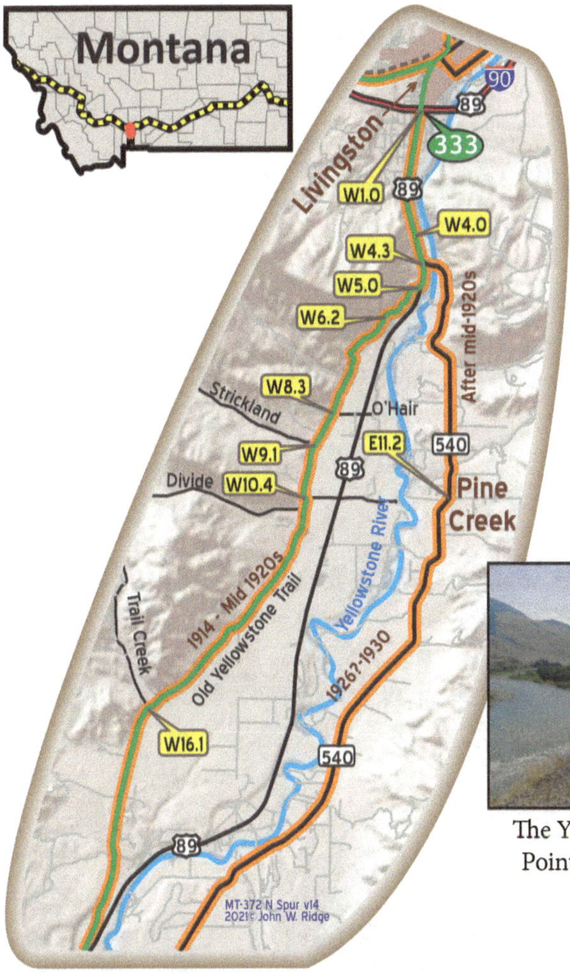

MT-W01.0 At I-90 south of Livingston

MT-W04.3

Intersection with MT 540, the later route of the Yellowstone Trail over Carter Bridge.

MT-W05.0

Junction of US 89 and Yellowstone Trail. There is a hard-to-see sign "old Yellowstone Trail N" on the west side of the road as you leave US 89. Notice Black Mountain and Mt. Cowen, tallest peaks of the Absaroka Range to the east.

MT-W22.1

Junction of Yellowstone Trail and US 89 just north of Emigrant.

MT-W23.0 Emigrant

Emigrant is at the base of pine-clad and snowy Emigrant Peak, 10,960 ft., and on the Yellowstone Trail. Turn west into Emigrant to see the **Old Saloon** at 210 Railroad Ln. Born in 1902 and out of business for some years, it is now serving three meals a day in an old west atmosphere of cool, dark wood interior.

The Yellowstone Trail is blocked going both north and south due to private property blocking, so you must return to US 89 here.

Early Yellowstone Trail and rail travelers would get to Chico Hot Springs Hotel from here, to the east.

Yankee Jim Road/Yellowstone Trail,
now an interpreted walking trail
Lee Whiteley

Rock work by prisoners on the YT

Yankee Jim
Doris Whithorn

Yankee Jim Canyon was named for an enterprising eastern pioneer (hence the name 'Yankee Jim') James George, who built a crude road through this narrow canyon and erected a toll gate in 1872. Since this was the main route to Yellowstone Park, it was a good money-maker. He was a real "character" and a cheerful tall-tales teller. The Northern Pacific Railroad tracks occupied his road in 1883 and the company was forced to build the colorful prevaricator another road farther up the hill, said W. C. McRae. The State of Montana completed its "project through Yankee Jim Canyon" for auto traffic in 1914, improving the road with the help of convicts ✿.

Rock slide resulting from the erosion of the bank of the Yellowstone River, just below. The areas above and below consist of unstable rocks making a repair difficult and expensive.

YT through Yankee Jim Canyon taken in the early 2000s, above the railroad bed

The Devil's Slide

HISTORY BITS

MT-W32.9

Junction of Old Yellowstone Trail and US 89. US 89 to the south crosses Yellowstone River and joins the eastern newer route of the Yellowstone Trail.

MT-W33.9

The Yellowstone Trail crosses the Point of Rocks. Great view of the river, old railroad bed, the road and mountains.

MT-W38.1 Miner

Just south of Miner, Tom Miner Creek Road (also National Forest Road 63) heads west for 15 miles to **Gallatin Petrified Forest**. Here is a layering of 27 or 30 petrified forests lying one on top of another, many of the trees standing. Today you can get a free permit to bring out a bit of petrified wood.

MT-W33.9

Just to the east is **Carbella Bridge**, nearly 100 years-old.

MT-W39.7-W40.9 Yankee Jim Canyon

Some of the original Yankee Jim road exists today as a hiking path just above the roadway built in 1924 providing a much improved road for the Yellowstone Trail. That route, in turn is just above today's Old Yellowstone Trail South which had been the Northern Pacific's track bed. It is this road that was closed by a rock slide in 2016.

MT-W40.72

Park here and walk. A few years ago we were able to drive the original route higher on the hillside. Today, the road follows the railroad grade which is much easier to negotiate. The National Forest Service has erected signs to help guide you through this complex area.

MT-W40.9

Sphinx Creek Interpretive Center (unmanned). A large interpretive sign describes the river, the railroad, the Yellowstone Trail and Yankee Jim's road.

MT-W43.7 Cutler Lake

Watch out for the gumbo around here.

MT-W45.9 Royal Teton Ranch

The Church Universal and Triumphant bought 25,000 acres surrounding the Yellowstone Trail and built a compound for members in 1986, calling it Royal Teton Ranch. It is reduced in size with only about 40 people tending the remaining acres where quarterly retreats are held. It was considered a Doomsday cult by many.

MT-W47.0 Bridge to Corwin Springs

The bridge to Corwin Springs, built in 2007, is uninteresting as a bridge. It replaced the old but interesting through truss bridge built in the early 20th century.

MT-W48.34 Devil's Slide

See that red streak down Cinnebar Mountain? That "Devil's Slide" marks the place where a coal stream burned out of the Triassic period sedimentary rocks. It is thought that there was

more oxygen on Earth 200 million years ago reacting with iron to create the red color. Those "dikes" you see sticking up are stratified rock tipped up on end.

MT-W49.4 Electric (and Aldridge)

Now, at best, archeology sites. At the settlement called Electric was the power plant built to supply electricity to the mines at Aldridge. At the turn of the 20th century, ovens at Electric produced 300-500 tons of coke daily from coal mines in Aldridge. The coke was shipped to Butte and Anaconda smelters to smelt copper ore to make copper wire for the booming telephone and electric wire industries.

Cinnabar in 1901
National Parks Service

MT-W50.4 Yellowstone National Park Boundary (Entrance and Arch are in Gardiner)

MT-W51.6 Cinnabar

Now just an archeology site. Excavations have revealed a blacksmith shop and the location of the railroad depot.

In 1883, the Northern Pacific Railroad built track from Livingston towards Gardiner, the north entrance to Yellowstone National Park. South of Cinnabar a dispute over some property kept it from continuing the last three miles to Gardiner. Thus, train travelers coming from Livingston were transported from Cinnabar to Gardiner to complete their trip in horse-drawn carriages. While the National Park entrance arch was being built, the Northern Pacific was able to extend the tracks to Gardiner, arriving in 1902, but with "limited services" apparently meaning it lacked a side-track. President Teddy Roosevelt arrived in Gardiner by train to dedicate the unfinished National Park arch in April 1903, but after dropping off the President, the train returned to Cinnabar with the presidential car and the President's entourage where there was a side track to store it while Roosevelt was in the Park. Thus, Cinnabar claimed to be the capitol of the U.S. from April 8-April 24 while Teddy was in the Park.

MT-W54.0 Tinker's Hill Cemetery

MT-E54.6 Gardiner

See Gardiner information, next page at MT-E55.6

MT-W54.9 (MT-E56.0) Yellowstone National Park Roosevelt Arch

SPUR - LIVINGSTON to YELLOWSTONE NATIONAL PARK - Eastern Side, page 1

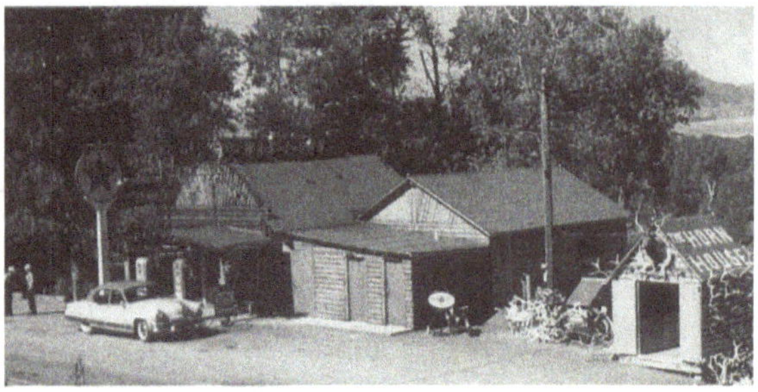

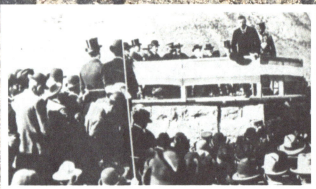

Wan-I-Gan
Doris Whithorn, in 1996

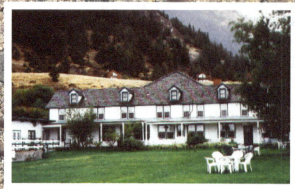

Across the river from Emigrant once stood a small compound of store, gas station, and 12 cabins called "**Wan-I gan**," built in late 1920s for "supplies along the river." Wanagan is a word meaning "supply craft for logging boats." Bill and Doris Whithorn ran this supply station from 1948 to 1976. It was more than that. It housed recovering patients in the cabins, it hosted wedding parties and Paradise Valley events, it welcomed returning fishermen and hunters. It was "home" to many. It is no more, but Doris preserved its memory in several books about every day life in Paradise Valley which you can find at the Yellowstone Gateway Museum in Livingston. ❂

MT

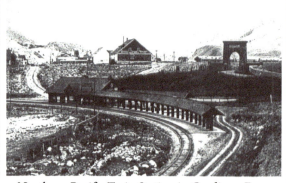

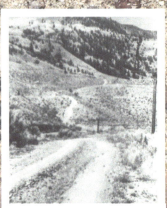

On April 24, 1903, Teddy Roosevelt laid the cornerstone of the unfinished arch "for the benefit and enjoyment of the people" with a band playing, a military presence and 4,000 cheering onlookers.

The Gardiner/Mammoth "Back Road"

The Yellowstone Trail ended when it reached the Roosevelt Arch. From Gardiner to Mammoth Springs in the Park, visitors used the "Gardiner Back Road" still usable but one way only today.

The early picture to the left is from the Park Photo Archives. To the right is a modern picture taken of the road. ❂

Chico Hot Springs

Northern Pacific Train Station in Gardiner. Four months after the cornerstone of the Arch was laid, the last rough-hewn log was set upon Gardiner's new, huge train depot's stone foundation. The last train to stop there was in 1956.

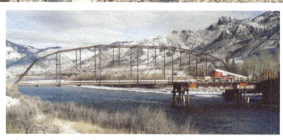

The modern bridge at Corwin Springs being built in front of the original bridge, now removed

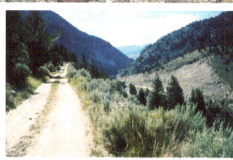

The YT near Gardner

When the original Yellowstone Trail arrived in Livingston there was little call for an auto road continuing to the Park; The Northern Pacific had excellent service there and autos were not allowed in the Park (until 1915).

However, almost immediately, Yellowstone Trail tourists from the East and Midwest began agitating to be allowed to use the Livingston-Gardiner wagon road and to be allowed to use their cars in the Park. The existing wagon road was routed on the west side of the Yellowstone River and ran, generally, along the tracks,.

There were many local pressures to have an auto road on the east side of the river, and over the period 1913-1928 such a road slowly took form.

Remember that the route of the Yellowstone Trail was not

determined by governmental agencies, but rather by use and, usually, local recommendations for Yellowstone Trail Association action. As bridges were built and roads constructed on the east side, some maps show a gradual movement of the route of the Trail to the east side to promote the use of better and safer roads. By 1928 the Trail was effectively moved and is now identified as US 89. The west-side route retained the Yellowstone Trail name, however, and today is known formally as the Old Yellowstone Trail. It moved slightly in many places with the construction of new roads and the taking over of the abandoned rail bed, but retains the historical aura.

MT-W01.0 At I-90 south of Livingston

MT-W04.6 Carter Bridge

The original Carter Bridge was a toll bridge made of logs built in the early 1880s. This one was built in 1919. The stories of this bridge and many others are told in *Montana's Historic Bridges, 1860-1956* by Jon Axline (Montana Historical Society Press, 2005).

MT-E11.2 Pine Creek Village

MT-E22.3 Pray

MT-E24.0 Turn off to Chico Rd.

This leads to **Chico Hot Springs**. Established 1900, it is on the National Register of Historic Places. Originally a hotel, then a medical facility, now it is a resort. It is a an appealing place with a big pool, saloon, hotel, cabins, and out-of-this-world cuisine. See **Trail Tale: Chico**, page 154.

MT-E24.6 Murphy Lane to Emigrant

MT-E26.1 Wan-I-Gan

See History Bits about the store that was once here. It was a welcome "home" to many.

MT-E36.1

MT 540 and US 89 join

MT-E39.2 Tom Miner Creek Road

MT-E48.1 Corwin Springs

Look for a glimpse of what remains of the site of Dr. Corwin's 1909 elegant Hot Springs Resort Hotel and Natatorium. Hot water was pumped from the LaDuke hot springs 2 miles south. Many came for the believed relief that hot springs afforded the ill.

MT-E55.8+ Gardiner

North of the Arch is the **Yellowstone Heritage and Research Center**. It holds 5.3 million items in its herbarium, archives and archeology lab. You are welcome to conduct research

there, however, it is not a museum for the tourist. [Note: The authors helped with moving the items from cramped quarters at Mammoth into the new building. Astounding collections!]

MT-E56.0 (MT-W54.9)Yellowstone National Park Roosevelt Arch

END OF SPUR SECTION

Roosevelt Arch
North entrance to the Yellowstone National Park

The July 23, 1915 Automobile Club of Seattle newsletter gave instructions to autoists planning to use the north (Gardiner) entrance to the park at the end of the Yellowstone Trail spur which was to officially accept autos. They specified the costs (1915 dollars) to enter: "runabouts and single-seated cars, $5.00; five passenger cars, $7.50; seven passenger cars, $10.00. All automobiles are operated on a strict running schedule within the limits of the park." See **Trail Tale: We Want In**, page 150. ✿

We Want In: Admitting Automobiles to the Yellowstone National Park

"We Want In" said the bronze-colored medallion we held. We were at the Livingston, Montana, Yellowstone Gateway Museum. Beneath those words was a picture of a tiny car at the Roosevelt Arch at the Yellowstone National Park north entrance. On the obverse was "Yellowstone Trail" with the famous arrow. What tale, we wondered, was this medallion telling?

We discovered that it was a watch fob issued by the Yellowstone Trail Association around 1915 to promote its position that the ban on autos in the park should be lifted. Autos had been admitted into the other six national parks so why not Yellowstone?

The Yellowstone Trail Association brought autos down the spur to the Park's north entrance.

The Trail Association was not alone in the push to admit cars, but the issue really struck at the heart of the purpose of the Association. This organization was named "Yellowstone" in honor of the park. The Trail itself was attracting hundreds (soon to be thousands) of auto tourists to the park which increased the urgency of this question of admission. The Yellowstone Trail was the only auto route to the north entrance.

You could rent a tent/cabin from Wylie Camping.

A few cars had sputtered into the park, but from 1902 they were officially banned. Why? Was it to keep out poachers, loggers, or miners? Was it for safety reasons? Was it for economic reasons? Auto roads would have to be built separate from the lanes of the horses. Or was it to protect the horse-drawn transportation business within the place?

Three major companies moved park visitors from train to hotel and ferried them about the park in a variety of carriages. They used an estimated 1400-1600 horses. Transportation and hotel concessionaires were, of course, averse to autoist "sagebrushers" who might camp and travel about freely – and free. Even President Theodore Roosevelt was not allowed to motor in the park when he vacationed there and dedicated the north entrance arch in 1903.

There were other reasons for the ban. The federal government saw the high cost of improving the winding roads to make them safe for autos, and they saw the cost of providing safe water, electricity, ranger protection, and telephones for campers. The Army, which administered the park at that time, worried about traffic congestion, safety, and control. The roads within the park were not ready for autos. They were unpaved, often steep, often one-way, and wide enough only for the slow horse-drawn coaches.

The ban didn't sit well with the public, however. Henry Merry crashed through the north entrance in 1902 at a breathtaking speed of 25 miles per hour, which caused horses to bolt. Merry paid his fine by taking park superintendent Major John Pitcher for a ride. The ban also stirred the citizens of Cody to petition to allow cars to enter via the east entrance. And story had it that AAA pathfinder A. L. Westgard would annually drive up to an entrance of the Park and shake his fist angrily. The issue was emotional.

The auto was the great democratizer. The admission of automobiles into the park would open the park's wonders to many who could not take long vacations or afford the five day slow carriage tours sponsored by elite hotels. The auto would permit visitors to see what they could in the time they had available. They wanted to be "sagebrushers," to camp, fish, hike, and enjoy. To many, auto admission represented a victory for the "average Joe."

The National Highway Association, the AAA, auto groups of every stripe and countless individual automobilists all pushed for auto admission. Park concessionaire, Wylie Permanent Camping Company, providers of wood-framed tents for the wealthy as a back-to-nature alternative to hotels, embraced the idea of this new brand of tourist that they could serve. Walter Fischer, the Secretary of the Interior in 1912, argued for auto admission "if the ⇨

Front side
Yellowstone Trail
Association watch fob

Back side
"We Want In"
with Roosevelt Arch

TRAIL TALES (150) **TRAIL TALES**

conditions were right." They apparently were not right for three more years.

Michael Dowling, future president of the Yellowstone Trail Association, concluded, after a pathfinding trip from Minneapolis to the park in 1913, that "automobiles would soon make the park accessible to every family, rich or poor." The Yellowstone Trail Association began to push for auto admission almost as soon as the Association was formed. At its third annual convention in March, 1915, a resolution was adopted.

The Association renewed its twice passed resolution asking the Honorable Secretary of the Interior to open the Yellowstone National Park to automobile travel under proper regulations. "We believe this to be in the interest of the public."

State chapters of the Yellowstone Trail Association distributed the "We Want In" medallions and undoubtedly did their share of letter writing. Franklin K. Lang, Interior Secretary in 1915, must have received these resolutions, among many others, for he complained, "I am in receipt of a considerable number of telegrams brought about by the very laudable and active influence of the automobile organizations." Indeed, the Secretary (no doubt exasperatedly) telegraphed Parmley assuring him that "arrangements would be made to allow automobiles to enter Yellowstone National Park."

Or, you could set up your own tent.

Come On In

So, the handwriting was on the wall. Acting Secretary of War, Robert S. Oliver, whose department managed the park, concluded that broadening the present road system was more economical than a second road system for autos. But he refused to upgrade the roads and permit autos. Even the letter from the governor of Colorado to President Taft could not budge Oliver's thinking. It probably was the enormous amount of public pressure that made Oliver eventually give up.

August 1, 1915, was the designated opening date for autos, selected late in the season to allow concessionaires time to prepare. A couple of dozen cars were admitted on July 31, ahead of the grand opening, supposedly to lessen the crush of cars the next day. First among them to pass through that celebrated arch was a Model T owned by Mr. and Mrs. K. R. Seiler of Redwing, Minnesota. Other reports differ. The first 10 days saw 321 cars enter the park.

The proposed ridiculous auto entry fee was $5 or $10, depending upon the number of seats in the car. In today's

dollars that would be about $125 or $250. The fee certainly would serve to keep autoists out. By 1921 the fee was $7.50. The Livingston Chamber of Commerce argued against any fee at all, declaring that federal taxes alone should pay for the park.

But There Were Rules

The rules of the road in 1915 were draconian. To accommodate carriages and autos on the same road, autos were to start measured trips 30 minutes before horse carriages. They were to adhere to strict time schedules, checked by guards. When meeting a horse carriage, the horse got the inside lane, and autoists were to stay 150 yards away from everything. Autoists were to "drive around the road system in a 'loop' in a direction opposite to the hands of a clock. Speed limits imposed: 10/mph going the 'up' road on the loop; 12/mph going the 'down' road; 8/mph when passing a horse; 20/mph on straight stretches. The reverse direction may be taken as follows:

Norris Junction to Mammoth Hot Springs, 11:00 a.m. to 1:00 p.m. and after 4:30 p.m.

Madison Junction to Norris Junction, anytime except 10:00 a.m. to 1:00 p.m. and 3:00 to 6:00 p.m.

Mammoth Hot Springs to Tower Falls, early enough to reach Tower Falls by 1:00 p.m."

The rules regarding auto engines, penalties, horse teams, speeds, etc., still filled a 1921 brochure, although the speeds were increased somewhat: "On straight open stretches when no vehicle is nearer than 200 yards the speed may be increased to 25/mph." Teams still had the right of way and "automobiles shall be backed or otherwise handled so as to enable teams to pass." A driver had to prove to park rangers that his auto had good brakes and that he understood that the average altitude of park roads was 7,000 feet and thus his auto's power required a leaner mixture of gasoline.

The rules were printed and widely distributed. As a service to those traveling the Yellowstone Trail, the Association distributed the rules along the Trail. President Joe Parmley, twelve days before the entry day, wrote to the park superintendent begging for more copies for the Association's travel bureaus.

The next year over half of the park's visitors came by car. Horse-drawn carriages were replaced by "auto stages" and by 1917 most of the cumbersome road rules were dropped. However, as late as 1928 the spacing rule remained, as did strict speed and auto equipment requirements.

Today

As we write this, we read of proposals to severely limit the numbers of autos admitted to the park.

Appreciation of the park's wonders today is muted by tangled traffic, foolish drivers and strained patience. The many who pushed for admittance 100 years ago would be victims of their own success today.

The watch fobs tell an important tale of conflict and tension to achieve the Roosevelt Arch promise - "for the enjoyment of the people." Today, tension seems to have risen again. ⚙

Hunter's Hot Springs Resort

The meeting was certainly a rowdy one at Hunter's Hot Springs resort, the site of the semi-annual Yellowstone Trail Association convention! The delegates were deciding the route of the Yellowstone Trail through Montana. It was hot in early August, 1914, long before air-conditioning. Opinions about the proposed route to Idaho were loudly expressed by most of the 200 members of the Association who had made the cross-country trip (some by train) to the famous resort. The Great Falls delegation just couldn't be silenced; they argued loudly for the highway to be routed through their town. Order was restored when George Metlen, Secretary of the State Highway Commission of Montana, rose to state that the route from Butte to Missoula to St. Regis was favored as a state highway by the Commission. Thus, the Association voted to route the Trail that way to Idaho, not to Great Falls. That decision would dictate their route through Idaho and entrance into and through Washington used for the next 25 years.

This two year old toddler of an organization made other important decisions at Hunter's: they changed the name to Yellowstone Trail Association from the cumbersome Twin Cities-Aberdeen-Yellowstone Park-Trail. Twin Cities referred to Minneapolis and St. Paul, the beginning of the Trail in 1912. They approved extension of the Trail to the Pacific, which caused the brouhaha about how to actually route the Trail to Idaho, much less the Pacific. They selected their logo - black arrow within a circle of yellow. They also - again - urged the Department of Interior to admit autos into the Yellowstone National Park.

Two months later the Association published an odd but interesting book. It contained the verbatim account of the speeches, arguments and civic bragging of the convention attendees. Advertisement pictures looked like an ancient Sears Roebuck

The Swimming Pool, now for a plunge (top)
The Solarium, sunny and bright (middle)
The Parlor, beautiful and inviting (bottom)

catalogue. Delightful reading. It was called *On the Yellowstone Trail: The First Year Book*. If they planned another yearbook, it never materialized.

Washout!

This important meeting about routes and highways got off to a rocky start. In fact, it didn't start as planned at all. It was scheduled to begin July 8, 1914, but a major rain storm over South Dakota and eastern Montana washed out parts of the Yellowstone Trail and other dirt roads. It was postponed until August 5.

Weekly newspapers along the trail between Minneapolis and Bozeman heralded the coming of the meeting at Hunter's, only 16 miles east of popular Livingston. There was to have been quite a procession of autos forming a caravan, had it not rained. The papers fleshed out the "amazing sociability run" with names of local participants, guides and activities. The June 25, 1914, *Livingston Post* announced that:

One fleet of cars will leave the Radison (sic) Hotel, Minneapolis, at 8 a.m. June 29. They will make their first stop at Montevideo and the second night at Aberdeen (SD). Several cars will join the fleet enroute. From Aberdeen they will be piloted by local drivers who have recently been over the route. They will leave Aberdeen July 1 and reach Hettinger (ND) at noon July 2. They will remain at Miles City (MT) July 3 and 4 for the wild west sports show. July 5 they make a stop at Billings and will reach Hunter's Hot Springs July 6. The 7th may be spent in sightseeing or fishing.

A very slow schedule has been prepared. Cars may be heavily loaded with camping outfits without danger. This being the first run over the trail, towns and county commissioners are requested to have their section well dragged.

The irony of it. A road convention washed out! Having been alerted to the change of date, newspapers cranked up their public relations machine and wrote enthusiastically all over again in July. Guesses varied wildly; the *Billings Journal* guessed that 250 autos would start off at Minneapolis, would be joined by many, "stretching out in a sinuous string of six to ten miles in length." Others guessed only 100 autos would start out. Economic visions danced in the heads of Trail town editors, salivating over the prospect of 1,000 visitors in their

YTA General Manager
Cooley at Hunter's

➡

hotels, restaurants, garages and camp sites. We do not know if such a "sociability run" ever transpired. Papers were mum on the subject.

The Dakota Hotel at Hunter's Hot Springs

Why Meet at Hunter's Hot Springs?

This was a grassroots organization with little money. Why would they pick such a fancy place? It was right on the Trail, literally, so the site satisfied the Association's requirement that all meetings be held on the Trail. As today's convention planners know, attendees like to go to high profile places and "see the sights" to get the most for their convention dollar. It was the same a century ago. The renowned hot springs offered such a diversion. It was the Disney World of its day. Its 100 acres were bordered by the Absaroka Mountains to the south and the Crazy Mountains to the north. It was a collection of small hotels, shops, stables, a pool, a golf course, medical facilities and even its own post office. One goal of the organization was to promote tourism and what better place to go than to a top tourist resort?

The resort chosen for this meeting was Western elegant, but it also had an interesting history. In 1864 Dr. Andrew Jackson Hunter observed Native Americans bathing in the hot springs, and he staked a claim to the area. In 1875 he built a wood-framed hotel and opened a health spa featuring the hot springs waters. In 1880 Hunter's son-in-law, Frank Rich, built another hotel nearby, not as competition, but to house the overflow. By 1885 the two were running a "free hack," transporting guests over what was to become the Yellowstone Trail, from Bozeman, Livingston and Springdale depots to their resort. Dr. Hunter sold his interest in the property in 1886. Frank Rich leased his property and moved into other occupations. In 1909, five years prior to the Yellowstone Trail Association convention, the luxurious Mission-style Dakota Hotel was

built on Frank Rich's old hotel site by James Murray. Business was booming.

In that day of limited medical help, people sought ease from pain wherever they could, even using now-outlawed ingredients. At the turn of the 20th century a cough syrup contained heroin, the popular Coca Cola contained a small amount of cocaine, and opium was used in vaporizers to treat asthma. Hot springs were believed to ease the pain of rheumatism and arthritis. A Hunter's Hot Springs brochure c.1916 assures such relief but also contains the shocking statement that, "Those suffering from liver and kidney diseases, stomach disorders and chronic constipation testify that much benefit is derived by having the system thoroughly boiled out."

Anxious to assure the public of the safety of the spa, the brochure asserts, "There is a regular physician in constant attendance …" and "… it is customary for those coming to the springs for their health to be examined before commencing their baths" and it spells out cautions related to hot baths. But people did not soak in hot mineral water all day. There had to be other attractions. This page from the Hunter's brochure (below) lists other activities available.

The huge pool, or "plunge," had 40 dressing rooms, the 400 foot long veranda looked out on a panoramic sweep of the grounds and distant mountains, the solarium was a 50 foot semi-circular glass structure. Beamed ceilings and paneled walls gave a feel of luxury, even on hard wooden chairs in the "parlor." One can imagine the Yellowstone Trail Association movers and shakers huddling in mini-meetings in the Solarium or the Parlor or even the pool, planning strategies which would ultimately affect 8,000 Trail Association members and 3,600 miles of their named highway. For $2.00 a day you could get a room with running hot and cold water and a toilet. There were tennis courts, riding horses, hunting and fishing possibilities. All this plus the servings of "curable" waters in the shade.

Resorting

The word "resort" conjures different cultural and geographic images. One hundred years ago the idea of vacationing at a big resort hotel was "in" among the wealthy in the East. Mother, children and servants would leave the stifling city for the summer and flee to the Adirondacks or the Catskills or Cape Cod. Father would join them for weekends. Tennis, croquet and sailing were enjoyed "in the proper dress." The emphasis seemed to be upon being seen rather than upon relaxing. In the Midwest, "going up north" to rustic resorts with cabins or camps was the thing to do. No dress code required ⇨

for canoeing and hiking, and you could take your meals at the resort's main lodge. In the West, many resorts were built around natural hot springs because proponents advocated their health benefits. Such was the belief of the healing powers of mineral-rich hot springs that railroads ran spurs to them and advertised them widely.

One such Western resort was Chico Hot Springs. Still popular today, it is much as it was 100 years ago. The Northern Pacific Railroad built a 50 mile spur from Livingston, Montana, to Gardiner to serve visitors going to Yellowstone National Park. At about the midpoint, at Emigrant, the "Chico Bus" met visitors and carted them the 3.5 miles to the spa. Other brave visitors drove their new automobiles to Chico on the still-primitive Yellowstone Trail which paralleled the railroad. Although auto tourists began to replace visitors using the Northern Pacific Railroad, both the Railroad and Hunter's Hot Springs advertised the spa as "only two miles from the Springdale depot."

Hunter's Hot Springs - an Epitaph

The Hotel Dakota burned to the ground in 1932, which spelled the demise of the rest of the resort. A Quonset hut was erected over the pool which continued to be used by locals until the late 1970s. Thirty years later the remaining buildings had been bull-dozed and the land had changed hands several times. It stands vacant now with a hot spring still visible. Hunter's Hot Springs resort is being forgotten.

So now we need to park on the gravel road near the remaining walls and trickling spring water, somewhat reduced in flow due to earthquakes. We try to visualize the ghosts of that 1914 convention. To listen to the officers' speeches. To watch the voting. To see the families in the "plunge." To imagine new 1914 cars parked diagonally in front of the Dakota Hotel. To move a bit to allow the motorized hotel hack to shuttle new visitors from the railroad station. To do a bit of shopping in the long-gone souvenir shop. To think about the passing of the passenger train, the coming of the auto and the Yellowstone Trail, and the advent of I-90 which took us into a new world and left Hunter's Hot Springs isolated and crumbling in the old. ✿

Chico Hot Springs

Ever been to Chico Hot Springs? Just off MT 540 (Yellowstone Trail after 1922) on the east side of the Yellowstone River at **MT-E024.0** is a great resort worth seeing. It was founded on land and springs that Native Americans and miners long ago visited for the springs' "healing power." Today one can swim in the "plunge" pool, fed by the hot springs behind the present hotel and eat really sumptuous meals. All surrounded by rustic lodge effects.

The reception lounge

looking up at the stars is an exotic plus for any resort. In 1973 Mike and Eve Art resurrected the place and turned it into a beautiful Victorian lodge retreat. The garden has been resurrected as a sunny quarter-acre plot with hothouse and hot spring water running beneath the vegetables and, of course, straw-berries. Our stay occurred on a cold (-30°!) winter weekend but we got strawberries!

In the late 1890s Percie and Bill Knowles opened a boarding house near the springs for working men in the area. One could get room, plentiful board and a big bowl of strawberries at every meal for $6 a week. In 1900 they opened the Chico Warm Springs Hotel. The two-story clap-board hotel with its dormer windows and veranda extending the length of the front of the building looks today just as it did then. A five-acre vegetable garden was kept in the early 1900s using the thermal water to irrigate plants and fresh strawberries, Percie's trademark.

Years passed and the mission of the place changed from that of Percie's health spa, to a dude ranch, then to a religious re-treat, and, last, to a roadhouse. In 1957 the roof over the pool fell in. It was never replaced, for floating in hot water and

Today, there are cabins, additional lodge rooms and a convention center. Besides the pool, amenities include horseback riding, live music on weekends in the Saloon, hiking and fishing, rafting on the Yellowstone River. In the winter there is cross-country skiing. Or you can skulk around the upper floor of the lodge, hoping to catch a glimpse of the reported ghost of Percie. ✿

Chico bus to the train

The original "plunge" with roof and its modern replacement at right

Historic Savenac Tree Nursery

with Maxx Handel and Dan Capps

Thank heavens the acres of seedling beds were irrigated. Thank heavens the seedlings were protected by the moist soil. They survived. But not so the rest of the 7,920 square feet of the U.S. Forest Service seedling nursery in the Bitterroots. The horrific 1910 fire storm, called the "Big Burn," destroyed over three million acres of timber, six small towns, 78 fire fighters' lives, and the Savenac Tree Nursery near Haugan - all in 36 hours.

Two year old seedlings moved to a transplant bed

President Theodore Roosevelt had been establishing many national forests in the face of lumber company opposition. The conglomerates succeeded in limiting funding for these National Forests. Thus, fire protection was inadequate.

In dry August of 1910 many small fires erupted. A cold front fanned the flames into joining together, becoming explosive all along the future Yellowstone Trail from near St. Regis, Montana, to Kellogg, Idaho, and westward. Terrible tales abound detailing the flight of hundreds, some flights successful, some not; of brave fire fighters, of the train which saved many but was so hot the paint ran off. Edward Pulaski, a forest service ranger, forced his crew of 45 into a mine tunnel in Wallace, Idaho, saving 40 of them. Later, he invented a handy tool for constructing firebreaks which is still used today; it combines an axe with an adze and is called (what else?) a Pulaski.

The nursery had been founded in 1907 by forest ranger Elers Koch, just three years before the onslaught of the flames. The young ponderosa pine and western white pine transplants would have been ready for shipment the next year had they not perished. Now, certainly, replacement seedlings and transplants were needed as never before. But it took time. Seeds were planted and two years later they were moved to transplant beds to grow for two more years. After four years they were ready to be shipped.

Fortunately, the seedling beds survived. The rebuilding of nine buildings, seed beds, transplant beds and irrigation ditches started immediately. By 1915 the nursery stocked three million transplants and three and a half million seedlings of several different species. And the numbers kept on growing. By the early 1940s, 12 million young trees annually were sent to reforest national forests across the country. Research and development resulted in hardy varieties of trees and shipping techniques still used today. It was the largest producer of seedlings in the nation.

Old YT sign at Savenac
Mineral County Museum

The Yellowstone Trail was up and running in Montana by 1915. In fact it was running right through the Savenac Nursery. A U.S. Forest Service brochure describes the presence of the Trail as "opening the nursery to automobile traffic and visitors, which in turn led to new improvements to the appearance of the nursery." Ornamental trees and shrubs were planted and an arboretum was built in 1916. Today's visitor can still see the concrete bridge over Savenac Creek that carried the Trail on the property. By 1932 the state of Montana had abandoned the Trail and built US 10 which now is a frontage road near the nursery.

In 1935 the Civilian Conservation Corps (CCC) did much to improve the site. The young men built a new administration building, more seedling beds, cottages, a seed extractory, cone shed, and packing plant. A new entrance and showplace to welcome visitors was constructed.

Bridge in Savenac carrying the Yellowstone Trail

In 1969 operations were transferred to the nursery in Coeur d'Alene, Idaho. Since then, the U.S. Forest Service has maintained Savenac as an educational and environmental site where various programs are put on for school children. It also is an interpretive center where the public can experience some of the history of the region. The kitchen and bunkhouse and cabins are available for group functions.

In 1996 Passport in Time (PIT) volunteers, "Friends of Savenac," and the Superior, Montana, Ranger District staff began the Herculerean task of restoring the site to its historic appearance. Bunkhouses and residences were painted, the arboretum was maintained, and the rental cabins and welcome center were refurbished. They are still at it.

Today a traveler on the Yellowstone Trail can see a wonderfully restored historic site carrying on the mission of forest preservation set more than 100 years ago. ✿

Yellowstone Trail at Savenac, then

Evelyn Cameron: Shooting the Old West

"I wish I could lead a life worthy to look back upon."
Evelyn Cameron

Christmas comes even to the stark prairie of eastern Montana. In the early 20th century it was a time for real celebration. Farmers hitched up the roan to the sleigh, bundled the family in blankets with heated rocks at their feet. They crunched through the blowing snow to the local gathering place - the school house. Monthly church meetings with the itinerant preacher, school programs, and important local events took place at the school house. It was the place to see neighbors and break the isolation. It was where Mrs. Marks, one of the few Jews in eastern Montana, gave out Christmas presents to the kids. In that treeless landscape it may have been the school that had the only decorated Christmas tree.

Ranches and farms were flung out like stars, broadcast across the wide expanse of the plains. The hundreds of new immigrant farmers with their government-issued half-section were hated by ranchers for their fences and their hopeless future without cattle on these dry lands. But all were united in their belief that they were pioneering individualists, away from any parent body.

The Enlarged Homestead Act of 1909 gave 320 acres of semi-arid land in eastern Montana to anyone willing to cultivate and put up a dwelling. Railroad companies needed population to accompany their westward expansion so they depicted land as marvelously fertile in their unregulated advertising. Thousands came. By the time the Yellowstone Trail was established there in 1913, that fertility was fragile, giving way to the dust of a four-year drought commencing in 1917.

Stories about this hardscrabble farming are familiar, but the lives of the families who peopled that backdrop are not. Thousands of these hapless, hopeful "Honyockers," ranchers, and cowboys and their way of life are now forever immortal-

Cameron carries her heavy
Graflex Camera
Carol Larsen,
Prairie County Museum

ized through the determination and patience of local rancher and photographer Evelyn Cameron. For almost 40 years "Lady" Cameron took amazing pictures of proud, unsmiling homesteaders in front of their humble homes, of cowboys at work on the prairie, and breathtaking close-up shots of animals and birds before the telephoto lens was invented.

Folks around Terry called Evelyn and her husband "Lord and Lady" Cameron in deference to her aristocratic British upbringing. Evelyn's early life could not have been more different from life in eastern Montana, but this adventurous, spirited, tough lady loved the land and the people. When they visited the area on their 1889 honeymoon, the limitless horizon, the peace, and the freedom apparently appealed to her and her impoverished Scottish husband, Ewen. By 1893 they were in their first ranch house near Terry and six miles from what would become the Yellowstone Trail. Ewen raised polo ponies to send back to the aristocracy of England and when that failed, he turned to his first love, ornithology, writing several respected books about birds.

Evelyn was left to run the ranch, but she once wrote, "Manual labor is about all I care about. I like to break colts, brand calves, cut down trees, ride and work in the garden." She enjoyed the solitude of the land and her outings to explore and understand it. Jonathan Raban's book, *Bad Land: An American Romance* (Pantheon, 1996) carries a wonderful eye-witness description of Lord and Lady Cameron at a dinner party in Ismay, Montana. She apparently had a "low, gruff, drawling voice. She regarded [a guest] this way, and then that way. She cocked her head to one side. She rose suddenly - a pillar of hairy, horse-smelling, checkered tweed and said, 'Marvelous face that one.' Lord Cameron offered cigars to

"Honeyockers" pose for Cameron
Carol Larsen, Prairie County Museum

the gentlemen and gave one to Lady Cameron, too. She later recited in her foghorn baritone a poem she had written. After she had left, a guest opined that 'Evelyn can be rather a trial.'"

Evelyn Discovers the Camera

To augment their dwindling income, Evelyn first sold vegetables to railroad section houses, remote ranches, and to cook wagons out on the range. Then she sent for a dry plate glass negative 5x7 Graflex camera and taught herself photography. She was often seen traveling for miles by horseback in ⇨

Cameron commuting to work clutching her camera
Carol Larsen, Prairie County Museum

a scandalous "divided skirt" with glass plates in the sad-dlebags, the heavy camera draped over her shoulder, and a tripod strapped to the horse.

The world of photography had progressed from daguerrotype to wet plate to the "modern" dry plate, Cameron's choice. You needed a big camera and big plates (8" x 4 ½") for large pictures. The camera needed daylight, so there were no twilight shots and there was no zoom lens. Her tripod weighed eight pounds.

Self-taught Cameron at work
Carol Larsen, Prairie County Museum

Evelyn became well-known around Terry so folks trusted her when she was at their ranch or range to photograph them. She posed people and animals outside for better light; it took several seconds for the proper exposure and kids never sat still, and smiles didn't keep smiling that long. She stepped back from her subjects to shoot in order to show the space and proportion that was Montana. Raban says she caught the emptiness and distance and disquieting character of western space. "Nearly all her people looked as if their presence in Montana came as a bewildering surprise to them …" She sold albums at $5.00 each for settlers and cowboys to send to family back home.

The Value of a Picture

Writers have declared her work to possess "spectacular attention to detail," to be a "stunning portrayal," or "startlingly clear." It was that and more. She captured the work-a-day faces and the action of work: of the shepherd driving his sheep, of the cowboys riding or branding, also of family gatherings, of hopeful faces in spite of the isolation and hard work. These photos, along with her detailed diaries, provide a black-and-white view of the reality of a way of life we see little of 100 years later.

The pictures preserve indelible images of American history in that under- reported period between late 19th and early 20th century. "The homestead period was in all respects a

compressed, 'final edition' of the Old West," wrote historian Grant Venerable. Helping to write that 'final edition' was the Yellowstone Trail, bringing the seduction of the outside world to Terry, Montana.

And Then?

When she died, Evelyn left all of her many diaries, 1,800 glass plates, 2,700 original prints, and all her equipment to her friend, Janet Williams. They remained in Janet's dry, dark basement for almost 50 years. Donna Lucey, a former editor of *Time-Life Books*, heard about them in the late 1970s and spent almost a decade going through Cameron's 35 years of diaries, plates, and photos. Six decades after Evelyn's 1929 death, Lucey published them in *Photographing Montana, 1894-1928: The World of Evelyn Cameron* (Montana Historical Society, 1991).

The Montana Historical Society, which now holds the glass plates and most of Cameron's photos, established a Cameron Gallery in downtown Terry, next door to the Prairie County Museum. The Museum is housed in a 1915 bank building at 101 Logan St. They also staff the Cameron Gallery next door in another 1915 building. The Museum has a collection of homesteading tools, a caboose, and rare historic photographs. And you've got to see this! There is a steam-heated, communal four-hole outhouse in the back yard of the Museum. There is an original Yellowstone Trail black "R" painted on the side of the Museum indicating that one had to turn right to follow the Trail. The Museum and Cameron Gallery are open Memorial Day to Labor Day. See pictures on page 138.

Here is an opportunity for personal discovery. Pull off of I-94. Go to the gallery and museum. Immerse yourself in her pictures. Drive around "Cameron country" and explore the expanse. Drive to Ismay on the Yellowstone Trail but gas up first. Discover your own eastern Montana.

And the one-room school house today? Most of them on the old Yellowstone Trail have fallen victim to the elements. A few have been turned into private homes or hauled to museums. They probably saw their last Christmas program around 1940 when school consolidation and busses took over. The next time you see an old school on the Yellowstone Trail, stop and walk around it. Peer into the black, gaping doorway or broken windows and you might still hear a faint "Silent Night" sung by long-ago children. ✿

Evelyn Cameron Gallery, Terry

The Knowlton Cutoff: A Tug of War for the Trail

Prologue

A storm had been threatening by the time we were less than half way across the railroad trestle bridge spanning the roaring current which raced 30 or more feet below. We were less than half way across the bridge, bumping carefully across the ties, with less than eight inches between the tires on one side and the abyss below, when the storm broke with intense fury. The first blasts were so strong that I feared we would be blown off the trestle, there being no guard rail or other protection. The wet rubber tires and the wet ties made our situation precarious, especially since a train was soon due in a direction opposite to that we were going. It seemed that we were hours jolting along since we entered the trestle. Then I heard the whistle of the train in a lull of the storm. I stepped on the accelerator with a prayer on my lips and the car shot ahead the short remaining distance of the trestle. With the aid of a small board the car cleared the track and landed in the ditch just as the train shot by with a scream and a roar which sounded unearthly.

That was A. L. Westgard's memory of crossing the Powder River near Terry in 1912. There was no auto bridge on the Powder River. As he said in his *Tales of a Pathfinder* (1920), he could have driven 50 miles further for a bridge at Mizpah, but he preferred to save time and chance it on the railroad track. Usually, wagons and an occasional auto would ford the mile wide and an inch deep Powder River but the spring rains made it far too dangerous for Westgard to ford.

Westgard had driven his big Pathfinder auto from New York to Seattle in his effort to "find" a northern drivable cross-country route when there were no marked auto routes – or even any really usable roads. Westgard named his New York/Seattle route The Northwest Trail. His trip was sponsored by the AAA, but little attempt was made to make the route a promoted, named trail.

Westgard's tale of his "white knuckle" crossing of the Powder River without a bridge made vivid the dilemma of many a Yellowstone Trail traveler trying to get to Miles City from Ismay or Terry.

In 1913, Eastern Montana Was Not Quite Ready for the Yellowstone Trail

The first known map of the route of the Yellowstone Trail in eastern Montana is in the 1914 *First Year Book*. It shows a very detailed route from North Dakota to Miles City. Detailed, but not entirely possible or, at least, practical. But it is an improvement over the 1912 overall vague plan of routing the Yellowstone Trail: from South Dakota head towards Puget Sound (Seattle), stop at Yellowstone National Park (its namesake) and follow the Milwaukee Road tracks, or others if necessary.

Often, across the country, there was a wagon road next to the railroad tracks and it became the Trail. Other places had major problems, illustrated well by the Marmarth (North Dakota)/Ismay/Terry/Miles City section. There had been,

The Powder River "An inch deep and a mile wide."

essentially, no auto traffic there. Indeed, J. E. Prindle, second President of the Yellowstone Trail Association and Ismay, Montana, resident had to take the train from Terry home to Ismay after a meeting in 1913.

The roads around Terry, and most other areas in the Northwest, developed through use, not construction. In the late 1800s and early 1900s wagons found paths to follow and left tracks in the prairie which were generally used as "farm to market" or to the railroads. The roads that early autoists had for use in eastern Montana were those tracks - the very ones that Westgard probably used. State and federal governments had no involvement, but counties built a few bridges and had "county roads." Long distance (or even relatively short distance) trips were made by train, not auto.

The "prairie trails" were unmarked and were constantly changed by washouts, land owner claims, and whatever, such as the county building of a bridge here rather than there. While the original government survey specified roadways along all section lines, the area terrain had rough areas and many gullies making many section lines impractical for roads. And many section lines were not needed as roads.

The detailed route was often left to local Yellowstone Trail Association members to determine with the expectation that changes would be reported to the officers of the Association so that formal action could be taken at the next executive meeting. It is safe to assume that not all detailed route changes were carefully reported and acted on and recorded. In fact, it can be assumed that locals just moved the route markers, if they existed, or simply directed autoists as they judged best. It must be remembered that no government agency maintained records of the routes of the old named trails.

Westgard rejected fording the Powder, probably remembering his unfortunate experience on the Yellowstone River where he was marooned by high water for 16 days. But fording rivers was a way of life around the unpredictable Powder River even though harrowing stories abounded, including the rumor, and apparently the fact, of quicksand. ⇨

The Mizpah Bridge, built 1926

Continued

1913–Michael Dowling Makes His Pathfinder Trip

In 1913, Michael Dowling, future president of the Yellowstone Trail Association, drove the Trail from his home in Minnesota to Livingston, Montana, and the Yellowstone National Park, acting as the official pathfinder for the Yellowstone Trail. He was accompanied by two other autos but was the driver of his own auto despite his handicaps. See **Trail Tale: Dowling**, page 239.

At Ismay, (the town already a major cattle shipping point and a town that residents believed was to become the Chicago of the West) Dowling had to chose to either follow the planned route of the Yellowstone Trail following rail tracks through Terry and on to Miles City (about 88 miles), or to head southwest through Knowlton to use the Mizpah bridge over the Powder River. That county bridge was long established as a local service bridge, but it was a long way from city or railroad. No services of any kind would be available for the entire 65 miles along poorly developed roads and no train to hale for help.

Nevertheless, the same lack of a bridge over the Powder River near Terry that challenged Westgard, also frustrated Dowling's entourage. Ismay's J. E. Prindle and the businessmen of Terry urged Dowling to drive through Knowlton, then over the existing Powder River bridge at Mizpah and then on to Miles City.

Those businessmen were well aware of the new $35,000 bridge under construction over the Powder just west of Terry which would be ready for service for the "touring season" of 1914. The Trail was then routed to follow the preferred way - along a railroad from Ismay, through Mildred to Fallon, then to Terry and across the new Powder River bridge, and on to Miles City; about 80 miles with no fording necessary and with greater safety.

The Knowlton/Mizpah Route Became the "Cutoff" and Controversy Lingered

But even after the Yellowstone Trail was established following the tracks through Terry, many local folks still preferred to head from Ismay to Knowlton and then over the Mizpah bridge to Miles City. They called the route the Knowlton Cutoff or, simply, the Cutoff.

The old Mizpah bridge was replaced in 1923, was washed out and replaced again in 1926 (to great huzzahs). ⇨

Route 446—Marmarth, N. D., to Miles City, Mont.—143.8 m.
Route Map, page 15.   Reverse Route, No. 1049.

Via Baker, Fallon and Terry. This is a section of the Yellowstone Trail. Poles are painted with a yellow band and black arrow pointing toward Yellowstone Park. Good graded road most of the way to Ismay. A mixture of graded road and good prairie trail between Ismay and Terry. Terry to Miles City good graded road most of the way. Tourists are cautioned not to take the Knowlton cut-off between Ismay and Miles City, even if they are advised to do so by local people. While this cut-off is shorter than the other road, it is forty miles away from a RR. and goes thru a desolate country, with very little chance for supplies or help in case of a breakdown or accident. By following this route according to the following directions the tourist is always close to the RR. and a source of supplies.

The official position of the YT Association was that the route of the YT was through Terry, not Mizpah. The Blue Book publishers got the word.

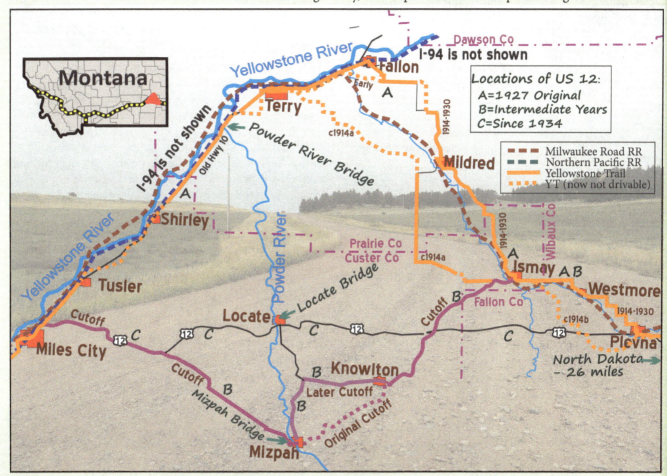

Between '23 and '26 "people forded the river one half mile north of the bridge site when the water was low" reported former Ismay resident Garry Schye.

It was directing Yellowstone Trail traffic to the Cutoff instead of the Trail through Terry that irritated Terryites no end, triggering a two-year newspaper war of accusations and counter-accusations: Ismay accusing Terry of guiding tourists to the northern Red Trail (Westgard's route) and Terry accusing Ismay of routing all to the Cutoff, missing Terry. Ultimatums were issued, vehement denials flew, derisive name-calling ("Phonograph Prindle") occurred. The *Terry Tribune* even lashed out at the Yellowstone Trail Association itself June 18, 1915, stating that Terry residents paid "hundreds of dollars in assessment dues upon the assumption that the Trail would pass through Terry and now find that they have been buncoed."

However, all of the publications of the Yellowstone Trail Association, from beginning to end, list the Terry route as the Trail. Interestingly, however, Gene Garber, a longtime resident of the Ismay area, unearthed from local historical records, a 1927 letter from Founder Joe Parmley to a Terry official. The letter indicates that Association Managing Director, Hal Cooley, apparently had declared that the Trail officially now used the Cutoff and the Terry folk had heard of his statement. After 12 years of relative quiet about the matter, here it cropped up again. Parmley, now in the South Dakota State Highway Commission, hotly denied that the Trail had been moved and acerbically described his growing anger with Cooley.

This modern sign by Gene Garber reads "The Yellowstone Trail Cut Off 1921-1935 From Ismay to Miles City Via Knowlton - Riverview"

The authors interpret the conflict as being the result of the differing outlooks of the two men. The older Parmley believed that an agreement once made was to be unbroken, that upright, honest behavior was sacred. The younger Cooley appears to have been the extraordinarily capable business person who gave priority to developing a successful, modern Yellowstone Trail, nationally known and based on meeting the needs of long-distance travelers. Ideally, the two outlooks could be melded, but the egos of the two successful leaders clashed and, combined with the emergence of government numbered routes, the organization began its slide to an end made real by the Depression.

> The cut-off between Miles City and Ismay is marked and saves 21 miles, but lacks supplies or service and is only advisable in dry weather. Inquire at C. of C. before starting. Gas at Knowlton and Mispah.
>
> *MH-1928* ✿

The controversy over the routes raged for decades, well beyond the life of the Yellowstone Trail Association. Even at the start of the 21st century, there were those who "know" that the "real" Yellowstone Trail was the Cutoff. Indeed, one elderly life-long resident of Ismay to this day still claims that the southern route was superior and was the true Yellowstone Trail. Possibly he heard tales of Michael Dowling going that way and that the 1915 relay race car went that way and because Cooley said so.

The modern Ismay-Terry Road

Epilogue

Westgard's route through North Dakota and west through Terry became known as the Red Trail. It was assimilated by the National Parks Highway in 1915 to compete with the Yellowstone Trail and much of Westgard's route eventually was designated as US 10 and then I-94.

The Yellowstone Trail route coming through Baker, Terry, and Miles City was designated US 12. It lost out on becoming an Interstate primarily because it could not include a state capital. US 12 was moved to its present route through Locate a few years later when the road was built.

The Cutoff was improved piecemeal over the years and during the 1920s took the US 12 name from the Ismay-Terry route. With the building of the 1934 Powder River Bridge at Locate, US 12 moved from both the Cutoff and the Yellowstone Trail alignments. Locate bridge was later abandoned but left in place and can be visited today. And Ismay died. Mostly. As we write this, buildings are actively collapsing and memories are being lost. Chicago of the West it is not. But driving the Cutoff remains one of the very best experiences to sense the past.

These tales might seem quaint to the modern reader. But quaint or not, they reveal a way of building auto transportation routes which is very foreign to us today. One hundred years ago everybody seemed to have "some skin in the game." Personal involvement, personal opinion, personal experience, personal allegiances and the natural environment all played more important roles. ✿

Mizpah Bridge today

North Dakota

Marmarth
Rhame
Bowman
Buffalo Sps
Scranton
Gascoyne
Reeder
Bucyrus
Hettinger
Haynes

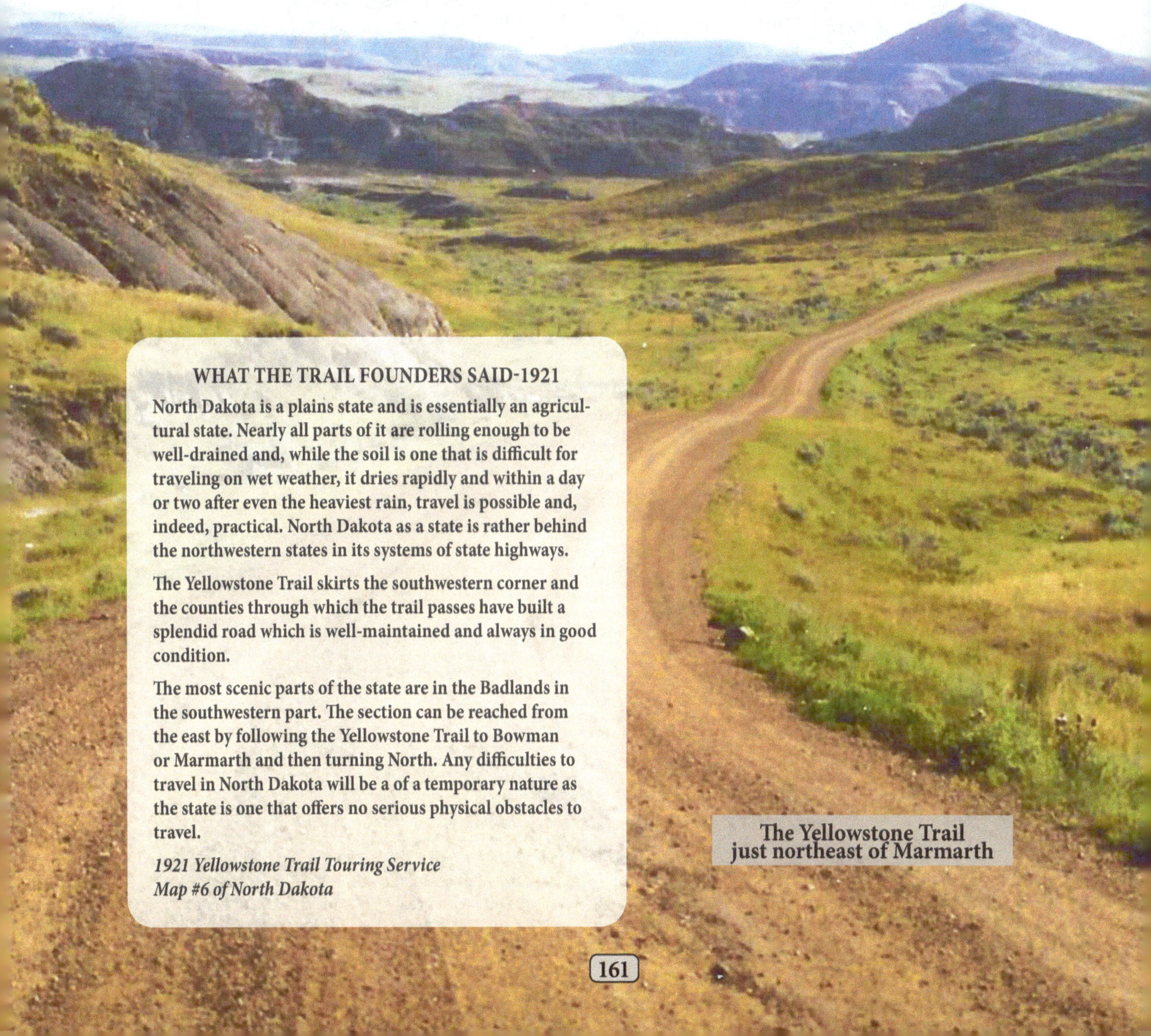

WHAT THE TRAIL FOUNDERS SAID-1921

North Dakota is a plains state and is essentially an agricultural state. Nearly all parts of it are rolling enough to be well-drained and, while the soil is one that is difficult for traveling on wet weather, it dries rapidly and within a day or two after even the heaviest rain, travel is possible and, indeed, practical. North Dakota as a state is rather behind the northwestern states in its systems of state highways.

The Yellowstone Trail skirts the southwestern corner and the counties through which the trail passes have built a splendid road which is well-maintained and always in good condition.

The most scenic parts of the state are in the Badlands in the southwestern part. The section can be reached from the east by following the Yellowstone Trail to Bowman or Marmarth and then turning North. Any difficulties to travel in North Dakota will be a of a temporary nature as the state is one that offers no serious physical obstacles to travel.

1921 Yellowstone Trail Touring Service
Map #6 of North Dakota

The Yellowstone Trail
just northeast of Marmarth

The formation of the Yellowstone Trail Association and its subsequent meetings were fodder for many newspaper column inches in small town weeklies. For instance:

February 28, 1913 Marmarth Mail announced a coming formative local meeting and spent a whole column visualizing better roads for their village, and later repeating Association assurances that "we may all expect to profit by the increased travel over this route by eastern money men." Excited pride in hosting later meetings and effusive adjectives abounded. ❁

Thomas Hall, Secretary of State, distributed on May 1st to the several counties of the state $12,062.60, the accumulation for the month of April for the motor vehicle registration fees. The money is placed to the credit of the county road fund and is expended under the supervision of the County Board Commissioners. To date there have been only 10,771 registrations of motor vehicles with the Secretary of State, estimated to be only about half of the motor vehicles in the state.

May 7, 1914 Adams County Record (Hettinger)

GOING EAST
YOU ARE ENTERING STATE OF N. DAKOTA
OVER THE

Americas oldest and best Transcontinental Highway

Organized 1912 Active in travel Ever since.

A Good road from Plymouth Rock to Puget Sound

DISTANCE IN MILES TO —

MARMARTH, N.D.	6	ABERDEEN, S.D.	325
BOWMAN "	38	MINNEAPOLIS, MINN	646
HETTINGER "	87	CHICAGO	1119
MOBRIDGE, S.D.	223	BOSTON	2188

YOU HAVE BEFORE YOU —

STANDARD STATE GRADED ROAD TO MOBRIDGE, S.D. THEN ALL MAINTAINED GRAVEL, OR PAVING. SEE NEXT SIGN AT S. DAKOTA LINE - 103 MILES

ROUTE FOLDER AND ROAD BULLETIN AT MARMARTH

WE WOULD LIKE TO HEAR FROM YOU

GOOD LUCK

THE YELLOWSTONE TRAIL ASSOCIATION 403 EVANSTON BLDG MINNEAPOLIS

Accurate reproduction of a picture of a 1927 sign at the Montana/North Dakota border taken by John Ridge's father

NORTH DAKOTA FIRST STATE TO MEET TRAIL ASSESSMENT

North Dakota came in for commendation at the recent meeting of the Yellowstone Trail Association at Minneapolis when C. W. Lewis, Executive Director from this state, paid in full $1,075, the amount of the North Dakota 110 mile Yellowstone Trail assessment for the year 1919, thus being the only state along the entire trail to meet its assessment in advance.

March 27, 1919 Adams County Herald (Hettinger)

WAYSIDE

About four miles north of US 12 (on Fort Dilts Road or 162 Ave.) between Marmarth and Rhame is **Fort Dilts State Historic Site**. It is marked with a red "D" on the map. There the visitor will find grave markers and the remains of a sod fortification thrown up in 1864. The cavalry and an immigrant wagon train traveling from Minnesota to the gold fields of Montana were surrounded by Sioux. With oxen and a plow, a six foot high two foot thick sod wall was thrown up. The siege lasted 16 days before help came. The fort was named after Jefferson Dilts, a soldier who died in the conflict. There are informative panels and an artist's interpretative picture at the site.

The present alignment of US 12 between Marmarth and Rhame was probably created in the early 1930s but may have carried the Yellowstone Trail for a short time before that.

Vista along the Trail in North Dakota

Fort Dilts with great views and a sense of history

INTRODUCING THE YELLOWSTONE TRAIL IN NORTH DAKOTA:
PEACE GARDEN STATE

"The highway is not simply a road. It is not simply a surface. It is the assurance of the civilizing influence of better communication between sections."

North Dakota Highway Commission

In *Scranton 1908-1983* (the town of Scranton's 75th anniversary book), the question is asked: Why did so many people move west? The authors of the book concluded that people responded to the many large advertising posters by railroads and land companies which described new horizons and opportunities possible on cheap land. In North Dakota's case it was the Milwaukee Road and the Western Land Securities Company advertisements that drew folks.

From the beginning it was well understood that the route of the Yellowstone Trail, as it was extended from its origins in central South Dakota, was to follow the route of the Milwaukee Road going through the many towns created by that railroad as far the Yellowstone River in Montana.

Thus, in North Dakota the Trail includes 100 miles across the far southwest corner of the state. The early settlers and representatives of the ten small towns along that 100 miles boosted the Trail early on. The question is: why did the few citizens, owning so very few automobiles and who were gathered together in towns little more than a decade old, get excited about supporting a transcontinental auto road through their 100 miles? Perhaps interest was raised when several drivers stopped at Marmarth while crossing the Badlands by auto in 1910.

One of their own, O. T. Peterson of Hettinger, compiled the data for the 1914 *First Year Book of the Twin Cities-Aberdeen-Yellowstone Park Trail Association*, the association for which he was Secretary-Treasurer. He wrote about North Dakota:

> The Trail through Adams County is in fair condition. One can drive a car through the entire county on high gear without once dropping into intermediate or low. Bowman County shows unusual Trail enthusiasm this year. The county commissioners let contracts for five miles; the citizens of the village of Bowman subscribed $1089 for the Trail.

> To guide the tourists, the Trail is marked mostly with stones painted chrome yellow, or telegraph and telephone poles have a band of yellow. Nearby White Butte, South Dakota, has used natural cone-shaped or columnar sandstone. They are about nine feet high. [Note: The geologic term for them is hoodoo.] Trail enthusiasm has reached a great height.

The route in North Dakota was among herds of cattle and flocks of sheep grazing on the hardy prairie grasses and scattered brown-topped buttes. Near the western end the route passes through the southern part of the Badlands where ever-changing colors and shadows still form a background of weird beauty. That route is, today, US 12.

Considering some dates is important here. The Milwaukee Road was extended through this area of homesteading in 1907-08. The towns were created primarily for the building activities and promises about the future by the Milwaukee Road. The Yellowstone Trail was extended here in 1913. Yet there were enough cars, brought in by the railroad, to get excited about a long-distance auto route! Change was dominant.

The Trail was described to the readers of the Yellowstone Trail Association's 1916 *Route Folder* thus:

> The road across North Dakota is particularly good, part of it being designated by road men as ideal country road. The road is splendidly marked the entire distance. The Little Missouri River is crossed just before entering Marmarth. In times of low water, fording is easy, and only cools the tires a bit. In times of freshet, a splendid ferry is on duty, and there are no troubles.

They did not produce a 1918 *Route Folder* (apparently because of World War I) but the 1917 and 1919 *Route Folders* say virtually the same with the language about fording the river replaced by the announcement of a "new steel bridge."

The Yellowstone Trail Association was able to progress in its goal of achieving better roads for tourists by pressing the argument of state aid, available to some extent, finally, to counties of North Dakota with a 1914 state constitution amendment. The Association then pressed the argument of federal aid available from the Federal Aid Road Act of 1916.

The WPA wrote about North Dakota almost 90 years ago and the descriptions they wrote then could easily apply to the North Dakota of today:

> A state of unbounded plains and hills and Badlands – elbowroom. Superb sunsets. High winds and tumbleweed. Little towns crowded on Saturday night, and busy cities shipping out products. Soft, fragrant spring days. The sad, slow wail of the coyote. Endless facets are apparent in the temper and tenor of life.

In 2013, the North Dakota state governor was motivated to officially recognize the Trail in Adams and Bowman counties by allowing Yellowstone Trail signs to be posted on those 100 miles. This was accomplished by fans of the Trail from Hettinger. ✿

YT in the
North Dakota Badlands

The shown mileage between Marmarth and Rhame is inaccurate because of the ambiguities of the early route of the YT in that area. The shown mileages still serve their primary purpose of coordinating places on the map with the mile-by-mile text.

Trail Day June 20, 1914 Marmarth, North Dakota

MARMARTH'S WORK ON THE YELLOWSTONE TRAIL

The national office of the Trail Association set May 22 as "Trail Day" along the whole Trail from the Twin Cities to the National Yellowstone Park. Whole towns were to go out on the Trail and drag it or patch it or even build bits to help the county.

June 12, 1914 Marmarth Mail

Note: And they did! Read more about Trail Day in **Trail Tale: YTA,** page 2.

The red "A" on the map identifies the location of this old directional sign with the words "Yellowstone Trail" and an arrow facing west. Some now interpret the sign as indicating that the Yellowstone Trail followed the road near the sign, but all old map evidence suggests the sign indicated the direction to travel to get to the YT from that sign.

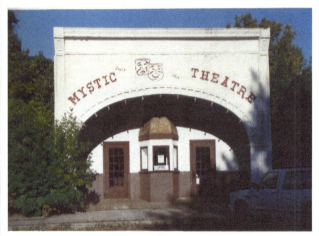
Historic Mystic Theater, Marmarth

MARMARTH IS TO HAVE NEW THEATRE BUILDING
NEW BUILDING GOING UP TO BE CONSTRUCTED ESPECIALLY FOR MOVING PICTURE THEATRE.

March 6, 1914 Marmarth Mail

MYSTIC THEATRE OPENS

It showed "Out of the Dust," a film based on Frederic Remington pictures that came to life and moved.

April 24, 1914 Marmarth Mail.

One 1923 source map suggests the YT was located at the intersection of modern 167 Ave. and 74 St. Generally, maps of the period do not definitively determine the historic alignment.

The original route of the YT west of Marmarth is not clear and the inspection of modern satellite views suggest several possible alignments.

When last we drove 83 St, we noted poor gravel, but like a 1915 road. Do not take when wet.

The drive northwest of Marmarth along or near the original route is a nice drive today, a semi-badlands in places. Many roads are not marked, just as in 1920.

Marmarth Tourist Camp

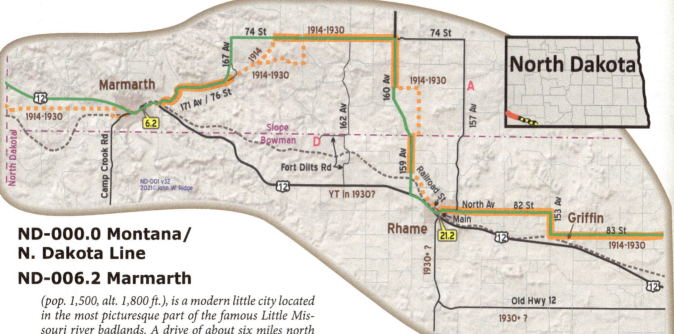

ND-000.0 Montana/ N. Dakota Line

ND-006.2 Marmarth

(pop. 1,500, alt. 1,800 ft.), is a modern little city located in the most picturesque part of the famous Little Missouri river badlands. A drive of about six miles north of town takes one to the foot of Pretty butte, one of the most fantastic badland formations. There are extensive camping grounds in Marmarth. BB1921-9

As the tourist nears Marmarth the Badlands of North Dakota are reached, these being one of the most curious natural formations; very interesting and picturesque. WPA-ND

Marmarth is at the confluence of Little Beaver Creek, Hay Creek, and the Little Missouri River. Known as the "city of trees," Marmarth is almost an oasis in the treeless Badlands country. The town had its inception in 1902, and grew rapidly following the advent of the Milwaukee R. R. in 1907. Proximity to the Little Missouri and its tributaries has not always been advantageous; the town has been flooded five times. Dikes have been put up around the town adjacent to the streams. WPA-ND

Marmarth is a shipping point for cattle brought overland from range grounds in this State, Montana, and South Dakota. The stockyards, which cover an area of 45 acres, and contain 86 pens and 15 loading chutes, are built on the site of the old O-X (0 Bar X) ranch. Nearby, on Hay Creek, still stands the squat old ranch house in which Theodore Roosevelt was once a guest. WPA-ND

It is a freight division of the C. M. & St. Paul R. R. Cozy Cafe is well liked. Marmarth Camp, 50c, wood stoves; a nice site on river.

ST. CHARLES HOTEL is best; 30 rooms, 6 with r. w., 3 with bath; sgl. $l-$2; dbl. $1.50-$2.50; with bath $3.

PHILIPS MOTOR CO., Ford, owner is master mechanic. Fine for all cars. Labor $1.50; phone 42 until 10 p. m. MH-1928.

In 1911 Marmarth was the largest city in North Dakota on the Milwaukee Road. By 1917 it was the only town in North Dakota to have natural gas piped in for both commercial and domestic use.

The problem of crossing the Little Missouri River at Marmarth yielded many a story including the fording of the river in 1913 by Michael Dowling and the fund-raising efforts of the Yellowstone Trail Association. For the stories and pictures of the crossing, see **Trail Tale: Marmarth Bridge**, page 174.

After a long period of stagnation, Marmarth, just south of the Little Missouri National Grassland, seems to be enjoying a renaissance of sorts. The *Bismarck Tribune* says,

> Population is 136 as of the 2010 census, but that doesn't take into account the folks who drive through on Highway 12, the oil workers who drift into town and the paleontology scholars and volunteers who participate in summer dinosaur projects.

305 First St. W (US 12/Yellowstone Trail). **Unique Antique Auto Museum**. The Unique Antique Car Museum showcases its 50 refurbished antique vehicles, a miniature car collection and a vast collection of old license plates from 1916, and a 1920s die cast toy collection.

51 Main St. The **Mystic Theatre** was built in 1914, and is now owned by the Marmarth Historical Society. It has a stuccoed exterior and seats 187 (another source says 109 seats). It was unusual for its time, as it was specifically designed for showing "motion pictures" 13 years before "talkies" happened. It opened April 22, 1914, and was packed.

It is listed on the National Registry of Historic Places. The Society still operates the theatre and hosts a cowboy poetry gathering in September of every year, along with local talent and visiting entertainers. In 2014 there was a big 100th birthday bash for the ediface.

118 N Main St. **Pastime Bar** (one block north of US 12/Yellowstone Trail) or, more formally, Pastime Club and Steak House. Don't be scared off by the name. It's just a cowboy bar that serves great food and has creative participatory entertainment. We ate there a few years ago and had the best, largest hamburgers we ever ate.

May 22, 1914 was decreed by Trail founder Joe Parmley and Association officers as "Trail Day," a day when all able-bodied men were expected to get out and work on the Trail - dragging, ditching, routing, using teams to build road foundations, and painting posts and rocks along the Trail yellow. Women were expected to feed the men. Bowman was particularly active that day. All stores were closed from 9 to 4 and about 40 women fed 500 men, including people "who just came to town." With few other entertainments available to rural villages, activities like this became excitement personified ⚙

The village of Bowman has raised a fund of over $1,000 to be used on the Yellowstone Trail.
May 7, 1914 The Ward County Independent (Minot, ND)

Bowman county expects to obtain $8,000 federal highway aid and will appropriate as much more from county funds, all of which is to be expended next spring in improving the Yellowstone Trail.
September 18, 1917 The Bismarck Tribune from Bowman

CITIZENS INTERESTED IN THE COUNTY AIDING TRAIL ASSOCIATION TELL COMMISSIONERS SO

A meeting was held in the courthouse Monday afternoon for the purpose of considering the county granting aid to the highway known as the Twin City - Yellowstone Trail. This amount to be expended in work on the trail in Bowman county. All present were in favor of the movement with the possible exception of the county board chairman who did not seem to know where he was at or when he got there.
May 29, 1913 Bowman County Pioneer

~~~~~~~~~~~~~~~~~~~~~~~~~~

The surveyors for the Yellowstone Trail have been working in this vicinity this week, and have passed through the town, coming from the east. They are placing stakes which show the route the Trail will follow.
June 26, 1913 The Rhame Review

~~~~~~~~~~~~~~~~~~~~~~~~~~

The Trail is now officially recognized by the National Highway Association and henceforth will be shown on all of their maps.
January 29, 1914 The Rhame Review

The Rhame Commercial Club has been planning to have a Trail Day May 22, when all those interested in building the Yellowstone Park Trail will come together and hear dissertations on road building.
May 19, 1914 The Bismarck Tribune
Note: Come to hear dissertations?! Those attending were in for a big surprise. May 22 was the date of the first Trail Day wherein townspeople along the whole Trail were encouraged to go out and help patch up or construct the Trail with teams of horses in their area. No mention of actual work to be done was made in that newspaper. *The Bismarck Tribune*, almost 200 miles from Rhame, certainly misunderstood.

YELLOWSTONE TRAIL MEET HELD AT RHAME LAST WEEK

... every town along the Trail in North Dakota was represented by the 65 attendees. D. W. Williams, Division Engineer of the State Highway Commission was present and promised considerable assistance in the way of state aid for the Trail next year.
December 9, 1920 The Rhame Review

BOWMAN COUNTY'S YELLOWSTONE TRAIL AUXILIARY [CHAPTER] HOLDS INTERESTING MEETING

E. E. Hogoboom gave a short address on the benefits of good roads, laying particular stress on the benefit derived by farmers. He showed that hundreds of dollars could be saved in the hauling of the farmers' produce to market alone. He also made the proposition that he would personally build one mile of the six miles connecting his farm with the Yellowstone Trail and make it according to specifications of the Trail, if the farmers in his neighborhood would build the other five miles.
April 9, 1914 Bowman County Pioneer

The men of Bowman turn out for Trail Day

ND

Marmarth Research Foundation in the Hell Creek Formation near Marmarth. Dr. Tyler Lyson of the Smithsonian has been digging for dinosaur bones and fossils in this Badlands area his entire life. His 501(c)(3) Foundation has attracted other professional university paleontologists. It is entirely private, but amateurs are invited to dig, for a fee, and careful attention is made to maintain scientific integrity. The site includes tents, a lecture hall/ dining facility and a lab. There is an office in Marmarth.

ND-021.2 Rhame

(3,184 alt., 356 pop.), named for M. D. Rhame, district engineer of the Milwaukee R. R. when it was established in 1907, has the highest elevation of any town in the State. It is in a high valley between two large, flat, scoria-capped buttes. WPA-ND

A 1924 Bulletin lists the Buttes Hotel and the Yellowstone Trail Garage.

Rhame's first post office (1908) was a derailed boxcar. Before this, the mail was brought by stage and placed under the rock ledges of Post Office Butte for people to pick up their mail. The townsfolk celebrated their 100th anniversary in 2008.

SE corner of Main & 2nd Sts. is a **log cabin** built in 1912 as a whimsical-style gas station. It was most recently used as a community museum. The walls were made of logs from a camp at Ekalaka where they were assembled before moving to Rhame. The roof is covered with scoria rock and extended on the west side so as to cover the service area. Note the height of the trees in that area in this picture. No car has approached the building in many decades (see picture below).

As you travel east from Rhame you will notice less of a "badlands" scene, fewer volcano-like buttes and more rolling hills and cattle. You might even see a few oil pumps.

Though rustic, a warm-hearted welcome

🚗 The record is unclear about the use of the road going south from Rhame and then east to Bowman, the old US 12. It is doubtful that it opened before the early 1930s and used by the YT.

ND-038.0 Bowman

A live town in a grain and cattle raising area. Meals at Rudolph Hotel. Bowman Motor Co. is modern Ford Agency. Free camp site, no shade. Good new pay camp to be built.

RUDOLPH HOTEL is partly modern; 3 rooms with bath, dbl. $2.75; dbl. without r. w. $1.75.

MH-1928. A 1924 Bulletin lists two more garages.

12 First Ave. NE. The **Pioneer Trails Regional Museum** is a regional research and repository museum reaching from within 100 miles of Bowman to include parts of Montana and South Dakota. As such, it has programs available on anthropology, archaeology, paleontology, botany, and others. Part of their mission is to conserve local historical artifacts and fossils. [Note: Western South Dakota and Western North Dakota are prime areas for organized dinosaur digging.] Guided tours of fossil sites are available as well as "hands on" digging. It is a sharp, energetic museum with a broad vision, a sod house, and a good book selection in its small shop. We stop in whenever we are in the area to view changing displays and their list of scientific guest speakers. Step into their small back yard and you will see a Yellowstone Trail sign.

If you are in Bowman in early September, you might see their annual Threshing Bee and display of 100-year-old farm equipment such as the huge Reeves Steam Tractor. Actual threshing happens and you can volunteer to experience what farming was like in Yellowstone Trail days.

Display garden of Bowman Museum
with modern YT sign near an original hoodoo YT sign

About 30 miles north of Bowman is an oddity of nature. The Burning Coal Vein is a badlands landscape still in the making. For at least 200 years and until very recently a fire was smoldering in the coal layer several feet underground. As the burning turned the soil above it to ash, it collapsed, leaving large cracks in the surface of the badlands. The phenomenon still occurs on occasion, but the U.S. Forest Service has a policy of mechanically extinguishing the coal veins where they're burning on the Little Missouri National Grasslands in order to prevent grass fires. A visitor might still see escaping gasses and slumping soil.

ND

Gascoyn boosters on parade

Written for Feb. 6 issue but necessarily omitted on account of lack of electricity with which to operate linotype. A delegation of Trail boosters from Marmarth traveled to Scranton to attend the annual state convention of the Yellowstone Trail Association and helped to mold legislation for the future conduct of this great Pioneer Transatlantic [sic] Highway. The entire delegation was shown through the huge briquetting plant. Then that indomitable worker, H. O. Cooley, the Association General Manager, gave a detailed and concise report of last year's business and outlined the work for the present year. Association President Wiley gave a talk on the benefits derived from the Trail.

February 13, 1920 Marmarth Mail

Gascoyne had two newspapers during the Yellowstone Trail era: the *Yellowstone Trail Pennant* and the *Gascoyne Gazette*. The latter published the following on Oct. 13, 1915: It is reported that with every 1916 Model Ford sold, two squirrels will be furnished to run along behind and pick up the nuts as they drop off. ✿

J. W. Parmley of the South Dakota Development League visited Scranton and viewed the new process of briquetting lignite coal. He was enthusiastic over the accomplishment and said "It is the greatest thing for the entire west in a generation."

May 10, 1917 Scranton Register

Note: Parmley also founded the Yellowstone Trail Association five years previously.

ANNUAL MEETING STATE TRAIL ASSOCIATION
Meeting to be Held at Scranton Oct. 30.

October 10, 1924 Marmarth Mail

SOUTHWESTERN COUNTIES WILL BE REPRESENTED AT ROAD MEETING

Plans will be laid at a meeting in Reeder to send delegates to the annual meeting of the Yellowstone Trail Association which will be held in Minneapolis October 24 and 25.

September 29, 1913 Evening Times (Grand Forks, ND)

Bargain Day in downtown early Scranton

GET BUSY ON TRAIL DAY

Great preparations are being made in North Dakota for Trail Day May 22. Gascoyne is having three miles prepared. Gascoyne is also having posts made for markers to be erected on Trail Day.

May 14, 1914 Bowman County Pioneer

~~~~~~~~~~~~~~~~~~~~~~~~~

Officers of the Yellowstone Trail Association have designated May 22 as "trail day," and have made a plea for as many men as possible to work on the trail that day, smoothing the road, etc.

May 15, 1914 The Christian Science Monitor (byline Reeder, ND).

Popular center parking in Scranton

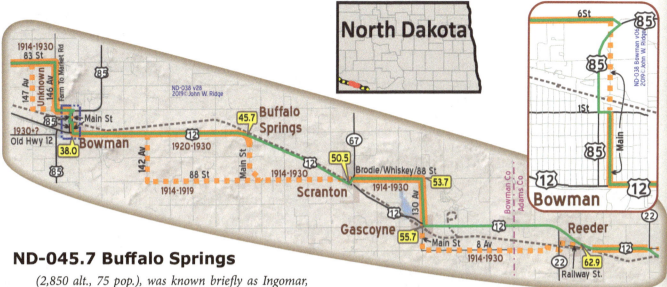

ND-045.7 Buffalo Springs

(2,850 alt., 75 pop.), was known briefly as Ingomar, but in 1907 received its present name, suggested by the nearby springs which once served as a watering place for the bison that roamed the plains. WPA-ND

gas, supplies and repair shop. Small free camp. MH-1928

ND-050.5 Scranton

pop. 450; in a grain district; has several active coal mines. Scranton Garage is best; open until 10 p. m. ALBION HOTEL not modern, but clean rooms; dbl. $1.50; water and bath in halls. Good meals 50c MH-1928

Named in 1907 for Scranton, Pennsylvania, because both were coal mining towns. Clay suitable for brick manufacture was discovered and today's Yellowstone Trail traveler may see remnants of 1907 brick work on downtown buildings. Briquetting lignite coal was a big operation.

Many grain elevators today suggest a major grain shipping center.

ND-055.7 Gascoyne

(2,759 alt., 97 pop.), Northwest of town is a railroad Reservoir (swimming and picnicking facilities). WPA-ND

pop. 90. Gas and small garage. MH-1928

Pause as you travel the Trail. Look at Gascoyne, population 12. They have erected a small memorial to the Trail. It is a limestone hoodoo, found easily in these parts, painted yellow with a new Yellowstone Trail sign attached, flanked by two flags. Not bad for a very small village!

Gascoyn's current memorial to the YT

The name of the town in 1907 was Fischbein, a hamlet founder, but was changed to Gascoyne, a railroad foreman, in 1909 because "Fischbein" was too difficult for Morse Code spelling.

The YT here in 1927 is but a "prairie trail."
B. Danielson from her father's travel diary

ND-062.9 Reeder

A typical farm center. Oelker's Hotel is best; not modern. Free camp with stoves and tables. OELKER'S GARAGE, Ford, and good on all cars. MH-1928

Reeder had a population if 181 in the 2000 census. It, like many other towns, got its name from a Milwaukee Road railroad employee. A strain of wheat has been named after the town.

Reeder citizens have repurposed their old school, which they say has retained its integrity from the first graduating class, 1916, to the last, 1993. It has retained the gym for physical workouts and transformed 12 rooms into motel-type rooms for hunting parties, wedding parties and any other overnight groups. Space is also available for quilting retreats, auction sales, etc. And what does this do for today's Yellowstone Trail traveler? You could stop in, shoot some pool, exercise a little and see what's cookin'. Quite a creative idea for a small town to stay vibrant. It includes the Dakota Prairie Enrichment Center, a 501(c)(3) organization.

🚗 Just to the west of Bowman 83 St. and 146 Ave. were, together, named "Farm to Market Rd." a general name given to early regional roads.

🚗 The 1921 ND maps seem to indicate that the main route (and thus the YT) followed 147 Ave., now not usable.

🚗 It is no longer possible to travel between 6th St. and the railroad on the Main St. route of the YT. So just south of the railroad, use 1st St. between Main St. and 1st Ave.

ND

Hettinger has a special place in the annals of the history of the Yellowstone Trail for this was the home of Mr. O. T. Peterson, the organization's secretary/treasurer in 1914. That year the organization published the Association's *First Year Book*. As it turned out, it was also its last. There are extant copies of this unique book - an amalgam of minutes of a 1914 meeting of the Yellowstone Trail Association and articles boosting the member towns. The many advertisements of 1914 products make the book look like an early Sears Roebuck catalog. We have republished this 96-page archival gem with annotations. ✿

The engineers have been busy during the week staking out the Yellowstone east of Hettinger. They have completed the work west of Haynes. Stones along the roadside have been painted yellow and the telephone poles along the way have been converted into Yellowstone Trail guide posts.
May 22, 1913 The Call (Reeder)

DR. JOHNS CONSIDERS CALLING GOOD ROADS MEETING IN NEAR FUTURE

Dr. Johns, the North Dakota member of the committee of four whose duty it is to provide ways and means for the construction of the Twin City to Yellowstone Park Trail, is considering calling a Good Roads convention at Hettinger to increase the enthusiasm and to work out more minutely plans under which the proposed highway may be built and for starting agitation for state and national aid for this particular highway.
December 12, 1912 Adams County Record
Note: This was two months after the Lemmon meeting at which they wrote bylaws, and only eight months since Joe Parmley called an initial group together at Ipswich, South Dakota. This shows the perceived urgency in getting a through road, and how large a role private individuals played in the Trail's ultimate success.

In 1912 the only national aid possible would be through post road aid (RFD mail). In 1916 post road aid was expanded to include many more auto roads.

Dr. Johns held his big meeting in Hettinger in 1912. There were at least six front page articles in three newspapers about the coming event and the summary conclusions. One had inch high letters screaming at the reader. Excitement was high at this first-of-a-kind event. Helping to construct a road and form a national road organization - being a cog in a great machine, yet benefiting your own village was effervescing stuff. ✿

Each member of the executive committee is expected to organize an auxiliary organization in each of the counties in his state through which the proposed highway passes, and with these organizations work out ways and means for the highway construction.
October 10, 1912 Adams County Record
Note: This article, written at the close of the Lemmon, South Dakota, trail association formation meeting, spelled out the job for each attendee. Hettinger's Dr. John Johns took that challenge seriously.

As happened in other Trail towns, the local newspapers engendered much excitement about the coming Trail Day wherein everybody living along the Trail was expected to get out on one day to patch it up or help with construction. About 700 people turned out at Hettinger for lunch and sports. But how many actually worked on the road?? Another Trail Day was decreed for September 3, 1920 resulting in the same bruhaha in the press, energizing the citizens.
May 21, 22 and June 18, 1914. Adams County Record

Trail Day workers near Hettinger on April 27, 1914

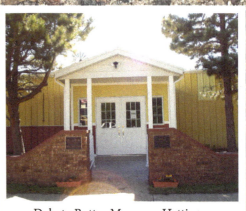
Dakota Buttes Museum, Hettinger

At the Yellowstone Trail meeting in Adams County a resolution was passed endorsing the bill in the legislature requiring road taxes to be paid in cash, and all road improvements to be done on contract.
January 28, 1913 Bismarck Daily Tribune
Note: Joe Parmley had been demanding that in 1907 when he was in the South Dakota legislature. He was hooted down.

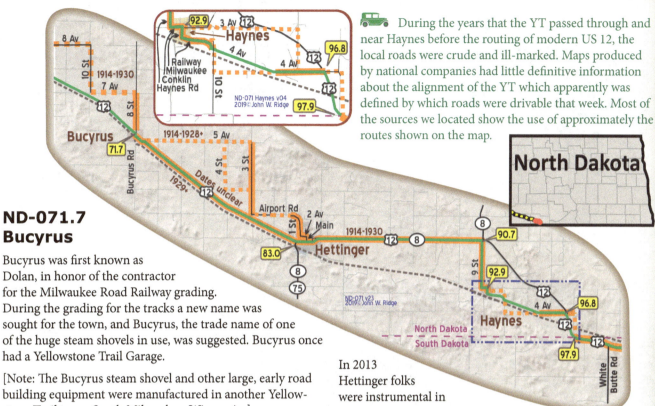

During the years that the YT passed through and near Haynes before the routing of modern US 12, the local roads were crude and ill-marked. Maps produced by national companies had little definitive information about the alignment of the YT which apparently was defined by which roads were drivable that week. Most of the sources we located show the use of approximately the routes shown on the map.

ND-071.7 Bucyrus

Bucyrus was first known as Dolan, in honor of the contractor for the Milwaukee Road Railway grading. During the grading for the tracks a new name was sought for the town, and Bucyrus, the trade name of one of the huge steam shovels in use, was suggested. Bucyrus once had a Yellowstone Trail Garage.

[Note: The Bucyrus steam shovel and other large, early road building equipment were manufactured in another Yellowstone Trail town, South Milwaukee, Wisconsin.]

The population of Bucyrus was 27 in the 2010 census. The town was struck by a wind-fueled wildfire on October 18, 2012. Thankfully two dozen residents of Bucyrus were evacuated before the fire and there were no injuries. However, much of Bucyrus was lost in the fire.

ND-083.0 Hettinger

(pop. 1,000, alt. 2,400 ft.). There are a great many interesting rock formations in this section worthy of note. On the north side of town are some high buttes capped with rock containing fossils of imprints of leaves, as perfect in outline as the day they were deposited there. There is a lake at the edge of town where a swim may be enjoyed. BB1921-9

THE YELLOWSTONE HOTEL steam heat and r. w. in all rooms; sgl. $1.50-$2; dbl. $2; 3 rooms with bath $3

[Note: There was also a Yellowstone Garage listed in 1924.]

THOMPSON AUTO CO. is best for heavy cars; skilled men and modern bldg. Labor $1; ph. 17 until 10:30.

HETTINGER AUTO CO., Ford; large and modern. Ph. 24 until 10 p. m. MH-1928

At Hettinger, one can get from the rocks on the buttes numerous beautiful imprints of leaves, also some fossils. On the side of the road east of Hettinger lie several petrified stumps. Sections of petrified trees can be found in abundance in this neighborhood.

As in the Yellowstone Trail days, the scenery here still offers the traveler broad plateaus, majestic buttes, rolling prairie and wide, windswept vistas. This book encourages the reader to experience the Yellowstone Trail as much as possible. Appreciating scenery is part of that experience.

In 2013 Hettinger folks were instrumental in getting state representatives to officially recognize the whole of US 12 in North Dakota (100 miles) as a "Memorable Highway in the State of North Dakota." The route is now marked with Yellowstone Trail signs. In the fall of 2016 the *Adams County Record* featured five articles which traced in depth the emergence of the Yellowstone Trail through Adams County and Hettinger "in an effort to increase awareness of this historical roadway."

400 11th St. S. **Dakota Buttes Museum** is a complex of four redesigned buildings and outdoor exhibits displaying more than a century of life and times in Adams County. While you are there, look at the Yellowstone Trail kiosk and ask about Mr. O. T. Peterson and Rev. George Kenniston, two very early officers of the Trail Association. Also, ask about the self-guided tour brochure called Buffalo Trails in the Dakota Buttes which takes in 10 historic buffalo sites as well as current buffalo ranches.

ND-092.9 Haynes

Nearing the status of a ghost town, Haynes is a pleasant place to explore a bit and see a well maintained Yellowstone Trail hoodoo marker in the center of town (below). A "hoodoo" is a wind-formed obelisk of sandstone. The community keeps it painted yellow.

ND-097.9 N. Dakota/S. Dakota Line

Haynes still proudly displays its YT marker.

The obelisk marks a time when humble Haynes had bragging rights. It was where the nation's first cross-country trail for automobiles entered the state on its torturous journey from coast-to-coast. Old timers told of taking teams of horses and wagons out to the buttes in search of rounded pieces of sandstone that had dislodged from horizontal formations. This "hoodoo" has endured over 100 years. As you face this hoodoo, look to your left and forward a bit. There you will see a small band shell, somewhat obscured, but still there after how many years!?

September of 2010, Bismarck Tribune

An original YT marker stands in Hettinger.

YELLOWSTONE TRAIL IS POPULAR WITH TOURISTS
MARMARTH, NORTH DAKOTA
Over 31,030 long distance tourists have passed over the North Dakota division of the Yellowstone Trail in 1922.
November 17, 1922 Bemidji (Minnesota) Daily Pioneer

TRAIL BENEFIT BALL A GREAT SUCCESS
They raised $600 to help build the Trail locally.
May 22, 1914 Marmarth Mail

October 14, 1921 Three or more newspapers all carried long explanations of the agenda of the North Dakota state meeting of the Yellowstone Trail Association to be held in Reeder November 7th. North Dakota's dues assessment would be reduced "owing to bad conditions in this section." This collection of newspapers shows the great interest newspapers showed in all things related to the Yellowstone Trail, and in a certain consideration for stressed members, whatever those "bad conditions in this section" were. ✿

There is an eighteen mile stretch of road on the North/South Dakota border of which there is some difficulty in construction owing to the splitting of section lines in South Dakota. The matter is now in the hands of the attorney general ... in the matter of whether or not this state line is suitable for public highways the same as any other section line.
June 11, 1913 Aberdeen Daily News

YELLOWSTONE CHANGE UP TO NATIONAL DIRECTORS
The effort made by Glendive and North Dakota towns along the Red Trail to have the course of the Yellowstone Trail changed was voted down by a unanimous vote.
December 13, 1923 Adams County Register (Hettinger)
Note: Glendive boosters had tried to steal the trail since 1914 but failed. Then, a Glendive booster had cried, "That trail will certainly never enter Montana through Fallon or Baker." The Trail certainly did enter through Baker.

Haynes once had the Trail Garage & Cafe. ✿

September 1952. A large celebration was held spanning the miles from Marmarth west to Baker on US 12 upon the occasion of that span of highway being oiled. Three thousand people showed up for the traveling celebration from Marmarth to the free food in Baker. 1952 and they are only oiling gravel on a reasonably major U.S. highway!! ✿

FIRE RAZES BUSINESS SECTION OF HAYNES
Five business buildings and their contents were destroyed by the flames. All structures on the east side of Main St., with the exception of the pool hall and the hotel, were wiped out.
March 12, 1926 Marmarth Mail

NATIONAL AID FOR PARK TRAIL THROUGH SLOPE COUNTY
PROJECT INCLUDES AN OVERHEAD CROSSING OVER MILWAUKEE TRACKS HERE

Some 32 miles of federal highway No. 12 in Bowman and Adams counties are to be graveled.

January 17, 1930 Marmarth Mail

Note: At last it seems that this forgotten corner of North Dakota gets some attention, but still only gravel in 1930, two months before the Yellowstone Trail Association dissolved.

FRANK MIELKE TO CARRY LETTER

Another Great Relay Race from Boston to Seattle to be staged by the Yellowstone Trail Boosters. The Yellowstone Trail Association is to stage another great Relay Event next month when it will attempt to get a letter through by automobile from Boston to Seattle in a time limit of 120 hours. … a challenge was issued to the Lincoln Highway or any other transcontinental line to enter into a contest with the Yellowstone Trail in such an event but the challenge was not accepted, and now the Trail Association has decided to stage the event alone.

August 25, 1916 The Marmarth Mail

Note: For a more full account, see **Trail Tale: 1916 Race**, page 416.

A large Bucyrus gathering near the YT garage (at left)
Mary Rowley

WAYSIDE

About 10 miles east of Hettinger on US 12 (Yellowstone Trail) is a roadside display overlooking the site of the Last Great Buffalo Hunt by the Teton Lakota Sioux in 1882. Some say that the 50,000 buffalo gathered on the then-bigger Standing Rock Indian Reservation to avoid white hunters and that Col. McLaughlin supplied the Sioux with rifles with which they killed 2,000 buffalo in one day, 5,000 total in three days in an area from Haynes to west of Hettinger and north. By 1883 only 10,000 buffalo remain of this herd.

By 1911 lengthy automobile trips were commonplace.
A History of the Automobile in North Dakota to 1911 by Carl Larson in the North Dakota History Journal of the Northern Plains, 1987, Vol. 54, No. 4.

Theodore Roosevelt killed his first grizzly bear a short distance west of Marmarth on the Little Beaver, and just north of the town on the Little Missouri he shot his first buffalo. Many years later, when he was campaigning for the Presidency, on an appearance in Minneapolis he met a Marmarth pioneer. When informed the man was from Marmarth, at the mouth of Little Beaver Creek, the President exclaimed, "A town there? Do you have boats tied to your back doors?" He had visited the site only at times of high water. WPA-ND ✿

2018 Celebration of dedication of new YT interpretive sign and hoodoo marker, Hettinger

Marmarth Bridge

The saga of the Marmarth bridge construction over the Little Missouri River is proof of the value of persistence.

Marmarth, North Dakota, on the Little Missouri River, had become a major cattle shipping point as the plains were settled, but its development was hindered by a lack of a wagon or auto bridge. In 1913, the Yellowstone Trail was pushing westward toward Montana, and the lack of this North Dakota bridge created a gap that threatened the integrity of the whole trail.

Fording across streams was a way of life. In dry times an experienced driver could ford easily. But this Little Missouri River was different. It was described as "rampaging in spring, unpredictable, turbulent, hiding a strong current" and capable of rising several feet in moments. There were tales of horses getting spooked while fording, throwing riders. Then there was a crossing attempted on a raft; twelve miles downstream it finally hit the bank.

Big party at opening of bridge over the Little Missouri River at Marmarth, 1916

"Marmarth needs a bridge" was the chant in the western side of the city from early 1909. A county bond issue was voted down in the autumn of 1912. It seems the "east enders" of the city were not buying the idea. Some disgusted Marmarthians built a "low water" plank bridge just 12 inches above the low water level. It was designed to be "temporary" and it was. It floated away with the first high water.

The Yellowstone Trail Association weighed in to close this gap in the Trail in early 1913 offering to raise $10,000. They would do this by laying a special assessment on member towns in the area. Newspapers along the trail in three western states carried frequent articles about the bridge crisis. Trail literature took up the cry. Trail members hosted "benefit balls" and "socials" to raise more money. But by June 1913 only $4,000 had been raised.

Rev. George Keniston, a charismatic Chatauqua speaker, was dispatched in 1914 by the Trail Association to raise the rest of their promised $10,000. He reportedly had raised $28,000 in pledges in short order for this project and the road project through the Standing Rock Reservation, just west of Mobridge, South Dakota.

Now here's the puzzle. In September, 1914, the Yellowstone Trail Association reneged on its promise. What happened? Were pledges not honored? "Doomed to failure" declared one reporter of the Trail offer. There was some grumbling in the *Marmarth Mail*, saying that the Association "fluked out," but that was all that was said. The project proceeded anyway. Bids were lower than expected, coming in at $13,000. But there was only the $5000 pledged from Billings County in the pot now since the Trail Association backed out.

In April 1915, a request for a referendum about the bridge was declined by the county board. All progress stopped. A ferry functioned for a brief period. It was a plank box with sloping ramps for cars to enter and exit. It was fastened to a steel cable stretched across the river and was propelled by the current. When it dropped a car into the river the ferry fell into disfavor.

The large Billings County divided and the newly formed Slope County board passed a tax levy for the bridge. "East-enders" brought an injunction against the bridge that was soon dissolved, but a new injunction tied up the tax levy for a year. The Little Missouri River physically divided the town but the differences between the "west-enders" and the "east-enders" may also have been cultural. To the east lay flat farm land. To the west lay the "city" and the badlands. Apparently the eastern farmers saw no future in dealing with city folk nor need to cross the river.

But somehow, a steel and concrete bridge was built. On June 20, 1916, a big dedicatory celebration was held featuring a dance on the bridge, free barbeque dinner, electric lights everywhere and great hoopla. J. W. Parmley and J. Prindle, present and past presidents of the Trail Association, were featured speakers, so the $10,000 debacle was apparently forgiven.

How dedicated, yet how foreign to us was this nickel-and-dime attempt to close the gap. Personal involvement can be seen at every step. This was true of the Trail west of Minneapolis. The Trail to the east used bridges already built. ✿

Crossing the Little Missouri at Marmarth
Probably from Michael Dowling's
1913 trip
1914 First Year Book

1916: the new auto bridge
(foreground) over the Little
Missouri River at Marmarth

TRAIL ASSOCIATION FLUKES ON BRIDGE FAILS TO HAVE MONEY FOR BRIDGE WHEN BIDS ARE TO BE LET BY THE COUNTY BOARD
Marmarth Mail

The "Boys" of the Yellowstone Trail Association

Most important in front row:
Joe Parmley (second from left), Michael Dowling (center),
and Hal Cooley (fourth from left)

Executive Committee at work, 1919 or 1920

As the founder, lead spokesperson, and tireless organizer of the Yellowstone Trail Association, Joe Parmley got most of the notoriety, but there was a plethora of people in the Association as dedicated as he. Space allows only for mention of a few of the many stellar gentlemen who cast their lot with this great road experiment. There was no expectation of payment. Getting a transcontinental highway through their town was payment enough.

Establishing a trail, these men worked with no computers, no cell phones, no television, no auto pay, no internet, no Google maps, no apps. Rural telephones had to be cranked and long-distance calls were pretty alien. Crystal radio sets were only on the horizon for rural folk. The telegraph was their fastest line of distant communication, although the U.S. postal service (RFD) seemed speedier than today. Few connected roads existed to get these automobilists to Association national or even state meetings. Although passenger train service was good, it was vexing to have to take a train to a good roads meeting.

Hal Cooley

Besides Joe Parmley and Michael Dowling (See **Trail Tale: Parmley**, page 208, and **Trail Tale: Dowling**, page 239), the most physically and intellectually engaged in the Association was Harold (Hal) Cooley, certainly a public relations expert way before the PR term was invented. He spent his whole career in civic, political, and road promotions, jobs

Hal Cooley, General
Manager extraordinaire

seemingly intertwined with the warp and woof of his Type-A personality. His was the public face of the Yellowstone Trail Association for 15 of the Association's 18 years.

Some years ago we interviewed Cooley's granddaughter and elderly son-in-law and we drew a picture of Hal consistent with newspaper accounts of his day. He was everywhere on the Trail speaking at all of the state and national Association meetings.

He appeared regularly in most of the Trail towns from Ohio to Washington to speak, but more importantly, to beat the drum for dues payments. It was a Sisyphean task. Son-in-law, Julius Maland, remarked that "Hal was never home." This popular speaker was also sought by civic organizations unrelated to the Trail.

Maland related a tale that Cooley liked to tell: Cooley and a line of cars got stuck in the mud. He worried that the Yellowstone Trail would get a bad name from this occurrence so he went from car to car to get people out, formed a big circle and led them in singing to raise their spirits until they all got pulled out. His favorite song was "There's a Long, Long Trail Awinding."

Cooley at Hunter's
Hot Springs

Dozens and dozens of newspaper clippings described a very entertaining speaker who was humorous, yet mesmerizing, with his almost eidetic memory of Trail facts, delivered rapidly because he usually had a limited time allotted to him on the program. This rapid-fire delivery of sometimes startling road or Trail facts, all laced with humor, kept his audiences awake and kept the ever-present press on their toes.

Cooley wore several hats with the Trail Association as his position evolved, but it all boiled down to General Manager. It was he who managed the Aberdeen, then Minneapolis, then, briefly, Fort Wayne, Indiana, and Cleveland offices while writing the *Arrow* newsletter, building a budget, handling correspondence, supervising the 15 Trail Bureaus, and supervising weather/road condition regional reports. It was Cooley who let loose over one million pieces of Trail literature in one year with a small staff, and it was Hal Cooley who wrote many articles for road magazines and newspapers.

It was Hal Cooley who, in 1926, braved the unthinkable. He published the names of people and organizations in South Dakota with the amounts of their pledged dues that were ⇨

in arrears! He wrote that "Since this is a public business operating without a profit, in each bulletin we will designate one or more towns along the Trail which owes the most." There followed a list of South Dakota "welchers." By May of 1927 he was able to report in the Aberdeen *American News* that "The Association is out of debt for the first time since 1920." The embarrassing ploy must have worked.

This heavy-handed approach was frequently garbed with the threat of pulling the signs off of a town's Trail and moving them away if dues were not forthcoming. That approach apparently worked. Yes, the Trail was moved in areas as new and better roads were built, but never was it removed for lack of payment.

And it was Hal Cooley who crossed swords with Trail founder, Joe Parmley. Beginning around 1927 Parmley began to disparage Cooley in speech and writings. We can only guess that it was a difference in management style that drove them apart at the end. Joe favored honoring old route commitments; Cooley favored moving to new, better routes. Cooley kept up his busy regimen even as late as December of 1929, three months before the collapse of the organization.

Rev. George R. Keniston

George Keniston had a much shorter career with the Yellowstone Trail Association, only a few months, but it was colorful. He, too, wore two hats: one hat as the financial agent for the Association in 1914, and one as the preacher for the Congregational Church at Hettinger, North Dakota, which he had served since 1907.

Like Hal Cooley, George Keniston was apparently a mesmerizing speaker, but with an entirely different style. Handsome Keniston depended upon "friendly persuasion" with a sincerely happy persona as he more gently prodded his audiences. He was a very popular preacher and Chatauqua speaker, possibly due to his sunny disposition and richly textured reasonings.

Keniston's job for the Trail Association was to raise funds for the badly needed bridge over the Little Missouri River at Marmarth, North Dakota, and to buy the rights-of-way for

Rev. George Keniston

the road through the Standing Rock Reservation in South Dakota. These were the two weakest links in the Trail. In March of 1914 it was thought that $50,000 was needed, $15,000 for the bridge and $35,000 for Corson County and the Reservation.

Keniston hit the road running. Quickly he raised $28,000 in pledges and was soon off to Washington D.C. to confer with congressmen. A bill was written for $50,000 for the Indians, but only $5,000 of it was eventually passed. In late March, the necessary funds had dropped to $40,000 with $10,000 promised to Marmarth. Billings County, North Dakota, sold $5,000 worth of bonds at 4.9% for the bridge. The Association reported in June that "the remainder of the funds will be raised by contributions guaranteed by different communities along the Trail." But next thing we read was that in September the Trail Association reneged on it's promise of bridge help. Nothing was said about the Reservation.

We are puzzled. George Keniston was so charismatic and so quickly raised a good share of the funds. Let's see. $40,000 minus $28,000 raised, minus $5,000 from Billings County leaves $7,000. Washington D.C. apparently would not come through with $5,000 for awhile yet. But success was on the horizon. What happened? Did people not honor their pledges? Was the saga of the Marmarth bridge repeated injunctions off-putting to the pledgers? We read nothing about him after June. Keniston's honesty was never in question. For more about the saga, see **Trail Tale: Marmarth Bridge**, page 174.

By spring of 1915 Keniston was reported "helping the Bismarck Commercial Club in its fundraising efforts for a bridge over the Little Missouri River at Medora." And, simultaneously, he left Hettinger and became the ⇨

Yellowstone Trail Their Highway in Life

Caricature of some YTA leaders 1920 Minneapolis Evening Tribune

preacher for the Congregational Church at Beach, North Dakota. We can only guess that he was offered a better deal from Bismarck and their road project with the National Parks Highway (Red Trail) than the $300 a month from the Yellowstone Trail Association.

Other Trail-ers of Note

Most Trail members received less notoriety, but were nonetheless tireless volunteers without whom the Association would not have thrived. Due to space limitation, we only mention three here who really deserve a longer personal narrative.

Marcus Beebe, founder of Beebe, South Dakota, was a friend of Joe Parmley's in Ipswich. Marcus served as interim president of the Association, October 1912 to February 1913, until the first national meeting was held. He was a quiet philanthropist and on the Board of Regents of the South Dakota University. The most memorable tale about him was his impatience with the Edmunds county board's slow action about road funding. That resulted in his marching in and plunking down $500 in cash with a promise of another $500 to come! It shamed the Board into action.

Marcus Beebe, philanthropist and 1912-1913 Interim President of the YTA

Judge (Magistrate) J. E. Prindle of Ismay, Montana, was the first elected president of the Yellowstone Trail Association, serving 1913-1914. He, like Joe Parmley, was a land dealer. This first year of the Association presented many problems faced by entrepreneurs today - deciding on a business plan, budget, and organizational structure in addition to creating marking symbols and dues structures.

J. E. Prindle, magistrate and 1st President of the YTA

He also had to shoulder the burden, along with other founders, of persuading folks to accept the new idea of a national highway, and to look beyond their local RFD route.

R. B. Anderson was the father of the idea of Trail Day. That idea was not necessarily original, but it was new to the Trail Association in 1914 when it was first decreed. All citizens in towns along the Trail from Minneapolis through Montana were to get out and work on bettering the Trail on the same day with members of the press on hand. It worked! Newspapers along the Trail loved it.

Two members' names may ring a bell with modern readers: Asahel Curtis, famous Washington photographer, and vice-president from 1925 to 1928, and John Willys of Willys Overland autos in Toledo, member of the Executive Committee.

It would be easy to assume that these and other Trailmen portrayed a picture of self-importance and posturing, what with their "smokers" after each meeting and their many pronouncements to an accommodating press and eager townsfolk. Actually, they seemed like sincere guys who wanted the best for their communities and wanted to be part of something that they recognized as historic. They may have seen the scope of this project as requiring boldness, and a certain foolhardiness. Perhaps it was a combination of Mary and Oscar Handlin's observation that, "Voluntary associations proved essential to give the individual a place in a fluid society" and architect Daniel Burnham's 1900 admonition: "Make no little plans; they have no magic to stir men's souls" that also moved these men. They were characters with character. ❀

Where is that Road? Oh, for a Map!

Railroads were beginning to deliver automobiles to nearly every nook and cranny of America at the time the Yellowstone Trail was founded. New auto owners wanted to "drive somewhere." Big problems became apparent. Roads reasonably suitable for driving from one town to another were rare. There were no maps to consult, few guidebooks to buy, no helpful directional signs, and no established and marked routes. And nothing to tell the driver if the road ahead was even passable.

In practical terms, to make the Yellowstone Trail succeed, the Association had not only to motivate the construction and maintenance of the roads used for the route but it also had to motivate (or create) some way for people to know it existed and know where it was and where it went. In modern times, road maps with US, state, and local roads carefully shown, either paper or digital, inform about where a route travels and where it is.

To show the progression of road map-making, MAP 1 through MAP 5 show the area near Ismay (Is) and Baker (Ba), Montana.

MAP 1. There were early maps, of course. Counties of the period created maps showing roads (but not routes) for their own official uses. There were plentiful railroad maps for rail travel planning but they were of no help to the auto driver. And there were US Post Office maps like that below from 1911. The mail routes were mostly railroads and local wagon roads as rural free delivery spread across the county. ⇨

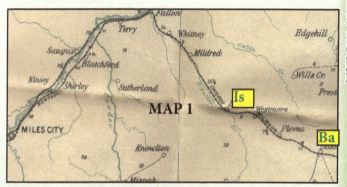

MAP 1

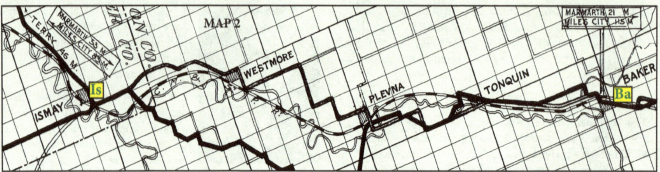

MAP 2. The Association published their first major publication in 1914, the *First Year Book*. In addition to an historical record of some interesting aspects of the Trail's first years, the *First Year Book* included maps of the Trail covering the then active section from St. Paul, Minnesota, to near Three Forks, Montana. Apparently it was based on county maps from along the route. Today those maps remain the best available of the early route.

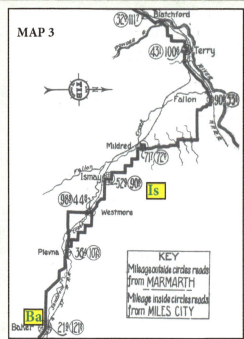

MAP 3. Probably the most helpful early guides to finding one's way were the voluminous books containing mile-by-mile documentation of roads using turn left/turn right instructions. See **Trail Tale: Guidebooks**, page 362. For a few of the major long-distance auto routes, "strip maps" were published by auto clubs or commercial services. One of the later is shown to the right.

MAP 4. Before the era of named auto Trails, several major, nationally based map companies were making, printing, and distributing railroad maps showing the cities and the rail lines connecting them. As named auto trails made their appearance, some map companies attempted to meet the need for an auto route map by adding free-hand drawn major auto routes on their railroad maps. They were often drawn crudely and with errors and great ambiguities. On the example shown here, the locally promoted version of the Yellowstone Trail is marked "Yellow" and just to the west of Baker it is marked "Trail". With imagination, the user could see those obscure green words that indicated the Yellowstone Trail. The maps were of little help for mile-by-mile travel.

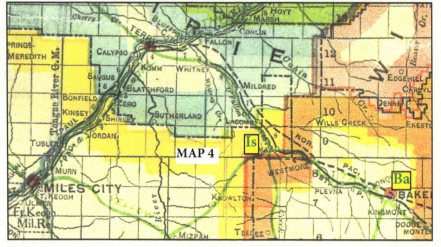

MAP 5. After Wisconsin's idea of state-specified route numbers and matching state road maps it was adopted across the country, and usable road maps became ubiquitous. They rather quickly supplanted the dominant guidebooks because of their cheapness and ease of use without a navigator in a passenger seat. But those numbered routes were designed to replace named highways, so fewer and fewer maps showed named routes.

The free service station state maps were introduced to motivate autoists to buy the advertised brand of gasoline in exchange for the map service. Not until the widespread use of GPS gadgets did the free service station map disappear. ✿

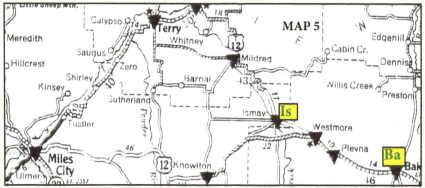

South Dakota

Map labels (along the Yellowstone Trail): White Butte, Lemmon, Thund'r Hwk, Keldron, Morristown, Watauga, McIntosh, McLaughlin, Wakpala, Missouri River, Glenham, Java, Roscoe, Ipswich, Andover, Holmquist, Webster, Ortley, Mobridge, Selby, Bowdle, Beebe, Aberdeen, Groton, Bristol, Waubay, Summit, Marvin, Milbank, Big Stone

WHAT THE TRAIL FOUNDERS SAID-1921

The state of South Dakota is an easy one in which to travel by automobile. For the most part, the state is well-drained and the soil is one that is well adapted to good dirt roads. In extremely wet times, the mud of South Dakota is very heavy and varies from thick muck to a light greasy gumbo. In all parts of the state, however, the soil dries rapidly. Within the last 2 or 3 years, South Dakota has been making rapid strides through the State Highway Commission in developing a state system of highways built and maintained by the state. The Yellowstone Trail crosses the entire northern part of the state and from the trail, easy connections are made to reach any part of the state.

One of the best summer resorts sections of the Northwest is at Big Stone Lake in the northeastern part of the state reached by the Trail. There is a lake section from in and about Sisseton, extending east, west and south for 100 miles.

The most scenic bit of South Dakota is the Black Hills in the extreme southwestern corner in and about Deadwood, Rapid City, and Hot Springs. This section of the state is best reached from an eastern destination by following the Yellowstone Trail to Mobridge or Lemmon and from one of those two points south to the Black Hills. Aberdeen on the Yellowstone Trail in the northern part of the state and Sioux Falls in the southeastern part of the state are the two largest cities and commercial centers of the state.

The roads of South Dakota are not guaranteed to be all good roads but they show, that under ordinary circumstances, the automobilist can go in safety and security. We advise consulting one of our information bureaus if you contemplate travel in South Dakota.

1921 Yellowstone Trail Touring Service Map #5 of South Dakota

County 12W between Mina and Aberdeen over the original alignment of the Yellowstone Trail. It all started here.
Toshio Koshimizu

INTRODUCING THE YELLOWSTONE TRAIL IN SOUTH DAKOTA: GREAT FACES, GREAT PLACES

South Dakota is Home to the Yellowstone Trail

Ipswich is well north of the Black Hills, the Bad Lands, and Mt. Rushmore, the best known attractions of South Dakota. Ipswich does not benefit directly from the hundreds of thousands of tourists who flock to those nationally known symbols. But little Ipswich can claim to be the home of a great force in transportation history, the major leader in the creation and operation of the Yellowstone Trail. The agricultural world of Ipswich and environs had little to attract tourists, but from Joe Parmley came the energy to establish a group to forward the idea of the great transcontinental auto highway that quite quickly opened the Northwest to auto tourism. He provided leadership in the building, financing, and marking of long-distance highways. The highway was his idea, but it was an idea whose time had come. For a more full story, see **Trail Tale: Parmley**, page 208, and **Trail Tale: YTA**, page 2.

History of Auto Roads in South Dakota

Parmley's good roads group echoed the feelings of millions of citizens across our nation and the almost14,000 South Dakota auto owners to "get us out of the mud." Roads in 1912 were spaces made available for your horse and wagon, sometimes improved by a drag but mostly they were prairie trails. To make them useful by the auto they needed improvement beyond the co-operative improvements by nearby land owners.

They would require government financial support. Townships and counties might provide occasional help. States provided nothing. Federal aid for connected roads was years in the future. The state legislature depended upon counties to build the dirt roads. Thus, in 1912 Parmley and crew aimed their appeals for Trail Association membership at individuals and town leaders and county boards along their proposed route. There was no support from eastern industrialists, the kinds of which supported the Lincoln Highway during its creation the following year.

In a slow change of thought, the South Dakota legislature

Road work on the Yellowstone Trail near Mobridge, South Dakota, 1915.

established a State Highway Department in 1913. There was no provision in the road laws of the state for state aid, no funds being provided. By 1916, the only federal money in sight for roads was a small amount for RFD mail routes. The Federal Aid Road Law of 1916 offered aid "for roads which are used to transport mail or may in the future be used to transport mail." In effect, that covered almost all auto roads. However, the amount available was minimal. To avail themselves of any federal aid for roads, states first had to amend their constitutions which had prohibited "internal improvements." South Dakotans overwhelmingly accepted the amendment in November, 1916.

Then South Dakota, and all states, had to create a State Highway Department to carry out any federal laws, and to set a budget. Simply stated, the federal government offered to pay one-half of the cost of roads with the state and county paying the other half. Of course, there are many complicated addenda to this offer. The state legislature appropriated $30,000 for fiscal 1917 for state road aid to counties. For the next four years the federal government increased appropriations and South Dakota created a new Highway Commission with power to oversee the distribution of the slowly increasing federal funding and the proposed road projects involved.

Role of the Yellowstone Trail in South Dakota Roads

By 1916 the Yellowstone Trail Association was accepted as a force for getting roads constructed. The State Highway Commission Report to the Governor said that,

> ... trails and highways were agreed upon and endorsed by the people of the counties through which the highways pass. State highways will be through routes connecting more than one county.

Connected highways is what the Yellowstone Trail Association wanted - one road linking to another county to create a single route across the state, then the nation.

In that same report, the Trail received official permission to mark its road through the state:

> This Commission will not interfere with any road markings with respect to color, emblem or design, adopted by any organization or community, provided that the markings of any one Highway shall not conflict with the markings of any other Highway within this State. Your Commission believes that all markings of Highways within the State will be most satisfactory by painting on such objects as may be available.

The state declared that gravel was too expensive in 1917, so dragging and draining dirt roads sufficed as "surfacing." At this early date, "paving" meant graveling. In May, 1922, *North Dakota Good Roads Magazine* complained that "No hard surfaced roads had been constructed in South Dakota as it has been figured that they are too expensive at the present time." Concrete was decades away. Gravel or no gravel, the Yellowstone Trail was designated an "arterial route" by the state, meaning that at intersections, the Trail traffic had the right-of-way. Well, yes, if the other driver had heard about that rule! ⇨

Why Did the Yellowstone Trail Go Where it Went in South Dakota?

A railroad could make or break a town. If the railroad was not coming to your town, people literally picked up their house and moved it to a town that would have a railroad. Parmley did that. The Milwaukee Road served Ipswich from the Twin Cities and on to the west. The Yellowstone Trail was routed near the route of the Milwaukee Road for practical reasons: railroads found or created the path of least resistance, help was near in case of need, and towns were created along the route. You had to get your product to the buyer and your supplies to your field. These town leaders formed the network Parmley needed to create and support the Yellowstone Trail.

Ah, but for the details. The railroads had all the money they needed, one way or another. Decision-making was centralized. They managed to get the land they needed with government help. The Yellowstone Trail Association had to choose a

The "Steel and Yellowstone Trail
thru Edmunds County, South Dakota"
1914 First Year Book

route over existing roads – or convince the local governments to build roads. No one had the wherewithal to buy land, so usually the free section line rights-of-way had to be used but they all are oriented north/south or east/west, resulting in the familiar stair-step route to stay near the railroad following its curving purchased route. See, for instance, the Trail's route near Java.

Routing the Trail through the Standing Rock Reservation in western South Dakota had been an ongoing problem for the Association. This land was federal and that fact introduced a whole new set of concerns about the rights and treatment of Native Americans before a successful Trail could be created. For a more full story, see **Trail Tale: Standing Rock**, page 212.

Although the route through the eastern two-thirds of South Dakota appears to be an easy straight line on a map, geology played its trump cards, too. Bridges had to be built (and paid for) across rivers to replace fords and ferries. Some grades

had to be cut down, shallows had to be filled in. The glacial lakes had to be circumvented. The glacial lakes in the Waubay area are especially interesting today as they flood and wane in the glacial debris. These lakes and many other geological route influences are presented in understandable terms in *Roadside Geology of South Dakota* (Mountain Press 1996) by John Paul Gries.

Suffice it to say that at least four periods of glaciation covered eastern South Dakota beginning about two million years ago and ending about 10,000 years ago. As the glaciers moved south, the material transported consisted of ground-up rock and boulders called glacial till. Any deposit of glacial till is called a moraine. Where stagnant ice melted, a stagnation moraine formed. The surface is hummocky and irregular. Stagnant ice buried in the ground moraine melted last, leaving pot hole lakes. The Trail through eastern South Dakota rests upon distinct geographic areas created by glacial till and by Glacial Lake Dakota. As a result of this action millennia ago, the area of Waubay was left with lakes that have no natural outlet. Thus, when rain exceeds drought, the lakes expand. The last decades were just that way; wet cycles exceeding dry cycles. Bitter Lake, south of town, has grown from five to 32 square miles and Waubay Lake from eight to 27 square miles. A few years ago Waubay received three to five inches in 90 minutes. Folks have left the community; some have raised their houses on stilts. Farms are inundated. US 12 was raised. Go to Google maps for pictures of the current situation.

We have driven the Trail in South Dakota many times over the past two decades of research and found it to be a pleasant, comfortable trip for the most part and even an exciting one. The eastern two-thirds of the route feature small towns with friendly people who have invited us to barbeques, who are proud of their town's history and museums, and who welcome discussion about the Trail. Aberdeen's Dacotah Prairie Museum especially has an active program and knowledgeable staff. So we invite you to enjoy the Trail through the state that gave it birth. ✿

SD

Modern glacial lake high water problem near Waubay

THE YELLOWSTONE TRAIL

The action taken by the good roads conference at Lemmon this week to promote an interstate highway leading from the Twin Cities through Aberdeen to the Yellowstone National Park is most aureative. There is no reason why the project should not be carried to completion and result in trementous advantage to Minnesota, South Dakota, North Dakota and Montana.

October 11, 1912 Aberdeen Daily News

At Lemmon recently a check on the traffic going over the Yellowstone Trail showed an average of considerably better than 100 foreign (out-of-state) cars and close to 300 South Dakota cars per day passed over the Trail.

September 25, 1925
The Marmarth Mail

NOVEL TRAIL MARKER

White Butte township, South Dakota and Gilstrap township just across the line in North Dakota are enthusiastic over the construction work and will have their stretches of the Yellowstone Trail completed this fall. The people of these two townships have secured natural sandstone pillars and planted them along the trail. These pillars measure from six to ten feet long, being from twelve to eighteen inches through at the base. They have been worn round and smooth by the action of the waters of centuries and make ideal markers when painted yellow with the words "Yellowstone Trail" painted in black letters on them.

June 11, 1913 Aberdeen Daily News

TRAIL DAY BRINGS OUT
LARGE NUMBER
SCORE OF LEMMONITES DEVOTE
MAY 22 TO LABOR ON THE TRAIL

From the Falls of St. Anthony (MN) to the Yellowstone National Park this will be the greatest day of road-building that the Northwest has ever known. The 7 or 8 miles of road which the city of Lemmon is looking after had scores of workmen and teams upon it.

May 29, 1914 Lemmon Herald

In 1928, in Lloyd's Model A, we drove to Lemmon on the Yellowstone Trail to see the area's first talking picture show at the Lemmon movie theatre.

Diary of Merlin Miller, Hettinger, North Dakota ✿

ASK LEGISLATURE'S AID TO BUILD
YELLOWSTONE TRAIL

It was decided to ask the next legislature of North Dakota to pass a bill providing for the cooperation of this state with South Dakota in building this road on the state line. Owing to the asinine policy of the old administration of North Dakota, the state line portion of the Yellowstone Trail is the worst piece of road on the entire Trail from Plymouth Rock to Puget Sound.

July 27, 1922 Adams County Record

BOARD MEETING

We hereby designate Monday, February 3, 1913 at 2 o'clock p.m. at the Commercial Club rooms as the place for holding a convention for the purpose of establishing the route of the proposed Twin Cities-Aberdeen-Yellowstone Park Trail ... and to elect delegates to the interstate convention in Miles City February 17.

January 29, 1913 Perkins County

One hundred representatives of the Yellowstone Trail Association from Montana, North Dakota and South Dakota met at Lemmon to discuss completion of grading and graveling of the Trail, doubling the information signs, getting out 100,000 route folders, and putting information bureaus at diverting points in the three states. Only two cities in the three states had paid their dues so far.

March 16, 1928 in 2014 Mobridge Tribune:
Yellowstone Trail Guide

The original Yellowstone Trail in western SD was located on or near the State border from Thunder Hawk to White Butte. Little of that routing can now be followed, except for Railway St. a bit east and west of Lemmon. Between Lemmon and Petrel (a railroad maintenance location) several maps show the route about half way between the border and present US 12. On-ground evidence is lacking.

Petrified Wood Park in Lemmon

SD

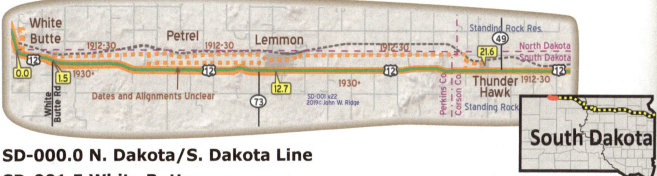

SD-000.0 N. Dakota/S. Dakota Line

SD-001.5 White Butte

(85 pop.), the last town in South Dakota on US 12, is a typical Western movie village, its few houses evidently built without much idea of the town's coherence. Since it is a railroad town with a favorable location as a stock shipping point, it is a familiar sight to see cows or sheep dodging behind houses as the herds are driven to the stockyards for their long journey to market. WPA-SD

One of the
Trail markers at
White Butte

A village; rooms; small garage; free camp space. C. A. SAMP-SON'S GARAGE leads; has good name and good mechanics. Labor $1.25; ph. 15 until 11 p. m. MH-1928

White Butte is the first town in South Dakota going east and the last going west on the Yellowstone Trail (now US 12). It was founded in 1909 and named after the white limestone butte nearby. In Yellowstone Trail days it was a stock shipping point with many businesses to support the ranches in the area. When the Milwaukee Road railroad left, White Butte shrank, like many other small towns abandoned by railroads.

SD-012.7 Lemmon

(2,567 alt., 1,785 pop.), was named for "Ed" Lemmon, pioneer and cattleman who for years was foreman of the large L7 cattle outfit. The town is the trade center for a large territory in both North and South Dakota, which produces grain, cattle, horses, and sheep. Thus, it is one of the few towns in the United States where cattlemen, sheepmen and farmers meet on a common ground. Situated on the North Dakota Line, part of the town is actually in the adjoining State.

Attempts at farming in the immediate vicinity have resulted in much distress during recent drought years, although the soil is exceptionally fertile. WPA-SD

pop. 1,300; YELLOWSTONE HOTEL is now best; 4 rooms with r. w. All rooms to be made modern; sgl. $1.25; dbl. $2.

LEMMON AUTO CO. Ford, large and modern; has best mechanics for all cars. Open to 10 p.m. labor $1-$1.25; ph. 29 for tow car. MH-1928

When you get to Lemmon you know you are on the prairie – the Great Plains. Windswept and glorious in the sunlight,

one can just imagine the early explorers and wagon trains lumbering slowly, pushing our nation west. Lemmon is near Grand River National Grassland and Cedar River National Grassland and the area is characterized by rolling hills dominated by mixed grass prairie with scattered outcrops of badlands. "Lemmon and surrounding area offers a way of life you can't find anywhere else. It is the way of life of the Northern Plains, of the prairie and of the Yellowstone Trail." *Highway 12 Guide 2005.*

Lemmon figured large in the story of the Yellowstone Trail. Oct. 9-10, 1912 Good Roads folks invited the Ipswich founding group to Lemmon to form an association. It was here that ByLaws were written and the long moniker of "Twin Cities-Aberdeen-Yellowstone Park Trail" was hung on their invention. It would be shortened to "Yellowstone Trail" later. Lemmon would remain a faithful contributor to the Association for its entire 18 year run.

It is also the starting point of a cross-state run in a Studebaker Six in May of 1915 by Trail founder Joe Parmley. His run ended at Big Stone City, 349 South Dakota miles, 800 pounds of South Dakota mud and 16 hours later. See **Trail Tale: Parmley's Trip**, page 214.

On US 12 (Yellowstone Trail) the **Grand River Museum** displays an interesting mix of local homesteaders' lives along with geological and paleontological artifacts such as dinosaur bones of T-Rex Sue and a triceratops. Depictions of Native American culture, cattle branding and Lewis and Clark's trek all bear credibility because of the proximity of those events to Lemmon. An interesting statue of a triceratops stands outside of the museum. It is made entirely of scrap metal!

On Main St. is the amazing **world's largest petrified wood park and museum**. It covers a whole city block, is outdoors and is free. You probably have not ever seen so much petrified wood in one spot before. It looks like the TV town of Bedrock with Fred Flinstone popping up among these "rocks". There is a 300 ton castle with turrets, also round balls, monuments with Yellowstone Trail printed on them, and cones tall and small. All man-made. Look closely and you will find dinosaur tracks and fossils. The "castle," built entirely of petrified logs, contains the gift shop where you can buy - what else? petrified wood bits.

SD-001.5: Before US 12 was given its modern alignment the highway ran directly north of White Butte, on a now abandoned road.

The Standing Rock Reservation is located in north Central South Dakota in Corson County. The Yellowstone Trail Association had much trouble with its plans to mark the Trail through the Reservation. It was on federal land, and the federal government had little interest in improving wagon roads there. Corson County, just across the Missouri River from Mobridge, had been a problem for the Trail Association for all of the Association's life of 18 years, first in getting a road built and then in maintenance. Claims often were published that the state ignored the county's road needs. Almost the whole of the county lay on the Standing Rock Reservation and, although sections were open to sale, most was not subject to taxation, being federal land. Jurisdiction clashes probably entered into road construction. This interruption in the route of the Trail was a serious problem for the integrity of the Trail. ✿

PARMLEY ROAD FOR McINTOSH?

Surveyors are at work surveying a highway from Mobridge to McIntosh, thence west to Thunder Hawk. It is the plan that this highway will be an extension of the "Parmley road" now being constructed from Aberdeen to Mobridge. A good roads meeting is called to be held in Lemmon October 9th for the purpose of having the "Parmley road" run west along the railroad track into Montana.

September 27, 1912 Morristown World

Note: They moved fast in those days! Note the date. It is only five months since the subject of a road was first brought up in Ipswich; now they spoke cavalierly about reaching Montana, 294 miles from Ipswich. The group didn't even have a name yet; they called it the "Parmley road," a name Joe Parmley demurred back in April in Ipswich.

🚗 Just west and south of Watauga at GPS: 45.92021, -101.54882 is a highway bridge on a disused road. It is directly in line with US 12 from the east and was undoubtedly used by the YT before US 12 was moved to north of the tracks to avoid a railroad crossing here and near Morristown.

🚗 Just east of Watauga at GPS: 45.92042, -101.47282 is a YT hoodoo route marker just north of US 12 on the fence line. A hoodoo is a vertical sandstone bullet-shaped route marker with the words Yellowstone Trail painted on it vertically. Northwest of the hoodoo appears to be a highway bridge in good condition in the middle of a field. It needs some research!

HIGHWAY CONSTRUCTION NEEDED

The county dads were in session Monday and Tuesday on road matters. They arranged to advertise for bids for the construction of five miles of highway between McIntosh and Watauga. The Yellowstone Trail Association will now take hold of the matter, and we dare say before the year is over they will spend close on to $10,000 in this county to complete this project.

May 23, 1913 Morristown World

Note: A misconception appears here. The Yellowstone Trail Association did not fork out money to build a highway. It only persuaded county boards to spend their road funds on the single road that the Association would choose to mark as the Trail.

President Parmley of the Trail Association and J. D. Harris of Mobridge plan to mark the Trail across Corson County as soon as the weather permits. The importance of marking the Trail so that it cannot be lost by travelers cannot be overestimated. The officers strongly urge every locality to see that their Trail is well marked.

March 27, 1914 Morristown World

🚗 The original route just west of Keldron is open to question. The curves to the east and west and the railroad overpass would certainly be dated to after the YT's formation. It is quite conceivable that the original road followed a straight line connecting the US 12 to the east and to the west.

INSPECTOR REPORTS

W. H. Doherty, who was appointed the inspector for the Yellowstone Trail for this section reported that ... the 20 miles between McIntosh and Morristown is really the best 20 miles on this section as steel drags are being used to keep the road in the best shape. No other part of the Trail is using steel drags.

May 28, 1915 Morristown World

HEAVY TOURIST TRAVEL

Tourist travel over the Yellowstone Trail has been the heaviest this season than any previous year. Automobiles carrying tourists from nearly every state in the union have passed through here east and west bound. According to figures from Aberdeen, 894 interstate touring parties went through here during the month of July.

August 11, 1916 Morristown World

SD

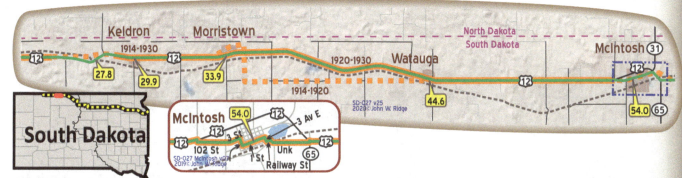

SD-021.6 Thunder Hawk

(100 pop.), has a general store where on Saturdays commodities, politics, and gossip are exchanged over the cracker and pickle barrels. WPA-SD

Thunder Hawk is on the western edge of the Standing Rock Reservation.

The STANDING ROCK INDIAN RESERVATION, covers the eastern half of Corson Co. in South Dakota, and extends into North Dakota, with the Agency at Fort Yates, N. Dak.

There are 3,828 Sioux Indians on the reservation roll, 2,565 of which are listed as full-bloods by the agency superintendent. The native bands within the Sioux Tribe on this reservation are: Hunkpapas, Yanktonai, Teton, Minneconjou, Itazibeo, Oohenupa, Sihasapa, Ogalala, Sicungu, and Isanyati. The native language is used by 90 percent of the people over 40, and by half the children of pre-school age, little by school children. Rodeos are held at irregular intervals during the summer months. WPA-SD

SD-029.9 Keldron

SD-033.9 Morristown

(2,240 alt.,.235 pop.), named for the C-7 ranch proprietor, Nels Morris. It supplies the surrounding ranchers with such supplies as they do not get from mail order houses.

A village in a wheat and flax growing district; three garages. Stadel Garage leads. No camp. MH-1928

SD-044.6 Watauga

pop. 100; wheat, flax and barley are the principal crops. Fair country hotel. Simon-Thompsen Garage is best. Open camp space. MH-1928

Watauga, Corson County, is located 10 miles west of McIntosh, the county seat. It is on the main line of the Chicago, Milwaukee, and St. Paul Railway and on the transcontinental highway, the Yellowstone Trail. The community surrounding this prosperous village is noted for its mammoth growth of prairie grass, affording pasture and hay for thousands of stock, and with rich deposits of Lignite coal which can be purchased at from $1.00 to $2.00 per ton. The community has RFD, telephone lines, and radio receiving sets. *Excerpted from Watauga Commercial Club publication 1923.*

On the corner of 2nd Ave. E and US 12, the northwest corner, you will see another small "hoodoo" painted yellow with

black vertical lettering of the Yellowstone Trail. It is across 2nd Ave. from **Brenda's Tumbleweed Café** at 22870 US 12.

Four miles east of Wautaga on the north side of the road about 20 feet from the road is a bullet-shaped hoodoo Yellowstone Trail marker painted white with a yellow stripe.

SD-054.0 McIntosh

Between Mcintosh and Lemmon the rolling country breaks into occasional sharp buttes and grassless mud flats. This land was once the paradise of cattlemen; it still is, but in a different sense. The cattleman must rent his land today; yesterday it belonged to anyone or no one. Here, where there are few towns and the roads are impassable in wet seasons, the temptation to go to town is less. Men and women are wind-burned the year around, and children are virtually raised in the saddle. WPA-SD

Wheat and sheep raising are the main sources of revenue. Boots Cafe is best. H. & C. Motors is reputed good. Mcintosh Motor Co., for Fords. Free camp space, cold showers. MH-1928

There was a Trail Garage there in 1924.

Native Americans of Standing Rock Reservation put on shows for tourists in Yellowstone Trail days.

McIntosh is the county seat of Corson County which contains much of the Standing Rock Reservation. Present county officers were much interested in the Yellowstone Trail. Sadly the offices burned down, preventing further research there. The Reservation also straddles the border into Sioux County, North Dakota. Lakota Sioux Indians populate the South Dakota portion. It is the sixth-largest reservation in land area in the United States with a land area of 3,571.9 square miles. McIntosh was laid out and parcels sold in 1910 by the Milwaukee Land Company, a division of the Chicago, Milwaukee, St. Paul and Pacific (The Milwaukee Road) Railway.

McIntosh, as a boom town, marched to the rhythm of the railroad: pool halls and cafes never closed. In 1912 there was [sic] six stalls for engines in the yard and six being built. Three hundred houses stood south of the railroad track where railroad workers lived. Many houses in town with a spare room had a boarder. When the First World War came, three shifts went on in the yards. In the thirties people were forced to turn to the railroad for coal - bits stolen, mostly. Stock was shipped out of the country by rail for decades. The railroads have changed now. High speed steel and diesel trains carry big loads across country without a stop. Morristown World June 1958.

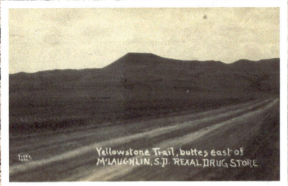

YT on Standing Rock Reservation

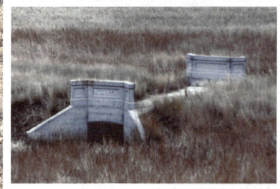

Remains of original box culvert bridge on YT, Standing Rock Reservation

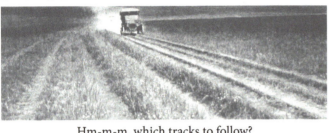

Hm-m-m, which tracks to follow?
The Trail near McLaughlin.

STATE TAKES OVER YELLOWSTONE TRAIL

The State Highway Commission took over the Yellowstone Trail in Corson County as a state highway, and the maintenance of the trail in the future will be under the supervision of the State Highway Commission and the cost to come out of the state funds.

The taking over by the state of the maintenance of the trail through Corson County, a stretch of nearly 100 miles, will be quite a relief to the County. Corson County has spent thousands of dollars annually on the upkeep of the road, in addition to the original cost. It is safe to say that the Yellowstone Trail, all told, has cost Corson County close to $100,000.

February 28, 1924 Morristown World

Note: Popularity has its costs.

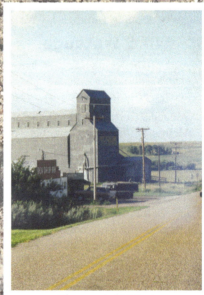

TRAIL GARAGE CO.

PREPARED TO DO MACHINE WORK OF ALL KINDS

VULCANIZING

TUBES AND CASINGS

SPECIALTY

ALL KINDS AUTO SUPPLIES

FREE AIR

MOBRIDGE SO. DAKOTA

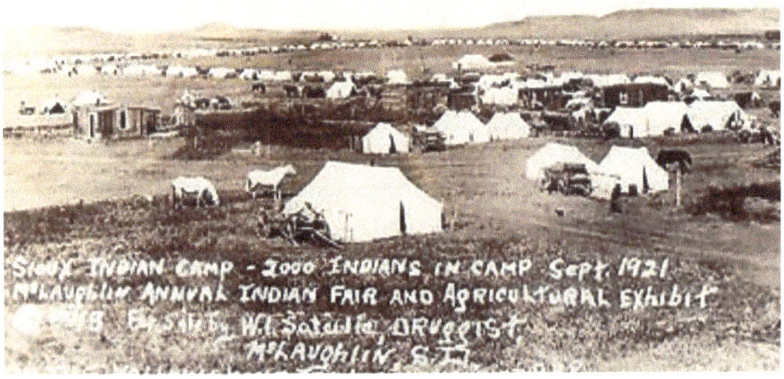

McLaughlin Indian Fair 1921 drew 2000 participants.

Downtown Mahto

SD

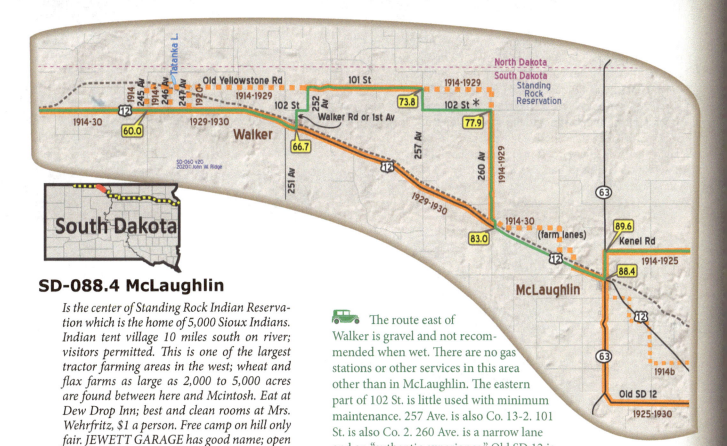

SD-088.4 McLaughlin

Is the center of Standing Rock Indian Reservation which is the home of 5,000 Sioux Indians. Indian tent village 10 miles south on river; visitors permitted. This is one of the largest tractor farming areas in the west; wheat and flax farms as large as 2,000 to 5,000 acres are found between here and Mcintosh. Eat at Dew Drop Inn; best and clean rooms at Mrs. Wehrfritz, $1 a person. Free camp on hill only fair. JEWETT GARAGE has good name; open 24 hrs.; labor $1;phone 12 for road service. MH-1928

(1,633 alt., 200 pop.), is a settlement of whites and Indians. The one-street village, of frame buildings and a bright new community hall, has board sidewalks. A modern, brick schoolhouse contrasts with log cabins and tents in the wooded outskirts of the village. WPA-SD

The route east of Walker is gravel and not recommended when wet. There are no gas stations or other services in this area other than in McLaughlin. The eastern part of 102 St. is little used with minimum maintenance. 257 Ave. is also Co. 13-2. 101 St. is also Co. 2. 260 Ave. is a narrow lane and an "authentic experience." Old SD 12 is made of packed clay.

Routing the Trail through Corson County was always a problem for the Yellowstone Trail Association, almost the whole of the county being on the Standing Rock Reservation. In 1916 Joe Parmley and others laid out a route. Before that the Trail ran along unimproved prairie trails. As late as 1938, US 12/Corson County boosters were begging for oiling their road, evidence that the Trail was still not much improved.

Traveling from the west, the land gently descends from the uplands as the road enters the Missouri River valley. Trees are scarce, visible only lining the length of creeks or planted in yards.

312 Main St., three blocks south of US 12 (Yellowstone Trail). Major James **McLaughlin Heritage Center**. You could stop to see if this interesting, little museum is open. It might not be. The Center was named for James McLaughlin, Indian Agent for the Standing Rock Reservation in the late 1800s. The small Center features a Major James McLaughlin family display and historical documents, early local settlers' memorabilia and hand made Indian articles and art.

The 1887 Dawes Act allowed Native Americans to divide their reservations into individual parcels or allotments which they were expected to farm and, thus, to conform to white patterns of thought. Paul Glad wrote in *The History of Wisconsin Vol;. V, 1990* that, "It opened the way for land-hungry whites to buy reservation land. This policy threatened the cohesion of tribal associations and tribal identity." Today, travel through the Standing Rock Reservation reveals this amalgam of white and Native land owners. ✿

The 1914 *First Year Book* shows the route of the Trail between McLaughlin and the Missouri River following section lines. However, the area had not been well surveyed and marked before the route developed in the area. An undocumented map in the Court House at Selby showed a more realistic original meandering road; a fair length of it remaining in Section 22 today.

DIFFICULTY IN CORSON COUNTY

A committee was appointed at the Aberdeen meeting April 16 and 17 to solicit funds in the east for the construction of this road through Corson County and also for the erection of the bridge across the Little Missouri River at Marmarth.

June 11, 1913 Aberdeen Daily News

The gravel Mahto Road is on scenic unchanged grassland, isolated, windy, and quiet. Generally, it follows Oak Creek. The mouth of Oak Creek is now a bay of Lake Oahe, the dammed section of the Missouri River.

Just east of Mobridge the YT wandered about north of present US 12, documented today by graded remnants and an abandoned concrete bridge (on private property.)

SD-119.1: The original US 12 followed the 1925-1930 route of the YT between McLaughlin and the 1924 Missouri River Bridge.

WORK GRADING NEW TRAIL UNDER WAY

Work of grading on the new route of the Yellowstone Trail from Wakpala to McLaughlin is under way.

The completion of this road will bring the Yellowstone Trail from the Missouri river bridge to McLaughlin without crossing the Milwaukee railway, the road running the entire distance on the south side of the track. Between Wakpala and the Missouri River the Grand River is crossed. This stream was bridged two years ago when the road from the Missouri River to Wakpala was finished.

Surveyors are now at work running the survey between McLaughlin and McIntosh, the last link in the new route of the Yellowstone Trail through South Dakota. The route from McLaughlin west will follow the south side of the railroad to a point near McIntosh where the tracks are crossed on an overhead bridge.

April 8, 1927 Morristown World

Major James McLaughlin was an Indian Agent in the Dakota Territory in the Standing Rock Reservation in 1881. Like most Indian agents of the day, McLaughlin believed that his mission was to "civilize" the Indians by forcing them to adopt white ways. Thus, while he worked hard to improve Indian living conditions, he simultaneously promoted the use of English and the adoption of sedentary farming.

Sitting Bull, famous for his role in Custer's defeat, was assigned to this reservation and his disdain for white ways was well known.

In December, 1890, McLaughlin ordered the arrest of the old chief, believing this might calm the tense situation on the reservation which was fanned by Sitting Bull. Unfortunately, during the arrest, a fight broke out and McLaughlin's Indian policemen killed Sitting Bull. The murder only exacerbated the climate of fear and mistrust.

Major McLaughlin wrote a very long and complete report to the Office of Indian Rights Association in 1891. However, he reported that the followers of Sitting Bull shot first from the crowd and hit the Indian police who were arresting Sitting Bull. Indian police were charged with the task, not the military in an effort to keep peace. In the melee, it was the Indian police who shot Sitting Bull.

"3 New Perspectives on the West: Archives of the West" PBS, September 1996 ✿.

SD

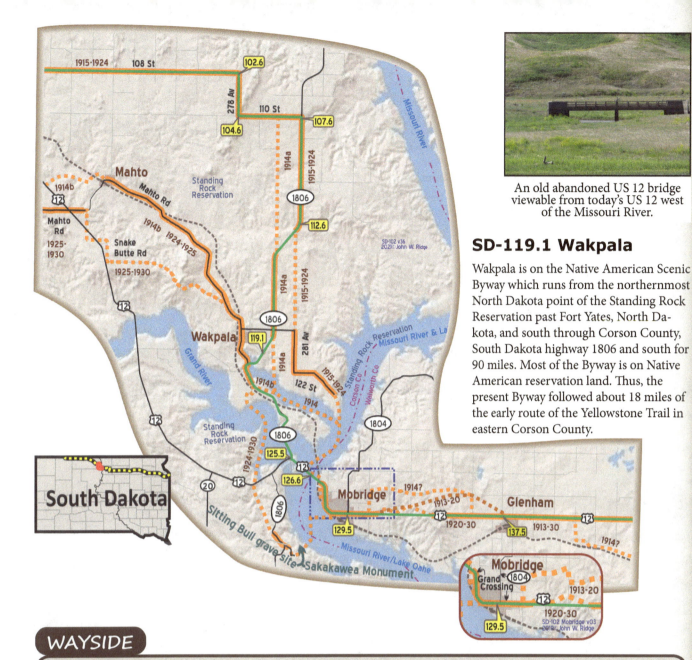

An old abandoned US 12 bridge viewable from today's US 12 west of the Missouri River.

SD-119.1 Wakpala

Wakpala is on the Native American Scenic Byway which runs from the northernmost North Dakota point of the Standing Rock Reservation past Fort Yates, North Dakota, and south through Corson County, South Dakota highway 1806 and south for 90 miles. Most of the Byway is on Native American reservation land. Thus, the present Byway followed about 18 miles of the early route of the Yellowstone Trail in eastern Corson County.

WAYSIDE

Travel south from Wakpala on Co. 1806, the Lewis and Clark Highway, for about 12 scenic miles and you will come to the **Sitting Bull grave site**, and a little further, the **Sakagawea (Sakakawea) Monument**. Or you can get there from Mobridge by going six miles west of Mobridge on U.S. 12 and four miles south on 1806. This is the final resting place of the great Sioux warrior.

Sitting Bull is mostly remembered today as a brave and wise leading figure in battles against whites, in the Battle of the Little Bighorn in which Custer died, and as a leader of the Hunkpapa Sioux. He is also remembered as part of the famous Buffalo Bill Cody's Wild West Show. He was killed in 1890 on the Standing Rock Reservation on which stands this memorial. He was buried at Fort Yates, North Dakota. Sixty-three years passed. The grave at Fort Yates had been neglected and poorly marked. With permission of his relatives, a delegation of men from Mobridge Chamber of Commerce quietly arrived at Fort Yates in April, 1953, and disinterred the bones. He now rests in a steel vault with 20 tons of concrete on top of it on a bluff overlooking the Missouri River/Lake Oahe. Sculptor Korczak Ziolkowski, who began the Crazy Horse Mountain carving near Mount Rushmore, agreed to sculpt the bust of Sitting Bull. GPS: 45.51696, -100.48521.

Variously spelled Sacagawea, Sakakawea. and apparently 15 other ways, not one with a "j", is a memorial to Lewis and Clark's Indian guide. Controversy still whirls around her life story. Her birth date of 1787 meets with less controversy than the date and place of her death and burial. Tribute is paid to "Bird Woman" with this monument which is a few miles away from the Missouri River site where Lewis and Clark once camped. Oddly, the memorial looks more like the Washington monument obelisk in Washington D.C. than a Native American design. GPS: 45.51588 -100.48811.

Information from *November 10, 2011 Native American Culture: "The First Scout"* by Dakota Wind. thefirstscoutblogspot.com

The town of Mobridge was only six years old when the Mobridge Commercial Club invited "good roads" men from Ipswich and Aberdeen to map an auto route to their railroad town in June of 1912. They suggested that the visitors "all come in cars so as to familiarize themselves with the need for road improvement." There was not a mile of that road improved between Aberdeen and Mobridge. The Yellowstone Trail Association had no organization nor even a name yet. Mobridge was just far-sighted in seeing the value of an auto road and, since the county and state were doing little, they saw a future in private endeavors. The 100-mile trip, a "Sociability Run" of 42 trembling Ts, wobbling Wintons, unsteady Studebakers, and assorted others, along with state engineer S. H. Lea, mapped a possible route from the rolling prairie down the precipitous drop to Mobridge and the Missouri River valley. A meeting resulted in a nucleus of the Yellowstone Trail Association. Four months later, October 9-10, saw the formalization of the Twin Cities-Aberdeen-Yellowstone Park Trail Association in Lemmon. ❀

1912 Sociability Run to Mobridge

YELLOWSTONE TRAIL BOOSTERS HOLD ENTHUSIASTIC MEETING AT MOBRIDGE

The second annual meeting of the Yellowstone Trail Association held at Mobridge last Friday and Saturday was attended by about 200 people from the towns along the trail from Billings to Minneapolis.

February 27, 1914 The Marmarth Mail

~~~~~~~~~~~~~~~~~~~~~

Friday evening of last week 100 businessmen from Walworth, Corson, Edmunds and Brown counties gathered at the city hall for the purpose of promoting the Yellowstone Trail. The main purpose was to secure the cooperation of Walworth and Corson counties in building a three mile stretch of road from the [railroad] bridge to Oak Creek.

March 1,1917 reprinted in
The Mobridge Tribune March 1, 1997

Glen Shillingstad, a longtime resident of eastern Mobridge reminisced about the Trail and Mobridge. The Trail swung up across his land, circled and came down again, not in a straight line, beginning about where present US 12 meets his long driveway. He said:

> Highway 12 used to be north of this land when they changed to US 12 in 1925. There is a box culvert up over the hill in the pasture where you can still see the indentation of the Yellowstone Trail in the pasture grass. My uncle did road repair for the county. He had a team, dump wagon and scrapers. The Yellowstone Trail was gravel. All other roads were dirt. ❀

Mobridge has been selected as the place for the annual meeting of the South Dakota region of the Yellowstone Trail Association. Nov. 9 is the date set for the meeting.

October 6, 1921
Dakota County Herald
(Dakota City, Nebraska)

Milwaukee Rd on RR bridge, Mobridge

Standing on old YT box culvert bridge on Shillingstad Farm on east edge of Mobridge

Sitting Bull Grave

After big uproar, a new sign was made by YT boosters.

Misleading sign near Mobridge luring Yellowstone Park travelers off the YT and through the Black Hills

SD-129.5 Mobridge

As the division headquarters for the Pacific extension of the Milwaukee Railroad, the town grew rapidly. A large railroad yard still remains. An excellent collection of Indian relics taken from Ankara village sites near Mobridge is displayed on Main St. In Mobridge are seen ranchers with ten-gallon hats and cowboy boots, and Indians in overalls or shawls. WPA-SD

At Yellowstone Trail and Main St.; pop. 3,000; the live trade center for a big territory, also an important freight and passenger division. Best meals at Pierce Cafe, lunch 40c. City camp, 25c.

BROWN PALACE HOTEL all rooms outside, light and with toilet; dbl. $2.75-$3; with bath $3.75-$4. Cafe in conn.

PIERCE HOTEL is second best; 29 rooms with r. w. and steam heat, 2 with bath; sgl. $1.25; dbl. $2; with bath $3.

S. ERDAHL in Buick Garage on Trail, is reputed best mechanics; labor $1.25; emergency night work; ph. 410 for 24 hr. road service.

DARLING AUTO CO., Ford, is large and modern. Phone 440 until 10 p. m. MH-1928

There was a Yellowstone Garage in 1924.

In May of 1906 work began on the railroad bridge which was to become "the mightiest bridge built anywhere across the Missouri" according to the *1981 Mobridge Tribune 75th Anniversary Special Diamond Jubilee Section*. There was no town until the railroad company established one three miles south of the bridge. They used the railroad telegrapher's abbreviation for Mo. bridge as the name of the new town. It became a major division headquarters with a 26-stall roundhouse. Like other railroad towns, folks moved to the rhythm of the railroad, its major employer. The bridge was replaced over the wider Lake Oahe, created in 1962 now spanning 2349 feet of water.

Main St (YT) Mobridge 1920s
Klein Musem

Auto bridge with Mobridge in background in 1924. The Missouri River here is now Lake Oahe.

Sakakawea Monument
thefirstscoutblogspot. com

Mobridge (Bridge City) is surrounded on three sides by Lake Oahe which was created in 1962 by a dam on the Missouri River near Pierre. The lake swallowed the much narrower Missouri River. Thus, today one sees huge bays and sweeping bridges and a small town making the most of its watery kingdom by attracting tourists and fishermen to this "Walleye Capital." As you look at maps in this book and read about ferry boats and a 1924 auto bridge at Mobridge, you must remember that the distance a bridge had to cover before 1924 was about 1800 feet, not the vast expanse of Lake Oahe created in 1962. For a discussion of Mobridge's ferry boats, the 1924 bridge, and the Yellowstone Trail, see **Trail Tale: Missouri River**, page 210. See also the map on page 212.

Even today people in Mobridge and area are aware of the Yellowstone Trail. There is an area school athletic conference called the Yellowstone Trail Conference, a ranching association called Yellowstone Trail Livestock Improvement Association and even a quilting group called Yellowstone Trail Quilters. Into the 1970s there was still a Trail Café and a Yellowstone Trail pheasant farm. A Yellowstone Trail Café again appeared in the early 2000s.

1820 W Grand Crossing (west US 12; the Yellowstone Trail). **Klein Museum**. European and Indian cultures are both on display in western antiques and in Sioux and Arikara Indian artifacts and beadwork. Typical early scenes such as a post office, dentist's office, and railroad memorabilia are displayed. Living history tours provide hands-on events for children.

212 Main St. **The Mobridge Auditorium (Howe Arena)**. Ten murals, 16' tall X 20' wide, depicting Sioux Indian ceremonies and history decorate the interior walls. Voice narratives accompany viewing. All were painted by the late Oscar Howe, world renowned artist and South Dakota Native American. The auditorium is on the National Register of Historic Places.

301 N Main St. **The Brown Palace Hotel**. Now called the Brown Palace Apartments. Opened in 1918 by A. H. Brown who said, "The people of Mobridge would have a beautiful hotel, as well as public restrooms on Main Street." It took around three years to complete the three-story 110-room building. It also contained a barbershop, lunch room, dining room, and eight apartments. Today, the hotel's exterior appearance remains much the same as in 1918. This building represents an important piece of Mobridge's history.

WAYSIDE

A walking trail along the shores of Lake Oahe is located just south of town.

River bluffs and rugged buttes to the west across Lake Oahe, and rolling plains to the east seem to protect Mobridge down at lake level. One can imagine buffalo by the thousands on the prairie grasslands. One can imagine Mobridge as the big cattle shipping site which it once was. A packing plant was needed, but people objected to the possible smell. "People all came from small farms. It's funny how that smell is bad when you move to Main St.," said resident Mrs. Dale Shillingstad.

Mr. Amerpol in *Bowdle Diamond Jubilee 1886-1961* said,

One has to use imagination to picture this country during the early days of pioneers. At the turn of the century there were still no roads, no trees, just rolling plains and prairies. With no trees, birds made nests on the ground. With no roads it was easy to get lost.

He and others put up markers in every direction showing the number of miles and direction to Bowdle out as far as 20 miles. ⚙

SELBY WILL BOOST FOR BIG TRAIL
ENTHUSIASTIC BOOSTER MEETING HELD AT SELBY LAST EVENING - RESULTS

A most enthusiastic booster meeting was held for the purpose of getting down to brass tacks and arranging a plan whereby the thirty-eight miles of the Twin Cities-Aberdeen-Yellowstone Park Trail through Walworth County could be constructed this year. J. W. Parmley, the main promoter of the trail, was tireless and relentless in his enthusiasm. He had stereoptican views of various sections of the road. All enthusiastically pledged their support. The Walworth County Commissioners pledged $4,000 in addition to the pledges of Selby, Mobridge, Java and Glenham.

April 26, 1913 Aberdeen Daily News

The Yellowstone Trail Garage sold Chevrolet and Dodge cars.

1921 Bowdle Business Directory

The city made a donation of $125 to the Yellowstone Trail Association.

1922-1923 Bowdle Centenniel 1886-1986

TO EXTEND THE YELLOWSTONE TRAIL

A contract has been let April 13 for the construction of the Yellowstone Trail through Walworth County, which is a part of the work laid out by the Yellowstone Trail Association.

Nearly half a million dollars will be spent in graveling the trail through South Dakota this summer. More than thirty-five miles of highway will be put in permanent condition.

May 27, 1920 Ortonville Independent

Note: Do they mean 35 miles in Walworth County or 35 miles out of the 350 across all of South Dakota? It is now seven years after Selby's first meeting and still no gravel in Walworth County?

Businessmen have started work on that section of the Yellowstone Trail which passes through Java.

June 28, 1913 Aberdeen Daily News

Work was begun on the Twin City-Yellowstone Trail where it passed through Bowdle. Contractor Sampson began work on the 3-mile stretch from Bowdle to the Walworth County line. The grading is being done at a cost of $50 per mile to the contractor. The state will build one mile of the road through the state lands east of Bowdle, thus leaving 8 miles in the Bowdle division under the supervision of Mayor Kelles.

June 5, 1913 Bowdle Centenniel 1886-1986

Every telephone pole on the south side of the Yellowstone Trail from Bowdle to the county line three miles west wears a yellow band a foot wide since "Trail Day" May 22. The markings were made equally well for nine miles east by the evening of that day and we understand have since been connected with the markings of Roscoe, making them continuous to Ipswich.

June 4, 1914 Bowdle Centenniel 1886-1986

GRAVEL JOB NEAR SELBY WINDS UP
BIG IMPROVEMENT IN YELLOWSTONE TRAIL MADE IN WALWORTH COUNTY WHICH ADDS MUCH TO ROAD.

February 25, 1925 Aberdeen American

A number of crews are at work at various points on the Yellowstone Trail through Walworth and Edmunds counties to the Brown county line. From there east the Trail is graveled. After next year it will then be possible to drive a motor car from the Missouri River wagon bridge at Mobridge to the Atlantic Ocean on a graveled or paved Yellowstone Trail every foot of the way.

July 24, 1924 Bowdle Centenniel 1886-1986

The 1914 *First Year Book* shows the YT route heading due west of Selby and turning north to present US 12 about three miles east of Glenham. Other maps show the later route (now US 12) only.

SD-150.7 Selby

Cattle and horse raising is carried on extensively as well as farming. Although Selby is several miles from the Missouri River, nearly every spring one resident builds a houseboat, pulls it to the river, floats down to New Orleans for the winter, sells his boat and returns to build another. WPA-SD

The crest of the Missouri River breaks is reached in the area, with a view of the river and bottom-land stretching N. and S., fringed with cedar, willow, and cottonwood trees. Here farming and livestock-raising are carried on together, and proposals for large irrigation projects are made annually. WPA-SD

pop. 800; a wheat area; many German inhabitants. Free camp space on Trail.

HOTEL AUBURN is clean. Dbl. $2; meals 50c. MANKE AND TAYLOR GARAGE, is best equipped; owner a fine mechanic. Labor $1.20; open late. MH-1928

This is the county seat of Walworth County. It wasn't easy, though. Bangor had been the county seat for 20 years, but Selby won a Circuit Court judgement and was the county seat briefly. After several differing court judgements, Selby finally won and a court house was built there in 1913.

4304 4th Ave. **County Court House**. Go take a look at the 100 year old building which looks like a midwestern court house should. Built about the time the Yellowstone Trail reached Selby.

One hundred years ago travelers on the Yellowstone Trail may have camped overnight at the city park. It's still free today.

Corner of Scranton and Main Sts. (SD 103/Yellowstone Trail) **Chesky Auto Co.** You can't miss it. The name is prominently displayed over the entry. In 1917 a frame garage was erected on the site, called the Yellowstone Garage. In 1925 Wm. G. Chesky bought it and by 1928 it became Chesky Garage in the brick building that you see. Today it is used only for storage.

3409 Main St. **Selby Opera House**. Built at $12,000 in 1908. Traveling theater companies put on plays, movies were shown, the Commercial Club was formed there and today, at over 100 years, it is still going strong.

SD-158.4 Java

pop. 330; grain and stock are chief support; country hotel. Spiry & Sons Garage is good Ford agency. MH-1928

The little town had an intriguing name. Story has it that it was named for a really good cup of coffee at a track-side shack for railroad crews. The town was a railroad town settled by people of German and Russian descent in 1900 and got its streets graveled in 1925 in a novel way: money was transferred out of the "liquor fund" on a monthly basis and utilized for the betterment of the streets and walks. No doubt one of those streets was Main Street, the Yellowstone Trail.

The "stair step" route of the Yellowstone Trail that you see south of Java on the map is a good example of the way roads were routed in the early 1900s. Farm section lines determined the route.

By 2000 most of the buildings were dismantled and folks had moved away, allowing time for prairie grass to begin to return, crowding over the once-bustling town.

SD-173.4 Bowdle

pop. 900; mostly German; rooms but no hotel; Bowdle Sales Co. Garage leads. Good meals at Carlsons. Free camp with cook house. MH-1928

There was a Yellowstone Trail Garage in 1924.

Bowdle was settled by farmers of German and Russian heritage and named for Alex Bowdle, a townsite agent for the Milwaukee Road railway. Bowdle became a large grain milling and shipping center because that was the terminus of the railway. Like its neighbors, Bowdle had a municipal light plant in 1911 giving unreliable and limited service until 1925 when the Northern States Power Company stabilized the utility.

Near Java, as elsewhere, the first route of the YT followed the least muddy section line right-of-way. Some became good roads, others became farmers' fields. Several combinations of section lines were used here, apparently.

The YT route just north and west of Selby is now gravel, perhaps poor. A Clason SD map of the period indicates that the route north of Selby ran one mile east of and parallel to 370 Ave.(From "Clason on disk").

SD

The first Electric light and power plant was built in 1916. Power was on from 6:00 AM to 12 PM "with certain days for washing and ironing".
Roscoe-The First 100 Years

In 1918, 25 people died of the influenza epidemic.
Roscoe-The First 100 Years

Chesky Garage, Selby,
corner of Scranton (YT) and Main

Right after World War I citizens of Ipswich built a large arch to span Main St. to honor their fallen boys and other veterans. It was made of wood with a painting of a World War I soldier and a Civil War soldier on the pillars. When traffic required it be moved, it was placed over present US 12 (Yellowstone Trail) in 1928 where the "traffic of the continent would pass under it." It was later destroyed by a tornado and completely rebuilt, this time with I beams and reinforced concrete and covered by donated stones from all over the world - Jordan, Siberia, Alaska, and the Philippine Islands. There is even a meteorite and petrified wood. A sealed metal box containing a copy of the Louisiana Purchase and Indian artifacts, among other items, was buried in the south pillar. Bronze plaques commemorate the dead of World War I and honor J. W. Parmley. In 1974 it became necessary once more to move the Arch. And so you see it here in Collier Park. ✿

Selby Opera House

The Ipswich Arch

Java YT boosters were there 100 years ago

John Spitzer and Ben Mayer purchased the Yellowstone Garage from Jake Schumacher in 1924. They had the dealership in Fords, Fordson Tractors and Durant cars, adding Case machinery in 1925, and changing Case for John Deere in 1927.
Roscoe-First 100 Years
Note: That dealership may have been located on the Yellowstone Trail, present US 12, where there is a Deere dealership today.

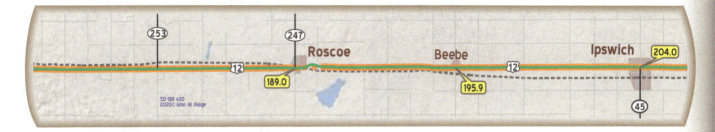

South Dakota

SD-189.0 Roscoe

(1,826 alt., 540 pop.), is a trade center for a farming community, not unlike the small towns of the movies, with pool halls, tall red grain elevators, general stores, square houses, and large frame churches. WPA-SD

The Homestead Act of 1862 drew many immigrants to the promised 160 acres of land at $1.25 per acre. There were farms, but no surveyed town until 1883.

Roscoe was the first home of Joe Parmley, founder of the Yellowstone Trail. He arrived from Wisconsin in April, 1883, having walked the 40 miles from the railroad end in Aberdeen. Upon his arrival, he joined fellow tenters (there was no town there) Sam Basford and Chas Morgan. The three named the "town" Roscoe after Morgan's father's friend, U.S. Senator Roscoe Conkling of New York. Parmley and Henry Huck established a newspaper, the *Roscoe Herald*, on Huck's printing press. Parmley moved his house (literally, with horses and rollers) to Ipswich when the train arrived there in 1885. He continued to publish the paper until 1910 when it became the Ipswich *Tribune* after Parmley had moved to that city. For more on Parmley's life and the Yellowstone Trail, see **Trail Tale: Parmley**, page 208.

SD-195.5 Beebe

Marcus P. Beebe founded the town and was its first banker. He was a friend of Joe Parmley of Ipswich and was a "founding father" of the Yellowstone Trail Association in 1912, and served as its interim president to February 1913 when a first election was held.

The Milwaukee Road railroad arrived in 1886 and served the community until 1982. Once a thriving town with hotels, a post office, churches, and schools, the town of Beebe served as a protection for people traveling the Yellowstone Trail in the winter blizzards. Today there isn't much left of Beebe to see as folks started to move away in 1942.

Work on the YT between Roscoe and Bowdle
1914 First Year Book

Good Roads Are Shortening Distance to Market

Typical Good Roads Movement promotion

STUDEBAKER CARS

While this is an ad from the Todd-Beaver Company in Billings, Montana, the advertised Studebaker seemingly was one of the favorites in these parts (except for the Ford, of course.)
1914 First Year Book

EDMUNDS COUNTY PLAYS THE LEADING PART IN A MOVE FOR BETTER HIGHWAYS

The cost of building the 26 miles between Aberdeen and Ipswich was explained: 03¢ a yard to move dirt for the main grade; cost of moving with wheel scraper 05-12¢ a yard. Cost of gravel "is expensive."

July 25, 1912 The Ipswich Tribune

Note: A major part of this newspaper was devoted to retelling the tale of the meeting about good roads Joe Parmley had called for April 23 and the June 20 "sociability run" to Mobridge. For a more full story, see **Trail Tale: YTA**, page 2.

Welcome to the home of the YT

GRAVEL ROADS IN EDMUNDS COUNTY

President Parmley [of the Yellowstone Trail Association] has donated 2,000 yards of sand and gravel and a large force of men and teams will commence work this week. Forty cents per hour will be paid for man and team.

December 8, 1914 Aberdeen American

I remember well the first year I went to school in the first schoolhouse built in this part of Edmunds county. One day we were all outside when someone noticed a man walking through the grass toward the school. As he got nearer we seen that it was Joe Parmley, Superintendent of Schools for Edmunds County. We all ran for the schoolhouse and took our seats, thoroughly frightened, and looking back now, I cannot see any reason for us being scared. He had started south from Ipswich, then east and back by way of Mina making the trip on foot. *Author unknown. c.1920.* ✿

Ipswich YT Garage

Parmley was elected to the state legislature in 1905 and 1907. 1909 was one of the boom periods and land seekers came flocking in on the trains. J. W. Parmley's Land Office escorted 34 men with eight teams and several autos out to see land which was for sale.

Ipswich 75th Anniversary Book - 1883-1958

In Yellowstone Trail days the town of Mina was "the trade center of a large territory." It boasted of two large general stores, two grain elevators, a bank, a lumber yard and a busy pressed brick factory with a long list of large buildings built with their product, including Joe Parmley's "concrete" fireproof house. [Note: To quote Peter, Paul and Mary, "Where have all the young men gone?" There is nothing much left of the former energetic, hopeful Mina today.] ✿

In March 1917 businesses advertising were, among others, the Yellowstone Garage run by Lass and Lass and the Yellowstone Restaurant run by M. D. Sheldon.

Ipswich: The First 100 Years 1883-1983

Note: Until recently there was a Yellowstone Trail Restaurant on Main St.

Joseph Parmley's Land Office Museum, Ipswich

Joseph Parmley, founder of YT, House Museum, Ipswich

SD

SD-204 Ipswich

The promotion of the Yellowstone Trail (US 12) from "Plymouth Rock to Puget Sound" was begun at Ipswich by Joseph W. Parmley, and the organization, now known as the U. S. No. 12 Association, still maintains its national headquarters here. A World War memorial arch spans the highway, bearing the name of the Yellowstone Trail and its founder. WPA-SD

pop. 943; a grain and stock raising center. The St. James Hotel is not modern, but best. Yellowstone Garage reputed good. Motor Sales Co. is open late. Camp 35c at serv. sta. on highway. WPA-SD

Ipswich is known as the "Home of the Yellowstone Trail" because it was there that resident Joe Parmley founded the Yellowstone Trail Association. Parts of the Yellowstone Trail in Ipswich (8th St. to Broadway) finally got paved with concrete in 1937, but the town itself still has side streets of gravel.

During the summer of 1883 the Chicago, Milwaukee, and St. Paul Railroad built 26 miles west of Aberdeen and stopped. The name of the stopping point was selected by a Milwaukee Road official who was from Ipswich, England. Thirty years later Ipswich was "one of the important shipping points on the Milwaukee Road."

If you visit Ipswich in June you may have the luck of viewing their "Trail Days" a weekend of celebrating the Yellowstone Trail which they have had, on and off, for the last 100 years. Parades, pie contests, bull riding (real bulls), and much more.

319 Fourth St. **J. W. Parmley Historical Home and Museum**. It is on the National Register of Historical Places. The museum was the original home of J. W. Parmley, built in 1919. The home is built of cement, brick and plaster, thought to withstand the many prairie fires that occurred during the early days of Ipswich. Parmley had suffered a house lost to fire before. Active in the Anti-Saloon League, Parmley suffered the loss of his house to a suspected pro-saloon arsonist. There are even a cement bath tub and cement floors. There are two stone fireplaces, which include stones and fossils from all over the world, collected by Parmley during his extensive travels.

115 Main St. **The Parmley Land Office Museum**. Joe Parmley was a land and abstract agent. He sold land to settlers, knew much about agriculture and was a "dreamer" in that he saw and worked for projects to better people's lives. His land office is in a 1900 stone block building. It offers a large map of the entire Yellowstone Trail, views of early Ipswich businesses, and yet another fireplace built of interesting memorabilia and rocks. For a more full story of Parmley's life, see **Trail Tale: Parmley**, page 208.

Between 8th and 9th streets along US 12, the Yellowstone Trail, there is a **memorial arch** standing in Collier Park. That arch has quite a history and is worth seeing.

120 Main St. **Marcus P. Beebe Memorial Library**. Beebe was a banker, philanthropist, and early Trail Association booster. Two other buildings of note are the Marcus Beebe home across the street from the Parmley Home Museum and the First Baptist Church. They are all built of fine fieldstone of the Dakota Territory. The library has a Medicine or Prayer Rock in its front lawn. Found in Mobridge, this petroglyph on a glacial boulder contains the hand prints of a Native American and was considered a symbol of great power.

SD-217.9 Mina

US 12 crosses the neck of Mina Lake, formed by damming Dry Run Creek. Construction of the dam was started by private subscriptions from Aberdeen and Ipswich residents who wanted a recreational site. It was completed with the help of the State Game and Fish Department and Federal relief agencies. The lake is stocked with game fish, and is a State game reserve. Another arm of the horseshoe-shaped lake is crossed over a rock spillway. WPA-SD

Mina Lake (Lake Parmley) Recreation Area, now a state park, is a lovely recreational site with camping, swimming, boating, picnicking and hiking. The lake is horseshoe shaped with the land between the two arms the state park. There was no lake there in Yellowstone Trail days. The Trail crossed one arm of Snake Creek, a wet slough north of Mina, and a bridge crossed the other arm. In 1930 Joe Parmley and others were looking for a way to bring in additional recreational water because a nearby lake was almost dry. Parmley suggested a dam at the fork of Snake Creek. By 1934 that dam was completed and a lake of 20 to 30 feet deep was created. Today, US 12 runs on top of that Parmley Dam. The lake is officially named Lake Parmley, but in general parlance it is Mina Lake. The dam is called Parmley Dam.

Edmunds County has appropriated $800 towards the construction of an eight foot concrete culvert near Mina. This culvert will be of reinforced concrete of the arch design, and will be the first piece of concrete work put in along the Trail in this section.

June 19, 1913 Aberdeen Daily News

SD

Historic Capital
Theater, Aberdeen

HEADQUARTERS ARE OPENED
GENERAL AGENT COOLEY OPENS NATIONAL HEADQUARTERS FOR YELLOWSTONE TRAIL

The Yellowstone Trail national headquarters have been opened in the Mueller Block, 114 South Lincoln Street, and they are very attractive quarters. When one stops to remember that this is the headquarters and managing office for the Trail from Boston to Seattle, this distance being something over 4,000 miles, they will realize that the work done here is considerable.

April 3, 1916 Aberdeen Daily News.

2nd floor housed first HQ of
YTA 1916-18,
114 S Lincoln Ave., Aberdeen

BURNING UP YELLOWSTONE TRAIL

A new record has recently been made for the distance from Minneapolis to Aberdeen, 337 miles, over the new Yellowstone Trail. Eleven hours and thirty minutes was the running time. Average speed for the trip was 29 miles per hour; 21 miles to the gallon.

January 1917 Ford Times

1928 Aberdeen Ward Hotel,
now Aberdeen Ward Apartments

BEST STATE ROADS MEETING

Fourteen of the principal towns along the route of the Trail were represented and … they voluntarily raised the subscription for that work from $3,100 to $3,900 and pledged that amount to carry forward the work.

February 27, 1919 Aberdeen Daily News

Friday night at Melgaard Park where the Yellowstone Trail Free Camp is located, about 12 tents were pitched …Most of the tourists arrived yesterday afternoon and on account of the rains they decided to stay over for a day or two until the roads dry up a little. Last season 11,381 persons registered at this famous camping ground.

June 10, 1922 Aberdeen Daily News

TO ADVERTISE ABERDEEN IN COLLIERS MAGAZINE
TRAIL AND TOURIST GROUNDS TO BE PRINTED WITH STORY IN COLLIERS IN AUGUST

July 9, 1921 Aberdeen Journal

…The first two miles west of Aberdeen is the worst stretch of road upon the whole of the Yellowstone Trail. It is asserted that a day's work by able-bodied businessmen of Aberdeen, a few cars of gravel and a lot of elbow grease would make it the best two miles.

October 17, 1913 Aberdeen American

HUB CITY'S HISTORY BY THE NUMBERS

83 automobiles carrying 285 people from 16 states passed through Aberdeen during the first three weeks of August 1921 part of a tour of the Yellowstone Trail. The tourists registered at the Yellowstone Trail Information Bureau in Aberdeen.

August 1921 Aberdeen American News
[reprinted July 20, 2010]

The Aberdeen Commercial Club has asked for bids for the placing of 36 signs in Brown County advertising the route of the Yellowstone Trail. These signs … will be substantially placed on iron posts five feet above the ground and will be imbedded in concrete 12 inches deep in the ground.

November 12, 1913 Aberdeen American

SD-231.6 Aberdeen

pop 18,000 BB-1921

At the Milwaukee R.R. stockyards, trainloads of cattle, sheep, and hogs from North and South Dakota and Montana are unloaded for rest, water, and feed on their way to packing centers farther east. From 200 to 2,000 carloads of stock pass through the yards each month during the fall shipping season. The yards are interesting by night as well as by day, when trains unload under bright lights. WPA-SD

Business center of northern South Dakota; sometimes called the "Hub City" of the Dakotas. It is situated in the center of the James River valley which is the largest artesian water basin in the world. Road information at the live C. of C, also at booth on Trail. Ward Coffee Shop is best, lunch 50c; Comb's Cafe is Amer. and popular. The Melgaard Tourist Camp, about one mile south, is in a beautiful park covered with Cottonwood trees, 50c per night. MH-1928

[Note: Melgaard Park is still there today.]

It became known as "Hub City" because five rail lines converged there. Five historic depots are located throughout the city.

It was the home of Hal Cooley, the consummate PR man who was the secretary of the Aberdeen Commercial Club when he gravitated to the Yellowstone Trail Association as General Manager in 1916 for 14 tumultuous years. For more about this energetic, creative dynamo, see **Trail Tale: The "Boys"**, page 175.

114 South Lincoln St. **The Yellowstone Trail Association Headquarters 1916-1918**. The headquarters site was at Parmley's Land Office in Ipswich from 1912 to 1916. Parmley then placed the day-to-day affairs in Cooley's hands and the headquarters moved to Aberdeen. It remained there for two years before moving in 1918 to more visible quarters in Minneapolis. The Aberdeen office remained as one of 15 "information bureaus" which acted like today's AAA in giving out maps and information about the Trail.

21 S Main St. **Dacotah Prairie Museum**. Aberdeen's prodigious past is displayed in pioneer life, wildlife, Native American culture, and railroads. A prairie diorama, children's exhibit, and the Telephone Pioneer Museum are also there. This 1889 building is on the National Register of Historic Places.

1 N Main St. **The Chicago, Milwaukee, St. Paul and Pacific (The Milwaukee Road) Station** is completely restored, showing its 1911 Craftsman/Prairie style influences of the early 20th century. It houses the Convention and Visitors Bureau which is well aware of the Yellowstone Trail. It is on the National Register of Historic Places.

104 S Main St. **Alonzo Ward Hotel**. Alonzo R. Ward built his hotel in 1928. Some 76 years later, in 2004, the building was restored. Ninety of the original hotel rooms were converted into 15 luxury condominiums on floors 3-6. The original restaurant, coffee shop, lobby, and commercial spaces were all restored. The exterior still looks like a 1928 building which

original Yellowstone Trail travelers would recognize. It is on the National Register of Historic Places.

Highlands Historic District - Comprised of 17 historic homes built between 1885 and 1952. The area is called "highlands" because the land is about three feet higher than the rest of the town. In flat South Dakota, three feet commands notice. They are mainly on North Main St. between 12th and 15th Aves. NE and S Kline.

415 S Main St. **Capitol Theatre**. It was built in 1926 as a premier vaudeville/silent movie house. Today it is the home of Aberdeen Community Theatre April through November. It also shares its stage with Northern State University productions. From December through March newly released Hollywood films are shown.

Sixth Ave. (Yellowstone Trail) between Dakota and Jackson Sts. is **Nicollet Park**, Aberdeen's smallest park at three-tenths of an acre. It was originally named for Nicollet Ave. which is now Sixth Ave. "Tourists made use of this park from the time the Yellowstone Trail went past it," according to the 1980 *Brown County History*.

Between 17th Ave. and Melgaard Ave. (19th Ave.) end of State St. is **Melgaard Park**. Twenty-five acres were donated to the city in 1909 by Andrew Melgaard. It was frequented by Trail travelers. In 1924 the Commercial Club put up 65 signs along the Yellowstone Trail and the Sunshine Highway directing tourists to the park. Today, after 100 years, it still features campgrounds, but also basketball and volleyball courts, a skate park, and aquatic center.

WAYSIDE

Wylie Park. While Wylie Park is not on the Trail, it is something fun to see along US 281 in northwest Aberdeen. Beyond expectations for a city park, it has over 200 acres of water sports, go-karts, a zoo, and a large campground. Storybook Land and Land of Oz are there, two large areas featuring themes from the Wizard of Oz. L. Frank Baum, author of the Oz stories, lived in Aberdeen from 1888 to 1891 and the community has never forgotten him.

During the heyday of the "trolley," or interurban electric light-rail cars, there were often parks at the end of the line to give people a reason to ride. Wylie Park was one of them. For a more full description of trolleys, see **Trail Tale: Trolleys**, page 393.

TRAIL OFFICE HAS MANY INQUIRIES

Last week more people inquired at the local Yellowstone Trail Information Bureau than inquired at the Fort Wayne, Minneapolis, Missoula, Miles City, or Spokane Bureaus. Milwaukee Bureau was the only one along the entire trail that had more tourists ask for information than did the Aberdeen office.

July 23, 1920 Aberdeen American

SD

Although the town of Bath was about a mile north of the Trail, citizens immediately claimed the Trail as theirs, working on it during Trail Days and, apparently, working to repair it during a devastating flood in 1922. ✿

The new bridge across the Jim [James River] on the Yellowstone Trail is being put in now. The span is an 80-foot one. The old bridge was shipped to Mansfield.
May 7, 1914 Aberdeen Weekly News

Because the gravel highway from Aberdeen to Redfield was in good condition in 1926, fire fighters from Redfield were able to reach Aberdeen in forty-one minutes - a distance of forty-two miles - when fire broke out at the Ward Hotel.
1926 reported in Brown County History 1980
Note: Most roads were still dirt at that time, and as late as 1956 only 128 miles out of 492 miles of highway in the county were black topped.

1884 Groton Trinity Episcopal Church

Until recently there was
Trail Chev on US 12, Groton

On the Twin City-Aberdeen-Yellowstone Park Trail, the first one to move dirt on this great highway was E. J. Mather, who has taken a mile that he intends to put in fine shape. After completion he will put a stone monument, painted yellow with the word 'Trail' in black letters on the corner of his farm.
June 27, 1913 Aberdeen Daily News
Note: Note the personal participation and "ownership" in maintaining the Trail.

WARNING TO SPEED FIENDS:
MAYOR CAMPBELL CALLS ATTENTION TO SPEED LIMITS
Automobile drivers, taking advantage of the splendid Yellowstone Trail through the city, have been speeding through Groton in excess of the speed limit of 15 miles per hour.
June 25, 1915 Aberdeen American

YELLOWSTONE TRAIL IMPASSABLE AT JIM:
WASHOUT COVERS QUARTER OF A MILE OF TRAIL AT YELLOWSTONE TRAIL
A washout on the Jim [James River] just west of the bridge over the Yellowstone Trail [sic], last night has rendered about a quarter of a mile of the trail impassable. Laborers were at work in an effort to save the new earthern dike which was built by the county along the Jim River last year as a part of the Yellowstone Trail. The Trail at that point was reported under water yesterday afternoon.
April 11, 1922 Aberdeen Journal

~~~~~~~~~~~~~~~~~~~~~~~~~~~

WILL COMMENCE WORK ON RAISING THE YELLOWSTONE TRAIL THIS WEEK
May 15, 1922 Aberdeen Journal
~~~~~~~~~~~~~~~~~~~~~~~~~~~

TWENTY CARLOADS OF GRAVEL EVERY DAY TO BE PLACED ON YELLOWSTONE TRAIL
The situation at the James River has been aggravated this year by more water than has been known in this territory in the last twenty years.
May 17, 1922 Aberdeen Journal

Olde Bank Building
(now a floral company), Groton

SD

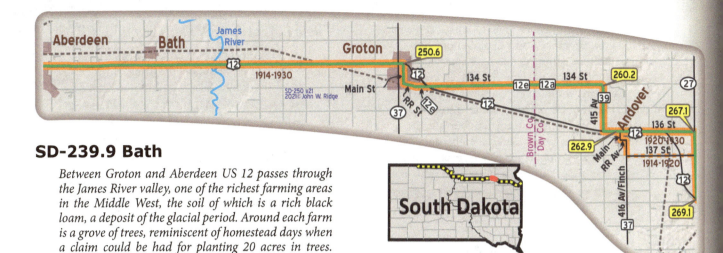

SD-239.9 Bath

Between Groton and Aberdeen US 12 passes through the James River valley, one of the richest farming areas in the Middle West, the soil of which is a rich black loam, a deposit of the glacial period. Around each farm is a grove of trees, reminiscent of homestead days when a claim could be had for planting 20 acres in trees. WPA-SD

The Bath Meteorite. John Paul Gries in *Roadside Geology of South Dakota* (1996) reports that a meteorite fell near Bath in 1892. He describes it colorfully thus:

People watched in amazement as a meteorite that weighed 46 pounds fell near Bath in a blazing fireball on the afternoon of August 19, 1892. Searchers had no difficulty finding it on the silty surface of the sediments deposited in Glacial Lake Dakota, which are certifiably free of rocks. Most of the meteorite is stony, composed of chondrules about the size and shape of bird shot with some metallic nickel-iron. Several of the large museums in the United States have spectacular polished slices on display, as does the British Museum of Natural History.

SD-250.6 Groton

(pop. 1,200, alt. 1,301 ft.), is an attractive little city situated in the center of a level, alluvial plain that in prehistoric times was the bed of the glacial lake Dakota. More than 1,000,000 bushels of wheat have been marketed in Groton in a single season. It is also fast becoming famous as a purebred Holstein center. Pheasant hunting is especially good along the James River, and the bright-colored ring-neck pheasants are to be seen any day, any season, somewhere along the highway. BB1921-9

GROTON, at bank; pop. 1,300; in center of the richest farm land in South Dakota. Country hotel. Ford Garage is best. Fine free camp in city park. MH-1928

210 3rd St. N. Small white **Trinity Episcopal Church** was built in 1884 and restored in 2009. Yellowstone Trail travelers must surely have stopped at this lovely, peaceful place.

SD-262.9 Andover

(alt. 1,475. Pop 324) was first known as Station 88 by railroad graders, but when the town was platted in 1881 it took its present name from Andover, Mass. This market town for a rich farming region has a large, old-fashioned hotel, the Waldorf. WPA-SD

Waldorf Hotel, recently demolished, Andover

The **Waldorf Hotel** was a memorable place. Its size stood out in this small community and it was clearly visible from the Yellowstone Trail (US 12). It is no more today. In 2000, residents of Andover tried to restore the 1902 "best hotel between Aberdeen and Minneapolis" but to no avail. Social life once centered around the hotel and Yellowstone Trail travelers certainly visited the three-story landmark on the prairie with its wide, curved front porch. As the population dwindled, resources faded and interest in preservation for so few also faded. It is now only a grassy space with lots of memories.

Small as it is, Andover still is the site of the annual James Valley Threshing Show. Steam engines, antique tractors and everything historic about farming is featured for the large crowds that gather the first weekend after Labor Day.

SD

> ## WAYSIDE
>
> 40161 128th St., Groton. **The Granary Rural Cultural Center**. Directions: East on US 12 to 402nd Ave. North on 402nd Ave. for 5 miles. West on 128th St. for ½ mile. The Center is composed of a 1928 granary building housing five art galleries and a restored 1912 town hall which can be used for meetings or presentations. The best way to describe this site is to say "art space in action." You can see local artists at work, browse the art galleries or become an artist for a day yourself. The Center is operated by the Dacotah Prairie Museum of Aberdeen.

Bristol still has a "Commercial Club" today. Most towns now call that civic organization a Chamber of Commerce. The interesting thing about that name, Commercial Club, is that that was the name of such civic groups over 100 years ago. Commercial Clubs would sponsor Trail events like Trail Days, cross-country races, local camping parks on the Trail, information bureaus, etc. Fast forward 100 years and you find Chambers of Commerce in some towns supporting the efforts of the new Yellowstone Trail Association to publicize the Trail. ✿

TRAIL BEING GIVEN NEW FEDERAL MARKING THRU STATE

Under the federal enumeration, the Trail, which has been No. 16 under the South Dakota plan, is now US 12. Upon the metal background shaped like a shield the words 'South Dakota' and 'United States' are printed.

June 8, 1926 Aberdeen Evening News

BOOZE RUNNERS MAKE ABERDEEN THIS CITY A WAY STATION AND YELLOWSTONE TRAIL MAIN ROUTE FOR RUNNERS

The Yellowstone Trail from Aberdeen east to Minneapolis has been the route for auto runners carrying on a traffic in booze hauled in from across the Canadian border.

August 17, 1920 Aberdeen American

WEBSTER GOOD ROADS BOOSTERS ARE IN LINE

The Webster Commercial Club is getting in line to boost for the Twin City-Aberdeen-Yellowstone Park road through this city and will hold good roads meetings in the near future. A representative has been sent to the meeting of the association in Miles City, and letters pledging the support of the businessmen of this city sent to the officers.

February 17, 1913 Aberdeen Daily News

Note: Miles City held the first annual national meeting of the Yellowstone Trail Association.

 Determining dates of the routes of the YT is often frustrating. Webster provides a good example. Early in our research, we found that the YT is authoritatively documented within the 1914 *First Year Book* to follow the route running south of Webster. Sources dated 1925 and after show the use of the northern east-west route. The availability of the 1916 and 1923 ABBs (Western volumes) show the route through town nw/se. The now impassible 12th Ave. route was included in a request to the State by Waubay citizens in 1923. Leaves room for error!

TO BOOST YELLOWSTONE TRAIL

The Day County Yellowstone Trail Association has been organized to push the building of a highway across the county from east to west to be a part of the Twin City-Aberdeen-Yellowstone Trail.

March 12, 1913 Grand Forks (ND) Daily Herald

WILL STATE AND NATION HELP CITY?

The state highway law does not authorize the expenditure of highway funds upon the streets of any city, but it is also held to be a reasonable theory that the law can be amended so that highway funds may be applied in the improvement of any municipal street which is a part of a charted public highway.

May 30, 1922 Aberdeen Daily News

Note: The article raises the question: if a state and national "charted and designated" highway runs through a town and needs repair, who pays for it?

PATROL TRAIL IN DAY COUNTY

Not only has the Trail been graded and built to perfection with gravel, but now it is going to be patrolled west of Webster and kept in perfect repair. Three men will be required to cover three patrol districts and bids are being asked for the work.

February 3, 1922 Aberdeen American

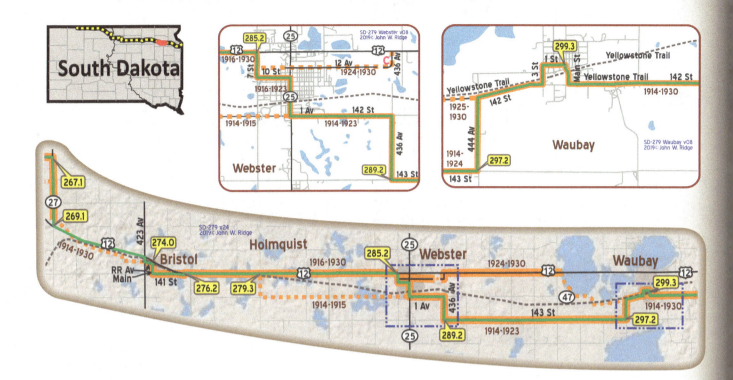

SD-274.0 Bristol

(1,775 alt. 624. pop.) has the largest creamery in the region, the farms around having large dairy herds. The town was named for Bristol, England, in 1881, when it became the terminal of the Milwaukee R.R., but it was not until 1921 that it was actually incorporated. WPA-SD

Between Bristol and Andover the range of hills dwindles to level prairie, and large wheat fields spread out in all directions. Occasionally early in the morning coyotes are seen on the hills near the road, and in the spring large flocks of geese feed in the cornfields along the highway. WPA-SD

BRISTOL, at bank; pop. 650; noted for being an alfalfa seed center; has fine creamery. McGarry hotel is good, not modern. Bristol Motor Co., Ford, has fine reputation and works on all cars. Free camp space among trees south of town. MH-1928

Bristol gas pump collector

Like many other midwest towns, Bristol was born as a result of railroad expansion and named by a person with British connections. See, for instance in this area, Groton, Aberdeen, Ipswich. Bristol became a real rail center in the 1880s with seven tracks and many trains traversing through town carrying settlers west. The Yellowstone Trail ran down Main St. and brought improvements of gravel and street lighting. Parts of the Trail are still visible and used today.

Bristol once sported two hotels which catered to traveling businessmen arriving on the new railroad and to Yellowstone Trail travelers. One hotel, the Brokaw Hotel, was built by a great-grandfather of former TV news anchor Tom Brokaw. It has been removed. **The McGarry House** still stands at 77 Main St. but is repurposed as a seed company.

At 2nd Ave. and 3rd St. you will see a display of **old fuel pumps** on private property.

May, 1997 Highway 12 Guide. "Parts of the Trail are still visible and used, but with the flooding of 1993, the portion immediately east of Bristol has been flooded. Some of the Trail west is still used by farmers."

SD-279.3 Holmquist

(85 pop.), has three large white houses, pretentious in the 1890s, and identical in appearance. It is a safe wager that every third person in the community is named Holmquist, Olson, Peterson, Johnson, Helvig, Sundstrom, or Jensen. WPA-SD

Just east of Webster (point "C" on the city map) (GPS: 45.33772, -97.48949) marks a cut off corner on the original US 12 and the 1925-1930 route of the YT, suggesting the high traffic volume there before the completion of the modern US 12 alignment.

The late Harry Tesch, a long time resident of Waubay and a knowledgeable person about the Yellowstone Trail having grown up on it, recalled for us the story of his father helping to rebuild the Yellowstone Trail in front of their farm four miles east of Waubay in 1917. He recalled the huge casting machines which sliced off the dirt in the ditches and rolled it up to be moved to low places in the road. Sixteen mules pulled the machine with about 15 men in the crew. Such deep ditches allowed good drainage, but were very hazardous to drivers. Later in life, Harry built three miles of road over Rush Lake. Harry worried about the rising water, fearing for the life of the former Yellowstone Trail.

Waubay is pinched on 3 sides by lakes often above flood stage and has been troubled for several decades. Waubay is in a closed basin with no natural outlet for the lakes for above-normal rain and snowfall. Bitter Lake south of Waubay has risen 25 feet in the last 20 years.

Harry may have been right to be concerned about the Trail. ✿

A contract for fifteen miles between Summit and Twin Brooks on the Yellowstone Trail was let yesterday to Dodd Brothers of Watertown for $40,000. The contract calls for extensive grading of the road. It is reported that with the completion of this job, the Yellowstone Trail to Big Stone Lake will be the best highway in South Dakota.
June 29, 1921 Aberdeen Journal

The county commissioners have appropriated $325 for the betterment of the Yellowstone Trail west of Summit.
August 10, 1914 Aberdeen Daily News

WAYSIDE

Roslyn is 12 miles north of Webster but deserves your attention for two reasons:

1.) There is **The International Vinegar Museum**, 502 Main St., run by a most unusual man and is worth your short trip off the Trail. There is more to see and learn about vinegars of the world and about Lawrence Diggs, the curator, than we can tell here.

Mr. Diggs, aka the Vinegar Man, has served as a consultant/connoisseur everywhere about vinegars. Did you know that there were dessert vinegars? He has been featured in *American Profile*, *Bon Appetit* and too many others to name. He is a native of San Francisco, but found a summer home in tiny Roslyn, South Dakota, where he conducts tours, cooking demonstrations, a parade, and shows you how paper is made with vinegar!

2.) Mr. Diggs went on a tour of the Yellowstone Trail some years ago and broadcast the Trail even though Roslyn isn't quite on it. He hoped to encourage communities to work together to create a consciousness of the Trail as a tourist destination. He was on local radio programs and newspapers in the East with his message of broadcasting the existence of the Trail. The new Yellowstone Trail Association received telephone calls from all along the Trail wondering about the Trail and Mr. Diggs after he had visited their towns. Just go to Roslyn!

County and city histories often reveal the flavor of the times. Here is a sample of quotes taken from the local weekly newspaper, *Reporter & Farmer*, and printed in *Webster …As It Was* (1989).

- April 23, 1925. A speaker for the Ku Klux Klan held forth at the opera house Monday evening to a good sized crowd. We fail to find many who were greatly impressed with the necessity for such an organization.

- June 9, 1926. Sprague is erecting a new filling station. This new station will make three stations within two blocks on the trail.

- February 7, 1929. Rural mail patrons are strongly urged to open up roads through the snow, at least make passable for teams, and all road supervisors should organize this work among the patrons living along the rural routes to maintain open lines for the rural carriers.

- July 27, 1929. The Stop and Go sign at the intersection of Main Street with the Yellowstone Trail was removed this week and the trail through Webster is now an arterial highway.

- 1931, the year after the Yellowstone Trail Association closed its doors, the Webster book reported the closure of three banks in the area. ✿

South Dakota issued the first metal license plates in 1913 to 14,000 autos. Before that, "plates" were fashioned of leather or wood to identify one car from another (all cars were black). There were no dates on plates until 1916. In 1926 plates began to have county numbers on them, numbers issued according to the counties' populations. The first two digits were county identifications. Grant County, for instance, was #26, but got booted down to #29 as other counties surpassed them in population, according to Arvel Trapp, Milbank license plate collector. ✿

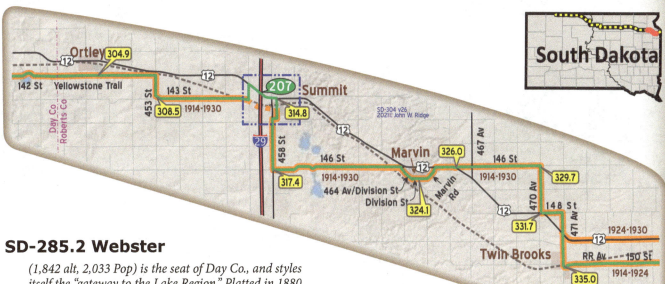

SD-285.2 Webster

(1,842 alt, 2,033 Pop) is the seat of Day Co., and styles itself the "gateway to the Lake Region." Platted in 1880 and named for the first settler, J. B. Webster, the town attracted young businessmen to the new farm frontier. A prosperous, civic-minded town has developed until now; it has a paved main street and two newspapers, one of which, The Journal, is widely known in journalistic circles for its rhyming headlines. WPA-SD

WEBSTER is the county seat of Day County. Best meals at Knapp's Cafe; lunch 50c. Compton Park, a free city camp on Yellowstone Trail, in a beautiful box-elder grove. COMMERCIAL HOTEL popular and well managed. sgl. $1.25-$1.75; dbl. $2; with bath $2.75. DAY COUNTY AUTO CO. best for heavy cars; has only wrecker; labor $1, or flat rate. Phone 228. Rush Lake; good duck hunting. MH-1928

The Glacial Lakes region of northeast South Dakota was shaped by the moving of glaciers over 20,000 years ago, leaving behind rolling hills and numerous (120) lakes. That is great for the locally promoted recreational fishing industry.

760 W US 12. **Museum of Wildlife, Science, and Industry.** The 23-building museum complex, open May-Oct., honors South Dakota's agriculture, pioneers, and history with Native artifacts and displays of an historic village. They have a 1920 map showing the Yellowstone Trail paved from Webster to Aberdeen. The map shows that stretch as "highly improved" and other roads not so improved. The nature of the "paving" was not described.

SD-299.3 Waubay

(1,813 alt., 976 pop.), is the English corruption of the Indian word "wamay" (where wild fowl build their nests), first given to the chain of lakes NW. of Waubay. The town is popular with the Indians, one of the few towns in which Sioux Indians actually reside. On the streets are Indian women in shawls and blankets, old men in moccasins. Having been founded in 1880, Waubay has many frame buildings, holds square dances with old-time music as often as modern dances, and nearly every male resident is a good fisherman. Blue Dog Lake is to the north. WPA-SD

RUSH LAKE, so called because of its tall rushes and boggy marshes. Muskrat houses are in the water; ducks also nest during the spring and summer. Often in spring great white pelicans are seen. Hunting clubs from the East have lodges here for fall duck and goose hunting. WPA-SD

WAUBAY MOTOR CO. Ford, but work on all cars; open 6:30-10 p. m. Storage 50c. Phone 46 for tow car. MH-1921

There was a Yellowstone Garage in 1924.

A great place for fishing, Waubay is the center of several above-flood-stage lakes which offer fishing. The National Wildlife Refuge includes more than 4,500 acres of wetlands which provide nesting places for more than 100 species of birds.

Lake waters seem to be rising in Waubay, closing some streets, 142nd St., for instance. US 12 (Yellowstone Trail) has been raised.

SD-304.9 Ortley

(168 pop.), is gradually moving toward the highway to take advantage of the tourist traffic. An Indian celebration is held here each June. WPA-SD

SD-314.8 Summit

(2,000 alt., 503 pop.), is the highest point along the railroad in the Coteau range, about 1,000 ft. above Big Stone Lake. Because the town had an altitude greater than any other between the Mississippi and Missouri Rivers, it was named Summit. Each year a celebration is held to observe the anniversary of the opening of the Sisseton Indian Reservation. The celebration occurs the latter part of June. WPA-SD

pop. 500; a farm settlement. Summit rooms, not modern, but clean. Larson Brothers are best mechanics. Small free camp in center of town. MH-1928

So named because it is the highest point in SD.

Authors find an apparently original
YT marker rock at Marvin

Pharmacist-turned cigar manufacturer, Nels Frederick Nelson, produced cigars in Milbank for around 12 years. He received patent #18624 on December 26, 1915 for registering the label "Yellowstone Trail" on his cigars. "Be a Man. Smoke Cigars" was his motto. The recession of the late 1920s brought an end to the business. At one time there were 34 employees producing the trademark Yellowstone Trail and Ariston cigars.

The 100-year-old Yellowstone Trail cigar box shown here was a gift from Trail friend Lance Sorensen. ✿

Grant County Museum, Milbank

1921 Annual Report South Dakota Highway Commission to the Governor. FEDERAL AID PROJECT #3. Milbank-Big Stone Road (Yellowstone Trail). "This project is 11.83 miles long." ✿

Contract for grading and structures was awarded to Scholberg and Kane of Marvin in the fall of 1918. Total amount of contract was $24,512.17. No work was started until June, 1919, and very poor progress was made by the contractor, as the work was in charge of a superintendent who had very little or no experience in highway construction. ✿

All along the road between Marvin and Milbank crews are at work on the Yellowstone Trail. In that part of the Trail which lies in Osceola Township, [they] are working industriously with a few others who are working out their taxes.

June 20, 1913 Marvin Monitor

The Milbank Commercial Club has completed the graveling of four miles of the Twin Cities-Aberdeen-Yellowstone Park Trail east of Milbank. This is the first stretch of graveled road along the Trail in this state.

October 1, 1913 Aberdeen Daily News

MAKE AUTO ROAD OF OLD MILWAUKEE GRADE

A movement is on foot at Big Stone to secure as part of the Twin Cities-Aberdeen-Yellowstone Park Trail the abandoned Milwaukee railroad grade through the hills in this section of South Dakota. The grade, being perfectly level, could easily be converted into an ideal automobile highway. It extends from Big Stone to Milbank, is already graveled, and all that it needs is widening somewhat to make it one of the best automobile highways on the continent.

February 11, 1913 Aberdeen Daily News

TRAIL DAY MONDAY WAS A BIG SUCCESS WEATHER PERFECT

Eleven teams, a tractor, and some 50 persons made up the roster. More than 100 loads of gravel were hauled by the close of the day on the stretch between the old depot at Big Stone City and the little red bridge crossing the Whetstone River. There was not the desired number of teams on the job because of the corn planting season and for this reason another Trail Day is being talked of.

May 27, 1920 Ortonville Independent

There was once a Yellowstone Trail Garage in Marvin where the Post Office now stands. ✿

Milbank

🚗 An aesthetically pleasing view of the Marsh Rainbow Arch bridge can be seen from the US 12 bridge between Big Stone City and Ortonville, MN. See Ortonville on page 219 for more information. The deteriorating bridge is now used as a footbridge along the old YT route and is worth exploring.

SD-324.1 Marvin

(1,657 alt, 136 pop.) There was a Marvin safe in the railroad office and a local punster suggested that Marvin was a "good, safe name." WPA-SD

Between Marvin and Summit, US 12 winds into the Coteau des Prairies, "hills of the prairies", so-named by early French explorers. From the crests of the hills are splendid views of Big Stone Lake, Lake Traverse, and far into Minnesota. WPA-SD

MARVIN; pop. 150; a village. Meals, gas and supplies. Westley's garage leads. Camp proposed. MH-1928

About midway between Marvin and US 12 on Division St./464th Ave. Look northeast to find an apparently original

Trail marker. In 2001 it looked like the picture. Since then it has been repainted dark yellow/orange by some good-hearted citizens making it less authentic but easier to find.

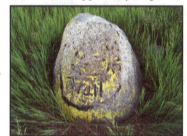

GPS: 45.26229, -96.91898

SD-342.8 Milbank

(1,148 alt, 2,549 pop.), was named for Jeremiah Milbank, a director of the Milwaukee R.R., which was extended through the city in 1880. A windmill, once used to grind grain from the surrounding country, has been moved to the center of the city, Left of US 12 (YT). WPA-SD

pop; 2,600; county seat of Grant County; an exceptionally attractive and substantial-looking little city, in the heart of a noted dairy section. St. Hubert Cafe leads. City camp in the court house yard 50c.

HOTEL ST. HUBERT has good beds and running water in all rooms; sgl. $1.25-$1.50; dbl. $2; with bath $3.

ROGGENBUCK GARAGE, is reputed best for repairs; light mech. work until 11 p. m. Labor $1. Phone 87. MH-1928.

As was true in many towns, Milbank had a Yellowstone Trail Garage in 1924. The city's "mascot" is a **large windmill**. According to their website, this 1882 windmill once powered a grain mill that supplied the town of Milbank with sustenance until 1907. It has been moved around the city, but it is now on display along US 12 (Yellowstone Trail). It has been completely renovated and a current announcement states that the mill will offer tours, and will be a working mill, one of only 50 in the country.

The corner of Third St. and Third Ave. **The Grant County Museum** is in a former Carnegie Library building. It houses Grant County memorabilia and artifacts.

[Note: There is a misleading sign at Hardees restaurant on US 12 calling US 12 the Yellowstone Trail "coast to coast." US 12 does not and never did go "coast to coast;" it ends at Detroit. Today, highways that now fall on top of or are near the old transcontinental Yellowstone Trail are numbered variously, 14 U.S. numbers, 25 state numbers, two Interstate numbers and a myriad of county numbers or letters, certainly not a single number such as US 12.]

SD-353.8 Big Stone City

(979 alt., 675 pop.), overlooks the lake from which it takes its name, and, in addition to being a summer resort center, has a brick factory, corn cannery, and granite quarry; During summer and fall the population becomes considerably larger. WPA-SD

Big Stone City is at the eastern end of the South Dakota leg of the Yellowstone Trail. It lies at the southern tip of Big Stone Lake. Originally the county seat for Grant County, the county seat was moved to Milbank in 1880 after a much heated battle between the two towns.

Around the time the Yellowstone Trail went through, the town was considered a summer resort center for the surrounding area. Trail travelers no doubt visited Big Stone Lake, a narrow freshwater lake and reservoir and source of the Minnesota River which today, 100 years later, is still a good fishing and great recreational site. There is also a nature reserve here.

SD-356.1 S. Dakota/Minnesota Line

Joe Parmley: The Time Had Come

Stuck again! The mud of Helgerson Slough between Aberdeen and Ipswich, South Dakota, did a number on anyone trying to drive that "road," including Joe Parmley. Anyplace where the grass was worn off was called a "road" in 1912, and woe be to the person who tried it in wet weather.

Henry Ford had been cranking out his Model Ts for at least four years and now couldn't keep up with the demand. The black beauties were delivered to dealers by the trainload. Yet the proud owner had only limited space in which to show off his prize. Technology was there to build roads, yet the will of governments was not; there was no need, they felt. A metaphor would be like demanding local space landing stations today for interplanetary travel. Engineers probably could do it, but why? Chicken or the egg conundrum then.

The South Dakota legislature established a State Highway Department in 1913, but roads were administered either by counties or townships. No funds were provided.

The first mile of a concrete road had been already laid three years ago near Detroit and here they were with dirt roads. Parmley was so disgusted by that slough experience and the lack of governmental action at any level that he called men of vision together for a good roads meeting to do something about the crisis. There had to be a better way. The time had come!

The press called that wet April 23, 1912 meeting another good roads group. Actually, it was the beginning of the formation of the Yellowstone Trail Association, a massive effort to get a coast-to-coast, long-distance road built, county by county. The creation of this Association most affected the eventual 8,000 members dramatically and the millions of people who traveled all or parts of those 3,600 miles perhaps tangentially, but gratefully. See the history of the Trail in **Trail Tale: YTA**, page 2.

Parmley the Man

Who was this prescient, common man with uncommon energy? A native of Wisconsin, after college, this tall, thin young man eagerly went west to seek his fortune like many did in 1883. He and two others founded the hamlet of Roscoe, South Dakota, where he started a newspaper and other endeavors. He also noted the problems that farmers had getting their products to market, let alone getting to a railhead miles away. When the Milwaukee Road railway reached Ipswich, 15 miles to the east, Joe moved there, literally; he put his house on rollers pulled by a team.

Farming just outside of Ipswich was only one aspect of his very multi-faceted life. He studied law and was admitted to the bar (but did not practice law), got married, and acquired Edmunds County Abstract Company, all in 1887. As a Land

Agent, he traveled daily the rural "roads" of Edmunds county, showing land to immigrant farmers, and experiencing once again the road problems. Was it here on the prairie that he began dreaming about profound social changes that a road could bring? He knew that it cost the farmer more to get his crops to a railhead than it did to ship them to Chicago. He knew that people in Roscoe and Ipswich had to travel up to 40 miles to Aberdeen for supplies. A good road was an economic necessity. He also knew that even the county government charged with road maintenance was doing little.

So he became a Republican state legislator, elected in 1905 and again in 1907. He often spoke about the uncomfortable problem of roads. In 1907 he proposed the unthinkable: people should pay their road tax in cash, not "work out" their tax by leaning on a shovel for a day. The other legislators hooted him down righteously.

Parmley's car with the trail route in gold paint
Joe Trotzig

Parmley the Founder

The frustration at the lack of progress concerning roads lead to his formation of the Yellowstone Trail Association. The idea of a cross-country route was not new, but a coast-to-coast booster-supported trail association certainly was. He set in motion a conversation that others were anxious to participate in when he talked roads. The organizationally nimble Parmley harnessed the local boosterism that ran in the businessmen-farmer's veins. One could say that Parmley led the race toward the inevitable.

In those days, progress was accomplished mostly face-to-face. He had an exhaustive list of speaking engagements to audiences large and small. Joe Parmley visited the chapters of the Trail Association, traveling by train by necessity at the beginning. Early Chambers of Commerce, called Commercial Clubs, were the "movers and shakers" of communities and they heard from Joe —often. He appeared in ⇨

person in western Montana to confer with Highway Commissioner George Metlen and Trail boosters to select the best route. He did the same in Corson County, South Dakota, on the Standing Rock Reservation. Having been in the state legislature and having the prospect of a future on the State Highway Commission a few years hence, he knew which men to consult.

In 1915 he decorated his auto in a stellar way to make his many trips. He painted the route of the Trail, from Plymouth Rock to Puget Sound, in gold on his black Studebaker. Some said it was gold leaf. However, that was probably not characteristic of this practical man. The eastern terminus of the Trail, Plymouth Rock, is shown just beneath the windshield on the right side (passenger side) of the car. The yellow ribbon follows the contour of the body back around to the left side driver's window labeled Seattle. All of the major cities on the Trail were labeled. Today, millions of cars, trucks and buses bear advertisements, but it was certainly a bold statement then.

Beyond the Trail Association

His was not a one verse song. As an exponent of the spirit of progress, his mind seemed to dwell on visions of various ways to help common men. In 1915, while he was president of the young Yellowstone Trail Association, he was also president of two state development organizations, and the South Dakota Good Roads Association. But his favorite, along with roads, was the South Dakota Peace Society. With an equal fervor, he pushed for a Peace Garden located on the U.S.-Canada border. This idea was born early on, but did not reach fruition until 1932. That park is still located today between Dunseith, North Dakota, and Boissevain–Morton, Manitoba, adjacent to the southeast corner of Turtle Mountain Provincial Park. Main features of the 3.65 square mile park include gardens, an 18-foot floral clock, fountains, chimes, and a peace chapel. His dedication to the concept of peace may have suffered disappointment when his son made the Army his career.

He advocated the wise use of natural resources including soil and water conservation, diversified farming, hydro-electric power, and dam-building. One dam he backed, today called Parmley Dam, created beautiful Mina Lake out of two streams near that hated Helgerson Slough.

Add to this the fact that he ran for Congress (lost), and was nominated to various state commissions and boards by seven different governors. To the average person, this looks like he spread himself thinly with his achievements so widespread.

What Was He Like?

So what kind of a man can juggle many civic balls at once, in addition to holding his farm and job? Remember, no computers then. Also, no secretary and just one typewriter and the first telephone in Ipswich. What kind of man can inspire men to help create a better life beyond their immediate horizon? He probably had a very organized and categorizing mind accompanied by protean energy.

Encomiums abounded about his unselfishness: He owned ponies which he "loaned" to farm boys for them to get to the

country schools, a problem he observed as Superintendent of Edmunds County schools. A horse-watering trough and gazillions of zinnias in Ipswich were courtesy of him. He loaned the county his road drag to smooth out the dirt roads. He bought paint to mark the Trail.

"Humility, mid-west moderation, dignity, restraint and reason" were all words used frequently in descriptions of him. His speeches showed these characteristics. Perhaps these were the attributes which allowed him to be so successful for the 18 years of the life of the Trail Association. From the beginning, he eschewed the idea of naming the Trail "Parmley's Road" or any claim to ownership. Reason won over many counties reluctant to spend money on a road which would "draw people out of their county," forgetting that that same road would "draw people to their county." Ingenuity of argument was his.

He was a vocal teetotaler. Tempers flared on that volatile topic and someone torched his house just before the 18th Amendment (Prohibition) was passed. Parmley long suspected the arsonist to have been an anti-Prohibitionist. He was never caught. As a precaution against that happening again, his new 1919 house had poured concrete floors, even on the second floor, concrete stairways, a metal roof and even a concrete bathtub. Melissa, his wife, commented that after leaving a hot bath from that tub, the concrete stayed warm for hours. The house today serves as one of two Parmley museums in Ipswich and is on the National Register of Historic Places.

He was not without humor. He took his visiting brother-in-law out duck hunting and then got the county game warden to arrest him and put him in jail on a trumped up charge. It wasn't until Joe bailed him out that the cooked up hoax was revealed.

The Yellowstone Trail Association lasted until 1930 when a perfect storm occurred among the coming of federally numbered roads, the Depression, and a management disagreement between Parmley and the Association General Manager, Hal Cooley.

Parmley and his split log drag

Continued

Parmley Forms Another Trail Association

But Joe Parmley was loathe to close the book on the Trail. After all, it still existed. Indeed, even though the concrete bore different names or numbers, in the popular parlance that route was still called the Yellowstone Trail until well into the 1940s with many streets still named Yellowstone Trail today.

So he created the Yellowstone Highway Association in 1930, peopled the offices with old comrades from Trail days and staked his claim through South Dakota to central Minnesota. They sought membership dues as of old days. It followed much of present day US 12. Unfortunately, time had marched on. People liked the new numbering schemes of highways. They liked the lack of personal interaction needed in

highway development. The Depression also marched on and Parmley's last highway gasp faded into graceful degradation around 1935.

States and the federal government now do the heavy financial lifting for road construction, a legacy of the influence of the Yellowstone Trail Association and many other groups. The Yellowstone National Park still admits autos, thanks to the push of many in 1915, including Parmley's boosters. The Peace Garden is still drawing hundreds to its peaceful floral setting. The horse watering trough is gone, but if you look carefully, you may still find a few of Joe's zinnias in Ipswich.

This common man with uncommon foresight embraced a Western culture of self-reliance and energy. He left a legacy on several fronts, but it was as the founder of the Yellowstone Trail for which he is best remembered. ✿

Crossing the Missouri River

Getting across the Missouri River at Mobridge was filled with strife for the Yellowstone Trail autoist in 1912. He could bump along on the ties of the Milwaukee Road railroad bridge, hoping a train was not due. Or he could chance it on the short lived, seasonal-only pontoon bridge. His best bet would have been the $1.00 ferry, if he could catch it before 6:00 PM and if ice or low water didn't impede the trip.

Before the 1924 Mobridge bridge, a pontoon bridge served, but not in the winter

Joe Parmley must have been pretty disgusted when he reached the Missouri River ferry too late. He chose to settle down in his Studebaker for an uncomfortable night, as he told all who would listen. He could see the campfires of people across the river, compatriots in the misery of life with no bridge there. Lacking a bridge there compromised the probity of the Yellowstone Trail which was Joe's primary concern.

There were two Mobridge ferries in Yellowstone Trail days plying the Missouri with its shifting sands. The southern ferry, run by the Larson family, was located just south of Mobridge. The more northern ferry, run by the Jacobson family, was a bit north of Mobridge, closer to the Milwaukee Road railroad bridge. Most importantly, the northern ferry was on the Yellowstone Trail. Both ferries had been in business from the beginning of the 20th century. Business was good as many farms and ranches were on the west bank of the river and did business in Mobridge on the east bank. Over 4,000 Trail cars used the Jacobson brothers' ferry, the "Evalyn," in the 1922 summer alone. Parmley was willing to give up the 10¢ per Trail car that the ferrymen paid the Trail Association for an expedient, reliable bridge. According to the Jacobsons' ledger, held by the Klein Museum of Mobridge, $532.28 was paid to the Trail Association for the seven months' season of 1922.

The Mobridge News of September 23, 1910, told a story that demonstrated a risk of taking a ferry:

A peculiar accident occurred at the ferry Wednesday. Mr. Buholz drove his machine on to the ferry. It failed to respond to his touch and could not be stopped. It leaped overboard into Big Muddy with Mr. Buholz still at the lever. The latter was fished out and, with great difficulty, four horses removed the machine and he went on his way rejoicing.

A 52-boat pontoon bridge was employed for a brief period. The Mobridge Bridge Company tested its creation by hauling heavy loads of lumber across it and declared that "the boats that supported the bridge did not go down into the water but very little." Problem was that the thing had to be dismantled when winter came!

A Bridge is Planned

Five bridges had been proposed to cross the Missouri at five different sites in South Dakota. In 1921 Governor Norbeck had suggested a small property tax to pay for the five bridges to build each bridge in turn. All completed in about 15 years. Parmley and Walworth County commissioners couldn't wait that long. They and legislators devised a plan whereby bonds could be sold to acquire money in advance, investors getting paid back from the state as taxes were ⇨

The ferry Evalyn loading at Mobridge

accumulated. These obligations would provide ready money for immediate construction. The state legislature passed the bill as part of the Bridge Act of 1923. Trail towns in Walworth, Edmunds, Brown and Campbell Counties, plus Corson County on the west bank, sold the bonds in record time, raising 58% of the $282,000 needed for "their" bridge. It would be the first of the five bridges to be built, completed in November, 1924. It stood considerably south of today's US 12 bridge.

The span needed to cross the Missouri then was only 1300 feet (plus approaches) as Lake Oahe was not formed until the Missouri was dammed at Pierre in 1962. See map on next page. The darker blue represents the original Missouri River. The lighter blue is present Lake Oahe. The bridge had five steel spans and six concrete piers rising 52 feet above the low water line. It would withstand the ice, was the promise.

At Last

Bridge dedication day, November 12, 1924, was a day to behold. Mobridge resident, Glen Shillingstad, remembered, "When the bridge was dedicated, I went. It was really something!" Featured were processions of dignitaries, a long parade with floats, speeches by the governor, by Parmley and by the chief engineer who assured all that the bridge would last 500 years. Six bands played, a carnival entertained, prayers and poems were read.

The "wagon bridge" represented a great rise in stature to Mobridge, joining east with west South Dakota. To the Yellowstone Trail Association it gave truth to their motto of "A Good Road from Plymouth Rock to Puget Sound." To founder Joe Parmley it was the realization of a long cherished dream.

And what of the western end of the bridge? Unfortunately, westward Yellowstone Trail travelers were dropped from the sparkling new bridge onto the Standing Rock Reservation with no clear direction to the Trail. The Trail wandered over the grasses in several directions over the years. Since major road building was lacking, the Trail Association was hard pressed to declare its route, and thus, it remained acutely obscured.

One year after the bridge was completed, the problem remained. In a 1925 speech Association Managing Director Hal Cooley said, "The lack of a road connecting up the Mobridge bridge with the Trail west of the river will also be taken care of next year and the difficulty experienced by tourists as they left the Missouri bridge this year, in being unable to find their way back to the Trail will be overcome."

Parmley's hard-fought-for bridge lasted almost 40 years, but in 1962 Lake Oahe was formed and it demanded a new span of 1 ½ miles as the water rose and slowly drowned a popular riverside resort, fields, ferry boat landings, and the Yellowstone Trail. ✿

A YT Sociability Run on Mobridge auto bridge

Resort now under Lake Oahe

1924 Mobridge Auto Bridge

Crossing the Standing Rock Reservation

Everywhere, it was tough finding roads usable enough to string together to form a national highway. But just west of Mobridge, South Dakota, there were a couple of major problems: how do you reliably get across the Missouri River and then, just across the river, how could the Yellowstone Trail Association chart a route across the Standing Rock Reservation? Success for most trail associations lay in cajoling county boards into improving extant roads or building new ones that a trail association could call its "own" and advertise that route. But what do you do when your transcontinental trail is stopped dead by another "nation" and a major river?

The river problem had to wait. A ferry had been operated since 1907 by the Jacobson family, but floods, ice and low water made the trip risky. And, of course, if you were young and foolish, and trusted railroad timetables, you could drive on the ties on the Milwaukee Road railroad bridge (Mobridge) with your fingers crossed.

Problems! Problems!

The first problem, though, was getting a road through the Standing Rock Reservation in Corson County that was usable by autos. One 1913 approach was to follow the 66 foot rights-of-way between surveyed sections that federal regulations reserved for roads here as elsewhere in the Northwest. That would mean a 115 mile route made difficult because the contours of the land and the river didn't follow section lines. The other choice was an 87 mile diagonal road that followed the contours, but land ownership complicated that choice. And nineteen miles of that 87 just west of the Missouri River were extremely difficult to build on: soft clay, gumbo, and large hills with 12% grades.

The federal government was mightily involved in Corson County/Reservation administration and, in this era, they had no great interest in road-building anywhere. Tribesmen owned most of the land but did have the right to sell to anyone (1887's Dawes Severalty Act). That opened the way for non-Natives to secure title to reservation lands. Federal aid was barely visible, $75,000 for the whole of the U.S. post roads in 1912.

In early 1914, the Yellowstone Trail Association appointed member Rev. George Keniston to the task of raising a reputed $35,000 to buy the rights-of-way from land owners (whites, Native Americans, railroad companies) across the reservation and build seven or eight bridges. Soon he was in Washington, D.C. pushing members of the Public Lands Committee and the Indian Bureau for funds. In May 1914 several senators and congressmen placed $50,000 into the Indian Appropriation bill for the project. They actually got only $5,000. We don't know if the Association ever raised their promised $35,000.

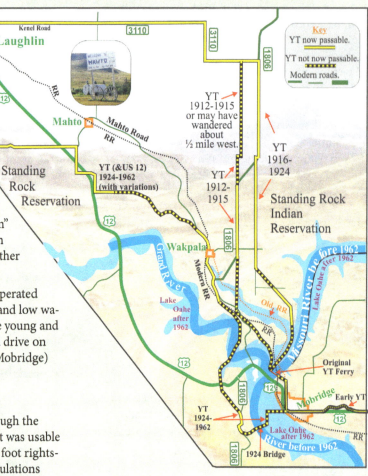

In July of 1916 *The Morristown World* (Corson County) reported that Joe Parmley, county board members and surveyor, and the superintendent of the reservation were all out tramping on "unbeaten paths," looking for a "permanent route" for the Yellowstone Trail. Indeed, 1916 maps show a new route, probably little improved dirt, still following section lines. Purchase of rights-of-way apparently was dropped in favor of following "free" section lines.

Parmley pushed for an auto bridge at Mobridge which was finally built in 1924. A major shift in the road location was made over a period of a few years, now with federal ⇨

Native Americans on parade

aid. Parmley had also pushed for dams along the Missouri. In 1962, 22 years after Parmley's death, the dam forming Lake Oahe was complete and sections of the Trail, along with the railroad, were flooded out.

The present alignment then developed and this route of the Trail was designated US 12 when the U.S. route numbers were adopted.

Study the map to see the wandering route of the Trail over the years. ✿

Native American women in McLaughlin 1921

WANTS FEDERAL AID FOR TRAIL

G. N. Keniston of Hettinger, North Dakota arrived at the capitol this week in the interest of the Yellowstone Trail. Considerable work, largely of a local character, has been done to establish a fairly good trail upon which autos can pass between Minneapolis and Helena, [sic.] Montana. Keniston wants the Bureau of Indian Affairs to give a right-of-way across the Standing Rock Indian reservation in South Dakota and will also ask the government to contribute its pro-rata share of the cost of fixing up the trail covering the mileage across the Indian reservation. The work that has already been done has been beneficial to the farmers and tradesmen at the different towns.

May 8, 1914 Marmarth Mail dateline: Washington, D.C.
Note: Apparently Keniston caught the ear of some. Read on; two weeks later:

~~~~~~~~~~~~~~~~~~~~~~~

INDIANS MAY HELP
BUILD THE TRAIL
BILL IN CONGRESS WOULD APPROPRIATE
$50,000 FROM INDIAN FUNDS FOR
YELLOWSTONE TRAIL PROJECT

Appropriation for the construction of a portion of the Twin Cities-Yellowstone Park Trail through the Standing Rock reservation of South Dakota probably will be included in the Indian appropriations bill.

May 22, 1914 Marmarth Mail dateline: Washington, D.C.

AID FOR YELLOWSTONE TRAIL

The government appropriation bill contains an item of $5,000 for the benefit of the Yellowstone trail to assist in improving that transcontinental highway acoss the Standing Rock Indian reservation in South Dakota. This item is there because of the recognized value of the Yellowstone Trail as a transcontinental road, and the money counties and states and individuals are putting into the improvement of the road.

Sept 8, 1916 Tensas Gazette, St Joseph, LA.

TO BUILD THROUGH BIG RESERVE
PARMLEY IS ON THE SCENE

County Surveyor Jagor, and chairman of the board of county commissioners of Corson County, J. Shirley, County Superintendent of Reserve, and J. W. Parmley President of the Yellowstone Trail, and Superintendent of the Standing Rock Indian Reservation, C. E. Covey were in conference and spent the afternoon inspecting feasible routes for the permanent location of the Yellowstone Trail from the Missouri river ferry to McLaughlin.

Heretofore there have been three or four different routes through the reservation, fairly good in dry weather but heavy in the spring and rainy season.

Superintendent Covey expects to commence work at once with two traction engines and full road making equipment.

The new route for the Yellowstone Trail traverses historic ground. At the Oak Creek crossing near the Missouri are still to be seen the remains of the Aickaree Indian village. Here Lewis & Clark stopped in the fall of 1804 and purchased corn, potatoes, turnips and pumpkins. ... In this immediate locality Sitting Bull and many noted chiefs held full sway. At Bull Head, Sitting bull was shot while resisting arrest during the Messiah craze.

July 22, 1916 Aberdeen Daily News

Native American women in Mobridge

Parmley's Splendid Trip Across South Dakota

Ever mindful of the value of advertising, and aware of the excitement engendered by auto races and similar stunts, Joe Parmley embarked on a race-against-time across South Dakota to show the practicality of the Yellowstone Trail. Three hundred and forty-nine miles in 16 hours! That's an average of 21.8 miles per hour, without stops for meals and repairs. Could it be done? Parmley's point was that anyone with a good car could do it because the Trail was in good condition.

Over the Yellowstone Trail
Across South Dakota (349 Miles) in One Day
SAT., MAY 15, 1915
PRESIDENT J. W. PARMLEY
of the Yellowstone Trail Association
will make this trip, accompanied by Newspaper Men

The Car
Used is a **STUDEBAKER SIX**
Under the direction of W. C. NISSEN, Distributor, Aberdeen, S. D.
The one car making the entire run. Car is equipped with Racine Country
Road Tires and carrying appropriate banners.

"Anyone" did not have a specially equipped car, a professional driver, relief drivers at the ready, roads cleared for their race, a mechanic, or "mechanician" as they were then called, on board, pit crews, and the press clocking their every inch and telegraphing their progress to the next town. And the crowds at each town were complete with brass bands! Parmley made meticulous plans for the attack.

The route was to be from Lemmon in the far northwest of South Dakota to Big Stone City on the state's east border. The day selected was a Saturday to maximize crowd attendance. A single car, rather than relay cars, was selected "to make it more interesting." The car chosen was a heavy Studebaker Six supplied by W. C. Nissen, a Studebaker dealer from Aberdeen. When the trip was planned, the car was stripped of its windshield and top and was covered about its body with a canvas cover on which was painted signs.

The driver was M. B. Payne who had driven in two Glidden tours, cross country runs sponsored by AAA. Telegrams were to be sent to all Commercial Clubs (predecessors of Chambers of Commerce) along the Trail as the car proceeded. All was in readiness - except for the weather. It had rained the day before and sporadically that day. Apparently the party was loathe to postpone such an adventure, and/or they had faith in the Trail shedding water, because Payne and Parmley set off as planned at 4:00 a.m. from Lemmon along with J. H. McKeever, Editor of the *Aberdeen Daily American* and a "mechanician".

Excited newspaper accounts of the trip used such hyperbolic terms as "skidding through," "streaking by," "tearing along," "flying trip" and "wild ride." The speedometer did hit 60 at one point, a remarkable feat. The breathless accounts may have titillated the readers, but the present day reader gets a picture quite different. The Studebaker plowed through mud four to ten inches deep in some places. Parmley later described their progress as looking

In front of his Land Office, Parmley prepares for his Splendid Trip across South Dakota.

like a torpedo boat, throwing wings of mud like a marine manure spreader. Chains applied to the tires broke repeatedly. Parmley intended to use a dictagraph to dictate observations on the trip; after the first severe bump, all thoughts of dictating were gone. Coming out of Mobridge they were obliged to back the car up a muddy hill out of the Missouri valley on a crumbling road. An unmarked road cost them two miles; misdirection around a slough cost them more time until they drove right through it. The hundreds of people who lined the streets were a mixed blessing. They certainly served to publicize the Trail, but they crowded the car, especially during pit stops.

Dr. Joseph Trotzig, grandson of Joe Parmley, recalled a family story of his grandmother, Melissa Parmley, standing out on the Yellowstone Trail with a container of coffee to throw at Joe when he whizzed through Ipswich. She threw - and missed, apparently hitting the side of the car and splattering coffee everywhere.

Still, they made it to Big Stone City in 16 hours and 15 minutes, only 15 minutes late and certainly a record. In spite of the mud, to Parmley the trip was a success because it showed him faults with the marking of the Trail, and "that the Trail is a great highway and that it is really all that has been said of it."

And the Studebaker? It performed well, needed no repair and did not get scuffed up. It got a bath to remove the 800 pounds of encrusted mud, and was driven back to Aberdeen the next day by another driver since Mr. Payne was "stiff and sore" from his 16 hours behind the wheel. The Studebaker was immediately sold to an observer of the race. ✤

PARMLEY CROSSES THE STATE ON YELLOWSTONE TRAIL BUT FIFTEEN MINUTES BEHIND HIS SCHEDULE
FORGETS HIS DICTAGRAPH THE FIRST TIME CAR HITS BAD BUMP, BUT CLINGS TO CAR THROUGH TRIP GREAT ENTHUSIASM FOLLOWS PARTY ALONG TRIP – BIG OVATIONS AT ABERDEEN AND ORTONVILLE
May 16, 1915 Aberdeen Daily News

Minnesota

Ortonville
Odessa
Correll Appleton
Milan
Watson Montevideo
Wegdahl Sacred Heart
Granite Falls Renville
Danube Olivia
Bird Island Hector
Buffalo Lake Stewart
Brownton Glencoe
Sumter Waconia
Norwood Young Am. Victoria
Excelsior Minneapolis
St. Paul
Lakeland

The Yellowstone
Trail in
Excelsior,
Minnesota

INTRODUCING THE YELLOWSTONE TRAIL IN MINNESOTA:
LAND OF 10,000 LAKES

"I came to believe that every little road leads to even littler roads and that destinations are not very important. Grandfather was really saying, 'I wonder what we might find along the road.'"

Ben Logan in *Wisconsin Rustic Roads 1995*

Minnesota: Yellowstone Trail Association Headquarters

The beginnings of the Yellowstone Trail Association were clearly centered in Ipswich and Aberdeen, South Dakota. But very soon in the life of the organization there was a need for business services in scope far in excess of those locally accessible. The Association early on needed printing services for such things as the thousands of the annual *Route Folders* and the 1914 *First Year Book*, a major printing and distribution project. The need for communication services, primarily the U.S. Post Office for intercity communication and phone service quickly exceeded those available in a small city. And the state of Minnesota was setting up provisions for the state to be involved in financing and controlling roads whereas South Dakota had yet to take such a step.

While train service between Aberdeen and the Twin Cities (Minneapolis and St. Paul) was frequent, it did not provide the close relationships between Association personnel and the needed services. Moreover, the initial name chosen for the Association was Twin Cities - Aberdeen - Yellowstone Park Trail Association. And the leaders of the Association sought close relationships with the emerging State Highway Commission. So the offices of the Association were moved from Aberdeen to Minneapolis, the 9th floor of the Andrus Building (again renovated in 2018) and other locations through 1930. The change no doubt marked the entry of the Yellowstone Trail Association into the Big Time.

Why the Trail Goes Where it Does in Minnesota

H. O. Cooley, apparently the first paid employee, is quoted in the 1914 *First Year Book* saying,

> ... from the very inception of the Yellowstone Trail movement, when it was adopted ... the Yellowstone Trail should follow the Yellowstone River from Gardener to Miles City, and the Milwaukee & St. Paul Railroad from Miles City to the Twin Cities ...

No records of official action appear to exist in support of this statement, yet, if the founders of the Trail living near Aberdeen, South Dakota, in 1912 thought about routing a road to the only big population center to the east, only one way presented itself: follow the established route of a railroad. And indeed, the Yellowstone Trail was mapped on existing local roads to closely follow the Chicago, Milwaukee, and St. Paul tracks through South Dakota and in Minnesota through Ortonville to Norwood, and then along tracks laid by the Minnesota and St. Louis Railroad from Norwood past Victoria. Because Waconia and Excelsior were recreational/resort areas for Twin Cities residents, it is probable that good roads from which to choose existed from there into the Cities.

The initial selection of roads from Excelsior into Minneapolis followed what is now Manor Road, Vine Hill Road, and Minnetonka to Lake Calhoun, as shown in the 1914 *First Year Book*. All subsequent maps from any source show the Trail moved to Excelsior Blvd. in that area. Part of Excelsior Blvd. was later moved, placing the Trail on Main St.

From the Cities to the east, the railroads had no straight route directly to Wisconsin, but there did exist the straight Hudson Road to the auto/wagon ferry over the St. Croix River to Hudson, Wisconsin.

Pioneers in Establishing Roles for State Government in Roads

Initially, the state government of Minnesota, as in most states, assumed no role in road building or maintenance because their constitutions forbade expenditures on "internal improvements" such as roads, leaving it to the land owners ⇒

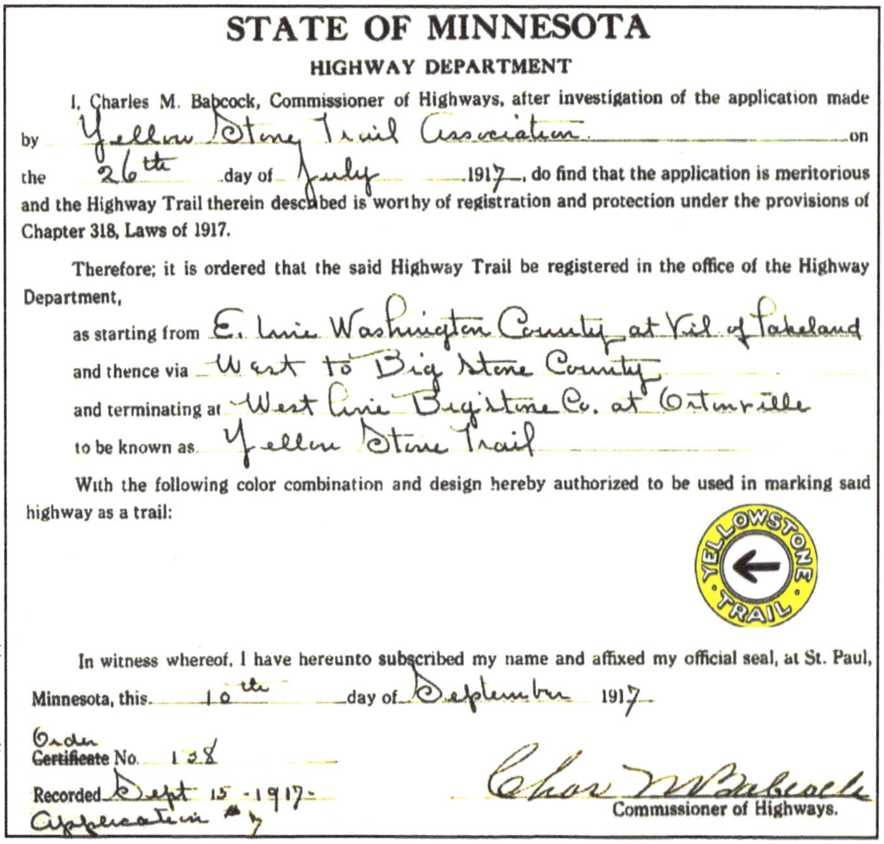

STATE OF MINNESOTA
HIGHWAY DEPARTMENT

I, Charles M. Babcock, Commissioner of Highways, after investigation of the application made by *Yellow Stone Trail Association* on the *26th* day of *July* *1917*, do find that the application is meritorious and the Highway Trail therein described is worthy of registration and protection under the provisions of Chapter 318, Laws of 1917.

Therefore; it is ordered that the said Highway Trail be registered in the office of the Highway Department,

as starting from *E. Line Washington County at Vil. of Lakeland*
and thence via *West to Big Stone County*
and terminating at *West line Big Stone Co. at Ortonville*
to be known as *Yellow Stone Trail*

With the following color combination and design hereby authorized to be used in marking said highway as a trail:

In witness whereof, I have hereunto subscribed my name and affixed my official seal, at St. Paul, Minnesota, this *10th* day of *September* 1917.

Order Certificate No. *138*
Recorded *Sept 15 -1917-*
Application # *3*

Chas M Babcock
Commissioner of Highways.

YT Registered by the State of Minnesota - July 1917

adjacent to the road, the townships, or the counties to build the improvements.

As a product of the Good Roads Movement, the prevailing thought changed to include state responsibilities. The Minnesota constitution was changed to allow the state to build selected roads and bridges in 1889. A State Highway Commission was created in 1905, which gave some aid to counties for roads but with the only real concern being "farm to market" roads.

Burgeoning interest in autos led to replacing, in 1917, the Commission with the Minnesota Department of Transportation (also known as the Highway Department) with a broad concern for transportation and especially longer distance auto roads. Charles M. Babcock was appointed to be the first head of this department. Babcock worked closely with the "boys" of the Yellowstone Trail organization to integrate the route of the Trail into state planning. A good working relationship was established. In fact, the Yellowstone Trail was "registered" and the logo accepted by the Highway Department in 1917. [See the copy of the Registration on previous page.]

Faced with the federal "use it or lose it" proposition for federal aid, they hustled to pass the Babcock Amendment in 1920 which allowed for a system of 70 trunk highways. The fight was led by Babcock, now head of the newly named Minnesota State Department of Highways. Sure enough, a huge bond issue was passed for roads! And they designated 70 longer routes that would constitute the State Highway System, and moreover, gave each a "Constitutional" number.

Road Numbering Advances and Confusion Over the Years

Constitutional Route 12 (this is not US 12) was designated to include three major segments of the Yellowstone Trail route: from Norwood to Montevideo, from south of Excelsior to Minneapolis, and from St. Paul to the Wisconsin border. Both state and commercial maps used the "12" to mark the whole Constitutional Route 12.

Alas, with the arrival of U.S. route numbering in 1926/27, Constitutional Route 10, a route running a more northern route from Minneapolis to Ortonville through Willmar, was designated US 12. Two highways 12 would never work! So the Norwood to Montevideo part of the Yellowstone Trail was made a U.S. route and designated US 212. At the time of this writing, some still assume that when 12 was "moved" north, so was the Yellowstone Trail. Well, it was not. Well, mostly not.

In fact, at the regional meeting of the Yellowstone Trail Association held in Olivia, Minnesota, on July 26, 1929, Manager H. O. Cooley made a point of announcing that the Association had distributed one million folders in 1928 to promote tourism on the Trail and that as long as the Minnesota towns on the Trail contributed, in dues, their $1,000 annual assessment, "the route will never be changed."

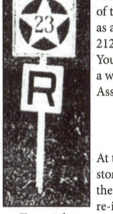

Turn right with Minnesota Trunk Highway Number 23

When J. W. Parmley attempted to re-ignite the recently deceased Yellowstone Trail Association in the early 1930s, his new Yellowstone Highway Association published a folder announcing that the Trail was rerouted both in Montana between Baker and Miles City to the new alignment of US 12, and in Minnesota to from Ortonville through Willmar, Wayzata, St. Paul, and on to Wisconsin also on US 12.

Cooley's commitment apparently died when the original Yellowstone Trail Association went out of business in early 1930. We assume that this rerouting, after the demise of the Yellowstone Trail Association and after the implementation and acceptance of U.S. route numbering, had little practical effect.

Stepping into more recent times, a new statute was instituted. Minnesota Statutes 1997, Chapter 161, Subdivision 9. Yellowstone Trail. "The highway now marked and known as US 212 from the Wisconsin state line to the South Dakota state line is hereby named and designated as the 'Yellowstone Trail,' and the commissioner of transportation shall adopt a suitable marking design with which the commissioner shall mark or blaze said highway to carry out the purposes of this subdivision." [Note: This was all well and good as an historical honor except for the small fact that US 212 did not carry the Yellowstone Trail east of Norwood Young America nor on the far west end. That route as a whole was never designated by the Yellowstone Trail Association.]

Resurgence of Interest in the Yellowstone Trail in Minnesota

At the time of this writing (2021), a group, the Yellowstone Trail Alliance of Western Minnesota, from along the western sections of Minnesota's Yellowstone Trail is re-instituting the Yellowstone Trail "brand" to promote local cultural and economic development. They hope to motivate tourism, involvement in the arts, preservation and use of historic buildings. They are revitalizing Yellowstone Trail signage and the knowledge about the Trail.

Their success has ignited interest in others to consider the development of an Alliance of Eastern Minnesota, thus following the groundswell approach of the original Association. ✿

BIG VICTORY FOR YELLOWSTONE TRAIL

The Minnesota state highway commission yesterday afternoon adopted a resolution designating a road following the Chicago, Milwaukee & St. Paul railway as closely as possible from the Twin Cities to Ortonville, as a state highway, and naming this road as part of the Twin Cities-Aberdeen-Yellowstone Park Trail. This means that this road will be constructed and maintained by the Minnesota commission and will furnish the shortest possible route from the Twin Cities to Aberdeen. This is about the last link in the interstate Trail …

March 29, 1913 Aberdeen (SD) Daily News

AUTOMOBILE RACE AGAINST TIME
O. A. PALMLUND WILL CARRY BANNER IN
OVERLAND *[a brand of auto]*
TO ORTONVILLE.
June 10, 1915 Olivia Times
Note: Read about the race from Chicago to Seattle in
Trail Tale: 1915 Race, page 302.

Rainbow Arch Bridge today
near Ortonville
Lance Sorenson

By 1920, the mileage of gravel roads in southeastern
and central Minnesota finally exceeded the mileage of
railroads there. ✿

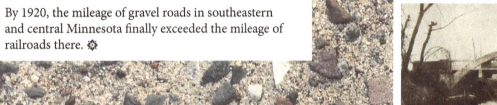

Rainbow Arch Bridge, 1920

BANDITS HOLD UP PASSENGERS
ORTONVILLE: In brief, bandits held up passengers on
the Milwaukee Road railroad obtaining $200. "When the
train slowed down for the stop here, the hold-up men
jumped off and ran toward the Yellowstone Trail where
a slowly moving automobile was boarded. No trace of it
has been found."
September 22, 1920 Willmar (MN) Tribune

ORTONVILLE: At a meeting for the Twin Cities-Aberdeen-Yellowstone Park Trail, there was a large attendance
and stirring addresses made on this great proposed highway through Minnesota, South and North Dakota, and
Montana.
March 13, 1913 Aberdeen (SD) Daily News

🚗 There is some indication that in Appleton the YT
followed a north-south street a mile east of the marked
route.

1913 Odessa jail

Ortonville Trail Day Workers at lunch May 22, 1914

ORTONVILLE: Overalls and
jackets were much in evidence
here on 'Trail Day.' Clergymen,
lawyers, doctors and merchants
participated in the largest single
good roads event launched in
western Minnesota. All worked
on the Yellowstone Trail from 6
a.m. to 6 p.m.
May 31, 1916
The Warren (MN) Sheaf

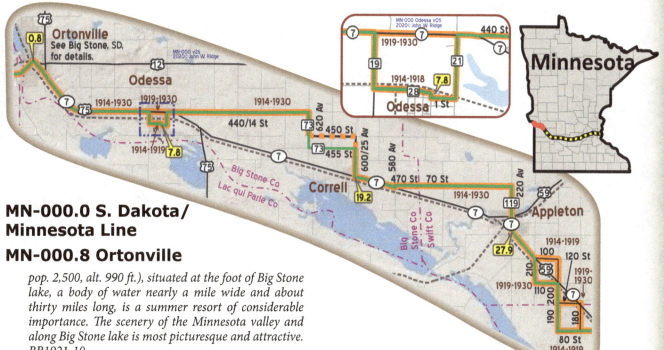

MN-000.0 S. Dakota/ Minnesota Line

MN-000.8 Ortonville

pop. 2,500, alt. 990 ft.), situated at the foot of Big Stone lake, a body of water nearly a mile wide and about thirty miles long, is a summer resort of considerable importance. The scenery of the Minnesota valley and along Big Stone lake is most picturesque and attractive. BB1921-10

COLUMBIAN HOTEL modern and well kept; all outside rooms. A. P. $3.25; with bath $3.75; breakfast 50c; lunch or dinner 75c.

H. J. McDOWELL GARAGE services all cars and reputed best. Open late. Ph. 24-J. MH-1928

Today the town is known for its granite-quarrying and canning industries. Seven large quarries operate throughout the year and provide an income to hundreds of families. WPA-MN

The Big Stone Lake Area comprises Ortonville, the Big Stone Lake and Park, and crosses the state line to Big Stone City, South Dakota. The area jointly features many outdoor activities connected with the lake. There is also hunting and a corn festival. The lake is the headwaters of the Minnesota River. From here to Granite Falls you are in the Minnesota River Valley.

Between Ortonville and Big Stone Lake is an abandoned **Marsh Rainbow Arch bridge** which crosses the Minnesota River. It once carried the Yellowstone Trail. The bridge is a fine example of a now rare concrete bridge type. It can be seen from the US 12 bridge, and you can get closer by taking County 37 which turns off of US 12 and walking a bit. It is a footbridge now. Similar bridges near the Yellowstone Trail can be found in Anaconda, Montana, and Chippewa Falls, Wisconsin.

Big Stone County Historical Museum Jct. Hwys 12 and 75. You can't miss this. There is a huge coat hanger-like sculpture set in concrete in the yard. It is called Paul Bunyan's boat anchor. The museum features wildlife collections. Note the Yellowstone Trail sign displayed in the front yard. See also the 1909 "Muskegon Boat" that once plied the waters of Big Stone Lake.

Ortonville Commercial Historic District 2nd St., Madison and Monroe Aves., between Jefferson and Jackson Aves. GPS: 45.30611, -96.44639. Long-serving commercial district is noted for its uniform Victorian buildings. It is representative of the region's small towns but unique for their purple granite trim, and the district contains 19 properties built between1879 and 1922.

A downtown landmark, the 1892 Columbian Hotel, burned down in 2012, another historic loss for the traveler on the Yellowstone Trail.

MN-007.8 Odessa

Odessa and towns south (Correll, Appleton, Milan) are prime sites for bird watching: white pelican nesting colonies, flyway zones, and shorebirds which have been migrating through the area for eons. Yellowstone Trail travelers of 100 years ago may have watched just as present travelers are now doing. **Big Stone National Wildlife Refuge**, just south and east of Odessa, is home to 230 bird species.

Main Ave. and 2nd St. GPS: 45.25973, -96.32894. **Odessa Jail** is Odessa's oldest public building, built in 1913. It is a rare surviving example of the freestanding brick jail houses once common in small Minnesota towns (also seen in Montana).

MN-019.2 Correll

pop. 180; garage, gas and supplies. Small pay camp, 25c. MH-1928

MN-027.9 Appleton

pop. 1,700; a grain growing and dairying center. Brown's Hotel has running water; dbl. $1.75. APPLETON AUTO CO., Ford, finely equipped and best for all makes. Labor $1; phone 235 for tow car until 10 p. m. MH-1928

Bordering the river in the northeastern section of Appleton is a beautiful park, formerly a slum district. It was recently laid out and constructed as part of a Federal relief program. WPA-MN

All of its 32 streets, except Minnesota St. are named for local veterans who died in combat.

RR underpass (a little north of Milan) that
replaced the YT level crossing south of Milan

RECOUNTS HISTORY OF THE TRAIL

State Trail Meeting at Montevideo. H. O. Cooley, General
Manager of the Yellowstone Trail Association, reported
that in 1913 only three autos passed over the Yellowstone
Trail into the Yellowstone National Park; in 1919 there
were 10,000. He was pointing out the tremendous value
of marking a trail. Minnesota invested about $3,000 to-
ward the maintenance of the Trail. In 1919 the actual cash
revenue brought to the state was $204,620.
February 19, 1920 Glencoe (MN) Enterprise

APPLETON: The 12th annual meeting of the Yellowstone
Trail Association was conducted here.
November 8, 1922 Warren (MN) Sheaf

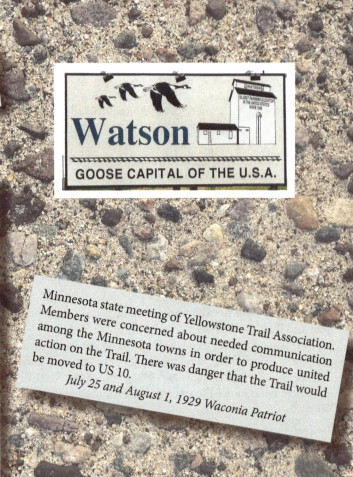

MONTEVIDEO: Plans for a model highway from the
Atlantic to the Pacific are to be considered at the annual
national meeting of the Twin Cities-Aberdeen-Yellowstone Park Trail Association which met here today. A year
ago it was decided to extend the road from the Twin Cities
to Seattle. Now it is proposed to build a transcontinental
highway eastward from the Twin Cities to the Atlantic.
February 18, 1915 Yuma (AZ) Weekly Examiner

~~~~~~~~~~~~~~~~~~~~~~~

The *Aberdeen (SD) Daily News* added that the group
shortened the unwieldy title to just the Yellowstone Trail
Association and adopted as its motto 'A Good Road
From Plymouth Rock to Puget Sound.' Resolutions urging that the Interior Department admit automobiles to
Yellowstone Park were adopted. Resolutions were left to
Dr. H. F. Marston and E. S. Hillweg of Minneapolis as the
selection of the most desirable route from Minneapolis
to Chicago.

Note: They decided on the Marshfield-Oshkosh route
through Wisconsin.

Minnesota state meeting of Yellowstone Trail Association.
Members were concerned about needed communication
among the Minnesota towns in order to produce united
action on the Trail. There was danger that the Trail would
be moved to US 10.
July 25 and August 1, 1929 Waconia Patriot

The Minnesota branch of the Yellowstone Trail Association has pledged to help finance the construction of Minnesota's unit of the Yellowstone Trail to cost $2,000,000. It
is proposed to build a hard-surfaced highway faced with
either brick or concrete across the state.
April 1917 The Road Maker
Note: The Association did not provide funds for road
building. It persuaded counties to build "their" road
which connected to the next county and the next, etc.
By "pledged to help finance," read "pledged to persuade
others to kick in."

Lance Sorenson showing a 1914 Model T
and a modern YT sign near Hector, MN

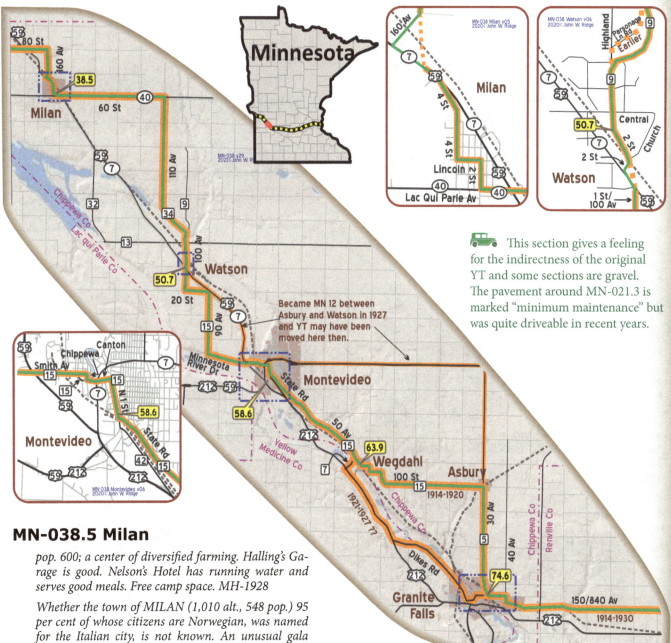

MN-038.5 Milan

pop. 600; a center of diversified farming. Halling's Garage is good. Nelson's Hotel has running water and serves good meals. Free camp space. MH-1928

Whether the town of MILAN (1,010 alt., 548 pop.) 95 per cent of whose citizens are Norwegian, was named for the Italian city, is not known. An unusual gala event, the Lefse Fete, is held in Milan in August. WPA-MN

Today Milan is still a leading center of Scandinavian culture and ethnic arts.

🚗 Route of YT on 2nd in Milan is uncertain.

MN-050.7 Watson Goose Capital of the World

WAYSIDE

Running just south and west of the Yellowstone Trail along the Minnesota River between Ortonville and Watson are various state and federal wildlife management areas known for bird watching. Just north of the Lac qui Parle Mission and about two miles west of the Trail is Lac Qui Parle State Park, known as a stopover for thousands of migratory Canada geese, bald eagles, pelicans, and other waterfowl. GPS: 45.02370, -95.86860.

Lac qui Parle Mission chapel

WAYSIDE

Just west of Watson and south of Milan near the junction of Co 13 and Co 32 at the Minnesota River is Lac qui Parle Mission. The site was established in 1835, where the first Dakota dictionary, grammar, and gospel were completed. A chapel built by the WPA features artifacts and exhibits related to the Dakota and missionaries who worked with them.

Railroad relics at Milwaukee Road Railroad
Heritage Center, Montevideo

Montevideo Depot with mid-century
Hiawatha Beavertail car

The Volstead house,
Granite Falls

The Swensson Farm

Danube Depot Museum
Steven Hill

Very early "motel" (cabins),
Danube

Sacred Heart Auto Club
Lance Sorenson

MN-058.6 Montevideo
Between Montevideo and Granite Falls the route is in the valley of the Minnesota River.

pop 4,900; a county seat and has beautiful 30-acre park on Chippewa River; a great shipping point for hogs and milk-fed chickens. Eandguard's Cafe is best. Pine camp site in park.

HOTEL RIVERSIDE modern and very well kept; sgl. $1.25-$1.50; dbl. $2; with bath $2.50-$3.

CLAY MOTOR CO., leads by far; 24 hr. serv.; Labor $1; phone 165. MH-1928

(922 alt., 4,319 pop.), seat of Chippewa County, was named for the capital of Uruguay; Smith Park, on the western edge of town, is a 35-acre Tourist Camp (free kitchen facilities). The bluffs of the city offer a remarkable panorama of the merging valleys of the Minnesota and Chippewa Rivers. WPA-MN

151 Pioneer Dr., Jct. of Hwys 212 & 7 **Chippewa City Pioneer Village**. Here is a "must see." About a mile north of Montevideo you will come upon Historic Chippewa City. It was platted in 1868. Then Montevideo was platted in 1870 and Chippewa City ceased to exist. Today one can see it rebuilt in 24 buildings preserved or period buildings moved in from various locations in the county. It is operated by the Chippewa County Historic Association. It's fun to stroll there through yesteryear.

Along the Minnesota River is the **Lagoon Park**, there since 1919 and now a modern camp ground with all of the current facilities.

301 State Rd (Yellowstone Trail). **Milwaukee Road Heritage Center Museum** at the restored 1903 Milwaukee Railroad Depot. The place has equipment, memorabilia, and facilities to show what transportation was like in Montevideo for almost a century.

MN-063.9 Wegdahl

MN-067.5 Olof Swensson Farm Museum

John Swensson turned his father's original farmstead into a museum. The farmstead consists of 17 acres, an 1880s timber-framed barn, grist mill remains, family cemetery, and a 22 room brick farmhouse. Constructed in 1901, the house contains original furnishings from this unique Norwegian/Swedish family. We were surprised to see a sizeable family chapel within the farmhouse. It is listed in the National Register of Historic Places.

MN-704.6 Granite Falls

pop. 1,800; in midst of fine stock and grain farms. Keegan Hotel has rooms with running water. Winter Garage is largest. Free camp on river, is fair. MH-1928

(922 alt., 1,791 pop.), is on a boulder-strewn bluff overlooking the Minnesota Valley. In the valley Archean granites are exposed; these rocks belong to the oldest era of geological history. The founders of the town were attracted by the power possibilities of the falls. WPA-MN

At the **hydro dam**, if you are there in early summer, notice the beautiful American White Pelicans in residence when the water is high. With large, black tipped white wings, these great birds dive gracefully and live seemingly cooperatively.

On the northern edge of town, running NW to SE is **Dikes Road**, a gravel road on top of dikes. The Yellowstone Trail of 1921-30 ran on this road.

163 Ninth Ave. **Volstead Museum**. This was the home of Congressman Andrew Volstead, most known as the author of the Volstead Act which enforced the 18th amendment to the U.S. Constitution which banned the production of alcohol (known as Prohibition). It was ratified in 1919 and repealed in 1933 with the 21st amendment. He also authored the important "Cooperative Act" which allowed farmers to band together to bargain with companies for a fair price. Agricultural "cooperatives" still stand today.

At MN 23 and MN 67 near the Minnesota River is the **Yellow Medicine County Historical Museum**. This museum's displays tell a story of the geology and archaeology of the Minnesota Valley, Native American history, and pioneer life in the county. Ask them about the oldest granite in the world, granite gneiss about 3 billion years old, that is visible in the area.

Yellow Medicine County Historical Museum, Hanley Falls

MN

SPARSTAD GOES AS DELEGATE TO ABERDEEN APRIL 16-17

A good roads meeting was called at the village hall. ... It was decided to send a delegate to the Yellowstone Park Trail convention to be held at Aberdeen, S.D. on April 16th and 17th. Mr. Sparstad was chosen. He departed Wednesday for that western city.

April 18, 1913 Sacred Heart Journal

Note: Note the date. The Trail Association was only six months old and finances needed to be mapped out, Corson County (Standing Rock Indian Reservation in South Dakota) needed discussion, and a national organization needed a business plan. That was an important convention.

Letter to the authors from Loren Schroeder of Danube: "From the Danube Council minutes of the meeting of Nov. 7, 1921, we see 'Motion to pay $25 to Yellowstone Trail Assn.'" ✿

A dicey practice was described to the authors by a Bird Island farmer. It seems that some farmers would keep their road very muddy to make a good business of hauling cars out of it with their teams at the ready. One farmer "was seen having to water down to keep his holes pretty wet." The going price was $1.00 to $5.00, depending upon the difficulty of the haul. ✿

Note: As we crossed the country researching the Trail, we heard similar tales countless times. *Motor Age*, a national magazine, carried an exposé on the subject in 1915.

Plans are being laid at Bird Island to electrically light the Trail to Olivia on the west and Hector on the east.

June 4, 1914 Olivia Times

Note: Wonder what came of this plan. That's 13 miles!

GOOD ROADS TRAIL DAY

June 12th has been designated as the second Trail Day by the Yellowstone Trail Association. A great deal of work has been done along the Trail on its first Trail Day, but owing to rainy weather and busy farmers, another day has been set.

June 4, 1914 Olivia Times

Renville County Board designated the street known as Lincoln Ave. through Olivia to Ninth Street along the course of the Yellowstone Trail as a portion of the State Road to the recommendation of the Highway Commission.

April, 1919 Buffalo Lake News

Note: They hope that now maintenance costs will be shared with the state.

Barry Prichard in Olvia
with his grandfather
Dowling's plaque

Renville Museum.
Formerly a school c.1888.
Michael Dowling was teacher and principal.

THE TRAIL IS SURE; IT WILL PASS THROUGH RENVILLE

RENVILLE: ...strong pressure to divert it through Kandiyohi and Swift Counties by way of Willmar and Benson but strong delegations from this route pulled it through. It will bring advertising and trade to the towns along the way.

April 4, 1913 (unknown newspaper)

Dowling's Bank (with clock) and Garage on left.
Lincoln Ave., Olivia
Lance Sorenson

YELLOWSTONE TRAIL HEADS IN SESSION IN OLIVIA

Plans for the next year for Minnesota's Yellowstone Trail were discussed and reports were received on the budget, committees, marking, road improvement and legislative programs. A unique memorial of the late Michael Dowling was held. Members were to relate the happiest incidents they remember of the late Mr. Dowling.

November 10, 1921 Bemidji Daily Pioneer

Note: Dowling was president of the national Yellowstone Trail Association 1917-1918 and died in 1921.

MN-084.7 Sacred Heart

pop. 800; named by the Indians, not a Catholic town; has some of largest quarries of best granite in the state. Free camp space in City Park

SACRED HEART HOTEL most pleasant and claimed best between Aberdeen and Minneapolis; sgl. $1.25-$1.75; dbl. $2; with bath $2.50. Breakf. 50c; dinner 75c; no lunch.

STAVNE'S GARAGE, is best for repairs; labor 75c; open until 11 p. m. MH-1928

The 1914-built **Sacred Heart Hotel** on the main drag is still there! The Sacred Heart Historical Society won National Register of Historic Places status in May, 2018 and is in line to receive grants from the Minnesota Historical Society to preserve the building for reuse.

300 5th Ave. W (US 212) **Sacred Heart Area Museum**. It is in a Lutheran church built in 1916 and displays and preserves the history of the Sacred Heart area.

MN-091.5 Renville

202 N Main St. **Renville City Historical Museum** in a late 1800s schoolhouse. The museum features many materials regarding former resident Michael Dowling, an amazing man who, despite triple amputations, was a "Good Roads" leader, teacher, and newspaper publisher. He later moved to Olivia where he was a banker, garage owner, president of the Yellowstone Trail Association 1917-1918, and friend of President William McKinley. For Dowling's inspiring biography, see **Trail Tale: Dowling**, page 239.

Gravel on the Trail near Danube

MN-097.1 Danube

pop. 300; country hotel; Service Garage leads. MH-1928

Danube Depot Museum. After 30 years of life near Olivia, Minnesota, the depot was rolled back into Danube and settled in the shadow of the Water Tower, near its original site. It houses railroad and local history. The traveler today should look up to see the water tower and follow it to find the historic depot.

There recently was formed "The Yellowstone Car Club" to honor the historic highway that ran through Danube.

"Corn Capital of the World" 50 foot monument at Olivia

Minnesota

MN-105.2 Olivia

pop. 1,800 in the midst of many fine farms and dairies. YELLOWSTONE CAFÉ is liked, inquire here for good rooms. Small free camp space.

IKE'S REPAIR SHOP, Ford; is far best; well equipped; phone 200 until 9 p. m.; after 9 ph. 170 for wrecker. MH-1928

Designated as the "Corn Capitol of the World" by the Minnesota Senate, that motto is borne out by the startling 50-foot tall ear of corn statue. The area has the highest concentration of seed research companies of any place on the globe. "Corn Days" are celebrated the last weekend in July which we have attended, representing the Yellowstone Trail Association. Fun!

Dowling's Bank next door to his garage, Olivia

801 E Lincoln Ave. (MN 212, Yellowstone Trail) corner of E Lincoln and 9th St. S. Here stood the **Olivia State Bank**, Michael Dowling, President, and next door was **Dowling's Garage** at 803-807 E Lincoln Ave. You already met Dowling if you read about Renville, 14 miles west of Olivia.

500 East DePue St. The historic **Renville County Courthouse**, built in 1902, is architecturally significant as a fine Victorian monumental building with a mixture of French, classic, and Georgian styles. The newly renovated building with its copper domes is worth seeing.

MN-108.3 Bird Island

Hill's Unique Gifts, Hector, MN

The YT is still dirt near Hector

YT Marker in Hector

Hector Tourist Park 1926

The season of the automobile tour over the Yellowstone Trail has begun. Several cars with camping outfits carrying Illinois and Ohio license tags have come through. The best of these to camp at our village campgrounds was a party with two cars enroute from Minneapolis to Seattle Tuesday night.
1913 Buffalo Lake News

A modern section of the Trail near Buffalo Lake looks like the old days

TRANSCONTINENTAL RACE PASSES THROUGH HERE ON YELLOWSTONE TRAIL

A large crowd gathered last Wednesday evening to see the auto go through here in the Automobile Transcontinental race against time over the Yellowstone Trail. The tour was for the purpose of demonstrating the condition of the Trail across the country. The distance covered between Plymouth Rock and Seattle was 3,685.5 miles in 120 hours. The distance mapped out was as near as possible to 51-mile relays.
September 21, 1916 Hector Mirror
Note: Read more at **Trail Tale: 1916 Race**, page 416.

BUFFALO LAKE 100% TRAIL TOWN

As reported from the Yellowstone Trail Association headquarters, there was a total of 33 towns on the Yellowstone Trail from Washington to Indiana which have sold their quota of memberships for this season of 1923. Among these are Buffalo Lake and Hector.
April 20, 1923 Buffalo Lake New

The grading outfit from Olivia that will build the new road from Buffalo Lake to Stewart on the north side of the railroad passed through Hector last Friday. They had some 50 head of mules and horses and a lot of other trucks.
April 17, 1919 Hector Mirror

AUTOS REQUIRED TO PARK IN MIDDLE OF STREET

Posts have been erected on Main St. and electric light globes adorn the tops of the posts. Parking in the middle of the street and rules for traffic have been adopted by the Village Council.
July 31, 1919 Hector Mirror

Modern Trail Day with a Model T, Hector
Lance Sorenson

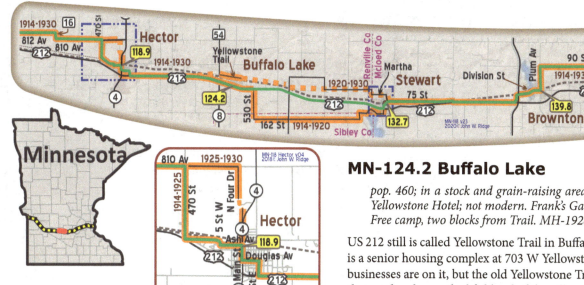

![Minnesota](state map)

MN-118.9 Hector

pop. 900; a farming community; rooms in homes. Hector Motor Co. leads, has wrecker. Good free camp in park. MH-1928

(1,018 alt., 864 pop.), is in a region formerly known for excellent water-fowl shooting. While extensive drainage eliminated much of the game, Mongolian pheasants, recently introduced into the locality, are now quite numerous. A free Tourist Park. WPA-MN

Look for the Yellowstone Trail road signs and the great yellow rock with the Trail logo in the north west corner of town, 5th St. W 200 block.

206 S Main St. is **Rural American Bank**, built in 1916. And the building is still recognizable as pure Prairie School.

US 212 E (Yellowstone Trail). **Hill's Unique Gifts**. You've got to stop here. It is a delightful tourist trap. We mention it because it once had large, yellow Yellowstone Trail signs out front, but now they are somewhat muted. There are thousands of unique items you don't need but would find kooky. See for yourself. Hill's is the Yellowstone Trail's answer to the kitsch of Highway 66.

MN-124.2 Buffalo Lake

pop. 460; in a stock and grain-raising area. Rooms at Yellowstone Hotel; not modern. Frank's Garage is best. Free camp, two blocks from Trail. MH-1928

US 212 still is called Yellowstone Trail in Buffalo Lake. There is a senior housing complex at 703 W Yellowstone St. Many businesses are on it, but the old Yellowstone Trail Hotel, on that road and once the life blood of the village, is no more.

MN-132.7 Stewart

(1,063 alt. 541 Pop) on the eastern edge of a 50-mile undulating plain covered with rich glacial drift. West of the lakes scattered in the eastern part of this expanse, the horizon is broken by moraines. WPA-MN

pop. 550; rest room at community hall; country hotel, small garage, free camp space. MH-1928

MN-139.8 Brownton

pop. 650; stock and grain raising supply principal revenue. Commercial Hotel is best, not modern. Yellowstone Trail Garage has best mechanics. Free camp space two blks. from trail. MH-1928

MN-145.6 Sumter

MN-152.0 Glencoe

pop. 1,750; an old and substantial town; a cattle-shipping point; best rooms in homes; Sweet Shop for lunch. Beneke Garage has good mechanic. Nice free camp in oak grove. MH-1928

Glencoe was named for its resemblance to a valley in Scotland. City Hall, County Courthouse, and Carnegie Library all were built at the turn of the 20th century (thus probably seen by Yellowstone Trail travelers) and all are on the Register of Historic Places.

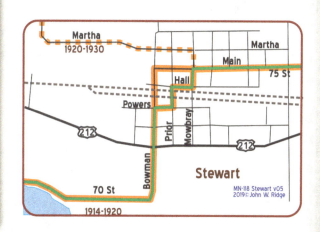

HECTOR BUSINESSMEN OPPOSE CHANGE IN ROUTE OF TRAIL

The Club Room of the Village Hall was crowded with citizens to discuss a matter it having been reported that the State Highway Commission was to change the route of the Yellowstone Trail. The Club voted unanimously against such a proposed change, and voted to pay Hector's allotment for the upkeep of the Yellowstone Trail.

November 6, 1919 Hector Mirror

Note: A state highway commission does not "move the Yellowstone Trail;" it declares a different highway a state highway and it is up to the Yellowstone Trail Association to move its signs to the new, better highway. This threat seems to have jarred the group into paying their dues.

MN

TRAFFIC ON TRAIL STAYS VERY HEAVY

Vehicle counters were stationed one mile east of Glencoe to count autos, trucks and horse-drawn wagons on the Yellowstone Trail. The Yellowstone Trail carried 8,466 vehicles in a week, almost three times the total of two other highways combined.

September 24, 1920 Stewart Tribune

Hector will be represented at the annual meeting of the Yellowstone Trail Association in Minneapolis February 3-4. Among topics of discussion will be the route from Chicago to Plymouth Rock.

January 21, 1916 Hector Mirror

MACHINE DASHES THROUGH GLENCOE

CONVEYING LETTER FROM CHICAGO'S MAYOR TO THE MAYOR OF SEATTLE OVER THE YELLOWSTONE TRAIL

June 17, 1915 Glencoe Enterprise

Note: This was the announcement of the 1915 relay race the Yellowstone Trail Association held to prove the strength and utility of the Trail to the public.

For a more full story, see **Trail Tale: 1915 Race**, page 302.

100 GATHER AT GLENCOE CONFERENCE

The important point at this meeting was the fear expressed by Granite Falls and Waconia that they will lose the Yellowstone Trail because the state is redesigning some state roads that may miss those two towns and the Trail may go with them.

November 22, 1922 Glencoe Enterprise

WILL SPEND $75,000 ON YELLOWSTONE TRAIL

ENTIRE TRAIL THROUGH CARVER COUNTY TO BE BOULEVARDED

Federal aid will happen. Waconia's share will be $1500, including liquor license money.

March 29, 1917 The Waconia Patrio

WACONIA WILL OIL VILLAGE STREETS

It seems that the Studebaker oiling machine cost $675 and the Ladies Welfare Club raised $350 for the oiler by throwing dinners and benefit functions.

May 24, 1917 The Waconia Patriot

The North Star Hotel had 35 rooms at $3 per day or $25 per week.

1930
Waconia Patriot

Note: Such a deal! Hmm, I'll take the daily rate if you don't mind and save $4!

STATE MEETING OF YELLOWSTONE TRAIL ASS'N HERE OCT. 26

October 15, 1925
The Waconia Patriot

MN

YELLOW TRAIL GARAGE
HECTOR, MINN.

Is still offering you in its second call the following list of used cars at bargain prices:

1 FORD TOURING 1 REGAL TOURING
MODEL 25 MAXWELL TOURING
MODEL 31 BUICK TOURING
HUPMOBILE TOURING

In new cars I am offering you
ELGIN, OLDSMOBILE AND STEVENS
all built by old established manufacturers and guaranteed to give good service.

Now is the time to change the oil in your motors and clean the crank case thoroughly, and replace the broken down oil with Zenoil of proper grade.

Remember in tires and tubes I have on hand the following brands to offer you, all new stock:
FISK, BRUNSWICK, BRAENDER, HARTFORD AND ARCHER.

A large assortment of automobile accessories carried in stock at all times.

HUGO BESKE
Phone 155 Hector, Minn.

Billy Wicks of Stewart who patrols the state road between Stewart and Hutchinson was operating a new "boom plane," 16 feet long by 8 feet wide, weighing a ton. The blades carry the dirt for some distance, filling depressions and cutting down hummocks. The contraption is pulled by a small caterpillar tractor and is being used on the trail.

July 1, 1920 Glencoe Enterprise

Note: This replaces the beloved King Drag and horses.

TRAFFIC REGULATIONS ON YELLOWSTONE TRAIL

...the Minnesota Highway Department, in a letter to the Enterprise says: Please notify the public that Trunk Highway No. 12 (Yellowstone Trail) between Excelsior and Norwood will be closed to gross loads over three tons in order to protect the road bed during the period when the frost is going out.

April 5, 1923 Glencoe Enterprise

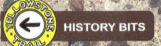

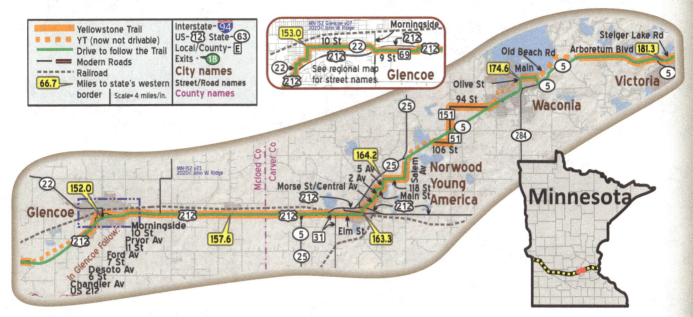

MN-163.2 Norwood Young America

Norwood pop. 550; a village; country hotel. Lunow's Garage is reasonable and has skilled mech. Free camp space; no conveniences. The Grivelli house has rooms and serves excellent home-cooked meals, 60c. Good Buick garage. MH-1928

Norwood Eastbound leave Highway No. 12 and follow the Yellowstone Trail.

Note: No. 12 via Chaska has fewer turns and better surface but the Yellowstone Trail passes many beautiful lakes and is much prettier and a little shorter. MH-1928

Norwood and Young America became one city on January 1, 1997.

Elm and Hazel Sts. (Elm is the Yellowstone Trail.) **Winter Saloon**. GPS: 44.76791, -93.929036. A c.1890 saloon with attached living quarters, Norwood's oldest and best preserved drinking establishment and a prominent feature of its downtown. In the 1890s the second floor was used by fraternal organizations. It is also known as Harm's bar since it was in the Harm family for three generations. The price of a liquor license in 1891 was $2.08, $1,500 in 1954. On the National Register of Historic Places.

224 Hill St. **Norwood Methodist Episcopal Church**. GPS: 44.76793, -93.92818. Built 1876, this small, architecturally interesting church looks freshly painted white with red trim. It appears to be in active use, cared for, and welcoming.

MN-174.6 Waconia

pop. 1,000; a pretty little town on Lake Clearwater. This famed lake, together with Paradise Isle, is one of the outstanding beauty spots of Minn. Boating and fishing at its best. Hotel North Star has clean rooms, not modern. Menzel Garage is good and has wrecker. MH-1928

The 1928 *Mohawk-Hobbs Guide* is interesting because it calls the lake "Lake Clearwater" when it seems that it was always called Lake Waconia, and, although the name of the island in the lake was called "Paradise Island" in 1927 and 1928,

that name lasted only for a brief time and reverted back to "Coney Island."

Yellowstone Trail travelers, no doubt, stopped to see Lake Waconia 100 years ago just as you can see the lake, beach and park today. Coney Island Resort, formerly a drawing card to its famous Coney Island, is now gone. At present, Carver County is working to eventually return the island to a recreational and historical site.

9 W. First St. **Waconia City Hall**, a red brick civic building designed in 1909 to accommodate city offices, fire station, library, senior center and public hall. It is noted for its locally unique architecture.

555 W 1ST St. **Carver County Historical Society Museum**. This museum is on the move and they know about the Yellowstone Trail. Much preservation work occurs, along with activities in the museum itself. It's a jumpin' group. Ask for directions to the Andrew Peterson historic orchard farm which the Society owns.

48 W. Main St. (Yellowstone Trail). **Mock Cigar Factory and House**, nicely painted green and white. It was a false-front factory and attached Italianate house (c.1875) owned by E. H. Mock, proprietor of an early Waconia industry, and is on the Register of Historic Places because the property is associated with important American history events.

The YT just east of Waconia

ANNUAL MEETING OF TRAIL ASSOCIATION

The 1923 state meeting of the Yellowstone Trail Association will be held at Excelsior on August 22.

August 20, 1923 Buffalo Lake News

WAYSIDE

3517 Raleigh Dr. St. Louis Park. The Pavek Museum of Broadcasting. 1.4 miles west of Lake Calhoun on Excelsior, north two blocks on Monterey Dr., north on Raleigh Dr. You've got to see this! The Pavek Museum preserves and presents the history of recording technology and electronic communication. There is the Jack Mullin Collection, documenting the history of recorded sound, as well as the Joe Pavek Collection of antique radios, televisions, and broadcast equipment, and telephones. A few of these items were popular even during the Yellowstone Trail era! Truly a one-of-a-kind museum. We were there just recently and received a wonderful tour by a very knowledgeable guide.

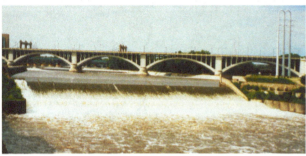

Terminus of the YT 1912-1915, St. Anthony Falls, St. Paul

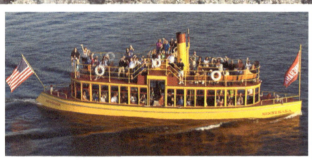

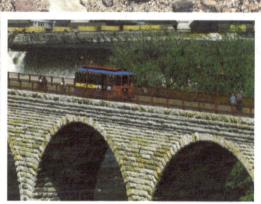

Stone Arch Railroad Bridge, Minneapolis. Now a walking trail.

The restored "Minnehaha" on Excelsior's Lake Minnetonka

MN

In 1959 US 212 was designated Yellowstone Trail and green highway signs with white letters were placed along 212, but seem to have disappeared. This state-designated route was not everywhere the Yellowstone Trail. The Trail became 212 only between Granite Falls and Norwood Young America. Elsewhere in Minnesota it became MN Hwys 7, 5 and I-94. Before 1925, trail associations "designated" route names, not state legislatures. ❂

Excelsior streetcar today

September 1996. A long-ago letter to the authors from an 'old codger' pictures for us a slice of life along the Trail:

> I was born in 1908 on a farm 100 feet off the dirt road that became the Yellowstone Trail. By 1915 it was graded by an elevated grader pulled by 16 to 20 mules. My dad's farm was called Yellowstone Trail farm. My dad had a sign on the barn door and one by the road with that name on it. My dad graded the dirt road to Bird Island once a week in the summer with a King Drag and horses. The road was graveled by farmers and wagons with dump boards about 1916. The mailman drove a surrey with snow runners in winter and two sets of horses; half way through the mail route he'd change horses which were kept by friends. ❂

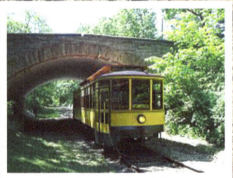

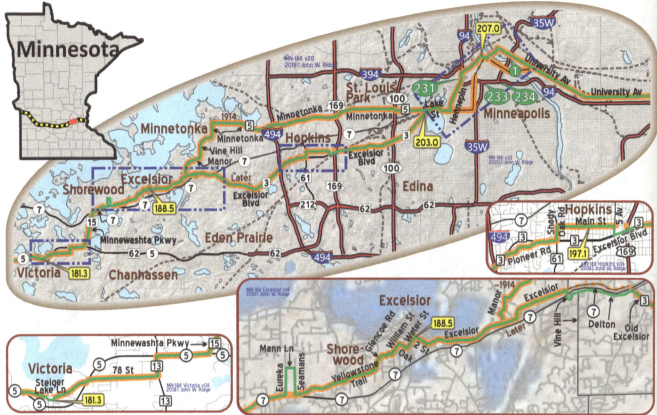

MN-181.3 Victoria

The City of Victoria is known as the "City of Lakes and Parks." It is surrounded by lakes and borders the University of Minnesota Landscape Arboretum and Three Rivers Park District's Carver Park Reserve.

Just east of Victoria, watch for the jog between Steiger Lake Rd. and 78 St. along MN 5. Traveling from the west the turn to the north to Steiger Lake Rd. is hard to see. It is just east of the Dairy Queen! For several blocks in the middle of Victoria the original YT cannot be followed, but now Steiger Lake Rd. can be followed. However, west bound travelers will need to work around a few blocks of one-way streets.

MN-187 Shorewood

Today there is still a street named "Yellowstone Trail" running on the original alignment through Shorewood. Yellowstone Press is located on this winding, hilly street amid an area of lovely homes. The western end of this section requires a detour because of the modern intersection with MN 7.

MN-188.5 Excelsior

305 Water St. **Excelsior/Lake Minnetonka Historical Society Museum.** Turn off of MN 7 at County MN 19 then right at Water St. "The hub of all activity in this quaint little town," said a reviewer. The Society runs the 1906 (restored) Steamboat Minnehaha on Lake Minnetonka tours. The Society's mission is "to preserve, document, and classify the physical history of the Lake Minnetonka area."

37 Water St. The **Museum of Lake Minnetonka** is an all-volunteer organization that maintains and operates the 1906 **Lake Minnetonka "streetcar" steamboat, Minnehaha**. Take a ride. You will hear about the place in history the Minnehaha

held in the early 1900s as you travel from Excelsior to Wayzata. The steamboats were not converted streetcars; they were constructed and painted to look like one as they transported vacationers to their lake cottages. After 1921 automobiles and better roads did the job. Four steamships were eventually scuttled, including the Minnehaha, and three were scrapped. Raised in 1980, the Minnehaha sat for 10 years before being totally restored and returned to service in 1996.

The **Excelsior Streetcar Line** near US 7. The Line's station is between 3rd and George Sts. The electric trolleys reached Excelsior in 1905 after regular railroads such as the Milwaukee Road and the Great Northern ceased running tourists to resorts west of Minneapolis. Those trolleys were running when Yellowstone Trail travelers toured the area. Board at the Water St. stop between 3rd and George St. or at Old Excelsior Blvd. near Minnetonka Blvd. Reservations are not required. Cars are restored historical artifacts more than 100 years old. "We do not operate them in the rain. Occasional mechanical problems may force us to alter or cancel our schedule," they say.

MN-197.1 Hopkins

pop. 4,000; a factory suburb of Minneapolis. Sustained largely by the Minneapolis Threshing Machine Co. which employs nearly 1,000 men. Hopkins Motor Co., Ford, is good on all cars. Free camp at Fair Grounds. MH1928

703 Excelsior Ave. (the 1921 Yellowstone Trail) **Yellowstone Trail Garage**. Now site of Hopkins Honda Collision Center.

907 Main St. (earlier Yellowstone Trail) **Hopkins Historical Society**. A resource center of over 10,000 photos and other collections depicting the history of Hopkins and area.

The annual meeting of the Yellowstone Trail Association is hereby called to meet in Minneapolis, Minn. on the third and fourth days of February, 1916, convening at 10 o'clock. The headquarters of the officers of the Association will be at the Hotel Dyckman and the place of the meeting will be bulletined in the lobby of such hotel.

January 7, 1916 The Marmarth Mail

THE TRAIL EXHIBIT

Space was provided in the Twin City Automobile show held February 4-11 for an exhibit and information booth of the Yellowstone Trail Association. On display was a section of the Trail across the continental divide near Butte, crossing the main range of mountains with only a 4% climb.

March 1922 Western Magazine

Radisson Hotel 1914

Hennepin Ave. 1916

Andrus Building, 500 Nicolet Ave. 1918-1923 9th floor Headquarters of the YTA

BURNING UP THE YELLOWSTONE TRAIL

A new record has been made for the distance from Minneapolis to Aberdeen, South Dakota, 337 miles over the new Yellowstone Trail. Eleven and ½ hours was the running time. The Minneapolis Ford dealer, Ned Spaulding, drove the buyer home to Aberdeen, averaging 29 1/4 mph, the fastest time which has been made by a motor car.

January 1917 Ford Times Vol. 10, No. 6

Interior of Mill City Museum

YELLOWSTONE TRAILSMEN ANNUAL MEETING
MET AT DYKMAN HOTEL MARCH 9

Eight states through which the Trail travels were represented.

1918 Northwestern Motorist

Mill City Museum, Minneapolis

When in Donaldson's Department Store, you could have visited their Tea Room

MN-207.0 Minneapolis

Minneapolis, situated on both sides of the Mississippi River, is one of the most beautiful cities in America. Its wonderful lakes, splendid boulevards and many parks are most enjoyable. A trip through the huge flour mills is very interesting. The high-class Auto Club is at 13th and LaSalle Ave. Municipal Tourist Camp, 50c, at Minnehaha Park, on Miss. River (southeast part of city). MH-1928

HOTEL RADISSON well managed and high class. Large and luxurious rooms; outside ones best. Sgl. $2-$6.50; dbl. with toilet $4-$5; with bath $5-$10.

CURTIS HOTEL the largest and one of the best liked in the Northwest. All rooms with bath; all rooms light. Sgl. $2-$3; dbl. $3-$4; twin beds $4.50-$6. Lunch 60c; dinner $1.MH-1928

As is true of large, old cities, there are too many historic buildings to point out here. The National Register of Historic Places lists at least 100 places. Since the Trail flowed right through downtown Minneapolis, many 100-year-old "skyscrapers" are visible there. Those sites described below surely would have been visited by the Trail's travelers.

500 Nicolet Ave. **The Andrus Building.** Main office of the Yellowstone Trail Association from 1918-1923. From 1924-1926 the office was at 816 2nd Ave. S and finally from 1927-1929 it was at the "Evanston Building." From these offices flowed hundreds of thousands of maps, weather reports, newsletters, research statistics and letters to individuals. Unfortunately, only a few original pieces of information remain. The organization ceased operation in 1930. Most official records and all undistributed publications were lost when the office was closed.

821 Marquette Ave. **Foshay Tower.** Set well back from the street and closer to 9th St. is a 1929 "skyscraper," its 32 floors with the name FOSHAY emblazoned on the top are still easily visible today. Built to resemble the shape of the Washington Monument, it was finished just in time for the 1929 Stock Market crash. Story has it that some businessmen jumped from the tower at the prospect of financial ruin. Today it serves as a 4.5 star hotel called W. Minneapolis -The Foshay Tower. Do see the museum on the 30th floor.

704 S 2nd St. **Mill City Museum** is a Minnesota Historical Society museum and a "must see." It opened in 2003 built in the ruins of the Washburn "A" Mill next to Mill Ruins Park on the banks of the Mississippi River. Every working day, approximately 175 railroad cars of wheat were processed at

the Washburn "A" Mill during its heyday. The area's historic milling district used the power of falling water at St. Anthony Falls. Flour milling boomed and numerous mills along this stretch of river changed the way food was produced, marketed, and distributed.

The Mill City Museum focuses on the founding and growth of Minneapolis, especially flour milling and the other industries that used water power from St. Anthony Falls. The mill complex, dating from the 1870s, is part of the St. Anthony Falls Historic District. We include this site because of its powerful story-telling displays of the history of the Twin Cities. You can see the Stone Arch Bridge and St. Anthony Falls from the roof. GPS: 44.97870, -93.25750.

1 Portland Ave. **St. Anthony Falls Visitor Center and Lock and Dam**.

St. Anthony Falls figured largely in early Trail literature. Exhibits at the visitor center provide information about the falls and its place in Minnesota history.

100 Portland Ave. **Stone Arch Bridge**. Built by railroad baron James J. Hill in 1883, the bridge allowed for increased movement of people and goods across the Mississippi River. It served as a working railroad bridge until 1978, but is still seen as a symbol of the railroad age.

201 3rd Ave. S (Yellowstone Trail). **Chicago, Milwaukee, St. Paul and Pacific (The Milwaukee Road)** Minneapolis' oldest surviving **railway station,** built 1897–9, with an earlier 1879 freight house. They are also significant for their architecture and association with the milling district. Now a commercial complex known as The Depot.

Before you leave Minneapolis, relax and spend a little time driving around the city's many lakes. Find peace and solitude from this otherwise urban environment. After all, Minnesota has 10,000 lakes and some are right here. Lake Nokomis, Cedar Lake, Lake of the Isles, Lake Harriet, Lake Calhoun, (now called Bde Maka Ska) all have their eponymous parkways, bicycle, and walking lanes.

Find Minnehaha Parkway on the southside to reach Minnehaha Falls, Minnehaha Park, Longfellow Gardens and a replica of Henry Wadsworth Longfellow's home in Massachusetts. Minnehaha Falls was a big attraction in Trail days. The 1917 *Automobile Blue Book* describes the Falls as "unrivaled for picturesque beauty. No cascade has ever been so celebrated in song and story and none claims a surer charm for the visitor." Near the Falls you will see a bronze statue of Hiawatha and his love, Minnehaha, placed there in 1912. Also nearby is Lake Hiawatha.

Longfellow's epic (22 chapters) poem, *The Song of Hiawatha,* is a fictitious and tragic love story of two Indians set on the southern shore of Lake Superior, but many claim that this falls was mentioned in the poem. Minneapolis and the Cult of Hiawatha, found in Historyopolis.com, says, "Minneapolis claimed the verse as its own, even though it was set 'on the shores of Gitchee Gumee.' The urban landscape was reshaped by the poem's iconography. Minnehaha Park was christened in 1889; Lake Amelia became Lake Nokomis in 1910; Rice Lake was reborn as Lake Hiawatha in 1925.

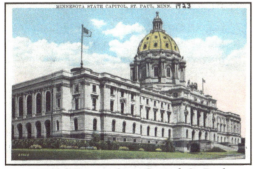

1923 Minnesota State Capitol, St. Paul

The Yellowstone Trail Bridges Over the Mississippi

Travelers on the Yellowstone Trail have used three different crossings of the Mississippi River, all within the City of Minneapolis: the Central Ave. Bridge, the Hennepin Ave. Bridge, and the Washington Ave. Bridge. Each of these areas is now interesting to explore. The walks, parks, and old mill tours provide fairly unique experiences.

1.) The Central Ave. Bridge (or the Third Ave. Bridge) previously known as the St. Anthony Falls Bridge was completed in 1918. It is a concrete arch bridge with curves to line up with streets at either end. Ongoing maintenance has kept it in service now and for the foreseeable future.

2.) The existing Hennepin Ave. suspension bridge was built in 1990 to replace the steel arch bridge which had been in use from 1891, thus in use during Yellowstone Trail days.

This bridge was preceded by two suspension bridges, the original crossing opened as a toll bridge in 1855, and is believed to have been the first permanent span across the Mississippi at any point. The same location is thought to have been a traditional crossing for Native Americans.

3. The present Washington Ave. Bridge, built in 1965, replaced the 1891 iron truss bridge in use during the Yellowstone Trail period. The 1965 bridge was just south of the 1891 bridge it replaced and the alignment with Washington Ave. to its west was significantly different due to the west bank development, especially I-35W.

For the first two years the Yellowstone Trail Association was named the Twin Cities-Aberdeen-Yellowstone Park Trail Association and detailed maps of the Trail did not exist. The first map by the Association, in the 1914 *First Year Book*, shows the Trail starting in St. Paul at Union Station, passing the state Capital, following University Ave., and crossing the Mississippi into Minneapolis on the Washington Ave. Bridge. Other sources show that the main route of traffic used the Hennepin Ave. Bridge.

Automobile Blue Books, the primary source of route information before road maps became common, specify the use of the Hennepin Ave. Bridge from 1912 through 1919, but sometimes giving the Washington Ave. Bridge equal billing. From 1921 through 1925, the books specified that the Yellowstone Trail used the Central Ave. Bridge. In approximately 1926 the route throughout Minneapolis was changed. See the small Minneapolis map on the previous page. The bridge of choice became the Washington Ave. Bridge.

A caution to those wanting to further research these bridges and their use: The Third Ave. Bridge name refers to the street followed to the south. The Central Ave. Bridge name stems from the modern name of the street followed to the north. However, Central Ave. from the north used to turn to the (now) Hennepin Ave. Bridge and the name Central Ave. is likely to show up as the name of the street crossing the Hennepin Ave. Bridge. Good grief! ✿

St. Anthony Falls (3rd Ave.) Bridge
at the time of the YT

The Hennepin Ave. Bridge at the time of the YT

An Interesting Stop at MN-210.7

On the south side of the Yellowstone Trail at 2550 University Ave. W., 1,000 feet east of Minneapolis just into St. Paul, is a large building built just as the Trail was formally extended past its door in 1915. It was the **Willys-Overland Motor Co. auto distribution center** serving the Northwest. The building, looking much the same, is open today as a retail and commercial center. Visit it to have a cup of coffee while contemplating its history which provided a backdrop for decades of Trail travelers passing by.

It added an aviation school during World War I and then, in 1920, it was the site of the 1920 National Automotive Show, an ad for which describes it as the

> largest, most complete, most brilliant and most entertaining Automotive Show the universe has ever known. Nothing New York, Chicago or even Europe has ever known in an automotive exposition can approach this tremendous show …

See pictures on page 236 and **Trail Tale: Auto Shows**, page 237. ✿

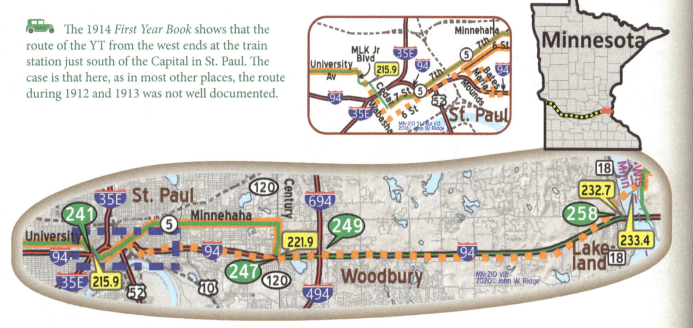

The 1914 *First Year Book* shows that the route of the YT from the west ends at the train station just south of the Capital in St. Paul. The case is that here, as in most other places, the route during 1912 and 1913 was not well documented.

MN-215.9 Saint Paul

population over 300,000; is located on terraces running back from the Miss. River. It is the capital of the state, the oldest city in the Northwest and is a very import-ant industrial and distributing center. The Ford plant covers 186 acres. Visit the magnificent State Capitol, Cathedral of St. Paul, Como Park and the noted city market. The Auto Club is at 4th St. and Smith Ave. Alverdes Restaurant is good, lunch 65c, dinner $1. St. Paul City Camp, in beautiful Cherokee Park, overlook-ing the Mississippi, 50¢. MN-WPA

SAINT PAUL HOTEL is finest. Has air of distinction. Splendid large lobby. Sgl., $3-$3.50; dbl. $4-$8; suites up to $15; all baths. Unexcelled dining; lunch 60¢-$l; dinner $1.50; coffee shop. MH-1928

350 Market St. **St. Paul Hotel**. From 1910 until today, the St. Paul Hotel has been regarded as one of the nation's premier hotels. The famous, from Charles Lindbergh to John F. Kennedy, have stayed there. It displays century-old charm and decor along with the modern.

The St. Paul Grill has a startling display of beverage bottles in the bar.

200 Tower Ave. **Fort Snelling**, originally known as Fort Saint Anthony, was a military fortification located high on a bluff at the confluence of Minnesota and Mississippi Rivers. Built in 1819 to ward off any Canadian or British invaders, the Fort stayed active until 1946. The Fort is a National Historic Land-mark. During the summer, costumed personnel interpret life at this early post. GPS 44.89360, -93.18690.

193 Pennsylvania Ave. E. The **Minnesota Transportation Museum** In the 1907 Jackson Street Roundhouse, is a fully functional railroad roundhouse, one of the last of its kind in the country. It is highly interactive, offering train rides and hands-on exhibits about surface transportation history of Minnesota. This site has been used for rail transportation since the first railroad came to Minnesota in the 1860s.

75 Rev. Dr. Martin Luther King Jr. Blvd. The **Minnesota State Capitol**. (The Yellowstone Trail ran along the west side of the capitol building.) The 1905 domed capitol build-ing, the third and final building for the capital city, features a large, gilded statue of four horses in front of the main entrance. They represent the power of nature: earth, wind, fire, and water.

10 E Exchange St. **Fitzgerald Theater** (that's F. Scott Fitz-gerald). The Fitzgerald Theater is the oldest active theater in Saint Paul. Built in 1910, it gets rave reviews for "not a bad seat in the house."

214 Fourth St. E. **Union Depot**. Begun in 1917 and completed in 1923 (World War I intervened), this station replaced the original 1881 structure which saw as many as 150 trains a day. In 1971, the station saw the last of railways and stood idle. In 2005, the Ramsey County Regional Railroad Authority renovated the station as an intermodal transit hub served by Amtrak trains, Metro Transit light rail, and intercity bus lines. Since its renovation in 2012, the place has hosted special events. Go look at the marvel-ous space.

240 Summit Ave. **James J. Hill House**. The rugged stone, massive scale, and ingenious mechanical systems of this magnificent Gilded Age mansion recall the powerful presence of James J. Hill, builder of the Great Northern Railway. The 1891 house has13 bathrooms, 22 fireplaces, 16 chandeliers, a reception hall nearly 100 feet long, and a two-story, skylit art gallery. It was once the largest private residence in the state. GPS: 44.94540, -93.10930. Pause and enjoy all of the neighborhood. Many old, large historic houses call Summit Ave. home.

MN-232.7 Lakeland

MN-233.4 Minnesota/Wisconsin Line

Establishing the Route Between St. Paul and Wisconsin

Before there was the Yellowstone Trail there was the Hudson Road, just another dirt road but it ran due east from St. Paul crossing the scenic St. Croix River using a ferry between Lakeland and Hudson, Wisconsin. That route was chosen in 1915 when the Trail was extended to Chicago. A bridge replaced the ferry and the route became a major cross-country thoroughfare. Ultimately, for much of the way, it was paved over by I-94 and hidden by commercial development. Some of the changes it underwent are noted here but little remains to explore.

If you are not so much interested in digging out the old route variations, you might skip the details in the paragraphs below and, instead, drive to Guardian Angels Catholic Church just on the north side of I-94 and just west of Exit 250 of I-94 (GPS:N44.949722, W92.940222) and ferret out a stretch of the old road between the church and I-94. An old cemetery is part of the scene.

The Official Route

If you are still with us, note that the original route of the early Yellowstone Trail as published in the 1914 Yellowstone Trail Association *First Year Book* came through Minneapolis, down University Ave. past the state Capitol, and ended at the St. Paul court house on Wabasha St. From there the record to the east is sketchy and often contradictory. The Yellowstone Trail Association published just one (apparently) good map of part of the route. That was in 1920. It clearly shows the route from Minneapolis following University Ave. to the state Capitol, bearing southeast on Wabasha St. for a block, bearing east to the front of the Capitol, southeast on Cedar St. to 6th St. Then it turned to the northeast on 6th St. past the Ryan Hotel with its Yellowstone Trail Free Information Bureau, bearing right at Arcade St. still on 6th St. until turning to the north on Johnson Blvd. and then east on Minnehaha St. The route apparently then turned south on Century Ave. (undocumented) to the original Hudson road, thence to Lakeland, Minnesota, which is across the St. Croix River from Hudson, Wisconsin. The 1919 Goodrich Guide agrees with this routing.

The Varying Blue Book Routes

The next most informative and reliable sources are the *Automobile Blue Books*. They give different routes for the Yellowstone Trail going east from St. Paul. In 1918, it stated:

> ... starting at the court house, proceed northeast on 6th St., jogging a bit [about three blocks east of the modern jog!], following a long viaduct over the railroad tracks to Maria Ave. Following Maria Ave. and the trolley to the southeast and then turn to the east, with the trolley on Hastings Road.

It then followed the established road, over "winding grades" over rolling country to Lakeland. Just north of that town the route followed the toll bridge to Hudson. 25 cents per car, 5 cents for each additional passenger. The name Hastings Ave. disappeared, in part, in subsequent years and appears to become, Hudson Way in places.

The 1916 and 1919 *Blue Books* are much the same as the 1918, except the turn from Maria is onto Plum St. "with the trolley" to Hastings Ave. ❁

The 1921 *Blue Book* makes another adjustment! Instead of leaving 6th St. at Maria, the route turns southeast on Mounds Blvd. and then onto Hastings. The 1922 and 1924 routes leave 6th St. at Bates Ave., then onto Hastings.

Ah, by the 1926 *Blue Book* the route is back on Mounds Blvd., Plum, and Hastings. This route carried on through 1929, one of the last *Blue Books*.

The Driving Line

All those *Automobile Blue Book* routes for the Trail, now much hidden and confused by decades of development, are no longer much fun to explore. Our recommended "Driving Line" shown on the maps is based on a route given by less authoritative historical sources but used because it is not under a freeway, it is easier to follow, it uses much of the "official" 1920 Yellowstone Trail Assocation route, and it passes through a neighborhood not much changed from 1920. And it uses Minnehaha Ave. which might motivate you to look up and enjoy the history and stories associated with that name! ❁

Along the shore of the St. Croix River, now on private property, are some remaining foundations of the large toll bridge, built in 1913 to replace a ferry which carried the YT. They can be found about one-half mile north of I-94, along the hard to find Old Toll Bridge Rd., off of Rivercrest Rd. just to the east of MN 95.

Below is a view of the Willys-Overland Motor Co. described on page 238. Above is a recent photo of the building looking much as it did 100 years ago. It was the site of the major auto show described in **Trail Tale: Auto Shows**, page 237.

AUTOMOTIVE EXPOSITION

10 ACRES of EXHIBITS

"Come on In"
NATIONAL AUTOMOTIVE SHOW

Jan 22, 1920 Colby (WI) Phonograph

Auto Shows Along the Yellowstone Trail

The way to get good roads is for the government to present every intelligent man with a Ford. The owners of cars are our best road builders. Let a man buy a machine and he is ready at any time to get out and work for highways that are a credit to the state. *Northern Wyoming Herald* (Cody), August 20, 1915.

Ah, yes! They are of a piece, those two, car and road entwined like two lovers, needing each other. Henry Ford had been mass producing his Model Ts for seven years by 1915, priced "for the common man." It was R. E. Olds, incidentally, and not Henry Ford, who built the first operational automotive assembly line. His runabout, also known as the Curved Dash, was the world's first mass-produced car, built between 1901 and 1907. Any number of other brand names came rolling out of factories to ever voracious buyers. This former "rich man's toy" had taken hold of the nation's fancy.

It may have been fine cruising around town at the regulated eight miles per hour, or driving out to the farm at 15, avoiding chuck holes. Detroit even had a bit of concrete. There was a big desire to go distances with the new black beauty on a respectable road. But outside of towns it was a different story. So, lacking that, an auto show was the next best thing to actually going somewhere for boys with their toys.

Preparing the Davenport Hotel for auto show, Spokane 1915
July, 2000 Notalgia magazine

1900 auto show at Madison Square Garden
Historic Vehicle Assn. website

The world's first auto show, the Paris Motor Show in 1898, was founded after the French Automobile Club created an international outdoor motor show that required exhibitors to prove their "seriosity" by driving their cars from Versailles to Paris, says the Historic Vehicle Association Timeline website. Some other major auto shows in the U.S. during the Yellowstone Trail era were listed by the Historic Vehicle Association:

1900: An American horseless carriage show was held in Madison Square Garden and drew roughly 10,000 spectators at 50 cents each (about $13 in today's money). Among the highlights was the appearance of Ransom Eli Olds' prototype for a new body style known as the "runabout." It wasn't the first automobile show held in the United States. It wasn't even the first held at Madison Square Garden. But it is considered the first modern automotive show. The week long event, sponsored by the Automobile Club of America, featured 66 exhibitors displaying 31 newfangled autos and a variety of accessories to pimp the ride.

1901: The Chicago Auto Show opened for eight days in the Coliseum Exposition Hall. Over 4,000 spectators attended. Prices for exhibit space on the main floor ranged from $1.00 to $1.50 per square foot.

1907: The Detroit Auto Show, renamed the North American International Auto Show in 1989, was first held at Beller's Beer Garden in Riverside Park.

1910: Detroit's first Auto show was held at the light guard armory in 1899, but the 1910 show was something of a landmark. It was the first time that many of the vehicles were exhibited complete with all of their equipment for the customer. In 1924, a new convention hall was completed at Woodward and Canfield in Detroit. "Some automotive historians said that the hall contained more exhibition area on one floor than any other showplace in the country," wrote Robert Tate in *The Detroit Auto Show: A Brief History of Style and Innovation* published on the Internet 1/29/2020.

1912-1913: The first detachable steering wheel and electric headlights drew a curious crowd at the Detroit Auto Show.

1915: Davenport Hotel, Spokane, Washington

1917: Billings, Montana

1919: Milwaukee at the state fair

Billings, MT auto show, 1917
May, 1917 Northwestern magazine

1920 January: 2550 University Ave. between Minneapolis and St. Paul is the large Willys-Overland building built in 1915 for automotive shows. It was modestly billed as "the largest, most complete, brilliant and entertaining Automotive Show in the universe." Today the remodeled building houses offices.

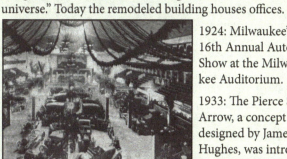

Milwaukee auto show
March/April, 2012 Wisconsin Trails

1924: Milwaukee's 16th Annual Auto Show at the Milwaukee Auditorium.

1933: The Pierce Silver Arrow, a concept car designed by James R. Hughes, was introduced at the New York Auto Show.

Motor Age listed the coming auto shows and contests for 1914. Six of the 17 shows were held in Europe and Canada, and 13 of the 34 contests were not in the U.S. (mostly in France). But that list shows a veritable boiling pot of interest in everything auto on two continents.

Headlines such as STATE FAIR AUTO SHOW THIS YEAR A $1,000,000 DISPLAY heralded the coming of the 1919 auto show at the Milwaukee State Fair appearing in newspapers in 1918. The ads allayed fears of shortages caused by World War I, saying, "Despite rumors that have been given nationwide circulation, production of passenger cars will be continued at an output as nearly equal to the demand as supply of labor and material will permit." Continuing on, the ad added, "The State Fair Auto Show … will be held in the Automobile Building as usual. It is impossible to make the Auto Show any bigger this year than last year, for the reason that the display of motor cars is confined to the Automobile Building, the largest structure on the Fair grounds, no other space being available for expansion." *Colby Phonograph* (Wisconsin) September 5, 1918.

A widely advertised auto show as "the world's exhibition of automobiles" was the 1920 National Automotive Show between Minneapolis and St. Paul in the Willys-Overland Motor Company building. $6,000,000 in displays, 10 Acres of Exhibits sang the headlines. "Largest, most complete, better, grander" were just some of the hyperbolic encomiums littered about by the press to describe something more than just a show of autos. Farm equipment, Vaudeville acts, live orchestras, style shows and, to attract the ladies while their husbands ogled the new Oldsmobiles or Packards, washing machines, food shows, vacuum cleaners, etc. You get the picture.

The Twin Cities did not act in a cooperative way until 1918 at the Willys building. Previously, each city had held its own event. The joint enterprise became very successful, advertising "double the exhibits."

We do not know if the Yellowstone Trail Association produced an exhibit in other auto shows held along the 3,600 miles of Trail,

Ad for Twin Cities auto show 1925
October 18, 2018 Park Bugle (MN)

but we suspect they did. Not many publicity opportunities were missed by General Manager Hal Cooley. The Association did make it to a Twin Cities show because Cooley profusely thanked them for display space in the following paragraph in the 1922 *Western Magazine*:

Due to the courtesy of the management, space was provided in the Twin City Automobile Show held February 4-11 for an exhibit and information booth of the Yellowstone Trail Association. On display was a section of the Trail across the continental divide near Butte, the majestic Rocky Mountains being worked out in bold relief, and showing the New Davis Grade crossing the main range with only a 4% climb. Photographs by J. E. Haynes Co. of Yellowstone National Park were shown through their kindness. The rest of the exhibit was made up of a display of Trail literature, markers, and publicity features. The Association desires to express its gratitude to the Automobile Show for the kindness shown.

Today, the famous Detroit auto show was canceled for 2020, perhaps for the first time in its over-100 year history, due to the coronavirus. Now called the International North American Auto Show, *Wikipedia* described it as, "… among the largest auto shows in North America and is regarded as the foremost venue for [car] manufacturers to unveil new products." It will resume in June, 2021 in Cobo Hall where it has been for 55 years.

Two major car shows beat the coronavirus: Los Angeles in late November, 2019, and Chicago in early February, 2020, just before all gatherings were canceled. New York's show scheduled for late August-early September, 2020, has been canceled. The reader may conclude that public health concerns beat America's 120-year love affair with the auto. ❀

A Mystery at the Museum

[A note about researching the Yellowstone Trail]

While researching the Yellowstone Trail, our visit to the Hennepin History Museum in Minneapolis, Minnesota, yielded an unexpected and mysterious short article: "The Yellowstone Trail Markers." It is in the Summer, 1963 issue of *Hennepin County History*, p. 23. The article is a report, with pictures, of a "recent" visit to several nearby Yellowstone Trail route markers. The pictures in the article were taken from along West 22nd St. along Blaisdell and at Pillsbury and Pleasant Avenues. Our modern boots-on-the-ground search found no trace of those markings.

The mystery? Our inspection of all available Yellowstone Trail Association publications and papers always had reported a Hennepin Ave.

route, as did several Automobile Blue Books.

Bewildered, we re-opened the search for the Minneapolis route. By that time we had collected later *Blue Books* and they showed the Blaisdell route. "Officially" or not, the route had been, *de facto*, changed to the "new" route on Lake, Blaisdell, and Nicollet (pronounced Nick-o-let locally). Mea Culpa.

Oh, and the General Manager of the Yellowstone Trail Association might easily have followed the newer route between his home and his office in downtown Minneapolis. Just sayin'. ❀

Trailblazer Dowling - Thank God I'm not a cripple!

It was cold and raining that April day of 1921, but that was to be expected in spring in Minnesota. The weather didn't matter to the hundreds who had come to stand silently outside of the house on Olivia's DePue Avenue. What mattered was that a good man had died and they were there to pay their respects.

Michael Dowling had cast his net widely in his 55 years. He had become known in the worlds of politics, good roads, education, newspapers, banking, innumerable charities, wounded WWI veterans, and the Yellowstone Trail Association. A true Renaissance Man, he.

Tragedy

In truth, he should have died 41 years earlier when, as a boy of 14, he got caught in a blizzard and froze both his legs and left arm and some fingers of the right hand. In that rude farmhouse where he sought refuge, gangrene set in, forcing the doctor to saw off the affected limbs below the knees and elbow. But he didn't die. Instead, he boldly asked for and received false limbs and a year at Carleton College and swore he would not be a ward of any county for the rest of his life.

Dowling driving, apparently in front of his source of "artificial limbs" in the Twin Cities
Minnesota State Historical Museum

His accomplishments would take pages to recite. They are detailed in his papers held at the Minnesota State Historical Society. We will mention only two aspects: politics, and good roads and the Yellowstone Trail Association. He was a fearless Irish advocate in all the causes in which he believed, with a ringing voice and a ready wit. His life was an inspiring one; his mantra, "Thank God, I am not a cripple!"

Dowling's Political Life

Politically, he was a Republican, becoming Speaker of the Minnesota Assembly, then secretary of the National Republican League and, thus, came to the attention of President McKinley. The Spanish-American War (1898) was a war against Spain's colonization of the Philippines which the U.S. joined. Later (1899-1901) the independent-minded Filipinos fought the American intrusion. In 1900 Dowling went to the Philippines at the request of McKinley to investigate the school systems there and prepare a plan for schools which the U.S. Army could carry out. There was a whiff of suspicion about that mission, implying Dowling was to spy for the U.S. which he vigorously denied.

Dowling's six months there resulted in 10 articles for the *Minneapolis Journal* and many letters home. Barry Prichard,

Dowling's grandson, has produced a valuable book, *Bolos, Bandits, and Bamboo Schools* (Richards Pub. Gonvik, MN, 2009), which is a compilation of those writings and a good history lesson. The Philippine experience also produced a comic opera based upon a true story of Dowling's appearance before Sultan Sulu. The Sultan was not attending to Dowling's discussion of schools, so Dowling slowly removed one of his false legs. That got only a glance from this "self-made king." Dowling removed the other leg. This got a longer glance. Then off came the right arm and a twist of his neck as though to remove his head. The Sultan finally laughed and attended.

Michael Dowling
about 1919,
Renville County
Dowling-for-Governor
Club, Olivia

On the surface, his political career after his stint in the Minnesota Assembly may look like failure. He did not win his run for the U.S. Senate seat, nor the Governor's chair, nor a close run for Congress vs Andrew Volstead (author of the 18th amendment, Prohibition). However, these forays led him to meet and work with people like himself, "movers and shakers" of the broader issues he cared about.

Meeting of the Sub-committee of the Executive Committee of the National Republican League of the U.S. President McKinley on the left, Dowling on the right.
Renville County Historical Society and Museum

A Good Roads Man

As an auto dealer in Olivia, Minnesota, and owner of the first car sold in Renville County in 1902, Dowling had foreseen the role of the auto in the development of 20th century America. He knew the value of roads as an absolute economic and cultural necessity which the federal government was ignoring. For instance, in 1910, before the Yellowstone Trail Association was born, Dowling directed Renville County's winning participation in two "Best Roads" competitions. The *Minneapolis Tribune* sponsored the ⇨

events as a way to inspire localities to drag their roads, drain their ditches, and push for graveling. The reward was bragging rights and a trophy.

The Yellowstone Trail Association caught Dowling's imagination. He determined to drive the Trail along the whole of its barely discernible 1913 route from Minnesota to the Yellowstone National Park. He wanted to be the first to "blaze" the route that the Association had drawn on a map, to advertise it, and prove it could be done. It then consisted of grassy wagon trails, farmers' muddy section lines, and mountain grades, with only about 120 miles graveled. Predicting that such a trip would be "safe, easy to traverse, and affordable" was stretching optimism remarkably.

So he piled his wife and three daughters into his especially equipped (right hand wheel and electric starter) Oakland 660 and, with two other families along, led a three-car caravan to the Park. Fording streams, wading through mud, and fixing punctures occupied the party, but they did it! They returned to welcoming ovations in Olivia. Such travel was considered extremely dangerous.

The Renville County $1,500[!] trophy.

Recalling that trip five years later, this great optimist quipped, "If a man with one arm, a wife and three daughters could make such a trip, anyone could."

Although the Association would not be expanding its route to the east for a year or two, Dowling jumped the gun and "blazed" the idea of a trail to Plymouth, Massachusetts in 1914. He took short cuts, but he did get the lay of the land. He shipped his car through the Great Lakes to Buffalo, New York, and began looking for a space to locate the Trail on the popular Rochester-Albany-Boston corridor. He was told that "there was no more room for colored markers on poles on that route." Indeed, eleven different trail colors festooned some poles already. He then traced a more southern route: southern New York to Hartford, Connecticut to Plymouth Rock. This was the route taken by the relay teams in the 1916 race from Plymouth Rock to Seattle. Dowling's grandson, Barry Prichard, published the detailed notes and pictures kept by his mother about those two historic trips in *We Blazed the Trail* (Richards Pub. Gonvik, MN, 2009). See the "Shop" in www.yellowstonetrail.org.

During his tenure as Yellowstone Trail Association president (1917-1918), Dowling oversaw the establishment of at least ten tourist bureaus which gave out information to Trail travelers; he approved the incorporation of the association; he saw the northern route through the east, which was refused to him in 1914, become a reality; and he spoke at all state and national Yellowstone Trail Association conventions.

The calamity which would have diminished lesser men brought out Dowling's strength of character. He led an incredible life, and was an integral part of creating and popularizing the Yellowstone Trail. This remarkable man invigorated the Yellowstone Trail Association as no other had. His very appearance inspired resolve among the membership as he repeated, "Thank God I'm not a cripple!"

The authors wish to thank Barry and Michael Prichard, Michael Dowling's grandsons, for their assistance. ✿

Heading West with Dowling, 1913
Barry Prichard

The Trailblazers Return, Olivia

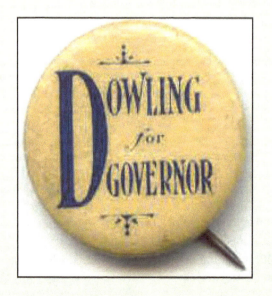

TRAIL TALES (240) TRAIL TALES

Travel Diaries and Hoopla in the Press

July 1:   12:00 p.m. Bought Ford
          4:30 p.m. Wish I hadn't bought it

July 17: 4:30 a.m. We get up and repair tires. By 6 o'clock
          we are on our way

          8:30 a.m. Sunday morning when we should be
          praising the Lord, we are praising a flat

          12:00 noon St. Paul, Minn. It's high time we
          were fixing a flat tire … again.

July 18: 5:30 p.m. There is a mule colt in the road ahead
          of us. No, beg your pardon, it's a jackrabbit.

July 19: 9:00 a.m. Just crossed the Missouri River at
          Mobridge. Rough detour on dirt road. These
          roads are like sponges in wet weather and rocks
          in dry.

          8:30 p.m. We are driving in the face of a bad
          looking thunderstorm. The prairie is fiery with
          lightening and we are trying to make it to the
          next town.

          9:30 p.m. The storm has broken and we are
          marooned on the prairie. Both the wind and
          rain are terrific and our old bus is about ready
          to topple over. We manage to skid along under
          the shelter of some hills where we spend the
          night with the wind howling like a hungry
          coyote.

B. J. Danielson wrote this diary during his 1927 camping trip west in his Ford named Rocky. His full diary exposed a man of humor and infinite patience.

For centuries, hand written accounts of people's experiences were more than just words. Writing style, drawings, and blood, sweat and tears left on paper gave detailed insights into the writer. The same can be evident in a trip diary. Letter-writing and journaling seemed more popular and necessary one hundred years ago, so keeping a diary while traveling was probably more naturally done. Today, cell phones can record a travel moment visually and audibly with just a click; a phone call can replace written description. A Twitter communique of only a few characters can transmit the basics of who, what, where, when. But to see what the traveler saw requires words, an attitude, and a mood of the diarist.

To the student of history, diaries are golden primary sources, written close to the action. One hundred years ago writing took time and a more active participation with words, possibly revealing more than intended by the writer. Long-distance travel was fairly new then, so trips that were made were sort of an understood benchmark in that family's story, demanding a more full account. However, trip diaries did not always assure complete accuracy. Some may have exaggerated the dangers due to fright at the moment. Some, because of frustration or anger, may have exaggerated the number of flats they had that day or the ferocity of rain. Waiting for three days for auto repair parts to arrive could surely make one frustrated. In their own words, long ago travelers on forgotten roads teach us about our culture.

The trip diaries kept along the Yellowstone Trail that we have come upon in our research showed us that trip "diaries" come in various forms. Some were kept literally day-by-day, some appeared as a series of post cards sent home, some abbreviated diaries appeared in newspaper articles submitted by returned travelers or were sought after by reporters. Some formed the bases of articles written as advice to potential travelers.

All of the diaries that we found referred to traveling to or from the west. No one seemed to have written about their travels east. Could it be that the roads were better there and, thus, not worth writing about? Picture post cards of historic sites seemed more important to verify one's trip east than hardships on the road.

Whatever the form of the missive, the diaries we have seen seem to gel around a few themes. The leading topics were problems (with auto, road, or lack of map), descriptions of surprising events, or of the scenery.

Problems, Problems

Paul G. Hoffman, president of Studebaker Corporation, told about a "long" 60 mile trip from southwest Chicago to Hobart, Indiana, in "America on Wheels," a chapter of Winifred Dixon's *Westward Hoboes* (1921). He, his parents, grandpa and aunt were well equipped for the journey with extra spark plugs, inner tubes and casings, springs, tools, and lunch. They started on a Saturday morning, but never made it to Hobart. Hoffman wrote:

> I tried to shift from third to second gear to climb a hill and failed. When the car was out of gear there was no service brake. We started to roll backward. My aunt screamed, tossed out the lunch basket, and followed it herself in a flying leap. … we reached a fork in the road, and we had no maps. We went right. We should have gone left. It began to rain. Considerable time was lost in putting up the curtains. The road became a bog into which we sank. I cut brush to give the wheels traction. We got out of the first mudhole, in a short way we sank again.

They stayed at a friendly farmer's home overnight, turning toward home the next morning having gone 45 miles. Grandpa seriously gashed his forehead on the radiator. Crankcase oil leaked out and the engine froze. The ladies got on a streetcar and went home. ⇨

Dad and Grandpa doing what they often did! Near Bozeman, Montana.
Bob Evans

The Ross family account of crossing Snoqualmie Pass before the Yellowstone Trail arrived included:

> This required the car's seven passengers to hoist the vehicle up the steepest grades by hand via a pulley system devised with 200 feet of rope and the sturdiest tree we could find.

In the Marmarth, North Dakota area, we read from Arthur Williams that:

> ... that was a dirt road. You shouldn't travel it in the rain. Not even our old Model T could get through. That gumbo mud built up on our wheels and it was just like you had the brakes on.

The tale of gumbo was repeated countless times on and off the Yellowstone Trail. Tales of tipping over, meager camping facilities, negotiating hills backwards (to favor the gravity-fed gasoline supply), and treeless North Dakota and eastern Montana garnered the most ink along with road and auto troubles in diaries.

THREE GIRLS MAKE 8,000 MILE TOUR
WITHOUT MISHAP THEY TRAVEL BY AUTOMOBILE THROUGH THE WEST

The girls from Milwaukee, Fond du Lac, and Oshkosh, Wisconsin returned home Friday after a 10 weeks' motor trip of 8,000 miles.

September 14, 1920 Stevens Point (WI) Gazette

And Yet They Endured

The Yellowstone Trail seemed damned about as much as it was praised in diaries. Allen Cooper, speaking about South Dakota's Standing Rock Reservation, said:

> The road traveled was the Yellowstone Trail. None of it was paved; all of it was poorly marked. In many places the only markings were smears of yellow paint on fence or telephone post.

And R. S. Spears wrote in *Outing Magazine* Vol 68, 1916 about his motorcycle trip to the Yellowstone Park and his problem of no Yellowstone Trail signs in Minneapolis:

> I do not know of any more trying experience than seeking a road out of a city with such picturesque and winding streets as those of Minneapolis. With a map of both the Twin Cities before me, I am quite unable to discover my route. I saw no signs for the Yellowstone Trail and people could not give me understandable directions for finding it. I know I crossed the Mississippi twice! "Just keep a-goin'" until I run into the Lakes, or Lake Ave. or something. Or "You can't miss it. Not after you turn right, go around the lake then hit, let's see four? blocks out. Then you're all right." Oh for some signs!

Conversely, we read from Mrs. Anna McKee of Minnesota about a 1920 trip through northern Illinois and Iowa:

> I am proud of the Yellowstone Trail as it is the best highway I have traveled on. The Jefferson and Lincoln High-

ways are good roads but work on the latter trail necessitates constant detouring. We passed over hard surface roads for a distance of 40 miles in some instances.

And Edgar Wilcox, in *Haggerty's Car Culture* 1923 announced that:

> The Yellowstone Trail is well marked - a yellow square (about 16" square) bearing two black circles between which are the words "Yellowstone Trail" and in the center a black arrow pointing to the Park. The sign came to be a faithful guide and friend to us in the hundreds of miles that we followed the trail to Spokane.

Troubles seemed to overshadow the descriptions of the beautiful scenery or the Yellowstone Trail, but yet they saw things. Descriptions allow us to see what travelers saw and endured.

Descriptions

An unknown (to us) writer recalled a trip in 1922 from Cheyenne, Wyoming, north through western Montana and Washington, then down to their new home in California. This diary mentioned Butte, Missoula and camping at a small town on the way to Spokane. They were most likely on the Yellowstone Trail. He wrote, "My mother wrote such an excellent account of the trip west in those times that I shall not cover it. This is her wonderful account of our trip." The following is just a bit of her description.

> Sat. eve drove thro' mountains and mountains, around curve after curve & hairpin turns - one place where just as we reached the bottom of one hill it turned and went down in just the opposite direction & big cars all have to stop and back a little to make the turn. Fords and Maxwells can make it without. Of course there's a sign before you get there telling you it's coming & there's a railing around it so you can't jump off. And the figure 8's and S's we did cut. Such roads - but it's certainly wonderful that they can make roads at all in such places.

Notes from an August, 1914, trip from Minnesota to the Yellowstone National Park were submitted to the *Winona Republican-Herald* upon the family's return by E. M. McLaughlin:

> From Huron, South Dakota, we went to Aberdeen. There we got on to the real trail to the park, called the Yellowstone Trail. It is marked with yellow posts and

⇨

RIEDMANS START ON AN EXTENDED AUTO TRIP

F. C. Reidman and family left July 4 for an extended auto trip that will end on the Pacific coast, where they will attend the world's fair [Panama–Pacific International Exposition] at San Francisco. Their equipment consisted of a Cadillac touring car and Detroit trailer to carry the tents and baggage. The Yellowstone Trail will be followed.

Mr. Reidman will leave the family in California and return here in September, and then go back and spend the winter in the warmer climate. [Mr. Reidman had just sold his John Deer dealership and retired.]

July 8, 1915 The Weekly Times-Record (Valley City, ND)

---

across the prairie with yellow stones. The roads are good in Minnesota and eastern South Dakota. In the western Dakotas and eastern Montana there are only grass trails with lots of stones and holes. Lots of new roads are being made across Dakota and Montana, so the trail takes temporary routes, sometimes fifty miles from a railway and fifteen to twenty from a house. The Little Missouri River has to be forded at Marmarth, but when we crossed, it was so swollen by rain that it could not be forded by teams to say nothing of autos, so we crossed on the railway bridge.

William C. Bettis had a different goal from most for keeping a diary in 1921. He was apparently a professional traveler who sold his travel booklets and who appeared on the lecture stage. Mrs. Bettis took notes, noting the good and the bad. A trip to the Pacific Coast carried the reader with them from Toledo to California. The booklet is heavy on description and advice, but there is little bad about the Yellowstone Trail, except to say that there are several detours due to road work. One exciting description of his trip, written as though to experienced travelers, follows:

There are a lot of experiences you would have had by this time also. For example, you may have been high up on a shelf road, one of those roads cut into the side of a mountain. You are away up among the clouds, a sheer mountain road towering over you on one side and a drop of hundreds of feet on the other. This road may be wide enough for just one car with nothing to prevent you from driving into the chasm. With both feet on the pedals and a death grip on the wheel you are swinging in and out around short, sharp curves, and suddenly you see a sign that reads PREPARE TO MEET THY GOD. No matter how experienced you are, this will send a shiver up your spine.

MAKES TRANSCONTINENTAL TRIP ON ONE PINT OF WATER

F. A. Goodrich completed a trip of 7,000 miles from Syracuse to Seattle and then south. The first time the radiator cap was removed was in Miles City, Mont. and a short pint filled it to overflowing.

Goodrich is enthusiastic over the part of the trip that followed the Yellowstone Trail, believing it by far the most scenic of all the transcontinental tours.

November 24, 1918 Tulsa (OK) Daily World

Unusual Tales

When something unexpected happened, the diarist was sure to include it. Chances are that the surprises are what people remembered the longest. This tale hit the *Antique Motor Cycle* magazine, summer 1999, about something that happened back in 1922, as told to his son by Allen Cooper (again). It revealed a happening on the open road - stranded parties. Cooper was on his 61-inch Harley-Davidson. We excerpt his tale here of stopping in western South Dakota as an example of kindness on the road 100 years ago.

There were few habitations and fewer gas pumps in the stretch between the river and McIntosh. Miles out on this barren and deserted road a parked car showed up. Four men in work clothes flagged me down. Their old Chevrolet touring car bore Pennsylvania license plates. Their car had quit on them suddenly, "like we had turned off the switch." They were laid off coal miners on their way to the Butte mines for work. It was plain they were on a close budget. None of them seemed to know anything about a car except how to drive it. The prospect of a big towing or repair bill could not have depressed them more. I asked to look at it. They readily agreed. It appeared that it was ignition failure. A wire had broken off right next to the battery. A few minutes' work stripping off some insulation and clamping the bare wire under the cable clamp completed the circuit. I had never seen four happier fellows. They insisted they owed me something, but my reply was perhaps they could pass on the favor to someone in trouble.

A diary kept by Montana's Spencer "Bill" Lauson c.1921 suggests that long-distance travel wasn't quite as we expect it to be today.

My brother Dwight said I was welcome to ride with him and his family from Billings to Chicago. I looked out the door and saw that the reconditioned Studebaker was filled to the roof with baggage, with only a small space left for the family dog.

In addition to the three members of my brother's family, an oversized lady with her teenaged daughter planned to ride for the first 150 miles - all five of them jammed in the front seat. I didn't fancy myself sitting on the fat lady's lap. 'I think you could sit on the front fender' my brother casually suggested.

If I were to save money on my travel, this would have to do.

I carried no luggage - there wasn't any room - except for a towel, soap and razor which I had hastily stuffed into my pockets. I had little idea how futile these cleanup efforts would be in the war against dust, grit and mud.

Shortly after we passed the outskirts of Billings it began to rain. We were following the old Yellowstone Trail which would take us to Chicago. The road turned into a slippery gumbo, and the old Studebaker would slide and fishtale as it hit a stretch of the unpredictable mixture of clay and rain. I hung on to the fender with white knuckles, trying to dodge clumps of mud that were thrown from the car's wheels.

The last unusual happenstance occurred in 1923 and was recalled by Lydia McKay. She and three other women were returning east to Brainerd, Minnesota, in a Star automobile after a 13-state tour. Two women occupants of another car were traveling west, beginning a tour.

As was the custom then, McKay stopped to chat with the other woman driver. What a surprise! They were all from Brainerd and met purely by chance on the Yellowstone Trail in South Dakota. Pictures were taken of the surprising event, tales of broken tie rods and poor roads were told, and tires were kicked. Attesting to the generosity of people, ⇨

Brainerd, MN girls meet by chance in SD
Wally McKay

Frank Wentworth and Lizzie
On the Road with Lizzie by Frank Wentworth

McKay reported that at one point the foursome saw a rainstorm approaching on the prairie. They simply drove into a nearby farm and asked to spend the night on the farmer's porch out of the rain. Consent was cheerfully given, followed by dinner and breakfast for the travelers.

Hoopla

Because long-distance travel was not usual, when a touring party reached town, frequently there was a big greeting awaiting them. There was the crowd greeting the Michael Dowling party of three cars as they arrived home from their 1913 Yellowstone Trail trailblazing trip. See **Trail Tale: Dowling**, page 239.

Some local newspapers seemed more intent upon recording the local greeting offered the travelers than upon the trip reported by the travelers. Only a year before the Yellowstone Trail arrived, we see in the *Minneapolis Tribune* of Aug. 30, 1911, how an auto tour was received in Minnesota:

> Officials of the St. Cloud Automobile Club piloted the tour to Clear Lake where the pilot car stopped for tire troubles. At Anoka, R. A. Cooper and Dr. E. A. Lyman in the pilot car were met by a delegation of five automobiles from Minneapolis. Among those who welcomed the visitors were H. J. Clark, president of the Minneapolis Automobile Club and G. Roy Hill, secretary. A special car from the Minneapolis Tribune met the tourists first, giving them copies of the morning editions in which were full telegraphic accounts of the tour. Officials of the Veerac Motor Company piloted the tourists through the factory where the ladies were given roses and the men cigars.

After such a reception given the tour group in Anoka, we can only guess about the hoopla which awaited the group in Minneapolis. We have no information.

From Diaries into Books

Frank L. Wentworth turned his six year camping trip into a fascinating 436-page book, *On the Road With Lizzie* (his affectionately named Model T). Frank crossed the nation several times between 1924 and 1930, seemingly choosing the route as his mood and the weather dictated. He moved about unhurriedly, spending weeks at single campsites, absorbing the environment and those who moved about him. Wentworth thanks his three daughters for help in preparing the book. Considering the amount of minute detail and the names of people he had met, he must have kept a careful diary which his daughters may have unraveled with him.

Another interesting book appeared in 2008. Dorothy was just a girl when her father, Yellowstone Trail trailblazer Michael Dowling, took his family west in 1913. She kept a diary, complete with pictures. Her son, Barry Prichard, and she turned that diary into the book, *We Blazed the Trail*. The reader can get a good view of that exciting adventure along uncharted tracts of land through pictures and through the eyes of a 13-year-old.

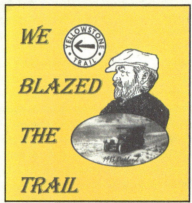

Earnest N. Smith, writing in *American Motorist*, December, 1925, described his latest run from Vancouver, B.C. to Chicago, one of several transcontinental trips he had taken. He concluded with this poignant paragraph:

> But best of all it [the trip] helped me see our country as I had never seen it before. It had given me a schooling, a patriotic education. There came to mind the sentiment of the ancient traveler of Rome who, returning after a long absence, said:
>
> I am a part of all that I have seen
>
> And all that I have seen is part of me. ✿

"4:30 a.m. We get up and repair tire. By six we are on our way." A bit later, another significant tire repair by the side of the road.
B. J. Danielson

Wisconsin

Hudson, Roberts, Hammond, Woodville, Knapp, Menomonie, Chippewa Falls, Bateman, Stanley, Thorp, Owen, Abbotsford, Colby

Baldwin, Hersey, Wilson, Eau Claire, Cadott, Boyd, Withee, Curtiss, Unity, Hewett, Auburndale, Junction City, Stevens Point

Spencer, Marshfield, Blenker & Milladore, Whiting, Plover, Amherst

Waupaca, Weyauwega, Readfield, Dale & Medina, Appleton

Fremont, Menasha, Neenah

Oshkosh, Van Dyne, Fond du Lac

N Fond du Lac, Byron, Lomira

Theresa, Nenno, Addison

St. Lawrence, Richfield, Slinger

Menomonee Falls, Milwaukee, Cudahy, Oak Creek, St. Francis, Milwaukee

WHAT THE TRAIL FOUNDERS SAID-1921

The stranger will find Wisconsin the easiest state in the country in which to find his way about. This is due to a very thorough and systematic marking of the state trunk line highways under the auspices of the State Highway Commission itself.

The roads are designated by a system of numbers of the state trunk line highways passing through that town. While the system may seem somewhat confusing to strangers, it will be found very easy and workable as soon as it is actually experienced.

The Yellowstone Trail is the short road across the state of Wisconsin connecting Chicago and the Twin Cities. It traverses central Wisconsin and is a good road throughout the entire distance. Wisconsin is an automobile outing state and offers such a selection of good things for the vacationist that no attempt can be made to describe them in detail here. The state abounds in lakes and good lake fishing is the common thing rather than an exception.

The state is well equipped with facilities for taking care of vacation trade and the conveniences of a home are always available nearby and yet there are portions of the state in which the primitive is still enough in evidence to satisfy the call of the wild.

Information bureaus of the Yellowstone Trail Association at Chicago, Milwaukee and the Twin Cities are all prepared to give detailed information about the state of Wisconsin.

1921 Yellowstone Trail Touring Service Map #10 of Wisconsin

Along the Yellowstone Trail at
Lake Wissota near Chippewa Fall, Wisconsin

245

INTRODUCING THE YELLOWSTONE TRAIL IN WISCONSIN:
THE BADGER STATE (AND VACATIONLAND)

"Old roads gossip. They pass along secrets about where lovers park and which settlers sleep the long sleep in country churchyards. The traveler who pauses to listen to the whispers is caught up in the sweet harmony of nature and time."

Bill Stokes in *Wisconsin's Rustic Roads 1995*

The YT brought economic development to its communities. Early 1920s log cabin filling station, Chippewa Falls.
Chippewa Valley Museum

The founders of the Yellowstone Trail adopted the ambitious motto "a good road from Plymouth Rock to Puget Sound" very early in its history. But the first years, 1912 -1914, were filled with the work to establish the organization and to define and develop the route between St. Paul, Minnesota, and a point near Three Forks, Montana. That was a route of more than 1,000 miles of roads, very few of which were in any way ready for the automobile.

By 1915, however, the Yellowstone Trail was known nationally, had huge support along the way in the west, and had tourists by the hundreds heading west, many to explore Yellowstone National Park now that it was open to autos. The Association was ready for more action. The decision was made to extend the actively managed part of the Trail west into Washington and east through Wisconsin to Chicago.

> ## SELECT ROUTE FROM MINNEAPOLIS
> ### EAST ROUTE OF YELLOWSTONE TRAIL TO CHICAGO WILL BE PICKED BEFORE LONG
>
> At the meeting last evening of the Yellowstone Trail Association, particular stress was placed on the necessity of selecting a route of the trail from Minneapolis to Chicago in order that it may be advertised along with other features of the trail.
>
> Two routes have been under consideration, one by way of Winona, Minn., crossing the Mississippi river at Lacrosse, and then on to Chicago by way of Madison and Milwaukee, while another is through Eau Claire.
> *March 24, 1915 Aberdeen (SD) Daily News*

The Association's choice to extend and actively manage the Trail through Wisconsin triggered and supported significant changes for both the Association and the state.

For the Association, the change was an acceleration of the transition from its primary concern with better roads (as part of the Good Roads Movement) to its concern for local economic development through tourism. In short, in Wisconsin the Association had less direct clout toward road improvement but significant ability to garner resources to increase auto tourism and thus the economies of member cities.

For the state, the success of the Yellowstone Trail as a long-distance route through Wisconsin gave legitimacy to the argument that roads were not just of a local concern for local use, needing only local financing, but rather that roads, when pieced together to form long-distance routes, were a concern for the whole state and needed state support.

More important, travelers over the Yellowstone Trail could follow the route because of the familiar yellow markers. The Yellowstone Trail markers certainly triggered Wisconsin's innovative marking of long-distance state routes with signs showing route numbers. Those signs, a triangle symbol, were erected across the state in May, 1918, on state designated routes.

The Background Story of Wisconsin Roads

Wisconsin roads began as they began everywhere: animal paths, native paths, horse rider trails, postal trails, and wagon roads, none "engineered." In 1830, Wisconsin benefitted from a Congressionally appropriated $2,000 for a "military" road running south from Green Bay. An interesting start, but during 1850-1860 the great development of railroads dissolved any interest in long-distance roads.

But then came the auto. Beginning in 1871 with Dr. Carhart's two cylinder steam engine auto and the 1875 auto race sponsored by the Wisconsin State Legislature, the cat was out of the bag. Entering the 20th century, interest in auto use and manufacturing in the state became surprisingly virile. See **Trail Tale: Hot Wheels**, page 282.

The Progressive Movement around 1903-1911 dictated that improving life for citizens become a political priority, particularly in Wisconsin. In 1908, Wisconsinites voted to allow the state to "appropriate money for the construction of highways," thus changing the state constitution which had prohibited such "internal improvements." Such constitutional changes marched across the country.   ⇨

Model Ts poured into Wisconsin via rail adding to local production and magnifying the need for roads useful to autos.
Mike Kirk

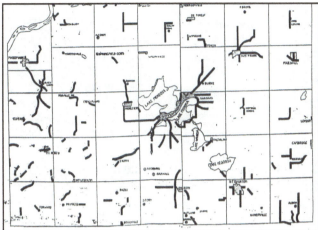

State/federal supported roads in 1917 before the state trunk system, Dane County, Wisconsin

The Wisconsin Good Roads Movement developed in parallel with the development of the motor vehicle. And, of course, as autos increased in number, the demand for better roads increased.

The capstone of the Progressive Movement for roads was the passing of the State Aid Law of 1911 stating that the financing of highways was to be a co-operative effort among the state, the counties, and the townships. But even then, the thought of creating routes over connected roads, even short ones across a county, apparently did not occur to officials. As a result, most roads were only farm-to-market roads.

But citizens saw the need for long-distance routes and responded with a wave of "named highways." From 1911 to 1917 there was an epidemic of unofficial laying out and marking of routes.

First, named routes were established by local tourism advocates and state autoist organizations to make auto travel easier and attract tourists. One noticeable example was the Blue Diamond route in the vacationland of northern Wisconsin.

And, second, there were interstate organizations like the Yellowstone Trail Association anxious to mark their routes in the state. They had legitimate goals of supporting local business.

Then, third, apparently new opportunities always attract the scammer. Many a local government or fraternal organization heard pitches for a grand new trail through the town that would bring economic success to the town. The bill was paid

OFFICIAL STATE TRUNK HIGHWAY MARKER

STATE TRUNK HIGHWAY
92
WIS

and the organizer was never seen again. These acts tainted the concept of named highways seemingly forever.

Indeed, the dishonesty of some "trail associations" apparently is remembered even today, 100 years after the fact. When we sought information about the Yellowstone Trail in Wisconsin from the State Historical Society Library, we were surprised to hear the librarian sneer, "trails!" We failed to prod her for the back story of her attitude, a failing we have regretted.

It was, no doubt, knowledge of those "scammers" that lead to resistance to the Yellowstone Trail. It had been in the state for two years by 1917 when it faced significant negativity, mainly at the hands of Frank Cannon who railed against the Yellowstone Trail from his bully pulpit magazine, *Good Roads for Wisconsin*. See **Trail Tale: Cannon**, page 288. Unfortunately, Cannon apparently had the ear of several legislators and, thus, his sweeping condemnation of all trails including the Yellowstone Trail, affected the thinking of men of prominence. But, the reality was that the Yellowstone Trail had proven itself to most people to have created something good and progressive - it had joined several roads into a route across the state, something that had not existed before. Towns had fought to get on the Trail. Honest service was rendered to member towns along this marked and promoted route. It soon became the most used route, requiring more maintenance than others, which became an argument against it, ignoring the fact that its use meant pronounced social and economic growth.

In the face of the proven value of a long-distance road, a common argument raised against the Trail in Wisconsin 100 years ago (and in other states as well) was that, "A road through the state will take people from Chicago out of the state to Minneapolis." We were startled to hear a similar argument from a Convention and Visitors Bureau official against reviving the Yellowstone Trail. Some people seem to forget that a through route also brings people into your state.

During 1916, Congress enacted the first federal aid highway act which required that the state adopt a state-wide system of roads. In response, in 1917 Wisconsin adopted a state trunk highways system of 5,000 miles with the requirement that the routes be marked, that counties in the aggregate are ⇨

WI

22,000 automobiles were routed through Wisconsin on the Yellowstone Trail in 1920. And those tourists spent an estimated $724,000 in Wisconsin.
February 11, 1921 Eau Claire Leader

WOULD LICENSE DRIVERS
MILWAUKEE PROPOSAL TO LICENSE DRIVERS ATTRACTS ATTENTION

Much comment is being heard relative to the ordinance proposed before the city council providing for the licensing of Milwaukee drivers ... a physical and temperamental examination as well as a test of the ability to drive a machine are to be made before a permit is issued.
January 11, 1917 Kenosha Telegraph-Courier

NEW YORK TO EMULATE WISCONSIN

New York is the latest to emulate the example of Wisconsin's standardized road numbering system. The Empire State was one of the first in the union to start a road program, long before Wisconsin, and marked its roads with bands of different colors on telephone poles. The state, however, has decided to adopt the numbered Wisconsin system.

Unknown source

required to provide an amount equal to the state, and state "Patrolmen" patrol sections of those state roads. During January of 1918, the decision was made to use numbers to mark that state trunk system. Route number markings were erected over the entire system in May of 1918. Wisconsin is thus credited with creating the first numeric (and alphabetic, in counties) route markers with a corresponding state road map showing those routes, an idea that spread across the country.

The modern highway system was being created.

Single lane YT
southeast of Junction City

The Yellowstone Trail and Early Wisconsin Roads

The Trail gave an immediate boost to tourism and the accompanying economic benefits. It was received well by tourists and the towns through which it passed. The dominant auto map producers, primarily Rand McNally, produced modern maps with the Trail prominently shown. The *Automobile Blue Books* publisher identified the route to guide cross-county travelers. The State of Wisconsin produced official state road

The 1919 *Rand McNally* Wisconsin maps adopted the Wisconsin numbering system including the exception offered the YT.

maps, actually printing the route numbers on maps to help autoists, the first to do so.

The 1918 and following state maps did not show the Yellowstone Trail because of the desire to make the state's numbering system "the" route identification system. Nor did they assign a single number to the Yellowstone Trail over its whole route.

In fact, the 1917 Wisconsin Session Laws (Chapter 175, Act 13b) stated that, "it is illegal to mark any route unless it coincides exactly with the state trunk highway system." Then Act 15 stated that, "it is illegal to erect any signs on the trunk highway system." Bewildering!

Then, another Bill was proposed prohibiting any markers on Wisconsin highways other than the marks for the numbered Wisconsin Trunk System. All towns along the Trail were urged by the Trail Association officers to contact their legislators. Result? The Bill was amended to read "all markers except the Yellowstone Trail markers."

The Yellowstone Trail was a heavily used route. For instance, in 1920, only eight years after the beginning of bourgeoning auto sales, 70,000 individuals in 22,000 auto parties, entered Wisconsin on the Yellowstone Trail. Almost all of the Trail became part of the state trunk system and because of its heavy use, by 1929 the Trail became the first completely paved cross-state route. Beginning in 1926, the federal numbered highway system, based on Wisconsin's 1918 ⇨

Before and after dragging in Waupaca County
Wis. Geological Natural History Survey Bulletin 3XVIII PL VII

WI

WI 77 with triangular road marker to the left
Wis. DOT

YELLOWSTONE TRAIL IS BEING REROUTED THROUGH HIGHWAY 95

State trunk highway 95 is known locally as the Oshkosh road. It is a more direct route than the old. The new trail leaves highway 18 just east of Fremont and takes them into Oshkosh on highway 95 by way of Butte des Morts, a road partly concrete. The yellow markers are now being switched to this more direct route. See Map, page 269.

August 28, 1924 Waupaca County Post

innovation, extended across the nation.

Travel Bureaus were established by the Trail Association. The Pfister Hotel at Milwaukee was the largest of the eventual 15 bureaus charged with giving out maps, road condition reports, and information to guide tourists to the next bureau.

Why the Trail Went Where It Did in Wisconsin

The route of the Yellowstone Trail in Wisconsin was chosen by members of the Automobile Club of Minneapolis along with Yellowstone Trail Association trailblazer Michael Dowling, as documented by the minutes of the Trail meeting in Montevideo, Minnesota, February 19, 1915. Throughout Wisconsin the distinctive yellow and black directive colors went up on telephone poles, fences, and even silos.

It seems safe to presume that a straighter and shorter route along a diagonal from Hudson toward Chicago would have been considered. However, they chose a route through Stevens Point east to Appleton, then south, looking like a big digit 7 on maps. But consider the criteria that were important at the time. First, the population and industrial centers of Wisconsin ran south, closer to Lake Michigan. That area had the better roads because of the population density. Second, the diagonal route would have included large areas of hilly, sparsely populated land and great areas of bogs and other difficult land on which to build roads. In addition, because railroads tied together population centers (the railroads might even have created those centers) and provided transportation services for necessary auto repair parts, and occasionally rescued stranded motorists, the route of the Trail usually followed rail lines. For the most part, the chosen route clung closely to the major rail lines.

Note also that the expenses of the Yellowstone Trail Association were paid by businessmen members and city members through their annual dues. There were few cities along the diagonal line through Wisconsin.

The route of the Trail did change in several places during its life, the most pronounced relocations being near Appleton and Oshkosh. In every case, those relocations were undertaken to take advantage of road improvements, especially the concrete construction undertaken from about 1924 to 1929. Most Trail markers were moved to follow the modified routes. After 1927, when many state highways were renumbered with U.S. route numbers, the Trail was unaffected.

Wisconsin is known for its beer, cheese, Green Bay Packers, and Harley-Davidson Hogs. But it would be good to be known through its interesting economic and social evolution as presented in the history of its highway development. Through the periods of Native trails, ox cart and wagon roads, to the Yellowstone Trail, to the modern arteries, that history is writ large. It is to the good roads of the last 100 years, built on the backs of years of governmental malaise, that people should give thanks for their beer, cheese, Packers, and Harley Hogs. And especially for the influence of the state's auto industry, a phenomenon that few can now recall.

The State Highway Commission showed remarkable prescience in 1916 when it wrote of the Yellowstone Trail that "In one way, this trail marking is an interesting indication of the present trend of thought in that these markings disregard town and county lines and concern themselves only with the best roads on which to get between two points …thinking in terms of states and the nation rather than small units of government." ✿

WI

TRAIL MEETING WELL ATTENDED; ASSOCIATION FORMED
June 3, 1915 Waupaca Record-Leader

Anywhere, any time
Chippewa Valley Museum

1913 bridge and causeway
across St. Croix River
St. Croix County Historical Society

Historic causeway, Hudson

Nov. 3, 1916, the Hudson Board of Trade
took out a membership in the Yellowstone
Trail Association. ✿

The 1913 bridge toll ticket

In May, 1922, Hudson's
Yellowstone Trail was opened
for its eighth summer season
by officials of the Yellowstone
Trail Association. Members
of the St. Paul Chamber of
Commerce visited and toured
the new tourist park. H. O.
Cooley, general manager of the
Yellowstone Trail Association,
spoke to the Hudson Com-
mercial Club, claiming that the
Yellowstone Trail Association
was making an industry of
summer touring. ✿

Headline story of the early days of autoing in the *Hudson Star-Observer*: "TWO SEPARATE AUTO PARTIES
FORMED A SOCIABILITY RUN TO HUDSON FROM
ST. PAUL." A sociability run was a social event of a
caravan of cars all going to the same destination just for
fun. However, in the same article: "A Hudson car was
rear-ended by a Minnesota hit-and-run driver who was
apprehended." ✿

25,000 tourists were routed over the Trail through Hudson
in the 1921 tourist season according to Trailman O. E.
Lyksett. That figures out to be 75 cars per day for 90 days,
each with 3.7 persons per car. The Yellowstone Trail Association issued the 3.7 passenger figure for all car counters
along the Trail nationally to standardize their estimates of
Trail tourist usage. ✿

In Hudson, a portion of the Yellowstone Trail (present WI
12) beginning at Vine and Ninth streets and running east
for three and a half miles was concreted with federal and
state aid and opened to traffic in October, 1920. A great
celebration was held; 2,000 attendees, speeches by the Trail
Association general manager, city and county officials, a
Congressman, a picnic and dance. This celebration was "a
recognition of the importance of the problem of the country highway as an artery of commerce," said the *Hudson
Star-Observer*. ✿

A traveler today may be familiar with a Woodall travel
guide. In July 1915 Mr. Woodall himself came through
Baldwin on the Yellowstone Trail to prepare a travel guide.
The July 9, 1915, *Hudson Star-Observer* said:

> Mr. Woodall is engaged in carefully measuring distanc-
> es between towns, stopping where supplies can be pro-
> cured, noting all the places of interest to motor tourists
> both on the trail and at distances removed therefrom.
> He is employed by the Yellowstone Trail Association on
> this particular trip. ✿

YELLOWSTONE TRAIL MEETING HERE

The gist of the meeting was to consider if the Trail should
move out of Wisconsin and into Iowa instead, due to
many towns in Wisconsin in arrears of their membership
allotments, the threat coming from the Yellowstone Trail
Association General Manager, H. O. Cooley.
January 14, 1921 Hudson Star-Observer

Hundreds came to the KKK open meeting just west of
Knapp to "get Protestants back into the pews." A hood-
ed parade preceded speaker, Mr. Rush, who spoke against
parochial schools, against Negroes and intermarriage,
and against Jews who control 70% of the money in the
U.S."

September 5, 1924 Baldwin Bulletin

BALDWIN HAS AN AUTOMOBILE CLUB

June 26, 1913 Hudson Star-Observer

Autoists had the Baldwin
Motor Club as early as 1913,
created "for social purposes, to promote good roads,
and the general welfare of
the automobile game." One
wonders what was meant by
"the automobile game." ✿

A public ladies room was established in the basement of Carnegie Library in 1921. "Hudson people
are requested to direct travelers to the rest room
for information and comfort. Mrs. Livermore,
restroom matron, has been supplied with a quantity
of Yellowstone Trail maps which can be had for the
asking. The Commercial Club has also provided
an employment bureau at the rest room." *Hudson
Star-Observer*. ✿

Dick's Bar on site of old
Yellowstone Trail Buffet, Hudson

WI-000.0 Wisconsin/Minnesota Line
WI-000.0 Hudson

is situated on beautiful Lake St. Croix, which divides the states of Wisconsin and Minnesota. From Prospect park, overlooking the city, one has a splendid view of the surrounding country. Free kitchen and dining rooms are maintained in this park for tourists. BB1921-10

US 12 crosses the Minnesota Line on a toll bridge (15¢ for auto and driver; 5¢ for additional passengers) over the St. Croix River, 16.9 miles east of St. Paul, Minnesota. WPA-WI

Hudson, A railroad division, it has car shops. Free Camp is at Prospect Park, free kitchen, dining rooms. Ford garage is best. MH-1926; BB1920

In 1915 the Yellowstone Trail entered Wisconsin from Minnesota across the St. Croix River on a toll bridge and adjoining causeway, or "dike" as it was locally called, built out to meet the toll bridge in the middle of the St. Croix River. The opening of the bridge, June 14, 1913, was cause for great celebration, speeches by officials of everything, ending in a big dance on the bridge. The city-owned bridge tolls allowed the Hudson residents the privilege of paying extremely low property taxes from c.1913 to 1951. Today the "dike" serves as a pleasant place to stroll or fish.

111 Walnut St. **Dick's Bar** is just a block up from the river where many steamboats moored. It has been a bar/saloon from 1853. "J. B. Gage has adopted a new name for his refreshment buffet, the Yellowstone Trail Buffet" (*1915 Hudson Star-Observer*). Today, stop in and say you are on the Yellowstone Trail. They know!

426 Second St. Just south of the Yellowstone Trail is the **San Pedro Café**, site of the former Yellowstone Café. "The place of business of the Yellowstone Café under the ownership of Koenig Brothers has been moved to 426 Second St." (December 30, 1926, *Hudson Star-Observer*).

Third Street Historic District consists of 17 historic homes on Walnut and Third streets. Travelers can obtain an Historic Walking Tour map from the Chamber of Commerce 502 Second St. Four houses that saw the Yellowstone Trail are most interesting:

1. 1005 Third St. Phipps House. Queen Anne style, built in 1884, now the **Phipps Inn B&B**.

2. 1004 Third St. **Octagon House**. It is eight-sided, built in 1855, and is on the National Register of Historic Places. It is a museum owned and maintained by the St. Croix County Historical Society complete with gardens and carriage house.

3. 915 Third St. **John C. Spooner House**. Built in 1878 of Italianate design for lawyer and three-term U.S. Senator Spooner. It is a T-shaped house with gable roof and large paired brackets along the cornice. Private residence.

4. 727 Third St. **Boyden House**. Victorian Gothic style, built in 1879. Private residence.

It isn't easy, but getting to **Prospect Park** on a high hill is worth it. 3rd Ave. south becomes Laurel, on to north on Blakeman to enter Prospect Park. It was created in 1885 overlooking the city. It features gardens, picnic pavilions, and playground areas. Adjacent to the park at its south end was a tourist camp, opened in May, 1922, that was used by many Yellowstone Trail travelers. Diaries of Trail travelers speak of "driving up the steep hill to the camp and enjoying the view of the town and river below." The newspaper reported regularly the numbers of campers (4,628 in 1923) and the amenities supplied by the proud city.

WI-011.4 Roberts
WI-017.7 Hammond

820 Davis St. On the corner where the Yellowstone Trail (present US 12) takes an abrupt 90-degree turn was the Hammond Hotel. Built in 1879, it survived 135 years in business, when the business was replaced in 2014 by **Cheap Andy's Saloon**. The hotel was also the headquarters for the annual Llama Run on the Yellowstone Trail.

WI-021.5 Baldwin

Baldwin Free camp at park. Good Country hotel.

Camp maintained by Community Club in park on Main St. near creamery. Accommodations for 5 cars, 20 people. Opera House with moving pictures twice a week. MH-1926

WI-026.1 Woodville

Woodville was incorporated in 1911. Lights came in 1914 and a water system in 1920. First newspaper in 1913.

The Wisconsin Highway Commission in 1923 reported: The traveled route of state trunk highway 12 through the Village of Knapp, Dunn County, contains four right angle turns, and there is an abrupt turn in the road which it is desirable to eliminate. The reason for those angles was because that area in Knapp was a swampy lake. Those sharp angles remained until 1930 when a new US 12 was built straight through Knapp and the swampy lake. ✿

Dangerous railroad crossing at top of hill just west of Menomonie
Wis. DOT

KEEP OFF THE NEW CONCRETE

A. Larson has again purchased the tacks and put them on the road to Hammond. He has also had signs made reading 'Fresh Concrete' and 'Look out for punctures.' The signs should do the business, and if not, the tacks will.

August 19, 1927 Baldwin Bulletin

Yellowstone Trail on Wilson Creek bridge, Menomonie

In the 1920s the Yellowstone Trail in the town of Spring Brook was marked by "little yellow signs." It was also claimed that a man named Weston passed through, "walking the distance on that road." It might well have been W. Warwick who was employed by the Yellowstone Trail Association to put up Yellowstone Trail markers along the Trail. ✿

Mabel Tainter Theater, Menomonie

Yellowstone Trail just west of Menomonie
Wis. DOT

A BADGER AND A MOTHER OF TWO HELD FOR ELOPING
March, 1920 Baldwin Bulletin

167,843 GIVEN LICENSES FOR 1924 IN WISCONSIN
Mar. 28, 1924 Baldwin Bulletin

Invented in Menomonie: Jeremiah Tainter invented the Tainter gate, a rocker-shaped device to raise and lower water levels for controlling water in a dam spillway. This 1886 invention is still used today in dams around the world. ✿

Knapp, Stout Company was the largest lumber corporation in the world in 1873. James Stout was a philanthropist, senator, and forward thinker about roads. ✿

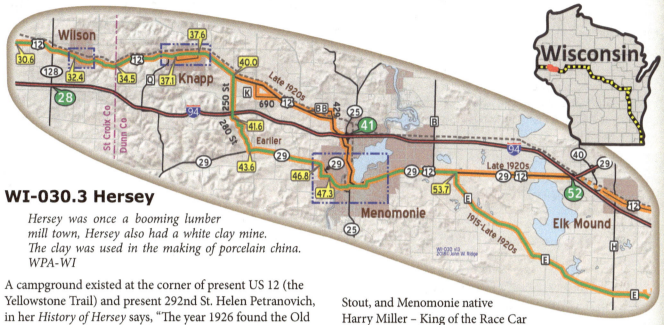

WI-030.3 Hersey

Hersey was once a booming lumber mill town, Hersey also had a white clay mine. The clay was used in the making of porcelain china. WPA-WI

A campground existed at the corner of present US 12 (the Yellowstone Trail) and present 292nd St. Helen Petranovich, in her *History of Hersey* says, "The year 1926 found the Old Yellowstone Trail becoming US 12. The old graveled road was widened and became a cement paved road. The Old Yellowstone Trail was at that time a main thoroughfare for horse jockies and gypsy caravans as they traveled westward."

WI-032.4 Wilson

Free camp space at Gas station. MH-1926

WI-034.0

Between Wilson and Knapp (Dunn County) is Knapp Hill. It is not now as scary as it was when folks were driving the Yellowstone Trail. No need now to back up the hill to keep gas running to the engine. Story has it that slow-moving trucks could slow down the traffic righteously, leading a trail of exasperated drivers of underpowered flivvers. Between Wilson and the county line, the route was subject to much straightening. You might look for the old route weaving in and out.

WI-037.4 Knapp

Good garage and country hotel. Free camp space on highway. MH-1926

WI-047.3 Area of Old Brickyard

Menomonie had at least one brickyard on Brickyard Road (the early Yellowstone Trail). Millions of bricks were once manufactured by seven companies using the outstanding nearby clay. In 1968 the last surviving brick company closed, a victim of modern plants. There are still hundreds of bricks lying about.

WI-048.8 Menomonie

A prosperous little town, supported by flour mills, brickyards, a piano factory and the successful dairy farmers of the territory. Hotel Marian; splendid new hotel. Best meals. Sgl. $1.25, dbl. with bath, $4. The C & O Garage is best. Labor $1. Tourist camp, 25¢, level and in a nice grove. MH-1926

1820 Wakanda St. **Russell Rassbach Heritage Museum** in Wakanda Park. Good exhibits have included local James Huff Stout, and Menomonie native Harry Miller – King of the Race Car Builders. It is open year round.

932 N. Broadway (Yellowstone Trail after 1925). **Skoog's Restaurant**. In Trail days a gas station stood on this spot, followed by other restaurants and motels for decades. What makes this place a stop for today's Trail traveler is that they have preserved some items from that era. It is a typical Wisconsin "supper club." It is now called Wilson Creek Inn.

901-999 N Broadway St. **Sanna Park**, called Menomonie Tourist Park in Yellowstone Trail days. In the 1920s the 10 acre park had camping, boating, dancing in pavilions, and comfort stations. It was a popular stopping place for Yellowstone Trail travelers. Today, the only remaining evidence of its past is the small stone pillars at the entrance.

205 Main St. **The Mabel Tainter Memorial Theater** is worth a stop. Built of sandstone in 1890, it is a beautiful 130-year-old Victorian theater which presents performing and cultural arts. There are two galleries devoted to Tainter Estate furniture, fittingly displayed in this "Guilded Age" building.

101 Wilson Cir. (on S. Broadway, the later Yellowstone Trail). **Wilson Place Mansion Museum**. It was built in 1859 by lumber baron William Wilson. It stayed in the family through three generations and endured three different architectural styles -Victorian, Queen Anne, and Mediterranean.

603 S. Broadway (the Yellowstone Trail before 1925). **Raw Deal Café** near UW-Stout campus. A funny little place where all the food is raw! It has healthy fruits and veggies and surprising treats and guest performers.

712 S. Broadway. **University of Wisconsin-Stout** began as the Stout Manual Training School in 1891 founded by James Stout. He was a wealthy lumberman, state senator, and a member of the UW Board of Regents. In 1898, as a Good Roads enthusiast he financed and built a half-mile section of the "road of the future" He personally oversaw the construction of a "seedling" half mile of a model multi-lane road that included two earth roads, a stone road, a walking path and a bicycle path. It has been overlaid by the road used by the Yellowstone Trail.

At **WI-067.0**: Fred and Flora Rossow farmed along here at the turn of the 20th century. They said:

> All the telephone poles were marked with a band of yellow and went clear out west, and they called this the Yellowstone Trail. About this time of year (summer), day after day, people would stop here and ask if they could pitch their tents and get water from us. We always let them. ✿

There are references to two campsites in Eau Claire, both on the Trail, although neither site is a camp or park today. One occupied almost a whole square block between the streets of Omaha, Spring, Birch, and McDonough. A later campground was in a park closer to the junction of Birch Street and Hastings Way, perhaps "at the foot of Mt. Tom." ✿

From Margaret Wethern, March 28, 1990:

> Among my very earliest memories is hearing someone say, 'Here comes Quilling!' and we would rush to a window or out on the porch to see Mr. Quilling go by in his 'horseless carriage.' He was a prosperous gentleman who lived west of us and he may have had the first car in the area — but it was like a two-seated carriage with a tiller for steering instead of a wheel, and no top. ✿

YT on 1924 Madison St. bridge, Eau Claire
Chippewa Valley Museum

Concrete! YT Eau Claire to Chippewa Falls built 1919
1921 Wis. DOT

From the minutes of the February 7, 1919, meeting of the Wisconsin Highway Commission:

> The road in question connects two important cities and is a connection for travel north and south and east and west. The cities of Eau Claire and Chippewa Falls are connected by two steam railways and one electric railway. On the State Trunk Highway there are nine grade crossings with these railways.

Good Roads for Wisconsin in 1920 reported "The new road is a splendid 18 foot concrete highway with all the grade crossings eliminated." ✿

The electric trolley was introduced to Eau Claire in 1889, the fourth city in the United States to use electricity for a mass transit system. It ran from Eau Claire to Irvine Park, Chippewa Falls. The turn of the 20th century saw the heyday of electric trolleys in towns across the country. There is no sign of the trolley tracks today. The only structure remaining from the trolley system is a small shelter at the southeast corner of Irvine Park which marked the end of the line. The last electric trolley ran on August 7, 1926, as a result of bus competition. See **Trail Tale: Trolleys**, page 393. ✿

Amber Inn - early days
Amber Inn Facebook page

Amber Inn now
134 years old, Eau Claire

Tourist Park near YT in Eau Claire

Standing in Eau Claire at the corner of Madison and Putnam streets watching for the car in the 1916 Yellowstone Trail Association auto relay race against time (coast to coast) was as exciting as it was for the 1915 race (Chicago to Seattle). On the evening of Sept. 13, 1916, as Dr. Cunningham was racing from Chippewa Falls to Eau Claire, he apparently got confused about the turn at this corner. He turned sharply and totaled his Oakland Six by wrapping a wheel around a telephone pole. He came through unscathed. Fortunately, his was only the backup or "trailer" car. The lead car, driven from Stanley by J. W. Galbraith, continued to speed toward the nearby corner of East Madison and North Barstow Street where he passed on the message being relayed to Allan Redmond who sped west to Baldwin. The point of the race was to cross the continent in 120 hours to show the War Department that the Yellowstone Trail could be named a military road if we would enter World War I. It took 121 hours to drive 3,700 miles. The Trail was, indeed, named a military road when the United States entered World War I. See **Trail Tale: 1916 Race**, page 416. ✿

WI-064.7 Elk Creek Lake

WI-072.6 Eau Claire

An important manufacturing and jobbing center. Beautiful residence district. The Eau Claire Hotel Barstow St. (sgl $2, dbl. with bath $4.50-$8.00) coffee shop.

Union Auto Service Co. Never closed. At Barstow and Gray Sts.

Tourist Camp, on Birch St., about one and a half miles from the center of town, 25¢. MH-1926

Hotel Galloway. BB1927

The Gillette Tire Company, once the largest employer in Eau Claire, flourished from 1917-1992, its large factory now repurposed as housing for over 150 small businesses. We mention this company because, as a Gillette company, their tires were sold everywhere and Yellowstone Trail travelers may well have been riding on those famous tires.

On the west side of Eau Claire is 100-year-old **Carson Park**, home of the **Chippewa Valley Museum** and **Paul Bunyan Logging Camp**. The lumber industry and early Eau Claire stories are told in the Museum with "hands-on" displays and many year-round activities. Summers at the Logging Camp one sees what loggers endured 100 years ago.

517 S Farwell St. **Schlegelmilch House Museum**. Built in 1871 and lived in by the family until 1948, the house is now owned by the Chippewa Valley Museum and is filled with period furnishings.

514 W Madison St. (Yellowstone Trail). The **1903 home of Norwegian newspaper writer Waldemar Ager**. He founded the *Reform* newspaper, written in the Norwegian language. He did so because he feared the loss of the language and also to voice his progressive political views. Some original furniture and copies of the *Reform* and other works may be seen.

Madison Street Bridge Area. Phoenix Park on the east side of the Chippewa River at Madison Street is a pleasant new park with concerts and a farmers' market. Yellowstone Trail traffic crossed here on a wooden bridge. It burned down in 1924 and was replaced by a concrete arch bridge, used until the present bridge was built in 1974. Across Madison St. (Yellowstone Trail) from the park is **Stella Blues Restaurant** in a renovated historic building.

316 Wisconsin St. **The Livery Restaurant**. The Livery is a country music bar and restaurant located in an 1893 horse stable, listed on the National Register of Historic Places. The stable now stands saved, intact and restored with ceiling beams exposed, antiques throughout and a working old elevator which the Oleson brothers used to haul buggies and autos (and horses?) up to the second floor. Not everyone owned a horse and buggy, necessitating a livery stable and its rent-a-horse business. The number of livery stables in Eau Claire fell from 13 to four in 1920 and this stable became an auto shop. The building represents, through its three morphings, the cultural history of Eau Claire - horses, autos, present renewal of the historic.

840 E Madison St., For 145 years the **Amber Inn Bar and Grill** has been a place of refreshment for the locals. Called by other names, the last 35 years with the same family, it has been the Amber Inn. During Prohibition the "root beer" was spiked with whatever alcohol was at hand. The historical integrity of the original two-story rectangular shape building is intact, in spite of the very small 10 foot addition. There are even pictures of old Eau Claire on the walls. Keep an eye open for Yellowstone Trail signs on streets as you go through this area.

Oleson's 1893 livery stable, now The Livery Restaurant, Eau Claire

WI-073.7

Along Omaha St. is the **Sacred Heart Cemetery** with a seldom noticed small, ornate chapel built in the 1800s and now listed on the Register of Historic Places. Across the street is the site of the former Eau Claire Tourist Camp which, in 1925, would have hosted Trail travelers.

February 9, 1920. Chippewa Falls hosted a Western Wisconsin state Yellowstone Trail Association convention. The eastern section met in Oshkosh February 11. ⚙

GASOLINE WAR IN CHIPPEWA FALLS

Filling stations today were selling gasoline at 9 cents a gallon, a drop of 2 cents overnight. As soon as the news spread, the stations reported a rushing business, almost everyone owning cars bringing in several containers. The price war started about three weeks ago when a garage announced a reduction from 23 to 22 cents a gallon.

May 6, 1927 Baldwin Bulletin

In Chippewa Falls it was "a dark and stormy night" at 1:47 a.m., June 16, 1915, when a Hope-Hartford auto careened along Canal Street and screeched to a halt, throwing the baton at George Murphy who was anxiously awaiting the speeder, gunning the engine of his Maxwell 6. He took the baton and vanished into the lightning-lit night toward Eau Claire. This drama was part of the 1915 Yellowstone Trail Association relay race from Chicago to Seattle, and they did it in 97 hours non-stop with 22 drivers passing the baton to the next driver. The next year, the Yellowstone Trail Association sponsored another relay race but this time it was from "Plymouth Rock to Puget Sound," around 3,700 miles. See **Trail Tale: 1915 Race**, page 302. ⚙

Lake Wissota was created when a large dam and power plant were built across the Chippewa River beginning in 1916. It was fully filled by 1918, creating a new recreation area of 6,300 acres. In the movie "Titanic," Leonardo DiCaprio's character, Jack Dawson, said that he grew up in Chippewa Falls and swam in Lake Wissota. The town still laughs at that today because the Titanic went down four years before the lake was even begun. It was the second largest hydroelectric dam in America. ⚙

WAYSIDE

About two miles south of Co. Hwy X (Yellowstone Trail) at 4271 220th St. is **Cabin Ridge Rides**. They offer horse-drawn, historical vehicle rides such as in a surrey, cutter, stagecoach or sleigh through 400 acres of woods to historic sawmills and logging camps. We mention this because of the historic interest of the experience.

Twilight on YT at Lake Wissota near Chippewa Falls

1897 Leinenkugel Brewery with tours, Chippewa Falls

Rare Marsh Rainbow Bridge, Downtown Chippewa Falls

Original 1918 Trail pavement, Greenville St., Chippewa Falls

The late Glenn Barquest told the tale of his school, located at the corner of county highways X and K in Bateman. At recess, in the winter of 1925, a Model T candy sales truck tipped over in the rutted, frozen road in front of the school. The kids grabbed all they could. His sister squealed on him and he caught heck at home for stealing.

Barquest's next tale gives us a vivid picture of the transportation problems of the times. In 1929 his parents traveled eight miles to visit relatives for the day. Glenn and his sister were in school. As the kids arrived home, a blizzard came up, trapping their parents at the relatives' home. Due to 10-foot drifts, snow plows couldn't get through. Their parents had to remain there for a few days for a crawler tractor with bulldozer blade to come through. The folks got home by way of a sleigh to the hamlet of Anson, train to Chippewa Falls, and bus to Bateman. All this for eight miles! ⚙

WI-085.8 Chippewa Falls

(alt. 866 ft.), once having the largest sawmill under cover in the world, is now a thriving manufacturing city. It is situated on the Chippewa River, which, with Wissota Dam, has one of the greatest hydro. electric plants in the northwest. The city boasts of a large and beautiful park, covering about 300 acres, with splendid drives throughout and a collection of native and imported animals and birds. The state home for the feeble-minded and the county insane asylum are also located here. BB1921-10

Beautiful and picturesque little city. Second largest shoe manufacturing city in the state. Follow trolley north to the tourist camp in beautiful Irvine Park. Fine kitchen with gas stoves. Tennis courts. Hotel Northern, modern throughout. BB1920

Keep an eye open for modern Yellowstone Trail yellow signs as you go through town. These signs do not mark the authentic route because they take you across the river, twice, to attract you to the business center today. Today, you will go past the Chippewa Area Visitors Center, 1 N. Bridge St., where you can pick up area information.

WI-085.0

Greenville Street was the Yellowstone Trail in 1915. It has the original width, 18 feet, and the concrete dates to 1915–18. This street was part of the effort to make the Wisconsin portion of the Yellowstone Trail, 409 miles, all concrete by 1929.

Trail travelers may well have frequented the following current places which were standing in 1915 even though the Trail itself did not cross the river:

236 W River St. **Sheeley House Hotel and Restaurant**. If you are on the Trail (Park St./Hwy J) take the bridge (Main St.) across the river. Directly in front of you at the end of the bridge is the Sheeley House. Through various owners from 1868 to the present, the Sheeley house has been a boarding house in one way or another with a tavern on the ground floor, restaurant on the second and sleeping quarters above. Today the tavern is the only remaining business.

124 E Elm St. Follow WI 124 North to 1 Jefferson Ave. **Jacob Leinenkugel Brewing Company**. The brewery was established in 1867. The fifth generation of Leinenkugels manages the brewery and, although it is now owned by Miller Brewing, it still makes its own seasonal and specialty beers. Leinie Lodge sells souvenirs, conducts tours and provides samples of beer.

WI 124. **Irvine Park and Zoo**. 300 acres across from Leinenkugel Brewery is Irvine Park, a popular attraction here year round with picnic areas, Glen Loch dam, trails and playgrounds. And the trolley station is left over from Yellowstone Trail days when trolleys ran to Eau Claire.

505 W Grand Ave. **Cook-Rutledge Mansion**. Built in 1873, remodeled in1887, its high Victorian-Italianate architecture, red brick exterior with hand-carved ceilings and woodwork draw many to tours. It is on the National Register of Historic Places.

123 Allen St. **Chippewa County Historical and Genealogical Society**. In the former Notre Dame Convent (1883), the museum contains genealogical resources and local historical exhibits. The Historical Society has marked the Yellowstone Trail throughout Chippewa County with official yellow signs.

21 E. Grand Ave. **Chippewa Falls Museum of Industry and Technology**. We include this recent museum because of its general interest to today's tourist. See the history of modern technology, including the original Cray supercomputers made in Chippewa Falls, once the fastest computers in the world.

Spring St. and Rushman Dr. **Marsh Rainbow Arch Bridge**. Built in 1916, it is the only one of this once common bridge design remaining in Wisconsin. It crosses Duncan Creek. Foot traffic only. We would remind you that the Trail did not actually go to downtown Chippewa Falls. We include this bridge because of its historicity and because Trail travelers may have come into the city for respite and interest and may have viewed this bridge. Other Rainbow Arch bridges along the Yellowstone Trail are found in Ortonville, Minnesota, and Warm Springs, Montana.

WI-086.3

WI 124 (Park Ave.) is the **Chippewa Spring House**. Since the early 1700s, water from this spring has been extremely pure. It is the source of the name of Eau Claire, 10 miles to the south. A great place for a watering trough and a water source for the radiator in Trail days. Just across the street is a county historical marker featuring the Yellowstone Trail.

WI-089.2 Lake Wissota

The Trail skirts beautiful, manmade Lake Wissota. (See the historic note to the left.)

WI-091.6 Bateman

19990 Co. X (Yellowstone Trail). **Butch & Jackie's Bar**. This 100-year-old building was built as a cheese factory.

The following seven small communities all share the Yellowstone Trail, Co. X, in both Chippewa and Clark counties and they offer a buffet of little gems to see. Under the auspices of the Highway 29 Partnership, they unveiled the marked 37 miles of Trail that they share in 2006 with the help of then-Lieutenant Governor Lawton.

WI-098 Cadott

On the corner of Co. X and MM is the **Yellowstone Cheese Factory**. Jeremy and Heidi Kenealy knew about the Trail before they built the factory on Highway X and chose the name of the place accordingly. Try the Yellowstone Crunch cheese—with chocolate bits!

Painting the YT sign on Cadott telephone pole
Cadott Historical Society

CONCRETE ROADS VOTED DOWN IN CLARK COUNTY

November 4, 1926 Owen Enterprise

~~~~~~~~~~~~~~~~~~~~

CLARK COUNTY BOARD VOTES TO COMPLETE PAVING HWY 29

… and the Board should be highly commended by all tax payers.

August 9, 1928 Owen Enterprise

Note: Apparently it took two years for the populace to appreciate concrete.

BUS CO. TO PLOW HWY 29 WITH AID OF VILLAGES

Jan. 27, 1927 Owen Enterprise

Note: There still was no tax money available, apparently. Individual citizens and businessmen ponied up the cost of plowing snow for 16 miles.

Ads in 1921 BB

1920 Withee Tourist Camp

Stanley was the home of a huge apiary in the early 1930s with 800 bee colonies producing clover honey. ❀

Owen facts -- signs of the time:
1924: Pork chops 25¢ lb.; beans 18¢ can; codfish 35¢ 1 lb. can; apples 12¢ lb.
1925: Danielsen's farm completely electrified
1926: Owen radio 9ARE
1926: Willys Overland touring car $500
1929: 45 mph rural, 15 mph town, 20 residential ❀

Garage in Stanley still named Yellowstone, now an implement company

In the early 20th century, the Chippewa Valley Electric Railroad ran a heated electric trolley to Electric Park in Hallie, now the site of the Eau Claire Press Company's Electric Park printing plant. ❀

Thorp Parade

Thorp renamed park

Owen's Woodland Hotel now and then

Yellow "R" told YT turned right in Owen

Woodland Hotel in Owen. John S. Owen built the Woodland in 1906 to house the brokers, salesmen, and buyers of the lumber trade who arrived by train to this small, isolated town. The hotel was so well built that over 100 years later it still stands whole. It featured hardwood floors and real wood paneling. It had hot and cold running water, steam heat, and electric lights in 1906! There was a writing room, dining room, and large kitchen. The parlor was a "man's" room with spittoons handy. Huge breakfasts were served for 30 cents. As auto travel burgeoned, the Woodland prospered because it was on the first completely concreted cross-state auto road - the Yellowstone Trail. A high point between 1955 and 1974 of the Woodland was the advent of the popular Sunday night buffets. People came from as far as 135 miles for the famous 100-item spread. Today, the three new owners are looking to resurrect this historic centerpiece of downtown Owen. ❀

WI-103.4 Boyd

801 E Patton St. **St. Joseph Catholic Church** was built in 1928. Its claim to fame is the priceless stained-glass windows and three-dimensional glass sculptures. They were created from mouth-blown antique stained glass imported from Munich. Later, during World War II, the Munich studio was destroyed.

WI-109.2 Stanley

Intersection of First Ave. and Broadway. The Royal is a good, clean country hotel, serves meals.

Miller-Thornton Ford. Tel 21. Small free camping space, water. MH-1926

219 E First Ave. (Yellowstone Trail). **Yellowstone Implement**. The building with the square glass blocks was built in 1917 by Armond Christopherson as the Yellowstone Garage. Partner M. R. Shock sold Dort, Dodge, Chevy, and Durant cars beginning in 1925. He was a member of the Yellowstone Trail Association. His son, J. A. Shock, has run it as an implement company. Tragically, shortly before we interviewed Mr. Shock, he had cleared out his father's Yellowstone Trail Association materials.

Just a few yards to the west of Yellowstone Implement and across the street from the post office in Soo Park is a small **Chippewa County Historical Society marker** featuring the Trail.

Corner Franklin and First Ave. A Yellowstone Trail sign was posted here for several years. In 2007 this **large yellow boulder** you now see (painted by school children) was placed here as part of the Yellowstone Trail celebration marking seven communities along the Trail on Co. X, the Trail.

228 Helgerson St. **Stanley Area Historical Museum**. Outstanding historical displays of farming and logging are there, also a 1906 Cadillac in pristine condition.

Just west of town is **Chapman Park**, created in 1922 on the site of a former lumber company. The mill pond now is an attractive lake. Yellowstone Trail travelers may well have stopped here.

WI-115.9 Thorp

Small country hotel; Dell's Station downtown existed in the 1920s if not earlier. MH-1926

Corner Stanley Street (Co. X, the Yellowstone Trail) and Co. M is **Bob's Corner Service Station**. When the gas station was called 'Dell's' in the 1920s and 1930s, Al Capone, the famous Chicago gangster, stopped there frequently on his way to his hideout in northern Wisconsin.

100 S Washington St. Same intersection as Bob's Station is the present **Heritage Court Motel** and its adjoining 1891 home. It is quite homey and has repeat customers on their way "up north."

Stanley St. **Yellowstone Trail Park**, so named because it is on the Trail. The park was renamed due to a resurgence of interest in the Trail.

WI-126 Withee

Black River Tourist Camp, free, in a nice grove. Supplies and gas. MH-1926

For the story of the Krueger Boys, pacifists during World War I, see **Trail Tail: Draft Dodgers**, page 286.

WI-127.8 Owen

Lumber mill and box factory. Two small free camps, four blocks from town. Woodland Hotel, modern and well managed. Dining room. MH-1926

246 Central Ave. **Pippin's Pub and Grub**. At the corner of Central and Fifth Street is a local watering hole, operated under various names since c.1907. There is a large yellow "R" on the side of the building, which owners keep painted. That "R" is the only original Yellowstone Trail marker known to remain, outside of museums, in Wisconsin. It stands for "the Yellowstone Trail turns right at the next corner."

207 Central Ave. **Woodland Hotel**. At this writing the Woodland Hotel is being revived after some years of neglect. The Woodland Hotel was built for the John S. Owen Lumber Company, which established the city of Owen. See History Bits to the left for more about the Hotel.

607 W 3rd St. **Mauel's Ice Cream and Dairy**. They have produced dairy products since 1919 and, no doubt, Yellowstone Trail travelers stopped there.

134.2 Between Owen and Curtiss on Willow Rd. (Yellowstone Trail) is a small **Norwegian church**. Used regularly until 1953. Built c.1916 of red brick, it is a simplified Gothic style with arched door and windows. It is opened for one service a year, on the last Sunday in July, but the church is open and some come daily to pray.

Vlander Oil, Stanley

The YT near Abbotsford on WI 13 in 1920
Wis. DOT

The late Les Bowen remembered walking to school on the Yellowstone Trail (County X) every day. He also remembered the Revival tent on the corner of County X and E where the Yellowstone Trail turned. ✿

From *Colby Centennial 1873-1973.* Wm. Will, Jr., liveryman, is the owner of an automobile. It is a Ford and was bought at Dorchester. He forgets once in a while and hollers, "Whoa!" ✿

Abandoned home of famous Colby Cheese, Colby

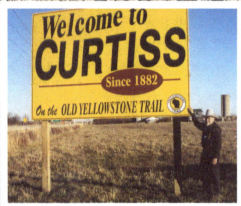
The late Les Bowen and his sign

July, 1920, Western Magazine. The Town Courteous. This was a relatively long letter from a person who was rescued after car trouble near Abbotsford. He described in detail the kindness of strangers in trying to repair the damage, building a drag to haul the car, and in housing the party overnight. He wrote: "[They treated] … us like honored guests. It was a revelation when one considers the usual 'bleeding process' applied to tourists." ✿

DON'TS FOR BALDWIN CAR DRIVERS

Don't turn in the middle of the block.

Don't back your car out on Main Street before looking to see if someone is coming.

Don't park your car facing the wrong direction.

Don't park your car on Main Street on Wednesday and Saturday nights if you live in the village.

April 18, 1924 Baldwin Bulletin

The YT south of Unity still gravel today

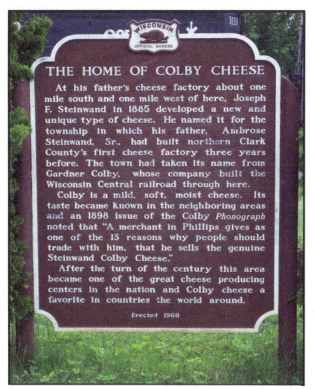
Plaque at abandoned original Colby Cheese plant

WI-135 Curtiss

813 Meridian St., Co. E. The **Old Curtiss Hotel** built c.1905, is now called Our Place Bar and Hotel.

WI-141.8 Abbotsford

Abbotsford Headquarters for Wisconsin cheese Producers Ass'n. Small garage, but no hotel. MH-1926

Camp 1 blk s. 5 cars, unlimited # of people, open field. AAA.

The town is entered from the west on Spruce Street. WI 29 lies on top of the Yellowstone Trail here. Downtown, on the corner of Spruce and 1st St., we join WI 13, the Trail.

Abbotsford, Colby and Unity, all on the Yellowstone Trail (WI 13), share a unique fact: they straddle the line between Clark and Marathon counties, no doubt complicating city governments.

At about WI-150, the route connecting Fairhaven Ln. and Lasalle St. varied, but Century Rd. is one known to have been used on the early route.

WI-144.3 Colby

Niehoff is a good country hotel. Ford garage. MH-1926

This is the home of the world-famous **Colby cheese.** In 1885 Joseph Steinwand left more curd and whey in and pressed it into molds for up to three months, leaving a tasty, mild, soft cheese. It was the only natural cheese native to the U.S. After the turn of the century, this area became one of the great cheese-producing centers in the nation and Colby cheese

became known the world around. The original cheese factory, now closed, is a bit southwest of town on, logically, Cheese Factory Road. You can drive down the road about a mile to see the closed, historic, small factory.

Adams and North Division Sts., just off WI13. (Yellowstone Trail). The **Rural Arts Museum** is a collection of buildings that tell the story of the railroad, dairy industry, and other past Colby history, complete with a depot and a furnished log home. Of note is the piece of meteorite that fell near Colby on the 4th of July, 1917.

WI-148.3 Unity

Free camp space one mile east. Good meals at Unity hotel. Garage across track is reliable. MH-1926

WI-162.8 Spencer

An Amish family on
Willow Road today (YT)

TRAIL ASSOCIATION ORGANIZED AT MARSHFIELD

May 27, 1915 Record Leader
(Waupaca)

YELLOWSTONE TRAIL MEETING WILL BE HELD IN MARSHFIELD

Activities for 1929 call for a re-marking of the Trail and the establishment of information bureaus in at least four state cities.

January 29, 1929 Marshfield News-Herald

St. Charles Hotel, Marshfield

FAST AUTO TO BLAZE NEW YELLOWSTONE TRAIL

An automobile bearing messages from the mayor of Chicago to the mayor of Seattle will speed from Milwaukee on June 15 to blaze the new Yellowstone Trail. The auto is scheduled to arrive in Seattle 100 hours after it leaves Chicago. It will be the fastest trip ever made to the Pacific coast from Chicago.

May 26, 1915 Milwaukee Sentinel

Note: For the full story, see **Trail Tale: 1915 Race**, page 302.

YELLOWSTONE TRAIL MEETING

January 14, 1921 Marshfield Herald

Note: Hal Cooley, General Manager of the Yellowstone Trail Association, spoke, centering on cities not paying their dues and threatening to move the Trail to Iowa and out of Wisconsin.

Story has it from an old Marshfield duffer that he drove his new 1926 Ford back to the Ford dealer to ask about the brakes with which he was unfamiliar. He coasted toward a stop a little fast, jumped the curb, hit the building, walked in and asked. ✿

Remember that the Yellowstone Trail Association sponsored a cross-country auto relay race in 1915? The Association sponsored another relay race against time in 1916. This race ran from Plymouth Rock to Puget Sound, some 3,600 miles. This time the race was run to show the Army that the Yellowstone Trail could be used as a military route for the coming World War. This time a packet held letters from Secretary of War Baker at Plymouth Rock to Fort Lawton, Seattle. They did it in 121 hours, averaging 30.4 mph. On the Yellowstone Trail at Hewitt a Buick, driven

The YT near Hewitt still gravel today

in the 1916 race by A. J. Clements, was coming from Stevens Point to Marshfield. It blew a tire; it flew off the rim. The mechanic riding along with the driver jumped out here at Hewitt to find the tire. The driver didn't stop. The last four miles to Marshfield were made on bare rim. Nothing stopped these daredevils. A considerable crowd had gathered at the Blodgett Hotel in Marshfield, where Mr. E. Blodgett waited to grab the packet and race west. The mechanic who was left in Hewitt found the tire; he later caught a ride into Marshfield with a passing motorist. With the tire repaired, he and the driver returned home to Stevens Point through a "sea of mud" while the letters flew west. ✿

Marshfield's Round Barn

Credit must be given for the system of marking the trail. For every turn left or right the yellow disk is in plain sight. The roads near Stevens Point were sandy with deep ruts. We found the Blodgett Hotel at Marshfield with a really truly carpet in the dining room - a good hotel, clean and comfortable. ... One scarcely ever sees evening dress about the hotels in the West, especially among tourists, and never among their distant cousins, the Fordists.

It Might Have Been Worse: A Motor Trip From Coast to Coast by Beatrice Massey (1919)

WAYSIDE

M222 Sugarbush Ln, three miles north of Marshfield. **Jurustic Park.** You've got to see this! It's a hoot. Take Co. E three and a half miles to **McMillan Wildlife Marsh**. Turn west on Sugarbush Lane. 250 mythical swamp creatures jokingly said to have existed in adjacent McMillan Wildlife Marsh millenia ago are made of metal. Rusted metal creatures ranging from six-inch spiders and mosquitoes to 45-foot, 4,000-pound flying dragons, plus turtles, birds and plant life, all in clever settings. The creator's studio is on the grounds. Open summers. We note this because it is clever and fun.

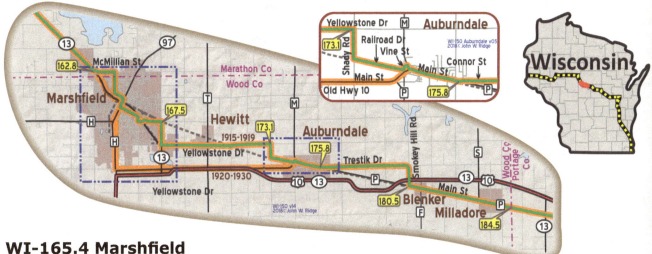

WI-165.4 Marshfield

Prosperous and lively. Free camp at Fair Grounds. Charles Hotel, most modern, forty-five rooms, half with bath. MH-1926

(pop. 6,000, alt. 1.271 ft.). The greatest cheese market in the Union. There are within a radius of forty miles nearly three hundred cheese factories which produced more than $10,000,000 worth of cheese last year. The C. E. Blodgett butter and egg company and the P. J. Schaefer company are reputed to be the largest wholesalers and exporters of cheese in the world. The fair grounds of the Central Wisconsin fair association are located in Marshfield and their stock exhibit barn is the largest round barn in the world. Central avenue, the main street of the city, is the widest paved street in the state, and is the pride of the city. BB1921-10

Blodgett Garage half a block from hotel. Victory Garage. BB1920

Today's Yellowstone Trail driver will find the route through Marshfield marked by Yellowstone Trail signs through town and on eastward on Yellowstone Drive. Eight historic buildings are downtown near Central Ave. including the 1901 Tower Hall, library, the old depot, and others. There are five historic residential districts.

103 S Central Ave. **Thomas House Center for History**, significant because it is in the restored Thomas House, originally a hotel built in 1887, so Trail travelers may well have stayed there. The Center has featured rotating historic displays.

212 W Third St. **Upham Mansion**. The restored home of former Wisconsin Governor William Upham is of mid-Victorian architecture with original furniture. This white house is inviting with a large, sweeping porch and rose garden.

513 E 17th St., south of downtown Marshfield, **World's Largest Round Barn**. Built in 1916, it stands in Central Wisconsin State Fair Park. The huge barn has 250 stanchions. The large arena for cattle shows is unique for it has no supporting beams. It is used for various events.

WI-170.4 Hewitt
WI-170.5

Yellowstone Recreation Park is just past Main St. on Yellowstone Dr. Local citizens have created a park along the old Yellowstone Trail, now named Yellowstone Dr.

WI-175.1 Auburndale

Dairying. Small free camp space two blocks from town. Good country hotel on Main St. Overland garage is best for repairs. MH-1926

Auburndale runs east/west along the Wisconsin Central RR with its businesses along the track.

M181.0 Blenker

Meals and rooms over Post Office. MH-1926

The post office is still in the same building as in the 1920s.

WI-184 Milladore

The old Clark's Garage now Hughes, Milladore

Bray's hotel. Clark's garage is said to have reliable mechanics. BB1926

[Note: Note the cobblestone face on Hughes Ford Garage. Undoubtedly the same building as Clark's Garage described in the BB1926.]

WI-188.7 Junction City

Free camp space at school. Farming village. Small country hotel and garage. MH-1926

East/west tracks intersect with north/south tracks, thus the "junction."

WI

STATE MEETING OF YELLOWSTONE TRAIL WILL BE HELD HERE

Stevens Point membership assessment for 1922 is $235.

October 12, 1921 Stevens Point Gazette

~~~~~~~~~~~~~~~~~~~~~~~~

NEARLY 100 NEEDED FOR Y TRAIL

August 23, 1922. Stevens Point Gazette

Note: It is now eight months into 1922 and Stevens Point was still $94 short of its assessment that was announced Oct. 1921.

Note: The Yellowstone Trail Association held a Trail Day once a year wherein citizens in each town along the Trail were asked to go out to fix up the Trail, all towns on the same day. The press was invited, politicians showed up for photo ops, picnics, and games abounded. Small towns closed up and everybody went out to the Trail. Stevens Point's newspaper said:

TRAIL DAY A HUMMER

Trail Day produced more than 200 bankers, physicians, lawyers, artisans, and laborers with teams, wagons, plows and shovels, putting in a full day's work improving the road. They spread 225 loads of gravel, had a picnic dinner and their good fellowship proved such a satisfaction that similar work spread to other parts of the state.

June 4, 1915 Stevens Point Gazette

Stevens Point owed the Yellowstone Trail Association for two years worth of dues in 1920, $300. They were in danger of losing the Trail, although the Association never did move the route from any town over the issue. Seeing its opportunity once again to get the Trail moved to their city, the city fathers of Grand Rapids (present Wisconsin Rapids) attempted to wrest the Trail from Stevens Point, even to the point of directing traffic from Waupaca to Grand Rapids via large signs. They had tried in 1915, 1917, and again in 1920. They offered to pay Point's arrears and an extra $1,000 for re-marking and re-mapping the Trail. The Association did not go for it, and Point kept the Trail, eventually paying their dues. [Note: In 1920 28,000 automobiles were routed over the Trail from Minneapolis by way of Stevens Point. This fact helped Stevens Point pony up its $300.] ✿

STILL ON THE JOB
SCHOFIELD SPEED COP HOLDING DRIVERS DOWN TO 15 MILES AN HOUR

August 23, 1922 Stevens Point Gazette

BONDING PLAN TURNED DOWN
PLEAS FOR CONCRETE FUTILE

Oct. 28, 1919 Stevens Point Gazette

Note: Headlines that same day proclaimed that Prohibition had commenced. Could it be that people were just mad at the world?

In the early 1920s Stevens Point's Clark Street Bridge, which carried Yellowstone Trail traffic across the Wisconsin River, kept catching fire due to the creosote-treated wood and oil on the wooden deck. Finally, the 20th time, May 30, 1923 was the last; it burned completely. A ferry served travelers until January 1,1926. ✿

Strongs St. (YT), Stevens Point
John Anderson collection

Joe Parmley's description of his ride on the Yellowstone Trail Association 1915 relay race from Chicago to Seattle: "The sandiest stretch from Plymouth Rock to Puget Sound must be near Stevens Point." And again in the 1920 Yellowstone Trail Association *Route Folder*: "From Waupaca to St. Point the road is sandy." Apparently cars got stuck there regularly. Today the area is called Golden Sands and produces millions of potatoes and other vegetables. ✿

Tourist campground, Stevens Point

Notice was given that Yellowstone Trail road condition maps and *Route Folders* were available at the Chamber of Commerce.

August 3, 1920 Stevens Point Gazette

Clark Street bridge
John Anderson collection

The *Amherst Advocate* newspaper was busy in 1915 recording the doings of the newly-arrived Yellowstone Trail. May 20, TRAIL GOES THROUGH AMHERST is followed by June 2 announcing the postponement of Trail Day, followed by TOMORROW WILL BE TRAIL DAY on July 1. The next excitement was in 1921 with REGIMENT MAY COME OVER THE YELLOWSTONE which announced an army movement from Ohio to Fort Snelling, Minnesota. The troops were expected to pass through Amherst on the way. ✿

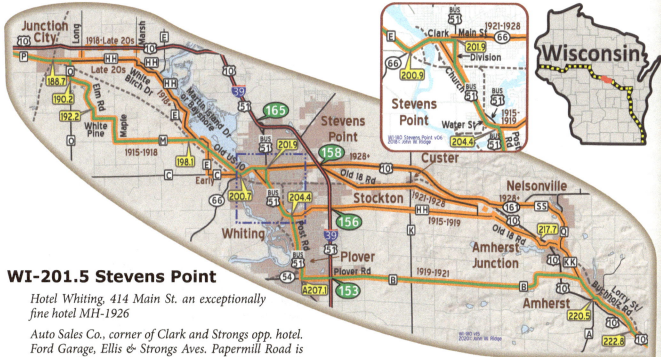

WI-201.5 Stevens Point

Hotel Whiting, 414 Main St. an exceptionally fine hotel MH-1926

Auto Sales Co., corner of Clark and Strongs opp. hotel. Ford Garage, Ellis & Strongs Aves. Papermill Road is also sought by autoists. Goes to paper mills just south of city limits. Wis. River Mill & Plover Paper co. Automatic self-rocking cradles are made in Stevens Point exclusively. Free camp at fair grounds. Better accommodations at the Yellowstone Camp, about 1 mile east of town on Trail [Route after about 1920]. Level and in a grove. 50¢. Three cabins $1.50 to $2.50 each (BB,1920); 40 acres. 200 cars and 1000 people. Toilets. MH-1926

They say they are the "potato capital of the world." The language they speak among themselves is often Polish. WPA-WI

As you cross the Clark Street Bridge, (old US 10/Yellowstone Trail) you will pass over the **Wisconsin River**. In the early days of Stevens Point, the river was often filled with logs as the lumber industry was prominent. The tar on the roadway of the bridge caught fire, closing it down in the 1920s. Today, a large mural (which you can see from the Clark Street Bridge) titled "Rivermen" celebrates this history. Many historical murals are throughout the downtown district.

38 Park Ridge Dr. (later Yellowstone Trail). **Silver Coach Diner**. This 1903 Smith and Barney train car may have started out just as a bar. The exterior does not look like a diner, and the original train car has been swallowed up by the addition, but its still there.

1408 Strongs Ave. at Clark St. **Old Whiting Hotel**. This 1900 Spanish Revival architecture hotel was on the Yellowstone Trail. The hotel became the main attraction in downtown Stevens Point and the place where travelers went for Trail information. Today it is called Whiting Place Apartments. The hotel was placed on the National Register of Historic Places in 1990.

2617 Water St. **Point Brewery**, has been in continuous operation since 1857. Daily tours.

In June, 1915, on "Trail Day" wherein local citizens all along the Trail pitched in to help maintain it, Point Brewery

donated a team of horses. Bet you thought they should have donated a few kegs.

WI-204.4 Whiting

To travel from Stevens Point to Whiting, a suburb, you will be on Post Road. Post Road is so named because it was originally designated for the transportation of mail.

WI-A207.1 Plover

The Comfort Inn on the 1918–20 route features a Yellowstone Trail Pub with modern decor but historic pictures and maps of the Trail. It is just west of I-39 and north of County B. This crossroad is the intersection of two national driving routes, Yellowstone Trail and US 51.

Corner of Washington and Willow Dr. in Plover. **Heritage Park**, run by the Portage County Historical Society, is an historical village of buildings from early Portage County. There is the last cabin surviving from Yellowstone Hotel and Tourist Court built on the 1928-1930 Yellowstone Trail route (present US 10) in Stevens Point.

WI-219.5 Amherst

The Amherst Inn. Yellowstone Garage on main route BB1920

Amherst Inn, Amherst

Amherst at the intersection of Co. B and Co. A.

303 Main St. (Yellowstone Trail). **Amherst Inn Bed-and-Breakfast**, a 1887 Victorian Gothic-style house was a popular stop for travelers in the heyday of both the Inn and the Trail. Now private.

WI-224.6

The Yellowstone Trail crosses the Ice Age Trail near Pipe Rd.

WI

Erle Whipple of Waupaca was on the executive committee of the YTA in 1919 and very active in the years before. He helped set up the YTA 1915 relay race -Chicago to Seattle, and the 1916 transcontinental relay race "From Plymouth Rock to Puget Sound." ✿

In June, 1915, the YTA sponsored a relay race against time from Chicago to Seattle. They made it in ninety-seven hours! People lined the road all along their route. The relay went on nonstop day and night. With only dim headlights in those days, it was very hard to see at night. The people of Weyauwega understood that and, since drivers would be going through their town at night, they lit "A Mile of Torches," as they called it. Fire lined the road, providing light and outlining the smiling faces of the cheering crowd. ✿

REPRESENTATIVE OF YELLOWSTONE TRAIL MEETS WITH OUR BUSINESSMEN
NEW TRAIL WILL HIT THIS CITY; ROAD WILL BE USED BY THOUSANDS OF TOURISTS EVERY YEAR CONDITIONS WILL BE IMPROVED FOR FARMERS AND WILL BENEFIT EVERYONE

May 20, 1915 Waupaca Record-Leader

Note: Mr. O. T. Peterson, traveling rep for the YTA, apparently did a bang-up job of convincing the businessmen of the value of the Trail and at an apparent small cost to the community.

YELLOWSTONE TRAIL IS BEING REROUTED THROUGH HIGHWAY 95

The Yellowstone Trail is being rerouted in Wisconsin to follow state trunk highway 95, known locally as the Oshkosh road. This is a more direct route than the former trail, which was marked through Medina, Appleton, Menasha and Neenah and followed highway 15 from Appleton to Oshkosh. The new trail directs travelers to leave highway 18 just east of Fremont and takes them into Oshkosh on No. 95 by way of Butte des Morts, a road partly concrete. The yellow markers are now being switched to this more direct route.

August 28, 1924 Waupaca County Post

Note: "No. 95" is now "broken up" into Co. II, Riverview Dr. and others. See on page 269.

YELLOWSTONE TRAIL ASS'N TO MEET NOV 7 IN STEVENS POINT

One important matter to be discussed is whether the Yellowstone Trail should be abandoned west of Yellowstone Park and east of Chicago in order to equalize expenses with income.

October 30, 1924 Owen Enterprise

Edwin West, farmer four miles south of city, bought a plane to go to town to shop, do his business and get back before neighbors have even cranked the Ford.

July 20, 1923
Waupaca Record-Leader

The late 1920s brought fanciful filling stations

Hotel Fremont now

Hotel Fremont then

Weyauwega's 1915 opera house

WAYSIDE

Chain O'Lakes. About three or four miles to the west of Waupaca on Wis. highway 22 is a marvelous string of twenty-two interconnected spring-fed glacial lakes of pristine clarity. See www.WaupacaMemories.com for information about the many lakes, etc. It really is beautiful, restful, and worth the wayside trip.

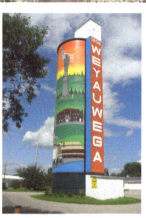

Weyauwega Silo

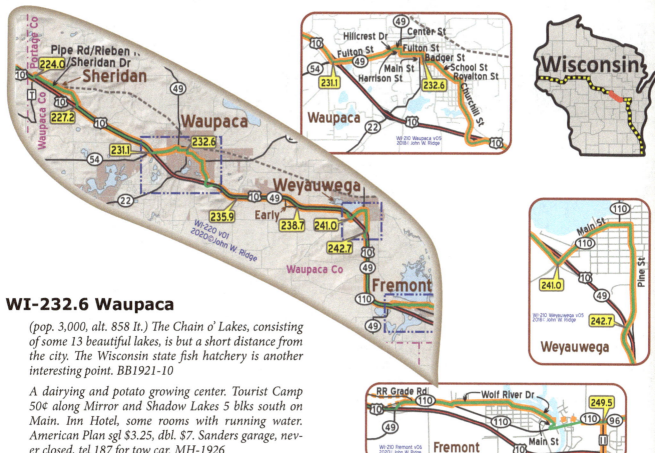

WI-232.6 Waupaca

(pop. 3,000, alt. 858 lt.) The Chain o' Lakes, consisting of some 13 beautiful lakes, is but a short distance from the city. The Wisconsin state fish hatchery is another interesting point. BB1921-10

A dairying and potato growing center. Tourist Camp 50¢ along Mirror and Shadow Lakes 5 blks south on Main. Inn Hotel, some rooms with running water. American Plan sgl $3.25, dbl. $7. Sanders garage, never closed, tel 187 for tow car. MH-1926

Delavan Hotel, on Yellowstone Trail and Main St across from Bank. Central stop on Yellowstone Trail between Chicago and St. Paul. BB1920

Keep your eyes open for **Yellowstone Trail signs** throughout Waupaca. Some locals feel that the Yellowstone Trail followed the Hillcrest Dr./Granite St./Main St. route from WI-232.0 to WI-232.6, just north of Fulton. However, the guides of the period, such as various *Blue Books* and *Mohawk Guides*, specify not Granite, but Fulton St. (with the trolley tracks) as the route in that area.

112 Granite St. In 1917 Dayton Baldwin leased the 1909 garage and called it the **Yellowstone Garage**. In 2016 the former Yellowstone Garage and Oakland dealership was bought by John Gunnell, automotive author and restoration expert. John owned a 1917 Oakland and felt that the 100-year-old car belonged in his 110-year-old garage in Waupaca. In 2018, Gunell sold his Waupaca garage and his 1917 Oakland to a Milwaukee collector who plans to retain the garage as an historic site.

321 S Main St. **The Holly History and Genealogy Center**. Located one block south of the Yellowstone Trail. The Center, in a 1914 Carnegie library building, is the headquarters of the Waupaca Historical Society and houses a local history and genealogy library.

The Historic Hutchinson House Museum. 1854, located at the south end of Main Street within South Park, having been moved from Fulton Street and refurbished in Victorian style. The Hutchinson House is one of the oldest surviving homes in the city of Waupaca.

WI-241.7 Weyauwega

Producer of dairy, cheese, butter. MH-1926

Weyauwega Historical Silo is just one block off the Yellowstone Trail which runs along Main Street. Built in 1855, it is a rye grain elevator, and the last one still standing in the United States. It has murals of old Weyauwega as well as the Yellowstone Trail logo painted on it. It's tall. You can't miss it.

WI-248.9 Fremont

(778 alt., 387 pop.), on the Wolf River, Thousands come from Wisconsin and Illinois to drop their baited hooks into the water here. WPA-WI

Fremont has been a magnet for fishermen for eons. The bridge over the Wolf River in downtown Fremont is no more. It was the route of the Yellowstone Trail. You can get to the other side of town, but you have to drive south a bit and take WI 110. Much road building has obliterated the Trail on the east side of town, but the citizens of Fremont have honored the Trail by marking it with large yellow signs.

Hotel Fremont on Wolf River Dr. (Yellowstone Trail). Built in 1895, it housed many a Yellowstone Trail traveler. The renovated hostelry has an ice cream parlor and historic pictures of Fremont are on the walls. The guests in the eleven-room hotel share three bathrooms, just like in Trail days.

WI-254.5 Readfield

WI-258.5 Dale

WI-260.5 Medina

Appleton Historical Society & Museum at the "Castle"

The Trail at Julius Rd. near Medina

WIS. PLAN FOR YELLOW TRAIL

The article reports the Wisconsin state meeting in Oshkosh where they discussed the 50 miles of the Trail being in concrete with plans for 100 miles more.
February 2, 1917
Marmarth (South Dakota) Mail

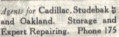

Valley Motor Car Company ad, Menasha
1921 Automobile Blue Book

Neenah, Menasha and Appleton will be retained as points on the trail, although a route 14 miles shorter could be obtained and one-third of the committee voted for the change. The three cities are retained because they offer a better road and also have much needed hotel accommodations.
March 1920 Wisconsin Motorist Magazine

Harry Houdini (1874-1926), whose real name was Ehrich Weiss (Weisz?), was born in Appleton, the fifth child of a Jewish rabbi. His parents had fled to America from Budapest after a duel in which Dr. Weiss was reported to have killed a gentile. Ehrich first manifested the skill that later made him famous as a magician by picking the locks his mother kept on her pastry cupboard. Pies and cookies frequently disappeared. Whenever a circus came to Appleton, Ehrich immediately visited the side show where the magician performed, and spent hours practicing the feats he had observed. After his twelfth birthday Ehrich ran away from home. WPA-WI ✿

VOTE AGAINST TRAIL
APPLETON AND OSHKOSH NOT PAYING MEETING ASSESSMENT
February 15, 1922
Stevens Point Gazette
Note: Apparently Oshkosh had a change of heart for it is still listed in Trail literature through 1928.

December 1921 *Good Roads for Wisconsin* reprinted from the *Neenah Daily News*. Losing Interest in the Yellowstone Trail. The article said that Neenah had not sent representatives to the latest state Trail meeting and appears to be withdrawing support from the Association. "It is felt that with the complete state highway marking system, the Yellowstone Trail has outlived its usefulness." ✿

WISCONSIN MAY LOSE GREAT AUTO TRAIL
The Yellowstone Trail may be rerouted to exclude Wisconsin because cities through which it passes are failing to respond to appeals for funds.
March 10, 1921 Wisconsin News (Appleton)

Along WI 96 about four miles east of Medina, is Julius Drive, the original 1915-1919 Yellowstone Trail. At this corner (WI-264.5) there is a small power substation converted into a **Yellowstone Trail display.**

Steve Nagy and members of the Greenville Urban Forestry Board built a rock garden with a huge yellow rock on top. Along Julius Dr. you will see several Trail signs, an authentic Trail marker stone excavated from Nagy's driveway with the original yellow paint on it, an avenue of some 120 shade trees, and a growing list of YT signs. ✿

WAYSIDE

In 1922 Roy, Clarence, Newell, and Leonard Larson cleared a landing strip on their father's farm near Larsen, WI. They purchased a Canuck (apparently a 1918 Curtiss JN-4 "Canuck"), built a hanger in 1924, and instructed students and gave pleasure air rides. They barnstormed and became well known. Aviators used this airport to refuel. These early pilots pioneered aviation in Wisconsin on this spot which now is just a quiet farm field near Larsen.

Hearthstone House, Appleton

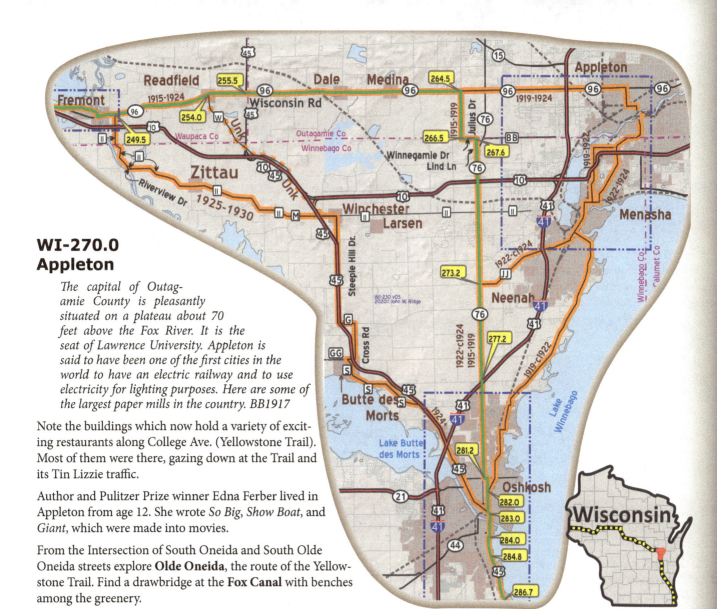

WI-270.0
Appleton

The capital of Outagamie County is pleasantly situated on a plateau about 70 feet above the Fox River. It is the seat of Lawrence University. Appleton is said to have been one of the first cities in the world to have an electric railway and to use electricity for lighting purposes. Here are some of the largest paper mills in the country. BB1917

Note the buildings which now hold a variety of exciting restaurants along College Ave. (Yellowstone Trail). Most of them were there, gazing down at the Trail and its Tin Lizzie traffic.

Author and Pulitzer Prize winner Edna Ferber lived in Appleton from age 12. She wrote *So Big*, *Show Boat*, and *Giant*, which were made into movies.

From the Intersection of South Oneida and South Olde Oneida streets explore **Olde Oneida**, the route of the Yellowstone Trail. Find a drawbridge at the **Fox Canal** with benches among the greenery.

330 E. College Ave. (Yellowstone Trail). **Outagamie Historical Society**. "The History Museum at the Castle," is in a Norman Revival-style 1924 Masonic temple. Appleton native Harry Houdini (Ehrich Weiss) exhibit, hands-on activities, and Appleton's heritage displays are featured. Look across the street at Lawrence University.

625 W Prospect Ave., corner of Memorial and Prospect. **Hearthstone Historic House** built in 1881. It was the first residence in the United States to be incandescently illuminated by hydroelectric power. Remnants of this original electrical system are intact, giving us a rare glimpse into the early technology used in residential electrification. The beautiful home has original light switches and electroliers that still operate.

Vulcan St. **Hydroelectric Plant**. In 1882 a group purchased two Edison K water driven dynamos. It began operation with a direct-current generator that lighted 250 sixteen-power lamps, each equivalent to 50 watts. A water wheel operating under a ten-foot fall of water turned the generator that operated at 110 volts. This was the first hydroelectric plant.

425 W Water St. **Paper Discovery Center**. The paper industry looms large in the Fox River valley which once boasted of 42 paper plants between Menasha and Green Bay. The Discovery Center is chock full of hands-on experiences. Make your own paper to take home.

WI-A276.7 Menasha

Menasha Tayco St. Bridge Tower Museum. BB1925

WI-A277.6 Neenah

Queen Ice Cream Parlor on Main Route (BB 1920); Valley Inn (on Lake Winnebago and Fox River) (BB 1923). Riverside park, Shattuck park, the Fox river and the lakes, all right in the city limits, are most interesting and beautiful. The great paper mills, wood-working plants, foundries, are also worth attention. BB1921-10

347 Smith St. **The Octagon House** houses the Neenah Historical Society. This eight-sided house was built in 1856. The belief at the time was that octagonal houses were a more healthful shape.

165 N. Park St. (Yellowstone Trail). **Bergstrom-Mahler Museum**. Housed in a vintage mansion on Lake Winnebago, this museum has the world's largest glass paperweight collection.

701 Lincoln St. **Doty Cabin**, once the home of Wisconsin's second governor, James Doty, 1844-1845. During summer, costumed guides re-enact the era.

AN UNUSUAL SMALL HIGHWAY BRIDGE

"A small concrete highway bridge is to be built. Located near the city of Oshkosh, on what is now the state trunk highway (Yellowstone Trail). It is in low, flat, rich agricultural country with Lake Winnebago within 500 feet on one side and the Oshkosh Country Club grounds on the other side." They are describing what became the current Kurt Graf Bridge which carries golfers to the Paukatuk Golf Course. That bridge once carried transnational traffic. The article gives, specifics of the consistency of the concrete, balustrades and measurement for approaches. In September, 1920, the bridge became a memorial to Graf, "a local soldier who was killed in the World War and who displayed unusual bravery."

May, 1917 Good Roads for Wisconsin

February 11, 1920. Oshkosh hosted an eastern Wisconsin state Yellowstone Trail Association convention. Note that as of this year Wisconsin divided the state into an eastern and separate western division for state Yellowstone Trail Association meetings. The western section met in Chippewa Falls February 9. Statistics about the Trail in Wisconsin were given: Six out of every ten cars moving from Chicago to Minneapolis travel the Yellowstone Trail although there are 54 different routes between those two points. 19,700 cars traveled the Trail. ✿

Kurt Graf Bridge carried transcontinental YT traffic, Oshkosh

1915 YT relay participants, Oshkosh

Oshkosh was a loyal supporter of the Yellowstone Trail Association over the fifteen years the Trail Association was active in Wisconsin, and it was the site of two important state meetings of the Yellowstone Trail Association. ✿

WI

A story told by the late Langdon Divers of Fond du Lac: A local man, Edward Doheny, moved to California early in the 20th century and became rich opening oilfields. In 1919 he purchased a beautiful, custom-designed Pierce-Arrow car. The car came with a chauffeur. Shortly after, the car, the chauffeur and Mrs. Doheny disappeared. This shows the power of a car. ✿

Lookout Lighthouse, Fond du Lac

This is the *Cushion Sole* Overall

Good practical Oshkosh overalls were found around the world during the life of the YT. They later became known as Oshkosh B' Gosh overalls.

WAYSIDE

3000 Poberezny Rd., Oshkosh. Experimental Aircraft Association. Site of the **EAA AirVenture Museum**, **Pioneer Airport**, and **EAA AirVenture Convention**. The Convention is the world's largest sport aviation event, drawing over 10,000 planes and over 600,000 enthusiasts every August. Historically significant aircraft are often on display showing the colorful heritage of aviation.

"... upwards of a thousand auto tourists camped at the [Lakeside] park from as far away as California."
1920 Good Roads for Wisconsin
Today, Fond du Lac's 400 acre Lakeside Park, Lookout Lighthouse, and Lakeside Park Marina are found in town on the southern shore of Lake Winnebago. Many events and activities are held there. The 63-foot Lakeside Spirit cruise boat offers rides on Lake Winnebago. ✿

WI-283.1 Oshkosh

(pop. 38,000, alt. 744 ft.) is situated on the west shore of Lake Winnebago and on both banks of the Fox River, which here enters the lake. Steamboats ascend from Green Bay to this city and can pass in other directions to the Mississippi river by means of the Fox and Wisconsin Rivers. Oshkosh is a flourishing commercial center with vast lumbering business interests. BB1921-10

Oshkosh Home of Oshkosh B' Gosh overalls. Alma's Restaurant on Wangoo St. serves excellent meals. Oshkosh Camp, 50¢. Winnebago Auto Co., Fords stored 40¢ per night. MH-1926

Three miles north of Oshkosh at 4100 Treffert Dr. is **Winnebago Mental Health Institute**, formerly the Northern Asylum for the Insane. It contains an interesting museum, the Julaine Farrow Museum in the Old Superintendent's House. It chronicles the early pioneers of mental health and the visitor can get a picture of the treatment of mind diseases during the time of the Trail.

100 High Ave. **Grand Opera House**. Built in 1883, it is the oldest operating theater building in Wisconsin. The fight to 'Save the Grand' lasted 20 years. After a $3.5 million restoration, it opened again but structural problems were found in original 1883 elements. In 2010, after a $2 million fund raising, it opened again, now hosting nearly 100 public performances each year.

1410 Algoma Blvd. **Paine Art Center and Gardens**. The Paine is a 1920s mansion looking like a Tutor Revival castle. It has historic interiors, art exhibits and hands-on activities. Go in the summer when the gorgeous gardens are in bloom.

1331 Algoma Blvd. **Oshkosh Public Museum**. Interesting changing exhibits tell of the settlement of the Lake Winnebago region of Wisconsin.

800 Algoma Blvd. **University of Wisconsin-Oshkosh**.

2413 S Main St. (& Doty St., the Yellowstone Trail). **Ardy & Ed's**. Stop at a delightful old-fashioned drive-in, Ardy & Ed's, probably from the 1950s, at the south end of Main St. Car hops in skates! It is not of the Yellowstone Trail era, but it will bring back memories to older drivers and is a prized historic site in Oshkosh.

WI-286.7

The old Kurt Graf Bridge just a couple of dozen feet west of WI 45 on West Ripple Avenue. The bridge once carried the Yellowstone Trail with its cross country traffic. Now, in its retirement, it carries golfers to the Paukatuk Golf Course.

WI-293.0 Van Dyne

N9564 Van Dyne St. (Yellowstone Trail). A lovely Tudor Revival cottage style gas station of perhaps the late 1920s fronts a country market. Note the steep, gabled roof. There was, apparently, no garage attached.

WI-299.6 North Fond du Lac

(749 alt., 2,244 pop.), changed from a small farming community to a bustling railroad center when the Soo Line and Chicago & North Western Ry, transferred their shops here in the early 1900'S. WPA-WI

When they moved WI 175 (now Co. RP) some years ago within North Fond du Lac, a block-long triangle of grass was left between Minnesota Ave. and Co. RP (Van Dyne Rd,) and between Garfield and Winnebago. The city fathers created **Yellowstone Trail Park** there in 2002. The park acquired a train caboose, reminding the viewer of the strong influence of railroads upon this community. Park your car and enjoy the area and the large Yellowstone Trail sign identifying the park.

Right across the street from the Yellowstone Trail Park is the old Yellowstone Garage building, now **Northern Battery** at 602 Iowa Ct. See History Bit on page 272.

WI-301.3 Fond du Lac

(pop. 27,000, alt. 800 ft.) lies at the foot of Lake Winnebago, the largest body of fresh water lying wholly within one state. Here is the largest tannery in the United States, and is a division center for the Northwestern and Soo Line railroads, and it has a summer resort. BB1921-10

From the modern concrete highway skirting the edge of Lake Winnebago the traveler may turn and in a few miles climb to a wooded hill which will permit an unobstructed view of 25 miles. BB1921-10

City Center. Hotel Retlaw. Kruger Bros. Auto Service, 30 E. First St., Crescent Motor Co. 56-60 N. Main. Ph 62. Free camp in Lake Side Park. BB1920

South of FOND DU LAC appears the Niagara escarpment, a long ridge patched with farms and woodlots; as the highway climbs a ridge spur, Hamilton stone shows. Flaked off, the dull yellow rock is used as facing in modern houses. WPA-WI

193 N Main St.(Yellowstone Trail). **Aetna No. 5 Fire Station**, with its tall bell tower, used for observation and for drying hoses, watched over the Yellowstone Trail. The word Aetna was used by fire stations in the 1870s, when the station was built. It referred to the volcano, Mount Aetna, in Sicily which was appropriate for this Italianate style. The building is privately owned now.

1 N Main St. Present **Retlaw Plaza Hotel** has had quite a history. Built in 1923 as the Retlaw (Walter spelled backwards) Schroeder Hotel in Yellowstone Trail days. Then it became the Ramada Plaza, closed in 2015, and now is back to the refurbished Retlaw. This historic landmark still retains some of its early features and elegance of 100 years ago.

336 Old Pioneer Rd. **Galloway House & Village**. Within the area are 30 buildings, including the Blakely Museum. The Galloway House began as a simple farmhouse and evolved into a 30-room showplace of history, gracious living with hand-carved woodwork and etched glass. **CCC Barracks Museum** (Civilian Conservation Corps from the 1930s) is on the grounds.

276 Linden St. **Historic Octagon House**. This house was built in 1856. The house features nine secret passageways including an underground tunnel used as a safe house for escaped slaves using the Underground Railroad. This is a private residence.

Mowbray's YT Garage then,
North Fond du Lac

Van Dyne then

YT Garage now, North Fond du Lac

YT Park at North Fond du Lac
with its founder Jim Mowbray

The **Yellowstone Garage** in North Fond du Lac built in 1920 changed ownership several times before Jim Mowbray ran it from 1949 to 1966. Sometime in the 1920s individual hand-carved wooden letters spelling "YELLOWSTONE GARAGE" were added over the large front door. Jim's son, Mark, tells many homey tales of the renamed Mowbray's Yellowstone Garage in his booklet, *History of the Yellowstone Garage.* Mark follows some automotive changes through warm tales of his family and the "family of friends" who frequented the place. A favorite tale concerns the fact that there was only an old clunker of an oil furnace in the garage corner, so in the winter they would burn a small amount of drained auto oil (mixed into the fuel oil) and use an old car fan to blow the heat through the garage. We call that recycling today. Other "Yellowstone" businesses once at that corner: McArdle's Yellowstone Auto Sales (1950s–1970s) was just next to and north of Mowbray's. The Yellowstone Tavern, across the street from Mowbray's, held its name from the 1930s to about the 1960s. Note the names. Thirty and forty years after the demise of the Trail, the name lingered on. See www.yellowstonetrail.org to find Mark Mowbray's full story of his father's garage. ✿

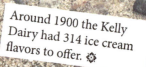
Around 1900 the Kelly Dairy had 314 ice cream flavors to offer. ✿

Old Yellowstone Trail, Addison

WAYSIDE

About 20 miles east of Fond du lac on WI 23 is the **Wade House Historic Site**. It is a former stagecoach inn built in 1848-51. Today the inn, which is listed on the National Register of Historic Places, is a historical museum operated by the Wisconsin Historical Society. There are nine other buildings on the property including the Jung Carriage Museum which exhibits a large collection of 19th-century American horse-drawn vehicles, a blacksmith shop and a sawmill.

The Trail in Byron
Byron Historical Society website

WI

WI-333 St. Lawrence

The **St. Lawrence Roman Catholic Church**, built 1880-82, is immediately visible with its tall steeple and Germanic style.

4900 WI 175, corner of WI 175 (Yellowstone Trail) and Co. K. **Little Red Inn**. This place has been a place of hospitality since the late 1880s. There are historic pictures in the place to prove it. Taverns were popular then as now. For about 75 years this was a tavern only, until about 1960, when a restaurant was introduced.

WI-311.1 Byron

(1,058 alt., 39 pop.), flanks the highway, a one street village where fields creep up to back doors, where a single building combines post office, general store, and filling station, where every house has a weathered barn. WPA-WI

WI-315.5 Lomira

The highway passes through the oldest section, for most of Lomira has moved eastward to follow a shift in railroad lines. WPA-WI

M320.3 Theresa

Pretty village. No camp. Small Hotel & garage. MH-1926

Ford Garage. Rooms and Meals in Connection. BB1920

As you drive through town notice the large rock wall on the east side bearing the town's name. A Yellowstone Trail marker is at the foot of that wall. At the top of that wall is the 1847 **Historical Society Museum/Solomon Juneau House**. He was the founder of Milwaukee and of Theresa, named after his daughter. The Museum is open summers.

214 W Henni St. **Widmer's Cheese Cellars** has been there since 1922; Trail travelers possibly stopped here. Founder John Widmer came from Switzerland. You can watch the cheese being made. They are still using the 1922 real bricks to press the brick cheese. Widmer's has been interested in the Yellowstone Trail and its history. Tours.

WI-326.4 Nenno

WI-328.2 Addison

Some years ago WI 175 was rebuilt just to the west of Addison, vacating its former location through Addison. Suzanne Fish, a friend of the Yellowstone Trail, ran a bed-and-breakfast on the old route. She grasped the opportunity and worked hard to get her street renamed Yellowstone Trail, the name it had almost 100 years ago. It meets WI 175 at Watercress Rd. on the north. At the south end the driver must finagle a bit on WI 33 to continue on the Trail (WI 175). An interesting little half mile on the Trail.

WI-336.2 Slinger

Small free camp ground at City Hall. Kohl Hotel is best for tourists. MH-1926

Commercial Hotel. BB1925

Originally named Schleisingerville after the founder, State Senator Baruch Schleisinger in 1857, it was shortened in a referendum in 1921; 169 votes for "Slinger," 25 blank votes, one for Vim City, and four votes said "Yes."

The **Kettle Moraine Scenic Drive** is just that – scenic. The last glacial period gouged and built. The result is rolling hills and "kettles." The Drive goes through Slinger, as does the Ice Age Trail. Hikers can access the Ice Age Trail at Slinger City Park.

100 W Washington St. **The Slinger House Pub & Grille**, built in 1857 and later run by the Roth family for 90 years. The Roths built a larger hotel and tavern on the existing sturdy field stone foundation utilizing locally produced cream city bricks. The new building "had the latest modern amenities, including gas lighting throughout." The place changed hands regularly from 1957 to the present, but it always remained a tavern serving food. In 2012 it was restored to its warm, historic self.

Washington County Concrete 1925

The jitney line furnished auto service from Theresa via Mayville and Horicon to Beaver Dam. The 24 passenger car ran every hour. "With traffic increasing, the village decided to purchase a motorcycle and hire a cop to patrol the road. Many arrests for speeding were made. This venture brought bad publicity."

July 18, 1922 Mayville News

Original YT sign
held by John Bodden

WAYSIDE

About 7 ½ miles west of Theresa is **Horican Marsh**. Yes, it is off the trail, but it is a worthy wayside. This "Little Everglades of the North" is unusual in a state composed of granite and pine trees. It is the largest freshwater cattail marsh in the U.S. within a state. It is a rest stop for hundreds of thousands of migrating birds in October. Boat tours give a nature lover or birder or photographer a close-up view of heron and egret rookeries.

Look at the original Yellowstone Trail sign that John Bodden found near Theresa. It has a few bullet holes in it, showing it to be the victim of target practice. Story has it that metal signs were frequently stolen from telephone poles to be used for patches for holes in barn walls and corn cribs. ✿

(968 alt., 214 pop.) Richfield was founded in 1842 by Philipp Laubenheimer, who proved an exception to the adage that lightning never strikes twice in the same place. Laubenheimer spent two weeks building a log house, only to learn that it was in the path of the Milwaukee-Fond du Lac road that Solomon Juneau was planning. So he built a tavern at what he considered a safe distance away, but inexorable road builders moved up and forced his second building off their right-of-way. WPA-WI ✿

Widmer Cheese Co., Theresa

The Bub Body Corporation, Milwaukee, has been incorporated with a capital stock of $50,000 by Elmer, Herbert and Arthur Zwebell, to manufacture automobile bodies, specializing in sport and speedster types. Plans have been prepared for a plant costing about $25,000 to be erected at Schlesingerville, [now Slinger} near Milwaukee.

November 11, 1920 Iron Age

Note: Made racing bodies for Model T's!

WAYSIDE

WI-337.1: WI 60 leads five and a half miles west to 147 N Rural St, **Hartford**, a bit off the Yellowstone Trail, but it is the home of an important museum of Wisconsin autos, **The Wisconsin Automotive Museum**, where you can see a collection of Kissel Kars, including a rare Kissel Gold Bug. It is the largest such museum in Wisconsin showing 110+ old vehicles. The Nash is featured, first built in Kenosha in 1916. Open summers. See **Trail Tale: Hot Wheels**, page 282.

Hartford is also the home of the **Kissel Car Company** begun in 1906. An historic marker at Hwy. 60, intersection of Sumner St. and Marine Dr., tells the history of the gasoline powered Kissel Kar. Nothing remains of the factory.

Whittlin Garage in Menomonee Falls, 1917

Wisconsin

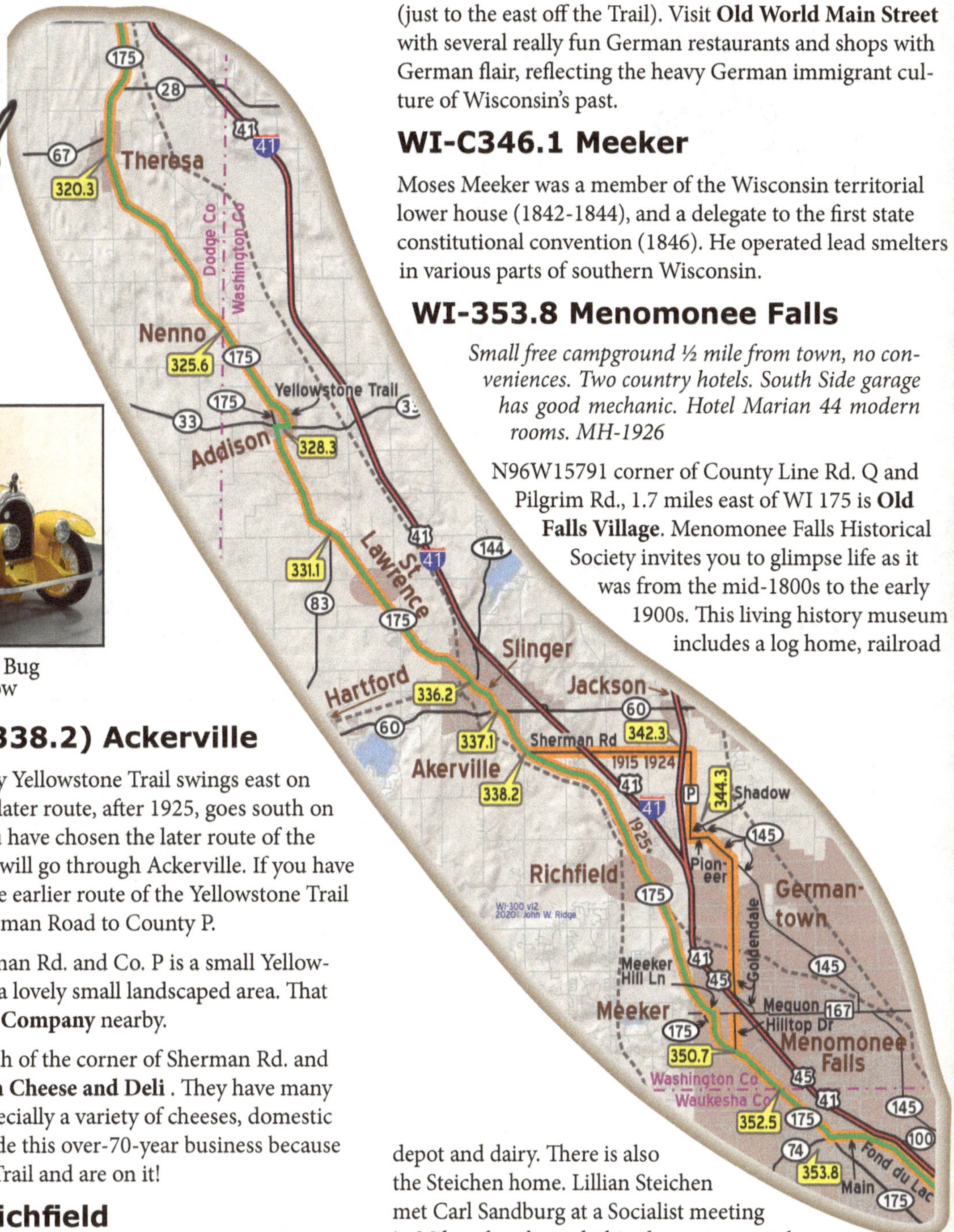

(just to the east off the Trail). Visit **Old World Main Street** with several really fun German restaurants and shops with German flair, reflecting the heavy German immigrant culture of Wisconsin's past.

WI-C346.1 Meeker

Moses Meeker was a member of the Wisconsin territorial lower house (1842-1844), and a delegate to the first state constitutional convention (1846). He operated lead smelters in various parts of southern Wisconsin.

WI-353.8 Menomonee Falls

Small free campground ½ mile from town, no conveniences. Two country hotels. South Side garage has good mechanic. Hotel Marian 44 modern rooms. MH-1926

N96W15791 corner of County Line Rd. Q and Pilgrim Rd., 1.7 miles east of WI 175 is **Old Falls Village**. Menomonee Falls Historical Society invites you to glimpse life as it was from the mid-1800s to the early 1900s. This living history museum includes a log home, railroad

1911 Kissel Gold Bug
at Iola Car Show

WI-338.2 (C338.2) Ackerville

Here is where the early Yellowstone Trail swings east on Sherman Rd., but the later route, after 1925, goes south on present WI 175. If you have chosen the later route of the Yellowstone Trail you will go through Ackerville. If you have chosen to stay with the earlier route of the Yellowstone Trail you will go along Sherman Road to County P.

At the corner of Sherman Rd. and Co. P is a small Yellowstone Trail sign set in a lovely small landscaped area. That marks **Lamm's Floral Company** nearby.

3271 Hwy P (Just south of the corner of Sherman Rd. and Co. P). **Bieri's Jackson Cheese and Deli**. They have many delicious goodies, especially a variety of cheeses, domestic and foreign. We include this over-70-year business because they know about the Trail and are on it!

WI-C343.2 Richfield

WI-347.1 Dheinsville. N128W18780. Drive one mile to the east off the Trail on Holy Hill Road and you will come to Dheinsville Settlement Park, operated by the village of Germantown. It is located at the six corners where Holy Hill Rd., Maple Rd., and Fond du Lac Ave, (WI 145) converge. The hamlet has retained all of its twenty-two original German structures, many having undergone extensive restoration. There are three museums there: Christ Church Museum of Local History; Wolf Haus Museum and Genealogy Research Center; and the Bast Bell Museum. The Bell Museum is within an old barn and contains more than 5,000 bells from all over the world. All open summers only.

WI-349.5 Germantown

While negotiating the twisting Co. Y to get around the US 41 exit, you might take a short side trip to visit Germantown

depot and dairy. There is also the Steichen home. Lillian Steichen met Carl Sandburg at a Socialist meeting in Milwaukee, brought him home to meet the parents and married him.

N92W17387 Appleton Ave. (Yellowstone Trail). **Wittlin's Service Station**. Although it doesn't look it, this family owned business is 11 years old. In 1907, just a few blocks south of the present station, John B. Wittlin began his blacksmith and auto repair business. In 1909, Wittlin's became a Ford dealership before starting up the gas station at the present location in the mid-1920s. And a gas and auto service station it has remained. Undoubtedly, Yellowstone Trail travelers stopped here.

Coming into Milwaukee from Waukesha via Fond du Lac Avenue (Highway 175) it takes some imagination to see it as it might have looked when this was the Yellowstone Trail 100 years ago. It is totally urbanized today. The Trail founders would wonder what happened to their tranquil gravel road.

St. Josapaht Basilica, Milwaukee

Harley-Davidson, Milwaukee

Free maps at the progressive Milwaukee Journal. Municipal camp in Lake Park, free. Plankinton Hotel ranks first, suites up to $12. Antlers Hotel, 3 floors reserved for women or families. The Sixth St. Garage at 186 Sixth St. collects and delivers your car to your hotel— no charge and no tipping. Hotel Pfister, on Wisconsin Ave. BB1925.

Note: Free maps at the "progressive" Milwaukee Journal. For more information on the person responsible for those road maps, see **Trail Tale: Brownie,** page 287.

MILWAUKEE TAKES IMPORTANT PART IN YELLOWSTONE TRAIL PROMOTION. DIRECTORS HOLD MEETING HERE
ASSOCIATION HELPS ATTRACT MANY MOTOR TOURISTS TO WISCONSIN

The organization brought 22,000 cars, or about 66,000 tourists through Wisconsin on motor tours to the great northwest. Ray Smith, proprietor of the Republican House, is vice-president of the Trail Association.
February 22, 1920 The Milwaukee Sentinal

~~~~~~~~~~~~~~~~~~~~~~~~

YELLOWSTONE TRAIL WILL BE TRAVELED BY RECORD NUMBER

More than $100,000 have already been appropriated for improvements. Recognizing the importance of the northwest to the Trail, a separate Association office will be set up in Seattle.
February 28, 1920 the Ellensburg Daily Record
Note: The newspaper was reporting the meeting of the previous week in Milwaukee. That $100,000 does not come from the Yellowstone Trail Association. It is the amount states would be paying for Trail repair that year.

~~~~~~~~~~~~~~~~~~~~~~~~

YELLOWSTONE TRAIL OFFICIALS BELIEVE 1920 WILL SET NEW TRAVEL RECORD

March, 1920 Wisconsin Motorist
Note: The magazine was reporting the previous meeting in Milwaukee. They had travel bureaus who kept count and reported: 30,000 travelers on the Yellowstone Trail in 1918, 60,000 in 1919, and predicted 100,000 in 1920. These are not all through Wisconsin.

For the second year the Yellowstone Trail Association will conduct a free information bureau for tourists in this city. Last year 5,300 touring parties were served by the Trail bureau, more than half of them coming from outside of the state. David Rellin is in charge, in the Hotel Pfister.
June 1920 Wisconsin Motorist magazine

~Golda Meir, Israel's first woman prime minister, came from Milwaukee. Ingrid Bergman played her in the movie A Woman Called Golda, 1982.

~The typewriter and electric guitar were invented here.

~The weather station in Milwaukee was begun in 1901 by Increase Lapham at Water and Michigan Streets with official three-day forecasts for the North Atlantic. ✿

IMPORTANT MEETING
BIG ROADS CONVENTION AT MILWAUKEE AT TURNER HALL

Sept. 8, 1908 The Stanley Republican
Note: The nation-wide Good Roads Association had state chapters, all pushing for government help with roads, which would not come until 1916,.

MILWAUKEE AUTO SHOW TO HAVE FORD EXHIBIT

Ford will have a special exhibit in connection with the 16th annual automobile show at the Milwaukee Auditorium.

January 6, 1924 The Milwaukee Journal
Note: That date means that auto shows began in 1908, well before the Yellowstone Trail arrived in Wisconsin, but for nine years Yellowstone Trail travelers may have stopped to see the magnificent hall and new models of cars.

WI-369 Milwaukee

(pop. 500,000, alt. 636 ft.), the most populous city of Wisconsin is situated on the west shore of Lake Michigan at the mouth of the Milwaukee river. Its natural waterways and harbor have made Milwaukee one of the chief manufacturing and commercial centers of the northcentral section of the Union. BB1921-10

[Note: Its nickname, "Cream City," comes from the cream-colored brick manufactured there in 1800s and sold world-wide and can be seen on houses throughout southeastern Wisconsin.]

There is more to Milwaukee than Germans, motorcycles, and beer. In Trail days, Milwaukee produced 1/3 of the industrial output of the state. The Lake Michigan waterfront is essentially one long band of parkland from historic Third Ward north for miles and encompasses several individually named parks; most were available to old Yellowstone Trail travelers.

The Trail on Water St. skirts the Third Ward, an area which is south and west of Interstate 794. An intriguing mix of shops is in this historic warehouse district. It has a high concentration of art galleries, antique shops, and theaters. For a walking tour, see www.historicmilwaukee.org.

1030 N Old World 3rd St. **Usinger's Famous Sausage Company**. Four generations of Usingers have led their German sausage into world-wide fame from 1880 to the present day.

1041 N Old World 3rd St. **Mader's Restaurant** is across the street from Usinger's. Absolutely great German food and atmosphere. Mader's opened in 1902 mainly as a beer hall, which pleased the large German population. When Prohibition landed, they turned to serving German food. Today, the third generation Mader has kept up with the times. Order the tangy sauerbraten.

424 E Wisconsin Ave. (Yellowstone Trail). **Pfister Hotel**. The lobby held a Yellowstone Trail Association Bureau where maps, weather, and road reports were given out at no cost. Bad times befell this beautiful lady after World War II until Ben Marcus raised it like a Phoenix from the ashes in the 1960s to the elegant hostelry it is today, much as it was 100 years ago.

400 W Canal St. just off South Sixth St. (the Yellowstone Trail) is the popular **Harley-Davidson Museum**, with displays of historic motorcycles that were an important part of the Yellowstone Trail years. It began in 1903, making the bikes known as "Milwaukee Iron." The museum has "outrageous customs, personalized gear and pop culture." We toured the York, Pennsylvania, Harley plant and marveled

at all the robots.

2333 S Sixth St. At Lincoln and South Sixth (Yellowstone Trail) is the **Basilica of St. Josaphat**, Magnificent 100-year-old landmark designed after St. Peter's in Rome. Built by Polish-Americans between 1896 and 1901. Stained glass and murals show Milwaukee's heritage.

144 E Wells St. **Pabst Theater**. The Pabst Theater is the centerpiece of Milwaukee's downtown theater district. Built in 1895 by Frederick Pabst, it features a variety of programs. The original monster organ is still there. Today it is a National Landmark and Wisconsin Historical Site.

800 W Wells St. **Milwaukee Public Museum**, chartered in 1882. It has exhibits on the natural environment of various parts of the planet. This place has many activities always on - always changing. They include an IMAX theater. It is regarded as one of America's top natural history museums.

2900 S. Kinnikinnick Ave. **The White House Tavern**. Built in 1891 as a Schlitz tavern; more than just a tavern, it was a neighborhood gathering place and institution. At 130 years old it is still going strong.

1037 W Juneau Ave. and 901 W Juneau Ave. **Pabst Milwaukee Brewery & Taproom**. Best Place at the Historic Pabst Brewery. The old Pabst Brewery complex has been renovated into interesting sites. The Best Place is named for the 1840s brewery founders, Jacob and Phillip Best.

Blue silk was tied to each bottle, reminding all that the beer once won a blue ribbon. The Taproom also offers a tour and food. Pabst beer is once again brewed (as a microbrewery) on the first floor of the old church. The second floor is the Taproom.

WI

"Today, visitors to South Milwaukee can find many of the old buildings along the Yellowstone Trail still in use. Still, if one would stand at the corner of 10th and Milwaukee Avenues to gaze down the road once traveled by so many, so long ago, you can almost hear the sounds of the Flivvers and Tin Lizzies as they sputter past, in those heady, early days of automotive travel in America." Nels Monson ✿

Old Engine House #3, Racine

Underground railway. Before the Civil War, Racine was well known for its strong opposition to slavery, with many slaves escaping to freedom via the Underground Railroad passing through the city. In 1854 Joshua Glover, an escaped slave who had made a home in Racine, was arrested by federal marshals and jailed in Milwaukee. One hundred men from Racine, and ultimately 5,000 Wisconsinites, rallied and broke into the jail to free him. He was helped to escape to Canada. Glover's rescue gave rise to many legal complications and a great deal of litigation. This eventually led to the Wisconsin Supreme Court declaring the Fugitive Slave Law of 1850 unconstitutional, and later, the Wisconsin State Legislature refusing to recognize the authority of the U.S. Supreme Court. ✿

Historic White Brick Motel, Kenosha

South Milwaukee early on joined the Yellowstone Trail Association. Local historian Nels Monson has written: "City leaders were quick to realize the importance of improving street conditions to meet the increased traffic demands. On May 21, 1921, the city paid its $50 'assessment' to the Yellowstone Trail Association." ✿

Before the Yellowstone Trail arrived in Wisconsin in 1915, Racine witnessed its first automobile race. A. J. Horlick in a Locomobile and Robert Hindley in a Winton. The course was over the 14 unpaved miles to Western Union Junction (Sturtevant) and back. About a mile out of town Hindley overtook the lead from Horlick who became stalled. When Horlick was able to resume the race it was too late and Hindley was declared the winner after about six hours on the road. ✿

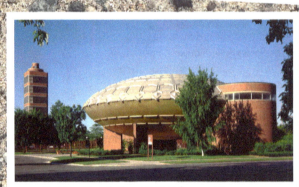

Golden Rondelle at S.C. Johnson Company

Supper Club on YT near Racine

WAYSIDE

The Golden Rondelle Building is the starting point for a tour of the S.C. Johnson complex, maker of Johnson's Wax products. The Golden Rondelle Theater was designed by Taliesin Associated Architects, the successor firm to Frank Lloyd Wright, and built in 1964 for the New York World's Fair. The Administration Building and Research Tower were designed by Frank Lloyd Wright. The 1950 Administration Building has received world-wide recognition. Its "Great Work Room" with its one-half acre of floor space and 31 foot ceiling houses desk workers. To preserve the shiny "Johnson's Wax" floors, desks and three-legged chairs were designed to have minimal contact with the floor.

Simmons Library, Kenosha

WI-374.5 St. Francis

The city took its name from St. Francis Seminary, founded by Milwaukee Archbishop John Henni. It is a quiet town, and bears 14 Trail signs along Lake Drive, the Yellowstone Trail. You can't get lost there!

WI-376.6 Cudahy

A factory suburb of Milwaukee. The Cudahy Packing Plant is located here. BB1920

The city has embraced the movement to resurrect the fame of the Yellowstone Trail so watch for the Trail markers through Cudahy.

West Layton Ave. and Applewood Ln. One can see the famous **Patrick Cudahy Meat Packing Company** which was moved to Cudahy by Patrick Cudahy, town founder, from Milwaukee in 1893. Today, Cudahy is still known primarily as a meat-packing town.

4647 S. Kinnickinnic Ave. **Cudahy Historic Depot**. The Chicago and Northwestern Railway stopped here from 1893 to 1940. When freight service was discontinued, the doomed depot was saved by the Cudahy Historical Society. Visitors will see a beautiful, fully renovated train depot.

5133 S Lake Dr. **Sheridan B & B**. This is truly a boutique hotel. In 1920 it was called The Sheridan Hotel. It changed names mid-century, now has been completely renovated and returned to its original name. Expect excellence. For more on that name, see **Trail Tale: Sheridan Road**, page 284.

WI-380.5 South Milwaukee

Bucyrus Co., made steam shovels that dug the Panama Canal. 10th Avenue. BB1920

Camp 1 mile ne, 60 cars, bathing in lake. AAA

Economically a part of Milwaukee, South Milwaukee has 17 industrial plants. WPA-WI

A number of Yellowstone Trail signs marks the Trail through South Milwaukee.

100 Hawthorne Ave. **Grant Park** at the Lake Michigan lakefront in northern South Milwaukee. It is 400 acres of wooded bluffs, paths and beach. According to its history posted at the park: "Created at the behest of the Wisconsin Highway Commission in 1921, the tourist camp was a popular resting point for those traveling the Yellowstone Trail highway in the early days of cross-country automobile travel."

The city is very proud of Grant Park. Stroll where Trail campers strolled over 100 years ago.

1970 10th Ave. **Caterpillar Global Mining Company Museum** at Heritage Building. The museum opened in 2009. Bucyrus, then Bucyrus-Erie, now part of the Caterpillar Company, makes huge mining equipment and dredges with drag lines. Seventy-seven of Bucyrus' steam shovels

went to Panama to dig the canal in 1904–07. One 1960 model was the largest self-powered land vehicle built. Some of the original buildings can be seen at1100 Rawson Ave.

WI-383 Oak Creek

WI-394.6 Racine

The Belle City on the Lakes. Hotel Racine, new and elegant. $2-$6. 200 rooms, 160 baths. William Becker Garage, 339 Wis. St. is best. MH-1926

Horlick malted milk. Home of Mitchell and Case automobiles and J. I. Case Threshing Machines, Exide Battery Station , 3rd St Garage. BB1920

231 Main St. (Yellowstone Trail). **Ivanhoe Restaurant**. Built in 1891 and once owned by Frederick Pabst, this place has been a restaurant of one kind or another for 129 years. Trail travelers may very well have dined here. Some original interior decor remains such as the stained glass windows. There is even an antique player piano there from the nineteen-teens.

1841 Douglas Ave. (Yellowstone Trail, WI 32). **O&H Danish Bakery**. They know that they are on the Yellowstone Trail, and they are history buffs. Stop in for kringle, a yummy Danish pastry for which they are famous worldwide. Racine is known for kringle and several bakeries make it, but this one is right on the Yellowstone Trail so it is special. Try the almond.

701 S Main St. (Yellowstone Trail). **Racine Heritage Museum**. Three floors of changing, interesting exhibits tell of historic Racine products such as Horlick's Malted Milk, Hamilton Beach, and Johnson's Wax. Racine was a well-known destination for escaped slaves during the Civil War. Pick up a walking/driving guide to the Underground Railroad, which helped escaped slaves get to Canada. The museum also has a local history research center.

700 Sixth St. (Yellowstone Trail). **Old Engine House #3 Museum**. This museum is a former Racine Fire Department station which was active from 1881 to 1968. The Fire Station housed a horse drawn steamer and hose cart (1882-1918), and a Motorized Fire Engine (1918-1943). The building has been preserved to reflect the early 1900s and it displays artifacts from that period.

2200 Northwestern Ave. Former home of the world famous **Horlick Malted Milk Company**. Horlicks is a malted milk-based drink originally created as a supplement to babies' formula. The two Horlick brothers began production at the turn of the 20th century. It grew to an international company with a branch in England where it is still popular. Operations were shut down in 1975. The 1902 castle-like buildings are now occupied by a variety of small firms.

1525 Howe St. at 14th St. **S.C. Johnson Company**, makers of Johnson's Wax products. See the Wayside on the previous page for more information.

Wisconsin Motorist magazine declared in its March, 1919, issue that "Six thousand tourists were put through Wisconsin during 1918, according to the Yellowstone Trail Association. A greater number would have passed through the Badger state if the condition of Sheridan Road between Milwaukee and Chicago had been more favorable to transcontinental automobile travel." For the story, see **Trail Tale: Sheridan Road**, page 284. ⚙

Kenosha Public Museum and Civil War Museum

Kenosha was home to five famous auto brands in 110 years: Rambler, Jeffrey, Nash, and American Motors. Finally, it became the home of Chrysler engine plant for a while. See **Trail Tale: Hot Wheels**, page 282. ⚙

1915 Jeffrey. The year the YT came to Wis.

Mitchell Motor Car Company. Established in 1902, by 1910 the company employed 2,000 people, and cars were shipped by rail to their destinations. Racine-built Mitchell Motors' popular touring cars traveled the Yellowstone Trail in the Trail's earliest days. The company closed in 1923, bankrupted; it was later bought by Kenosha's auto maker, the Nash Motor Company, in 1925. ⚙

KENOSHA OFFICER FINDS
DAMP HOTEL BASEMENT
John Scholey, whose one-man raids made him notorious, raided the State Line Hotel on Sheridan Road on Saturday afternoon finding, it is alledged, 25 barrels of mash and two cases of whiskey in the basement. Owner John Schmidt was ordered into court for having liquor in his possession.

January 9, 1925 Baldwin Bulletin
Note: Hang on, John Schmidt. In eight years it will all be legal again.

Readers of a certain age may remember that Johnson's Wax sponsored the very popular 1940s radio comedy called "Fibber McGee and Molly." ⚙

HIGHWAY 15 OPENED WITH
ENTHUSIASTIC ACCLAIM
The long, heraldic article described the big whoopla which accompanied the opening. Caravans of cars peeled out onto the highway from each town: Kenosha, Racine, Milwaukee and all towns to Appleton had parades, bands (even a "motorcade band"), speeches by mayors and locomotives with whistles welcoming the motorcade. The parade then moved on to Green Bay and the Yellowstone Trail veered west.

September 1922, Wisconsin Motorist.
Note: State Highway 15 was the Yellowstone Trail from 1921.

The Coffee Pot, Racine

WI-405.7 Kenosha

(pop. 30,000, alt. 611 ft.) Kenosha has a fine harbor and a U. S. life saving station. It has extensive fisheries, and an active business in shipping. Its factories include the Simmons Mfg. Co., Nash Motor Co. (automobiles), Alien's Sons Tannery, and Macomber-Whyte Rope Co. There are many small and pretty lakes nearby, whose shores are inhabited during the summer by aristocratic Chicagoans and others. Kemper Hall is one of the best known girls' preparatory schools in the west. BB1921

Hotel Dayton Sgl. $2, Dbl. with bath $4.50-$6. Sheridan Rd. Garage. Open all night. MH-1926

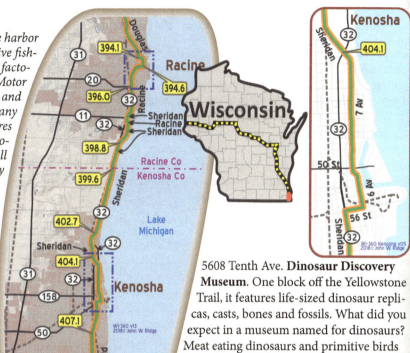

Five famous auto brands span 110 years in Kenosha: Rambler/Jeffrey/Nash/American Motors/Chrysler engine plant.

973 N Sheridan Rd. **White Brick Motel**. Notice the cabins. They were there, no doubt, during the Yellowstone Trail era. Cabins gradually changed to motels after connecting roofs were built between cabins for auto storage. The White Brick represents an early motel.

220-51st Pl. **Kenosha History Center** on historic Simmons Island in Kenosha's harbor. It features the Rambler Legacy Gallery with changing Kenosha automobile exhibits.

5117 4th Ave. Simmons Island Park, 50th Street and Lighthouse Drive (4th Ave). The **Southport Light Station Museum** is composed of the 1866 historic lighthouse and the adjacent 1867 historic Lighthouse Keeper's home. The Light Station Keeper's House opened in May 2010 as a maritime museum featuring artifacts, maps, and information about Kenosha's important 19th century harbor. Both floors of the Lighthouse Keeper's home have been restored to a 1908 time period. Want to climb the 72 steps to the top of the lighthouse? It is operated by the Kenosha County Historical Society.

5500 First Ave. **Kenosha Public Museum** in Harbor Park. Right next door to the Civil War Museum. Natural exhibits include a mammoth skeleton and world ethnology. All exhibits are carefully explained and many are interactive.

5400 First Ave. **Civil War Museum**. It is unusual in that it displays a Midwestern perspective on the war with stories of regional people who played a role in that war as well as the manufacturing and agricultural contributions to it.

Roughly bounded by 59th St., 7th Ave., 61st St., and 8th Ave. **Simmons Library National Historic District**. GPS: 42.58072, -87.81947. An elegant park and buildings worthy of a stroll. It was created in 1900 by mattress maker Zalmon Simmons, maker of Beautyrest. The library has much about Simmons and the history of Kenosha within this delightful mausoleum-like building.

5608 Tenth Ave. **Dinosaur Discovery Museum**. One block off the Yellowstone Trail, it features life-sized dinosaur replicas, casts, bones and fossils. What did you expect in a museum named for dinosaurs? Meat eating dinosaurs and primitive birds also make their appearance.

598 58th St. Only a couple of blocks off the Yellowstone Trail, **Frank's Diner** is locally recognized as an historic landmark and great breakfast and lunch joint. It might not look like it from the outside. Featured on the Food Network series "Diners, Drive-ins and Dives," and numerous TV specials, Frank's is now nationally famous. The diner is the oldest continuously operating lunch car diner in the U.S. In 1926, six horses pulled the diner to the spot where it stands today. Celebrities have visited the place.

Kenosha's **Electric Streetcar**. Five restored electric streetcars travel a two-mile loop providing a scenic tour of the Lake Michigan shoreline, Harbor Park, and other sites. It makes 17 stops along the route. From 1903 to 1932 electric rail was the regular mode of transportation in Kenosha. In June, 2000, quiet, electric streetcars returned to service.

4914 7th Ave. (Yellowstone Trail). **The Coffee Pot**. A quaint little coffee shop and diner. We mention it here because of its old fashioned appearance and hospitality of staff which reminds one of 100 years ago on the Trail since they are really right on the Yellowstone Trail. They have expanded and also added the "Garden of Eatin'" for outside dining. Breakfast and lunch only, more's the pity.

The Yellowstone Trail exited/entered Wisconsin on Sheridan Road, now highway WI 32. In some WI 32 highway signs you will see small red arrows. That honored the Wisconsin Red Arrow Army Division organized in 1917. It was originally made up of National Guardsmen from Wisconsin and Michigan. Men from the 32nd served in some of the fiercest battles in WWI. In WWII the 32nd was one of the first to be called. They subsequently spent 654 days in action in the Pacific Theater. The Division was de-activated in 1946. This highway has been dedicated to that Division for 104 years.

WI-412.2 Wisconsin/Illinois Line

WI

Hot Wheels in Wisconsin

People don't usually think of Wisconsin as a hot bed of auto manufacturing, but since the first car steamed out of Dr. Carhart's barn in 1871 until 1915 there had been 141 brands of vehicles coming out of barns in Wisconsin, according to the Wisconsin Society of Automotive Historians. Most lasted less than a year. Some have lasted over 100 years. In spite of early restrictive laws designed to curtail the growing popularity of these "devil wagons," and in spite of farmers' initial remonstrances, the auto with its internal combustion engine prevailed.

In the Beginning

In 1871 Dr. J. W. Carhart, a medical doctor and Methodist minister of Racine, designed and operated what may have been the first steam-powered, self-propelled vehicle in the U.S. The belching monster enraged citizens and scared to death a horse. Carhart later described his inaugural run of his "Spark" thus: " The noise of the exhaust which escaped through the stack, and which shot smoke and cinders fully 15 feet into the air, was terrific and startling."

The "Spark" consisted of a small upright boiler, a pair of slide-valve engines on high buggy wheels, developing four horsepower. Steering was done by a chain and drum gear which turned the entire front axle. He usually had the street entirely to himself as he ran about town. He did not take out a patent nor did he manufacture any more. He just enjoyed the experience for several years.

Carhart's "Spark"
Motor Age, March 19, 1914

Although the Duryea brothers of Massachusetts are given credit for creating the first workable gasoline-driven car company in 1896, Gottfried Schloemer had already scared and scattered the crowds with his auto wagon's gasoline engine roar on Milwaukee's West Water Street in 1892. He built a carburetor with wicking to prevent flooding (for which he received a patent in 1892). Because of a lack of spark plugs, he created a "make and break" system of two small steel points which struck up a spark to ignite the gas. The one-cylinder, two-speed vehicle was not pretty; it was just a place to sit with an engine in the rear.

Others thought it was just not practical. Schloemer toodled around town in his "auto wagon," even appearing in a parade,

Schloemer Motor Wagon,
1892 Auto Industries
Wikipedia

until July of 1920 when he sold it, still running well. He had turned his attention to gasoline-driven tractors in 1896, creating probably the first one ever made. If only he had found a backer to manufacture more autos he would have beaten the Duryeas by years.

The 1878 Race

The "Spark" invention of Dr. Carhart inspired an automotive vision in the state's 1875 legislature which proposed an endurance auto race of 200 miles with a $10,000 prize for the winner. The Legislative Act read in part, "An Act to encourage the invention and successful use of steam or other mechanical agents on highways." Chief among the many rules for the race was that the machine should prove to be a "cheap and practical substitute for the use of horses."

It took three years and a rush of creative energy in many barns to respond to the challenge of a race from Green Bay to Madison. Finally, in 1878 only the "Green Bay" and the "Oshkosh" vehicles lined up. One eye witness said, "Talk about your excitement! Barnum's circus was no greater attraction and horses could not be kept anywhere near the highway when it [steam motor car] came along." Newspapers along the route estimated that thousands watched, proving that the contest evinced a considerable interest in "road wagons."

The "Green Bay" was of a horizontal fire box boiler type. It had a considerable number of gears, and a front axle steering knuckle similar to the ones that exist on automobiles today. It had three speeds forward and one reverse speed.

The "Oshkosh" machine had one forward and one reverse speed. It had a vertical boiler with a box heater at the bottom. Two engine cylinders were attached on top of the heaters. The propelling device was a sprocket pinion on the crank shaft. The driving chain was similar to that used on motor trucks years later.

A few miles from Madison the "Green Bay" was shipped back to Green Bay, the "Oshkosh" continuing on to Madison and the prize. The little engine that made it through without a breakdown was made in Oshkosh for threshing machine power and work only. The commission found nothing of sufficient value to the people of Wisconsin to justify the reward of $10,000 or even a part. It was not a cheap and practical substitute for horses. The next legislature grudgingly awarded $5,000 to the winning crew in 1879 without realizing that this was probably the first horseless carriage race ever.

Autos and roads were all of a piece. The somnolent state government needed these "auto shocks" to consider road building as within their purview. Because of these auto events, ⇨

Jeffrey Plant in Kenosha

it became clear to legislators where the interest of the public lay, and road improvement soon followed. Four years after the State Highway Commission was formed in 1911, the Yellowstone Trail Association was putting its signs on Wisconsin roads.

Rambler/Nash plant in Kenosha
Nash website

The Jeffrey

Thomas B. Jeffrey began building his auto in a bicycle shop in Kenosha where he had brought out his popular bicycle, the Rambler. In 1902 he sold upwards of 1,500 of his one-cylinder, eight horse power car, the "Rambler." By 1909 "one thousand workers labored around the clock in two 12-hour shifts," reported writer Dan Jensen.

After Thomas Jeffrey's death in 1910, son Charles took over the company, bringing out the famous four-wheel-drive Quad truck which eventually became the World War I workhorse of the American Army in France. By 1913 Jeffrey was producing 13,000 vehicles a year.

In 1916 Charles sold the company to then-General Motors President, Charles Nash. In 1917 the name Jeffrey was dropped from the auto and renamed Nash.

The Nash Ambassador was the first convertible produced after World War II, it being the first to be called a "compact car," the first to offer seat belts, the first to introduce the "unibody" structure which is used by the auto industry today.

Nash merged with Kelvinator in 1936 which merged with Hudson Motor Company in 1954, forming the American Motors Corporation which was bought out by Chrysler in 1987. Financial complications arose resulting in the Fiat-Chrysler LLC company being formed. The final Chrysler plant (an engine plant) was closed in 2010.

The Kissel

"A hard-top that one could remove, exposing a roofless touring car," read the Kissel Kar All-Year ad in *Motor West*, Oct. 15, 1917. By that year the high-end, custom built automobile was selling well, reaching a capital stock of $1,000,000 in the 1920s. Designs way ahead of their time made the Kissel unique and popular. Louis Kessel and sons founded the Kissel Motor Car Company in June of 1906 in Hartford, Wisconsin. The company built custom, high-quality vehicles -- automobiles, hearses, trucks. Each car cost $1,850; a windshield and other parts were extra. They called their product Kissel Kars (the German spelling of cars) until World War I when they dropped the word Kars. Because each car was hand-made, they were able to provide quality touches, but were a low production company.

A Kissel Kar became a prized auto, especially when a yellow model of a speedster came out. It was dubbed the "Gold Bug" by the populace. It had cutaway doors, wire wheels, and pull-out drawers on the outside containing a fold-up seat! How frightening was that, sitting outside of the car?! It didn't hurt business when movie star Anita King drove a Gold Bug across the U.S. in 1915. Hollywood stars soon became owners of this expensive, hand made eye-catcher. You might recognize some names: Fatty Arbuckle, Mary Pickford, Douglas Fairbanks, Al Jolson, Jack Dempsey, and aviator Amelia Earhardt.

During World War I Kissel manufactured 2,000 four-wheel-drive, 3 ½ ton trucks under license from the Four Wheel Drive company in Clintonville, Wisconsin. The company reached its peak in the 1920s, with the White Eagle Speedster, priced from $1,500 to $45,000, and still years ahead of the industry in design. Kissel autos were made until late 1930 when the family business could no longer compete against assembly-built cars and the Great Depression. In 1942 the business was sold to West Bend Aluminum Company. Of the 35,000 automobiles built by Kessel, only 150 are known to exist today. The Wisconsin Automotive Museum of Hartford displays several of these remaining cars, including a Gold Bug (see picture on page 275).

The Mitchell

Henry Mitchell, wagon maker, and son-in-law, W. T. Lewis, auto maker, joined forces and by 1903 Mitchell cars were winning speed and endurance races. They made three, five, and seven-passenger cars and limousines. The Racine plant covered nearly 30 acres. Organizational and financial difficulties plagued the company. After it folded in 1923, Nash Motors bought the factory in 1925.

Ad for a Mitchell

Four Wheel Drive (FWD) – Clintonville

Story has it that it all began when William Besserdich and some others got stuck in deep sand in 1906. Upon pushing the front wheels forward, Besserdich noticed how easily the car moved out of the trap. The combination of force to all four wheels suggested to him an invention. By 1908 they had a patent for four wheel drive.

The company reached an international market during World War I, producing over 14,000 trucks for the U.S. government. After the war, the company built trucks and highway building equipment, earth-moving machinery, and fire trucks. World War II once more brought prosperity to the company. But, mergers and acquisitions brought an unfortunate end to this successful Wisconsin company in 2003. The Four Wheel Drive Foundation maintains a museum in Clintonville.

And do not forget that the Harley-Davidson Motorcycle Company is a Milwaukee company! The Yellowstone Trail Association worked for the roads necessary to carry the lightning-fast speed of the auto industry in Wisconsin. ❁

Sheridan Road

with contributions by Sam Teske

Before the Yellowstone Trail Association routed their Trail on Sheridan Road from Wisconsin into northern Illinois in 1915, that route already had old roots. First, a path by Native Americans to a French trading post in northern Illinois, then a mail route from Fort Howard (Green Bay) to Fort Dearborn (Chicago) in 1832 by Act of Congress. Railroads and water routes also linked Green Bay with the new town of Chicago. Sheridan Road then became the eastern-most route between Illinois and Wisconsin, running along the shore of Lake Michigan. By 1915, it was the main route through that populated area and, thus, was chosen by the Yellowstone Trail Association.

> ## IT IS "SHERIDAN ROAD"
> ### CHICAGO'S NEW DRIVE HAS A NAME
> The North Shore Improvement Association voted to bring to fruition the north shore drive and called it Sheridan Rd.
> *February 24. 1889 Chicago Daily Tribune*

The road running in front of 1880s Fort Sheridan, named for Civil War Union General Philip Sheridan, was aptly named Sheridan Road. Today, Sheridan Road in Illinois is a major north-south thoroughfare that leads from Diversey Parkway in Chicago north, passing through the elegant towns along the shore until it reaches the Illinois-Wisconsin state line. It is known for its historic sites such as Fort Sheridan, lakefront parks, Great Lakes Naval Training Center, and gracious mansion homes including three designed by Frank Lloyd Wright. Sheridan Road kept its name in Illinois.

In Wisconsin, Sheridan Road became several things. It entered Wisconsin about 35 years before the Yellowstone Trail Association placed its signs upon it. After Wisconsin numbered its roads in 1918, the Trail and Sheridan Road found themselves entering Wisconsin on WI 17 until 1920 when the road was renumbered WI 15. It was the easternmost north-south through street, closest to Lake Michigan from the Illinois border north to Green Bay. At Milwaukee the Yellowstone Trail and Sheridan Road turned northwest along with state WI 15 until they parted company when Sheridan Road and WI 15 went east to Green Bay and the Yellowstone Trail went west toward Stevens Point.

Sheridan Road before improvement,
Town of Pleasant Prairie, Kenosha County
Wis. DOT

Road development proceeded slowly and unmethodically in the early 20th century in Wisconsin as road responsibility shifted from township to county to state. There was no state trunk highway system established in 1915 in Wisconsin when the Yellowstone Trail was routed there. There was $1,250,000 available in state aid to counties, but this aid resulted in scattered road improvement, determined by local government based on local consideration, not connectedness.

The Yellowstone Trail Association, the State Highway Commission, the Good Roads Association, and the Sheridan Road Association were all interested in the development of that well-worn trade thoroughfare. Progress on improving that road for heavy auto and truck traffic became stalled in the two townships of Somers and Pleasant Prairie in Kenosha County, Wisconsin, and the town of Zion in Illinois. The story of developing that road is a trenchant social commentary upon road-building as local governments stumbled through the evolution of funding the inevitable.

First, There Were Two Townships

Milwaukee County saw the advantage of an improved Sheridan Road to Chicago and promptly worked to that end, moving its paving crews south to the Racine County line. But there was an area in Kenosha County abutting the Illinois border that chose to ignore the fervent entreaties of the Yellowstone Trail Association *et al*. That area consisted of the two townships, Somers and Pleasant Prairie.

In 1915, groups that wanted to see road improvement could not force their township or county to apply for state aid, which demanded matching funds, and the state trunk highway system would not be created for another two years. What could groups do to raise money as a motivator for a better road? They went hat-in-hand.

News articles named various townships as having raised money for improvements, but the fact that individuals and good roads enthusiasts had raised $5,000 in Racine County and that the Racine Motor Club volunteered to keep their portion of Sheridan Road maintained, shows us that responsibility for roads was not expected of local governments.

By the time the Yellowstone Trail Association put its signs on Sheridan Road, there was already an active Sheridan Road Association in Milwaukee County facing the problems with Somers and Pleasant Prairie townships to the south. Ray Smith, president of the Milwaukee organization (and future president of the Yellowstone Trail Association in 1921-1922) held a meeting in Chicago with Sheridan Road enthusiasts to address the Wisconsin townships' problem. The July 29, 1915, Kenosha *Telegraph-Courier*, noted that representatives of Somers and Pleasant Prairie townships in Kenosha County did not attend.

In late 1915, to circumvent the state law which prohibited "forcing" road improvements, the Kenosha Automobile Club offered to give money to the two townships if they raised an equal amount, and if the boards voted to accept the gift. ⇨

KENOSHA NEXT- NEW ROAD SLOGAN
BIG GATHERING OF ROAD EXPERTS IN MILWAUKEE ON SATURDAY PLAN WORK SOON SHERIDAN ROAD MILWAUKEE TO BE FIRST TO HAVE CONCRETE HIGHWAY ALONG OLD ROAD.
December 2, 1915 Telegraph-Courier (Kenosha, Wisconsin)

The idea was promulgated by A. R. Hirst, chief engineer of the Wisconsin Highway Commission. This differed from state aid, presumably, because many other stipulations were avoided. The auto club planned to raise the money by garnering "a couple of hundred" new members of the Sheridan Road Association. President of the Kenosha Auto Club, Dan Head, gave a realistic prediction, reported in the October 28, 1915, Kenosha *Telegraph-Courier*: "These contributions will relieve the towns of just that much expense, as every town board knows that, sooner or later, this permanently improved road must be built."

In late November, 1915, the Milwaukee County portion of the Sheridan Road was completely concreted, and, to much fanfare, ribbon cutting, and banqueting, the road was declared open. Apparently Racine County had promised to proceed apace because the cry at the party was "Kenosha next!" The Kenosha *Telegraph-Courier* of December 2, 1915, said,

> It is expected that $15,000 will be spent on the Sheridan Road in the town of Pleasant Prairie. If the town officials will be able to aid, it is probable that a considerable sum will be raised by subscription for the building of the road.

We see, once again, individual citizens taking responsibility for this "almost impassable" road.

More hoopla was to come a year later. Sept. 26, 1916, saw a large meeting of Sheridan Road Association enthusiasts at the state line. Their point was to raise a ruckus and pressure politicians to move forward on road improvement. Wisconsin's Governor E. L. Philipp and Illinois Congressman George Foss spoke, the songs "On Wisconsin" and "Illinois-Illinois" were played. "Moving picture machines were clicking along." Interstate schmoozing galore. The group then drove to the cities of Kenosha and Racine, in the two counties with the most road work still left to be done. Officials, swept away by the moment, promised that "nothing would be left undone to promote the highway."

SHERIDAN RD BUMPED IN SOMERS
VOTERS OF THAT TOWN TURN DOWN PROPOSITION TO ISSUE BONDS BY NARROW MARGIN OF FIVE VOTES
September 7, 1916 Telegraph-Courier (Kenosha, Wisconsin)

However, Somers township voted down a proposed bond issue. Pleasant Prairie township passed a $45,000 bond issue with the understanding that the county would issue a like

amount and the state is expected to contribute $30,000. At last! State aid is apparent. Road boosters declared that they would again pass the hat to help Somers township.

Finally, the Federal Aid Act of 1916 was approved by the Wisconsin legislature in 1917. It took an act of the federal government to finally solve the problem. However, the authors cannot find an official map of the state trunk highway system of Wisconsin from 1918 to 1923 that shows Sheridan Road fully concreted from Milwaukee to the Illinois border. Did it really take six years more to complete the project?

Wisconsin Motorist magazine declared in March, 1919, that six thousand tourists were put through Wisconsin during 1918, according to the Yellowstone Trail Association. "A greater number would have passed through the Badger state if the condition of Sheridan Road between Milwaukee and Chicago had been more favorable to transcontinental automobile travel." ⇨

Sheridan Road in orange

Continued

And Then There was Zion

The saga of Zion, Illinois, was similar to that of Kenosha County in that persuasion and foresight about roads did not prevail. Zion City, as it was originally called, was founded by a religious zealot and faith healer, John A. Dowie. The community, industries, and institutions revolved around his Christian Catholic Apostolic Church. He was called the "dictator of Zion." He had argued that if an interstate road was wanted, Wisconsin could pay for it. Meanwhile, Dowie began calling himself Elijah, preaching that the Earth was flat, and building a huge tabernacle, a 25-room mansion and a Chicago townhouse all paid for by his believers world-wide. Upon his death in 1907, Wilbur Glenn Voliva took over. He began the years-long task of getting the group out of bankruptcy. Unfortunately, he carried on the strict discipline established by Dowie, allowing no freedom of thought, "hacking" elections and, again, bleeding the parishioners, and amassing a personal fortune of $5 million. He asked Milwaukee, Racine, and Kenosha counties to launch a drive in 1920 if they wanted a road. Then he came up with $90,000 and said he would pave one-half of a mile in downtown Zion City, but somebody else would have to build the rest. Apparently, that "somebody" was the county and state of Illinois, wresting away local power.

In Illinois, the route was first shown on official maps in 1924. In 1925, Route 42 was realigned to include all of Sheridan Road in Illinois; the route continued south to the Indiana border at Hammond. Sheridan Road was marked as Route 42 until the highway was removed from the state highway system in 1972.

By 1929 Sheridan Road and all of the Yellowstone Trail in the two states were concreted. After World War II, in honor of the famous 32nd Wisconsin Infantry "Red Arrow" Division, the road from the state line north to near Sheboygan was re-numbered WI 32. Today one can still find Sheridan Road so named along WI 32 from the Illinois border north through Pleasant Prairie township near Kenosha and on north to downtown Racine where the name Sheridan Road stops and Racine St. begins. There is a Sheridan Avenue in Milwaukee.

The completion of Sheridan Road marked a momentous occasion for the Yellowstone Trail. A good road now existed from Milwaukee to Chicago. Besides becoming a main thoroughfare for the transport of goods and services, the Yellowstone Trail and its supporting businesses on Sheridan Road also benefited from its development, opening southeast Wisconsin to Trail promotions. ✿

The Draft Dodgers of Withee

The entrance into World War I placed a pall upon our country which subsumed thoughts of travel. Gasoline was not rationed as it was in World War II, but the numbers of travelers was down. The Yellowstone Trail Association did not produce their famous *Route Folder* for 1918.

When the United States entered World War I in 1917, neutrality faded and outward shows of patriotic fervor commenced. Congress amended the Espionage Act in May, 1918, widely broadening the definition of espionage to include uttering disloyal language against the government, showing disrespect for the flag and evading the draft. Disloyal language was very broadly defined and brought fines of thousands of dollars and a jail term. Draft evasion only resulted in immediate induction. Pro-war hysteria was just as fervent in Wisconsin as elsewhere, despite Wisconsin Sen. Robert LaFollette voting against it. Wisconsin had a large German population. Some of the best Milwaukee breweries were owned by German families. German was spoken fluently and in some schools, English was taught as a second language. Some churches held two services Sunday mornings - one conducted in German and one in English. Tensions were higher than need be. Neighbors became close-mouthed.

In Withee, Louis and Leslie Krueger registered for the draft. Brother Frank was too old and Ennis too young. Neither claimed conscientious objector on the form, but both were influenced by their mother's strong religious view that war was wrong. She had preached that to her boys from little on. A new draft law was enacted which broadened the age category. Ennis at 19 and Frank at 37 were now eligible. They did not register and, thus, became draft dodgers.

In September, 1918, (two months before the war ended) a U.S. Marshall, armed with a posse of disorganized, angry locals and police, came to arrest the boys. Apparently no one in the posse knew what to do and a display of random shooting resulted from this apparently leaderless mob. They fired first with three boys answering with fire from the barn. Much gunfire ensued, resulting in the death of one officer, the capture of Caroline Krueger, the boys' mother, and the wounding of Frank. Louis had fled west before the shoot-out. Ennis and Leslie escaped, but Ennis was supposedly shot by officers

The posse at the Krueger Farm near Withee

days later and Leslie was captured in Minnesota the next month. Mystery surrounded a body which may or may not have been Ennis. Sixteen years later Frank and Leslie, who had been incarcerated for "mental illness," were set free and were eventually reunited with Louis and Caroline back at the Withee farm, or what was left of it, just south of Withee.

The home still stands (with bullet holes extant in 1998 from the shoot-out). Jerry Buss has written a meticulously researched and fascinating book about this complicated case, titled *A War of Their Own* (Badger Books, 1998) from which the above information was taken. He leaves no doubt that the entire event could have been better managed with much less bloodshed. The shock to Buss was that even in 1998 when he sought information about the case from the Justice Department, the FBI would not release the full story, and he asks, "Why? After 80 years, why?" ✿

Brownie's Call of the Open Road

with contributions by Ben Johnson

"Brownie" was not a frog. He was a newspaperman. However, the drawings accompanying all of his writings did feature a frog with a driving hat, goggles, a pipe, and, often, an upside down triangle. William Wallace Roland picked up the moniker "Brownie" as a *Milwaukee Journal* mail boy at age 12. He became a fantastic auto pathfinder for Wisconsin. He popularized those routes by writing a column for the *Milwaukee Journal* newspaper from 1915. Brownie became the official word, the very last word, in auto travel and road conditions in Wisconsin. He mapped and then popularized routes throughout Wisconsin.

Iconic Brownie caricatures appeared on all of Roland's writings.

But before that, William Wallace "Brownie" Roland was a sportswriter for the *Journal*. In 1901 he developed a belief in the automobile as the way of the future and he drove some of the first newfangled machines seen on the streets of Milwaukee and environs. Sometime before 1915 he began writing an automotive column each Sunday for the *Journal* based upon his weekend discoveries of road conditions, good and bad, and his map-making. Soon he was regarded as a pathfinder for "sociability runs" which were social gatherings of auto owners who all drove to a destination for fun and to show off the new black beauty.

The *Journal* recognized a good thing and ordered Brownie in 1916 to "get out there and give the people directions they need." And he did, writing his humorous Sunday automobile touring column for 25 years. Soon he realized that the *Blue Book* directions of "turn left at the red barn" were not good enough because red barns got painted or the barn disappeared altogether. So Brownie had

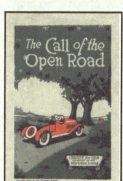

Cover of Brownie's 1918 booklet

hundreds of wooden signs painted with "Milwaukee Journal Route to [city name]" and a large arrow pointing in the direction of that town. These he would nail to trees.

The Call of the Open Road guide booklet came out in 1916. It was a collection of his Sunday column maps and advice. The introduction stated Brownie's purpose: "This collection of road maps would be of real benefit to motorists generally, and motorists in and about Milwaukee

particularly." For the next 17 years that remained paramount in his annual guides - to be of help. By providing markers and guides, navigator Brownie did just that. He was out in the state directing the blazing of trails through the woods and marking directions. All this while he loudly plumped for numbered highways.

Brownie's trips produced an interesting narrative in his writings. The characters and actions had two levels of meaning: 1) discovering new routes and mapping existing roads for a driving audience; 2) showing how bad most roads were to encourage public arousal and action.

Brownie didn't travel alone. Long-suffering sidekick, W.T "Poor Cuss" Cuddy, traveled the thousands of Wisconsin miles with Brownie. Poor Cuss was Brownie's "everyman" in his writings, some of which he wrote in the voice of the Poor Cuss. They traveled in autos loaned to them by auto agencies for the advertising fame. How many miles did they travel? Hard to estimate, but it would probably be in the hundreds of thousands in Wisconsin and neighboring states. In the beginning it was just weekends, then they were gone for 30 days on some trips, Brownie telephoning in his weekly articles. In 1923 he traveled 32,000 miles, mostly in Wisconsin. Poor Cuss once joked about a forthcoming trip of 7,000 miles saying, "More mud to shovel."

"Brownie" and "The Poor Cuss" at the start of a 10,000 mile inspection tour of Wisconsin highways
Concrete Highway Magazine (1925)

The meteoric growth in popularity of the free *Call of the Open Road* guides led to the establishment of the "Milwaukee Journal Tour Club" in 1920, staffed and located in the lobby of the Journal building. Folks who paid their 50¢ membership for a Tour Club Kit (later it was $1.00 or $1.10 if ⇨

Milwaukee Journal Tour Club Membership Card, 1928
Florence Ridge Collection

An embossed car emblem
Harvey Ridge Collection

mailed) received a copy of the latest *Call of the Open Road*, route maps, and an embossed car emblem to hang on the car's radiator. In 1930 you also got trip maps, a sectional map for a 100 mile radius of Milwaukee, road logs, and a one-page Wisconsin map with all roads eliminated except main roads to eliminate confusion. In 1929 some auto dealers were giving away Tour Club Kits to their customers.

Throughout the Roaring Twenties his pamphlets and its maps were a standard reference for 20,000 intrepid member drivers in 1923, and 30,000 in 1924 from 43 states. The Journal Tour Club staff answered more than 200,000 inquiries for tour information in 1924. By June of 1925 "the annual *Call of the Open Road* sold to the extent of 85,000" averred Brownie in *Concrete Highway* magazine of that year. In 1929, 30,000 signed up for membership, including members in six foreign countries.

The thing that got Brownie's goat was speed traps which he thought were just unfair for the average driver. There were no uniform speed limits, but some cities set them at 8 miles per hour and some counties at 25 miles per hour in rural areas. "These are foolish and everyone cheerfully ignores them. As long as the motor cop is paid by the number of tickets he issues, speed traps will exist. Speed traps are less than useless. They only give a town a bad name," wrote Brownie. His solution was education of the driver and more realistic speed limits. He railed on this topic in his invited speeches around the state.

Sometime before 1929 a weekly radio program, the Journal Tour Club Ramblers, was heard on Sunday nights at 7:15 to 8:15 on WTMJ. It was an aggregation of merrymakers, Russ

Winnie, Jack Turner, and Bill Benning, and a 16-piece band who made musical jaunts to Wisconsin towns on a mythical bus.

The Club lasted until 1933 by which time the state had numbered highways and had issued its own official maps and information for 15 years.

Much credit is given to Brownie's influence in the state adoption of a numbered highway system in 1918, the first in the nation. He had maintained close contact with the Wisconsin Highway Commission and local road authorities,

Wisconsin Hwy Commission adopted Brownie's famous "upside down" triangle signature for its new 1918 road signage.

so is it a coincidence that the first road numbers issued by the Wisconsin Highway Department were displayed on roads in an already-recognized upside down triangle? We think not.

The *Milwaukee Journal* was his podium and Wisconsin and beyond was his beat. When

he died in 1944 there were many encomia written, the best being, "He meant so much in the lives of so many persons that no one can put his portrait in words that will be fervent enough for all who knew him."

Brownie may have been from Wisconsin, but his travels and club alerted the whole nation to highway needs and action. ✿

Frank Cannon Discredits the Trail

with contributions by Erica Shrader

Not everyone was pleased with the idea of private organizations influencing county boards to build roads, and charging fees to towns and individuals for advertising. Some folks felt that a national trail could be a "sometime thing," moving the route on a whim and subverting state efforts. Frank Cannon of Wisconsin was one of them.

The Good Roads Association-Wisconsin had an over-eager secretary who regularly used that association's newsletter as his "bully pulpit" to disparage the very existence of the Yellowstone Trail Association. Francis (Frank) Cannon viewed the Yellowstone Trail Association as the enemy of the State Highway Commission and the state's new highway numbering system, even though the Commission allowed the Trail to exist.

The nation-wide Good Roads Association and the Yellowstone Trail Association sought the same ends: better roads for autoists and tourists. They worked from different premises, but the two national organizations were friends. That is, everywhere but in Wisconsin. The Trail Association worked

Frank Cannon, Secretary, Good Roads Wisconsin

from the premise that, since governments were not doing much for roads, private organizations should, and they should boost tourism. The Good Roads Association in Wisconsin, in the person of its Executive Secretary, Frank Cannon, chose to lobby the State Highway Commission for better roads. Two paths to the same end. Both saw the need for connected roads. Wisconsin in 1916 had 4,000 miles of highway - in 3,000 pieces. But Cannon chose to excoriate the Yellowstone Trail Association at every turn in the *Good Roads for Wisconsin* magazine. He also carried on a terrific arraignment against the Townsend Bill which sought a national highways system, saying that that system would "demoralize state highway efforts." So, did Cannon hate the Yellowstone Trail Association because he believed in the autonomy of the state? Most likely.

The two organizations were more alike than not. The Good Roads Association charged a membership fee as did the Yellowstone Trail Association. Apparently, Cannon was paid by the membership dues as was the Yellowstone Trail Association General Manager, Hal Cooley. Cannon ⇨

was not elected to any office, did not speak with any authority other than that from the private organization he represented. Same with Cooley. If Cannon claimed to speak "for the Wisconsin Highway Commission" it was only through his own imagination.

Frank Cannon's problem with the Yellowstone group was not personal. He hated *all* trail organizations. He averred that anything related to highways should be the sole responsibility of the Wisconsin Highway Commission. He used a wide brush to paint all trail groups as crooks, but he specialized in the Yellowstone Trail Association, bashing it relentlessly for about nine years. From the get-go, when the Good Roads Association was formed in Wisconsin in 1915 and the Yellowstone Trail had arrived in the state, Cannon was on the Trail Association's case.

Some of his arguments did accurately describe scoundrel trail groups who preyed upon the public, who made promises, collected money, and disappeared. Cannon also said organizers routed trails to the highest-bidding town. Neither argument was true of the Yellowstone Trail Association.

Cannon's diatribes all appeared in his *Good Roads for Wisconsin* magazine. Since none of Cooley's answers were printed in Cannon's magazine, his responses appeared in many newspapers, speeches, and Yellowstone Trail Association releases and are paraphrased here.

Hal Cooley of the YTA
*Jane Vinger,
granddaughter*

■ Cannon: It is fundamentally wrong to lay out a road between any two points and determine its layout by the willingness of the cities between the two points to 'come across' in a financial way.

Cooley: The Yellowstone Trail in Wisconsin was laid out by a Minnesota group before the Yellowstone Trail Association arrived to promote it. Of course, a road would be laid out according to population centers. Cannon had it backwards. The route was laid out first, *then* towns were approached for membership.

■Cannon: Any trail association is doomed to failure because town or county units, those units approached by trail groups, are interested in looking after local needs. Trail groups in Waukesha and Kenosha, for example, have failed to make north-south road progress because those counties want to build east-west local roads and only the state had the power to control county plans.

Cooley: This is exactly what the Yellowstone Trail Association is all about, getting people to see the need to lengthen and join roads, forming a route. [Note: At the time of this argument, 1917, the Yellowstone Trail Association had been in the state for two years and had attracted much attention because of the idea of connectedness, an idea the state had not yet publicly embraced.]

■ Cannon: The Yellowstone Trail is popular, thus higher maintenance is needed for which the state must pay.

Cooley: Exactly! That was what the Trail Association hoped for. By providing more traffic and demanding more maintenance, the Trail would benefit all. Cannon forgot that Wisconsin resident taxpayers also used the Trail and Wisconsin businesses benefitted from the tourists. The Trail is the popular route but there is no reason for its being the popular route except for the work of the Yellowstone Trail Association. The road is somewhat better but that goodness has been caused by the fact of the density of travel it carries during which time the Yellowstone Trail Association has been making its program of selling and directing travel. The communities on the Yellowstone Trail are well satisfied with their investment.

■ Cannon: Their route ushered people *through* the state not *to* state destinations.

This thought troubled Joe Parmley 100 years ago. How do you get people to act locally and think globally (to use a current phrase)? He felt that once people saw tourists coming and using local garages, hotels, restaurants, and campsites, local folks would broaden their horizons some and realize that these guests had come from *somewhere else* to *their* town. If there was a tourist attraction in that town, a connected road was needed to deliver the tourist. If the tourist was on his way to another site, he passed through that town on his way, dropping his tourist dollars as he went.

The *Hudson Star-Observer* (Wisconsin) August 6, 1920, headlined "Yellowstone Trail is Agency for Wide Thought on Highways." The article pointed out that,

> The Yellowstone Trail Association gives the value of national thought. Motor transportation is changing a man's thought from interest in his local road to interest in travel and roads in the next county or even the next state, over which he exercises no control. This brings about state and national thought as applied to highways. The Yellowstone Trail Association offers an agency through which this national thought can be expressed and by which wise public policy can be applied. The people in the east can learn of the methods of people in the west and can unify their efforts so that it becomes an agency for constructive thought on a national basis. This alone justifies the existence of the Yellowstone Trail Association.

[Note: This article and others of the *Star-Observer* are reprints of earlier Association press releases that had been circulating throughout seven states for at least six years; repetition apparently was another way to get people to think globally.]

■ Cannon: The Yellowstone Trail Association does not build roads nor repair them.

Cooley: The Yellowstone Trail Association never claimed that it did. The Good Roads Association also does not build nor repair roads.

■ Cannon: People who pay taxes should not have to pay a private organization for road improvement.

Cooley: Cannon travels the state gathering memberships for the Good Roads Association. Were the members not paying this lobbyist organization to influence highway improvement? If not, what were Good Roads memberships buying?

■ Cannon: Trail organizations take credit for expenditures made by state governments on highways, expenditures which would have occurred without trail makers even existing.

Cooley: We take credit for prodding governments into building or maintaining a road and we publish the expense incurred through our persuasion, without which the maintenance would not have occurred. Yes, they published road-creation and maintenance figures along the Yellowstone Trail, but it was to celebrate their sweat-equity successes and to report to the present and potential membership. They did not claim that the Yellowstone Trail Association itself spent that money on a road. The existence of the Yellowstone Trail in Wisconsin laid the foundation for the idea of connected highways. By persuading counties to connect roads to each other to form a longer road, people could see the advantage of such a system. That idea preceded the state highway commission's actions by three years. This occurred in state after state along the Trail. Then the Association had to maintain vigilance to push for road maintenance on the county level. This was done through local Trailmen who leaned on county boards to effect the repairs. This was carried on before the state's idea of Patrolmen appeared.

H. O. COOLEY WRITES
TO FRANK CANNON
SUGGESTS A RUNNING DEBATE FROM
HUDSON ACROSS THE STATE
Jan 21, 1922 Eau Claire (Wisconsin) Leader

In January, 1922, Cooley challenged Cannon to a series of public debates to be held in various towns along the Yellowstone Trail in Wisconsin. Cooley even offered to pay Cannon's travel expenses. Cannon did not respond. Cooley took the high ground in his written and oral rebuttals, saying that his Association never had a quarrel with the Wisconsin Highway Commission or the Good Roads Association, and never met such vehement opposition in any of the other 12 states through which the Trail ran. He iterated that the Yellowstone Trail Association applauded all efforts at road improvement. He argued in the Stevens Point, Wisconsin *Gazette* September 21, 1921, that "to deny a community the right to join private efforts is to deny any communities the right to do something for themselves" and "... by encouraging travel on a certain road that is interstate in character and by succeeding, the Yellowstone Trail Association has insured that the road gets better maintenance. Is that not a good investment for communities on that road?"

In 1918, Wisconsin became the first state government in the United States to number its highways, mark each state highway with that number, and publish road maps showing those numbers. The Wisconsin Highway Commission and Cannon were anxious to clear all state and county roadsides of trail markers, leaving only official state road numbers

and directions. But State Highway Commission reports for the years 1918 to 1923 reveal a confusing picture. All signs of smaller trails were ordered removed in 1918, but not the Yellowstone Trail's signs. A 1919 *Rand McNally* map shows the Yellowstone Trail as the only marked trail in the state. In 1921 a proposed road-marking Bill would have removed Yellowstone Trail signs. After a blitz of letters to legislators, the Bill was amended to exclude the famous yellow and black markers. The highway commissioners muttered at their 1921 and 1923 meetings that "trails ought to be discouraged" but no action was taken and the 1923 *Rand McNally* map still noted the Trail in Wisconsin.

After 1924 Cannon's vitriolic writings and the marking issue faded. Perhaps his view about trails was tempered by, ironically, his membership in a trail organization - the National Parks Highway Association. Or his interest may have shifted as the federal government entered the scene beginning in 1925, clouding his defense of the "autonomy of the state." The newly formed American Association of State Highway Officials (AASHO) and federal highway officials met to create national route numbers. The process took two years until federal road numbers went up on state trunk highways in 1927. The Yellowstone Trail signs themselves began to disappear in the late 1920s, not by decree but by kids using the famous metal markers for target practice and by farmers mending holes in their barns with them. ✿

COOLEY ATTACKS
FRANK A. CANNON
IN ROAD DEBATE

Accuses Wisconsin Good Roads Man of Knocking Yellow-stone Trail

In a leter to the Journal, H. O. Cooley, general manager of the Yellowstone Trail association, sharply arraigns F. A. Cannon, secretary of the Wisconsin Good Roads association, for alleged malicious statements regarding the Yellowstone Trail.

Both men were recent speakers here, Mr. Cannon at a Chamber of Commerce dinner at the Parish house and Mr. Cooley at the Strand theater.

Source unknown

Winthrop Harbor
Zion
Beach Park
Waukegan
North Chicago
Lake Bluff
Lake Forest
Fort Sheridan
Highland Park
Glencoe
Winnetka
Kenilworth
Wilmette
Evanston
Chicago
South Chicago

Illinois

WHAT THE TRAIL FOUNDERS SAID-1921

The state of Illinois is developing a marked system of trunkline highways and, while at the time of this writing the marking system has not been developed to an extent where the traveler can be guided by it alone, it will be found to be of great help. It passes right through the city of Chicago.

Travel in Illinois depends very largely upon the weather conditions, it being difficult and very wet weather. Road conditions are rapidly getting better as the roads are being constructed and better drained.

It is not difficult to find one's way by automobile either into or out of Chicago. The route of the Yellowstone Trail through Chicago is comparatively simple, although the Association has not been able to secure permission to place its marks through the city.

1921 Yellowstone Trail Touring Service Map #11 of Illinois

State Street, Chicago
National Archives
#30-N-34126

INTRODUCING THE YELLOWSTONE TRAIL IN ILLINOIS:
LAND OF LINCOLN

"Thanks to the Interstate highway system, it is now possible to travel from coast to coast without seeing anything."
Charles Kuralt

The 1915 list of duties demanded of the Chief Highway Engineer and staff of the Illinois State Highway Department reveals a wide scope including advanced knowledge and use of state aid, even used wholly for some highways and bridges. The western states which carried the Yellowstone Trail were still grappling with the availability of such aid while Illinois was already pouring concrete in Chicago. To be fair, western Trail states had fewer taxpayers and more miles to cover. Also, other parts of Illinois had as much mud as South Dakota on its roads.

Joy ride in Illinois

Chicago was certainly a transportation hub from early on. Railroad yards, stock yards, Lake Michigan shipping docks and wagon roads all contributed to making that city a thriving "toddling town" according to Frank Sinatra. But the addition of a national auto route was probably of less importance than almost anywhere else.

The Yellowstone Trail saw little of the prairie immortalized by Carl Sandburg's poetry. It did see Frank Lloyd Wright's "prairie style" architecture in the northern suburbs. From Wisconsin to Indiana, the Trail occupied fewer than 100 Illinois miles. And those miles were, generally, either through urban areas or hugging Lake Michigan, not out in the prairie. Little interest was shown by Chicagoans in yet another

> Under the provisions of the law enacted in 1905, state highway work in Illinois is in the hands of a State Highway Department composed of the three members of the State Highway Commission, the Chief State Highway Engineer, the Assistant State Highway Engineer and various subordinates. The law passed in 1913 provided for the appointment of the three members for two, four, and six year terms. Each must be a competent civil engineer and experienced in highway construction and maintenance.
>
> *August 7, 1915 Good Roads: Illinois*

trail when the Chicago Motor Club had already mapped 12 major routes in and out of the city by 1920. However, the Yellowstone Trail Association pursued, marked its route and established a successful Bureau at 215 W. Washington St. in Chicago. Their bureaus operated like the AAA today, only a traveler did not have to be a member of the Trail Association to receive free maps, guides, and weather and road information.

> At the coming general election the people of Illinois are to vote their approval for the issuing of $60,000,000 of bonds for the building of hard surface roads that shall cover the state in all directions - roads that once built, will stay built. When interviewed, Governor Lowden cautioned:
>
> "If the war is still on when the bonds are voted on in the fall, I wouldn't think of marketing those bonds immediately. You wouldn't get the labor without paying prohibitive prices and you wouldn't get the materials without paying prohibitive prices. ... But most economists predict a very serious depression when our troops are released from the trenches and come back home. Men will be available and with the cessation of all these multiform activities which have come as a result of the war, many men will be thrown out of employment. You would not only build roads cheaper, you would hold things steady, furnishing employment."
>
> *September 1, 1918 Western Magazine*
>
> Note: We wonder if the bond issue passed. Look at the date. World War I ended 2 ½ months later. Did Governor Lowden's prediction come true? Roads were and still are often held hostage by crises or perceived crises by lawmakers.

Why Did the Yellowstone Trail Go Where it Went in Illinois

There was not much choice for the Yellowstone Trail Association! Starting from the state line just south of Kenosha, Wisconsin, and proceeding east as soon as possible, what choice did they have? Hug Lake Michigan, go south and around it to Indiana. Just pick the best, most used roads to and through Chicago!

One of the best roads was Sheridan Road south from Wisconsin to mid-Chicago. Sheridan Road, based on an old Indian trail, was the eastern-most route between Wisconsin and Illinois, running along the shore of Lake Michigan. It was the best available route between Kenosha and Chicago. It was named for Civil War Union General Philip Sheridan, as was also a fort just north of Chicago. Before the Yellowstone Trail arrived in 1915, Sheridan Road had a booster Association in Milwaukee which was active in efforts to get that road improved because it was a busy thoroughfare. Two townships curtailed that effort in Wisconsin in a day when there was no way to force a township to cough up matching funds, and there was no state trunk highway system yet.

⇨

IL

Early road making in Illinois

NEW TOURING BUREAU
The Yellowstone Trail Association has opened a new loop touring bureau at 215 West Washington St. with A.L. Slade in charge. Maps and reports covering not only the popular northwest trail, but national highways generally, are available free of charge in the new bureau.
June 19, 1921 Chicago Daily Tribune

In Illinois, a similar interruption of the Sheridan Road's progress occurred in Zion. Two states, three counties, and two trail associations could not budge the city of Zion to improve their portion of Sheridan Road. See **Trail Tale: Sheridan Road**, page 284, for the trials and tribulations of that road funding.

Enjoy your ride south from the Wisconsin border to Chicago. Enjoy the Jack Benny Center in Waukegan if you remember his radio and television programs. The past several generations never heard of him. Are you a navy vet? Enjoy the Great Lakes Naval Museum in North Chicago. Highland Park has several homes by Frank Lloyd Wright. See the lovely homes in Wilmette and Evanston. Apparently, the lovely home in the film "Home Alone" was located in Evanston which is also the home town of the Women's Christian Temperance Union (WCTU).

Following the Trail through Chicago can be a challenge. Obviously, a large city does not stand still for 100 years. There is very little to remind the driver of the Trail what with Interstate highways and various Throughways and Expressways. No time to ponder. We mapped the Trail through Chicago several times early on Sunday mornings, before the city was fully awake.

The Open Road. Where one is free to drive at will. Where a scene can be surveyed and a picture taken while standing on the road without fear of losing life or limb. Where driving at 20 miles an hour bothers no one. Well, the Yellowstone Trail in Illinois didn't then/ doesn't now quite make it.

But there is history to be seen, some beaches to be enjoyed, beautiful homes to be envied, several world renowned museums to learn from, some incredible architecture to appreciate, and lots of "things to do." If you are following the Trail for a "sense of accomplishment," head out on a Sunday morning with your maps and you may find it. The Trail follows no Interstate here and few high speed routes. Expect the Chicago area to consume nearly a full day. At the end of that day you will have a sense of having "done it."

Or, plan for an "exploration" that allows time to think about what you are seeing. Imagine transportation in this area in 1920. How have the various areas around the Trail developed over the years? How did people get to work?

If the city is intimidating or if time is of the essence, just take the expressways and avoid the city, but you are missing the heart of the Yellowstone Trail. ❀

The magnetic truck

USE MAGNETS ON HARD ROADS
More than 600 pounds of nails, tacks, bolts and pieces of scrap iron were removed from a seven mile stretch of the Yellowstone Trail in Illinois, affording motorists great saving and relief as the puncture hazard was eliminated. The truck was driven back and forth, the magnet positioned four inches above the surface of the roadway and supplied with current from 72 cells of the locomotive storage type, lifting jagged bits of metal from the loose stone covering with ease. Many of them were so small that persons walking slowly along the road could not see them.
1926 Science Magazine Vol. 64

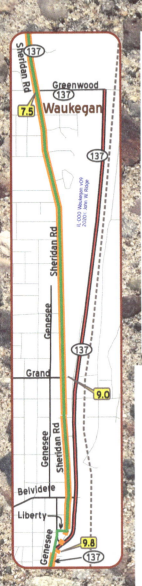

Zion Home, on Elijah Ave., a gray frame, block-long building erected in 1904, serves as a hotel and divine healing home. A ground-floor porch extends along the entire front exposure. Zion Home, the only available eating place on Sunday, strictly observes the ban on oysters, clams, and "swine's flesh," offering for the latter a substitute called "Zion beef bacon." The square, gray frame Zion Administration Building, across the street from the Home, houses the offices of Zion Industries, Inc., and serves as the general administrative quarters for the town. WPA-IL ✿

Beatrice Larned Massey, in a 1919 memoir entitled *It Might Have Been Worse: A Motor Trip From Coast to Coast*, described her drive through Zion thus:

Driving down its main street was like a funeral. The houses were closed, the buildings seemed deserted and the only evidences of life were two men, a horse, a stray dog and a wagon. ✿

Home of Zion founder, John Dowie

WAYSIDE

IL-003.0 Illinois State Beach Park makes six miles of Lake Michigan beach available to the visitor. No doubt travelers on nearby Sheridan Road (Yellowstone Trail) viewed the lake and perhaps frolicked on that beach 100 years ago.

HISTORY BITS

MILE-BY-MILE

IL 000.0 Wisconsin/Illinois Line
IL-000.9 Winthrop Harbor

is located midway between Waukegan and Kenosha, directly upon the famous Sheridan road. It has a splendid shore line and is surrounded by wooded plateaus, bluffs and picturesque ravines. Here, are located, among other industries, the Winthers Motor Co. and the Linga Carburetor Co. The town is served by the C. & N. W. and the C. & M. electric road. BB1921-10

(598 alt, 661 pop.), grew out of the acquisition in 1892 of 2,700 acres of dairy farm land by the Winthrop Harbor and Dock Company, which planned to develop a harbor and establish an industrial town. With the collapse of the plan, dairying continued as the chief occupation of the community, and today its sole industrial plant is an ultra-modern dairy near the North Western station. WPA-IL

IL-003.2 Zion

(pop. 5,000, alt. 938 ft.) is the seat of the singular religious community founded by John Alexander Dowie in 1900, 6,000 acres being purchased by him here at that time. The principal industrial feature of this town is the Zion lace manufactory, which was conceived and founded by Dowie, he being the first man to import a general line of lace machines and skilled lace weavers and designers from England into the United States. The industry was purchased by Marshall Field & Co., of Chicago, several years ago, and they have since greatly enlarged the plant until it is now the greatest and largest of its kind in the world. Zion City has three fine parks. Beulah park, one mile north of the city, on Sheridan road, is one of the most beautiful wooded ravines between Chicago and Milwaukee. BB1921-10

(633 alt., 5,991 pop.) Zion was founded by a man who believed the world to be flat despite his having taken a trip around it. The town enforces one of the most stringent sets of blue laws in the country. WPA-IL

In 1899 Chicago real estate offices were buzzing with rumors of a big land deal on the North Shore. On the night that marked the end of the nineteenth century, the man behind the deal revealed himself as John Alexander Dowie (1847-1907), Scottish faith-healer who, four years before, had founded the Christian Catholic Apostolic Church. He announced his plan for the city of Zion, a community where the tenets of that church would govern every phase of life. "Our motto," affirmed Dowie, "the unalterable and unassailable truth that where God rules, man prospers … our object, the establishment of the rule of God in every department of the government."

Zion had not, until recently, modified the essential structure of theocratic government. The church owned all industries and commercial establishments but one. The use and sale of liquor, tobacco, playing cards, oysters, pork, and clams are prohibited. No trains stopped in Zion on Sunday. In

The route of the Yellowstone Trail was also known as Sheridan Road. Sheridan Road extended many miles south into Chicago. To read more, see **Trail Tale: Sheridan Road**, page 284.

IL-005.1 Beach

IL-009.0 Waukegan

(pop. 16,069, alt. 596 ft.), is located on Lake Michigan, 35 miles northwest of Chicago and 48 miles south of Milwaukee. Waukegan and North Chicago, in all except municipal administration, are one community, and the center of activity for the large number of naval training station men off duty. The harbor is used as a home port for many of the gun and training boats under command of the Great Lakes naval training station, which immediately adjoins the community. There are many beautiful ravines hereabout which are rapidly being bought up and improved by the Waukegan park board for the benefit of the public. BB1921-10

The shops and residences of Waukegan are on a bluff overlooking Lake Michigan. The lowlands between the base of the bluff and the waterline of the city harbor are jammed with factories that back the piers and railroads. Here are produced gas, tool steel, locks, chemicals, machinery, sausage, babbitt, envelopes, asbestos products, outboard motors, refrigerating units, ornamental and industrial steel fences, ignition contacts, and pharmaceuticals. Coal, coke, and raw materials comprise the bulk of the cargoes landed at Waukegan. WPA-IL

Lincoln spoke at Waukegan in 1860. Jack Benny was born here 39 years ago. [Note: Jack Benny fans would get the joke.]

1917 N Sheridan Rd. (Yellowstone Trail). **Waukegan History Museum** is in the 1843 home of former Chicago mayor, John C. Haines. Exhibits, photographs, and artifacts tell the history of Waukegan. Among the most noted objects is the bed that Lincoln slept in when visiting Waukegan.

1800 N Sheridan Ave. **Jack Benny Center for the Arts** in Bowen Park. It is possible that Jack Benny knew the Yellowstone Trail because when the Trail arrived in Waukegan about 1915, Jack was 21 and forming various performing groups before moving on to fame and fortune with comedy and a violin.

203 N Genesee St. **Genesee Theatre**, 1927. As it is one block west of Sheridan Rd., it may have been visited by Trail travelers. Recently renovated for $23 million, it now hosts Broadway shows, comedians, and more.

Between IL-009.5 and IL-007.5, IL 137 follows a newer multi-lane road while the YT followed Sheridan Rd. At the south end of this stretch, for three blocks, follow Liberty and Genessee to detour around the closed old route.

1939 Wilbur Voliva, Dowie's successor, lost his control as overseer; titles to real estate were being transferred to individuals; other modifications of the theocratic government and managed economy seemed imminent. WPA-IL

Left on this road is the entrance to Dunes Park (adm. 10c), 0.5 m., 1,500 acres of duneland along three and a half miles of beach. This typical dune region, with pine and oak woods, cactus, juniper, and bearberry clinging to windblown sandhills, has been kept in its natural state. WPA-IL

1300 Shiloh Blvd. **Shiloh House**. An elegant 25 room mansion built at the turn of the 20th century by Zion's founder, Rev. Alexander Dowie. Now it is owned by the Zion Historical Society.

IL

IL-011.7 North Chicago

(673 alt., 8,466 pop.), North Chicago and Waukegan constitute a continuous industrial area with 65 diversified industries manufacturing more than 200 commodities. Along the lake-shore east of the business district is Foss Park (May 30-Sept. 15; camp sites 50c a night or $2 a week, including stoves, tables, chairs, and running water), a 34-acre recreational tract. The stretch of wooded bluffs and sandy beach has complete playground equipment, with facilities for boating, tennis, baseball, dancing, and swimming. WPA-IL

The GREAT LAKES NAVAL TRAINING STATION, (9 to sunset; guides at entrance gates), only major naval unit in the Middle West, is one of four in the United States. In 1937, 2,943 recruits, ranging in years from 18 to 25, trained here. About 245 men leave the station each month, after 12 weeks of intensive training, for assignment to ships or naval trade schools. The station was first designed to accommodate 1,500, but during the World War (1918) the area and structures were increased to receive and train 50,000 men. WPA-IL

Sheridan Rd. **Great Lakes Naval Museum** just south of Waukegan. The Museum is located near the front gate at Farragut Ave., just off Sheridan Rd. (Yellowstone Trail). The museum's mission is to select, collect, preserve, and interpret the history of the U.S. Navy, featuring the Navy's only "boot camp."

The original 39 buildings (of the present 1,153) were standing when the Trail went by on Sheridan Rd. In 1917, just before the U.S. entered World War I, there were 165 acres and 1,500 sailors. Today, there are 50 miles of roads on the 1,628 acres.

IL-015.1 Lake Bluff

(pop. 1,000, alt. 683 ft.), is situated, as the name would imply, on the high bluffs of Lake Michigan, and is a favorite place with many Chicagoans, and particularly desirable as a family resort. There are many pretty summer homes located here, and bathing on the beach, one of the finest along the lake, is a popular pastime. Nearby is located the Great Lakes naval station. BB1921-10

One block off of Sheridan Rd. (Yellowstone Trail) is Lake Bluff's 1905 brick **Town Hall**. It overlooks the village green and gazebo. Its pocket commercial area was recently recognized as a National Register Historic District. Originally founded as a Methodist camp in the 1870s, current ads tout the friendliness, cohesiveness, and quiet of a small town. There are great mansions, but also small houses built in the days of the Methodist camp and Chatauqua. (Chatauqua were on-going cultural lectures occurring across America.)

Scranton Ave. The 1904 vintage redbrick **train station** with its castellated tower still serves commuters to Chicago. The Metrarail train (Union Pacific line) runs parallel and close to Sheridan Rd. right through town. One hundred years ago the Yellowstone Trail ran right through the middle of most towns.

IL-017.4 Lake Forest

(pop. 5,000, alt. 704 ft.), situated on the shores of Lake Michigan, 28 miles from Chicago, is a city of beauti-

ful homes and surroundings, its site being diversified by picturesque ravines and bluffs. Many Chicagoans make their summer home here, while others are all the year round residents. It contains the Lake Forest university and Lake Forest academy, two leading educational institutions. BB1921-10

(713 alt., 6,554 pop.), is known as the wealthiest of the North Shore suburbs. Magnificent estates, many surrounded by high iron fences, border both sides of State 42. Large groves of timber outline beautifully landscaped lawns; statues, formal gardens, pavilions, and stone benches are placed with an eye to beauty and functional use; occasionally a tennis court or swimming pool is visible from the road. The architecture of the costly homes, many silhouetted against the blue waters of Lake Michigan, ranges from the elaborate pre-World War styles to the straight-line modernity of Frank Lloyd Wright. WPA-ILw

This affluent city is one of several comprising the "North Shore," a geographical area known to all.

555 N Sheridan Rd. (Yellowstone Trail). **Lake Forest College**, founded in 1857, is a four year coed, residential, private liberal arts college.

700 N Sheridan Rd. Across Sheridan Rd. from the college stands the **Presbyterian Church**. The bituminous limestone used in the construction of the present 1886 building was salvaged after the 1871 Chicago fire from the Second Presbyterian Church in that city.

 Between IL-018.9, at Westleigh Rd., and IL-020.1, at Old Elm Rd./Simonds Way, the route of the YT is not well documented. It is hypothesized without evidence that it followed a now obscured route nearer the cemetery.

IL-021.0 Fort Sheridan

built a quarter of a century ago, c.1890, it is beautifully situated on Lake Michigan and is, at present, the largest general hospital in the United States, having a 5,000 bedding capacity for patients. During the war it was a training camp for officers, and since the armistice its work has been devoted entirely to the reconstruction and rehabilitation of wounded soldiers. BB1921-10

Separating the "town" of Fort Sheridan from the military Fort is difficult. The Fort Sheridan website says that Fort Sheridan is a residential neighborhood spread among Lake Forest, Highwood, and Highland Park in Lake County. It was originally established as Fort Sheridan, a United States Army Post named after Civil War Cavalry General Philip Sheridan.

In 1984 parts of Fort Sheridan were designated a National Historic Landmark District by the National Park Service as the site "possesses national significance in commemorating the history of the United States of America."

When the main fort was officially closed by the Army in 1993, the majority of the property was sold to commercial land developers. Approximately 90 acres of the southern end of the original post were retained by the Army; there the Army now operates the Sheridan Reserve Center and recruit training center complex.

IL-023.0 Highwood

Highwood is situated just west of Sheridan Rd. Highwood is a quiet North Shore residential community with lovely homes built from stone, brick, and masonry by local Italian stonemasons. Highwood is also a community shaped by Fort Sheridan; Highwood's business district was once so notorious for its bars and taverns that its knickname was "Whiskey Junction." From Evanston to Kenosha, Highwood was the North Shore's only wet community.

IL-023.4 Highland Park

(691 alt., 12,203 pop.), one of the largest residential suburbs of the North Shore, stands on the site of two Potawatomi villages. White settlement began with the construction of the Green Bay House (1834), a tavern on the Chicago-Milwaukee post road, now Waukegan Road.

On Sheridan Road, opposite the entrance to Lake Shore Country Club, is an Indian trail marker, a bent tree that the Potawatomi twisted as a sapling to mark one of their trails. WPA-IL

Hotel Moraine on Yellowstone Trail & Sheridan Rd. BB1925

Like other North Shore towns, Highland Park sits on top of a high bluff running along 6 miles of Lake Michigan shoreline with deep, wooded ravines extending up to 1 mile inland.

Pioneering architect, **Frank Lloyd Wright**, designed several "Prairie Style" homes here with some, like the Willits house, on the National Register of Historic Places. A mansion owned by basketball star Michael Jordan and designed by Wright is located just north of Highland Park. Oak Park, to the west, can claim the most homes by Wright in one place, at least 17.

In addition to several houses designed by Wright, the National Register lists homes in Highland Park designed by other prominent architects.

200 Ravinia Park Rd. **Ravinia Festival Park**. A few feet off of Sheridan Rd. is the oldest outdoor music festival in the country. It started in 1904 as an amusement park to lure riders to the newly founded Chicago and Milwaukee Electric Railroad. No doubt Yellowstone Trail travelers stopped here. The tradition of live annual open-air summer musical performances continues to today. We went when the weather was absolutely perfect.

326 Central Ave. **Highland Park Historical Society**. It is housed in a 12 room Italianate Victorian house which preserves the history of Highland Park and surrounding area.

IL-028.2 Glencoe

(673 alt., 6,295 pop.), was first settled about 1836, and was incorporated as a village in 1869. The name is a compound of "glen," suggestive of the site, and "Coe," the maiden name of the wife of Walter S. Gurnee, one of the founders. The Gurnee House (private), a three-story yellow brick building with elaborate porches and gables, still stands on Green Bay Road, opposite the North Western station. It was built in the 1870s. WPA-IL

There are 9 Frank Lloyd Wright homes in Glencoe, two of which are on Sheridan Rd.

Glencoe is part of a unique walking/biking trail that runs along on the Old Green Bay Rd. to the North Shore villages. It is called the Green Bay Trail. The Green Bay Trail began as the road between Chicago and Green Bay, Wisconsin. At the end of the 19th century (1898), the North Shore Electric Railroad ran a line from downtown Chicago north to service commuters from the many developing suburbs. For most of the early 20th century, what is now the trail was used as the right-of-way for the North Shore Line. When the railroad abandoned the Shore Line route, the villages along the line cooperated in purchasing the right-of-way to be used as a walking and bike trail. Today, the trail is utilized by thousands of runners and walkers. The Old Green Bay Rd. runs parallel to and within a couple of blocks of the Yellowstone Trail for some of it.

375 Park Ave. **The Glencoe Historical Center and Eklund Garden** hosts exhibits, events, and a research center. At this writing they are featuring the end of World War I Centennial.

IL-029.7 In this area the Yellowstone Trail has a ravine and twists and turns with beautiful homes along the side. About as close to an open road that one can find in a city.

Ravinia Park then, Highland Park
Ravinia Festival Park website

"No Man's Land" is different from the rest of the North Shore. There is more of a Spanish life style here, colored stucco buildings with Spanish names - dancing, drinking, dining, and movies. Access to the lake and beach, exclusive elsewhere in the North Shore, may be had here for a nominal price. This bright spot, which on a summer's day contrasts strikingly with the quiet of the residential suburbs, is so named because a strip of lake shore frontage was not included in the corporate limits of either Kenilworth or Wilmette. WPA-IL

Note: No Man's Land (IL-032.7) was annexed to Wilmette in 1942. ✿

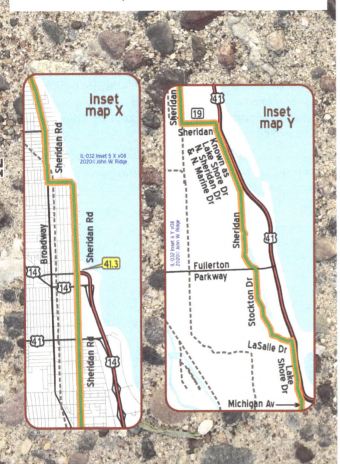

IL-030.8 Winnetka

On Tower Road, L. of the highway, is the Water Tower (1893) of the community-owned and operated water plant. The plant, at the base of the steep bluff on which the tower stands, is integrated with the municipal electric plant, resulting in numerous economies in the operation of both. WPA-IL

This affluent North Shore village is located approximately 16 miles north of Chicago. As you drive along Sheridan Rd., the Yellowstone Trail, note the many large, stately and beautiful homes with backyards that look upon the lake.

The Chicago, North Shore, and Milwaukee electric interurban railway was built through Winnetka and the North Shore in the first decade of the 1900s, and the line through Winnetka was removed in 1955. This is now the Green Bay Trail bicycle path.

411 Linden Ave. **Winnetka Historical Museum**. The collections of the Winnetka Historical Society reflect and document the development of the Village since the 1830s and include archives, over 3,000 photographs, and artifacts.

784 Sheridan Rd. **Christ Church-Epicopal**. "The Church on the Hill" is aptly named because of its location on a hill on Sheridan Rd. Dedicated in 1905, it was surely viewed by Yellowstone Trail travelers on Sheridan Rd.

IL-032.2 Kenilworth

(615 alt., 2,501 pop.), is named for Sir Walter Scott's novel, and many of the streets in its hilly residential section commemorate places or characters in the book. WPA-IL

15 miles north of downtown Chicago. As of the 2010 census it had a population of 2,513. It is the newest of the nine suburban North Shore communities bordering Lake Michigan, and is the only one developed as a planned community. In January 2011, Forbes named Kenilworth "the most exclusive neighborhood in the Midwest."

IL-033.6 Wilmette

(pop. 4,943, alto 614 ft.), is a pretty suburb 14 miles north of Chicago. Here many of the most prosperous business men of the city make their homes the year round, while others spend only the summer months. There are many very fine drives in and around this picturesque village that would prove most enjoyable. BB1921-10

The village is named in honor of Antoine Ouilmette, a French-Canadian fur trader.

The Village of Wilmette is a beautiful suburb, known for its "lakefront, tree lined streets, green street lanterns & brick streets," says the Wilmette website.

The North Shore Channel was constructed by the Chicago Sanitary District in 1909 and 1910 to control the flow of water from the Chicago River to the lake. Clay excavated from the channel was deposited nearby as landfill which became the Willmette Harbor and Washington (later Gillson) Park. The second major engineering project was the construction of Sheridan Rd. to replace the old Green Bay Trail. The

Yellowstone Trail route through the area was established in 1915 on Sheridan Rd. so that road was built by then, allowing Trail travelers views of Washington (later Gillson) park and the large harbor and Lake Michigan.

100 Linden Ave. at Sheridan Rd. The **Baha'i Temple** is one of only seven Baha'i Temples in the world and the only one in the U.S. They held their first religious service in the uncompleted building in 1922. After many pauses in its construction, it was finally completed in 1953. The beautiful, white lace-style exterior detail is set off by the lush landscaping and fountains. The white tower is visible as one drives along Sheridan Rd., and surely those travelers on the Yellowstone Trail viewed it abuilding.

609 Ridge Rd. **The Wilmette Historical Museum**. Besides chronicling local history, the history society sponsors an annual Spring Housewalk, celebrating the preservation of local homes.

The **Oak Circle Historic District** is a 2.4 acre historic district. It includes fifteen single-family homes representative of the Prairie School and Craftsman styles of architecture. The Oak Circle Historic District is on the National Register of Historic Places.

Ouilmette North Historic District is a 46 block area placed on the National Register of Historic Places for local significance. It extends from Chestnut Ave. on the north to Sheridan Rd. on the east to Lake Ave. on the south to 13th St. on the west.

1122 Central Ave. **The Wilmette Theatre**. Built in 1914, and after several renovations and changes in ownership, the theatre still thrives. From silent Mary Pickford to the "talkies" to "Pirates of the Caribbean" and art films, the Wilmette Theatre drew and still draws crowds. It is certainly historic.

IL-035.9 Evanston

(pop. 35,000, alto 601 lt.), one of Chicago's pretty and aristocratic suburbs, is located at Lake Michigan. It is the headquarters of the National Woman's Christian Temperance Union (WCTU), Northwestern University and Garrett Biblical Institute. BB1921-10

1730 Chicago Ave. **Frances Willard Memorial Library and Archives**. Northwestern University and Garrett Biblical Institute were both founded by strong Methodists who, long before Prohibition in the 20th century, voted Evanston dry in 1863 and so it remained until the 1970s. It is no surprise, then, that the

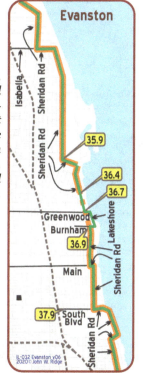

headquarters and president of the Woman's Christian Temperance Union, Frances Willard, were situated in Evanston.

1841 Sheridan Rd. might be the place to start if you want to visit the **Northwestern University** campus. This place has maps and undergraduate information. Like other huge urban universities, Northwestern is not just in one place. But a visit to view a slice of a major midwest university is worth the time.

225 Greenwood St. **Evanston History Center** in a chateau-style house built in 1894, once home to U.S. vice president Charles Dawes. It strives "to capture and teach Evanston's rich history," they say.

The YT route between IL-036.4 and IL-036.7 is now used by a parking lot with north bound traffic. Going south is detoured around the area, follow posted signs. The YT route between IL-036.7 and IL-036.9 is indeterminate.

State Street in the heart of the
shopping district, Chicago
National Archives
#30-N-34126

Lake Shore Drive in Chicago, 1925.
Note double-decker bus.

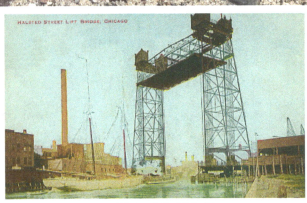
1894-1932 Halsted St. lift bridge over
south branch of Chicago River

The Tiffany Dome, part of a magnificent interior
at the Chicago Cultural Center

The Art Institute of Chicago
Automobile Blue Book 1924

IL

IL-050.1 Chicago

Chicago is today the second largest city in America as well as the largest railroad center in the world. Its population as given by the 1920 federal census is 2,701,705. Thirty-nine railways, including twenty-four great railway systems, about 40 per cent of the railway mileage of the U. S. terminate in Chicago, in addition to which there are a large number of belt lines, etc., greatly increasing the trackage within the corporate limits. Chicago has more than 11,000 factories; the output of its manufacturing zone is $6,500,000,000 annually. It is the distributing center of the U. S. and the financial center of the west, the metropolis of the richest agricultural section in the country and the focus of its primary facilities for industrial development. It also has the largest market for live· stock and is the first grain board in the world. Fifty million people live within one night's ride of this great city. BB1921-10

It is impractical to mention here the historical, manufacturing, artistic, or cultural attractions of Chicago and their location in relation to the Yellowstone Trail. There is no sign of the old Trail left to see in Chicago. In about 1915 when the Trail went through, the Yellowstone Trail Association found little support or interest by the citizens. This is not surprising and was portent to the things to come in major eastern cities. After all, they had roads to choose from in their cities. Should travelers wish to head west, there was the Yellowstone Trail Association Chicago bureau to supply them with maps and a connection to the next bureau in Milwaukee which would send them on to Minneapolis, etc. For a more full explanation, see **Trail Tale: YTA**, page 2.

The August 22-28, 1920, *This Week in Chicago* booklet advised visitors and residents to see entertainments that Yellowstone Trail travelers could have seen and could still be seen today: Grant Park, Academy of Sciences and the Zoo at Lincoln Park, Field Museum of Jackson Park, Newberry Library at Walton Place, Michigan Ave., and Clark St.

In 1922, one could select any of five tours of Chicago offered by T&S Tours for $1.00/hour. Four tours were within Chicago city limits; one tour to North Shore towns was all day for $5.00. "Just call Harrison 3566 or show up at their office 302 South Clark St."

But the Trail did go through Chicago on a long complicated route: Sheridan Rd. to Michigan Ave. zigzagging to Drexel, then to 57th St. where today it is under US 41. Then US 12 into Indiana. When we mapped and followed the Trail through Chicago for the first time, we found ourselves among the huge Esso gas tanks in south Chicago. The traveler today would do well to check the maps on these pages to find a more driveable route to avoid those gas tanks.

1601 N Clark St. **Chicago Historical Society**.

Monroe at State St. (two blocks west of the Yellowstone Trail, Michigan Ave.) **The Palmer House**. This historic hotel with an opulent frescoed lobby is very close to the Art Institute of Chicago and close to many famous sites tourists want to see. Surely, some Yellowstone Trail travelers stayed here.

The first Palmer House was opened on September 26, 1871

and burned down 13 days later in the great Chicago fire. Rebuilt on the same spot in1875, seven stories of iron and brick. Opulent again. Rebuilt in1923-25 to 25 stories and opulent. Surely the Yellowstone Trail travelers would have seen the tallest hotel in Chicago as they passed by two blocks away on Michigan Ave. Today it is called The Palmer House-A Hilton Hotel and has amenities unlikely in the 1920s.

7th and Michigan. (Yellowstone Trail). The Blackstone Hotel, now the **Renaissance Blackstone Chicago Hotel**, is housed in a 1910 beaux arts building across the street from Grant Park. This elegant hotel is 0.8 miles from the Field Museum. Since it was right on the Yellowstone Trail and near other tourist attractions in Chicago, it is no wonder that Trail travelers may have stopped here.

The hotel has housed many of the world's colorful, famous, and infamous from presidents to crooks in the past 100 years. Unfortunately, it became shuttered and bought and sold until 2008 when it reopened after renovation, the owners staying true to its historic elegance, while adding contemporary amenities.

Entry at 78 E Washington St. About 110 N. Michigan Ave. (the Yellowstone Trail.) **Chicago Cultural Center and its Tiffany dome**. *Atlas Obscura* says that this architectural wonder on Michigan Avenue, the former Chicago Public Library, should be visited to see the most magnificent Tiffany dome ever created. Colorful mosaics, 1,134 square feet of them, including 30,000 panes of glass is the largest of its kind in the world. Completed in 1897, the dome is estimated to be worth $35,000,000 today.

910 S Michigan Ave. **The Karpen Building**. Built in 1911 for a furniture store, then owned by Standard Oil; it now houses a bank. In Yellowstone Trail days it also housed a company that produced valuable auto road guides. The *Automobile Blue Books* were essential to drivers in this pre-road map era. Volumes covering 12 geographical areas of the U.S. were published every year from 1901 to 1929 guiding drivers, mile-by-mile, along various routes. Difficult to follow today when one is directed to "turn left at the red barn."

3301 S Indiana Ave. (between 33rd St, and Martin Luther King, Jr. Dr.) the address of the former iconic **Pilgrim Baptist Church**. The 1890 renowned church burned in 2006, almost entirely, rendering the landmark a shell. Fortunately, plans, backed by many organizations, made the shell a National Museum of Gospel Music in 2019.

IL-057.9: Between E Hyde Park Blvd. and S Lake Shore Dr., the YT followed E 55th St., which now is closed at S Lake Shore Dr. Using E 57th (near the Museum of Science and Industry) is advised. South of this point the actual alignment of the YT to 67th St. is obscure.

IL-064.1 South Chicago

The YT crossed the Indiana border on Indianapolis Blvd., which now is nearly under the I-90 Skyway. From Indianapolis Blvd. north the trail follows US 41 on Ewing Ave.

IL-065.7 Illinois/Indiana line

The 1915 Relay Race, with a Bit of Added Intrigue

"A Good Road From Plymouth Rock to Puget Sound" was the motto. Yet by the end of 1914 the Yellowstone Trail Association's active operations and useful signage installation only went from St. Paul, Minnesota, to just west of Bozeman, Montana. For 1915 the commitment was made to extend routing and operations from Chicago, Illinois, through to Seattle, Washington.

How better to celebrate and bring to the attention of the world the new progress and potential of this great highway than an attention-grabbing race? The Association had just confirmed the publicity potential of such exhibitions with Joe Parmley's well-publicized "Splendid Trip Across South Dakota" (see **Trail Tale: Parmley's Trip**, page 214). So, copious, detailed plans were laid for a major relay race of over 2,000 miles through eight states, a maneuver of enormity.

A relay of 21 successive automobiles carrying a banner and message from Mayor Thompson of Chicago to Mayor Gill of

The 1915 Relay Race Banner

Seattle would try to cover 2,445 miles in 100 hours. The fastest train schedule was 70 hours. Could they do it? The auto route was largely over dirt roads and a mixed bag of gravel roads.

Newspapers along the route trumpeted the coming event, describing the dragging of roads in preparation, and encouraging people to come out to view their local relay car set off. Excessive encomiums poured from the press, telling the world that a new epoch was starting in cross country travel over a route which some said was impassable nine months of the year. One unknown Minneapolis newspaper headline summed up the excitement with, "Magnificent Yellowstone Trail Across American Continent to be Given First Test; Racing Against Time in Dash From Chicago to Seattle."

Much Depends on the Road

That unknown Minneapolis paper continued,

> But it is not in cars primarily that the hope of the promoters of this run is based. It is on the road. To-day and every day from now until the car actually passes, men are working and dragging, fixing the bad spots, and banking the turns for the run. Across the state of Wisconsin the road is a new one in some places but a good one throughout. Across Minnesota the run goes over the award-winning Good Roads county of the state, Renville, and all of the road is being patrolled. Across South Dakota it is now a dragged turnpike, rain being the only thing that can stop a 30 mile an hour schedule through that state. At Aberdeen, the headquarters of the entire run, speculations, bets, and guesses are even now being registered, and the whole state is getting ready. Across North Dakota the message ⇨

Walter Beck of Missoula starts out.

"Chicago to Seattle Over the Yellowstone Trail in One Hundred Hours"

We believe that it is true that the Yellowstone Trail received the most effective and thorough test of its organization and excellence of a road, when on June 15, 1915, a car was started over it at 12 o'clock noon, carrying a letter from the mayor of Chicago to the mayor of Seattle, with the announced intention of delivering that letter to the mayor of Seattle in 100 hours, counting both night and day. The letter was carried over a system of twenty-two relays, a distance of 2,445 miles, and was delivered to the mayor of Seattle in ninety-seven hours and ten minutes from the time it left Chicago. So far as the Yellowstone Trail Association is able to find out, this is the only run of this kind ever undertaken, and the performance not only shows a thorough organization, but a road over which an average speed of 26.2 miles can be maintained day after day. The table appended hereto will show the manner in which the feat was accomplished much better than it can be done in words. It will be observed that a large variety of cars were used, there being only one racing car in the entire list, all the rest being touring cars. The running time of the Chicago to Seattle trains is seventy-two hours.

From	Manager	Driver	Car	Miles	Due	Arrived	Time	Ahead	Av pr Hr
Chicago	J. T. Brown	D. Boone	Moline-Knight	96	12:00 m.				
Milwaukee	Oscar Slegeman	Oscar Slegeman	Maxwell	84	4:00 p. m.	2:54 p. m.	2:54	1:05	33.1
Oshkosh	Paul Redeman	Walt Williams	Cadillac 8	79	7:40 p. m.	6:51 p. m.	3:56	0:49	21.3
Stevens Point	G. W. Andrae	H. A. Andrae	Pope Hartford	116	11:20 p. m.	9:40 p. m.	2:49	1:40	28.2
Chippewa Falls	G. E. Dee	Geo. Murphy	Mitchell 6	125	3:30 a. m.	1:47 a. m.	4:07	1:43	28.1
Minneapolis	H. F. Marston	H. F. Marston	Studebaker 6	103	8:10 a. m.	5:50 a. m.	4:03	2:20	30.8
Olivia	M. J. Dowling	O. A. Palmlund	Overland	104	12:25 p. m.	10:21 a. m.	4:31	2:04	22.8
Ortonville	R. G. Farrington	Emil Ostlind	Reo 6	128	4:50 p. m.	3:02 p. m.	4:41	1:48	27.3
Aberdeen	S. H. Collins	S. H. Collins	Ford	103	10:05 p. m.	7:15 p. m.	4:13	2:50	30.5
Mobridge	J. W. Harris	J. W. Harris	Ford	118	2:20 a. m.	11:27 p. m.	4:12	2:53	26.4
Lemmon	W. H. Doherty	E. E. Papke	Dodge	118	6:10 a. m.	5:58 a. m.	6:31	0:12	15.7
Marmarth	G. H. Sult	F. A. Bordwell	Overland	145	10:45 a. m.	9:47 a. m.	3:49	0:58	29.5
Miles City	G. E. Brown	J. Clifford	Haynes	157	4:35 p. m.	3:54 p. m.	6:07	0:41	23.5
Billings	W. McCormick	Lee Mains	Oldsmobile	130	11:00 p. m.	9:57 p. m.	6:03	1:03	25.9
Livingston	W. C. Busche	John Warner	Stevens-Duryea	137	4:20 a. m.	3:32 a. m.	5:37	0:48	23.4
Butte	E. J. Barker	M. E. Barry	Cadillac 8	131	9:55 a. m.	8:10 a. m.	4:38	1:45	29.6
Missoula	W. H. Smead	Walter Beck	Cadillac 8	124	3:15 p. m.	12:10 p. m.	4:00	3:05	32.7
Wallace	F. E. Stone	Ben Braham	Overland	86	7:20 p. m.	5:10 p. m.	5:00	2:10	22.8
Spokane	H. L. Olive	H. L. Olive	Overland	115	10:55 p. m.	7:57 p. m.	2:47	2:58	30.7
Coulee City	C. W. Gilbert	C. W. Gilbert	Case	121	3:40 a. m.	11:35 p. m.	3:33	4:05	31.6
Ellensburg	S. H. Kreidell	E. F. Schultz	Studebaker	131	8:55 a. m.	5:55 a. m.	6:20	3:00	19.1
Seattle					2:00 p. m.	11:10 a. m.	5:15	2:50	24.9

The above is submitted as being the best evidence of the possibilities for travel over the Yellowstone Trail. It is an accomplishment, not a claim.

will have clear sailing, and the evidence of some of the hardest and best road work in the country will be found in Montana. The Seattle Auto club writes that the Washington roads will be in good condition.

The distance was divided into approximately 100 mile segments. The relay cars running continuously day and night were to be followed by "trailer cars" to carry the banner and the letter in case of a relay car emergency. The first car left Chicago at noon, June 15.

The Race

Joe Parmley, founder of the Yellowstone Trail, had the privilege, of course, of riding in that first relay car as it left Chicago heading to Stevens Point, Wisconsin. He reported to the *Aberdeen American* (South Dakota) newspaper that:

> Along the beautiful boulevards of Lincoln Park we flew, our banner streaming in the wind. We soon saw that we were followed by a motorcycle policeman and the jig was up. I said to Boone, "Turn on the juice and let him know he has to go some if he arrests us." Up went the speedometer to 40, 45, 50 but the police gained. Boone said, "Show him your banner." As he closed up on us I did so and shouted, "We have right of way." He shot by smiling and shouted, "Follow me." He was a special police detailed to escort us out of the city.
>
> We rolled into Milwaukee 65 minutes ahead of schedule. The next car, a Maxwell, was waiting and we swept out. Two tires had to be replaced due to blow outs and we lost 35 minutes. Eight thousand people were out in Oshkosh. The small towns were out in force and as darkness came on, bonfires lit up the way.
>
> In the hurry of transferring across the Missouri River at Mobridge, the banner was left on the ferry. It was put on the fast coast train to be taken off at Marmarth, North Dakota, if the relay car had not left, but the train schedule was too slow and the banner continued on to Miles City, then to Billings and to Butte, but the driver was over the crest of the continent to Missoula in an hour and forty minutes faster than any previous record. The last hope was Spokane, and the letter in the car was still ahead. The only thing to do was to continue the banner by express train to its destination - the Automobile Club of Seattle.

"We felt sore at first over this break, but as the letter conveyed by human hands in automobiles traveling on earth roads kept outdistancing the fastest trains on steel tracks, we perked up a little and concluded that our trail wasn't so bad after all," wrote the Association later.

WARNER SMASHES RECORD
June 18, 1915 Livingston (MT) Enterprise

Newspapers, tales of local Trailmen, drivers, and Association public relations releases continued the commentary throughout the trip, several reflecting on the effects of the rain which had passed over 1,500 of the 2,445 miles of the route just before the run. Most local papers bugled "Auto Relay Ahead of Time" because it was true in all communities - coming into Seattle almost three hours ahead of time!

The race was not without mishap, but it had no major accident. And, of course, the promised "trailer cars" which were supposed to follow the relay car did not always appear. Between Bird Island and Hector, Minnesota, a run-in with a farmer's rig disabled the relay car and considerable time was lost in waiting for another car to be sent out from Hector as no trailer car appeared.

There was J. W. Harris who traversed the Standing Rock Indian Reservation in South Dakota at night and who got stuck in the mud. With no trailer car in sight, he walked and ran three miles to McLaughlin and got two automobiles to go back and pull his car out, losing two hours and 10 minutes in all.

Walter Beck was to drive from Missoula, Montana, to Wallace, Idaho. He was just a short distance from Missoula when he suffered a broken wheel. The Reo car which was following him took the letter and raced on to Wallace, arriving two hours ahead of schedule.

In spite of it all, they arrived in Seattle on June 19 having left Chicago 97 hours and 10 minutes earlier! Countless newspapers across the country blasted the news to their readers. Two hours and 50 minutes ahead of schedule! And without a serious accident. Well, maybe one.

YELLOWSTONE TRAIL PROVED FAST ROUTE
AUTOMOBILE FASTER THAN MAIL TRAIN
June 20, 1915 Aberdeen (SD) American

The Intrigue

The *Seattle Star* (Washington) and the *Tacoma Times* (Washington) each carried large headlines on June 19, screaming "Auto in Ditch; Man is Killed" and "Road Race Ends in Fatal Smash; Legislator Killed." Each outlined an accident which they declared occurred about one hour east of Seattle. The car, they said, skidded and ended in a ditch, upside down, "instantly killing state legislator George E. Dickson."

The *Aberdeen Herald* (South Dakota) picked up the tale and repeated the story on June 20. The *Waupaca Record-Leader* (Wisconsin) printed the story on June 24. We do not know how many other newspapers carried the death notice.

The Seattle paper wrote,

> George E. Dickson of Ellensburg, former member of the legislature, was killed instantly and John Keller of Ellensburg was injured when a Ford automobile, in which the last lap of the 100-hour race against time from Chicago to Seattle over the Yellowstone Trail was being run, skidded on a curve two miles east of Redmond, and turned over in the ditch.

Strange. The known, official driver arrived in Seattle a little later with appropriate celebration. What happened? H. O. Cooley, secretary of the Yellowstone Trail Association, set the record straight. The official driver's name was not Dickson. ⇨

The Seattle Star

PAY ONLY ONE CENT FOR THE STAR

The Only Paper in Seattle That Dares to Print the News

NIGHT EDITION

VOLUME 15   NO. 68.   SEATTLE, WASH., SATURDAY, JUNE 19, 1915.   ONE CENT

Cross-Country Relay Race Ends in Tragedy at Redmond
AUTO IN DITCH; MAN IS KILLED

Seattle Will Get Warship

The Best Note of All!

LEO FRANK DOOMED, IS BELIEF

BUSINESS MEN WILL DECORATE

Message Bearer in Chicago - Seattle Race Meets Death

It was E. F. Schultz who drove a Studebaker and not a Ford over the last lap of the relay, and S. H. Kreidell, and not Keller carried the message.

The saying that "rumor travels on many wings, truth but two" appears to have been as alive and well 100 years ago as it is today. The rush to print, to scoop, to be "first" too often trumps accuracy.

About 90 years later J. J. Johnson, of Waupaca, Wisconsin, found a refutation of the death story:

> **YELLOWSTONE TRAIL DRIVER NOT KILLED**
> **STORY CIRCULATED WAS FAKE - STARTED BY SEATTLE PAPER WAS ACCEPTED AS THE TRUTH**
> *July 22, 1915 Waupaca (Wisconsin) Record-Leader*

The Backstory

The backstory of the event was made clear by the *Cle Elum Echo* (Washington) newspaper of June 25, 1915. It seems that Clyde Gilbert, mayor of Coulee City, selected the official Yellowstone Trail race route from that city to Cle Elum. The route went west through Waterville, Wenatchee, and Blewett Pass, and west toward Cle Elum. That was the planned route of the Sunset Highway and also became the Yellowstone Trail in 1925. People living in the Vantage Ferry area criticized Gilbert's judgement in leaving out Vantage from the official race route. When he refused to make a change in the official route, they created a competing race route to include Vantage, where there was a ferry across the Columbia River. A number of their cars left Coulee City at the same time as the official car but they followed the competing route. The point of the unofficial race was to prove that a Vantage route to Ellensburg, Cle Elum, and Seattle was faster. It was their George Dickson who was thrown out and killed at a sharp turn near Redmond. Another unofficial driver carried on, arriving in Seattle over an hour before the Yellowstone Trail car.

So, the Vantage Ferry people proved their point that their route was quicker, but at the cost of a life. Column headings identified the incident as " Racing Auto Has Accident," and "Road Race Ends in Fatal Smash," leading the reader to believe that Dickson was an official Yellowstone Trail racer. Because of the massive advertising of the coming Yellowstone Trail race, it was natural for the reader to link the word "race" with the Yellowstone Trail. The true story was somewhat complicated for hurried reporters to unravel and still be "first." Later, buried paragraphs in papers did indicate that he was an unofficial racer. ⇨

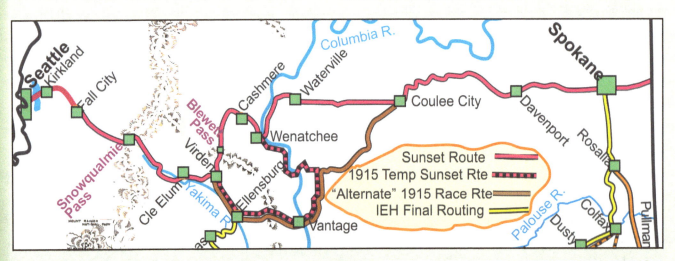

Sunset Route
1915 Temp Sunset Rte
"Alternate" 1915 Race Rte
IEH Final Routing

Continued

The Happy Ending

Soon after 1915, Blewett Pass was put in somewhat better condition for autos, and the Sunset Highway was moved to the Blewett Pass race route off of the reverse curve "temporary" route south from Wenatche. Little noted was the fact that at the time of the race, the independent decision was being made for the initial route of the Yellowstone Trail through Washington to follow the Inland Empire Highway rather than the northern Blewitt Pass route! It was not until 1925 that the Yellowstone Trail was moved to the race route over the Blewett Pass. ✿

The 1918 Spanish Flu and the Yellowstone Trail Association

Lydia Kohl, author Alice Ridge's mother, reminisced only once about the Spanish flu that hovered over their house in 1918 in Wisconsin when she was 18. She said,

> It started with my younger brother's cough. Then moved like lightening to my two other siblings and both parents. I never got it, so I spent days doing laundry and making soup for five people all headed for our one bathroom. My business college classes were canceled so I was home. Oh, my family all survived, but I remember it clearly, now decades later. Do you know that the mailman even stopped going down our block? He, literally, dropped the mail at the corner and we had to go pick it up.

I never asked her more about this ancient (to me) historical event. This was only one of possible millions of stories that could be told by flu survivors, and those told about the millions worldwide who died. Statistics showed that a very high number of the American victims were young adults, the numbers possibly skewed by soldiers fighting World War I falling ill.

It was called the Spanish flu because Spain was neutral in World War I and freely reported flu activity, whereas in the U.S., communications about the severity of the disease was kept quiet to keep up public morale in wartime. This, unfortunately, backfired because the populace was not warned sufficiently and people still gathered in public places like a Philadelphia parade which likely caused the deaths of 5,000.

What was this cataclysm, this "mother of all pandemics" and why did it spread so quickly world wide? *Remembering the 1918 Influenza Pandemic* by The Center for Disease Control and Prevention (cdc.gov/features/1918-flu-pandemic) provides much information, but questions about its origin, epidemiology and pathology remain. Modern science has been able to determine the genomic sequence of some of the virus's genes from autopsy tissue. The *New York Times* of October 6, 2005, announced that the deadly flu was actually the bird flu virus, H1N1, that jumped directly to humans and adapted.

Recent theory posits that Asia was the site of the beginning of the epidemic, but no specific country can be identified. Reported beginning and ending dates of this calamity vary. But all conclude that a person could be fine in the morning and dead by dark. It was spread by droplets in the air from a cough or a sneeze, settling in the lungs and breathing passages of the receiver, causing a sore throat, headache, and fatigue. Evangelist Billy Sunday said the cause was sin.

World War I was raging, troops were crowded in camps and troop transports, and the lack of vaccines and treatments helped spread the flu. The first cases in the U.S. were reported from Fort Riley, Kansas, in April of 1918. Within a week, the number of cases there quintupled. By May hundreds of thousands of soldiers were shipped to Europe. Some died on the ships before they even saw the war. Military doctors had to treat the war wounded and flu victims simultaneously.

Kansas Emergency Hospital 1918

Three distinct waves were identified: spring and August-October of 1918, and spring of 1919. Citizen efforts to stem the flood ranged widely: isolation from neighbors, quarantine, closure of public settings, mandatory use of face masks, and fines for people who did not cover their coughs. Baseball games were canceled; schools were closed, including our third cousin's rural school in Montana. And, apparently, as my mother had reported, mailmen did not have to go door-to-door. Scientists had not yet known about viruses. There were no antibiotics to treat the pneumonia that accompanied the flu virus. Even into 1920 it raged, with Chicago reporting 6,000 cases in January. The war had sucked up many doctors, leaving fewer at home. The relentless demands placed upon medical staff left at home took their toll. Citizens turned gymnasiums, schools, any large spaces, ⇨

even rooming houses into makeshift hospitals.

Fear and desperation drove some to desperate measures. A doctor in Montana was on his way to treat a patient when he was flagged down by a rancher who begged the doctor to attend his family. The doctor said he would on his way back from his patient. The rancher pulled out a "a wicked looking six gun" and the doctor complied ("No More War, No More Plague," *Montana the Magazine of Western History*, Summer 2018).

Just as the child's chant of "ring around the rosie" actually described the plague in England 400 years ago, a new chant was born in 1918:

> I had a little bird,
> Its name was Enza.
> I opened the window

Masked Seattle police

Philadelphia Parade caused 5,000 deaths among attendees.

> And in-flew-Enza

The Flu and the Yellowstone Trail

The flu certainly must have affected long-distance travel. We don't know whether it was due to the war, or out of fear of reprisal for being uncaring, or if the limited staff of the Yellowstone Trail Association fell ill, but there was no published Association *Route Folder* for 1918. These annual *Route Folders* encouraged travel, providing much information about Trail towns and maps. The three fledgling Information Bureaus recently set up in major city hotels and designed to help travelers along the Trail were probably closed. Vacation travel was far from people's minds.

The enormity of the consequences of the epidemic must have affected the 5,000 Trail Association members. Illness, death, fear of travel or lack of motivation must have taken their toll on travel and the Association membership. The Trail crossed 13 states. The 1918 autumn total of deaths in those 13 states

was estimated to be well over 100,000, most occurring in October alone. While these figures cover whole states, not just the Yellowstone Trail corridor, a picture may be drawn, nonetheless.

The Association officers may have been aware of what was happening in member towns, if Trailmen were communicating with them. Also, even small town newspapers along the Trail published their local tragedies. The fall of 1918 seemed the worst for Trail towns as for the nation at large. A few Trail town examples follow: Bozeman, Montana, and environs lost 87; 40 cases and two deaths were reported in little Marmarth, North Dakota, in October; tiny Ismay, Montana, declared two cases were in town, but gave no details other than a gloomy prognosis. The village of Baldwin, Wisconsin, not only listed its dead, but gave glowing obituaries of them. Eau Claire, Wisconsin, counted 44 deaths. McIntosh, South Dakota, on the Standing Rock Indian Reservation, listed 18 deaths, two in one family. In the end, an estimated over 50 million succumbed to the flu worldwide.

The National Institutes of Health has said that "almost all cases of influenza A worldwide at present have been caused by descendants of the 1918 virus." The pandemic virus, accompanied by pneumonia, continued to circulate seasonally worldwide for 38 years. The epidemics of 1957 and 1968 were somewhat different, being a human flu with a few genetic elements of bird flu. "This suggests that pandemics can form in more than one way," said researcher Jeffery Taubenberger of the Center for Disease Control. Today's flu shot may not cover all forms of flu, but it would, we hope, help ward off another "mother of all pandemics" and allow folks to travel the Yellowstone Trail.

To the Reader

This article was written before the 2020 pandemic of Covid-19. When we reread it for publication preparation of this book, we saw the awful similarities to that pandemic of 100 years ago. When governments try to cover up a health problem, no matter what the reason, be it a war or politics, the nation loses. Today, our CDC knows about viruses and the lingering threads they weave, apparently over 100 years. Vaccines have been found as we write, but probably the "silver bullet" will never be found to protect us from future epidemics. Viruses are slippery creatures, morphing and combining into something different every year.

The Spanish Flu produced its book of stories. Covid-19 will write another chapter. ✿

A Reeder, North Dakota, survivor's memoir described the sorrow of seeing parents dying, leaving orphaned kids, or volunteers sacrificing themselves by nursing the ill.
H. Erikson and D. Merwin, eds. *Prairie Pioneers: A Story of Adams County. (no date)* Bismarck, ND

The influenza epidemic of 1918 was a trying time for those at home [not fighting in the war]. Dr. Hill traveled night and day, getting his rest mostly while traveling from one patient to another. All nurses were pressed into assisting, as well as many volunteers. An emergency hospital was started in the Rooming House.
Ipswich, S.D., the First 100 Years 1883-1983, Centennial Book Group

Garages: The Stable Transformed

Have you ever considered the heritage of your garage? Think about it. Most likely, your garage is glued to your house so you don't have to go out into the elements. Some garages are half the square footage of a house. Most garages face the street more boldly than does the front door. But how did it get that way?

The word "garage" is derived from the French word "garer" which means "to store or repair automobiles." Early in the 20th century, people actually did store their cars in a public garage for a period of time. Today we use the word to mean "a place to repair cars" in addition to "a place to put my car overnight." Yet a third broader meaning is posited by Wikipedia when it mentions the tv show, "Jay Leno's Garage." Jay's program shows his and others' car collections, holds antique car conversations with other experts, and takes viewers on rides.

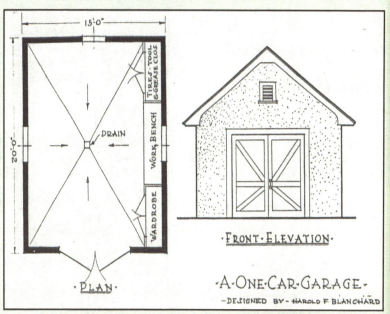

Plans for your garage. Scale as needed: 11' long for a Ford, up to 18' for your Rolls Royce
Motor Land, date unknown

An unknown (to us) source, probably from an early era, contained the following conundrum: a word wanted.

A selection of a correct word for a private collection of automobiles equivalent to "stable" seems to afford considerable difficulty. "Motorbarn," "motorome." "motorden," "motorium," "motorshed" and "motable" all have been suggested. The French term "garage" would be a good one if it was not used for designating a place simply for storage and repairing automobiles.

Garages for the Wealthy

Since it was the wealthy who could afford cars at the beginning of the century, it was the wealthy who concerned themselves with housing the beauty. And housing they did! Locating the garage far from the house because it was considered crude, they sometimes included chauffeurs' housing, a squash court, a repair parts room, a heating unit, and a repair pit in a concrete or stone fire proof building.

Believe it or not, there was a portable garage on the market for the wealthy to take along with them for their three-month summer vacation.

The Milwaukee Corrugating Company marketed the "Porto." Seven feet six inches wide and thirteen feet long, it came in galvanized steel and weighed about 845 pounds. Not very portable, it would seem.

Garages for Fords

For the more ordinary autoist, growing in number after Henry Ford came on the scene, there was a prefab model introduced in 1912. Rusk Auto House was making the sheet metal

parts that you could order and assemble. It came complete with galvanized steel pieces cut in two-foot widths, wood frame, and bolts, as reported by the North Dakota Historical Society in the "Editor's Choice" column of their newsletter.

Many owners chose simply to convert their stable into a garage. It was away from the house, thus not a fire danger. The door was big enough for a Ford, as was the length. It seemed that the Ford was the measuring tape, both for length and for width. Since most repair/tinkering was done on the premises, three feet of space was needed on each side of the Ford. There

The "especially popular Ford sized" Porto Garage shipped from Milwaukee features "Open Hearth Tight-Coat Galvanized Sheets" each corrigated, with all necessary hardware. 7' 6" x 13' 1"
Feb. 1922 Wisconsin Motorist ⇨

was a cartoon drawn in a 1913 newspaper showing a horse looking nervously askance at a comical Model T-like car sharing his stall. The horse did not have the blanket, the car's hood did.

Motor Land magazine (sometime before 1922) offered blue prints of designs for garages, noting that Fords needed:

> 11 feet from stem to stern, and the Locomobile, Rolls-Royce and Pierece-Arrow scaled about 18 feet from bumper tip to spare tire. A Cadillac is about 16 feet overall. A garage for a Ford might be made 12 feet by 7 feet.

An interesting comment was appended to the article:

> A garage 12 by 20 is quite satisfactory for a moderate sized house, the assumption being that the owner of this dwelling is likely to have a car in keeping. But for similar reasons, the larger houses should have larger garages 6 by 18 feet. Allowing a 3-foot strip all around the car, the building dimensions are found to be 12 by 24 feet.

This comment may have been added by an architect concerned about balance and lines of house and garage.

Leslie G. Goat has written a fascinating study of the garage in "Housing the Horseless Carriage: America's Early Private Garages" in *Vernacular Architecture Forum*, Vol 3, 1989. Goat says,

> The 1910s and 1920s brought a period of popularization and experimentation in garage design. There was the 'Hy-Rib' garage, a system of structural wire lath covered with stucco. The Van Guilder Hollow Wall process used special forms and quick-setting concrete in a continuous row-by-row process. By 1929 there would be one car for every 4.5 Americans. The impact on the American landscape was

"Favoritism". The new auto gets a quilt; Dobbin gets nothing.
Oct. 31, 1913 Marmarth (ND) Mail

dramatic as 'motor suburbs' sprawled across the countryside.

The garage became a necessary and integral part of the residential property. It moved out of the back yard and joined the house itself. That shows how much value is placed on automobiles and their care today. But it was a different kind of garage. Professional repair garages now had the technology, so auto owners didn't have to make repairs. Have you looked under the hood lately? It's all computerized! Nothing to recognize but the dip stick. There are even advertisements now that show how to share the automobile space with creature comforts such as for a man cave, or soundproofing for Junior and his loud garage band.

Drive down any suburban street today and you will see a plethora of three-car garages, some with stylish or creative themes. We've come a long way since Old Dobbin (a common name for a horse) was asked to share his stable with that clattering conveyance. ✿

The prefabricated Rusk Auto House was first advertised by George Rusk in 1912. Garages measured 18' long X 12' wide X 10' high and were constructed of galvanized sheets cut in two foot widths which were anchored to the wood frame with bolts. The metal shell consisted of 71 separate sheets. It was apparently manufactured until the first World War made sheet metal difficult to find and very expensive.
Bismarck Tribune, date unknown

Indiana

Winamac East Chicago
Gary Valparaiso Hanna
Mark Town Hobart Donaldson
Wanatah Hamlet Plymouth Bourbon Warsaw Pierceton Columbia City
Etna Green Winona Lake Larwill Harlan
Fort Wayne

The Yellowstone Trail just west of
Hamlet leading to the closed bridge

WHAT THE TRAIL FOUNDERS SAID-1921

It is generally regarded that of all of the central west states, Indiana has the best roads of any state. Whether or not this statement is true, it is a fact that Indiana has a splendid system of country roads and that they are being developed and kept apace with the times. The state is splendidly drained and it lacks the heavy muck that predominates in Illinois and Iowa. A person can practically travel to any destination in the state of Indiana without any serious inconvenience whatever. The Hoosier State Automobile Association located in Indianapolis will be glad to help automobile travel in the state and the Yellowstone Trail Association maintains one of its information bureaus at Fort Wayne in the northern part of the state. There is a very heavy north and south travel through the state of Indiana with people seeking vacation ground in northern Michigan.

The short route leading east from Chicago to reach any eastern destination and crossing northern Indiana is the Yellowstone Trail which leaves the Lincoln Highway at Valparaiso and takes the short cut to Fort Wayne where it again crosses the Lincoln Highway. Under ordinary circumstances, this is a splendid road, although being comparatively a small part of it hard surfaced. There is a large number of small lakes and lake resorts in the state of Indiana. Some of them nationally known, so that they are the objectives of a considerable automobile travel. The state of Indiana as a whole is not a vacation ground state but more of a place where people who want to take vacations live and make their money. It is in fact, as fiction has it, a state of corn, poets, and politicians.

From the 1921 Yellowstone Trail Touring Service
Map #12 of Indiana

INTRODUCING THE YELLOWSTONE TRAIL IN INDIANA:
CROSSROADS OF AMERICA

Almost at its founding the Yellowstone Trail was expected to become a transcontinental auto route; the motto "A Good Road from Plymouth Rock to Puget Sound" was first heard in 1912. It was 1915 when the route was formally extended east through Wisconsin, reaching Chicago on Lake Michigan. To get to Plymouth Rock from there, the Trail would have to go through Indiana, but no official action was yet taken.

After the great success of the 1915 Chicago to Seattle relay race, it was decided that 1916 would be the year to make the motto come true; they would hold a relay race from Plymouth Rock to Seattle! That forced a route decision.

A route had to be chosen but the choice was not made in time for it to appear in the 1916 *Route Folder*. By race time a route was chosen and it appeared belatedly in the 1917 *Route Folder*. Chicago to Plymouth was referred to as the "eastern section," not marked and for the most part used only for the 1916 Race. The *Route Folder* says, truthfully,

> The eastern section has only recently been added to the Yellowstone Trail, and is not as intensely organized as is all of the road west of Chicago. This route is shown on this 1917 Route Folder map more with the idea of the line that the Trail is going to follow, than with any claim that the Trail organization really extends there actively. Very little of this section is marked. During the summer and fall of 1917 the Association intends to mark this eastern section.

Through Indiana, the western entry point of the Trail was dictated by the 1915 extension of the Trail into Chicago. The reason for choosing the crossing into Ohio at a point northeast of Fort Wayne past Harlan toward Hicksville, Ohio, is unknown, but it does connect logically with the rest of the early route to Plymouth, Massachusetts. Guesses can be made that the decision was based on 1) the desire to avoid following the path of the Lincoln Highway which crossed Indiana on a northern route closer to Michigan, 2) the natural interest in passing through larger cities, in this case Fort Wayne, and 3) to follow the principle that the Yellowstone Trail be established along rail lines, in this case along the Pittsburgh, Fort Wayne, and Chicago railroad, an arm of the Pennsylvania Railroad at least as far as Fort Wayne. Railroads provided a source of help in auto emergencies and a means for obtaining replacement parts, often available only from far away providers, and they connected commercial centers along the straightest line possible.

1919 Route of the "Eastern Section"

Even when most of that first "eastern section" of the route of the Yellowstone Trail was changed to the final route in 1919, the part in Indiana remained the same. Today, determining the routing of the Yellowstone Trail in Indiana (as well as much of the "eastern section") is made difficult by the ambiguity of the routing by the Association and the tendency for map makers and editors of route guides to decide the route

for themselves. A review of the 1919 Rand McNally Indiana map shows several differences in the route near Gary and elsewhere, differences not found in the later versions.

The 1919 *Route Folder* listed The Anthony Hotel of Fort Wayne as the site of an Information Bureau of the Yellowstone Trail Association, one of 15 such bureaus across the country. A Trail traveler could get maps, weather and Trail road condition information and directions to the next Bureau, probably in Chicago or Cleveland. Those folks would then send the traveler to the next Bureau, and so on.

The rapid growth of the Trail Association in Indiana can be seen in the 1921 *Route Folder*. Seventeen "trailmen" from 21 Trail towns indicate that Indiana was finally an important Trail state. Trailmen were the eyes and ears for the national office. They reported local road changes and conditions, led local Trail Day activities and helped lost travelers.

Three years later Indiana is listed as having 298 of its promised 1,000 memberships. Membership numbers held up fairly well until the Association folded in 1930 due to the numbering of highways by governments and the presence of the Great Depression which made collecting membership dues impossible.

Later Years and the Lincoln Highway

Like other states, Indiana created a state highway commission in 1919 in response to the possibility of getting the recently announced federal aid for highways. States were required to meet certain requirements to apply for aid, including creating connected highways which would lead to county seats and larger towns, something the Yellowstone Trail Association had been dedicated to for seven years. The traffic generated by the Yellowstone Trail route was acknowledged and federal money was applied to it. Over the years the state straightened the Trail, improved the paving, and removed railroad crossings. In 1926, much of the general route was designated US 30, for being a part of a major cross-country route. The transition from the original Yellowstone Trail route to the more modern US 30 alignment was slow and piecemeal.   ⇨

The Yellowstone Trail and the
Lincoln Highway in Indiana

IN

The maps provided in this book do not report the process of that evolution. Add a realignment of the Lincoln Highway into the mix and a good bit of historical study is suggested to see recorded transition from discontinuous county roads to modern US 30.

The original Lincoln Highway connecting New York City and San Francisco crossed the Yellowstone Trail in two places, both in Indiana: Fort Wayne and Valparaiso. The Lincoln followed a looping route between them closer to Michigan through South Bend and Elkhart.

The year 1928 was a fateful year for the Lincoln. First, in that year the Lincoln Highway Association moved the Valparaiso-Fort Wayne alignment to generally follow the Yellowstone Trail corridor using the emerging major US 30 route. Second, the Boy Scouts of America undertook a project to mark and commemorate the Lincoln across the country with stone sign posts, and it did so on the southern Fort Wayne-Valparaiso section. Third, the management of the Lincoln Highway Association acknowledged the effects of state highway numbering and marking (with both state and U.S. numbers). They closed the Association and ceased operations. The Yellowstone Trail Association labored on until 1930 before the dual effects of government route numbering and the Great Depression forced its end.

The Forgetting

As famous as the Yellowstone Trail was in its day, by 1987 it was pretty well forgotten in Indiana. In the Knox, Indiana, *Leader* newspaper of September 23, 1987, the Director of the Indiana Department of Highways stated,

> Our agency does not have a map of the Yellowstone Trail. We have conducted some research in an effort to determine a source where such a map can be obtained. Unfortunately, we are unable to locate one ... the solution to the necessity to correct the route of the famous old trail and the type and acquisition of proper signs to designate the historical road across Starke County are still to be discovered.

In Indiana, as in most states, named sponsored auto routes were of little interest to the state after government numbered routes were established. ❈

YELLOWSTONE TRAIL TO BE CHANGED
EXCHANGE WITH LINCOLN HIGHWAY?

The annual meeting of the association was held in Minneapolis, Minnesota, at which new officers were elected. The association also decided to send H.O. Cooley, the General Agent, on the road from Chicago east to confer with local officers in different towns in reference to certain changes in the route. It is possible that the Yellowstone Trail will assume the northern route of the Lincoln Highway through Indiana and allow the Lincoln Highway to use the present more southern Yellowstone Trail route between Valparaiso and Fort Wayne. This would avoid their conflict of interest, benefitting both.

March 17, 1919 The Aberdeen (S.D.) Daily News

Note: The exchange never happened, but in 1928, just before going out of business, the Lincoln Highway did move to the Yellowstone Trail, then being reconstructed as US 30.

1919 ROUTE FOLDER 1919

You Don't Need a Log Book to Travel This Road—FOLLOW THE MARKS

The Yellowstone Trail

A Good Road From Plymouth Rock to Puget Sound

For Auto Business and Tourists

See America First By This Route

ONLY AMERICAN HIGHWAY GIVING PERSONAL SERVICE TO TRAVEL.

Free Information Bureaus at

Ft. Wayne, Ind....................Anthony Hotel
Milwaukee, Wis....................Hotel Pfister
Minneapolis, Minn...............Hotel Dyckman
Aberdeen, S. D...........114 So. Lincoln St.
Miles City, Mont.........Chamber of Commerce
Butte, Mont....................23 Broadway
Missoula, Mont.........Chamber of Commerce
Spokane, Wash.........West 410 Sprague Ave.

AT YOUR SERVICE

THREE NATIONAL PARKS ENROUTE
YELLOWSTONE—GLACIER—MT. RANIER

More improved highway—Better hotels and garages—More beautiful scenery—Better marked—Shorter than any other trans-America highway.

No desert—No stretch without water—Supply towns each twenty miles or nearer—A live representative in each town.

Weekly Road Condition Bulletins
For Information, Address
YELLOWSTONE TRAIL ASSOCIATION, INC.
916 Andrus Building
MINNEAPOLIS, MINNESOTA

FARNHAM PRINTING & STATIONERY CO. MINNEAPOLIS

[Above] The Yellowstone Trail Association issued *Route Folders* each year to inform travelers of the entire route of the Trail and facilities in the towns along it. The 1919 *Folder* says, "The section of road from Ft. Wayne to Valparaiso has lately been declared state market road by the Indiana Highway Commission, and is scheduled for improvement of a high class. Most of this road at this writing is well-constructed dirt highway, much of it surfaced with gravel. It passes through Columbia City, Warsaw (the location of Winona Lake with its famous Chautauqua), Plymouth, and enters Illinois at Hammond"

Modern view of a Marktown duplex home
Meyers Marsh Davis

Modern view, below, of Marktown single family homes -
no garages available!

Note: Tracing down the route of the Yellowstone Trail as it was routed from 1912 to 1930 was (and is) a demanding research question. We had help along the way, including extensive route finding research by Michael Koerner. His note to me illustrates the extent of his work. The area to which he refers is in Hobart, Indiana, where the Yellowstone Trail traveler was routed between Ridge Rd. (37th Ave.) and 39th Ave. just west of I-65.

He said:

> It took me nearly two weeks to determine that this cossover is at Missouri St. Nothing in the *Blue Books*, period maps, modern maps, and air photos was making sense here. I was re-re-re-examining hi-res air photos of that area and noticed that there is a very slight offset in 39th Ave. at its first intersection west of I-65. The road on either side was likely built at different times.
>
> Hmmm. 39th Ave.'s pavement is of a different width on either side of Missouri St.
>
> Hmmm, again. There is a noticeable broad curve in the paving at this intersection in its northeast quadrant. Right in front of the foundation of what looks like an abandoned gas station. Interesting indeed!
>
> I then reran all of the *Blue Book* lists [of distances] and, yes -- it fits!
>
> The Yellowstone Trail crossed over here. Checking in the field, I found nothing to counter that finding. Too bad that the northern of those two blocks [of Missouri St.] was obliterated when I-65 was built." ✿

Marktown

In the March 20, 1920 edition of *Chicago Commerce,* the headline announced that the Steel and Tube Company of America at Work on Great Undertaking and that it would "Build Home Town To Benefit Employees."

This article describes the plans of Clayton Mark, Sr. in devising a town for his 8,000 employees. As described, this former swamp land was to be quite Utopian: spaces for parks, public square, theater, shops, bank, school, library. Individual homes would rest on lots 40 by 50 feet. In some larger spaces, duplexes and fourplexes would rise two stories high.

However, the town was never completed as planned. Only 10% of the original design was built, terminated by aftereffects of World War I and the sale of the Mark Manufacturing Company.

However, the surviving homes reveal a picture of closeness and provide a sense of community.

There are efforts today to preserve the community, but to little avail.

When visiting **Marktown** it is easier to visualize the time period of the Yellowstone Trail: the dominance of big industry, corporation-employee relationships, home design, limited auto ownership (no individual garages), and even the role of new concepts of city planning. ✿

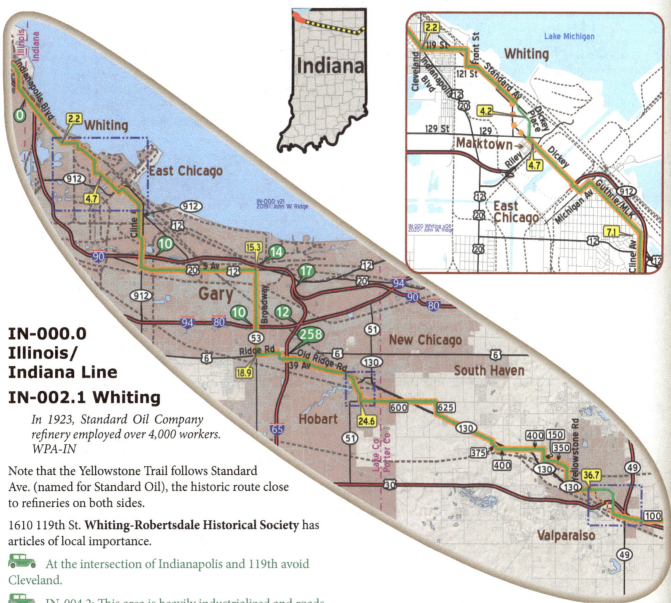

IN-000.0 Illinois/ Indiana Line

IN-002.1 Whiting

In 1923, Standard Oil Company refinery employed over 4,000 workers. WPA-IN

Note that the Yellowstone Trail follows Standard Ave. (named for Standard Oil), the historic route close to refineries on both sides.

1610 119th St. **Whiting-Robertsdale Historical Society** has articles of local importance.

🚙 At the intersection of Indianapolis and 119th avoid Cleveland.

🚙 IN-004.2: This area is heavily industrialized and roads have been and are being reshuffled to meet modern needs. You may have to explore a bit to find your way. The original YT may have more closely followed Dickey St.

IN-004.7 Marktown

For the heritage traveler, Marktown is a very unusual and serendipitous find. It is part of East Chicago, not a separately incorporated city, but it is isolated within a massive industrial plain.

Starting in 1917 the **Marktown Site** was built by Clayton Mark Sr. to be used as housing for his Mark Manufacturing (steel) Company employees. It was to include housing for 8,000 workers and all conveniences of a model village on 20 acres. In 1923, Mark sold his company with only a fraction (200 houses) of the community built.

Restoration and preservation are not thriving. Some of the 1917 houses are still standing today, but many are in decay. Surrounded by busy highways and petroleum smells and derelict steel mills, apparently fewer want to live there.

Check the Marktown website for information and tours.

IN-006.0 East Chicago

East Chicago with its port at Indiana Harbor became one of the great shipping centers of the Nation. The most important industry to enter the region was steel. Inland Steel had established a plant in East Chicago in 1893; and when US Steel Corporation decided in 1905 to erect its greatest mills on the sand dunes, the industrial future of the region was assured. WPA-IN

Here was the world's largest cement plant. East Chicago (western section) is separated from the Indiana Harbor section by a vast rail yard that served as the rail gateway to Chicago and the west. A canal system of waterways joins the Calumet River to Lake Michigan.

2401 E Columbus Dr. **East Chicago Historical Society** has useful information about this complex area.

🚙 IN-7.8: Cline St. and IN 912 south of East Chicago run parallel. Today's driver must switch from one to the other of those two roads by using one of the exits, probably 7.

🚙 IN-15.1: The YT followed 5th Ave. which is now one-way so 4th Ave. may be needed to be used.

IN

YELLOWSTONE TRAIL BEING MARKED FROM COAST TO COAST

... the official markers are now being placed up along the Yellowstone Trail passing through Porter county. It is expected the official marking committee will be in Valparaiso in a few days and that within the next two weeks the Yellowstone Trail will have been marked through Porter county.

July 12, 1918 Valparaiso Evening Messenger

Michael Buettner, author of "Together in Indiana: The Yellowstone Trail and Lincoln Highway and US Route 30," *(Yellowstone Trail Association, Arrow newsletter August 2012)* referred to the early "stair step" route of the Yellowstone Trail along section lines as,

...the ultimate road less traveled and, thankfully, places like Wanatah have memorialized this original version of the Trail with just enough signs to help modern tourists capture that wonderful feeling of roadway rediscovery. ⚙

This morning members of the state highway commission were taken over the Yellowstone Trail west to Hobart. They stated that if they found this road in as bad a condition as reported, and if it carried the amount of traffic also reported, they would recommend that it be taken over at once by the state from Valparaiso to Hobart.

May 17, 1923 Valparaiso Evening Messenger

~~~~~~~~~~~~~~~~~~~~~~

STATE WILL TAKE OVER YELLOWSTONE TRAIL

The Yellowstone Trail between Valparaiso and Hobart will be taken over and maintained in good condition this year, after which it will be hard surfaced, according to a report of the Valpo-Chamber of Commerce.

May 25, 1923 Valparaiso Evening Messenger

Two great highways crossed in Valparaiso

Porter County Museum of History, Valparaiso

Restored Memorial Opera House, Valparaiso

The Way Things Were: Early Hobart
Hoosier Happenings Blog

IN-015.3 Gary

Gary came into being when massive mills were built along miles of lakefront and tens of thousands of workers were brought in. With US Steel firmly entrenched as a magnet, other enterprises were drawn to the region. WPA-IN

220 W 5th Ave. **Gary Historical & Cultural Society** on US 20. They preserved Gary's first building - The Gary Land Company Building (1906) - and maintained it as an historical museum. Population, at this writing, has shrunk more than 50% of its former size with devastation visible along the Trail.

IN-20.1: Just west of I-65 the YT followed Missouri St. between what are now known as Ridge Rd. and 39th Ave. (was Old Ridge Rd.) Missouri St. is now partially overrun by an I-65 interchange. The existing parallel streets are poorly marked. Tennessee or Louisiana Sts. may be used today.

IN-023.1 Hobart

Hobart morphed from a major railroad and shipping hub in the late 1800s to a residential community for employees of area industries from the 1920s. Street railway service to Gary began in 1914, just before the Yellowstone Trail arrived.

Hobart is uncovering history by restoring the original facades, original brickwork and authentic architecture of downtown buildings. The historic district holds some preserved buildings which were on the Yellowstone Trail. Included are the **First State Bank** built 1888 (301 Main St.), the **Friedrich Building** built 1910 (614 E Third St.), and a neat **First Unitarian church** on Main St. built in 1874.

Deep River County Park is a beautiful, serene park featuring Wood's Historic Grist Mill, built in 1838 by John Wood and rebuilt in 1876 by his son, Nathan.

706 E 4th St. **Hobart Historical Society Museum** contains local artifacts.

IN-036.7 Valparaiso

Under Henry Brown's excellent management Valparaiso University became nationally known as the "poor man's Harvard," and in 1914-15 boasted a student body of 6,000, second only in size to that of the older Eastern university. WPA-IN

The Indiana Steel Company Plant (visitors welcome), in the northwestern part of town, produces 80 per cent of all the magnets made in the United States. WPA-IN

The Yellowstone Trail and the later routing of the Lincoln Highway run together for a short distance in Valparaiso. Author Michael Buettner says,

It is probably safe to assume that with the completion of the original US Route 30 alignment between Valparaiso and Fort Wayne, the Yellowstone Trail immediately relocated to match the federal route. The Lincoln Highway would make it a triumvirate of routes after its relocation in 1928. As a result, this is the only region in the United States where the two groundbreaking automobile trails shared a common corridor."

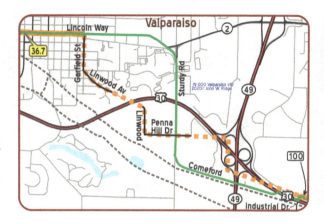

The route of the Yellowstone Trail from Valparaiso to Fort Wayne looks like a series of "stair steps" along section lines.

Glaciation has left numerous kettle lakes and knobs in this hilly area of northwest Indiana. Many glacial erratics can be found throughout the city.

The downtown square contains several historic buildings, preserved from the 1800s and on the National Register of Historic Places around, roughly, today's Lincolnway (the Yellowstone Trail) and Franklin St.

The **Porter County Museum of History** is one block from Lincolnway (the Yellowstone Trail), next door to the Memorial Opera House, on Indiana Ave. near Franklin. Housed there since 1916, the museum has an eclectic collection ranging from local historic tools to a World War II P-38 tough can opener, dubbed the "John Wayne." Also contained are Dr. Noah Amstutz' inventions which led to the cathode ray tube and TV. The rear of the building is an old jail.

Next door, 104 E Indiana Ave., is the restored 1893 **Memorial Opera House,** now called Memorial Hall. It featured John Philip Sousa at the turn of the century and the Marx Brothers in 1919.

IN-048.5 Wanatah

Wanatah is a farming village named for Wa-na-tah, an Indian chief who is said to have been noted for his laziness. WPA-IN

Keep an eye out for Yellowstone Trail markers on the well marked Trail in Wanatah.

West Cross St. (one block west of the Yellowstone Trail). **Wanatah Historical Society.** An active group, they promote awareness of the area's rich history. They have a fully restored 1888 wooden caboose filled with railroad memorabilia from more than fifteen different railroads.

Wanatah's caboose with local RR memorabilia

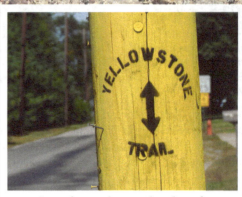
One of several recent hand-made
signs in Hamlet
Marilyn Goodrich

The modern Waymire Corner Tap

Three incarnations of Hamlet's
1915 Yellowstone Hotel

The Gundy Hotel
Marilyn Goodrich

The Yellowstone Hotel in 1919
Marilyn Goodrich

ROSS HOUSE
219 La Porte Street
PLYMOUTH   INDIANA

Stop at Ross House
for comfortable night's rset and good
things to eat. American Plan. Prices
reasonable. O. C. Himebaugh, Prop.

Remains of a YT bridge west of Hamlet
BridgeHunter.com

Recent sign, now removed, leading to
the bridge west of Hamlet. The sign
provided a memorial to the end of the
original YT

IN-058.8 Hanna

IN-068.0 Hamlet

HAMLET, (702 alt., 519 pop.), was platted in 1863 by John Hamlet. It owes its existence to its location at the crossing of the Pennsylvania and New York Central Railroads, and is a shipping point for the surrounding country. WPA-IN

4 W Davis St. **Waymire's Corner Tap** around the corner from Starke St., the Yellowstone Trail. The building, built c.1915, housed the former Hamlet Café and Hotel, also called the Yellowstone Trail Hotel. The Hamlet Café was reputed to be a stop for Al Capone; John Dillinger was also seen on the Trail.

Keep an eye out here, too, for Yellowstone Trail signs. There was an interesting hand-painted Yellowstone Trail sign on a telephone pole at the corner of Indiana and Starke Sts.

Hamlet is quite interested in the Trail, having hosted several annual "Yellowstone Trail Fests." Everyone turns out for the themed activities involving their portion of the Trail, including old car runs, foot races on the Trail and scrap metal sculpture. The Lincoln Highway is marked north of the tracks at N300E and N500E. It is Old US 30, which was the Lincoln Highway. It provides a good detour for the closed Trail.

Near Hamlet, between N400E (US 35) and N300E, the YT has long been abandoned leaving a bridge over Robbins Creek (GPS: 41.38943, -86.63514). The bridge, still standing, is described at http://bridgehunter.com/in/starke/robbins-600n/. Between US 35 and N500E the road is still formally known as the Yellowstone Trail and is driveable gravel but the intersection with US 35 may prove difficult. The signs that stood here and reflected the fate of the YT are now removed. They read: "Yellowstone Trail, Bridge Out, Dead End, Road Closed."

IN-076.7 Donaldson

There is another hand-painted Yellowstone Trail sign here on 8th St.

The YT follows a zigzag route across the tracks.

Plymouth sits at the intersection of five early routes, each celebrated in the Marshall County Museum

IN-084.0 Plymouth

(pop. 3,838, alt. 790 ft.), is a thriving town at the junction of three railroads. It has extensive manufactures of basket and box works and has beautiful streets and residences. At Twin Lakes, 3 miles southwest, is Pottawatomie Park, named for the Native American tribe who once inhabited this section. BB1921-4

The Yellowstone Trail runs along the tracks from Jefferson to Laporte and on Laporte between the tracks and Michigan. BB1924

123 N Michigan St. (Yellowstone Trail). **Marshall County Museum**. This vibrant museum really jumps. In addition to county and city memorabilia, interactive displays and guest expert presenters, they have a Transportation Center room. Five highways crossed Marshall County, the Yellowstone Trail being one of them. The history of those roads is told with audio stories, and the "Train Room" is a big draw, especially among the "train guys" who add to the moving display and manage it. Can one ever take the kid out of the man?

The **Michigan Street Bridge** across the Yellow River (one of 5 notable bridges) carried the Yellowstone Trail in downtown Plymouth. A blog entitled "Hoosier Happenings" described the bridge, saying that the Michigan St. concrete bridge was built in 1916-17 and that " It was constructed in place of the early metal Michigan Road bridge, probably in keeping with the construction of the Yellowstone Trail following the alignment and bringing additional vehicular traffic across the bridge."

IN-087.9: The intersections of US 31 with Co 12B and with Michigan Rd. are inadequately marked. Use care.

IMPROVE YELLOWSTONE TRAIL

One of the big motor trucks used by the state highway commission in caring for state roads is now at work on the Yellowstone Trail east of Columbia City and large quantities of washed gravel are being hauled in and placed on the road east of town.

January 22, 1921 Fort Wayne News-Sentinel

Two views of the Michigan St. Bridge in Plymouth. Above from c.1918. Below as renovated
Kurt Garner,
Hoosier Happenings Blog

STATE COMMISSION COMING
MAY RECOMMEND PAVING OF TRAIL

Members of the state highway commission are expected here Tuesday to inspect the Lincoln Highway and the Yellowstone Trail. The commission will recommend the paving of the Yellowstone Trail rather than the Lincoln Highway. The Yellowstone route, which is closer to Chicago, runs through such cities as Cleveland, Toledo, Fort Wayne, and west through Columbia City and Plymouth. It is considered the logical road to improve at this time.

May 15, 1922 Fort Wayne News-Sentinel

Marshall County Museum,
Plymouth

July 15, 1919. Letter from brand new Indiana chapter of the Yellowstone Trail Association to General Manager, Hal Cooley, says in part:

Be it resolved, that we, the delegates, representing the towns on the Yellowstone Trail in Indiana, from Valparaiso to Fort Wayne inclusive, hereby pledge ourselves to become a working part of the Yellowstone Trail Association as a state unit, and to help in carrying out the work of the Association in every way that we can.

Note: They also promised to pay at least $1,500 for the Association's program for 1919. ✿

STATE HIGHWAY COMMISSION DESIGNATES YELLOWSTONE TRAIL THROUGH PLYMOUTH

The local people made a hard fight to have the commission designate the trail from the Leesburg Rd. north through Plymouth and thence west through Hamlet in preference to a straight westward route from the Leesburg road through Knox.

June 18, 1920 Plymouth Daily Pilot

YELLOWSTONE TRAIL MEETING
MEMBERSHIP OF INDIANA MEETS IN BOURBON IN ANNUAL MEETING

January 31, 1924 Bourbon News-Mirror

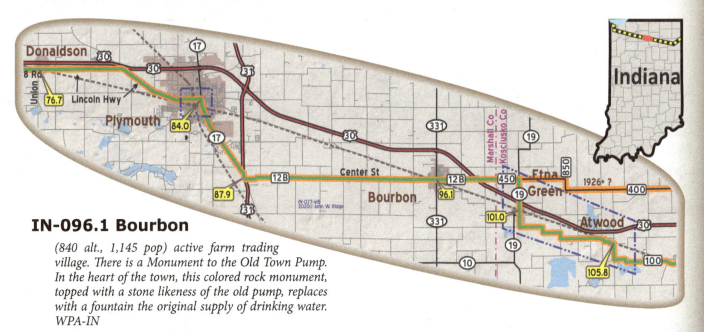

IN-096.1 Bourbon

(840 alt., 1,145 pop) active farm trading village. There is a Monument to the Old Town Pump. In the heart of the town, this colored rock monument, topped with a stone likeness of the old pump, replaces with a fountain the original supply of drinking water. WPA-IN

Bourbonites are very proud of the memorial to the town pump that now is located in **Sit Park** on the corner of Old US 30 and Main St.

IN-101.0 Etna Green

The right angle turns taken by the Yellowstone Trail in the area are good examples of the effects of rectangular surveys.

IN-105.8 Atwood

Several streets in Atwood are no longer driveable. Use Gault (east/west) and Wray (N200W) (north/south). The YT apparently followed (from the west) W200N past Wray, south on Harrison, east on High, south on Green, east on Gault to N650W. Note the curve between Green and High, an indication that it was used as a highway. These streets not labeled on this map.

IN-105.8 - IN-113.8: One source, the 1926 Rand McNally map, shows the YT running north of Atwood and east of Etna Green. on what became US 30. Had the Trail been rerouted there?

The Chinworth Bridge (41.24697,-85.91077) connecting the YT and the 1928 version of the Lincoln Highway just west of Warsaw is described in Wikipedia and BridgeHunters.com.

IN-110.3

The Chinworth Bridge crosses the Tippecanoe River between the old Yellowstone Trail and the 1928 Lincoln Highway, now called Old Highway 30. At almost 125 years old, the bridge now carries no vehicles, but hosts families out for a walk or just communing with nature. As it is near the site of the Chinworth Bridge Trailhead, it is also an inviting site for canoeists, picnicers and hikers at the nearby Tippecanoe Rest Park. The Kosciusko County Historical Society now owns the Park and leases the bridge.

The bridge is the last remaining Pratt through truss single-span bridge in the county, the kind once found throughout the country.

There once was a post with yellow bands and a "Y" in a black circle at the south end of the bridge marking the Yellowstone Trail, although neither the Yellowstone Trail nor the Lincoln Highway was routed over the bridge.

It is reported that the Yellowstone Trail has been marked through Chicago and will be marked east of that city and through to Fort Wayne in a few days.

July 9, 1918
Warsaw Union

YELLOWSTONE TRAIL FIELD REPRESENTATIVE IN CITY URGING COOPERATION

F. C. Finch, field representative for the Yellowstone Trail Association, was in Warsaw to work up interest in the Trail meeting in Fort Wayne November 16 so that the controversy over the route through Warsaw may be ironed out.

November 8, 1921 Warsaw Union

Beachwood Park at Hoffman Lake is experiencing a great boom due to the construction of the new Yellowstone Trail cement highway from Chicago. The new road passes within three blocks of the little lake. Chicago people are purchasing lots for $300 there which formerly sold for $50.

September 19, 1927 Warsaw Union

Dan Coplan, writing in *That's Life* published by the Winona Lake Historical Society, said, "But the Yellowstone Trail was much more than an avenue for a 1916 cross-country relay race, no matter how thrilling the event may have been. It was one of Koskiusko County's first important highways, and for more than a decade brought thousands of people – and their dollars to the county's lakes and the immensely popular summer programs and church conferences at Winona Lake. ✿

There was much excitement in the press the autumn of 1916 about the cross-country relay auto race against time on the Yellowstone Trail. See **Trail Tale: 1916 Race**, page 416.

A sample of headlines from the *Warsaw Union*:

August 12, 1916. Warsaw on Route of Big Relay Run

August 14, 1916. The Continent Over Yellowstone Trail

August 29, 1916. Yellowstone Relay Run to Start Sept. 11

September 8, 1916. Everything Now Ready for Trip Across Country

September 12, 1916. Lookout for Speeding Car

September 13, 1916. Yellowstone Car Passes Through 2 Hours Ahead of Schedule. ✿

Residents of Columbia City can now drive straight through to Fort Wayne over the Yellowstone Trail. This was previously impossible on account of a stretch of three miles in Allen county. Efforts to get Allen county to improve the road failed, so Sam Trembly, President of the Columbia City Commercial Club, arranged through that body to have the work done. Six teams and drags and wagons were furnished by the Whitley county men and the road was put in fine shape and is ready to travel.

May 5, 1920 Fort Wayne News-Sentinel

Representatives of the Yellowstone Trail Association passed through here [Columbia City] yesterday marking the trail through this city and Whitley county. The signs were placed on telephone poles and are yellow tin with a black arrow showing the direction of the trail.

August 23, 1920
Fort Wayne News-Sentinel

YELLOWSTONE TRAIL MEETING

There will be a meeting of the Yellowstone Trail Delegates at Columbia City Nov. 10th.

November 4, 1920
Bourbon News-Mirror

STATE ROAD MEET WILL BE HELD MAY 18 PROPOSITION OF SECURING YELLOWSTONE TRAIL WILL BE TAKEN UP

May 3, 1916
The Kosciusko Union (Columbia City)

HEAVY TRAFFIC ON THE TRAIL

A Whitley county farmer, residing on the Yellowstone Trail between Columbia City and Warsaw, has made a count of the automobiles passing over the highway. He reports that the average for week days is from 350 to 400 and on Sundays from 700 to 900

September 14, 1922 Warsaw Union

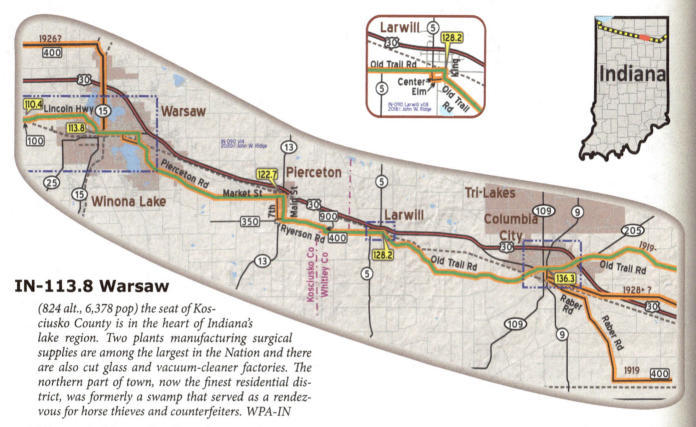

IN-113.8 Warsaw

(824 alt., 6,378 pop) the seat of Kosciusko County is in the heart of Indiana's lake region. Two plants manufacturing surgical supplies are among the largest in the Nation and there are also cut glass and vacuum-cleaner factories. The northern part of town, now the finest residential district, was formerly a swamp that served as a rendezvous for horse thieves and counterfeiters. WPA-IN

505 S Detroit St. **Warsaw Cut Glass Company, Inc**. In 1912 Warsaw Cut Glass opened for business. The building is constructed of rejected paving bricks from Warsaw's street department. The long, narrow building features many high windows to allow as much natural light as possible (there were no electric lights). One main shaft drives two floors of cutting with 55 workers. The shaft, and the original leather belts, are in use today as one of the last American facilities practicing the art of cutting glass.

121 N. Indiana St. **Kosciusko County Old Jail Museum**. Located in downtown Warsaw, this Gothic Revival building was built in 1870. On the National Register of Historic Places, it currently serves as the headquarters for the Kosciusko County Historical Society. The Old Jail Museum & Genealogy Library are housed here. The sheriff and his family lived in the jail building and the sheriff's wife provided the meals for the inmates.

IN-116.2 Winona Lake

Located around the eastern shore of Winona Lake, the **Winona Lake Historic District** includes various historic buildings that attest to the area's history as a Chautauqua and Bible conference hotspot. "Chatauqua" was a New York organization that sponsored Christian speakers nation-wide. Famed preacher and professional baseball player Billy Sunday lived here; famous photographers taught here; The Winona Lake School of Theology was located here from 1920 to 1970. Today some restored original structures make it an historic summer resort.

100 9th St. **Winona History Center** in Westminster Hall of Grace College has pictures of early autos and Yellowstone Trail-era photos and more about Chatauqua and Winona's significance.

IN-122.6 Pierceton

Many art studios and antique shops line IN 13, the Yellowstone Trail, in downtown Pierceton.

The 7th St. route of the YT has an unknown date.

IN-128.2 Larwill
IN-136.3 Columbia City

108 W Jefferson St. **Whitley County Historical Museum**. It is housed in the Columbia City home of Thomas Riley Marshall, Indiana Governor and 28th Vice President of the U.S. under Woodrow Wilson. The museum complex consists of the Marshall House, an Annex, and an outhouse.

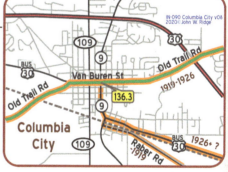

Van Buran and Walnut Sts. There is an old operating gas station with original canopy.

Van Buren and Main Sts. **Whitley County Courthouse**. Van Buren Street was the Yellowstone Trail. The 1888 courthouse accorded travelers on the Yellowstone Trail a good look at its sculptures of animals and birds.

An historic district, bounded by Jefferson, Walnut, Ellsworth, and Wayne Sts., contains historic buildings, repurposed and thriving.

IT'S GOING SOME

The war department message being relayed across country by automobile over the Yellowstone Trail, a coast-to-coast route, reached Fort Wayne at 5:15 o'clock this evening and was carried on to Warsaw, 45 miles distant, in an hour and one minute. The time set for the trip sets a record. The message was an hour and 55 minutes ahead of its schedule.

September 13, 1916 San Diego Evening Tribune
Note: For full story of the race across the country, see
Trail Tale: 1916 Race, page 416.

WAYNE HOTEL
"Special Attention Given to the Motorist"
121-123 West Columbia Street
FT. WAYNE   INDIANA

EUROPEAN PLAN, $1.50 and Up
A Thoroughly Modern Hotel of 120 Rooms, 40 with Bath. Running Water in Every Room. First Class Restaurant in Connection.   Reasonable Prices

---

HEAD OF YELLOWSTONE TRAIL
MAIN OFFICE IS NOW LOCATED
IN FORT WAYNE

Fort Wayne is, for the time being at least, the virtual headquarters of the Yellowstone Trail Association. The whole of the organization is keeping step with Fort Wayne as Mr. Cooley has announced that his headquarters will be here for an indefinite period.

July 29, 1918 Fort Wayne News-Sentinel
Note: Cooley was the General Manager of the Association who may have used Fort Wayne as his temporary headquarters, away from his major Minneapolis headquarters, as he pushed for boosters in the eastern states. The difference between the East and the West in Trail acceptance is apparent.

OFFICIAL SIGNS OF ALL HIGHWAYS
AND TRAILS COMPILED IN BOOKLET
BY CHAMBER OF COMMERCE

Motorists and others who have been puzzling their brains over the mysterious signs which appear on telephone poles in various parts of the city as well as on many county highways may set their worries aside for the good roads bureau of the Chamber of Commerce has published in pamphlet form a compilation of all the markings which are used to indicate the seven great national highways which pass through Fort Wayne.

April 14, 1919 Fort Wayne News-Sentinel

It appears that an early Fort Wayne route of the YT, from the east along Lake Ave., crossed the river on a previous bridge to Superior St. which it followed to Calhoun St. It then turned south to Main. A newer route apparently used a newer bridge running south of the first bridge, worked its way to Berry St., then north on Calhoun to Main.

Sam F. Trembly, state member of the executive committee of the Yellowstone Trail has returned to Columbia City from Milwaukee, Wisconsin, where he attended a two day session of the Yellowstone Trail Association. A recommendation was drawn up and sent to the government asking that the charge to tourists for entrance to the Yellowstone National Park be abolished because enough expense had been incurred [getting to] the park without an entrance fee.

The annual budget for the next year was placed at $22,000 and Indiana is assessed $1,400 to be apportioned to counties and cities along the trail route which is to be marked soon.

February 19, 1920 Fort Wayne News-Sentinel

In Fort Wayne, the YT is at its southernmost point.

STARTING CAMPAIGN FOR
DELINQUENT ROAD FUNDS
QUOTA IS $400 PER YEAR

Fort Wayne's share for the Yellowstone Trail Association treasury will be raised starting today by an intensive drive through the business district of the city by the Chamber of Commerce. The quota has been placed at $400. One hundred and fifty-four dollars of this amount was not raised last year, so it is the intention of the businessmen to collect the money along with the regular quota for the year.

August 12, 1920
Fort Wayne News-Sentinel
Note: They succeeded, but not easily.

TWO TOURIST BUREAUS HERE
YELLOWSTONE TRAIL AND HOOSIER
MOTOR CLUB PLAN SERVICE

…The Hoosier State Motor Club will open a branch office in the Anthony Hotel and the Yellowstone Trail Association will maintain an office in the Chamber of Commerce.

April 27, 1921 Fort Wayne News-Sentinel

YELLOWSTONE TRAIL SELECTED

The Yellowstone Trail was selected as one of the U.S. Highways from the Atlantic to the Pacific. They were selected by the joint board on interstate highways as "United States highways" to be designated with uniform markers.

August 27, 1925 Hobart News
Note: The marking never happened.

This Wayside is really worth the 27 mile drive north of Fort Wayne to Auburn. The most beautiful classic automobiles of all time are displayed on three floors of the 1974 **Auburn Cord Deusenberg Auto Museum** at 1600 S. Wayne St.

Over 100 antique autos are shown in the former Auburn Automobile Company building. These original Duesenberg, Cord, Auburn, Cadillac, and Rolls Royce beauties are so polished they hurt the eye. In 1926, Errett Cord, then the owner of Auburn Company, partnered with Duesenberg Corporation, famous for its racing cars, and used it for a line of high-priced luxury vehicles. He also put his own name on one of the first front-wheel-drive cars, the Cord L-29.

Wikipedia says "The Auburn Automobile Company administration building is part of the campus where cars were hand-assembled, rather than mass-produced. The showroom and administrative buildings were designed in Art Deco style." The facility's buildings were declared a National Historic Landmark in 2005. Because luxury cars were out of the question during the Great Depression, the company's doors closed in 1937.

The Museum once served as the factory headquarters of the company beginning in 1930. It's Art Deco decor is a fitting backdrop for these gorgeous cars. This is not a static museum. Each Labor Day weekend the autos are outside on parade - literally - which draws hundreds of spectators. Some exhibits have interactive kiosks that allow a visitor to hear the sounds the car makes and to see related videos.

Perhaps the best display of this Museum is a history of luxury cars and their need for good roads.

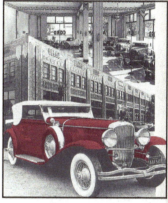

Auburn Cord Deusenberg
Auto Museum

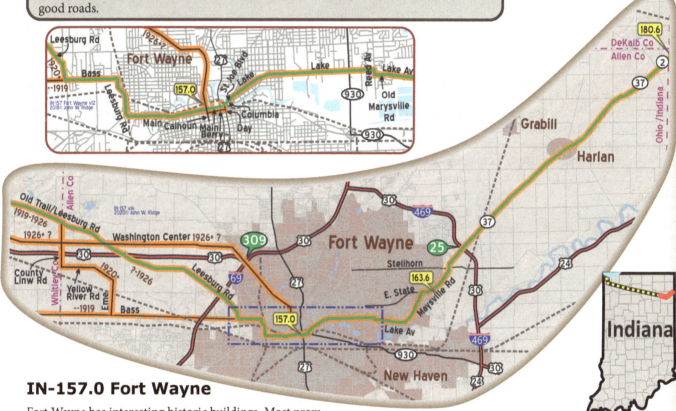

IN-157.0 Fort Wayne

Fort Wayne has interesting historic buildings. Most prominent are four churches, all built in the mid-1800s. Four Historic Landmarks are listed below:

The Pennsylvania Railroad Station, also known as Baker Street Station (1914)

2701 Spring St. University of Saint Francis, **John H. Bass Mansion** (1902)

216 E Washington Blvd. **Masonic Temple** (1926)

715 S Calhoun St. **Allen County Courthouse** (1902)

302 E Berry St. **The History Center**. Old castle-like 1893 building on the Yellowstone Trail. The Center also oversees the historic Barr Street Market (adjacent to the building), the oldest public space in Fort Wayne. Today the Center maintains a collection of more than 26,000 artifacts. The largest of these is the very building in which the society has resided since 1980-the 1893 City Hall building.

IN-181 Indiana/Ohio line

Before Filling Stations

by Holliday Ridge with contributions by Kendall O'Neal

"Service stations have sprung up like mushrooms in the last few years and many different types have been introduced." *Standard Oil Company*, 1922.

All-electric cars are a popular concept today, but they don't go very far without needing a long recharging time. In fact, running out of power is a big fear for people contemplating any alternative fuel car. A local poet once quipped "a battery low and 30 miles to go." The nation-wide distribution system to support alternate energy cars doesn't seem to yet exist. This insecurity of modern drivers was just the opposite of our motorist ancestors of 110 years ago who raised a hue and cry for better roads to go farther distances, seemingly without a care for where the next tank of gas would come from.

"A good road from Plymouth Rock to Puget Sound" was the motto and fervent desire of many. However, the ubiquitous stand-alone filling station was not developed until the nineteen teens, and not wide spread until the 1920s. So, how did the wheezing Winton, the Tin Can T and the muscular Maxwell get fed on long trips? How was gasoline transported, kept, and sold in pre-filling station days? The complexity of gasoline history involves dangerous aspects, and the invention of a new machine.

Distribution Systems

The answer lies with the common kerosene lamp of the 1800s. Oil was found in 1859 in Pennsylvania by Colonel Drake, and before that, it was imported. This oil was refined into kerosene and a relatively useless by product called gasoline. Bulk kerosene was distributed around the country in horse-drawn tankers to distribution centers. This business

Early bulk kerosene delivery wagon
petroleumhistory.com

was so big that the Supreme Court split up Standard Oil in 1911. Kerosene and its network paved the way for gasoline distribution. Standard Oil's breakup provided inroads for new, small companies to get in the distribution system of both kerosene and the growing gasoline trade.

Gasoline did have a few niche markets before automobile use, including solvents for cleaning and in chemical and industrial plants. But it was not uncommon for refineries to simply dump unused gasoline into waterways. As the demand for gasoline increased, the proportion of kerosene to gasoline distribution at bulk stations shifted from less than 10 percent

in 1904 to 40 percent in 1930. (Williamson et al. in Melaina). A well-developed network of kerosene distribution provided gasoline on demand to almost anywhere by the time Henry Ford was cranking out his black beauties.

The kerosene distribution system consisted of:

> ... more than 100 refineries and vast networks of bulk storage facilities and tank wagons. In 1906 Standard Oil operated nearly 3,573 bulk stations in the U.S. These storage facilities received barrels or tank wagons of petroleum products directly from refineries, and redistributed them to local populations (Willamson *et al.* in Melaina).

Fill'er Up

Purchasing gasoline along The Yellowstone Trail before stand-alone filling stations were created could have been accomplished from several types of sellers, none familiar to our modern understanding of the process. Before the more familiar pumping mechanisms located in front of stores, garages, and parking lots were created, gas could be purchased in cans, barrels, and at the depots themselves, where a barrel and dipper were mostly used. A can of gas could be found on grocers' and other retailers' shelves (Witzel). Even at drug stores. This method was preferred, even with the more unwieldy five gallon cans. Larger barrels of gas were often kept in repair garages and busy dry goods stores, where portions of it were sold to consumers by, in many instances, dipping a ladle in the barrel and pouring it into a pitcher to take to the thirsty car. Parking lots often sold gas, although in this age, a parking lot was more a storage area for cars in the middle of a town, if they were not used on a daily basis.

Once procured, there were many ways an early auto enthusiast could fill'er up. None of those methods was easy, convenient, or clean. And they were all dangerous. There were no pumps, hoses, or dedicated employees to do the work - at least not before around 1913, and even then the pumps took a while to spread across the country. Once the gas was ladled into a pitcher, or was in a small bucket or can, it was poured into a funnel placed at the opening of the gas tank in the car. Over the funnel one placed a cloth to filter out bits because the refining process wasn't as complete as it is now. Then, when one thought the tank was full or close to it, someone had to get very close to the opening and look straight ⇨

And then there were curbside pumps

down into the tank to see the level of the gasoline, and guess how much more to put in, breathing the fumes all the while. It took practice to judge by sound and sight when the typical five gallon tank was full. During this long process, gasoline covered the rag cloth, the funnel, the bucket or can, the riding cloak of the driver, probably some on the car itself, and fumes everywhere. And at distribution depots, an entire nearby building was also quite combustible. One accidentally lit match or cigarette was the cause of many horrific fires. Indeed, Montana's *Big Timber Pioneer* (Historic Review section, 1972) recalled that,

In 1916 the following article appeared: Sunday afternoon a young man drove to the Main Street Garage for gas. As one of the Newness brothers was pouring gas, the owner of the car suddenly struck a match and held it over the tank to see how much it contained and in the twinkling of an eye a fine blaze was the result.

Early Gas Pumps

An early pump was invented around 1883 to deliver gasoline more safely to autos. Sylvanius Bowser of Fort Wayne, Indiana, developed a pump with a plunger that would push kerosene up through a pipe. Just like drawing water from a well. The pump had a hand lever, an upright faucet lever and a dial indicating the quantity of gas pumped. The pump was placed on barrels of kerosene and rolled into grocery stores, hardware stores, drug stores and elsewhere. In 1898 John Tokheim of Cedar Rapids, Iowa, built a gasoline pump that lifted fuel from an underground tank up to a hose. Tokheim also patented the first self-measuring, "visible" gas pump in

Bill's Filling Station, on the Yellowstone Trail, Marmarth
O'Neill Photo (ND)

1901. A marked glass "dome" on top of the pump held the amount of gasoline being pumped (up to five gallons) and thus it could be accurately measured. By 1903 Tokheim adapted his pump and hose to dispense gasoline directly into an automobile fuel tank. In 1918 The Tokheim Company was sold and moved to Fort Wayne, Indiana, home of the Bowser pump.

As the Yellowstone Trail became more well developed and used in the 1920s, as with many other roads, travelers needed more than gasoline, so the newly independent filling station buildings expanded to include amenities for the tourists and travelers a long way from home (Steil). Snacks, clean restrooms, and free maps at first, then diners and motels were built adjacent to filling stations to give real comfort to travelers.

A fine history of filling station architecture can be found in *Fill'er Up: The Glory Days of Wisconsin Gas Stations* by James Draeger and Mark Speltz. (Wisconsin Historical Society Press. 2008.)

Today's filling stations are a far cry from 110 years ago when motorists along the Yellowstone Trail ran high risks of explosions and trusted on chance to find gasoline.

References:

Melaina, Marc W. "Turn of the Century Refueling". *Energy Policy* Vol 35, Issue 10, October 2007.

Steil, Tim. *Fantastic Filling Stations*. MBI Publishers, 2002.

Witzel, Michael Karl. *The American Gas Station*. MBI Publishers, 1998. ✿

Bowser gas pump from along the YT. Displayed in Butte, Montana at the World Museum of Mining

Pumps often carried the name of the particular route on which they were located. Note the YT logo.
Hal Meeks

A Sylvanius Bowser pump c.1883
Smithsonian Insstitution

Car Heaters in the Yellowstone Trail Era

Early cars with no windshield, open cars, and even closed cars without heaters, put a real bite on winter autoing along the early Trail. Many owners dodged the chilling experience and just put their cars up for the winter, opting for short trips with the horse and sleigh, probably equipped with buffalo robes and hot bricks. In mountainous areas, that furlough for the auto could take up to seven months.

As roads got better, autos were used more in the winter, bringing the issue of warmth to the forefront, especially by women. Clothing appeared that was designed for motoring such as storm aprons made from heavy rubber material, lap robes, long fur coats, and fur hats.

The heated brick wrapped in cloth placed on the floor for foot warming was popular for its simplicity and low cost. Good for short trips, anyway!

Margaret Wilcox of Chicago (Imagine that. A woman!) is credited with inventing the first experimental car heater. Patented in 1893, her car heating system directed air from over the engines for warming inside the auto. Her invention was well received, but the temperature could not be well regulated.

Portable galvanized iron heaters appeared in 1925 which were just advanced models of the hot brick. Brick-shaped burning coal was held in elongated foot rests. One could

$1.10 OUR HIGH GRADE MOMIE CLOTH LAP ROBE.

MATERIAL—Extra heavy momie cloth yarn, woven in fancy Jacquard pattern. A very beautiful design. COLORS—Olive green, old rose and light brown. Closely woven. SIZE—52x60 inches; weight about 16 ounces.

One of the first commercial car heaters

AVALON STORM APRONS

Affords complete protection against bad weather for cars and occupants. Made with openings for one to five persons. Openings can be closed if not used. Heavy rubber cloth--plaid black.

extinguish the heat with water. The use of exhaust gas heaters came next, in which air passed around bundles of tubes carrying the exhaust. They tended to leak a bit giving off an obnoxious odor.

By 1929, an attempt to heat the auto consisted of conducting the warmed air from the back of the radiator to the floorboard and deflecting it toward the passengers.

During the Yellowstone Trail days, there weren't good interior heating systems! It wasn't until into the 1930s that the popular system of directing some of the hot water exiting the engine cooling system to another radiator through which the auto's interior air is directed. It picks up the warmth from the engine and distributes it into the passenger compartment. Perhaps of interest was the 1937 introduction of a heating system by Nash Motors that directed warm air from such a radiator into the auto at a bit of an elevated pressure. That kept the drafts from the outside, out. With the addition of air conditioning and a good brand name, Weather Eye, it was used for nearly 40 years.

Today, our warm tootsies appreciate the efforts and good intentions of early engineers.

Note: Much of the above Information is from the Australian Society of Heating, Refrigerating and Air-Conditioning Engineers. ✿

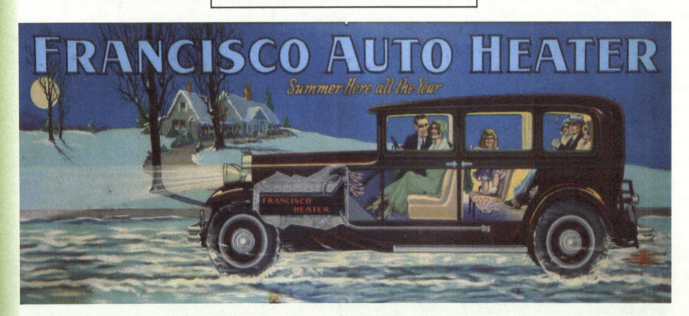

Ohio

WHAT THE TRAIL FOUNDERS SAID-1921

Ohio is one state that needs no writeup. Good roads lead all over the state and they are rapidly developing a system of paved roads. Some difficulty in finding roads from towns will be experienced because there is almost an entire absence of any marking in the state of Ohio. This condition, however, will be temporary as plans are already afoot which will make a complete marked system in the state of Ohio, possibly within a short time. The very best advice that can be given for travel in Ohio is to study the map carefully and then inquire your way from someone who is in a position to know. The Automobile Clubs in Toledo, Cleveland, Cincinnati. and Dayton maintain information bureau departments, and the Yellowstone Trail Association at its information bureau in the Winton Hotel in Cleveland will be glad to serve such inquirers as apply to them. Travel is comparatively long distance in Ohio. That is, 100 miles or more is getting to be customary and the usual thing, and a stranger to the state need have no hesitancy in starting even if they have nothing but this map for a guide. The Ohio river on the south and Lake Erie on the north afford some splendid vacation grounds.
1921 Yellowstone Trail Touring Service Map #13 of Ohio

The Union Building in Cleveland, 1922 Yellowstone Trail Eastern Headquarters

INTRODUCING THE YELLOWSTONE TRAIL IN OHIO:
THE BUCKEYE STATE

Extending the Yellowstone Trail through Ohio

The path of the Trail in Ohio is unique. It lies in an historic swath of land across northern Ohio known as the Western Reserve. Explained too simply, it was land owned by the state of Connecticut after the Revolutionary War. It was part of a larger swath westward from Connecticut to eastern Ohio between latitudes 42 and 41. Connecticut gave up most of its claims to the federal government so that the Northwest Territory could be created. However, it reserved the northeast corner of the territory for itself. This area came to be known as the Connecticut Western Reserve. Investors in the Connecticut Land Company sold parcels. However, only after the War of 1812 was settlement assured. The name "Western Reserve" is still visible today, 200 years later. See, for instance, Case Western Reserve University. The "Firelands" are part of the western edge of the Reserve. This land was reserved for Connecticut victims of fires started by the British in the War of 1812. The word "Firelands" is also still visible today, 200 years after the event.

Attempting to get roads built and marked in the early 20th century was an uphill battle in Ohio. See, for instance, the following from the September 18, 1912, *The Horseless Age*:

> PROPOSED ROAD AMENDMENT DEFEATED. After receiving the official vote from 88 counties of Ohio, it was found that the proposed amendment to the state constitution voted on September 3 providing for the issuing of bonds in the sum of $50,000,000 for the construction of a system of inter-county roads had been defeated. The greater part of the opposition came from counties which have improved their highways and the people did not feel like taxing themselves to build roads in other counties.

Eight years later in the July, 1920, *Western Magazine* we see a common problem:

> The outstanding feature of omission in Ohio is the great lack of road signs. We asked a Buckeye why they did not put up sign posts like other states. Here is his characteristic reply: 'Every road in Ohio leads to where you want to go, once you get on it.' But there is the rub, to get onto the right road one has to ask a thousand questions and every native has a favorite route.

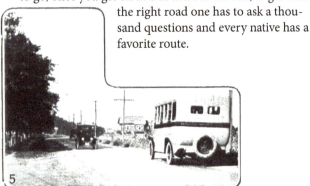

An early bus in Ohio

When the Yellowstone Trail Association (read Joe Parmley) announced that the successful relay race of 1915 from Chicago to Seattle would be expanded in 1916 from Plymouth Rock to Puget Sound, it was doubtful that he had any specific route in mind. Sitting in midwest Ipswich, South Dakota, he may have simply looked at a map and drawn a line across from Plymouth, Massachusetts, to Chicago irrespective of available highways and reality. The managers were to start the race at Plymouth, then go to Kingston, NY, then through southern New York to Olean, then, with no planned route in Pennsylvania, on to Akron, Ohio, then to Fort Wayne, Indiana, then to Chicago and on westward. This never became the official Trail. In 1919, when a presence of the Trail Association was finally acknowledged, the Trail was routed on popular roads near Lake Erie.

The yearly Yellowstone Trail Association informational *Route Folders* become quite tentative from mid-Ohio eastward. Precise directions for following the Trail fade and are replaced with compliments and pep talks. For instance, the 1919 *Route Folder* explains that "Following the south shore of Lake Erie in Ohio, one of the most intense industrial and commercial parts of the United States, the trail is passed through. There is no country anywhere that is doing more in the way of building permanent roads." And "The Yellowstone Trail is known to be a good road passing through a beautiful country and one that offers a splendid journey for travel from the middle west to the Atlantic seaboard."

Following this compliment, we learn that "the road is marked east as far as Sandusky with the regular Yellowstone Trail marker;" apparently, travelers were on their our own east of Sandusky.

Further in the *Route Folder* we read, "From Toledo west the Trail is designed to care for the immense traffic between the centers of population on Lake Erie and the foot of Lake Michigan, and thence to Chicago." The 1921 *Route Folder* continues on happily saying that "Most of the road between Cleveland and Conneaut is paved and requires no worry. All of the Trail will be found well marked through the state of Ohio with the exception of the route through the city of Cleveland." But no specifics are given.

Western Ohio residents, however, saw the advantage of a national highway as we can see from three newspaper items regarding Hicksville:

From the June 10, 1921, *Hicksville News-Tribune*:

> The Hicksville Chamber of Commerce is entering into the spirit of the Yellowstone Trail idea heartily. In inducing tourists to use the Yellowstone Trail it is found that a camping place is urgently needed and towns that have such are getting direct benefits. With this idea in mind the Chamber of Commerce is arranging to provide a fine camping spot three squares [blocks?] from the downtown district.

From the November [day unknown], 1921, *Cleveland Plain Dealer*:

> The Hicksville Chamber of Commerce will send a representative to Cleveland to attend a meeting of the ⇨

OH

Yellowstone Trail Association November 8th to discuss the extension of the Trail from Indiana east to Cleveland via Hicksville, Bryan, Toledo, Fremont, Sandusky, Cleveland and Conneaut, the eastern boundary of the state.

From the November 11, 1921, *Hicksville News-Tribune*:

F. J. Clemmer attended a meeting of the Yellowstone Trail Association on the 8th at Cleveland. Mr. Clemmer reported that they heard a good talk as to how the Association worked, and that they established a free Bureau of Information in each city of any magnitude and it is their duty to have a report daily as to the condition of the Trail and to furnish maps. Ohio will join in the Association, and improvements along this line will be pushed. The Bureau at Fort Wayne, Indiana, reported that 2,900 auto parties sought their advice last year, the first year of the Bureau's work.

The Ohio Department of Highways began operations in 1905. Its mission was to study the state roads and the science of road construction. The state granted aid to counties for the construction of certain roads designated as "inter-county." The state paid 50%, the county 25%, township 15%, and abutting property owners 10%.

The system of state highway numbering that appears on the Ohio maps of today originated in 1923. The most important routes in the state were given numbers from one to ten, including the National Old Trail Road (State Route 1), The Yellowstone Trail (State Route 2), and the Lincoln Highway (State Route 5), says researcher Michael Buettner in the Yellowstone Trail Association newsletter, the *Arrow*, May 2012. If you look at the Yellowstone Trail map, page 337, you will see that present US 6 closely follows the Yellowstone Trail from Sandusky to Cleveland, all in the Western Reserve. Buettner reports that the road was called the "Shore Road."

Buettner continues,

When the Yellowstone Trail first reached Ohio in 1916, it was more on paper than on the ground - drawn as a fanciful smooth line across the top of the state. The trail association map of 1919 traced a much more practical and historically popular route that connected larger cities on the shoreline of Lake Erie.

Just as the Association assured western-bound travelers of their safety (Native Americans no longer were hostile, gas was available, hotels existed), the 1921 *Route Folder* addressed eastern-bound travelers, saying, "Travel in the East may be made safely without any equipment at all. The tourists will not need to camp nor carry any supplies unless they desire to do so. At no point extra gasoline or water need be carried. Good garage facilities may be found each 20 miles or so."

In an effort to assure Ohio audiences of the Trail's authenticity and validity, Trail Information Bureaus and sub-bureaus were established, as they had been in other Trail states, to assist autoists with Trail information. The fact that most bureaus were located in Chambers of Commerce should tell the reader that businessmen saw the advantage of a national highway early on. Toledo, Fremont, and Sandusky Chambers of Commerce became sub-bureaus under the lead of the Cleveland office. Auto clubs also supplied information.

An eastern office of the Trail was established in Cleveland in 1922. This was a *bona fide* office with Trail Association General Manager Hal Cooley actually moving in to direct efforts. The Association realized that the East was different from the West in road development. The East was more "settled," expected more from state governmental agencies, and, thus, less interested in personal involvement in road development. A few towns from the Indiana border to Cleveland had joined the Association, but eastern Ohio remained aloof, rendering the state less than dependable for Yellowstone Trail support. ❁

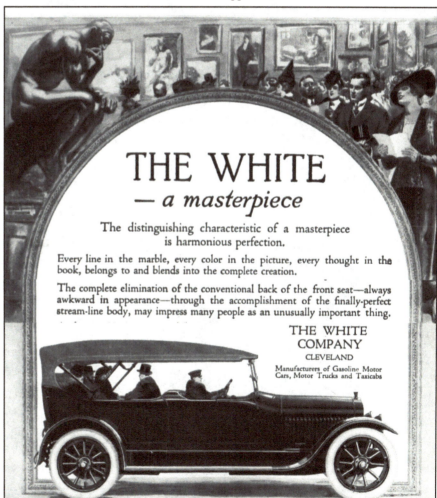

A National Geographic advertisement (abbreviated)

Allen Hilbert of Hicksville "pumped gas into many cars" on State 2 (the Yellowstone Trail) and shared his interest in the Trail with the authors a few years ago:

The first paved portions of route 2 were completed in 1926 (approx). The long-distance truck traffic, Mack semis, and the Greyhound buses used this route through Hicksville until the completion of Route 24-Toledo to Fort Wayne in the early '30s. A petition was circulated in 1919 proposing to rip up the four miles of road south of Hicksville built only a short time ago. This is true of all so-called stone roads as they soon go to pieces. Brick or cement on main lines of travel are the only roads that hold up. Once built, all expense is at an end for fifty years or more years, if built right. ✿

WAYSIDE

At 22611 Ohio 2, about two miles north of Archbold, is **Sauder Village**, a large living history site with costumed interpreters. We mention it because, although opened in 1976, well after the Yellowstone Trail era, it is dedicated to educating visitors about the history of northwestern Ohio and the former Black Swamp area. Erie Sauder was the founder of Sauder Woodworking, the well known maker of modestly priced ready-to-assemble furniture. Sauder's idea was to collect some historic structures and have people in these structures who could show guests how to use the tools like his grandpa had shown him and also engage in conversations about history. The living history village grew to 110 structures on 239 acres.

Courthouse in Bryan with an historical restoration with modern standards

HISTORY BITS

OH-000.0 Indiana/Ohio Line
OH-002.6 Hicksville

(754 alt., 2,445 pop) a busy shipping point for farm and dairy products in the center of a melon- and tomato-growing district. It supports a canning factory, a cigar factory, two wood-working shops, and two grist mills. WPA-OH

W High St. (Yellowstone Trail/US 2). The **Land Office** (1837). The Land Office is so named because in 1837 the Hicks Company of New York sent A. P. Edgerton to sell its 140,000 acres of land in Hicksville. He built a one-story square land office in the Greek Revival style and developed the land from swampy forests to good farmland. It currently houses Hicksville Historical Society collections.

OH-021.3 Bryan

(pop. 3,641, alt. 764 ft.), the county seat of Williams county, was established as such before any town existed here. The town is situated on a ridge which is supposed to have been at one time the shore of Lake Erie. Bryan is sometimes called the "Fountain City," because of its many flowing artesian wells. BB-1920v4

From west of Toledo to northwest Indiana to southern Michigan through Bryan extended the Black Swamp—a wasteland 120 miles long and from 20 to 40 miles wide, thickly forested and filled with malarial bogs and pools of water. Immigrants gave it a wide berth as they pushed on toward Indiana or Illinois. An early surveyor made this entry in his journal: Water! Water! Water! tall timber! deep water! Not a blade of grass growing, nor a bird to be seen. WPA-OH

Extensive reclamation work was carried on during the latter half of the century as farming proved a profitable undertaking on this virgin soil. Today the only reminders of the blight that once infested the region are the parallel rows of drainage ditches running across the fields like strings on a harp. WPA-OH

Communications from Fort Wayne, Indiana, through to Sandusky speak of the Black Swamp. The authors lived in the area for a year and saw nothing deleterious. All we noted was the rich soil and the vast tomato crops which drew seasonal pickers for the Heinz ketchup factory.

One Courthouse Square, corner of High St. (Ohio 2, the Yellowstone Trail, and Ohio 34,) and Main St. **Williams County Courthouse**. The Romanesque courthouse with its high clock tower was built in 1888 and is listed on the National Register of Historic Places, and it is part of the Bryan Downtown Historic District roughly bounded by Walnut, Beech, Maple, and Bryan Sts. A Residential Historic District is roughly bounded by Butler, Lynn, W. Wilson, Center, Portland, and Beech Sts.

400 N Portland St. **Spangler Candy Company**. Established 1906 first as a producer of baking powder, baking soda, and corn starch at 204 W High St. By the time the Yellowstone

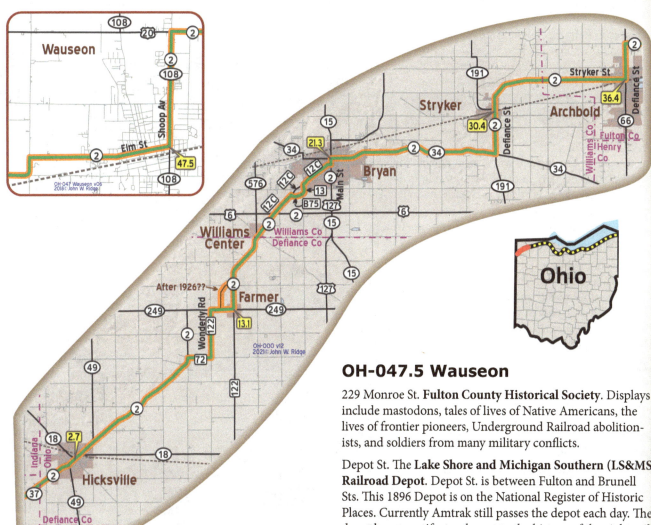

OH-047.5 Wauseon

229 Monroe St. **Fulton County Historical Society**. Displays include mastodons, tales of lives of Native Americans, the lives of frontier pioneers, Underground Railroad abolitionists, and soldiers from many military conflicts.

Depot St. The **Lake Shore and Michigan Southern (LS&MS) Railroad Depot**. Depot St. is between Fulton and Brunell Sts. This 1896 Depot is on the National Register of Historic Places. Currently Amtrak still passes the depot each day. The depot houses artifacts relevant to the history of the eight railroads that once traversed the county, and a large "O" gauge model train display.

S Fulton and Chestnut Sts. **Fulton County Courthouse**. On the National Register of Historic Places. Opened in 1872 and is still in use today.

OH-055.9 Delta

Trail passed by on High St. in 1916 travelers could also buy candy. Over 100 years later a traveler can now visit the Portland St. factory for candy and for a tour.

OH-030.4 Stryker

115 N Depot St. **Stryker Depot** built in 1900, is on the National Register of Historic Places. The Depot houses the Stryker Area Heritage Council Museum.

OH-036.4 Archbold

Be it resolved by the Toledo Automobile Club that this Club will assist in every possible manner the establishment of the Yellowstone Trail across the state of Ohio and east to the Atlantic Coast. *May 2, 1919.* ⚙

Already the proprietor was struggling with the problem of what to do with automobiles and what to do for them who drove them. He was vainly endeavoring to reconcile the machines with horses and house them under one roof; the experiment had already borne fruit in some disaster and no little discomfort.

The automobile is quite willing to be left out-doors overnight; but if taken inside it is quite apt to assert itself rather noisily and monopolize things to the discomfort of the horse. Stables - to rob the horse of the name of his home - must be provided, and these should be equipped for emergencies.

Two Thousand Miles on an Automobile by Arthur Eddy (publisher unknown, 1902)

[Note: And they were called garages two decades later.] ⚙

Old Lorraine Hotel,
now Lorraine Motor Hotel, Toledo

Old Monticello Hotel, now Davis Building, Toledo

Willys Overland Auto Co. headquarters, Toledo c.1915

A nice day's drive in Ohio

Toledo Museum of Art
Dustin Ramsey, Wikipedia

OH

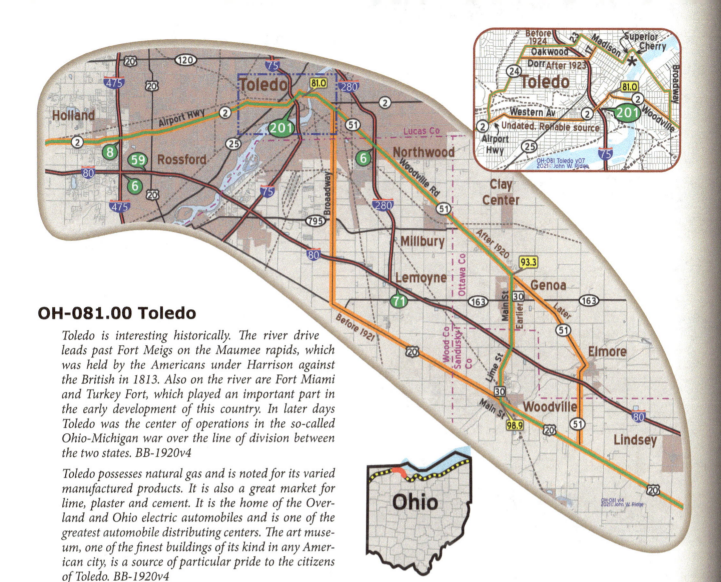

OH-081.00 Toledo

Toledo is interesting historically. The river drive leads past Fort Meigs on the Maumee rapids, which was held by the Americans under Harrison against the British in 1813. Also on the river are Fort Miami and Turkey Fort, which played an important part in the early development of this country. In later days Toledo was the center of operations in the so-called Ohio-Michigan war over the line of division between the two states. BB-1920v4

Toledo possesses natural gas and is noted for its varied manufactured products. It is also a great market for lime, plaster and cement. It is the home of the Overland and Ohio electric automobiles and is one of the greatest automobile distributing centers. The art museum, one of the finest buildings of its kind in any American city, is a source of particular pride to the citizens of Toledo. BB-1920v4

Toledo has been called "Glass City" ever since Edward Drummond Libbey came to town in 1888 and brought his New England Glass Works with him. Later, joining with glassmaker Michael Owens, the company of Libbey-Owens Glass became the leading glass company in the U.S. There were other glass companies, such as the Toledo Mirror and Glass Company, so the city lived up to its name. Even today it is commonly so called.

The Toledo of today would hardly be recognized by Yellowstone Trail travelers of 100 years ago. Downtown Toledo has mostly financial institutions and small restaurants. We saw few, if any, shops, unless they were hidden on the ground floors of skyscrapers. Mobile food stands provided lunch for the more budget-conscious office worker. Three hotels of the Yellowstone Trail era are still in business. While they were not on the Trail, we include them here because of their historicity and because they were available to Trail travelers as described in *Blue Books* of 1920 and 1925:

The **Waldorf Hotel** corner of Summit & Madison with the facade of lower floors covered nicely.

Hotel Monticello (now called the **Davis Building**) is well kept at Jefferson Ave. & Michigan St., houses miscellaneous agencies and businesses.

Hotel Lorraine (now called **Lorraine Motor Hotel**) offers low cost housing at Jefferson Ave. and 12th.

2445 Monroe St. The **Toledo Museum of Art** was founded by Edward Drummond Libbey who collected art works and opened the first museum in rented rooms in 1901. In 1912 Libbey moved the museum to its present location in the imposing columned building with the wonderful, wide entry steps. Today there are 30,000 pieces in 6 buildings on 36 acres with many programs that invite participation. Returning to its roots, the museum has added a Museum of Art Glass Pavilion.

2001 Collingwood Blvd. **Toledo History Museum**. Located in the historic Milmine-Stewart House, 1874, the museum offers a glimpse into Toledo's rich and diverse past.

OH-093.3 Genoa

OH-098.9 Woodville

Lime was first produced in 1872 in Woodville and still today there are at least three lime plants near Woodville. They call themselves the "Lime Center of the World."

107 E Main St. **Woodville Historical Museum**. Contains a collection of local historical items.

HO

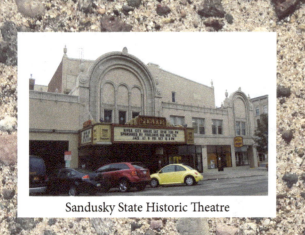
Sandusky State Historic Theatre

Rutherford B. Hayes house, Fremont

Gary's Diner on YT, Clyde

Rush Sloane House on Underground Railway, Sandusky

OH-115.0 Fremont

(pop. 12,500, alt. 630 ft.) abounds in historic memories from its earliest days. A British post was established here during the Revolution and, during the war of 1812, the one successful land battle on American soil was fought at this point. This is known as the battle of Ft. Stephenson. BB-1920 v4

Fremont was the home of Rutherford B. Hayes, thrice governor of Ohio and president of the United States. His remains lie at rest in beautiful Oakwood cemetery near this city. At the south edge of town in a beautifully wooded park stands his old home, known as Spiegel Grove, now the residence of Col. Webb C. Hayes, who has recently deeded it to the Ohio archaeological and historical society for use as a state park. In the grove is a handsome Hayes memorial library and museum building, erected by the state and formally opened in 1916. It contains the priceless 10,000 volume library of Americana gathered by President Hayes, as well as military, historic and personal souvenirs. This building is open to the public every week day afternoon. BB-1920v4

1337 Hayes Ave. Spiegle Grove. **President Rutherford B. Hayes Presidential Center**. Entrance to the Hayes Center is at the corner of Hayes and Buckland avenues. (GPS: 41.34187, -83.12666). Of the eight presidents associated with Ohio, two (Hayes and Garfield) lived near the Yellowstone Trail.

The facility consists of two buildings – the Hayes Home and Hayes Museum. The museum houses Hayes' personal belongings as well as documents from all U.S. Presidents. The Hayes grave site is nearby. The Library consists of 100,000 volumes of American history. He was president 1877-1881.

514 Birchard Ave. **Sandusky County Historical Society Museum**. A Victorian home built in 1884 houses artifacts of local interest. Rutherford B. Hayes was one of the Society founders.

OH-123.2 Clyde

124 W Buckeye St. **Clyde Museum**. The museum is in a white-steepled former church. The Clyde Museum features unique historical items such as Indian artifacts, pioneer to industrial era items, and stories of famous people from the Clyde area.

198 E Maple St. **home and museum of General James McPherson**, hero of the Civil War. (cor. of US 20 "McPherson Highway"/Yellowstone Trail, and Ohio 101). A National Register of Historic Places Property & Ohio Historical Society Marker Location. It is small with a small sign on a busy corner so it could easily be missed.

222 W McPherson Hwy. (Yellowstone Trail). **Gary's Diner**. A few years ago this diner was called the Yellowstone Trail Diner.

OH-134.4 Castalia
OH-141.4 Sandusky

(pop. 19,989, alt. 629 ft.) lies on the shore of Sandusky bay, the best harbor on the great lakes, large, land-locked [sic] and 18 miles long. This city commands a fine view of the harbor. The older portion of the city

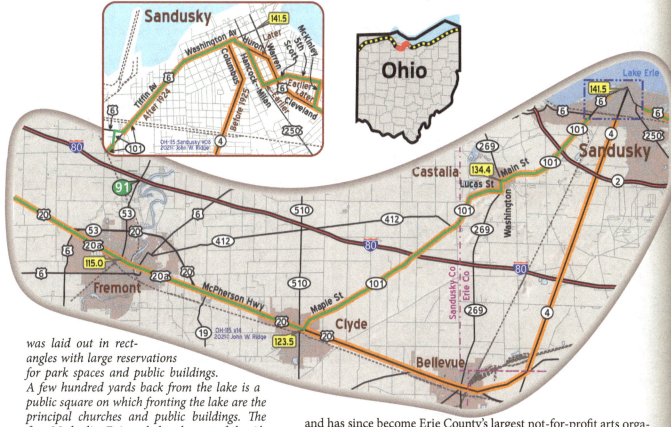

was laid out in rectangles with large reservations for park spaces and public buildings. A few hundred yards back from the lake is a public square on which fronting the lake are the principal churches and public buildings. The first Methodist Epicopal church west of the Allegheny mountains is still standing here. It is interesting to note that this church was built by an appropriation from Congress. BB-1920v4

Sandusky is the most convenient point of departure for the islands of Lake Erie, among them Put-In-Bay, the scene of Perry's victory, in honor of which a huge monument was recently erected. On the eastern of the two peninsulas which inclose the bay is Cedar Point, the "Atlantic City of the west." It is the largest summer resort on the great lakes, and can be reached by boat or automobile. BB-1920v4

1 Cedar Point Dr. **Cedar Point** is still there on the eastern peninsula, only now it is the "roller coaster capital of the world" on 364 acres of amusement park, hotels and restaurants. What would Yellowstone Trail era travelers think now!

404 Wayne St. **Follett House Museum**. Corner of Adams and Wayne Sts. Each of the four floors of the 1827 mansion tells the history of Sandusky. There are documents from "Prison Island" and the Civil War. It is on the National Register of Historic Places, and is in a neighborhood of great old houses.

1415 Columbus Ave. **Cooke-Dorn House State Museum**, built 1844. Sandusky is known for its collection of limestone buildings including this Greek Revival.

107 Columbus Ave. **Sandusky State Historic Theatre**. The Sandusky State Theatre has been in operation since 1928 functioning as a top Vaudeville theatre, movie palace, and world-class performing arts center. In 1992, the Theatre underwent a major renovation

and has since become Erie County's largest not-for-profit arts organization featuring live performing arts. It is on the National Registry of Historical Places.

403 E Adams St. The **Rush R. Sloane House** was a famous stop on the Underground Railroad during and before the Civil War. The house is not open to the public but just driving by might stir your interest in U.S. history.

The Yellowstone Trail ran close to Lake Erie. Thus, travelers on the Trail had many opportunities to view the lake. We can only surmise that travelers stopped at whatever marinas and lighthouses were there 100 years ago. That lake-hugging route along Lakes Erie and Ontario was popular among trail organizations – so popular, in fact, that the Yellowstone Trail Association was not permitted to put up its signs along the lakes in New York until after 1918 because of the plethora of 11 other trail "colors" that were present.

WAYSIDE

Ohio Blue Holes. From the 1920s to 1992 a favorite stop for travelers was the mysterious Blue Hole, just one half mile north of Castalia on the banks of Cold Creek. It was a road side attraction that kids looked forward to, having been bored to death by miles of flat Ohio corn rows. The Hole was mysterious and beautiful; a 75-foot pool of crystal clear water bubbled up from an aquifer of unknown depth. The Castalia Trout Club was formed to manage the property; they added bridges, paths, a water wheel, and water aeration for the added trout. However, its fame paled and another Blue Hole was opened an additional one half mile north. This one was owned by the state of Ohio which utilized the wonderfully clear water as a fish hatchery. The same source of water from that aquifer, now-known to be 60 feet down, feeds this newer Blue Hole which entertains a new generation of kids who find magic in fish idling by in deep, clear water.

Fort Stephenson, located on the banks of the Sandusky River, was garrisoned by Major George Croghan, a young Kentuckian 21 years of age, 168 men and one cannon, "Old Betsey." 8,000 British regulars sailed up the river and were joined by 2,000 Indians under Tecumseh. Against this force, Croghan battled for two days and maintained the fort in a glorious victory. His one cannon was shifted from place to place during the siege to give the impression of several. The original fort used by Croghan may be seen in Fort Park in the heart of the city … [with] soldiers' remains at the monument, and "Old Betsey." BB-1920v4. ☼

WAYSIDE

About 9 miles south of Huron is **Milan**, the birthplace of Thomas Edison at 9 Edison Dr. It is now a house museum, restored, and containing Edison artifacts, inventions, and memorabilia.

TO PUSH TRAIL PROJECT
LORAIN WILL BOOST YELLOWSTONE
HIGHWAY MOVEMENT

Lorain is going to get behind the Yellowstone Trail movement. This was the word given out today by Mayor William F. Grail and George Dudderar, Chamber of Commerce secretary, following their return from the Yellowstone Trail Association meeting in Cleveland yesterday.
November 10, 1920 Cleveland Plain Dealer

Liberty Ave. station of The Lake Shore Electric Railway. The LSE, formed in 1901, was an interurban electric railway that ran primarily between Cleveland and Toledo. The line served many communities along the south shore of Lake Erie, with innovative, high-speed transportation at a time of mostly horse-drawn vehicles on dirt roads. It helped to develop tourism as a major industry in northern Ohio. Business for the LSE was good until the mid 1920s, as it was for most interurbans. Around 1925, states and counties began paving roads and inexpensive cars began to be produced in growing numbers. Business for interurbans began to drop as a result, and by 1930 many interurbans had stopped operating. ☼

There once was a ship-to-shore radio station near the present Beaver Park Marina, Lorain. Ship captains received valuable weather reports from this service as well as sailing guidance to the various ports along the Ohio shore. ☼

HISTORY BITS

OH-151.0 Huron

(599 alt., 1,820 pop.), at the mouth of the Huron River, has a natural harbor that made communications with the interior of Ohio comparatively easy a century ago. When the completion of the Huron-Milan canal diverted shipping and building to Milan, the town's propelling force was lost. Decades passed before fishing, and later coal and iron ore transshipping, and finally the tourist business restored Huron to some semblance of its former self. WPA-OH

The Huron Lighthouse (visitors not allowed beyond the cement pier), opposite the end of N. Main St., was built in 1934 to supersede the lighthouse erected in 1847, which stands near by. It has an outer white light of 7,500 candlepower, visible for 17 miles. WPA-OH

The highway continues to follow the lake shore. Between Vermilion-on-the-Lake and Huron, a succession of resorts, tourist camps, dance halls, amusement parks, and institutional camps attract thousands of vacationists each summer. Hundreds of cottages dot the low wooded shore along miles of sandy beaches. WPA-OH.

Beach front cabins, cottages, trailers, lodges for rent for summer residents or year-round residents still dot the old Yellowstone Trail (US 6) today as they did about 90 years ago.

A word that the traveler will see on signs and hear is "Firelands." Here is the term's origin: Erie County had its origin in the Revolutionary War. Connecticut towns were burned in the historic raids of Benedict Arnold and British General Tyron; 500,000 acres of Ohio were awarded by the Connecticut Assembly in 1792 for compensation to the fire-sufferers. Those acres are now Huron and Erie Counties. This area is therefore known as "The Firelands."

333 Williams St. The **Huron Historical Society Museum** is located on the lower level of the Huron Public Library. There are exhibits about Huron and its waterfront history.

Main St. at the harbor. **Huron Harbor Pierhead Lighthouse**. A lighthouse was first placed at this point in 1847. Then in 1936 a new lighthouse was built using the "art-deco" style. Directions: From US 6 follow Williams St. north to the lake. It will end at Wall St. Turn right onto Wall St. and follow that for a short distance to Main St. Turn left onto Main St., and follow that to the end where there is a small parking area. You can now walk out to the lighthouse on the pier, but the last part is difficult -somewhat rocky. Although the lighthouse that the Trail travelers would have seen is not there, the view is the same. There is also a white pyramid lighthouse at the harbor.

120 Ohio St. (at Lake Park) **Christ Episcopal Church** built in 1839. On the Register of Historic Places.

Just northwest of OH-151.5 in Huron, the intersection of Main St. and Cleveland Rd. was rebuilt and relocated so following Williams St. for a very short distance is probably necessary.

MILE-BY-MILE

OH-162.0 Vermilion

(604 alt., 1,605 pop). Like many other towns along Lake Erie, Vermilion is both a fishing center and a tourist resort. Somnolent in winter, the town comes to life with the first touch of spring; all manner of boats come out of hiding, and the fields are webbed with great stretches of nets drying and undergoing repairs. Tourists are passing through the town in large numbers. An annual regatta is held here in August which attracts boating enthusiasts from the various lake ports. WPA-OH

Liberty Ave. (US 6, Yellowstone Trail). The downtown area is **Harbour Town**, an 1837 Historic District and the center of the community. It features old buildings repurposed as restaurants, shops, marinas, and more. Community-wide revitalization efforts have encouraged property owners to retain the unique charm of their businesses and homes.

13115 W Lake Rd. (US 6, Yellowstone Trail) 1.5 miles west of Vermilion. **Lakeland Lodges**. Although their website does not state the history of the place, we believe that it saw Yellowstone Trail travelers because a reviewer said that it "looked the same today as it did on a 1926 postcard." Also, their website encourages the reader to "step back in time to when life was simple …" and describes "cozy cottages and bonfires on the beach," certainly reminiscent of Yellowstone Trail days.

Two buildings of special note probably seen by Yellowstone Trail travelers are:

1.) 5581 Liberty Ave. **Old Vermilion Banking Company Building**. Built 1907 in early 20th century Beaux Arts style. Seems to be a newly refurbished wine bar.

2.)5780 Liberty Ave. **Old Pelton Home**. Built about 1820 by Capt. Josiah Pelton. Was once called Old Shore Inn. Not well maintained. A private dwelling.

There are 41 buildings on the National Register of Historic Places in Vermilion. Ten of them are homes of ship captains, which is not surprising because of Vermilion's connection with shipping on Lake Erie. Fourteen buildings are on or near the Yellowstone Trail.

51211 N Ridge Rd. Go about five miles south of Vermilion on Vermilion Rd. to Ridge Rd. **Benjamin Bacon House Museum and Carriage Barn** 1845 at Mill Hollow in Vermilion River Reservation. Bacon was an early settler. The museum features themes of daily living and includes the profound effect the railroad had on the economy and on people's lives.

OH-172.7 Lorain

(pop. 50,000, alt. 610), lies at the mouth of the Black River. Though comparatively new, it is an important point for shipbuilding, as for over 3 miles the stream exceeds 200 feet in width, with an average depth of 15 feet. It is now the fourth port on the lakes in receipt of ore and an important point for shipbuilding and steel making. BB1920v4

Annual production of sandstone in Lorain County alone totals approximately 700,000 cubic feet. In a landscaped ravine on Milan Ave. back of the town hall is Old Spring Park, with outdoor tables and benches made from large grindstones. WPA-OH

309 W 5th St. Black River Historical Society's **Moore House Museum**. It was the home of Mayor Moore and family in the 1920s. It has been restored to reflect life at that time period in the City of Lorain.

617 Broadway. **Palace Civic Center**. Rebuilt in 1928 after the 1924 tornado and called the Palace Theater, it featured silent films, vaudeville acts, the great Wurlitzer organ and more every evening. Gothic on the outside, opulent Italian Renaissance inside, sculptures everywhere. Apparently money was no object for Warner Bros., the owner. In 1977 the declining theater was purchased by the city, and after Herculean fund raising efforts, it emerged as the successful Palace Civic Center. It is worth taking a look, and Yellowstone Trail travelers may have.

The symbol many people have come to identify with Lorain is the 1917 **Lorain Lighthouse**, or the "Jewel of the Port." The lighthouse stands at the north end of the West Harbor Breakwater in Lorain Harbor. One must take a boat to tour the lighthouse. A museum and tour ticket office are located at 138 Alabama Ave. To get there, take US 6 (Erie Ave. and Yellowstone Trail) to the east end of the bridge over the Black River and then turn north from US 6 onto Alabama Ave.

Euclid Avenue is well paved in the city, but just outside there is a bit of old plank road that is disgracefully bad. Through Wicliff, Willoughby and Mentor the road is a smooth, hard gravel.

1902 Two Thousand Miles on an Automobile by Arthur Eddy (publisher unknown, 1902). ✿

By the 1920s many local restaurants and hotel dining rooms began providing entertainment. They began with social dancing during lunch, dinner, and after the theater and went on to host local radio shows broadcast from the premises. In 1925-26, some of these hostelries that doubled as radio "stations" included the Hotel Winton (with the Rainbow Room Orchestra), the Hotel Statler, and the Hollenden. ✿

Westlake Hotel
Now Cleveland Condominiums

Hotel Statler, now Statler Arms,
Cleveland

1927 Public Square, Cleveland
National Archives RG30-N

YELLOWSTONE TRAIL HAS OFFICE HERE

A Cleveland office has been opened by the Yellowstone Trail Association of Minneapolis, Minn. in the lobby of the Hotel Winton. W. E. Wootters, jr. manager, is distributing information to motor tourists and to those who plan to make tours.

May 19, 1921 Cleveland Plain Dealer

~~~~~~~~~~~~~~~~~~~~~~~~

In 1922 a Yellowstone Trail Association office was opened at 1836 Euclid Ave. in the lobby of the Union Building. It was to serve as an eastern headquarters office, charged with "getting things started to put over an intensive campaign through Ohio, Pennsylvania and New York. It is a subsidiary office out of the national headquarters in Minneapolis ... it should not take over two or three years before the eastern end of the Trail is as thoroughly organized as the western end ..."

January 1922 Western Magazine

Note: It never was.

Lorain will support the Yellowstone Trail move, a national highway from Plymouth to puget Sound.

Findley will establish a curb market as a measure to cut food prices.

November 19, 1920 The Mahoning Dispatch

Lobby of YTA
eastern headquarters, 1922

YTA eastern headquarters,
1836 Euclid Ave./YT

The **Yellowstone Trail Association office** moved to the Union Building, at 1836 Euclid Ave., in 1922, having moved from their 1921 location in the Winton Hotel. This appears to have been the eastern most outpost the Association had. With no local groups established to publicize or promote the Trail and no "boosters" from here to Plymouth Rock, the Association changed its mission from that of road building to that of a tourist agency, inviting people to travel to the "wild West"via the Yellowstone Trail.

Go through the front door of this imposing building and you will see a narrow lobby that looks like it probably did in 1922 when the Yellowstone Trail Association moved in: brass fittings, old elevator door and marble floors. Study the picture here of the warm colors and be taken back almost 100 years. The building is now under the care of Cleveland State University. ✿

OH-192.5 Rocky River/Lakewood
OH-199.5 Cleveland

West of Cleveland, US 20 (Yellowstone Trail) leads through a prosperous residential district. WPA-OH

Cleveland (pop. 880,000, alt. 580 ft.) At the southeast corner of the public square, Euclid avenue, one of the most famous streets of America, begins. This street was once renowned for its private residences, but is now the principal retail thorofare of the city. Four miles out on Euclid avenue, beyond East 107th street, is University circle, which intersects the Cleveland park system and is a beautiful spot for a moment's rest. BB-1920v4

"Road conditions from Cleveland to Buffalo are not so good, but travel is never seriously inconvenienced. When roads are bad, cars are shipped by boat at a small expense." *Yellowstone Trail Association 1919 Route Folder.*

1501 Euclid Ave. (Yellowstone Trail). **Playhouse Square**, 5 theaters, 10 production spaces located in downtown Cleveland, is the "world's largest theater restoration project." Abstracted from their website: "These theaters, built in 1920-21 for vaudeville and movies, were ultimately impacted by the rise of television and population flight to suburbia and by 1969 all but one were boarded up." Then a 20-year grass-roots effort restored them, one to its original 1920s elegance.

Euclid Ave & E 12th St. Hotel Statler, now **Statler Arms**. It is still a hotel with a nice lobby.

6709 Euclid Ave. **Dunham Tavern Museum**. Once a stagecoach stop on the Buffalo-Cleveland-Detroit post road, Dunham Tavern Museum today is the oldest building still standing on its original site in the city of Cleveland. The 1824 home of Rufus and Jane Pratt Dunham is now a designated Cleveland Landmark and is listed on the National Register of Historic Places. In stark contrast to the cityscape that surrounds it, the museum and its gardens offer a glimpse of history and insight into the lifestyles of early Ohio settlers and travelers.

19000 Lake St. foot of 1910 Detroit Ave. bridge over Rocky River Gorge. The **Westlake Hotel**. The hotel opened its doors in 1925, at a cost of $3.5 million. Interurban lines, then busses, stopped just across the street for a direct trip to downtown Cleveland. After years of ups and downs in fortune and a half-million dollar fire, the site became renewed as a nice-looking 98-unit condominium complex. [Note: The entrance lobby is beautiful - full of plants.]

3900 Wildlife Way. **Metroparks Zoo**. By 1910, Cleveland's Metroparks Zoo had started building exhibits where animals could roam freely outside of cages. In 2012, it opened the $25 million African Elephant Crossing, the zoo's two-story indoor Rain Forest. Visitors will find many more animals from Asia, Africa and the Americas than did Yellowstone Trail travelers 100 years ago.

Lakefront Reservation is made up of three very distinct properties, Edgewater Park, Gordon Park and E 55th St. Marina on the shores of Lake Erie, together called the "Emerald Necklace." The Emerald Necklace Centennial, 100th anniversary, was in 2017. In 1917, Yellowstone Trail travelers, no doubt, visited these parks, dipping a toe into Lake Erie to cool from long hours in non-air conditioned, dusty Model Ts.

Lorain Ave. and W 25th. **West Side Market**, established in 1912 and still going strong over 100 years later! Cleveland's oldest public market is home to 100 vendors offering all manner of foods.

10825 East Blvd. **Western Reserve Historical Society History Center**. Five miles east of downtown take US 6, Superior Ave. (Yellowstone Trail). Just across Doan Brook, turn south on to East Blvd. The museum has the state's largest collection of regional history. It also includes the Crawford Auto-Aviation Museum with 200 rare autos and planes. And a restored 1910 carousel.

Old Standard Oil Station
on Euclid Ave., the YT

HO

1824 Dunham Tavern Museum, Cleveland

OHIO STATE MEETING

A meeting of representatives from towns on the Yellowstone Trail in the state of Ohio was held at Cleveland on Monday, Feb. 27th. A good representation was present and all matters relative to the Yellowstone Trail in Ohio with particular reference to the program for 1922 was gone into. An assessment list for 1922 of $4000 was adopted, and a movement to relocate the route in Ohio was defeated.

March, 1922 Western Magazine

AUTO TOURS

To those traveling either East or West the ever popular 'Motor Steamer' trip in connection with C&B Line Steamers between Cleveland and Buffalo is very alluring. With the low round trip rate of $7.50 and special service provided for automobilists, the tourist is quick to take advantage of the opportunity of breaking the monotony of the land journey, enjoy a night of comfortable sleep on Lake Erie, make progress of 183 miles and awake refreshed and eager to resume his auto trip early the next morning.

August 6, 1919 Fredonia Censor (New York)

1812 Rider Tavern, Painesville

OH-218.1 Willoughby

(649 alt.,4,363 pop.), Originally called Chagrin, Willoughby was named for an instructor in the Willoughby Medical College. The school grew rapidly after its establishment in 1834 and had nearly 200 students when, in 1843, a Mrs. Tarbell discovered that her newly buried husband was not where he should have been—in his grave. The onus of blame for Mr. Tarbell's unseemly disappearance fell on the school. Virtually the whole town rudely invaded the college building, turned the rooms upside down searching for Tarbell's vagrant remains, bashed in furniture, and tossed fragments of cadavers through the windows. Evil days fell upon the college because of this episode, and in 1847 it closed its doors. Four teachers went to Cleveland to establish what later became the Western Reserve University medical school; others moved to Columbus and founded the Starling Medical School, now part of Ohio State University. WPA-OH ✿

The 19th century downtown district is on the National Register of Historic Places. As the downtown deteriorated, the residents saw an opportunity to reinvent the downtown, coupling historic preservation with a commercial center. Today the old buildings house new, thriving businesses.

30 Public Square (on US 20, Euclid Ave.,Yellowstone Trail). **Willoughby-Eastlake Public Library and History Center**. No museum, but research materials are available.

25 Public Square. **Indian Museum of Lake County Technical Center** - Bldg B Corner of River St. and Center St. near US 20 (Yellowstone Trail). Visitors can see prehistoric items, 10,000 B.C. to 1650 A.D. locally or statewide, also Native American crafts, 1800-2012.

2 Public Square. The **Willoughby Area Welcome Center** is open year round in the historic Barnes House, adjacent to the Willoughby City Hall. This 104 year old "Cobblestone Cottage" provides information about the historic aspects of Willoughby and Lake County and other visitor services.

OH-221.9 Mentor

8095 Mentor Ave. **President James A. Garfield National Historic Site** (Lawnfield). The home of the 20th President (inaugurated March 1881, assassinated in July, died in September) features his private study, library, memorabilia and many original furnishings. The visitors center, in the carriage house, contains permanent exhibits of Garfield's life and career.

OH-228.5 Painesville

(702 alt.,12,237 pop.) A fixed character discernible today in the prim elegance of its old houses, the Western Reserve's architect-builder, Jonathan Goldsmith, lived here 36 years in the 1800s. Painesville has several examples of Goldsmith's work. WPA-OH

Five of architect Goldsmith's 1800s designs still standing today are:

1.) 106 E Washington St. The **Gillette House**, built of red brick, has long round-arched windows, two of which have tiny iron balconies, a Classic-columned side porch, and corbeled chimneys.

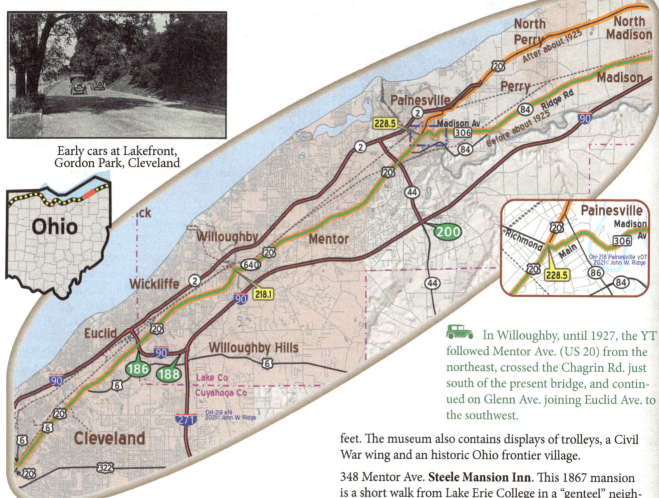

Early cars at Lakefront,
Gordon Park, Cleveland

Ohio

In Willoughby, until 1927, the YT followed Mentor Ave. (US 20) from the northeast, crossed the Chagrin Rd. just south of the present bridge, and continued on Glenn Ave. joining Euclid Ave. to the southwest.

2.) 792 Mentor Ave. (Yellowstone Trail). The **Rider Tavern**, once a stop on the Cleveland-Buffalo stage route, was built in 1812. It is patterned after Washington's Mount Vernon home. A two-story portico with square columns gives the tavern a stately beauty. This place on the Yellowstone Trail is still in business today as a Bed and Breakfast. It is known for its historically significant stop on the Underground Railroad. Of course, it is on the National Register of Historic Places.

3.) 497 Mentor Ave. at Washington St. **Lake Erie College**. A school for women was established in 1857. The school is patterned after Mount Holyoke College and has six buildings occupying a 40-acre campus. "Its varied program and individualized instruction carry out the ideal of its founders in furnishing to young ladies … a thorough education." The grounds are still beautiful.

4.) 470 Railroad St. **Railroad Depot**. Built in 1893 by the Lake Shore & Michigan Southern Railroad, the building was considered the jewel of Painesville. In 1914, it became part of the New York Central, and in 1971 the last passenger train pulled out of the Painesville yard. In 1997, depot owner Edward Dunlap donated it to the Western Reserve Railroad Association for restoration.

5.) 415 Riverside Dr. (Ohio 84) **Lake County Historical Society Museum**. It houses the only collection of 1900s music boxes in the state of Ohio. A collection of these "Magical Musical Machines" demonstrates home entertainment from the turn of the century and vary in size from one foot to several

feet. The museum also contains displays of trolleys, a Civil War wing and an historic Ohio frontier village.

348 Mentor Ave. **Steele Mansion Inn**. This 1867 mansion is a short walk from Lake Erie College in a "genteel" neighborhood. Now a small hotel and "Gathering Hub," the large home has been returned to its original looks. After the Steele family occupied it, the home became part of the College, then an apartment house. Walk in and enjoy the restored old carved trim and the authentic appointments along with modern accouterments.

The **Painesville City Hall**, northwest corner of the public square, was designed by George Mugate, and this Classic Revival style edifice was completed in 1852. The Mentor Ave. Historic District is bound by Liberty St. (east), Washington St. (south), Mentor Ave. (north) and terminating at the intersection of Washington & Mentor near Lake Erie College. This district, which includes 54 buildings, is significant both architecturally and historically.

OH-240.7 Madison

Cleveland Beach at Edgewater Park 1920s

OH

Unionville Tavern (The Old Tavern) under renovation

Hubbard House, Ashtabula Terminus for Underground Railway

Old Hotel Ashtabula, now a clinic

1915 bridge, Harmon Hill, Ashtabula

Ashtabula Maritime Museum

Stanford Inn near Conneaut. Now private home.

OH-243.1 Unionville

UNIONVILLE (305 pop.), old and history-laden in the Western Reserve. At the northwest corner of the town's crossroads is the New England House (tavern), an imposing three-story structure, first opened in 1805 as an inn. Here paused soldiers on their way to battle in the War of 1812; stagecoaches made overnight stops, and Negro slaves rested in their flight to Canada. During the 1830s and 1840s, when bog iron was mined in the vicinity, ironmongers and sailors rattled the 14-inch beams with their jollities. Old records and curios are on display. WPA-OH

Ohio 84 and County Line Rd. (Yellowstone Trail). The Unionville Tavern, described above, still stands as Unionville Tavern although it is popularly known as The Old Tavern. Beginning as two log cabins in 1798, this historic tavern was the first tavern in Ohio. It served as an inn before becoming known simply as the "Old Tavern." By the mid-nineteenth century Unionville Tavern was an active Underground Railroad Station. There is still a tunnel under the building through which escaped slaves may have traveled. It served as a functioning inn until the early 20th century and a restaurant thereafter. In 2011 the Unionville Tavern Preservation Society was created with hopes of returning the decaying Tavern to its former historical status. During 2019 it was undergoing serious renovation, but stop by anyway. Explore www.savethetavern.org to see great pictures of the renovation process of this historic tavern. Unfortunately, due to COVID-19, all work on the building has been suspended until further notice.

OH-247.4 Geneva

OH-257.2 Ashtabula

In 1831 it was incorporated, and carried on as a fishing and farm trading center. Strong abolitionist sentiment made it a key terminus on the Underground Railroad. On December 21, 1850, the Ashtabula Sentinel reflected the temper of the town on the slavery issue:

"Resolved, That we will not aid in catching the fugitive but will feed and protect him … and that we pledge our sympathy and property for the relief of any persons in our midst who may suffer any penalties for an honorable opposition or failure to comply with the requirements of said law." WPA-OH

The segment of the Yellowstone Trail from Cleveland, Ohio to Erie, Pennsylvania runs through a dairy and fruit country. The road is all concrete or brick, except two short stretches of macadam. 1926 Mixer's Route Guide and Strip Maps.

The Yellowstone Trail Association had trouble with Ashtabula's covered bridges in developing the Trail. It took several routes over the years.

Ashtabula has a strong maritime, abolitionist, and lake shore recreation history. It also promotes an amazing 18 covered bridges in the area. Locations of the bridges may be obtained by going to www.coveredbridgefestival.org.

1603 Walnut Blvd. **Hubbard House**. Built in 1841, the two-story brick house sits on the shores of Lake Erie. It served as a terminus for the Underground Railroad that

OH

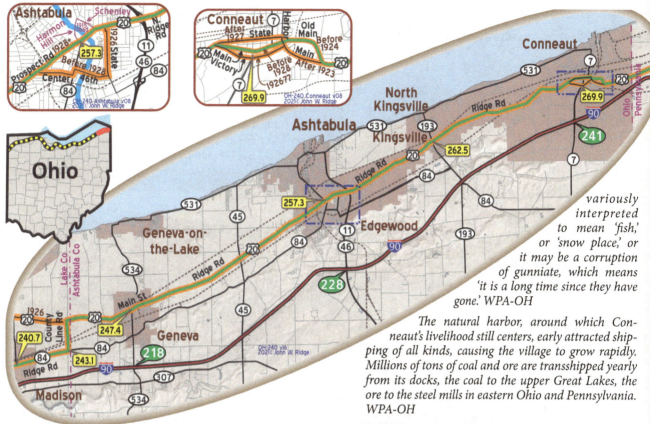

variously interpreted to mean 'fish,' or 'snow place,' or it may be a corruption of gunniate, which means 'it is a long time since they have gone.' WPA-OH

The natural harbor, around which Conneaut's livelihood still centers, early attracted shipping of all kinds, causing the village to grow rapidly. Millions of tons of coal and ore are transshipped yearly from its docks, the coal to the upper Great Lakes, the ore to the steel mills in eastern Ohio and Pennsylvania. WPA-OH

carried escaped slaves across the lake to Canada. Today, the house is a museum dedicated to the region's role in the abolitionist movement.

1071 Walnut Blvd. the **Ashtabula Maritime Museum**. Built in 1871 and located atop a cliff overlooking Ashtabula harbor, the museum is the former home of the Ashtabula lighthouse keeper and Coast Guard chief. The museum's seven rooms house thousands of photographs and artifacts that tell the story of Lake Erie and Great Lakes shipping - the good and the tragic.

4726 Main Ave. **Hotel Ashtabula**. Built in 1920, it now no longer functions as a hotel. Once the "pride of Ashtabula, new, fireproof, and modern. Offering excellent food and room rates from $2.00 up" according to *Mixer's 1926 Route Guide and Strip Maps*. The hotel ceased in 1965 but the restaurant ran until 1985. The building stood empty until 2014 when it was completely overhauled. On the National Register of Historic Places. Go look inside and see if any traces of the1920s remain.

West 5th St. from its 1200 block to the **Ashtabula River. Ashtabula Harbor Commercial District**. West 5th St. has also been known as Bridge St. because there is a bridge over the Ashtabula River at the end of it. The Ashtabula Harbor Commercial District is an historic district in the northern section of the city including 75 properties and buildings constructed largely between 1865 and 1878.

OH-262.5 N Kingsville

OH-269.9 Conneaut

CONNEAUT (ko'-ne-ot) (650 alt.,9,357 pop.), is at the mouth of Conneaut Creek. Its name is an Indian word

363 Depot St. **Conneaut Railroad Museum**. The railroad museum is housed in the old passenger depot (1900) of the New York Central railroad. The tracks are still in use. You will see trains, historical photos, a NYC video, and more.

230-238 State St. (US 20, the Yellowstone Trail). The Cleveland Hotel (c.1914), now **Cleveland Hotel Luxury Apartments** is on the Register of Historic Places. Writer Sharon Wick describes the renovated hotel today thus: "The Hotel has been brought back to its splendor and reminds us of the days when it was in its glory ... you are delightfully surprised to see the original mosaic flooring, the original ceilings and the original fireplace. There are 3 full floors above ground and the lower level of the hotel that all have been made into 28 condos ..."

246, 250, and 256 Main St. (Yellowstone Trail). **Harwood Block**, built in 1889, housed an opera house on its third floor until 1903. This was a major stop for touring companies between Buffalo and Cleveland. The third floor was then leased to the National Guard for drills, and after World War I became a dance hall. The stage is still intact. Several merchants now occupy the first floor.

"The historic architecture leads to the high Victorian Italianate mode. The cast-iron storefront was produced in Chicago and shipped to Conneaut on the Nickel Plate Railroad. With no instructions for its installation, Main Street was roped off and pieces assembled on the street, then attached to the building." *Gail Diehl, News-Herald, July 20, 1978.*

501 Sandusky St. **Conneaut Area Historical Society**. There are many displays that speak of the area's history as well as a research library.

OH-272.0 Ohio/Pennsylvania Line

OH

There are 16 covered bridges in Ashtabula County. Two covered bridges near Conneaut are:

1.) Middle Road Covered Bridge is a 136 ft. bridge which spans Conneaut Creek. It was built in 1868 and renovated in 1984. It is a single span Howe truss design and is located approximately 3.2 mi south of downtown Conneaut.

2.) Conneaut Creek Road Covered Bridge is located approximately 3.4 mi southwest of Conneaut, spanning Conneaut Creek. It was built in 1880 and renovated in 1994. It is 112 ft in length, and of single span Town truss design.

The route that became U.S. 20 [the Yellowstone Trail] has been in use for hundreds of years. During the 17th century, the then-five nations of the Iroquois pushed the Erie, Huron, and other Algonquin peoples west along this route in order to take control of the bountiful beaver population in the region. Later, this road became the chief avenue for Euro-American settlement of the Western Reserve. It was one of the primary east-west thoroughfares in the country. *Abstracted from David Bernstein.net "Current Projects."* ✿

Cleveland Hotel, Conneaut

Interior of Cleveland Hotel,
now Cleveland Hotel Luxury Apartments

Conneaut Hardwood Block Point
where Western Reserve began

COTTAGE, COOK HOUSE & GARAGE

CAMP GROUND

GAUKEL BROTHERS
State Line Garage & Tourists' Camp
EAST CONNEAUT, OHIO

COOK HOUSE
FREE CAMPING
REST ROOMS   **SINCLAIR** GASOLINE OILS
TENTS, COTS   STORAGE
GROCERIES SUPPLIES   ACCESSORIES
REFRESHMENTS   LOTS OF AIR
SHOWERS   SANITARY CONVENIENCES
MICHELIN TIRES   EVERYTHING FOR SELF AND CAR
                              GARAGE SERVICE

120 miles West of Buffalo   70 miles East of Cleveland
          Chicago - Buffalo or Yellowstone Trail
              PHONE 1378 MAIN.

Trailblazer A. L. Westgard

What is the measure of the debt of gratitude which the public owes to the men who have pioneered the ways that are now to become the great National Thorofares? The chief Pathfinder is A. L. Westgard ... the constant explorer of the ways from east to west, from north to south, mapping, publishing, making men appreciate what a country this is.

Dr. S. M. Johnson's philosophic Foreword in A. L. Westgard's fascinating 1920 book, *Tales of a Pathfinder*, reflected much of the public's thinking. Westgard was a household name by 1920, immediately recognized for his pathfinding. He published and spoke much about his adventures and accomplishments in finding routes (paths) for autos along the maze of wagon roads, prairie trails, and rock and stump strewn mountain roads. And many stories were written about his exotic calling; one might say that he had a really big fan club.

Westgard was a Norwegian by birth and an American by choice and his other early life choices led him to surveying, civil engineering, state maps and atlases creation, and, always, traveling by the newfangled auto. At the dawn of the automobile age, Westgard bought a rare road map in 1903 and grasped immediately the need for such maps, so he formed the Survey Map Company with the intent of developing maps for automobile use based on data in general atlases.

He soon found that atlases were fine for plotting a train trip but totally inadequate for auto drivers seeking long-distance travel. He joined the Automobile Blue Book Company and worked on the 1906 edition, the first to include maps to any extent. *Blue Books* relied on driving instructions in text rather than maps.

Typical "road" for Westgard

He saw the need for "boots on the ground" for adequate route-finding and map-making. He ventured forth for almost two decades without maps, without assurances of gasoline or housing, without dependable autos and without knowing what dangers might lie ahead. "Pathfinder" Westgard criss crossed the United States many times with a definite motivation: to find and map the best routes for future highways. More than that, the articles he produced for the many automotive and "outing" magazines, and the speeches he gave to travel-hungry audiences focused on the broader view of the important relationship between the motor car, good roads, and tourism.

Westgard
Tales of a Pathfinder

In addition to his work with the Automobile Blue Book Company he joined with the American Automobile Association (AAA) and worked with that organization the rest of his life as Field Representative and consulting authority. In 1913 he became Vice President and Director of Transcontinental Highways of the National Highways Association. He was also Special Agent for the Office of Public Roads of the Dept. of Agriculture, forerunner to the Federal Highway Administration.

Westgard's Remarkable Travels

His "boots on the ground" principle led him to extensive travel as a pathfinder.

In 1907-08 he traveled 50,000 miles for the Automobile Club of America "in the days when motors had dry batteries and spark-coils instead of magnetos and storage batteries, and before the demountable rim was thought of. He traveled when a man must needs be a mechanic, an engineer, and, like the Biblical Job, he needed patience as well as to be a skilled driver," wrote the National Highways Association in 1913.

In 1911 he made "A quick trip to Yellowstone National Park, after which he put his car on a flatcar and took the train home," said author Aubrey L. Haines in *The Yellowstone Story* (YNP 1977).

He then drove from Chicago to Los Angeles, the trip sponsored and publicized by AAA in fall as the "Trail to Sunset" or "Sunset Route."

Still in 1911, he drove a "pioneer Freighter" truck across the continent. It was a first. He represented the Touring Club of America. The truck was laden with camping gear, fuel, lumber for bridging creeks, and supplies. He demonstrated the usefulness of a truck as a freight carrier, good to know when we entered World War I six years later. It had chain drive, four gears, traveled seven miles per gallon, and weighed 14,000 pounds. He went from the west coast through Denver to New York City.

In June, 1912, he was the pathfinder of the Northwest Trail: Buffalo, Chicago, St. Paul, with connections to Yellowstone and Glacier Parks and on to Seattle. The *New York Times*, August 25, said, "For much of his route west of the Missouri River, pilots were supplied by AAA clubs, good roads associations, Boards of Trade [early Chambers of Commerce], ⇨

Westgard on the road
Tales of a Pathfinder

and public-spirited individuals." It was this trip that was of assistance to the Yellowstone Trail.

In the summer of 1912, he traveled east from San Francisco, through Salt Lake City, Cheyenne, Omaha, and Chicago, to New York City establishing the Overland Trail.

On Oct 1, 1912, he set out again and defined the Midland Trail through Philadelphia, Pittsburgh, Indianapolis, St. Louis, Kansas City, Denver, Salt Lake City, and Los Angeles.

Also in 1912 his accomplishments were enshrined as "Westgard Pass" between the White and Inyo mountain ranges in California in the Inyo National Forest.

He made two major trips during the summer of 1913: the Southern Route through lower Atlantic states and west to join his 1911 "Trail to Sunset." His second trip was to establish his Oregon Trail.

In 1920 he was asked by the National Park Service and Bureau of Public Roads to identify the best route for the National Park-to-Park loop to open an entire circuit of western parks for tourists. This was his 19th and last journey as Pathfinder. Immediately after mapping the route he left the group due to illness and died months later, April 3, 1921.

The Life of a Pathfinder

American Motorist magazine in Westgard's 1921 obituary says during those trips,

> He was occupied with not only charting the route, but noting details of topography, geologic features, and safety of the route. He also was pressed to speak to citizen groups where he roused the people to the importance of good roads. He was amiable, and an interesting conversationalist.

His kind of campaigning bore fruit. Not only was the AAA able to publish maps, but "conditions along the way have been vastly improved. Permanent bridges have been built, roads relaid." said the *New York Times* of May 4, 1913. Indeed, success with the Park-to-Park loop brought promises of immediate road work on that trail through federal, state and county cooperation.

The life of a pathfinder was an adventurous one. Following Native American trails, dusty wagon indentations in sand, or wild game routes in mountain passes, fording mountain streams, and hauling his sputtering auto over rocky terrain are bound to produce humorous or hair-raising tales, many of which he recorded in his *Tales of a Pathfinder*.

One such scary tale described an encounter with the Yellowstone River. Reports of flooding upstream lead to camping at a rancher's house on a knoll "near the lonesome station of Zero. There was more than irony in that name," he wrote. The river did, indeed, rise and continued to creep up and up, closer and closer to their camp, marooning them for 16 days! The knoll became a small island, the rancher's larder became

Westgard reported: Laborious and slow but counted as all in the day's work to take apart and reconstruct this bridge in Montana.
Tales of a Pathfinder

smaller, the chickens in the coop became fewer, the flour bin became empty. One day "mystery meat" appeared at the table. However, when they discovered that it was prairie dog, "The expression on the faces of us three Easterners seemed to show an utter lack of appreciation. Eventually, after arduous struggles across soggy river flats, we succeeded in getting to Miles City," he recalled.

Westgard's Routes

Westgard related another incident:

> After a rain storm in South Dakota, ... the whole inside of the car was wet and full of hopping, wriggling little black things which gave us all a creepy feeling. The road ahead and the ground in all directions just black with little frogs which jumped lively and frisky in all directions. There were millions upon millions of them. After putting on skid chains we proceeded slowly.

Your authors experienced something just like this in 1962 in South Dakota. We skidded around, unavoidably crushing a few thousands of them.

A humorous story is oft told about Westgard. It seems that he had made annual trips to Yellowstone National Park. Once, while the Army was still managing the park and before autos were permitted in 1915, he approached the eastern gate to the park in his auto. Upon being refused entry he climbed out of his car and shook his fist at the soldiers on duty, climbed aboard his car and drove away until another year rolled by whence he did it again. This particular version is related by Richard Bartlett in *Yellowstone: A Wilderness Besieged* (1985).

Westgard and the Yellowstone Trail

While Westgard was the biggest player in the nation-wide creation of named highways, he limited his work to pathfinding and he did little to specifically promote travel on his creations. The Good Roads Movement pushed for roads in general throughout the nation for years. Westgard produced specifics of exactly where potential transcontinental routes could be established. Both raised their voices in a common song. The Yellowstone Trail Association joined the chorus. Coming along in 1912, the Association was a beneficiary of Westgard's work through Montana, Idaho and Washington - the western part of Westgard's Northwest Trail. His route through Montana into Idaho was the one selected by the Association in its 1914 meeting, albeit the lack of other viable routes limited the choice! At that meeting was George Metlen, Secretary of the State Highway Commission of Montana, who must have been aware of the Northwest Trail. He supported the Trail Association's choice of route through Montana, declaring that the Commission had preliminarily decided to designate that route as a state highway. In fact, from Livingston, Montana, at the north end of the Yellowstone Trail spur to Yellowstone National Park, to Idaho there was no viable alternative.

Seemingly, a not often observed contribution of Westgard proved to be a boon to the Yellowstone Trail: Our research into the establishment of the Yellowstone Trail turned up numerous instances of acknowledging the source of road map data to Westgard. That attribution is found on AAA (or its affiliates') maps, often strip maps. More remarkable, the attribution was found on county surveyors' maps. Apparently, Westgard's travel notes were well done and useful to others.

A Lasting Legacy

Two fundamental differences can be noted between the operations and goals of Westgard and the Yellowstone Trail Association: First, Westgard had the backing of the nation-wide agencies, the AAA and the Bureau of Public Roads in Washington, D.C. Parmley and crew operated with coordinated county support and the popular promotions of its members. Second, Westgard's work seemed to end with the "finding" of the path; the Association's work sought to pave the path and people it with tourists. Because Westgard did not have local boosters to brand his routes with his chosen names, his trail names like the Trail to Sunset or Northwest Trail faded from public view.

One of Westgard's products

A seemingly natural extension of his road expertise was his line of products: Westgard Tire Co., Westgard Tire Chains, outing cream, hair cleanser, toilet kit "all for the needs of travelers during their journey."

Today, over 100 years later, the name Anton Westgard is hardly recognized, the subject of early auto pathfinding being regarded, if at all, as a quaint addendum to our nation's history. He was a major player in the early story of long-distance road development in the U.S., yet we do not regard him for a moment as we Americans drive thousands of smooth miles over his selected paths.

The nation is indebted to A. L. Westgard for his vision and practical application of transcontinental road expansions. He was a man with a vision. ❀

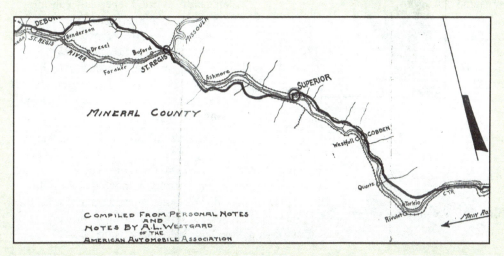

This shows a small part of a road project map drawn by a mining engineer in Wallace, Idaho, to prepare the YT for the onslaught of traffic headed to San Francisco for the Panama–Pacific International Exposition in 1915. Among many maps much of the data is attributed to Westgard, gathered in his 1912 trip. Note: 1) the Camel's Hump between Henderson and St. Regis, and 2) the Missoula River, now named Clarks Fork River.

Blood and Gore: Accidents on the Trail

"GIRL LOSES LEG IN AUTO ACCIDENT. Car Upsets Catching Right Limb Underneath Front Wheel … The Ford became unruly and climbed the bank of the road, turning over. The flesh was stripped from the leg from ankle upward. In the cuts and tears were dirt, sand and grease … Yesterday it was found necessary to amputate the limb."

An Indiana newspaper reported that:

> Harry Kirchner and an unidentified woman were killed when their automobile turned turtle on the Yellowstone Trail four miles west of Columbia City. Kirchner's jaw was broken and his skull crushed. The woman's neck was broken and her chest was crushed.

This graphic style of reporting accidents was popular in early 20th century newspapers along the Trail. Gory accidents were reported, seemingly almost daily, in the hundreds of newspapers we read while researching the Trail. Most articles were long, colorful, and emotionally embellished. It seemed that the mode was "the bloodier the better." Were papers pandering to the macabre instincts of their readership? Or did such tales simply sell papers? With the lack of 911 and ambulances, kind passers-by did what they could for the unfortunate accident victims. They piled the injured into their cars, broken bones and all, not realizing the additional damage they could be causing. It was even more interesting to read of victims with broken ribs continuing on their journey with no thought of medical attention.

The legacy of these many stories is a picture of a time of great danger on the Yellowstone Trail, much greater than today's traffic, and statistics bear this out. There was much nattering in the automotive press about standardization of traffic rules and railroad crossing safety, but there was no robust safety culture. The statistics were alarming. Traffic deaths recorded in 1925 were 21,250. At that rate of deaths per 100 million miles driven, 17.7, the number of deaths in 2004 would have been 499,000. It was 42,836. Better yet, the National Highway Traffic Safety Administration reported that in 2017 the death rate per 100 million miles driven was 1.16, totaling 37,133 deaths, in spite of a population almost triple that of 1925 and in spite of 263 million registered vehicles today.

There were many macabre jokes about, verifying the danger of automobiles. To wit:

> A telegraph pole never hits a motor car - except in self defense.

> Children should play on railroad tracks where it is safer than on roads.

A "turned turtle"
Wis. DOT

A bus leaves the trail
Lance Sorenson

The high death rate was the result of a mosaic of ignorance, carelessness, lack of uniform rules of the road, poor roads, auto construction, inexperience, and poor judgement. We hear of the many problems with short-lived tires, but they were not the major bedevilers of accidents.

By far, the most serous accidents of 100 years ago were between autos and trains at "grade crossings." Roads were built along railroad tracks, and crossed and re-crossed them whenever it made road construction easier. But most auto-train collisions make one worry about human genetics. Millions of words warned readers about the subject and still accidents happened. A November 1922 *Western Magazine* headline pointed to the "cause" of the problem: "Can't Make Railroad Crossings Fool Proof." Between 1917 and 1919, 70% of fatalities were caused at grade crossings.

Daredevils were convinced that they could beat the train, only to hit the engine due to a slight miscalculation. Getting stalled on the track was common. Some drivers actually hit the train that was standing stock still on the track. Some ignored the warning signs on the side of the road. Some rear-ended a stopped auto, pushing it onto the tracks. Some became distracted. Such accidents engendered really gruesome newspaper descriptions of "body parts dragged down the tracks." In 1925 a North Dakota driver drove around a stopped truck, through the barrier, ignored the flagman and drove into the moving train.

Some accidents were the fault of the railroad – the engine not running the headlight, or faulty signs at the crossing. Responsibility for signage at crossings was a decades-long argument: was the railroad company or was the town responsible? When trains became express, they sped through villages where once they stopped, creating more fatalities for the unwary driver.

Faulty auto construction was another major part of the mosaic. "Steering gear gave way; steering knuckle snapped, front springs broke, radius rod broke, brake bands broke" statements occurred repeatedly, causing drivers to lose control and cars to "turn turtle" (flip over onto their tops with wheels in the air). The glass of the windshield sliced up many crash victims as they were thrown forward through them. Tin Lizzies were not that strong and seemed to crumple easily, taking passengers with them.

Drivers were literally left in the dark for years. Some did not use their headlights, which were pretty dim anyway. Rules for driving in the right-hand lane were unclear even though a long history of moving in the right lane in the U.S. preceded the auto. Pennsylvania adopted the right side rule in 1792 and New York in 1804. The early central steering tiller didn't help the decision. Most ⇨

cars before 1910 placed the steering wheel on the right and intended the car to drive "curbside."

In 11 cities in the east, one blast of a policeman's whistle allowed east-west traffic to proceed, while in 14 other cities the same signal allowed north-south traffic to proceed. The idea of a centerline, created most probably in 1917, seemed to cause confusion. Big ditches on either side of the road forced drivers to head for the middle in the early years. This proved fatal to the fellow who crashed into an overhead bridge abutment placed on the centerline.

Shown is a "subway" after the addition of reflective warnings on the pillar. A driver then drove into it explaining "I thought we were to straddle the center line." This is from Wisconsin, but reflects the learning curve that was needed across the country.
Wis. DOT

In spite of countless newspapers along the Trail cautioning drivers, we see a 1919 Wisconsin news article which describes a common problem:

> Mr. Huhn had turned the corner but kept to the left of the road and at times turned partly to the right, confusing Mr. Bremmer as to just what side of the right of way to take. Both drivers became excited and turned toward each other, resulting in the crash.

As late as 1926 we see this from Colby, Wisconsin:

> Mr. Gocha was driving on the right side of the road. The approaching car was coming toward him in his lane. Folks thought that Gocha believed that the car was not going to turn to the proper side of the road, so swung his car to the left. The other driver turned at the same instant, coming together with a crash. [Both drivers died.]

Speed was always a problem. Still is. But one really has sympathy for drivers with headlines like this one from Wallace, Idaho in 1911: "Police on Watch for Autoists Who Violate Recent Six Mile Per Hour Law." Or the later 15 mile per hour law in urban areas. Farmers were the first to stump for the speedier 25 mile per hour limit in the countryside.

It doesn't matter whether it was speed, the road condition, or stupidity that caused this accident. The effect was an entirely preventable death. In 1922 a car that wouldn't start was being pulled by another. A young man rode on the running board of the dead car. The lead car swung widely around the corner. The rider leaned out and was killed by a telephone pole.

Another piece of the mosaic was the road itself. Slippery mud, gumbo, ditches, sharp turns, unmarked bridge ends, few danger signs, all haunted paved and unpaved roads.

Roads on section lines produced ninety degree turns. Grades and banks on curves provided a ride up the bank and off the road. A feature foreign to today's drivers was "the rut." Heavy farm machinery traveling on unpaved roads left deep ruts. Drivers complained of "getting in a rut and not getting out" or they said "I just followed the rut." In fact, we still say "getting in a rut" to mean lack of change. In winter, ruts froze, making life worse.

A rut almost caused an accident in this story from April 8, 1920 *Mineral Independent* (Superior, MT):

> A young fellow and his sister were returning in the wee hours from a dance in a neighboring town. He was driving a flivver. They were very tired and both dropped off to sleep. A heavy farm wagon had passed that way leaving heavy ruts in the mud which froze solid. The car got into those ruts and ran along them with no one guiding it for some time. The tracks finally turned into a farmyard and went into the barn. The fliv followed the tracks into the yard. It was going straight on and would have smashed into the barn door had not the girl waked in time to see the building looming up just in front of them.

Something more than printed newspaper articles had to happen. Granted, local governments posted some warnings, but uniform rules were needed to prevent others from stretching chains across roads as some local law enforcement officers did to slow down speeders. They also shot tires. In 1917 the Yellowstone Trail Association called for uniform hand signals. In 1922 the Trail Association worked with locals to eliminate as many as 119 grade crossings along the Trail in Montana.

In 1926 Herbert Hoover called for a National Conference on Street and Highway Safety which adopted a motor vehicle code for all 48 states. It only had limited success. From the Office of Road Inquiry in the early 20th century to the present Federal Highway Administration, federal offices have addressed highway safety. The present National Highway Traffic Safety Administration and its crash dummies have caused significant changes in auto, road and sign design which have lowered accident figures. But we have yet to see improvement in driver mentality. Perhaps the new "driverless cars," considered experimental at this writing, will save us from ourselves. Or maybe not. ⚙

A dangerous unmarked grade crossing ahead
Wis. DOT

TRAIL TALES

TRAIL TALES

Car Radios in the Yellowstone Trail Era

The Year 1912

1912 was the founding year for the Yellowstone Trail. 1912 was well within the period of technological development which aggressively changed everyone's everyday life in America. Railroads and canals had opened the country and revolutionized the economy. Electrification of city homes was well underway and indoor plumbing was at least a goal for many. Telephones were well along in development and use.

And, 1912 was elevated in history by the introduction of Oreo cookies.

And around 1912 was the great upturn in automobile production and use, tied to the declining price (of basic autos, at least) and their increasing quality, utility, and practicality. The overall cost and effort of the ownership and use of an auto became a match to a team of horses. So now the new owner of an auto wanted to go somewhere other than in to town for barbed wire. But those autos didn't do well on the wagon paths that existed. And governments were not very receptive to providing good roads.

With burgeoning numbers of autos and increasing miles of useable roads a great revolution was underway. In fact, it may be said that, perhaps, outside of computers, automobiles and good roads formed the biggest sea change of the 20th century.

And Radio Technology?

Some of the underlying technology for radio communication was understood at the opening of the 20th century and the first voice transmission was made in 1906. Early enthusiasts with their hand-made crystal sets and earphones would occasionally hear a voice or a bit of music from far away.

Some dedicated "broadcasters" began to create scheduled programs of talk or music for their far flung listeners. In turn, listeners were encouraged to send post cards to stations they listened to. This allowed the station to gauge its range

The 1920s Rice Lake, Wisconsin, high school radio club. The science teacher, Harvey Ridge, is on the right. That radio is not quite ready for use in an auto!

and give them bragging rights. In return, the stations would send return cards to listeners. Science teacher Harvey Ridge (to whom this book is dedicated) and his student Radio Club collected many such cards.

During 1917, the federal government forced most transmitters off the air due to World War I, pausing the medium's growth. The University of Wisconsin's station, 9XM (now WHA), was sending wireless telegraph agricultural reports to farmers in 1915 and then voice messages in 1917. Broadcasting got a big boost

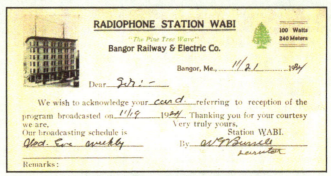

Typical broadcaster's acknowledgment card

after the War when thousands of amateur radio "stations" took to the air, most with a limited broadcast range.

So What's With Car Radios?

Thoughts of putting a radio in an auto percolated as early as 1904, but in a different way. Lee DeForest demonstrated radio as a means of vehicle-to-vehicle communications. Had that been perfected we could have carried out our "road rage" in a less destructive way! By the 1920s home radios were so popular that people wanted them in their autos also. The problem was that the usual noisy reception was subject to car electrical noise in a running vehicle and the constant tuning requirement made the radio unusable. Early attempts at car radios were frustrated by noise, a lack of adequate amplifiers, bad headsets, a need for large antennas and a separate battery. Radio installations were put anywhere they would fit – under the front seat, on the back seat, on the running board.

But slowly, the technical problems were made somewhat manageable and broadcast programing made the use of a radio more attractive.

A big turning point was the comedy program Amos and Andy, in 1929. It was so popular that it was a major factor boosting design and sales of auto radios. It was said that even President FDR would avoid scheduling his

Notice the elaborate wire antenna stretched between the two masts on this car, 1919
historydumpster.blogspot.com

famous "fireside chats" when Amos and Andy was on the air.

Historysdumpster.blogspot.com reported that, "in 1926, Paul and Joseph Galvin invented for Philco, what could be considered the very first mass produced car radio, the Transitone, and production began for the 1927 model year to be an option in Chevrolet sedans."

Just in time for the users on the Yellowstone Trail. ❁

North East
Erie
Fairview
Girard
West Springfield

Pennsylvania

Admiral Perry's ship SS Niagara

INTRODUCING THE YELLOWSTONE TRAIL IN PENNSYLVANIA: THE KEYSTONE STATE

In 1914 Michael Dowling traveled east to blaze an eastern section for the Yellowstone Trail Association, only to discover that his chosen route through northern New York was rejected because, as he reported, there were 11 trail colors already plastering telephone poles, etc. The Yellowstone Trail was left in limbo.

The 1916 cross-country relay race "from Plymouth Rock to Puget Sound," devised by the Trail Association, forced their hand. They had to determine a route for the racers. In Pennsylvania that meant that the popular, short, northern route through Erie was to be sacrificed for the less developed southern route through Sharon, Oil City, and Bradford. It would enter New York at Olean. The Trail would run along the southern border of New York, entering Connecticut at Salisbury, thence to Hartford and through Providence, Rhode Island, and on to Plymouth just south of Boston.

While received well by many of the included towns, it was undoubtedly little used. By 1919 their original choice of hugging Lake Erie became permanent and was published in the 1919 *Route Folder* map: enter Pennsylvania in the north from Conneaut, Ohio, on to Erie, to Buffalo, New York, Syracuse and Albany, across central Massachusetts to Boston and south to Plymouth. This route was incorporated into Rand McNally and other major maps as they were created. Some, of course, were a bit creative, putting the Trail where the editor thought it should go.

There were no organized groups of boosters in the East and the 1916 and 1917 Association *Route Folders* said that:

> The Yellowstone Trail Association makes no claim for having any extensive organization or special information relative to the Eastern section of the road, the intensive organization starting with the state of Ohio. The organization of the Yellowstone Trail is being pushed eastward state by state.

As late as in 1921 the *Route Folder* read,

> A tentative route east of Ohio has been adopted by the Yellowstone Trail Association [even though it had been marked on major maps for years] and is known to be a good road passing through a beautiful country and one that offers a splendid journey for travel from the middle west to the Atlantic seaboard. This route will be found marked in an incomplete manner with the regular mark of the Yellowstone Trail.

What was the trouble? Why was there virtually no membership in the Association east of Ohio? In the West, the Association was received with open arms because it bore the hope of better roads where there was mud, and the hope of a road where there was none. Such was not the case in the East. There were roads; there were experienced highway commissions and systems in place. These people did not need another "color" plastered on poles nor did they need to pay dues to an organization. They paid taxes. Thus, the Yellowstone Trail

Association became a touring promotion business in the far eastern states.

In 1925 a user-friendly system of numbering roads was established by Pennsylvania, especially for travelers. The system assigned one-digit numbers and a few two-digit numbers to major highways ("auto trails") across the state, with even numbers assigned to north-south routes and odd numbers to east-west routes. The system began by numbering nine auto trails that were far better known by name. The Yellowstone Trail received the route #9, proving that the Highway Department recognized the Trail as an important route even without boosters.

Shifting its focus from encouraging road building, as it did in the West, to encouraging tourism to and from the East, the 1921 *Route Folder* wrote in terms a Westerner would understand, should he be planning a trip to cities in the East. The Westerner was assured that,

> Travel in the East may be made safely without any equipment at all. The tourists will not need to camp nor carry any supplies unless they desire to do so. At no point extra gasoline or water need be carried. Good garage facilities may be found each 20 miles or so.

US 20 runs through the center of Erie. Before numbered roads became federally mandated in 1926, that route was called the Ridge Road, and later, the Yellowstone Trail.

Ridge Road has had a long history, dating from 1805 when it was first "opened," although then it was just a blazed trail through forests. The railroad came in the 1850s, ending the stage coaches on that road from Buffalo to Cleveland, but a number of short stage lines still remained in business for years and the Ridge Road was a heavily traveled thoroughfare. It was dotted with taverns, a hold-over from their role as a waystation for horses to be changed and travelers to rest.

In October, 1921, the Ridge Road was again dedicated, "today a perfect ribbon of concrete" and it carried the Yellowstone Trail. *Erie County Historical Society.*

By 1923 the route of the Yellowstone Trail in Pennsylvania was marked State 87 from New York state to Erie, the previously named Buffalo Rd. Between Erie and Fairview the route was marked State 272, part of the previously named Ridge Rd. From Ohio to Fairview the route was marked State 86, more of the Ridge Rd. State 86 went north from Fairview to Avonia and thence east to Erie; this raises the possibility that the Trail might have been moved to that through route.

Why Did the Trail Go Where it Went?

Within each chapter of the this book, it is customary to provide a brief discourse on the known or apparent reasons that the Yellowstone Trail followed the path it followed. For the route of the Trail in Pennsylvania, the authors found no record of reasons expressed by the founders.

We suspect that the founders, having chosen to route the Trail through Buffalo, New York, and Cleveland, Ohio, discovered that the shortest, best, and just about the only existing route through Pennsylvania between those cities was the well established Ridge Road. ❀

PA-000.0 Ohio/Pennsylvania Line

PA-002.5 W. Springfield

(712 alt., 250 pop.), a one-street hamlet of small frame houses interspersed with occasional older dwellings of red brick; is dependent on farming, poultry, and livestock. WPA-PA

At PA-3.3 at Steinberg Rd., across US 20 from the Home Tavern, the YT headed northeast on a now mostly obscured road which bore east to meet the present US 20 at PA-3.6.

PA-006.2 E. Springfield

(741 alt., 391 pop.), a rural tree-shaded borough, was named for fresh-water springs found here by early settlers. WPA-PA

PA-011.5 Girard

(831 alt., 1,554 pop.), a trading center and community for retired farmers and businessmen, is a quiet town, in many ways resembling an old New England village, inhabited before 1800; named for Stephen Girard, a Philadelphia merchant who owned land in the vicinity, it was incorporated as a borough in 1846. WPA-PA

The Soldiers' and Sailors' Monument, believed to have been the earliest Civil War memorial, was erected in 1865 by Dan Rice, famous circus owner and clown of that period. The 25-foot cylindrical marble shaft surmounted with draped flags and an eagle, occupies a prominent position in a traffic island on the main street. WPA-PA

The land in north Girard Township is generally rough, hilly,

and in some parts quite mountainous. In the western part, at what is known as "The Knobs," the hills reach a height of 2,230 to 2,280 feet, writes Roland Swoope in *History of Girard, PA.*

522 E Main St./US 20. (the Yellowstone Trail) **Hazel Kibler Memorial Museum**. Offers a Candlelight Ghost Walk through Girard Saturday nights, Memorial Day through Labor Day. Featuring an Underground Railroad exhibit and a 19th century circus clown, Dan Rice, memorabilia display.

436 Walnut St. three blocks south of US 20 (the Yellowstone Trail). **The Battles Museums**. Two house museums built by Rush Battles. The Battles Museum is next door to the Charlotte Elizabeth Battles Memorial Museum. Get a glimpse into 19th Century rural life, beautiful gardens and architecture. The museums are run by Erie County Historical Society. Rumors of ghosts abound in the museums.

PA-015.5 Fairview

(717 alt., 1,200 pop.), incorporated in 1868, is inhabited largely by retired farmers and Erie commuters. It has a basket weaving shop and a tool factory.

West of Fairview is clover hay country. The fragrance of clover fills the air in blossom time. Cultivation of strawberries, raspberries, gooseberries, and currants is extensive. WPA-PA

4302 Cor. Avonia Rd. and Water St. (PA 98). **Jeremiah and William Sturgeon House** built 1838, having acquired land in 1797. It is a museum, depository of local historical and genealogical data and a meeting place. The Sturgeons operated "coach stops and taverns" in the area for travelers after the first road was cut from Erie to Cleveland, Ohio, in 1805. The simple house was listed on the National Register of Historic Places.

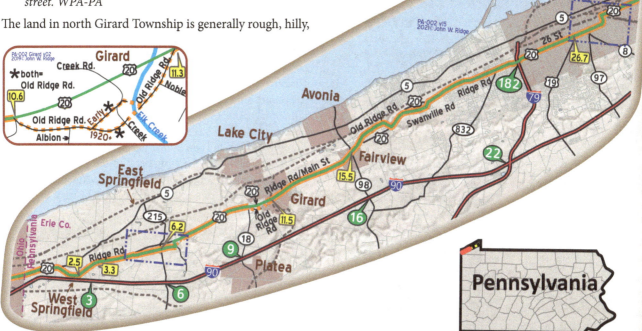

When the War of 1812 was declared, Great Britain had a series of military posts stretching along the Canadian border that gave her mastery of the Great Lakes. Early in the war the British captured America's only armed vessel in inland waters and were in a position to strike a fatal blow upon Lake Erie's south shore. Lieutenant Oliver Hazard Perry was sent to Lake Erie to take command of a small fleet then being hurriedly constructed. The enemy tried to bottle him up in Presque Isle Bay, but on July 19 Perry nosed part of his squadron out of the bay to engage briefly with the British until they withdrew. Later he conquered the fleet in a battle off Sandusky, Ohio. WPA-PA ✿

YELLOWSTONE TRAIL, SKIRTING LAKE ERIE
PERRY'S FLAGSHIP "NIAGARA" ATTRACTS TOURISTS
May 1925 American Motorist

Replica of Adm. Perry's ship Niagara
at the Erie Maritime Museum

Hagen Mansion Museum, Erie

Erie's historic Warner Theater

1928 Ford Hotel now Richford Arms, Erie

Erie has a long maritime history featuring a voluminous shipping past, plus the tales of the famous Revolutionary War General "Mad" Anthony Wayne, and the daring Lieutenant Oliver Hazard Perry's defeat of the British in Lake Erie during the War of 1812.

Foot of Ash St. The Wayne Memorial on the site of the American Fort Presque Isle, is a reproduction of the blockhouse in which 'Mad' Anthony Wayne died in 1796. The remains of General Wayne, for whom the State rebuilt the blockhouse as a memorial in 1880, lay buried at the foot of the flagstaff here until 1809, when the bones were removed to his birthplace, Radnor, Pennsylvania.

150 E. Front St. just off Bayfront Parkway between State and Holland Sts. Erie Maritime Museum and the Brig Niagara. This is a great experience. We roamed around the rebuilt ship of Commander Oliver Perry, seeing what it must have been like fighting the British in the Battle of Lake Erie, 1813. Visitors can tour, touch, and see a sailor's life of 200 years ago. Some parts of the ship are original, the sunken vessel having been raised and rebuilt. [See picture on first page of this chapter.] The museum tells the story of Erie's role in Great Lakes history. Open year round. ✿

Between North East and the New York border, the Yellowstone Trail probably followed (very early) Stinson and the partially abandoned Gulf Rd. and somewhat later followed Stinson and Gay. By 1923, the route was on the modern US 20.

PA-026.7 Erie

(pop. 110,000, alt. 713 ft.), located on Lake Erie, has a safe, land-locked harbor, which is four miles long by one mile wide, and is protected by the island of Presque Isle, on which lighthouses have been erected. The city contains many attractive buildings, but it is mainly of a commercial character, producing particularly large quantities of iron and steel. The blockhouse, which is a facsimile of the old French fort under which "Mad Anthony" Wayne was buried, may still be seen. Commodore Perry built his fleet which won the battle of Lake Erie here. BB1920-3

With its wide tree-lined streets, broad lawns, and pleasing architecture, perhaps no other feature so clearly marks Erie as its ample elbow room. Even in the city's eastern and less pretentious section, each dwelling has its plot of ground and a few shade trees. WPA-PA

The water front presents a scene of activity when the lake, ice-locked several months of the year, is open to navigation. Here 44,000 vessels annually warp into and away from the piers, carrying heavy cargoes of lumber, coal, petroleum, grain, iron ore, and fish; until 1925 more fresh-water fish were shipped from Erie than from any other port in the world. WPA-PA

811 State St. **Warner Theater** built 1930. It was used as a movie theater until 1976, when it was sold to the City of Erie. In the early 1980s, Erie converted the theater to a performing arts center, now a focus of a downtown revival. It is on the National Register of Historic Places.

356 West 6th St. **The Hagen History Center**, a three-plus building campus with a stone castle-like exterior. A very active museum with programs for all ages and a large research facility.

415 State St. **The Old Custom House**, 1839, for many years served as a customhouse, internal revenue office, and post office. It is now part of a five building complex of the Erie Art Museum, also on State St. It is on the National Register of Historic Places.

PA-034.3 Harborcreek

In the well-populated stretch between Wesleyville and Harborcreek the route crosses the western edge of the better grape-growing district. WPA-PA

This is wine country! There are vineyards all along the Yellowstone Trail in this area straight to the New York border.

PA-041.5 North East

US 20, the Yellowstone Trail, parallels the Lake Erie shore line across the only important grape-growing section of Pennsylvania; west of Erie the raising of cattle and poultry supplants fruit growing. In winter, frequent mists swirl in from the lake to blanket the countryside. WPA-PA

In North East is the WELCH GRAPE JUICE COMPANY PLANT (no visitors), 143 S Pearl St. In making juice, freshly picked grapes are inspected and cleansed before delivery to a stemming machine. After they have been heated in large kettles, hydraulic presses extract the juice, which is pasteurized and poured into five-gallon carboys for storage in cool dark cellars. At the end of three months, when the cream of tartar precipitate has settled, the juice is bottled. During the busy season, September and October, grape crops within a 20-mile radius are bought up, and more than 500 workers are employed. WPA-PA

25 Vine St., 1 block south of US 20 (the Yellowstone Trail). **North East Historical Society** in the Old Town Hall. The building was built in 1880 to be used for a town hall but it got sidetracked into being a fire station, complete with horses. Local history and a photo gallery are there.

31 Wall St. **Lake Shore Railway Museum** (4 blocks south of US 20). The 1899 passenger depot, used until 1960, is the museum with rail pictures. Eight restored engines, some passenger cars, and more have been collected.

PA-045.9 Pennsylvania/NY Line

State-maintained highways were given legislative numbers in 1911. These numbers were reference numbers that were useful for bookkeeping and documenting state highways. A more visible and user-friendly system was developed in 1925 for the driving public. ⚙

1926 Pennsylvania: Facts Motorists Should Know. Pennsylvania, Historic and Beautiful. Yellowstone Trail Route No. 9. "This thoroughfare enters Pennsylvania a short distance east of Conneaut, Ohio, passing through Girard, Erie, Harbor Creek and North East into New York state. It is entirely improved, except for a short section near the Ohio line." ⚙

The 1920 Old Ridge Rd. bridge across Elk Creek (near PA-11) was demolished in 2016 after decades of disuse. Contemporary maps (like the 1915 Goodrich) seem to show the previous crossing to be just north on the north branch of Old Ridge Rd. Seems ripe for some local research. GPS: 41.994125, -80.326203
Bridgemapper.com (Photo taken by Todd Wilson in 2008)

THE YELLOWSTONE TRAIL
[Route No. 9]

The great Yellowstone Trail, Route No. 9, skirts the shore of Lake Erie from the Ohio to the New York State line, through about forty-six miles of beautiful scenery dotted with historic landmarks.

Less than three miles east of Conneaut, Ohio, the motorist comes upon the fine concrete roadbeds of Pennsylvania. Near West Springfield and 1,300 feet above sea level, lies Conneaut Lake, the largest and most attractive lake in the State.

Leaving Erie via Elizabeth Street, the motorist passes through Wesleyville, Harbour Creek and North East. Wonderful vineyards have made this section famous. The New York State line is crossed four miles farther, where the Trail continues to Buffalo, other points in New York, Canada and New England.

This is a glowing description of the YT in Pennsylvania donated by a YT history fan.

PENNSYLVANIA TOURIST GLAD HE'S OUT OF NORTH DAKOTA "WILDS"

Apparently a disgruntled Pennsylvania tourist wrote to the *Ward County Independent* of Minot, North Dakota, and complained. Here is the response to the complaint: "A Pennsylvania tenderfoot made a number of misstatements that ought to be corrected. Allen Rishel said he reached Minot in snow. No snow has been reported yet in the state of North Dakota. Flowers are still blooming. He grew excited at the sight of our harmless Indians. He probably expected to see them in their war paint and tomahawks. He became so discouraged at the condition of the Minot roads that he sold his car and purchased a railroad ticket.

September 28, 1922 Ward County Independent (Minot, ND)

In 1925, the Erie Concrete Company proudly announced this concrete road.

A-Camping We Will Go

In 1921 there were eight of us camping from Tacoma, Washington to Minnesota. Two days out we went on until darkness fell. Dad said, 'The next spot we see, we're stopping.' Almost instantly we saw a lantern being extinguished in a tent. We stopped and pitched our tent in the dark. The next morning we awoke to see the fast flowing Columbia River at the base of a sharp drop very near our tent. There had been no lights, no barricade.

C. L. Wadsworth

By 1910 auto ownership was no longer the prerogative of the wealthy. Some owners now eschewed the expensive train and hotels and chose the auto and camping as the only economical way to go. Even if some could afford the comforts of a roof, steam heat, and indoor meals while viewing America, the tyranny of schedules was anathema. And to some, rich or poor, the open road represented freedom to be near wilderness and away from whatever bedeviled them at home. Perhaps it was the willingness of those individualistic Americans to meet the challenge of the wilderness that prompted them to go camping. Had not even President Teddy Roosevelt camped?

The emphasis in this Trail Tale is on camping in the west. As R. B. Anderson, Director of Bureaus of the Yellowstone Trail Association, wrote in *Outdoor Life* in 1924, "More tourist camps will be found in the west than in the east, due to the fact that the camping movement originated in the west."

Camping as Influencer

The interplay between the concept of camping and its influences on the culture of early 20th century is interesting. At first, camping was viewed with suspicion, and words such as "gypsies" or "tin can tourists" or "motor hoboes" were ascribed to campers. However, the power of the concept of camping eventually influenced the automobile industry to build larger "touring" autos to tote families and camping gear. Women's clothing was designed more for the outdoors where trousers were acceptable. The pattern-maker, Butterick, offered coat patterns with more choices of purpose. Gazillions of inventions popped up designed to ease food preparation and sleeping arrangements in the camp. The creation of local campgrounds became a necessity due mostly to the burgeoning availability of automobiles. State parks soon followed. More democratic attitudes resulted as campers rubbed elbows with other classes and nationalities, all drawn to the same campground in the same small town, and now, for at least one night, living under the same conditions.

Town retailers and camp managers soon saw the economic future and were influenced by women's choices and demands for clean camp sites, showers, and stoves. Competition from other camps resulted in improvements just to "keep up." Governmental rules to protect the health and safety of campers, and demands for better roads spurred modernization. Indeed, the camping movement was influential.

Camping by the Roadside

There were as yet only a few designated campgrounds, public or private, in the first decade of the 20th century. People just pulled over to whatever farmer's field looked flat and set up camp; even a wide space by any roadside sufficed. Few restrictions made one feel free of restraint on the road. "Thoreau at 29 cents a gallon," wrote Warren Belasco in *Americans on the Road: From Autocamp to Motel 1910-1945* (MIT Press 1979). Soon, however, the litter left by casual campers became a visible problem, especially to farmers.

All the comforts of home
Eastern Washington University Archives

Small communities without much hotel space grasped the fact that camping tourists leaked money for gas and food and, desiring to hold on to campers a bit longer, designated a free, empty space near (but not too near) town center as a campground. The town fathers welcomed the Yellowstone Trail, not only because of the promise of a better road, but also because visions of tourist dollars danced in their heads. And farmers were glad to be rid of these "vagabonds." At first, there was nothing provided but 10-15 acres of space. Campers, perhaps used to hotel amenities, made it known that they expected more from their free space.

The Crush is On

The 1915 Panama-Pacific International Exposition in San Francisco, as well as the opening of Yellowstone Park to autos, drew thousands west. World War I closed Europe to wealthy Americans used to "the Grand Tour." U.S. government appropriation of railroads for military transport limited vacation travel. So, many turned to the new sport of auto camping to "see America first," as the slogan went. "By 1919 more than 60,000 people visited Yellowstone Park, two-thirds of these came by private automobile. Nearly 60% who arrived in cars brought their own camping equipment. Only ten thousand people stayed in the Northern Pacific's expensive hotels that year" wrote Anne Hyde in *An American Vision: Far Western Landscapes and National Culture 1820-1920* (HarperCollins 1990). Even business tycoons camped. Perhaps you have seen that celebrated picture of President Warren G. Harding camping with his friends Thomas Edison, Harvey Firestone, Henry Ford, and naturalist John Burrows. Although they didn't have to pitch a tent, from all reports they really enjoyed their several experiences of the great outdoors just as others did. ⇨

Running boards often held camping gear.
Author's family scrapbook

By the early 1920s, public campgrounds in municipal parks appeared in abundance. An estimate of somewhere between 3,000 and 6,000 existed. Small towns offered a covered shelter with a stove or grill, water, lights, and "comfort stations." Community campgrounds became a source of pride. In the 126 campgrounds on the Yellowstone Trail, the local Trail-man was given the job of maintaining the camp. Newspaper accounts proudly listed the numbers of campers that took the Yellowstone Trail to their town for that week and announced what improvements had been added to the place.

Everybody Wanted In On the Act

Gas stations now rented out their spare grassy space in the rear. Along with their restaurant next to the station, they did well. Magazines carried camping equipment advertisements *ad infinitum*. Lists of necessary camping equipment and advertisements for such appeared everywhere. For instance, *Motor Age* in 1917 devoted nine pages to necessary items, instructions, and cautions about camping. The AAA in 1922 used 30 pages to do the same in their *AAA Official Camping and Campsite Manual*.

The ingenuity of designs for these items knew no bounds. Most advertisements in the early years centered on "tents" which meant just draping your tin lizzy with some sort of canvas covering and stretching it to cover a single bed on one or two sides of the auto, or any variation thereof. By 1920 free standing tents appeared everywhere. Running board "cages" held the outdoor equipment: the tent, the camp stove, and the Coleman arc lamp. (The famous Coleman camp stoves would come later.) Then there was the Tour-Tent. You slept on a bed stretched from the back of the rear seat to the steering wheel, all above the seats within the car.

Handling food was another major topic in camping literature. Our favorite was the fad of putting food on the hot exhaust manifold to bake while traveling. John Ridge (one author of this book) reported that his father baked many a potato that way during his travels. There was even a magazine called *Manifold Cookery and Recipes*. Ingenious ways of carrying food and strapping down dishes were myriad. Again, Harvey J. Ridge solved his food problem in the late 1920s and early 1930s by attaching a homemade pantry cabinet to his car's back bumper.

Pantry attached to the car
Author's family scrapbook

The auto was often used as part of sleeping arrangement.

tourist." They were proud of navigating the mapless dirt roads or snow-filled mountain passes. They became a "band of brothers" comparing road tales and useful travel information around the camp fire. Sinclair Lewis' 1919 story, *Free Air*, was based on his camping trip along the Yellowstone Trail from Minnesota to Seattle. In the book, a penniless camper repeatedly rescues two wealthy campers from peril. The meaning here was that merit was the measure of the man, not social class.

Trouble in Paradise

The free municipal camps had a short life. By the mid-1920s communities began to impose a small fee. The move was two-fold. First, free camps became overcrowded, noisy, and they attracted undesirable elements. Romani ("Gypsy") people, migrant workers, petty crooks, etc. camped for months without moving on, using up space and not shopping in the town's businesses. Second, competition in attracting campers meant upgrading facilities, a cost that some town councils would not bear. A small cost of 50¢ per car per night and policing the camp might solve the problem, they believed.

"The Jiffy"

Have you seen it? The box forms the table; the double deck bed accommodates FOUR. It is a "Home FOR FOUR PEOPLE." The most compact, lightest outfit on the market. If you want the BEST, HERE it is.

F. O. BERG CO.
REALTY BUILDING   SPOKANE, WASH.

Typical ad for camping gear

Campers wore their pride openly. Some even put tin cans on their radiator caps as emblems of their choice of diet and transportation mode; thus, the term "tin can

Central Park, Montana, learned to police its campground too late. In the autumn of 1920, two couples and three children camped there for over a month, living on fish caught and products of a trap line. One of the couples was killed and buried right in the campground. For three years no one knew of these "auto-tramp" deaths. Then the wife of the surviving couple named her husband as the killer. He was hanged for the deed. Later, on her death bed, she confessed to the crime.

What really solved the problem was the private campground. When communities began charging fees, the floor was leveled for private campgrounds who had struggled to compete with the subsidized community parks. Private operators could screen customers, could maintain decorum, and could set time limits. Resident camp owners had more reason to watch over their property.

The small fees that communities charged would not cover the expenses of further modernization. As a result, many community campgrounds closed and were reverted back to parks for day use for locals. It should be noted that today some communities still maintain small municipal parks with free overnight camping.   ⇨

Sometimes he lit the stove inside the tent!
Scorched the chimney hole a bit.
On the Road with Lizzie by Frank L Wentworth

mid-to-later 1920s campers took conveniences for granted, and, thus, the market itself closed unsafe camps.

What would the Trail founders think of camping today with the fading of tenting and the rise of 40 foot RVs - homes on wheels? They might wonder what happened to communing with nature, to trading travel stories around the camp fire, to feeding the bears in Yellowstone Park. We are safer now, but are we happier commanding, not communing with nature?

Another problem that beleaguered community campgrounds in the mid-1920s was the revelation of unsanitary conditions. Installing proper sanitation was too costly for some and so they closed. Health department investigations showed that some camps drew water from nearby lakes into which they also disposed of their waste. In the Yellowstone Trail states of Indiana and Minnesota, health departments discovered that about 27% of all campsites were affected by bad water. Serious dangers: typhoid, diarrhea, and dysentery. However, by the

The best thing about following the Yellowstone Trail today is the possibility of communing with nature on this now "back road" at places that don't require a 40 foot RV. And sometimes you will find clean, spartan cabins to shield you from the weather. ✿

Camping near Superior Montana
Mineral County Historical Society

Marking the Trail

It was a dark and stormy night. Carl Fisher, a founder of the Lincoln Highway Association, and two others were about 10 miles from Indianapolis in 1913. They came to a 3-way fork in the road with no road markers. There appeared to be a pole with a sign at the top. It was dark. Fisher apparently lost the toss and climbed the pole, lit a match (how could he in the storm?) and read Chew Battle Axe Cut Plug. This oft-told humorous tale demonstrated clearly the need for road markings.

It wasn't as if no one had suggested the idea before. The Romans marked the Appian Way to Rome. Later, signs with directional arms were introduced. In the U.S., the Automobile Club of America motivated a signboard movement in the eastern states in 1901 with iron strip signs bolted to iron posts.

In 1905, the Southern California Auto Club began erecting concrete mileposts on standard quality roads. By 1913, motorists had grown accustomed to seeing the blue-and-white enameled steel signs that marked the miles leading from Los Angeles to the Mexican border, Nevada, and San Francisco.

The *American Blue Book* series in their annual, thick guides and city maps (1900-1929) did their best to help the driver by saying such things as "In 3.4 miles turn left at the red barn, then in 2.3 miles turn right at the church." But there were no road markers to help.

Obviously, there was no governmental intervention, standardization, or interest in promoting road marking. At this time governments were not even interested in building roads, much less marking them. They had railroads to contend with. Asking residents the way to a distant destination often lead to frustrating confusion.

Types of Yellowstone Trail Signs

When the Trail was young, yellow painted rocks, rings of yellow paint circling telephone poles, daubing fence posts, silos, water towers, or anything handy along the road sufficed. There was no "official" marker for several years. The 1916 Yellowstone Trail Association *Route Folder* provided some direction toward a "standard" marker design which allowed markers to be duplicated and put up by Association members in their own locales:

Very early Washington YT sign near Denny Creek now maintained by the Forest Service

> The mark of the Yellowstone Trail is chrome yellow painted in a band around telephone poles and posts along the road, particular attention being paid to mark all turns and crossroads. An arrow is also used pointing toward the Yellowstone Park, the arrow being black on a field of yellow. The chrome yellow is also used on rocks on the side of the road, being placed in a disc. [Note: That is, the field of yellow should be circular with arrow inside.] Across the state of Minnesota, the yellow color has a white band above and below it. Tourists will have no trouble following the Trail if these marks are observed.

Note the confusion here. How can "bands around telephone poles" have the field of a yellow disc shape? Does the disc shape appear on rocks and bands on poles? If a

Recent picture of an original hoodoo sign near Mobridge

disc of yellow is the chosen design, why does Minnesota have white bands above and below the yellow band? Later instruction set the yellow band as five feet above the ground with a black arrow on the yellow band.

It was at the 1917 annual convention at Aberdeen that J.F. Alspaugh of Livingston moved that the organization officially adopt a 12-inch circle in yellow with a 6-inch black arrow in the middle with the words "Yellowstone Trail" on the outer edge, to be copyrighted. Motion passed.

Original YT metal
sign displayed at
Parmley House
Museum, Ipswich, SD

The subsequent 1917 *Folder* carried a more detailed and official description:

> The official mark of the Yellowstone Trail is the insignia shown on this folder, the background being in yellow and the arrow and lettering in black. This insignia is largely used on an iron marker fastened to telephone poles, fences, trees, etc., along the roadway. By the end of 1917 the entire Trail should be marked in this manner. Turns are denoted by "R's" or "L's" placed in the place of the arrow approximately 50 yards before a turn. Where the iron markers are not used, paint is used, the colors being chrome yellow and black arrow without any lettering, and the turns denoted in the same manner.

Note the words "Where iron markers are not used, paint is used." This is probably a nod to the obvious lack of trees and some telephone poles in the North and South Dakota route and treeless eastern Montana. Later, signs showing "S" for Slow, "X" for upcoming railroad tracks, and "D" for Danger were added.

Western Magazine, March 1922, reported yet another marker. "The present copyrighted marker is inserted in a container made of 20 gauge galvanized iron. The container is crimped on both sides and at the top, the marker being inserted from the bottom and bolted on a seven foot metal post. To change the sign, just unfasten the bolt, slip out the old marker and replace with the new."

Joe Parmley painted the route of the Trail on his car and suggested "chrome yellow paint at 13-16¢ a pound mixed

Joe Parmley's car with Trail route painted
around the car in yellow
Herrick Collection, Ipswich, SD

with linseed oil could paint vehicles" with the distinctive yellow sign. There was talk of painting bridges on the Trail yellow which Livingston did on the Harvat Bridge which crossed the Yellowstone River. To make up for the lack of trees in North Dakota and eastern Montana, the ingenious idea of using natural sandstone pillars was promulgated. Members found and placed the pillars along the Trail and painted "Yellowstone Trail" vertically on them in yellow paint. The pillars, also called hoodoos, were to be about 10-feet tall with a base of 12-18 inches and a top of 6-8 inches.

Sandstone hoodoo
YT marker
1914 First Year Book

Erecting the Signs

Having established an official image for Trail signs, maintaining consistency in signage was necessary. It appears that signs could be requested and paid for by a town and Joe Parmley would order the metal signs from the supplier to be shipped to that town where locals could install them.

Also, to insure accuracy of placement and maintenance of signs, the Association sent out "trailblazers" who either carried signs with them or received them at specified railroad freight offices. All did not go well at times as we see in the *Western Magazine*, July 1920:

> The only department of the Yellowstone Trail Association not going full steam ahead at this moment is in marking, due to delay in receiving a new invoice of markers. They were shipped in ample time, but we are the victims of the railroads. Tracing, telegraphing and swearing have all proven ineffective, and meantime, we have two idle marking crews, one at Morristown, S.D., going west, and one in Wisconsin, going east. If — mind the if — however, the markers are received in reasonable time, the marking both ways will be completed this year.

Over the years, several "trailblazers" passed through the marking department of the Association. Most of the blazers representing the Yellowstone Trail were in-house, such as Hal Cooley's son and J.W. Dassett, Director of Bureaus of the Association. Even the Boy Scouts of Baker, Montana, signed up to paint rocks. Problem was there was no paint donated, said the *Fallon County Times*. At times, teams would go out, one team covering the western portion of the Trail and another the east.

The *modus operandi* of blazers seemed to be that they would arrive at towns on foot where they would receive the signs or had carried signs, and post them. The town Commercial Club, or similar, would pay his expenses. Then the town was expected to find a ride for him to the next town. A 1921 letter to Yellowstone Trail Association General Manager Hal Cooley from the Secretary of the Billings Commercial Club says much: ⇨

Your son, Parl, arrived from Huntley last night and stopped at the Carlin Hotel. This morning I took up with him the matter of markers. He used 78 markers between Billings and Pompey's Pillar. I take it that he has in all about 290 markers.

He made the trip from Huntley part way by auto and got a fellow to bring his cards into town, he walking half the distance and putting up markers on the way. He was pretty well tired out, I guess, when he got to Billings so I took him to Laurel myself this forenoon. We marked the Trail between Billings and Laurel [16 miles] thoroughly and I left him there at noon. He expects to finish up at Laurel this afternoon and go on to Columbus.

Considering that the signs were metal and had to be affixed somehow to sturdy posts, we wonder at the speed of putting up signs described here as well as in similar reports of other trailblazers.

Also: the *Jefferson Valley News*, Whitehall, Montana of December 6, 1917, reported that:

Mr. Tait, manager of the Yellowstone Trail Garage in this city, very kindly donated a car and drove the Trail man to Butte [35 miles Whitehall to Butte]. Markers were placed on all crossroads and at intervals of not more than three miles where no crossroads appear. The markers are 9X9 inches, heavy enameled tin, yellow, with black circle and the words "Yellowstone Trail."

The signs mentioned above seem a little small considering the "official" sign voted on earlier in the year was to be a 12-inch circle. One assumes the task was completed in a day, again very speedy.

Getting the eastern leg of the Trail marked with signs "soon" was a promise made annually for years. Field Representative F. C. Finch called marking the eastern Trail as "more or less a vision" as early as 1922. Try as they might, they never could "perfect a working organization" east of Ohio. Although they did get permission to put signs up in New York by 1919, it is doubtful that any were actually put up, there being no local organization for support.

Professional Trailblazers

We wonder why young men would go into the trailblazing business when it involved such uncertainty. But, there were professional trailblazers. They put signs up along whatever trail an association had hired them to sign. Sometimes the "blazer" held two or three contracts at the same time if the trails were near each other. There was even an American Trail Blazing Association. The Yellowstone Trail Association did hire one hot shot of a professional blazer — William Warwick.

Warwick didn't just put up signs. He made a career out of it, alerting newspapers of his imminent arrival, speaking about trails at Chambers of Commerce or city council meetings, sometimes traveling with his wife and little daughter in a truck/camper which drew the press. Some scouting was also expected of him to find a better route, if possible, for the Trail. Newspapers would report his local route and treat him

as an important news story with big headlines. Newspapers would worry with him if a shipment of paint was late.

Iron YT sign (from a bridge?) displayed at Montana Hotel in Reed Point

Now here's a conundrum. Warwick carried a banner on his car which read "From Plymouth Rock to Puget Sound," implying that he marked the Trail thus. Exuberant newspapers also included mileages from the Atlantic coast in reports of his transcontinental trips. We are wondering about those signs. Did he actually put up signs that far in 1915? The Trail had only reached Chicago by 1915. The *Mineral Independent* (Superior, Montana) of July 27, 1915 wrote excitedly, "The famous trail is now marked so that auto tourists can make the entire cross-country trip without asking for any directions whatever." Apparently, some people were taking the motto as reality.

Problems in Eden

The Association hired trailblazers summers for sign maintenance for good reason. Signs were regularly defaced, used for target practice, removed by farmers to repair holes in barns, etc. Another problem was the disparity between sign placement and maps. Local citizens sometimes moved signs to new or better roads without telling the Association. It was not a malicious act, just enthusiasm. Nonetheless, blazers had to take notice of unauthorized changes.

And theft occurred. Perhaps it was just "boys being boys," but signs just disappeared. Obvious theft. And competing trail organizations may have just added their signs to the same post, stealing space.

Original YT right-turn sign maintained by a bar in Owen, WI

Around 1925, two years before the federal highway numbers went up in 1927, the Yellowstone Trail Association and Lincoln Highway Association argued to retain at least a single number for the length of their routes if they could not retain the name of their trails. They lost. The Yellowstone Trail became 14 federal routes, 25 state routes, innumerable county highways and, ultimately, two Interstates. But marking continued for two more years during this "crossover" period before the federal and state numbering programs, along with the Great Depression consumed all trails. Trail colors came down.

So it was that the Trail was marked by paint on silos, posts, sides of barns, yellow stripe within white stripes, small iron markers, and yellow metal with black arrow. But it was the lowly yellow stones along the Trail that impressed Harvey Ridge, John's father, on a 1927 trip west. Little did he know that his remembrances and photos would lead to this history 94 years later. ✿

Where Do I Turn? A Guidebook Would Help

With no or very few road maps or guides, how did the auto driver of the early 20th century find his way? Until then there had been little need for road maps or guides. Most trips were short, made by locals who already knew where they were going. Venturing farther meant traversing dirt wagon roads. Numbered routes didn't exist. Finding your way took time, patience and luck. It's little wonder that until then traveling between cities was done mostly by rail, not by auto. Railroad maps had become common. In fact, Rand McNally's first map, printed in 1872, was a railroad guide and it was well into the 1900s before they added roads.

As the numbers of autos burgeoned, and roads slowly improved, the need for guidance was met by a plethora of guidebooks for the autoist. Usually they displayed a small-scale (large area) map displaying numbers along roads which provided a key to the mile-by-mile instructions, listings of turns and features of the area – like railroad crossings and school buildings. They pretty much required a navigator in the passenger seat.

We acquired and used those guidebooks in our research by tracing out the mileages, turns, and listed features on modern digital maps. That determined the deviations from modern roads and provided information about the services and features in each town on the route. The book included stops where drivers could find gasoline and lubricants, or find a repair shop. The locations of camp sites and hotels were specified.

Three series of such guides (many others were visited) proved to be most helpful in the modern search for the Yellowstone Trail alignment:

The *Automobile Blue Book* (and others) approached the subject as the man on the street would if he had been asked directions. "Start at this railroad crossing, go straight for x miles until you get to the four-corners. Then turn right past the church ..." They might say at mile 58.5, "left-hand turn just before railroad," or "turn right away from poles." Their proclivity to use specific buildings, street car tracks, and other non-permanent features in their directions reduces the books' utility for today's research.

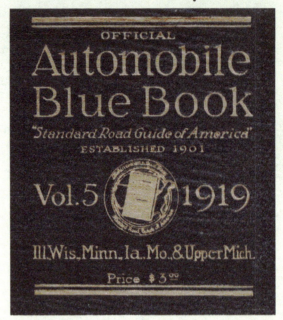

Standard cover. This volume has 1214 pages.

35.6	0.2	**Plevna.** Bank on far left. Turn left for 1 block and then right for 1 block.
35.7	0.1	End of road at church and school; turn left for short distance.
35.8	0.1	Turn right with road and take first left, immediately beyond away from travel. Ascend grade 36.0.
36.2	0.4	Fork just beyond cemetery; bear right, winding across prairie on fairly good road.

Instructions from Route 446 of Volume 5 of the 1916 *Automobile Blue Book*, a 1310 page volume

The Blue Books were very popular. Between 1901 and 1929 the books gave driving directions through the whole of the U.S., for some years filling 10 regional volumes each of 1000 pages each year.

Mohawk-Hobbs Grade and Surface Guide. This pamphlet style guide, sponsored by the Mohawk Tire Company, was unique in that it included an elevation profile of the road. Cut-away views of the road grade and surface along the route included: road surface information (asphalt, concrete, paved, gravel, dirt); condition of the road; assessment of garages; evaluations of hotels and campgrounds. All this was compressed into just a couple of lines per entry. There were no advertisements from other companies. In many areas Mohawk-Hobbs tried to mark the routes with signs along the road to guide the traveler – and direct him to a Mohawk Tire Company garage!

The Works Project Administration (WPA) was created by President Franklin Roosevelt's Administration to help alleviate unemployment during the Great Depression of the1930s. Men by the thousand worked on countless outdoor projects, artists were hired to paint, and writers created travel guides for each state through this Federal Writers Project. These guides, arranged geographically, included valuable information about the histories of each city, detail of hotels, restaurants, and garages in each city along various "Tours." Those listings provided the base for the city descriptions used in the Mile-by-Mile sections of this book. There were good city maps included.

The WPA guides began just a couple of years after the demise of the Yellowstone Trail Association. While the purpose of each volume was to document the history and current status of an entire state, they presented the information along auto routes, mile-by-mile. The guides provided the historic introductions to each place included in this book. Things had not changed enough from the heyday of the Yellowstone Trail to the publication of the WPA guides to make the historic or then-current information substantially inapplicable. The route of the Trail was still there, the history of each town was still true, and the evaluated hotels and restaurants were still there.

New York

Map labels (west to east along the trail):
Wanakah, Farnham, Silver Creek, Brocton, Ripley, Westfield, Fredonia, Irving, Angola, Buffalo, Le Roy, Batavia, Avon, Canandaigua, Geneva, Waterloo, Seneca Falls, Auburn, Chittenango, Wampsville, Sherrill, Illon, Little Falls, Palatine Bridge, Syracuse, Canastota, Oneida, Utica, Herkimer, St. Johnsville, Fort Johnson, Canajoharie, Fonda, Amsterdam, Scotia, Schenectady, Albany

Erie Canal and towpath

WHAT THE TRAIL FOUNDERS SAID-1921

For the past two years the active organizers have been seeking a favorable route east to the Atlantic Coast. Having much study of the route, Chicago, Fort Wayne, Toledo, Cleveland, Buffalo, Albany, Boston, Plymouth, it was adopted in June, 1919, as the Yellowstone Trail.

1919 Yellowstone Trail Association Route Folder
Note: This was a significant change from the route chosen and used for the 1916 Race.

INTRODUCING THE YELLOWSTONE TRAIL IN NEW YORK:
THE EMPIRE STATE

The Yellowstone Trail traveler of the 1910s and 1920s in New York was probably much like the Yellowstone Trail traveler of today. The Easterner followed the Trail west because it was a marked route through the state (or at least it was well defined on a road map like a *Rand McNally*). The traveler's goal was to "head west" often to visit Yellowstone National Park. The Westerner headed east on the Trail to the founding colonies of America. In New York is was easy, or at least possible, to travel across the state without being constantly lost. The experience would have been much like today, going east to find some of the history of our country.

While the roads were not much easier for the new-fangled auto, the population was well-settled by a mature society. In the Far West, society was just emerging and developing. Today, the traveler will find that the Yellowstone Trail leads him or her along a fine American Road Trip, making real the origins of America.

The Great American Road Trip in New York

There are many sites calling the tourist on this "Great American Road Trip in New York." About 10 miles south of Westfield is Chautauqua. Tour this former Methodist camp for Sunday School teachers - turned cultural center - turned recreational center. See Buffalo and its elegant hotels and museums. The Finger Lakes wineries (old and new) dot the Yellowstone Trail. See the Erie Canal and its various museums as it peeks out regularly in Trail towns. Walk the towpaths. The Freethinkers of Seneca Falls will make you think, especially around the100th anniversary of women's suffrage. Yes, even rusty old factories at waterfronts tell a story. You'll really want to see the Hotel Utica (now the Double Tree by Hilton). It's gorgeous inside. Small one-house forts in Johnsonville and nearby Fort Johnson speak of the bravery of Americans during crises. Beardslee Castle east of Little Falls speaks of quirky elegance. Small restaurants called Diners were (and are) a big thing in the northeast where they were born. And the arched bridges! Almost everywhere! They tell several tales - of transportation, of engineering, of people's desire to move. Even the Jell-O museum in LeRoy is interesting. For the science-minded there is the Case Lab in Auburn (home of the "talkie" movies invention); and the exciting home of GE history in the Schenectady Museum of Innovation and Science.

The Erie Canal has been widely associated with New York since its beginning as "Clinton's Folly" in 1817. Prosperity came to the towns along the 348-mile-long "folly" for 100 years, when, in 1918, the New York State Canal System modernized the old, obsolete canal system. This "Barge Canal" followed much of the old route, joining rivers and lakes into a complex chain of waterways which is still used today. Here and there, the original Erie Canal has been resurrected from obsolescence by volunteers to preserve it as an historic

presence. Reportedly, 80% of upstate New York's population lived within 25 miles of the Erie Canal.

The Yellowstone Trail runs fairly near the Barge Canal in places. We mention it but only as a famous backdrop to Yellowstone Trail towns Buffalo, Geneva, Seneca Falls, Syracuse, Chittenango, Canastoda, Utica, Herkimer, Little Falls, Schenectady, Amsterdam, and Albany.

Road Patrol Man, New York
National Archives

You will see mention of Dutch land offices a time or two. What was that all about? Well, the Holland Land Company speculated in American property on behalf of a Dutch consortium in early America. It was illegal for foreigners to own U.S. land in the 1700s. So, American agents, acting for the Dutch consortium, bought and sold great quantities of New York and western Pennsylvania in the name of the Holland Land Company. One of your authors, had a great-grandfather who bought his farm in New York through this system.

Why Did the Yellowstone Trail Go Where it Did in New York?

The initial Yellowstone Trail route between Indiana and Massachusetts was chosen on short notice to accommodate the Association's 1916 transcontinental relay race but little was undertaken to develop that route because the Association had all it could do to establish and manage the route between Seattle and Indiana from their offices in Minneapolis. That early eastern route ran through Connecticut, southern New York, Pennsylvania, Ohio, and into Fort Wayne, Indiana. Hal Cooley, General Manager of the Yellowstone Trail Association, explained to the *Aberdeen News* (South Dakota) that,

> This less known route was selected because it was possible to use the markers [Yellowstone Trail signs] on it, whereas these markers cannot be used on the northern route owing to the New York and Massachusetts roads already having all the markers the commissioners want. Trail markers have to be registered in these states and they have refused to register any more on that route.

The permanent route, formally determined in 1919 but undoubtedly preferred from the beginning, included   ⇨

> The further east we went the poorer the system of marking. The road from Buffalo across the Mohawk Valley into Albany was a wonderful stretch of oiled macadam. We took a few runs off the main roads into the side, but did not go far, for the side roads, as a rule, were very rough and narrow.
>
> *P. D. Southworth reporting on New York roads in October, 1921, Good Roads for Wisconsin*

ELMIRA ON BIG TRAIL MAP

A big road condition map sent out by the Yellowstone Trail Association has arrived at the offices of the Elmira Chamber of Commerce and been hung on the wall for the convenience of those wishing to look up the continental trip. The map gives hotels, garages, and places of interest all along the Yellowstone Trail which stretches across the country from coast to coast and passes through Elmira.

Elmira Star-Gazette. May 18, 1917.

Note: This route designated for the 1916 Race didn't last. In 1919 the route was established through Geneva, 55 miles to the north.

better established and improved roads through far more populated areas nearer Lakes Erie and Ontario.

We wonder if they ever did get permission to put up their signs in Erie, Buffalo, Syracuse, Utica, Schenectady, and Albany, their chosen route, or if they, exasperated, just moved their signs in 1919 to that northern route and managed to have the major map companies show that route.

One hundred years later that 1919 route of the Yellowstone Trail is now named NY 5 and/or US 20. The Trail danced a *pas de deux* with US 20, then NY 5, then US 20 again for much of its journey across New York. At times they are parallel, braided, or on the same path. Today, NY 5 (and US 20, when joined) is called "Main Street" all the way from Buffalo to Syracuse, a distance of approximately 155 miles, with only a brief interruption or two. This attests to the importance of this east-west route (US 20 having evolved from a 1799 wagon path) and, thus, to the importance of the Yellowstone Trail which followed this path before there were highway numbers.

It is appropriate to remind readers that the routes of named highways before the development of state highway departments were determined and marked by highway associations of businessmen, and the recording of routing decisions was not undertaken by any government. Without historic records of the associations, routes simply cannot be definitively, legally determined. In fact, the publications and maps from the Yellowstone Trail Association leave questions about many aspects of the route. This suggests differences of opinion within the Association or, quite likely, shifting plans. The most straightforward of those differences is the inclusion of Niagara Falls and Rochester on the route. These two cities appeared in some selected publications of the Association but no "boots on the ground" confirmed that route, and a preponderance of information suggested otherwise. Such differences made their way into *Automobile Blue Books* and thereby provided confusion. We assume that the emergence of road maps took over informing the traveler. *Rand McNally* and *Goodrich* set the route.

Finding specific information about the route through New York from the Yellowstone Trail Association itself was difficult. Their 1919 *Route Folder* was vague:

> Following a hard surfaced state road across New York state, the route passes through Rensselear, where Yankee Doodle was written, Albany, the state capital, and westward across the state through a country that marked much of the early Indian trouble and, especially interesting, in historical data, of the French and Indian War.

But detailed information about the Trail itself was missing.

The *Route Folder* of 1921 promised that the Trail

> will be active during the year 1921 in organizing and marking this road across New York and possibly as far east as Boston. Most of the road along this planned road is paved and the traveler has little to fear from weather conditions. Travel going from the east end of Lake Erie in and about the section of Buffalo is advised to follow this road to Albany and then turn south to enter Massachusetts.

A problem of the Association was with stirring up enough interest in the Yellowstone Trail in the East to form local booster groups. Roads were aplenty, so the original mission of the Association (encouraging road building) was moot. The Association changed its role, as a natural progression, to that of a tourism promotion/economic development agency, persuading the East to tour the unknown West. ❂

Lincoln's Funeral Trail Followed the YT from Chicago to Gary area, from Cleveland to Batavia, and from the Syracuse area (maybe Geneva area) to Albany. This demonstrates that auto routes followed established rail lines, even in the east. National Geographic, April, 2015

Frustration abounds in attempts to use the maps of the period to determine the route of the YT. Examples:

The *Rand McNally* road maps of the period are reasonably consistent in their routing and labeling of the Yellowstone Trail in New York, but several of the *Automobile Blue Books* listed the Trail going through Rochester and claim it is well marked! Makes research difficult.

The 1927 BB Highway Map of New York labels the YT with "YT". Fine, but from Albany east it is marked on State 45 (today's 35?) rather than the correct US 20.

CAR DEALER RECEIVES REPLIES

WHAT WOULD YOU DO?

Q: If your brakes failed going down hill? A: I would jump out and throw a rock under the wheels.

Q: On which side of a car going in the same direction must you pass? A: Always pass on the safest side.

Q: If your engine stalled on a train track, what would you do? A: Telephone my husband to come and fix it.

Q: When the car is parked, which side should be next to the curb? A: The side nearest the sidewalk

Q: When the battery runs out what must you do? A: Run after them or get new ones.

Q: What is the speed limit in the city? In the country? A: Not over 40 in the city. Slower in the country because the roads are bad. *Nov. 15, 1919 Batavia Times*

WAYSIDE

10 Roberts Ave. **Chautauqua Visitors Center**. About 11 miles south of Westfield on NY 394 is the town of Chautauqua on Chatauqua Lake. The Chatauqua Institution was founded there as a summer school for Methodist Sunday School teachers and quickly expanded into a national speaker and entertainment bureau in late 19th and early 20th centuries. Wholesome topics and musical performances were the order of the day and, with no movies or television, the arrival of a Chautauqua presenter in a small, rural town in the West was a very popular event. Yellowstone Trail Association Field Representative and fund raiser, Rev. George Keniston, was a popular Chautauqua speaker and an ordained minister c. 1914.

Chautauqua Institution. Today, for nine weeks each year, from late June through late August, the Chautauqua Institution offers an extraordinary blend of arts, lectures, opera, symphony, dance programs, and recreational activities. One can rent one of the many Victorian cottages and attend events or lounge around Chatauqua Lake. An **Athenium Hotel** is also on the grounds, dating from the mid 1800s.

Lucille Ball-Desi Arnaz Museum and Center for Comedy. Keep driving south about 19 miles farther on NY 394, then NY 474, then NY 60 to Jamestown and the Lucille Ball-Desi Arnaz Museum and Center at 2 W 3rd St. You are correct. They had nothing to do with the Yellowstone Trail, but the guide at Chatauqua told us that they were as much "Americana" as the Chatauqua lecturers and entertainers.

Costumes, memorabilia, and awards are only some of the things on display. Also, see the **Lucille Ball Memorial Park** in Celoron, NY, just minutes to the west. A new statue of Lucy replaces the 2009 one, considered by most to have been "scarey, looking totally unlike Lucy and hated."

WAYSIDE

Seven miles south of Brocton (take Co 380, then Co 58 east) is the tiny village of **Lily Dale**. Founded in the 1870s as a spiritualist mecca, it was very popular for those who rejected Darwinism and who "longed to believe in life after death and who wanted to contact the spirits of the dead," says Mac Nelson, author and emeritus professor at State University of New York - Fredonia. There were summer programs of lectures and other activities featuring authors and leaders in research into psychic phenomena. In his fascinating book, *Twenty West* (State University of New York Press, Albany, 2008), Nelson says, "Spiritualism survives today as an entertainment and a small formal religion." He reports that, "Even today, most of the residents are spirit mediums and if you are there on a Sunday, you might visit a service wherein a medium attempts to contact the dead." Perhaps Yellowstone Trail travelers stopped by.

HISTORY BITS

NY-000.0 Pennsylvania/NY Line
NY-003.1 Ripley

Ripley was for a long time the State's busiest hasty marriage site. Rival justices had large signs in front of their homes, neon-lighted at night and open for business 24 hours of the day: out-of-State couples could take their pick. But since the passage of the Todd 'anti-hasty' marriage law, requiring three days to elapse between the license and the wedding, the marrying business has evaporated. WPA-NY

At the time the Yellowstone Trail was routed through Ripley, its economy was built around grape-growing. Much of the recent economy of the town is based on growing fruit, especially Concord grapes.

10759 W Main St. (Yellowstone Trail/US 20). **Kelly Hotel**. This 1824 hotel had survived through thick and thin - through life as a stagecoach stop, through two visits from Abe Lincoln, through Prohibition and through the Great Depression. Unfortunately, it has not survived any longer and is up for sale at this writing. What will the seven reported ghosts do now?

NY-011.0 Westfield

(pop. 7,980, alt. 750 ft.), lies in the heart of the famous Chautauqua grape belt and is the home of Welch's grape juice factory. The Chautauqua grape belt comprises a two to three-mile strip running about 30 miles east and west of the town, and a drive thru the beautifully kept vineyards during the early summer or late fall is well worth while. In the town, on West Portage St., may be seen the principal office of the Holland Land Co., of which Wm. H. Seward, Lincoln's secretary of state, was the head. Opposite it is the old colonial home of the Sewards. Northwest of the village, about 10 miles on the old Portage road, is the quaint little fishing hamlet of Barcelona. This at one time was the Lake Erie port of entry and better known than Buffalo. The old lighthouse which still stands here was the first building in the state of New York to be lighted by natural gas. BB1921-1

The present main WELCH PLANT (open), N. Portage St., erected in 1910, produces 3,000,000 gallons yearly and employs about 500 men and women. Other local industries include the grape juice division of Armour & Company and auxiliary shops manufacturing grape baskets. WPA-NY

Many grape vineyards are seen along the Yellowstone Trail from the Pennsylvania state line to Westfield. Chautauqua County is the largest grape growing county outside of California. There are several winery tours and tastings available. *Road Trip USA* called Westfield the "Grape Juice Capital of the World." Resident Dr. Charles Welch introduced the product to the world in late 19th century and the rest is history. Today the headquarters for Welch Foods are still in Westfield.

MILE-BY-MILE

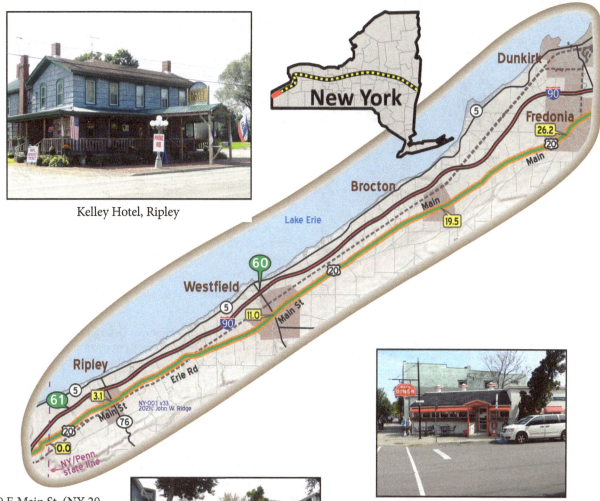

Kelley Hotel, Ripley

Main Diner, Westfield

Chautauqua, south of Westfield

40 E Main St. (NY 20 and Yellowstone Trail) **Westfield Main Diner**. Westfield and Brocton were hotbeds of diner manufacturing in the 1920s. The original lunch car portion of the diner (a 1926 Ward and Dickinson) has lunch counter seating and a kitchen area. An additional room was built on in 1983. This is the closest operating diner to Silver Creek, factory site of Ward and Dickinson diners in the 1920s.

20 E Main St. **Chautauqua County Historical Society and McClurg Mansion Museum**. The mansion was built in 1818 by pioneer James McClurg and contains period furniture, artifacts, and farm machinery. "Its grand salons and formal rooms stood in sharp contrast to the rugged homes of neighboring frontier settlers," says their brochure.

East Main Street Historic District is a national historic district encompassing 20 buildings and the Westfield Cemetery located along East Main St., the Yellowstone Trail. Within the East Main Street Historic District stand mid-nineteenth to early twentieth century residences.

E Main St. and South Portage. **French Portage Road Historic District** is a national historic district. It encompasses the nearly intact 19th century and early 20th century village core of 104 buildings.

NY-019.4 Brocton

(740 alt.,1,301 pop.), celebrates the memory of Deacon Elijah Fay by holding a grape harvest festival each autumn, with pageants, street fairs, and dances. Deacon Fay began experimenting with grape culture around 1811, trying several varieties that failed, but was finally successful with the Isabella and Catawba, and later with Concord, which has since become the favorite of the region. WPA-NY

Jct. of Main St.(NY 20/ Yellowstone Trail) with Lake and Highland Aves. **Brocton Arch**, a double arch over the street, placed on the National Register of Historic Places in 1996. Brocton Arch is an historic "welcome arch." It is a 1913 freestanding steel arch over a public thoroughfare bearing the community's name. It is a rare double span, four-way street arch.

41 W Main St. **Green Arch Restaurant** is a 1931 Mulholland diner, another long-standing reminder of the glory days of diners.

2 W Main St. **St. Stephen's Hotel**. According to Wikipedia,

The St. Stephen's Hotel has been a fixture at the center of Brocton since the mid-1800s. It was bought and sold several times... Recently (2012) local resident Al Seavy has bought it and has begun to return the St. Stephen's Hotel to its former glory.

NY

White Inn, Fredonia

GOOD ROADS
ROUTE 18 (PRESUMABLY THE YELLOWSTONE TRAIL)

...Assemblyman J. A. McGinnies says that the Highway Department have promised that the next letting of bids will include the stretch between Silver Creek and west to Roberts Road, and that the balance of the road west to Brockton will be let sometime this summer.

June 4, 1919 Fredonia Censor

~~~~~~~~~~~~~~~~~~~~~~~~~

And then 3 weeks later:

STATE ROAD DELAYED

In spite of the positive assurance that Route 18 would be undertaken this year, Highway Commissioner Card has received word from the State Highway Commission that nothing will be done west of Fredonia this year.

June 25, 1919 Fredonia Censor

GOOD NEWS FOR OUR MAIN ROAD
WILL BE PAVED FROM PENNSYLVANIA LINE TO SILVER CREEK

...there is now prospect that the much needed improvement of our Main road from Pennsylvania State line so that it will be a continuous pavement all the way to Buffalo will be accomplished... The space left is about 25 miles west of Fredonia and 10 miles east to Silver Creek.

March 28, 1917 Fredonia Censor

HISTORY BITS

NY-026.2 Fredonia

(pop. 6,000, alt. 767 ft.), is in the heart of the "grape belt," and often called the "Athens of Chautauqua" on account of its excellent schools. Here large quantities of nursery stock and grape juice are produced. It is the birthplace of the Woman's Christian Temperance Union. This park, in the center of the village, was named for Gen. Lafayette, who visited here in 1826. BB1921-1

[Families with] wealth from the grape belt have settled here, and their handsome homes do much to eclipse the grape juice and conserve plants, wineries, nurseries, and seed companies. Natural gas was discovered early in the nineteenth century and exploited almost immediately for lighting; the streets of the village are said to have been the first in the world to be lighted by gas. WPA-NY

[Note: The site of the first gas well is marked by a stone monument downtown.]

The **Fredonia Commons Historic District** was listed on the National Register of Historic Places in 1978. The U.S. Post Office was listed in 1988. And we are still in wine country.

52 E Main St. (Main at White. NY 20/Yellowstone Trail) the **White Inn** Bed and Breakfast. The building was built in 1868 as a private home for the Devillo White family and opened on June 1, 1919 as an expanded public hotel. Several rooms on the upper floors are part of the original structure as is the foyer and University Room on the main floor. It still exudes charm and elegance in a stately, pillared, huge white home. It was recently renovated. Melanie Gambino, present owner, was most interested in the fact that the historic Yellowstone Trail ran right past the front door. [Closed as of 2020?]

280 Central Ave., **State University of NY- Fredonia**. SUNY Fredonia is a comprehensive, public, residential, liberal arts university located in beautiful Western New York. Founded in 1826, the university is among the oldest in the SUNY system.

9 Church St., **Fredonia Opera House**, two blocks from the Yellowstone Trail. Built in 1891, this premiere performing arts center has a year-round schedule of live events, concerts, films. Guided tours are available.

NY-035.2 Silver Creek

(pop. 3,500, alt. 726 ft.), situated on Lake Erie, is widely known for its manufacture of grain- cleaning and canning factory machinery distributed thruout the world. BB1921-1

The grape belt here is five or six miles wide and extends to Harbor Creek, Pennsylvania, 55 miles away, comprising half of the grape acreage of the State, mostly Concord in variety. ... but the big grape boom began in the early 1890s. Businessmen, professional men, and everyone who could shake loose a down payment bought farms and set out vines; production swelled to such a degree that it pushed the bottom out of the market, ruining many who had invested their last dollar. By 1900 the grape juice industry, founded by Dr. Thomas

MILE-BY-MILE

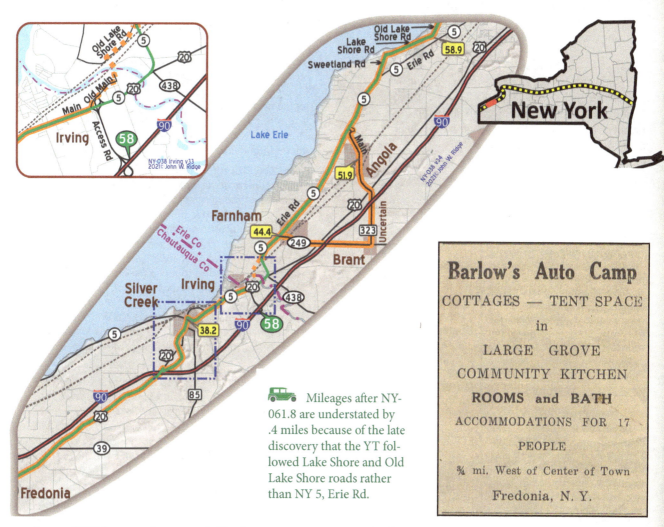

Mileages after NY-061.8 are understated by .4 miles because of the late discovery that the YT followed Lake Shore and Old Lake Shore roads rather than NY 5, Erie Rd.

Branwell Welch, got under way and offered a new market for the grapes. Today annual shipments from Chautauqua County average about 5,000 carloads of grapes, and about one third again as many are used locally in making wine and unfermented grape juice. WPA-NY

Silver Creek lies at the eastern end of Lake Erie and became an important shipping harbor before the advent of railroads. Today one can enjoy the recreational facilities and marina offered by the proximity to the lake.

From approximately 1907 to 1933 (roughly the Yellowstone Trail years) Silver Creek was on the Buffalo-to-Erie main line of the Buffalo & Erie Railway, a high-speed electric interurban railway. It was abandoned by order of the New York Public Service Commission to promote highway transportation.

1277 Central Ave. (NY 5/ Yellowstone Trail) **Dolly Dimples Waitress Statue**. She's about 12 feet tall and stands outside of Valvo's Candy store. It classifies as roadside kitch that the Society for Commercial Archeology would be interested in.

Diners were built here by Ward & Dickinson from 1924 to the late 30s, but we can find no museum dedicated to diners or address of the manufacturing plant.

NY-042.4 Irving

NY-044.4 Farnham

At Farnham the Yellowstone Trail trundled on straight east on what became modern NY 249 before turning north on what became modern NY 323 and joining what became NY 5. NY 5 was so numbered in 1924, just before the 1925-26 meetings of representatives of the federal government and states led to the Great Renumbering.

NY-051.9 Angola

8351 Erie Rd. (Yellowstone Trail). **The Evans Historical Society and 1857 Museum**.

NY-055.7 Derby

6472 Old Lake Shore Dr. (Yellowstone Trail). **Frank Lloyd Wright's Graycliff House**. Graycliff Conservancy preserved and restored the home built for Isabell Martin between 1926 and 1931. It is high on a bluff overlooking Lake Erie with views of Canada. See also Wright's Martin House Complex in Buffalo.

NY-062.8 Wanakah

A village on the shore of Lake Erie. NY 5 (Lakeshore Dr./ Yellowstone Trail) is the major east-west road which runs right through the village. The Township of Hamburg Park and Beach offers a stellar sand beach, swimming and boating opportunities. Yellowstone Trail travelers didn't have those amenities 100 years ago, but they did have the lake in which to rinse off the dust of gravel and dirt roads.

From the *Buffalo News*:

In 1927, world-renowned architect Frank Lloyd Wright designed a unique fuel filling station for downtown Buffalo. The station was never built. It featured a second story observation room with fireplace, restrooms, copper roof, gravity-fed gas distribution system for fueling cars, and attendant's quarters with a second fireplace.

Pierce-Arrow Motor Car Company was an American automobile manufacturer based in Buffalo, which was active from 1901 to 1938.

In 2002, Wright's filling station was built from his blue prints adjacent to the Pierce Arrow Museum as a complement to the museum. ✿

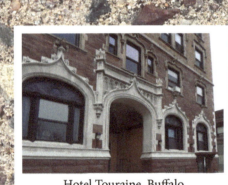

Hotel Touraine, Buffalo

HISTORY BITS

NY-074.5 Buffalo

Buffalo was laid-out in 1803-04 and became a military post in 1812. It extends along one side of the Niagara river, with Canada lying on the opposite shore. Along the entire length of this river were fought some of the fiercest battles of the war of 1812. Its rich historical sentiment, and the fact that at its northerly door are to be seen the world-famed falls of Niagara, has made Buffalo a mecca for the tourist. BB1921

(pop. 506,775, alt. 630 ft.), combines manufacturing and commercial facilities with delightful residential conditions. Though generally regarded as an inland city, it is in reality one of the great ports of the world. Buffalo has gigantic industries, made possible by the great hydroelectric development at Niagara Falls. The immense iron and steel mills and outlying coal elevators are interesting commercial features of the city, which also lays claim to possessing the world's greatest grain elevators. With the opening of navigation in 1918, Buffalo added to its already substantial transportation facilities one of the greatest artificial waterways in the world-the New York state barge canal. BB1921

It has a preponderance of asphalt paved streets and improved state highways extend in all directions. Among the most noteworthy thorofares are Niagara street, Broadway, Main street, [the Yellowstone Trail in 1920, presently closed] Delaware Avenue... On the corner of Genesee Street and Delaware Avenue may be seen the castle-like residence of President Millard Fillmore.

At 1168 Delaware Avenue, near Ferry Street, on September 13, 1901, President William McKinley died of 2 gunshot wounds fired at him Sept. 6. On the same avenue, at number 641, near North Street, at the Wilcox house, Theodore Roosevelt was sworn in as President. BB1921

There are about 30 museums in and immediately around Buffalo of interest to the traveling history buff. The following four were selected only because they were standing during the years that Yellowstone Trail travelers might have visited them. Check the web or an *AAA Tour Book* for the locations of others which might interest you.

263 Michigan Ave. **Buffalo Transportation/Pierce Arrow Museum**. The Pierce-Arrow Car Company is a symbol of one of Buffalo's significant eras of growth and prosperity. This museum preserves the company's long history.

1285 Elmwood Ave. **Albright-Knox Art Gallery**. Founded officially in 1862 as the Buffalo Fine Arts Academy. The Academy is the governing body of the Albright-Knox Art Gallery and is among the country's oldest public arts institutions in the United States. Since its inception as The Buffalo Fine Arts Academy in 1862, the museum has been dedicated to acquiring, exhibiting, and preserving modern and contemporary art. Its present stately building opened in 1905.

1020 Humboldt Pkwy. **Buffalo Museum of Science** is a science museum located at Martin Luther King, Jr. Park in the northeast of the downtown district, near the Kensington Expressway (NY 33). The historic stately building was opened in 1929, a little late in the life of the Yellowstone Trail

MILE-BY-MILE

New York

Historic Buffalo

recessed center looking quite imposing.

364 Pearl St. and labeled 2 Fountain Plaza. **The Genesee Hotel/Hyatt Regency.** The 1882 Genesee House was rebuilt as an office building in 1923, and became Hyatt Regency in 1983. Seemingly very sturdy for its description is thus: Renaissance-Revival building, steel frame, concrete slab floors, two floors of cast iron facade, and copper roof.

3165 Main St. (NY 5/Yellowstone Trail). **Lake Effect Diner.** According to their website, the Lake Effect Diner

is one of the last few dining car-style diners left in America. With old-fashioned milkshakes and a hearty menu of home favorites, Lake Effect has become a popular destination for locals and travelers.

262-274 Delaware Ave. **Hotel Touraine.** Erected in 1902, converted to apartments in 1982. Unique to Buffalo is this flamboyant Gothic Revival style with four-story annex (added 1923). The hotel originally had 250 rooms. One feature of the building was the installation of 100 bathrooms. Each room had a modern shower attachment. The tubs used were exhibited at the Pan-American Exposition and won a gold medal.

Lafayette Square (Washington, Clinton, Ellicott Sts.) **Hotel Lafayette.** The hotel opened in 1904 with two additions finished in 1917 and 1926 in a French renaissance style in red brick with trim of white terra cotta. It is now a boutique hotel and apartments with a smart black awning.

Association, but still available to Trail travelers. The excellent attractions include astronomy, the science of technology, and more about science.

1 Museum Ct. **Buffalo History Museum.** Housed in a stately 1901 building, its south portico meant to evoke the Parthenon in Athens. The museum serves to collect, research, interpret, and share the Niagara Frontier's rich history. It annually presents a wide array of programs and activities for all ages.

143 Jewett Pkwy between Woodward Ave. and Summit. **Frank Lloyd Wright's Martin House Complex.** Wright's Prairie Style design applied to a large residence, consisting of six connected buildings containing a collection of art glass and furnishings all designed by Wright.

140 North St. at Delaware Ave. (Three blocks off the Yellowstone Trail). **Hotel Lenox.** The hotel opened its doors in 1896 as a luxury-suite hotel for the prominent and wealthy.

1896 Hotel Lenox

It was renovated in 2005, but kept its historic charm. It is advertised as the only hotel in Buffalo that has been in continuous operation since the late 1800s. It is a large hotel with its two large wings and

Hotel Lafayette

Two Thousand Miles on an Automobile by Arthur Eddy (1902):

> Instead of turning to the northeast at Batavia and going through Newkirk to Rochester, keep more directly east through LeRoy, Avon, Canandiagua to Geneva; the towns are old; the hotels, most of them, good, the roads are gravel and country interesting.

Note: Seventeen years later this became the route of the Yellowstone Trail. ✿

C OF C TO OPEN ROADS

Chamber of Commerce has a committee to get the roads open from Batavia west to Buffalo and east to Rochester, so that travel on the state highways will again be possible. Many complaints have been received by the Chamber of Commerce owing to the condition to the state road, and it has been pointed out that with the possible railroad strike, it is deemed of great importance to have the main highway opened at once.

February 14, 1920 Batavia Times

Caledonia Fish Hatchery

Main St. and YT in early Batavia

Historic LeRoy House
and Jell-O Factory

Holland Land Office Museum, Batavia

BATAVIAN HAS PAPER
PRINTED IN 1800

Gives an Account of Funeral of George Washington.

Interesting Advertisements of Rochester: Man Offers Negro Wench For Sale.

November 15, 1919 Batavia Times

LIGHTING OF HIGHWAYS
A NOVEL PLAN
LIGHTED COUNTRY ROADS AN ADVANCED MOVEMENT –THE IDEA MAY SPREAD

May 29, 1920 Batavia Times

WAYSIDE

Although the great **Niagara Falls** area was not noted as being on the Yellowstone Trail in their literature or the many maps of the Blue Book Company or other contemporary mapping companies, it would be foolish to think that Trail travelers would not take a short side trip to the Falls.

Rochester, however, was noted by the YT Association as being on the YT on some early material but the Batavia route, used in this book, emerged as both the *de facto* and then the official route.

NY

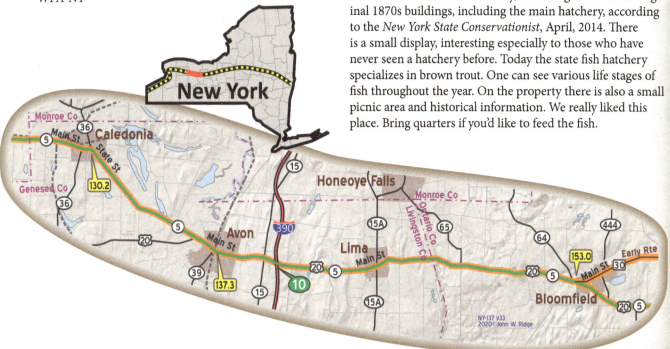

NY-113.1 Batavia

(pop. 15,000, alt. 890 ft.) is known as a thriving commercial and industrial hub as well as an historic town. Batavia is another name for Holland, just as Britannia is another name for England. Perhaps the most historic landmark in western New York is the old Holland Purchase land office, located at Batavia, which has been preserved as a museum and which contains the greatest of revolutionary relics. The two old guns in the front of the building were cast in New York state arsenal which manufactured arms in 1812. BB1921-1

131 West Main St. (Yellowstone Trail). *Holland Land Office Museum*. Built in 1804. Owned by the Holland Purchase Historical Society, the museum exhibits early farming tools, uniforms, and local records. The Holland Purchase included practically all of New York State west of the Genesee River, some 3,300,000 acres, sold in 1793 to a group of Dutch capitalists.

Joseph Ellicott surveyed it and was instrumental in the founding of scores of towns and villages, including Buffalo, but his pride was Batavia; "I intend to do all I can for Batavia because the Almighty will look for Buffalo." WPA-NY

NY-123.3 LeRoy

23 E Main St. (Yellowstone Trail). **The Jell-O Gallery and Historic LeRoy House**. LeRoy is the birthplace of Jell-O gelatin dessert, "America's Most Famous Dessert." It is at the rear of the Historic LeRoy House, an 1822 period house with three floors open to the public that interpret the house as it was used from 1830 to 1930. It contains a display of old transportation means - horse drawn sleds, carriages, an old Cadillac. The Gallery tells the story of Jell-O, from its rocky beginning in 1897 to today. "Jell-O advertising is a story of 100 years of American culture," says Gallery director Lynne Beluscio. About 10,000 people visit the little Gallery every year. General Foods closed the Jell-O factory in 1964; Kraft Foods now manufactures Jell-O in Dover, Delaware.

NY-130.2 Caledonia

3095 Main St. (Yellowstone Trail). **Big Springs Historical Society Museum**. Objects in the collection include those that represent the history of Caledonia's Seth Green Fish Hatchery (the oldest in the northern hemisphere), military artifacts, and rare paper broadsides.

16 North St. **Caledonia Fish Hatchery**, 150 year old descendant of the Seth Green Hatchery, still using some of the original 1870s buildings, including the main hatchery, according to the *New York State Conservationist*, April, 2014. There is a small display, interesting especially to those who have never seen a hatchery before. Today the state fish hatchery specializes in brown trout. One can see various life stages of fish throughout the year. On the property there is also a small picnic area and historical information. We really liked this place. Bring quarters if you'd like to feed the fish.

Avon Inn then
vintageviews.org

Avon Inn now

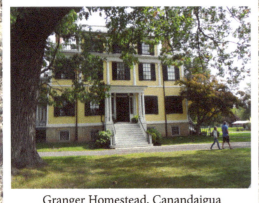

Granger Homestead, Canandaigua

Five Arch Bridge, Avon
Kelly Lucero (nyhistoric.com)

NY-137.3 Avon

(583 alt.,2,337 pop.), is a farming and canning center with a considerable milk industry. The region is a horse-breeding area, and the annual Avon Horse Show draws a large gallery of spectators. WPA-NY

Up to about 1860 Avon was a noted health resort. The United States Hotel and a dozen others were filled with guests who came to drink of the sulphur springs. Old registers carry the names of princes, dukes, and counts, Presidents and Senators. WPA-NY

55 E Main St. (Yellowstone Trail). **Avon Inn**. Built in 1820 and listed on the National Register of Historic Places, this beautiful Greek Revival mansion carries on a century old tradition of dining and lodging. The 200-year-old house has 14 guest rooms, and is decorated in ante-bellum style, not in Colonial period. A few years ago we stepped inside but did not stay there. The 2018 renovation was stunning.

On NY 39, about 2 miles south of Avon at 2078 Avon-Geneseo Rd. the Avon **Five Arch Bridge** is a remnant of a railroad bridge over the Conesus Outlet at Littleville. It was added to the National Register of Historic Places in 2012. It was built 1856-57 by the Genesee Valley Railroad to span the Conesus Outlet. The 200 ft. long x 12 ft. wide limestone bridge was part of the Rochester – Avon – Geneseo – Mt. Morris line. The line was electrified in 1907 with 13 runs daily. In 1941 the Avon – Mt. Morris section was abandoned and the rails removed. Today the bridge is in very good condition.

283 E Main St. **Tom Wahl's Restaurant**, a fun '50s place. Although not of the Yellowstone Trail era, this fast food restaurant apparently feels historic to the residents who list it right along with historic things to see in Avon. "It is not a fast food place," insists the retired owner. "It is a place that sells good food fast." We list it here because it is legendary to the residents and is on the Trail.

NY-161.6 Canandaigua

After purchasing from Massachusetts all of New York State west of Geneva and extinguishing the Indian title to a large part of the tract, Phelps and Gorham appointed William Walker as their agent and he opened here the first office for land sales in America. The first party of settlers, led by General Israel Chapin, arrived in May 1789, and within two years the town was overrun with emigrants from New England moving west over the Great Western Turnpike and up the Mohawk Valley. Here the Ontario Female Seminary, organized in 1825, was a pioneer in the education of women. WPA-NY

The ONTARIO COUNTY COURTHOUSE, top of the Main St. hill, is a two story gray brick Greek Revival structure built in 1858. Here was held in 1873 the trial of Susan B. Anthony and her associates, who had voted in a national election in Rochester. In 1937 women began jury service in this same courthouse where the pioneer suffragettes were found guilty of voting. WPA-NY

US 20 and NY 5 rise gradually out of the flatlands to the westernmost Finger Lakes town of Canandaigua. Iroquois legend has it that the 11 narrow finger lakes were created by

YELLOWSTONE TRAIL

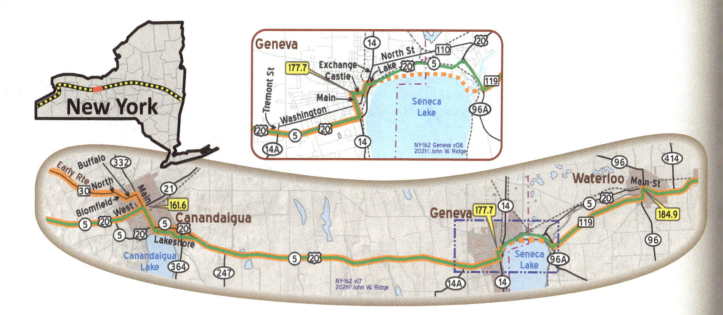

the hand of God. Five lakes bear the names of nations of the Iroquois Confederacy (Cayuga, Onondaga, Oneida, Seneca, and Tuscarora).

55 N Main St,. **Ontario County Historical Society**. Three exhibit galleries focusing on local history and a research library comprise this museum. Rotating exhibits spotlight life in various regions of New York. It is an elegant-looking building with tall, white columns.

295 N Main St. (Yellowstone Trail). **The Gideon Granger Homestead and Carriage Museum** 1814. Listen to stories of the four generations of Grangers who lived in this magnificent home from 1816-1930. Gideon was Post Master General under Jefferson and Madison. Over 50 horse-drawn vehicles are on display. Watch out, though. The arrow on Main St. is misleading. It shows an immediate left turn when it should show an arrow that points ahead for a block and then turn left.

151 Charlotte St. **Sonnenberg Gardens and Mansion State Historic Park**. Surrounded by 50 acres is a 40-room Queen Anne-style mansion built 1885-87 by Frederick Thompson, a New York City bank financier. Today, visitors can view many of its stately rooms of mixed architectural styles, and nine formal gardens.

Canandaigua Historic District, roughly Main St. (NY332/Yellowstone Trail) from Chapin to Saltonstall Sts. encompassing Howell, Gibson, Gorham, Bristol, Bemis and Center Sts. GPS: 42.88611, -77.28019.

There is a nice city park along the lake front.

You are entering the Finger Lakes wine country. Just east of Canandaigua in the small town of Flint right on NY 5/Yellowstone Trail, is the Amberg Winery, a good introduction to this large wine-producing area before you.

NY-177.7 Geneva

Among the foremost of the manufacturing establishments are the Geneva Cutlery Co., the largest razor factory in the world, the Standard Optical Co., United States Lens Co., and Fay & Bowen Engine Co. manufacturers of airplane and marine engines. Some of the largest fruit and ornamental nurseries are located here. Prof. William R. Brooks, a distinguished citizen of Geneva, has discovered more comets than any other man in the world. Geneva is an ideal stopping place for tourists, several pleasant drives into the surrounding country over improved roads radiating therefrom. BB1921

The **William Smith College for Women**, adjoining Hobart College on the west, was founded in 1906 by Geneva's philanthropist, William Smith, who, ironically, was a bachelor with little use for women. Smith students attend Hobart classes.

South Main Street Historic District has several buildings on the National Register of Historic Places. The street follows a long linear park, running along the shore of Seneca Lake. Although the Yellowstone Trail just skimmed the north tip of the lake, one could assume that the summer Trail travelers stopped for a quick frolic in the cool waters. GPS: 42.85774, -76.98176.

Cayuga-Seneca Canal, a New York Sate barge canal, connects Seneca Lake at its northern tip with the Erie Canal to the north east. It passes through Waterloo and Seneca Falls. It was approved by state voters in the early 20th century to compete with railroads.

Erie Canal and towpath

This area of New York was a "hotbed" of mid-nineteenth century radical social reform, making west-central New York a region of unprecedented social and religious foment. Ideas about free religious thought, abolition, birth control, woman suffrage, prison reform and anarchism bubbled. And then there was Robert Green Ingersoll, a "Freethinker." See his birthplace museum in nearby Dresden, 14 miles south of Geneva on NY14. He was a lawyer and popular orator whose favorite topic was religion. Known as "the great agnostic," he packed houses with comments like, "A fact never went into partnership with a miracle." Read more about Freethinkers in **Trail Tale: Freethinkers**, page 391.

Mary Ann M'Clintock House, Waterloo

**FINDS WAY TO MAKE
TIRES LAST LONGER**
FARM BUREAU AGENT PUTS ONE WORN
CASING OVER ANOTHER AND GETS
INCREASED MILEAGE
October 22, 1919 Seneca County Press

Statues of leaders of women's rights at the 1848 convention displayed in the Women's Rights Visitor Center, Seneca Falls

Amelia Bloomer (center wearing bloomers) introduces Susan B. Anthony (left) to Elizabeth Cady Stanton at 1848 convention, Seneca Falls

Restored Wesleyan Chapel, site of 1848 women's rights convention, Seneca Falls

NY

Gould Hotel, formerly The Clarence Hotel, Seneca Falls

55 Cayuga St. If you are into Victorian trappings, visit the **Seneca Falls Historical Society** in its 23 room Queen Anne mansion built in 1855. The ground floor is decked out in late 1800s style and you will get a glimpse of upper-class life of 165 years ago.

This is wine country … still. There are about three dozen **wineries** around Seneca Lake alone with dozens more around other Finger Lakes. Two of America's oldest wineries, O-Neh-Da Vineyard (1872) on Hemlock Lake and The Pleasant Valley Wine Company (1860) on Keuka Lake are not near the Yellowstone Trail. Did old Trail travelers seek them out? ✿

NY-184.9 Waterloo

Several churches and homes on the National Register of Historic Places are on Main St. (US 20/ Yellowstone Trail) and Williams St. one block north.

31E Williams St. The **Waterloo Library and Historical Society** (WLHS). The Queen Anne Victorian style building opened in 1881. The Waterloo Library was constructed specifically as a library and has operated continuously as a library in its original building under its original charter. An annex to the Waterloo Library, **Terwilliger Hall museum**, displays photographs and maps from as early as 1806 which give a sense of what life was like in the village at the turn of the 19th century.

14 E. Williams St. **The Mary Ann M'Clintock House** is part of the Women's Rights National Historical Park headquartered in neighboring Seneca Falls. On July 16, 1848, Mary Ann M'Clintock hosted a planning session for the First Women's Rights Convention. At this session she, Elizabeth Cady Stanton, and several others drafted a document they called the Declaration of Sentiments. It was ratified on the second day of the First Women's Rights Convention and signed by 100 men and women. Modeled on Thomas Jefferson's Declaration of Independence, this document proclaimed that "all men and women are created equal."

E Main St. **National Memorial Day Museum** tells the story of Memorial Day. Waterloo is the birthplace of that holiday.

Cayuga-Seneca Canal. The Seneca River, now the Cayuga-Seneca Canal, always has been an economic engine for the communities of Waterloo and Seneca Falls. The Seneca Lock Navigation Co., a private enterprise formed in 1813, dammed three sets of rapids and installed locks to allow goods to be transported to the Erie Canal. In 1818, a canal was opened between Cayuga and Seneca Lake. In 1825, a canal was begun to connect Seneca Lake with the newly constructed Erie Canal at Montezuma and the Cayuga-Seneca Canal was put into use in 1828. The Cayuga-Seneca Canal locks were modified in 1918 when New York State created the New York Barge Canal System.

NY-188.6 Seneca Falls

In the WESLEYAN METHODIST EPISCOPAL CHURCH BUILDING, corner of Fall and Mynderse Sts., now an automobile showroom, was held in July, 1848 the first American woman suffrage convention, which, presided over by Henry B. Stanton, Mrs.[Elizabeth Cady]Stanton's sympathetic husband, proclaimed that 'women have the right-or ought to have the right-to vote and hold office. WPA-NY

At the entrance to the Fall St. bridge is the SENECA FALLS HISTORICAL SOCIETY, which has several pieces of Mrs. Stanton's furniture, including her rosewood piano. WPA-NY

Seneca Falls is on Seneca River, part of the **Cayuga-Seneca Canal** and three miles from the head of Cayuga Lake. The Cayuga-Seneca Canal connects to the Erie Canal and upstate New York's Finger Lakes Region. The Cayuga-Seneca Canal is 12 miles long, built in c.1825 and combines the unique experience of inland water and deep-lake cruising.

The whole village is a buffet table for history buffs. Stand on the bridge over the Cayuga-Seneca Canal which once led to the Erie Canal. Seneca Falls was the model for the fictional Bedford Falls of the film "It's a Wonderful Life" and many civic activities remind the visitor of that fact. The mid-1800s hub of action for the women's suffrage movement was here. While the New England 1830s religious reform movement was going on just east of Seneca Falls, at the other end of the religious scale, one can visit agnostic **Robert Ingersoll's home** in nearby Dresden. See **Trail Tale: Freethinkers**, page 391.

136 Fall St. (Yellowstone Trail). **Women's Rights National Historical Park Visitor Center**. Women's Rights National Historical Park tells the story of the first Women's Rights Convention held in Seneca Falls on July 19-20,1848. It is a story of struggles for civil rights, human rights, equality and global struggles that continue today. Be sure to see the absolutely astounding group of statues of the 1848 inspiring thinkers and their words within the Visitor Center. The park includes: Wesleyan Chapel, Elizabeth Cady Stanton House, Hunt House, and Visitor Center.

Wesleyan Chapel is where the action took place. When we first visited Wesleyan Chapel in 1999 it was a sorrowful shell with only holes for windows and not even four complete walls. It was a joy to see it restored completely by 2015.

32 Washington St. **Elizabeth Cady Stanton House**. Part of the National Women's Rights Park. Stanton was instrumental in organizing the women's suffrage convention.

On E Bayard St., near the Ovid St. Bridge, is a very **life-like statue** showing Amelia Bloomer introducing Elizabeth Cady Stanton to Susan B. Anthony. An historic chance meeting on the street.

89 Fall St. **The Seneca Falls Heritage Area Visitor Center**. The Heritage Area's Visitor Center serves as an orientation point for local and regional history, providing a historical overview of the Reform Movements, specifically the Women's Rights Movement, and the development of transportation and water powered industry. An interactive exhibit gallery gives visitors a look at life in historic Seneca Falls and area.

Seneca Museum of Waterways and Industry is located within the Heritage Area Visitor Center. The Museum illustrates how the Seneca River and the Cayuga-Seneca Canal powered the rise of industry and fostered cultural development, helping to spread social reform movements.

108 Fall St. The **Gould Hotel**, 1919. It was called The Clarence Hotel for awhile. The Movie "It's a Wonderful Life" starring Jimmy Stewart and Clarence the Angel was shot in Seneca Falls, the town named Bedford Falls in the 1947 movie, which gets trotted out every Christmas. Revitalized in 2009 and again in 2018, the hotel now describes itself as a "modern boutique hotel and again a vibrant social center and premier destination." We hope this last renovation retained the hotel's unique historicity.

SENECA COUNTY RANKS HIGH
AN AUTOMOBILE TO EVERY SEVENTEEN PERSONS – STATE AVERAGE ONE TO EVERY 22
March 7, 1917 Seneca County Press

AUTOS FROM 35 STATES IN REGION IN PAST WEEK
July 26, 1922 Seneca County Press

WILL RUN AUBURN BUS LINE
J. J. Neil, 'the bus man' will have an auto bus running between Auburn and Seneca Falls during the coming summer...
April 24, 1918 Seneca County Press
Note: That would have to have been the route that the Yellowstone Trail Association would mark with their yellow signs, presently NY 5.

Harriet Tubman Home, Auburn

Harriet Tubman was a major "conductor" on the Underground Railroad. She was later a suffragist. Tubman lived in Auburn from 1859 almost to her death in 1913. She worked all her life to care for others who were unable to care for themselves, creating the Harriet Tubman Home for the Aged for indigent and elderly African-Americans in 1908. In 1911 she was admitted there herself and remained there until her death in 1913. ❀

NAMES HIGHWAY PATROLMAN FOR SENECA COUNTY
Highway commissioner Herbert Sisson has appointed patrolmen and helpers on state, county, and federal aid roads.
May 3, 1922 Seneca County Press
Note: Highway patrolmen were not policemen. They were ordinary citizens who were paid to help maintain roads by inspecting them and making minor repairs such as filling pot holes.

MANY TOWN IMPROVEMENTS ON FALL STREET
... the circus bills and dilapidated buildings that once greeted the stranger have disappeared and in their place we find stores newly painted and brightened up. The best and most noticeable is the new State Bank at the corner of Fall and Cayuga Streets. This handsome structure of granite and marble is just about completed.
July 26, 1922 Seneca County Press

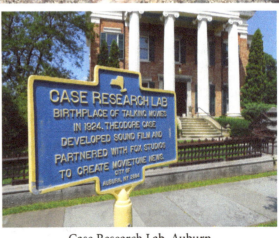

Case Research Lab, Auburn

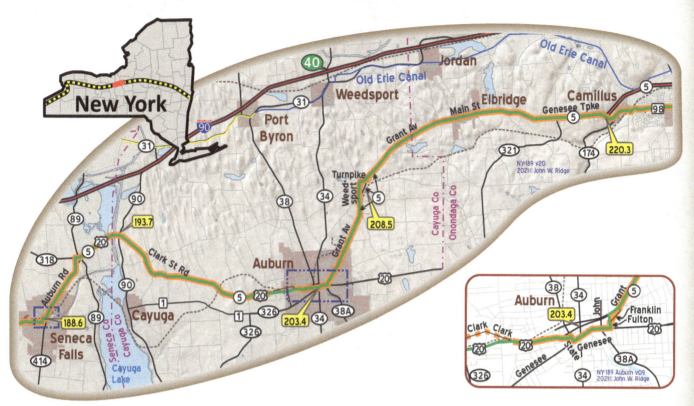

NY-A196.8 Cayuga (1920-1921 route of Yellowstone Trail)

The Cayuga Museum of History and Art. Shows the history of Cayuga, also featuring music, book clubs and movies. A jumping place.

Cayuga-Seneca Canal locks were modified in 1918 when New York State created the New York Barge Canal System. State engineers replaced five locks with a large two-flight lock having a 49-foot lift that required a great pool of water for its operation. This spelled the demise of the Flats area. Buildings were destroyed or moved to create Van Cleef Lake.

NY-203.4 Auburn

(pop. 36,000, alt. 643 ft.), an attractive summer resort, is situated in the beautiful Finger lake district. One can visit a different lake every day in the week and return to the city at night. On South Street is the old William H. Seward house, where the civil war secretary of state lived; he was instrumental in the purchase of Alaska for the U. S. There is a statue to his memory in Seward park. The town also boasts of several nationally known industries including the Columbian Rope Co., one of the largest rope manufacturing plants in the world, and the International Harvester Co. BB1921-1

33 South St. **Wm. Seward House Historic Museum** housed in a home originally built in 1816 but modified and expanded by Seward. Seward was a U.S. senator, a presidential candidate, and then Secretary of State under presidents Abraham Lincoln and Andrew Johnson. Seward is perhaps remembered for negotiating the 1867 purchase from Russia of Alaska, which became known as "Seward's Folly." The house is a National Historic Landmark.

180-182 South St. **Harriet Tubman Home for the Aged** and the **Harriet Tubman residence**. Both, along with her grave in Fort Hill Cemetery (located near South St./NY 34 between Tubman House and Seward House) have been designated as National Landmarks. Tubman was a "chief conductor" on the Underground Railway during the Civil War. The original Home still stands, but was renovated in 1953 by the African Methodist Episcopal Zion Church.

203 Genesee St. **Cayuga Museum of History and Art and Case Research Lab Museum**. The Museum's mission has become focused on the Case Research Lab and the history of Cayuga County and the Finger Lakes region. It is housed in the Willard-Case mansion, built in 1836 next door to the Case Research Laboratory.

The Case Research Laboratory is where Theodore Case invented the process of putting sound on film in the early 1920s, creating the "Talkies" for the movie industry. Visitors can tour the lab, see original equipment, and learn about this world-changing invention that came from a backyard laboratory in Auburn, NY.

South Street Area Historic District on the National Register of Historic Places. Roughly, South St. and adjacent properties from Metcalf Dr. to Lincoln St.

At least until about 1927 the YT entered Auburn on Clark St. from the west, as it does now, and followed the part of Clark which is now north of US 20. It is difficult to get on and off of that section of Clark. According to both the BB-1919 and 1927, Clark was called Aurelius.

NY

It had long been thought that a system of canals would benefit commercial and pleasure travel immensely. To that end, by the 1790s small canals were being constructed slowly in Pennsylvania, Virginia, Delaware, and the Potomac River in Maryland. Major problems seemed to be a lack of funds and a lack of experienced canal builders. Finally, in 1825 the Erie Canal was completed from Buffalo to New York City with the result that people poured west and trade exploded. Branches of the canal were built to connect small rivers to it, thus increasing its reach. With the arrival of the locomotive, the life of canals became moot. *The Erie Canal: A Brief History* (canals/ny/history) said, "Approximately 75% of the state's population still live within the corridors created by the waterways of the New York State Canal System." Today, the old mule paths alongside the canal in places serve as tranquil walkways and places to commune with nature. ✿

NY-229.2 Syracuse: The 1923-1924 highway map of New York published by the *Binghamton Automobile Club* shows, a "more" main highway from Syracuse to Chittenango following a route not unlike the modern NY 5, but there is no indication that it was used by the YT.

Chittenango Landing Boat Museum

Chittenango Landing

Erie Canal Museum, Syracuse

The Old Erie Canal was built from Albany to Buffalo, entirely with state money, starting in 1817. It was closed by 1917. A new Barge Canal opened in 1918, using rivers, lakes and enlarged sections of the Old Erie Canal. It is in use today and still run by New York State. ✿

WAYSIDE

Old Erie Canal State Historic Park runs along the Erie Canal from DeWitte, west of Chittenango to Rome, 36 miles to the east. It is a very skinny park designed for walking or bicycling and accessed from parking lots at the several cross-streets.

Old Erie Canal Historic Park, Canastota

NY

HISTORY BITS

YELLOWSTONE TRAIL

NY-229.2 Syracuse

(pop. 171,717, alt. 400 ft.), is an important commercial center. In 1798 salt works were established here and the manufacture of salt was its leading industry, but now its manufactories are diversified, including the construction of electrical apparatus, automobiles, typewriters and agricultural implements. The Solvay Process Works, at Solvay, west of the city, is one of the most extensive producers of soda products in the world. BB1921-1

Right from Syracuse on Milton Avenue to the Solvay Plant, 2.1 m., which here manufactures the well-known Arm and Hammer brand of soda. Facing the factories are the employees' small frame houses, their exteriors crusted with the ever-present limestone ash. WPA-NY

318 E Erie Blvd. (in the shadow of I-690) the **Erie Canal Museum** is a museum about the Erie Canal across New York. It is located in the 1850 Weighlock Building, the only remaining weighlock building in America. The lock was one of five stopping points on the Erie Canal where the state weighed the boatloads of freight to charge a toll.

There are 95 properties listed as being on the National Register of Historic Places in Syracuse. Several of these are on Genessee and James Sts., the Yellowstone Trail, but most are private homes and not open to view. However, the National Registry buildings on the **Armory Square Historic District**, bounded by S Clinton, S Franklin, Walton, W Fayette, and W Jefferson Sts. give one a view of a Syracuse of 100 years ago.

NY-245.4 Chittenango

1710 Lakeport Rd. **Chittenango Landing** is a mile north of downtown Chittenango. At the Landing is a **Canal Boat Museum** with information about canal boats. Outdoors is a restored 3-bay dry dock once used for repairing and building canal boats. Its an easy drive and very interesting.

NY-251.6 Canastota

(420 alt.,4,113 pop.), is noteworthy architecturally for the preservation of old canal buildings lining the canal. Another unusual feature is the number of wood Second Empire houses, with their flush board surfaces carefully chiseled to simulate stone jointing. WPA-NY

Canastota is within **Old Erie Canal Historic Park**.

122 N Canal St. **Canastota Canal Town Museum** is located in an 1860 canal-era building just across the street from Old Erie Canal Park's trail in downtown Canastota. The museum displays canal-related artifacts and exhibits on local businesses that thrived because of the canal. It contains a replica of a canal boat's cabin to give visitors a sense of what it was like to live on the canal.

NY-254.2 Wampsville

(480 alt.,280 pop.), is the smallest county seat in the State. It was selected as a compromise to settle a dispute between factions favoring Canastota and Oneida. The courthouse, with its dome and its Corinthian portico, lonesomely dominates its rural surroundings. WPA-NY

NY-257.4 Oneida

(437 alt.,264 pop.), geographic center of the State, a city of broad, shaded streets and well-kept homes, produces caskets, and period furniture. The establishment of Oneida resulted from a shrewd bargain made by Sands Higinbotham, owner of the city site, with the railroad whereby it received free right of way across his land, plus ground for a station, on the condition that it stop every passenger train at the depot ten minutes for refreshments at Higinbotham's Railroad House restaurant. Settlers came to this important stop, and Oneida became a thriving village. WPA-NY

435 Main St. **Madison County Historical Society** at Cottage Lawn, home of Oneida founder Sands Higinbotham. The museum is furnished with period pieces from the Higinbotham collection along with Madison County artifacts displayed throughout the 19th century home.

NY

Oneida Mansion House, Sherrill

The work of marking the Trail was carried through to Utica, New York, last year which will aid in increased tourist business in 1925.
January 16, 1925
The Marmarth Mail (North Dakota)

Hotel Utica in 1918 Scarborough Guide ad

Hotel Utica present elegant lobby

Hotel Utica today

Stanley Theater, Utica

NY-279.6 Utica:. The YT route south of the river in Utica cannot be followed as well as the northern (NY 5) route. However, on the southern route, the area near Turner St., with its giant abandoned factory that produced Savage Arms and became a huge shopping mall, is a fascinating area to explore, but rough and muddy and depressing. [Late August, 2020, the building was consumed by a gigantic fire.]

The recent intentionally invited influx of refugees from around the world into Utica is fueling a substantial recovery from "rust belt" days.

Note that Turner St. does not cross NY 55, thus interrupting the older YT route. You need to work your way through.

NY-259.7 Sherrill

At the T-junction with Sherrill Road, stand the Oneida Ltd., Factories (open, apply at office for guide), in which Community Plate, the 'silverware for brides,' is made. The conducted tour through the plant, a two-and-a-half-hour jaunt, follows the processes of manufacture from raw material to finished, boxed silverware. WPA-NY

Sherrill is more or less a suburb of Oneida.

The **Oneida, Ltd.** silver plating company rose out of the ashes of a cult known as the Perfectionists. They were a successful communal society which made silver plate until outside and internal pressures against their "religion" and culture broke up the community in 1881, leaving a company worth $600,000. Cult members were company shareholders, so, although the community dissolved, Oneida, Ltd. was retained and became one of the leading producers of silver plated tableware in the U.S.

170 Kenwood Ave., between Oneida and Sherrill. **The Mansion House**. According to their website,

> The Oneida Community (1848-1880) was a religiously based, socialist group of about 250, dedicated to living as one family and to sharing all property, work, and love. They called their 93,000 square foot home the Mansion House. Today, this National Historic Landmark houses a museum with permanent and changing exhibitions, a gift shop, residential apartments, overnight lodging, and banquet and meeting space.

NY-279.6 Utica

(pop. 94,000, alt. 800 ft.), is county seat and largest city in Oneida county and the commercial and industrial center for western section of the Mohawk valley. To the north, a short distance beyond the river and flats, are the picturesque Deerfield hills, beginning of the scenic highlands which stretch away toward the Adirondacks and the St. Lawrence river. WPA-NY

Utica has grown in population and wealth principally thru its extensive manufactures. It is clearly linked with the surrounding country by road and rail; and has interurban electric service. The section of which Utica is the center is one of the largest producers of dairy products in the state, and perhaps the most important eastern cheese market. BB1921-1

One enters here the Mohawk Valley that follows the Mohawk River and Erie Canal east.

1608 Genesee St. **Oneida County Historical Society Museum**. The Society was founded in 1876 and has served since that time to collect, preserve, and make accessible the past heritage of Oneida County and the upper Mohawk River Valley. Services center around a research library, a museum exhibit area, and weekly programs featuring guest artists, authors and historians. See the History of Transportation exhibit.

3 Rutger Park. **Roscoe Conkling House**, 1829. Conkling was a powerful, controversial Republican politician in a volatile political age, 1860s to 1880s. Conkling believed in

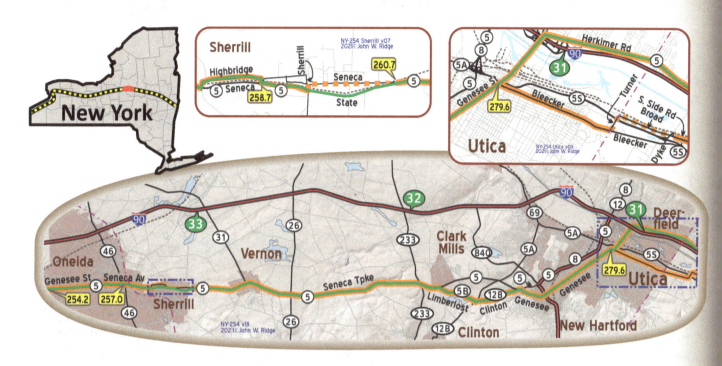

protective tariffs and was against civil service reform, preferring political appointments. It is on the National Register of Historic Places. At this writing the Conkling house is slowly undergoing a much needed restoration. Joe Parmley, founder of the Yellowstone Trail Association, was such a fan of Conkling's that in 1885 when Parmley arrived in South Dakota, he named his fledgling town Roscoe. The town is still there and is still so named.

Genesee and Bleeker Sts. are old streets, both on the Yellowstone Trail. About 10 properties are listed on the National Register of Historic Places in addition to the below. As you drive, note the gracious, historic buildings that were standing right there when the Yellowstone Trail travelers drove these streets 100 years ago.

Lower Genesee Street Historic District National Register of Historic Places. Roughly bounded by Genesee, Liberty, Seneca, and Whitesboro Sts. (both sides).

259 Genesee St. **Stanley Theater**. Originally built to be a movie palace, the Stanley opened on September 10, 1928 with 2,963 seats. On the Register of Historic Places, it now features live performers and community productions.

841 Bleeker St. (Yellowstone Trail). **Memorial Church of the Holy Cross** built 1891. This Episcopal Church right on the Trail may have been visited by Trail travelers 100 years ago. It is on the National Register of Historic Places.

102 LaFayette St. **Hotel Utica**. The date was March 11, 1912 when the hotel opened its doors. It was an era of prosperity and growth for our nation. Developers could afford to build with elegance. As their website says, "It was a time when gentlemen tipped their hats to ladies – a time when white-gloved hands held open doors with a welcome gesture. Saluting bellhops jumped eagerly for luggage and for tips.

It was a time when Judy Garland sang bird-like for guests from the mezzanine, and Mickey Mantle signed autographs out front for crowds. If the walls of this hotel could talk, they would tell the stories of Eleanor Roosevelt's visits to the kitchen to compliment the chef for his Bananas Foster, or perhaps of F.D.R.'s trips to the Gentlemen's Cafe to relax after the Democratic Convention."

We stayed recently in this great place which has managed to keep its historic aura in public spaces such as in its beautiful lobby. It is now a Double Tree by Hilton hotel.

NY-295.0 Herkimer

(pop. 7,520, alt. 406 It.), the seat of Herkimer county, in a picturesque section of the Mohawk valley, near the mouth of West Canada creek. Like many another Mohawk Valley town, Herkimer is an industrial center and a shipping point for dairy products. The principal industry is the manufacture of roll top desks. BB1921-1

The Standard Furniture Plant, at Washington St. and Eastern Ave. a six-story brick building covering an entire village block, is one of the largest producers of office desks in the United States. WPA-NY

The Erie Canal runs along the southern border of Herkimer. In 2000, the United States Congress designated the historic route of the Erie Canal, as the **Erie Canalway National Heritage Corridor**.

400-406 N Main St. at Court St. **The Herkimer County Historical Society Museum** traces 200 years of agriculture, industry and life in Herkimer County.

Herkimer Trolley Bridge (rear) over the West Canada Creek with NY 5/YT in front

🚗 NY-293.0 - NY-295.0: Southside Rd. (old 5 S) is a good, mostly rural road with no view of the canal.

🚗 NY-295.0 Herkimer: At GPS: 43.02874, -74.97377 is a tree-covered aqueduct of the old Erie Canal.

🚗 NY-302.3 through NY-304.3: The YT route is open only on the west end, but provides a glimpse of the old road construction and the canal and locks. Had a good picnic near the sewer treatment plant.

🚗 NY-308.6: New bridge going around old YT bridge.

THE YELLOWSTONE TRAIL

The Trail gets concrete in Herkimer County 1925

Lock E17 on Mohawk River/old Erie Canal

WAYSIDE

Saltsman's Hotel Restaurant. An historically interesting place about 10 miles north of the YT in Ephratah. Go north of Palatine Bridge and east of St. Johnsville at Ephratah. "Celebrating over 200 Years as a Destination Restaurant."

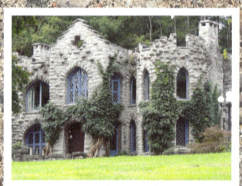

Beardslee Castle

Remnant of Erie Canal Lock #33

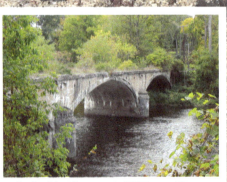

Arched bridge carried YT over Upper Canada Creek. Cloaked in grass today

WAYSIDE

123 Old State Rd. about 7 miles east of Little Falls is **Beardslee Castle**. The Beardslee family had a long history in New York, producing engineers, statesmen, builders, lawyers and investors. The "castle" was built in 1860. A small power plant was added and Third generation Beardslee, Guy, succeeded in mechanizing his farm and those around him. This was to become the first rural electric power in the country.

After a tumultuous 100 years including fires, repeated flooding, a failed eatery and on-and-off abandonment, it is now a beautiful restaurant with the bar in the "dungeon." One can view the whole valley through the second floor banquet room's floor-to-ceiling windows.

Unfortunately, Yellowstone Trail travelers would have driven right past the shambles in the 1920s. ⚙

About one mile farther east is an arched bridge which carried the Yellowstone Trail and then later NY 5 traffic over Upper Canada Creek. Workmen at the site with whom we chatted were interested in the fact that the Yellowstone Trail ran on that bridge before NY 5.

NY

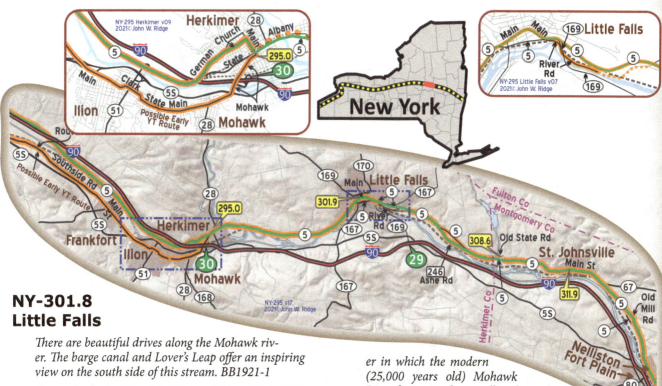

NY-301.8
Little Falls

There are beautiful drives along the Mohawk river. The barge canal and Lover's Leap offer an inspiring view on the south side of this stream. BB1921-1

Occupying both sides of the Mohawk River, Little Falls, (440 alt.,10,112 pop.), is an industrial city with dilapidated taverns on the canal banks and stately Victorian mansions on the crooked, hilly streets. A boom town of the old Erie Canal era, the city has never outlived the influence of that waterway; and its successor, the Barge Canal, remains an integral part of industrial and mercantile life. WPA-NY

The region became the largest cheese market in the country. Herkimer County cheese is still a favored trade name for the products of the middle western States. The ruined three-arch Aqueduct, foot of Bridge St., was erected in 1822 to provide access for boats from the Erie Canal on the south bank of the Mohawk to Little Falls on the north bank. The 70-foot central arch still stands; although the northern pier is fast disintegrating, the ruins are interesting as revealing the interior structure of the masonry. WPA-NY

The Little Falls Gorge is a rugged pass where the valley tapers down to a narrow cut. Two highways, two railroads, and the Barge Canal squeeze through between the sheer stone cliffs. The river here is a mad raceway, supplying water power to the factories that line its bank; the Barge Canal is a one-mile channel cut through solid rock. WPA-NY

In Little Falls at the corner of E Main St. and NY 5 turn south on River Rd., go 0.6 of a mile. There you will see old **Lock E17** on the Mohawk River/old Erie Canal. GPS: 43.03795, -74.84312.

319 S Ann St. **Little Falls Historical Society Museum**.

Little Falls Gorge at Little Falls is one of the great faults or dislocations of the earth's strata, which mark the southern Adirondack region. It runs from the south east side of Little Falls to the Pinnacle, 10 miles northwest and two miles north of Dolgeville. The bottom of the Gorge is the channel of the great Iromohawk River in which the modern (25,000 years old) Mohawk River has carved a smaller channel. The Gorge walls rise 300 feet. The Little Falls Gorge, with its exposed rock and strata forming a record of geological history and its evidences of titanic water and glacial forces, is a place of much interest to geologists. WPA-NY

NY-311.9 St. Johnsville

(360 alt.,2,283 pop.), is a mill town producing felt shoes and underwear and a farm shipping and trading center. The village displays several interesting Greek Revival houses, those at 30 Bridge St. and 11 and 13 Washington St. being especially notable. WPA-NY [Note: 11 and 13 Washington St. are half a block from NY 5/ Main St./Yellowstone Trail].

This is another town which owed its economic existence to trade on the Erie Canal.

Just east of the south end of the Bridge St. bridge over the Mohawk River is **Enlarged Double Lock No. 33 Old Erie Canal**, now filled in. It is an historic Erie Canal lock. It was built in 1824 and enlarged in 1840. The south lock was enlarged in 1888. It is built entirely of large cut limestone blocks mortared with hydraulic cement. Lock 33 fell into disuse after the opening of the New York State Barge Canal in 1918. Since 1997, it has been reclaimed and restored by local volunteers. When we saw it recently, it was filled in with soil but still recognizable as a narrow lock. It was added to the National Register of Historic Places in 2002.

Two miles east on NY 5 is **Fort Klock** (GPS: 42.98576, -74.64882). This is just a single fortified 1750 house built by Johannes Klock, not a fort in the Western sense with military barracks, etc. Citizens fortified their homes and sheltered their neighbors in times of crisis against Indians or the British, depending upon the year. This one contains 18th and 19th century exhibits and some antiques. A schoolhouse, Dutch barn, and blacksmith shop are also there.

NY

AN AUTO ENGINE HEATER

One of the troubles of the motorist who keeps his car in his own backyard garage is finding the tank frozen, or at best too cold to let the car start in the morning. A little electric warming-pad has just been devised to keep the engine warm all night. It attaches to an ordinary light-socket, and is only six inches by three in dimensions. It is slipped under the hood, the current turned on, and the car blanketed. It is said to keep the tank and engine warm at a small cost.

February 7, 1917 Seneca County Press

Erie Canal Lock #11, just west of Amsterdam

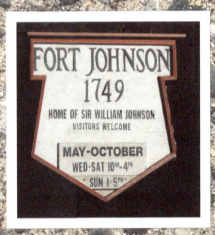

Roscoe Conkling Park, Utica

Fort Johnson

The terrain between the sharp slope up from the Hudson at Albany and the gentler slope down to the Mohawk at Schenectady is a sandy plain sparsely covered with scrub pine. Across this plain was built in 1830-31 the Mohawk & Hudson Railroad, the first in the State and one of the earliest in the country. The road had wooden rails covered with iron strips and laid on rigid stone blocks; between the rails was a path for horses, used on rainy days or when the locomotive boilers failed to generate enough steam. At the terminals the coaches, or wagons, were hauled up the steep slopes first by horses and later on inclined planes with stationary engines supplying the power. The crack trains of the New York Central still require an additional engine to help push them up the Albany grade. WPA-NY ⚙

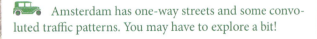
Amsterdam has one-way streets and some convoluted traffic patterns. You may have to explore a bit!

NY-332.4 Fonda

(300 alt., 1,120 pop.), is an important manufacturing village and freight transfer point. The main street faces on the railroad right-of-way, and the frame homes climb the hillside. The Fonda, Johnstown & Gloversville Railroad, which provides a freight outlet for the glove district, carries principally animal products and gloves. Fonda itself is a center for the manufacture of fabric gloves. In the summer its busses carry vacationists to southern Adirondack lake resorts. WPA-NY

Fonda was named for an ethnic Dutch settler, Douw Fonda, who was scalped by Indians during the Revolutionary War. Henry Fonda, the famous actor, wrote about his ancestors in his 1981 autobiography:

> Early records show the family ensconced in northern Italy in the 16th century where they fought on the side of the Reformation, fled to Holland, intermarried with Dutch burghers' daughters, retained the Italianate name 'Fonda.' Before Pieter Stuyvesant surrendered Nieuw Amsterdam to the English, the Fondas, instead of settling in Manhattan, canoed up the Hudson River to the Indian village of Caughnawaga. Within a few generations, the Mohawks and the Iroquois were butchered or fled and the town became known to mapmakers as Fonda. *My Life* by Henry Fonda (New York: Dutton, 1981).

NY-340.6 Fort Johnson

2 Mergner Rd., **Old Fort Johnson, Montgomery County Historical Museum**. Old Fort Johnson is the original 1749 limestone house, on the north bank of the Mohawk River, built by Sir William Johnson, the British Superintendent of Indian Affairs. A pallisade was built around the house during the French and Indian Wars, thus the name of "Fort Johnson." Like Fort Klock, this is just a house fort.

The Old Fort is a museum showing the social, cultural, military, and industrial past of the Mohawk Valley. The Old Fort has been the setting for many historical books. Read about its exciting history at www.oldfortjohnson.org. It is on the National Register of Historic Places.

NY-343.1 Amsterdam

The city of AMSTERDAM (288 alt.,33,640 pop.), straddles the Mohawk River at the mouth of Chuctanunda Creek, which has supplied water power to local industries. Guy Park Avenue, two blocks north, is in its western part a street of well-kept mansions on landscaped grounds. The rest of the city is given over to the frame and brick homes of workers and the heavy brick buildings bordering boisterous Chuctanunda Creek, within which are produced rugs and carpets, brooms, underwear, fabric gloves, linseed oil, and pearl buttons. In normal times more than 9,000 people are employed and large quantities of wool, silk, and flaxseed are imported as raw materials. More than half the population is mainly Italian and Polish. WPA-NY

Amsterdam hosts at least 15 properties on the National Register of Historic Places. It also shares the honor of the New York State Barge Canal on the Register with Canajoharie, Fonda, Glen, Minden, Mohawk, Palatine and St. Johnsville.

366 W Main St. (Yellowstone Trail) Guy Park, also known as **Guy Park State Historic Site and Museum**, is a house built in 1774 in the Georgian architectural style for Guy Johnson, the nephew and son-in-law to Sir William Johnson, 1st Baronet, the British Superintendent for Indian Affairs in colonial New York. [See Fort Johnson above, and yes, Guy married his cousin Molly.] It sits just behind railroad tracks off Main St. in the heart of Amsterdam. The mansion underwent substantial renovation due to Hurricane Irene in 2011.

Directly to the rear of Guy Park is **Lock No. 11 of the Barge Canal** where the locking of canal barges was once observed. The floodgates, or movable dams, were raised in winter to allow the ice free passage and were lowered during the canal season to regulate the flow of water.

The Mohawk Carpet Mills and Bigelow-Sanford Carpet Mills and others operated here for over 100 years due to easy canal transportation and water power supplied by the 300 foot drop in the rapidly flowing Chuctanunda Creek. Imports of wool, cotton, dyes and jute supported the employment of thousands, and the survival of an industry. By the mid 20th century the mills began closing, lured by newer factories in the south and cheap labor in China. Today the town is engaged in renewal efforts.

Just west of Amsterdam there is a viewing place for visitors to see the Erie Canal. Locks #12 and #11 are along NY 5. The old Erie Canal was a dug canal, but from 1909 to 1912 they "canalized" the Mohawk River, putting in locks and dams.

NY-357.5 Scotia: The YT Bridge over the Mohawk River has been redone. 1920 AAA strip map suggests it was more north/south than now.

The Abraham Glen house, Scotia

Proctor's Theater, Schenectady

The Schenectady Museum of Innovation and Science

Wellington Hotel 1924 ad, Albany

NY-357.5 Scotia

Erie Canal Lock #9. Continuing on NY 5W, about 3 miles west of Scotia, NY 103 S joins NY 5. The entrance to Lock 9 Park in Rotterdam Junction is just south of the intersection, before the bridge. The Erie Canal has been enlarged to encompass the Mohawk River.

1 Glen Ave. **The Glen-Sanders House**. Set alongside the Mohawk River, this historic home was built in 1658 by Alexander Lindsey Glen, Agent for the Dutch West India Company and fur trader. Astonishingly, the kitchen of this house, part of the original one room dwelling, still stands! He named this settlement "Nova Scotia," or New Scotland. Over the years, additional rooms were added to this substantial stone home by Glen and his son Abraham.

The Glen Family was host to many historical figures including General George Washington.

In 1765, Alexander Glen's great-granddaughter, Debra Glen and husband John Sanders became the sole owners of the Glen Estate. From that date until 1961 the house remained in the possession of the Glen family handed down from generation to generation. Today it is an inn.

14 Mohawk Ave. (NY 5/Yellowstone Trail). **The Abraham Glen** house was built in 1730 by the son of Johannes Glen from the Glen-Sanders Mansion. The house stayed in the family until 1842. Then the Collins family bought it and that is when Collins Park began. It is possible that there was an underground passage to escape Indian attacks or other enemies. Slaves also lived in the house. It is a rare surviving example in the region of a Dutch Colonial heavy timber frame house. It was extensively modified at the beginning of the 20th century but still retains its basic form and original materials. In 2004 it was listed on the National Register of Historic Places.

NY-358.9 Schenectady

Don Rittner, Historian of Schenectady County, wrote in the present Yellowstone Trail Association 2005 Fall newsletter, the *Arrow*, that "In Schenectady County, approximately 14 miles from three historic roads made up our part of the Yellowstone Trail: the 1663 King's Highway, the 1802 Albany-Schenectady Turnpike, the 1926 US 20/NY 5."

The Schenectady Times Union.com reported in December 27, 2005, that the city of Schenectady recently passed a resolution to designate that 14 mile section of Schenectady County as the Yellowstone Trail.

432 State St. (Yellowstone Trail). **Proctor's Theater**. Built in 1926 by F. F. Proctor, Proctor's on State St. in Schenectady was a popular vaudeville theater. In 1930, Proctor's hosted the first public demonstration of television with the help of General Electric. However, the Great Depression led to the decline of the theater.

After changing hands multiple times and almost being torn down in the 1970s, a group of concerned citizens banded together to save Proctor's. It re-opened in 1979 and since then, it has become the motivating factor for the revitalization of Schenectady's downtown area.

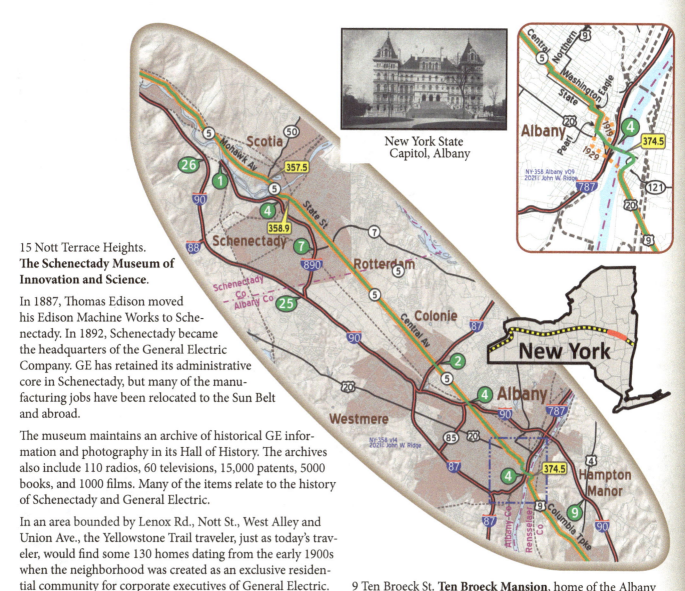

New York State
Capitol, Albany

15 Nott Terrace Heights.
The Schenectady Museum of Innovation and Science.

In 1887, Thomas Edison moved his Edison Machine Works to Schenectady. In 1892, Schenectady became the headquarters of the General Electric Company. GE has retained its administrative core in Schenectady, but many of the manufacturing jobs have been relocated to the Sun Belt and abroad.

The museum maintains an archive of historical GE information and photography in its Hall of History. The archives also include 110 radios, 60 televisions, 15,000 patents, 5000 books, and 1000 films. Many of the items relate to the history of Schenectady and General Electric.

In an area bounded by Lenox Rd., Nott St., West Alley and Union Ave., the Yellowstone Trail traveler, just as today's traveler, would find some 130 homes dating from the early 1900s when the neighborhood was created as an exclusive residential community for corporate executives of General Electric.

NY-374.0 Albany

Albany was the meeting place of the first Colonial congress, held 1754, to formulate a plan for a union of the several colonies. It was also the key to the primitive highway of central and northern New York which the French and Indian and revolutionary wars brought into new importance. During these conflicts military expeditions frequently passed thru en route to lake George, lake Champlain, Canada, lake Ontario and the Niagara frontier. WPA-NY

Between Albany (130,447 pop.) and Schenectady, State 5 is bordered by almost unbroken lines of small suburban homes occupied by commuters to the two cities. WPA-NY [Note: State hwy 5 was the Yellowstone Trail]

Nearly all departments of the state capitol are open to the public several hours a day; also the state museum. BB1921-1

In the Educational building (Washington avenue, nearly opposite Capitol) is the state library, one of the best schools for librarians in the U. S. BB1921-1

Albany exhibits a dramatic skyline with the capitol showing prominently.

9 Ten Broeck St. **Ten Broeck Mansion**, home of the Albany County Historical Association. Built in 1797-98 for the Ten Broeck family, then eventually given to Albany County in 1948. A variety of programs is given focusing on the history and culture of Albany.

State St. and Washington Ave. **New York State Capitol**. The Yellowstone Trail runs right past the iconic capitol building on Washington St. It opened in 1899 and was a show-stopper for the Yellowstone Trail travelers when they passed by around 20 years later.

Washington Park and neighborhood is designated **Washington Park Historic District** because of the many historic houses facing the park, each with its own story, and the story of the park itself. As far back as 1686 the park area was deemed public property by city charter and has been so used ever since. The park lies between Madison Ave. and State St., from Willett to Lake Sts., 81 acres including a lake. It was named Washington Park in the early 1800s.

547 Central Ave. (Yellowstone Trail). West Hill. **Jack's Diner**. Another diner, you say? Well, yes. Diners are an Eastern phenomenon and this one is on the Yellowstone Trail. We wanted to include Miss Albany Diner, which is on the National Register of Historic Places, but sadly, it is closed. Forever.

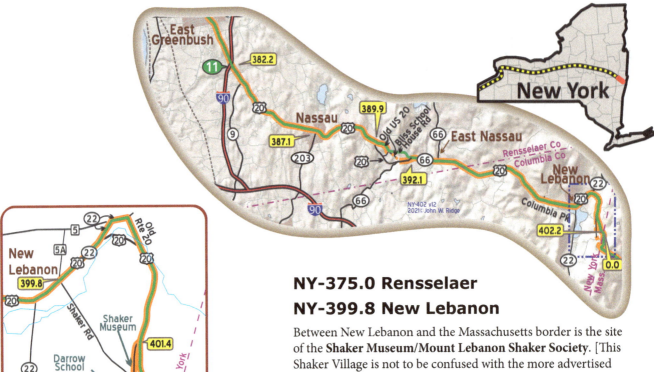

NY-375.0 Rensselaer
NY-399.8 New Lebanon

Between New Lebanon and the Massachusetts border is the site of the **Shaker Museum/Mount Lebanon Shaker Society**. [This Shaker Village is not to be confused with the more advertised Hancock Shaker Village a few miles to the east in Massachusetts.] It can be reached from NY-401.4 by following the original Yellowstone Trail running on Darrow Road or from NY-399.8 (at New Lebanon) running on Shaker Road.

This **National Historic Landmark** holds the remnants of a Shaker settlement of 1787. The United Society of Believers in Christ's Second Appearing is more commonly referred to as "Shakers" because of the very active singing and dancing related to their religious services.

Shaker Museum Visitors'
Center in 1838 granary
Trip Advisor

The website shakerml.org describes the religion thus:

> The Shakers believe in the millennialist principle of establishing "heaven on earth" through the practices of communitarian social organization, pacifism, celibacy, gender equality, and the public confession of sin.

There is still a Shaker community in existence in Maine.

The Museum's holdings span over 200 years related to all aspects of the American Shakers. The museum is in the 1854 Wash House and features special programs and events. The Visitors' Center is in the 1838 granary. Several buildings such as the Meeting House (1787), the Great Stone Barn (1860), the Poultry House (1870) and the Brethren's Workshop (1829) are in different areas of the property. Did you know that the first free lending library in the U.S. (1804) was here? Other religious retreat groups use some of the 10 buildings and 30 acres of the original village, as does a private boarding school, the Darrow School. Entry to the historic buildings is by guided tour only.

NY-402.2 NY/Massachusetts Line

🚗 At NY-401.4, there is an intersection of US 20 and Darrow Rd. Various of the *Automobile Blue Books* and other sources result in some confusion about whether the YT initially followed Darrow Rd. or the "new" road, now US 20, at the New York/Massachusetts border. It is probable, but not established, that the original route of the YT followed Darrow Rd. and intersected the modern US 20 at MA 000.9, at a point across US 20 at the east end of the existing wayside. *See USGS maps and Google Maps Earthview.

Driving Darrow Rd. today provides an up-close view of the Berkshires and an interesting visit to a lesser known Shaker village and its museum as well as an overgrown section of a pre-1900 road. Some of the historic Shaker buildings in this rural area house the Darrow School, a New England private high school (founded 1932), the Flying Deer Nature Center, and the Abode Mountain Retreat.

Seneca Falls Freethinkers

The Yellowstone Trail in New York

The role of the Yellowstone Trail Association in the western states was as a Good Roads advocate, developing a through route, and as a promoter of economic development through tourism. In the eastern states the role of the Association was primarily to develop travel to the Wild West on "their road" for the benefit of Trail member towns. Thus, the Association became a travel bureau, introducing the West to the East, assuring people that Indians did not scalp travelers anymore, that there was gasoline available, and roads to scenic wonders did exist. To that end, they competed for the very people who sought recreation and adventure in popular eastern places like the New York Finger Lakes area.

The Finger Lakes region has been a prime recreation and tourist location for well over a century. Chautauqua lectures now have been replaced by fairs, triathlons, wine festivals, and events remembering the movie, "It's a Wonderful Life," which was filmed there. But early outdoor activities of fishing, camping, and swimming are the same today. You can even take a boat ride on the Cayuga-Seneca Canal as they did almost 200 years ago.

Before 1919 the Yellowstone Trail traveler might have missed Seneca Falls because the original route of the Trail from Plymouth Rock to Ohio ran through Connecticut and the southern part of New York. In 1914, Yellowstone Trail Association member, Michael Dowling, had scouted New York state for a useful route upon which to place the famous yellow markers. The ideal route from Massachusetts was through central New York, including Seneca Falls, up to Buffalo, then along the shore of Lake Erie. Dowling was thwarted in his search, however. Highway officials claimed that there were too many "colors" of trails already on telephone poles and roads. One pole had 11 different trail signs on it. The Trail Association was forced to use a southern route, but by 1919 the Trail became blazed on its favored route and Seneca Falls was then visited by Trail travelers.

We tell this Trail Tale because in 1919 the Trail ran right down Seneca Falls' Fall Street, the main drag through that historic town. Trail tourists 100 years ago may have stopped to see the Wesleyan Chapel where a famous women's rights convention was held, but today's tourist will see much more since the site is now a National Park, and its history is told in brochure, preservation, and statues. The story rests on the word "freethinkers."

Freethinkers

Yes. They spelled it as one word.

In the mid-nineteenth century, west-central New York was awash in reformers and a hotbed of social, political, and religious innovation. Here "freethought" bloomed. Here speakers spoke freely to audiences about topics considered taboo elsewhere: abolition of slavery, birth control, prohibition, women's rights, agnosticism, prison reform. Here women dared to wear (gasp) bloomers! Freethought is a philosophical viewpoint that holds that

Freethinkers statue at Visitors' Center

opinions should be formed on the basis of science and reason, and should not be influenced by authority, tradition, or dogma. Mac Nelson, in his entertaining book, *Twenty West* (SUNY 2008), about US 20, the Yellowstone Trail's successor, says that what made the area so progressive was its "… freedom of thought and expression, its acceptance and nurturing of novelty and strangeness. That creative freedom led to … equality and justice."

It may be that such "progressive" socially rational thinking erupted in answer to the religious fervor of the 1830s in New York. Some of the fervor was "outside of the box" of conventional religious thinking. Most of this religious fervor, called the "Second Great Awakening," rejected rational skepticism, and accepted romanticism.

Robert Green Ingersoll may have been the "most remarkable American most people never heard of," as we read in his museum. His most controversial of lecture topics was religion. Known as "The Great Agnostic," Ingersoll defied the religious conservatives of his day saying, "A fact never went into partnership with a miracle." He championed causes like women's rights, racial equality, and birth control decades before their time.

Ingersoll Home, Dresden

Ingersoll's birthplace museum, 14 miles south of Geneva on NY 14 in Dresden, is an anchor on the "Freethought Trail" in New York, a collection of locations important to the history of freethought. It includes sites related to Mark Twain from Elmira, Andrew White, co-founder of secular Cornell University, and Margaret Sanger of Corning, founder of the birth control movement. A premier stop on the trail is Seneca Falls. ⇨

Amelia Bloomer (center) introduces Susan B. Anthony (left) to Elizabeth Cady Stanton (right)

Elizabeth Cady Stanton home

Continued

Women as Freethinkers

Seneca Falls pays homage to a women's rights convention held in the village in 1848, a meeting which historians called "the first wave" of organized protest and lectures about women's rights. Much of the town is in the Women's Rights National Historic Park. It is comprised of the Elizabeth Cady Stanton House on Washington Street, a Women's Hall of Fame, and the renovated Wesleyan Chapel where they had convened. Twenty bronze statues, the life sized portrayal of those early women's rights activists and male supporters,

1848 convention site
Wesleyan Chapel (restored)

are in the Visitors' Center near the Wesleyan Chapel on Fall Street.

Women, of course, were denied any hall, even churches, in which to speak about these issues. It was unseemly for women to speak anywhere in public. Lucretia Mott, Sarah Grimke (Quakers), Martha Wright, Mary Ann M'Clintock and Elizabeth Cady Stanton were the chief producers of a convention to discuss women's rights. The convention took place in the Wesleyan Chapel in Seneca Falls, home town of Stanton, in July, 1848. The big guns were there: Susan B. Anthony for women's rights and abolition, and Frederick Douglass and William Lloyd Garrison speaking on anti-slavery. Three hundred people showed up!

The organizers did not realize that what they were about would "change the world," as historians have described the event. They began the march toward the nineteenth amendment of 1920. Suffragettes worked hard during those 72 intervening years. The reader may recall pictures of thousands of women marching in New York City, and of others chaining themselves to the White House fence. Susan B. Anthony voted in the 1872 presidential election and was arrested. She was not allowed to speak in her own defense at her trial. The $100 fine was never collected by an embarrassed government.

The next time you find yourself on the New York path of the Trail, stop at Seneca Falls and ponder yet another chapter in our nation's book of freedom stories. ✿

Ahoogah Horns

First, lets make this clear. A horn, as in car horn, is a funnel-shaped object a bit like a cattle horn.

A car horn is a horn with a noise maker attached. Except a modern car horn often has no horn, just the noise maker. Sigh.

At the turn into the 20th century, this is really true! Autos were considered to be so dangerous to pedestrians that in some jurisdictions a person had to walk in front of the moving auto waving a red flag to warn folks of the oncoming monstrosity. The noise those things made was not enough? With quieter vehicles (especially, we assume, early electric cars) some way was needed to tell the pedestrian that he was about to be destroyed. They needed some modern technology.

So, first, there was the "sireno", a brand name for a siren. Sirens have a rotating fan (turned by a hand crank or electric motor) within a cylinder with holes which creates the pulses of air (sound) familiar to us all. One could hear it a mile away, but really, in front of my house? Frightened pedestrians would leap out of the way, pulling their dear ones with them. There was also the "Gabriel" which fastened to the exhaust pipe, giving out a novel sound.

Then there came, in 1908, Miller Hutchinson with his Klaxon, the real Ahooogo horn. You know the sound – gravelly and unmistakably related to antique cars. Friend Wikipedia says that,

the Klaxon horn's characteristic sound is produced by a spring-steel diaphragm [a circle of sheet steel] with a rivet in the center that is repeatedly struck by the teeth of a rotating cogwheel. The diaphragm mechanism is attached to a horn (the cow kind) that acts as an acoustic transformer and controls the direction of the sound.

There's an electric motor that drives it, but as the wheel comes up to speed you have that "ahoo," sound, and as it slows back down, that "gah" sound to it. The wheel was driven either by hand crank or an electric motor.

While the Klaxon had a mechanically driven vibrating diaphragm, Oliver Lucas, in 1910, improved upon the Klaxon by creating the vibration of the diaphragm electromagnetically. Think magnetic coils around a steel rod. Pretty much like creating the sound in the telephone, only bigger. The original had a horn that augmented the volume. Later, the diaphragm was big and bold enough to create sufficient air vibration (volume) to be used without a horn. Pretty common, yet, in the 21st Century.

Now, same diaphragm idea, with or without a horn, but with electronic/digital control of the vibration. Mechanically simpler and could be made to play tunes.

Even the auto horn is marching in the parade of technological history. But, the Klaxon horn never really disappeared. You can buy one today to adorn your antique black beauty and use to surprise pedestrians as you travel the Yellowstone Trail. ✿

Early Auto Horn
Lance Sorenson

Trolleys with Parks at the End of the Line

Clang, clang, clang went the trolley, ding, ding, ding went the bell. You know that trolley song. Well you do if you are our age. It was made famous by Judy Garland from the classic movie "Meet Me in St. Louis." Garland and friends were on their way to the 1904 World's Fair. That jaunty, lighthearted song pretty well described the feelings of early trolley riders across the country who were on their way to their local amusement park at the end of the line.

Trolleys had become a big part of the American transportation story before there were good roads and before family autos became common. They traveled, usually, down the middle of the busiest streets, so when intercity routes were established, like the Yellowstone Trail, they were frequently established along the trolley lines. Indeed, the *Automobile Blue Books* often gave directions to autoists to "follow the trolley tracks."

So What's a Trolley? A Trolley Park?

A trolley is a vehicle drawing electric power through a device attached to its roof (the troller) which reaches to the overhead power supply wires. Trolleys running on tracks are trams or streetcars (yes, spelled as one word). Trolleys running without tracks are trolleybuses. And of course there were early trolleys without a troller and pulled by real horsepower. All were light in weight (compared with a railroad car) and were usually operated by a single conductor.

Two-horse power for an early trolley in
Eau Claire, Wisconsin

Streetcar companies appeared across the country, many owned by the area electricity companies. To increase trolley ridership during weekends, electric companies often established a park or amusement park at the end of their suburban line. There are numerous examples of cities along the Yellowstone Trail that had their trolley-to-park entertainment feature at the outskirts of town. Let's look at five examples.

Chippewa Falls' Irvine Park. Eau Claire, Wisconsin, ran a trolley 10 miles to Irvine Park. Along the way the trolley stopped at Electric Park (now a golf course) with its dance hall, outdoor movie screen, and amusement rides. A 22-minute stop at Leinenkugel's Brewery (founded here in 1867) preceded it's final stop at Irvine Park with its small water falls, lake, band shell, and zoo. The trolley had a 28 year history of 15 trips a day, beginning in 1898 and ending in 1926. A small covered shelter which was at the trolley stop is all that remains today in Irvine Park of the glory days of family fun. But Leinenkugel's is still giving tours.

Ravinia Park in Chicago had (and still has) its Ravinia Park in a northern suburb, Highland Park. What started out as an amusement park to draw people to the Chicago-Milwaukee Electric Railroad in 1904 soon became the wonderful outdoor concert site it is today. Called Ravinia Festival, its first summer of 1905 it hosted the New York Philharmonic. It has held concerts every summer since, making it the oldest outdoor music festival in the U.S. The place seats 3,350 outdoors with two additional smaller venues on the grounds.

Big Island Park in Lake Minnetonka, just north of the Yellowstone Trail town of Excelsior, Minnesota, was created by the Twin City Rapid Transit Company (TCRT). Their trolleys provided transportation from the lake area to Minneapolis and St. Paul. To build weekend trolley traffic, the company built an amusement park on the "Big Island" in Lake Minnetonka. Big Island could not be reached by the trolleys, so steamboats were added at the end of the line at the lake. Beginning in 1905, you could ride a streetcar/trolley

Trolleys took riders to "streetcar boats" on Lake Minnetonka

to Excelsior and then "streetcar boat" to the Big Island. The steamboats were painted exactly like the trolleys - same canary yellow sides and red roofs.

Attractions at Big Island Park included everything from a roller coaster to a casino which featured musical entertainments.

The streetcar-to-boats proved to be very successful and profitable for many years. However, ridership on the trolley plummeted when roads were improved around Lake Minnetonka in the early 1920s. The TCRT discontinued all steamboat service on Lake Minnetonka by 1926. The boats were either scuttled, scrapped, or sold. The city of Orono reopened the island as a municipal nature park in 2006.

A "streetcar boat" on
Lake Minnetonka.

In 1979, diver Jerry Provost located the wreck of the Minnehaha, one of the scuttled steamboats, on the bottom of Lake Minnetonka. After nearly 20 years and many setbacks, the Minnehaha returned to passenger service in 1996. The Minnehaha steamboat has been a cruise boat on Lake Minnetonka ever since, operated by the Museum of Lake Minnetonka. ⇨

Columbia Gardens in Butte, Montana. From all descriptions, the amusement park called Columbia Gardens was a real Garden of Eden. William A. Clark, one of the "Copper Kings," built the marvelous park at the eastern edge of Butte. He and the Anaconda Company also owned the Butte Street Railway Company. It seems that the hated (by miners) Clark apparently had a warm spot for families and children. Each Thursday, rides on the trolley to the park were free for kids.

Aberdeen's first trolley, apparently just delivered by railroad. Also, a comment on the role of women?

Columbia Gardens streetcar was free on Thursdays.

Ivan Doig in *Work Song* (Penguin, 2010) described with warmth and excitement what the characters in his story saw in the park:

> We stepped off the trolley into an enormous amusement park with Columbia Gardens spelled out in a floral design against an entire hillside. Everything except the flowers seemed to be in excited motion. ...a roller coaster galloped through the tree tops, and beyond, a Ferris wheel against the sky, high flying swings, picnic groves, a merry-go-round, a zoo, a baseball diamond, a boxing ring, on and on. There was a huge central pavilion surrounded by refreshment stands.

You could pick the pansies in the pansy garden. And greenery! That was something one didn't ordinarily see in Butte because of the soot from the smelters. It opened in 1899 and closed 1937, sadly lost by the population as they watched the open pit mine get bigger and swallow up their beloved Gardens. One of the carousel horses survived and ended up in Missoula. It became the model for new, hand-carved horses that today adorn Missoula's famous carousel Caras Park.

Wylie Park. Trolleys had a short life in Aberdeen, South Dakota - 1910-1922. According to Jay Kirschenmann of Aberdeen News.com, November 17, 2019,

> The [trolley] service was called The Aberdeen Street Railway Co., and later, Aberdeen Railway Co.... There was a tiny depot, an exchange, where people could hop aboard the green and yellow cars that ran to Wylie Park daily during summer months and on weekends or days when baseball games and dances were scheduled in the Park.

Unlike amusement parks at the end of the line provided by power/electric vehicle companies, Wylie Park was, apparently, operated by the Aberdeen Park Board, but promoted by the trolley company. Today Wylie Park is a fine stop for travelers on the Yellowstone Trail. But what draws the most visitors to the park is Storybook Land, a world of imagination inspired by familiar nursery rhymes such as Humpty Dumpty and Hickory Dickory Dock, etc. And within Storybook Land is an area devoted to the Wizard of Oz. Frank L. Baum, author of the *Wizard of Oz* book and other stories, lived in Aberdeen for a while and the town never forgot. Complete with the Yellow Brick Road, the Scarecrow, Tin Man, and Cowardly Lion, children will learn of this timeless tale.

Kirschenmann concludes with a familiar story:

> But motor cars became more popular, and the streetcars were used less. Revenue declined, and in spite of a price increase from five to 10 cents per ride, the trolley system was shut down on July 31, 1922.

The Demise of the Trolley

Along with the rise of the automobile in everyday life came the entrepreneurs who extended the bodies of gasoline vehicles, called them buses, and took on the trolleys. Buses used public roads (not paid for by themselves) and avoided the capital costs (and associated debt) of tracks and electric wires. That efficiency and quite a bit of political shenanigans doomed most streetcar lines. Bus manufacturers and associated businesses succeeded in making the case for the use of buses and, after fierce legal and political battles, most of the trolleys were all gone by 1960 except in several large cities. In 1960 we discovered, to our sorrow, that Pittsburgh was one of those large cities. On a brief visit there we had accidentally parked our car with a rear wheel too close to the track. A streetcar could not simply steer past it. Returning to our car a few minutes later, we discovered a long line of traffic stopped behind a fuming trolley conductor. Our Wisconsin license plate probably confirmed Eastern attitudes about Midwesterners.

As you travel the Yellowstone Trail, enjoy the remaining "trolley parks" and check out their history. ✿

EAU CLAIRE-CHIPPEWA LINE READY TO QUIT

Passing of another interurban line as the result of bus competition was seen here Friday when the Northern Sates Power Co. filed with the city council a petition to discontinue its interurban line between Eau Claire and Chippewa Falls and to tear up its tracks.

March 26, 1926 Baldwin Bulletin

Massachusetts

Pittsfield
Lenox
Lee
West Becket
Chester
Russell
Huntington
Woronoco
Westfield
West Springfield
Springfield
Palmer
Warren
Brookfld
Spencer
Worcester
Leicester
Cherry Valley
Northborough
Marlborough
Auburndale
Newton
Weston
Boston
Quincy
Accord
Hanover
North Pembroke
Kingston
Plymouth

WHAT THE TRAIL FOUNDERS SAID-1919

No more fitting selection could be made for the start of such as a movement for the Yellowstone Trail Association than Plymouth, Massachusetts. The eastern terminus lies within sight of Plymouth Rock, and as it goes west, it follows the course of the progress of civilization in the nation. Crossing the state of Massachusetts on roads that permit one to travel according to taste, every moment one is in sight of scenes that are famous in the cradle of liberty days.

There is scarcely a place in this entire section but that has its claim to distinction in the history of the United States. So general is this, that we can mention only the outstanding features and give no details. The student or lover of history may have a new thrill in almost each mile. The road is paved or macadam of this entire section.

1919 Yellowstone Trail Association Route Folder

Wayside Inn near Sudbury
Fitzgerald Photo

INTRODUCING THE YELLOWSTONE TRAIL IN MASSACHUSETTS: THE BAY STATE

Across Massachusetts from its New York border to Boston, the Yellowstone Trail set the route for US 20 when federal numbers were established in 1927. But, that same pathway was famous long before the Yellowstone Trail Association placed its yellow and black signs on it. It was the way of the Native Americans, then the Boston Post Road, the way Washington marched to reclaim Boston from the British, the route where Franklin placed Post Office mile markers, the Knox Trail, and Jacob's Ladder, among others.

Between New York state and Springfield, Massachusetts, the Trail crosses the Berkshires. Part of that route is known as Jacob's Ladder. An unknown writer commented:

> Jacob's Ladder Trail traverses the scenic southern Berkshires. The scenic byway follows the same rivers and streams that guided Native Americans of the Mohican and Woronoake tribes as they traveled between the Connecticut and Hudson River valleys. In 1910, the road was opened as the first highway built specifically for the revolutionary new horseless carriages. Crossing the Berkshires as it does, it was dubbed "the First of the Great Mountain Crossovers." The Trail attracted automotive pioneers from far and wide to test themselves and their machines against the rugged terrain. Within a few years, Jacob's Ladder Trail had become a part of a continent-spanning highway linking Plymouth Rock with Seattle, Washington, known as the Yellowstone Trail.

Holly Angelo, writing for MassLive.com July 8, 2003, posted:

> The Jacob's Ladder portion of present Route 20 [the Boston Post Road/ Yellowstone Trail] is unique because its character has pretty much been preserved ever since the turnpike was introduced. There are no turnpike exits between Westfield and Lee and it is now a 33 mile scenic route from Lee to Russell.

As in the days of the Yellowstone Trail, this area is considered a major recreation area. Printed guides are full of announcements of plays, sports, festivals, fantastic restaurants and the arts. This is the playground of the state, just as it was in Yellowstone Trail days 100 years ago.

The rest of the route from Springfield to Boston follows closely the route established as one of the earliest long-distance roads in the nation – the Northern Boston Post Road, one road of the Boston Post Road "network." That roughly 400-year-old road was so named because it was part of the route the first mailman took from New York to Boston in 1673. See **Trail Tale: Boston Post Road**, page 417.

Today, looking at US 20 on a Massachusetts map you are seeing a good approximation of much of the Yellowstone Trail route of 100 years ago in that state.

P. D. Southworth, a Wisconsin county agricultural agent, traveled to New England in 1921, three years after Wisconsin had numbered and signed its highways. He reported his impressions of the Massachusetts roads. In part, he noted:

> Going into Massachusetts, the main highways were simply wonderful, especially through the Berkshire Hills. Many stretches of the New York and Massachusetts highways are brick paved with concrete borders to keep them in place … but when one attempts to get into country districts it is all hills and rough going. … An attempt had been made to mark the trails between the larger cities by different colored paints on the telephone poles, but between the lineman's spikes and the weather, the different paint markings were hard to distinguish. Going through the large cities it was a matter of guesswork to get out on the right highway. *Good Roads for Wisconsin*, Oct. 1921.

Why Did the Trail Go to Massachusetts?

Blame a motto! At the very beginning of the Yellowstone Trail, founder Joe Parmley, the active Good Roads man from South Dakota, was focused on getting his local roads in decent shape. It was remarkably soon that the publicity-minded friends of the Trail landed on the motto "a good road from Plymouth Rock to Puget Sound." Looking east and west from central South Dakota, those two end points defined a cross-county route through the northern tier of states with end points which were familiar to nearly everyone. With its major attraction, the widely known and exciting Yellowstone National Park, the route was nearly defined. Except for all the details. And except for that little bit from, say, Chicago to the town of Plymouth. The "boys" directing the Trail Association generally knew little about routes and roads in that "little bit."

To choose a route into Plymouth, Trail Association member, Michael Dowling, made a reconnaissance journey in July, 1914, to New York and Massachusetts to discover the very best potential route. For that trip he avoided the drive from Minnesota to New York by putting his car on a passenger boat in Duluth and he enjoyed the beautiful Great Lakes shipping route to Buffalo. There his goal of selecting a Yellowstone Trail route was thwarted by a plethora of local marked trails. Telegraph poles were overwhelmed with confusing trail markings. He visited relatives, had a great drive, and went home with no route to recommend but with a better understanding of the problems and potentials.

Until 1916 there was little urgency in defining that part of the route; there was enough to be done in the West. But in 1916 they forced their own hand by deciding to hold a relay race all the way from Plymouth Rock to Puget Sound. Their motto, "A Good Road from Plymouth Rock to Puget Sound" may have been informative and catchy, but it forced the eastern terminus to be Plymouth, and forced the founders to scramble to find extant main roads. Fast.

The Yellowstone Trail Race Route, 1916

The Yellowstone Trail had been formally extended east as far as Chicago in 1915. That means that the organization had established memberships and regularly dispensed travel information and involved members of the Association only up to Indiana. Their publications admitted that they had limited information beyond that point. We can only imagine a ⇨

committee sitting around a table reviewing what was available to them: Atlases, railroad route maps, the *Automobile Blue Books*. Directness would be a major factor. They hurriedly chose a route from Plymouth which headed southwest, then more or less straight west to Fort Wayne, Indiana, and then on to Chicago. That route became the Yellowstone Trail. Newspapers in towns along the way reported some excitement about being on the well-known Yellowstone Trail and about the impending transcontinental relay race. The 1916 relay race from Plymouth to Seattle was run with great success and wide publicity. Nevertheless, the Yellowstone Trail Association was not ready to "organize" that last part of their route until 1919. See **Trail Tale: 1916 Race**, page 416.

John Alden House in Duxbury, 1653

Why the Trail Goes Where it Does in Massachusetts, the 1919 Answer

By 1919, the leaders of the Yellowstone Trail Association had gained a better knowledge about "the East." And they apparently learned that an auto journey from Indiana to Plymouth might better take advantage of the better established roads, the kinder terrain, and significant population centers on a line through northern Ohio, a bit of Pennsylvania along Lake Erie, the center of New York state, and the developed historic Post Road in Massachusetts.

While the crowded utility poles undoubtedly still existed, the major map makers, especially Rand McNally, now showed highways on their maps rather than railroads, and the Yellowstone Trail was marked prominently as far as Boston, the *de facto* eastern end of the Trail. The Association's maps and information clearly placed the route through the center of New York, including the capitol, Albany. That forced the choice of entry point into Pittsfield, Massachusetts, and the existence of a state road from that point to Boston made the route choice easy.

So, during 1919 the Trail was clearly established through Massachusetts, but from Boston to Plymouth, the route of the Yellowstone Trail is not easy to document. Nothing recorded by the Yellowstone Trail Association was found by the authors. Two routes between Quincy and just north of Plymouth appear to be candidates: the first is the route closest to the ocean, much of it now designated as MA 3A, and the

Old postcard view of Elm St. in Worcester. Building on left is now condominiums.

second is the route through Hanover, now designated for much of the distance as MA 53. The latter route is labeled as the Yellowstone Trail on several commercial road maps found by the authors. It was the more direct, no doubt faster route, but the ocean route would be more appealing to tourists and was listed as a "main route" on early New England road maps.

What History Do You See Now?

There is little unique Yellowstone Trail history here. But so much American history remains and is visual in the East that today's traveler is able to experience what Trail travelers experienced 100 years ago. For instance: the Wayside Inn, near Sudbury, once had the Yellowstone Trail for its front driveway; Jacob's Ladder carried the Trail and is still there; the Adams homes compound on the Trail in Quincy is still there; countless historic homes, theaters, inns, and taverns may be visited; and there is always the traditional tourist attraction - the coastline of the Atlantic Ocean. ✿

OUT WHERE THE WEST BEGINS AS SEEN FROM MASSACHUSETTS

The Wallace (Idaho) Board of Trade receives many letters from the east seeking information regarding this section of the west, many of which display a surprising lack of knowledge regarding the industries, customs and character of the people who inhabit what was once known as the "far west." [This letter] was written evidently by an educated and cultured gentleman, and it is really a pity to disillusion one who is looking forward to thrilling experiences and hairbreadth escapes as he boldly advances into the land once known as the "wild and woolly." Here is the letter:

Springfield, Mass.
March 2, 1925
Gentlemen of the Wallace Board of Trade:

I am planning an auto trip across the continent during the months of July and August and expect to cover the territory in Idaho which lies along the Yellowstone Trail. Can you give me an outline of road conditions in your state as applicable to the trail; also information on tourists' camps —location, equipment, etc. Would there be any hotels or inns at which a man and his wife would feel secure in stopping for over night accommodation? Would you consider it advisable or necessary to carry firearms with us while traveling through the northwest, daytime only; need we feel anxious about disturbance on the road?

Please pardon the nature of these last questions; we are easterners, laden with only hearsay bits of gossip and quite inexperienced in western travel.

March 12, 1925 Wallace Miner

MA

The old road was through the Shaker village and contained grades which rendered it impossible for teams to draw any but the lightest loads. The new State road winds around and over the mountain at a grade nowhere exceeding five percent. It is a broad macadam and perfectly constructed. The disadvantage of having no intermediate-speed gears was forcibly illustrated. We had to make the entire ascent on the hill-climbing gear at a rate of about four or five miles an hour.

Two Thousand Miles on an Automobile, by Arthur Eddy, 1902, p.158 ✿

Melville's house, Pittsfield

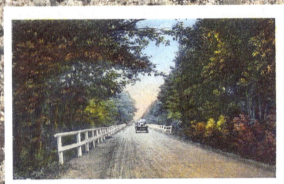
Looking west from near the NY border

Hancock Shaker Village, near Pittsfield

In the brochure **Historic Tours in Soconyland 1925** it says that Pittsfield is known for "beautiful homes and associations with the past". ✿

Concrete pavement in Berkshire Co., 1925

Hancock Shaker Village circular barn

WAYSIDE

297 West St. **Tanglewood**, the summer home of the Boston Symphony Orchestra and summer music school. Summer concerts, student recitals, chamber groups, and entertainers all perform classical, jazz, and folk music in the various venues on the campus. The 550-acre estate includes Hawthorne Cottage where Nathaniel Hawthorne wrote several books. The first concerts began in 1936, six years after the demise of the Yellowstone Trail Association, but this historic entertainment site is worth the side trip.

Tanglewood's main entrance is 1.4 miles west of Lenox on Route 183 (West St.).

MA-000.8: The probable original YT (now overgrown) headed west from Massachsetts into NY. Just within New York it passed the present Shaker Museum (not the Hancock Shaker Village in Massachusetts), which is just southeast of New Lebanon, NY, on Shaker Road. See blowup map and driving note near NY-402.2.

MA

MA-007.6 Pittsfield

The town was incorporated in 1761 and named in honor of William Pitt, Earl of Chatham.

The manufacturing industries of Pittsfield include at least twenty-six separate lines of industry, and comprise about 100 establishments. Chief among these is the plant of the General Electric Co., covering 133 ½ acres of land, with a large output of electrical machines and devices. BB1921-2

The old **Appleton Mansion**, girlhood home of the wife of Longfellow, is still standing on East street; it is now the Plunkett homestead. Longfellow spent several seasons at this house, writing there the "Old Clock on the Stairs" and other poems.

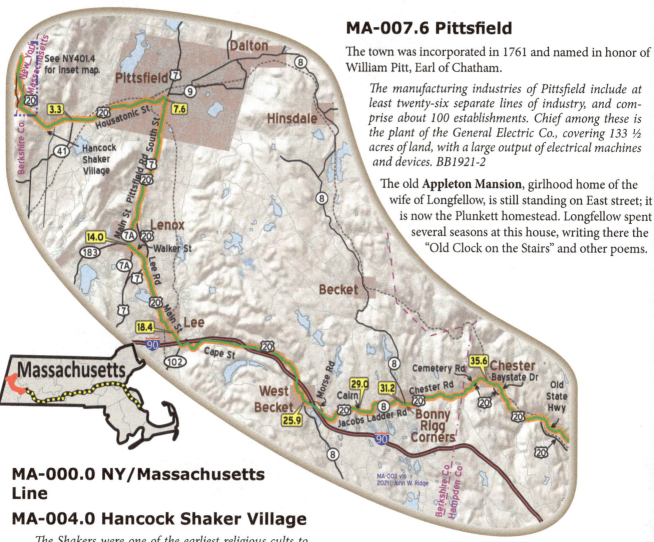

MA-000.0 NY/Massachusetts Line

MA-004.0 Hancock Shaker Village

The Shakers were one of the earliest religious cults to sprout in New York and Massachseetts. Its distinguishing tenets were celibacy, community of property, spirituality, and refusal to take oath or bear arms. The social unit was the large 'family' housed under one roof, but the men and women eating and lodging separately. The physical paroxysms accompanying their religious exercises gave rise to the name 'Shaking Quakers' later abbreviated to Shakers. WPA-NY

A combination of communism, industry, and inventiveness built a prosperous society during the nineteenth century. Wide markets were found for Shaker herbs, garden seeds, blankets, brooms, and chairs. They were called 'Shakers' because of their active dancing during services. This United Society of Believers in Christ's Second Appearing believed also in celibacy, so the sect's exclusive dependence upon converts and the adoption of orphans to recruit its numbers led to a slow disintegration until today there is only a handful of aged Shakers left. WPA-NY

1843 Housatonic St. (US 20/Yellowstone Trail). About 4 miles east of the New York border is **Hancock Shaker Village**. Established in 1783, Hancock Village thrived as an active Shaker community during most of the following two centuries. It brings the Shaker story to life with sixteen farm buildings, including the 1826 round stone barn. The Village is a National Historic Landmark.

780 Holmes Rd. **Herman Melville's 'Arrowhead' home** is the headquarters of the Berkshire Historical Society. The Society's website says:

From 1850 to 1863 Melville and his family called Arrowhead home. It was here he wrote some of the most influential American fiction, including *Moby Dick*. Surrounded by nature, friends Nathaniel Hawthorne and Oliver Wendell Holmes, and inspired by majestic views, Melville settled into domestic and professional peace if only for 13 years.

The artifact collection represents over 200 years of history, available for exhibit and research. The archives contain over 200 cubic feet of manuscripts, 170 linear feet of books, maps, 350 oral history tapes, and 14,000 photographic images.

39 South St. **Berkshire Museum**. Art, history, and natural science are combined in interactive displays with an emphasis on youth activities. Greek and Chinese art, and paleontological items are displayed.

Pittsfield is located in the far western reaches of the Berkshire Mountains, an area well advertised as a "foremost destination for cultural events and natural beauty." Some of the highlights are: Tanglewood, summer home of the Boston Symphony Orchestra; Jacob's Pillow Dance Festival; Norman Rockwell Museum; and various other festivals and museums.

WAYSIDE

Crane & Co. Museum of Papermaking, 66 Downing Industrial Park, is a little east of Pittsfield and off the Yellowstone Trail, but is an interesting historic place. Approach it from West Housatonic St. in Dalton. Crane has been producing special watermarked paper for the printing of money, bank notes, and postal notes since 1770 and still produces paper for the Bureau of Engraving and Printing in Washington, D.C.

The Road from Pittsfield to Lenox is just a broad, graded, and somewhat improved highway and on this Saturday morning dust was inches deep.

1902 Two Thousand Miles on an Automobile by Arthur Eddy (publisher unknown, 1902). ⚙

WAYSIDE

Stockbridge, MA. About five miles southwest of Lee on state hwy 102 is Stockbridge, home of the **Norman Rockwell Museum**. His paintings, especially those on the cover of the *Saturday Evening Post* magazine, reflected American culture and were popular world-wide. The museum displays many of the most popular pictures and explains how some of them were created. Most of his work was done post-Yellowstone Trail days, but this museum is included here because it is so much a picture of Americana in the 1930s and 1940s that it is a history lesson in itself.

 Near MA-026.8 is a short stretch of Morse Rd. which carried the YT and old US 20, that was overridden by the building of I-90.

🚗 Near MA-034.8 where Cemetery Rd. intersects US 20 is a bit of an old highway left when the newer US 20 smoothed the curve.

🚗 MA-007.6 (Pittsfield) to MA-031.2 (Bonny Rigg Corners): The Clason Maps for 1927 and other years show the route of the YT heading east from Pittsfield through Dalton, Hinsdale, and Becket and south to Bonny Rigg Corners. YTA materials never identify that route and always indicate that Lenox and Lee are on the YT. Note: Assuming the Scottish community of Bonny Rigg is the source of the name, the variants Bonnyrigg, Bonny Riggs and others are probably not correct.

Berkshire Trail along the Westfield River near East Windsor

WAYSIDE

Jacob's Ladder. The part of the Yellowstone Trail now called **Jacob's Ladder Trail**, begins just a few miles west of Lee in the Berkshire Mountains. It is a 35-mile-long Scenic Byway through historic rural landscape beginning here at Laurel Lake in the west and ending at Tekoa Mountain, near Russell, to the east in the southern Berkshires. As its name implies, the road climbs up into the lower Berkshire Mountains. The Yellowstone Trail traversed this route and, although today it seems a bit more "tamed" than 100 years ago, it still takes one back to a slower and simpler time of travel.

An old postcard scene of Jacob's Ladder

MA-014.0 Lenox

(pop. 3,000, alt. 1,270 ft) occupies a slightly elevated plateau in the midst of a scenic highland section, mostly covered with forests, sprinkled with attractive lakes and traversed by several picturesque streams. BB1921-2

Lenox is a quaint, prosperous town set in a pastoral area at the base of the Berkshire Mountains.

In the late 19th century wealthy families had summer "cottages" (mansions) here.

2 Plunkett St. Edith Wharton's home, "**The Mount**," is in the countryside, a little south of Plunkett St. This remarkable woman was a prolific writer and designer of homes and gardens. She designed "The Mount" and lived in it 1902-1911, but she spent most of her life in France. The home is a National Historic Landmark. She won the Pulitzer Prize for *Age of Innocence* in1920, the first woman to win in the fiction category. The home features her library, restored rooms and three acres of formal gardens.

6 Main St. **Curtis Hotel**. Built in 1829 on the site of an inn since 1770. It boasted many a famous guest, among whom were U.S. President Chester A. Arthur, Horace Greeley, William Tecumseh Sherman, and John Jacob Astor. The ground floor was restored historically, leaving it a stately colonial brick treasure. It is now senior housing.

104 Walker St. (Yellowstone Trail). **Ventfort Hall**. This 1893 Gothic-looking brick and brownstone 50-room mansion was built for J. P. Morgan's sister Sarah and it witnessed a number of influential visitors of that age. The movie "The Cider House Rules" was shot in and around the Elizabethan-style mansion. By 1997 the house was seriously damaged, but saved and returned to elegance and offered as a museum and tribute to "the Gilded Age" with tours, lectures, exhibits, and events.

10 Willow Creek Rd. (one mile east of Lenox) **Berkshire Scenic Railway Museum**. The restored 1903 Lenox Station contains exhibits about railroading and the economy it built for the region.

MA-018.4 Lee

(pop. 4,481, alt. 900 ft.). Paper making was established here at an early date and flourished on a large scale for many years. Though since exceeded in quantity of production by other cities in western Massachusetts, it is still the leading business. An important industry now is marble quarrying. Several hundred thousand headstones have been shipped from Lee to mark the graves of U.S. soldiers, particularly in national cemeteries. BB1921-2

85 Center St. **Joe's Diner** has been a western Massachusetts institution since 1939. It is claimed that Joe's Diner was the inspiration for Norman Rockwell's 1958 *Saturday Evening Post* cover,

"the runaway," the little boy runaway and policeman treating him to a snack at a diner. The magazine cover is prominently displayed. It is not a classic diner architecturally, but just a very small greasy spoon with a devoted clientele. Reviewers say, "What makes Joe's Diner special is that it is a slice of Americana. The walls are covered with photos of famous people who ate there."

25 Park Pl. **First Congregational Church of Lee**. This beautiful Italianate church was built in 1858 and has the tallest steeple in the country. It's white and can be seen from quite a distance.

Appalachian Trail Scenic Byway crosses Jacob's Ladder. (GPS: 42.29036, - 73.15557). That is about five miles east of Lee and about three miles west of West Becket. There will be a sign, but don't run over the hikers. It is called a Scenic Trail for good reason. This part of that scenic trail is especially beautiful through forests.

MA-025.9 West Becket

Nearby is **Jacob's Pillow**, a long-time dance academy mecca. The Jacob's Pillow Dance Festival is something truly special. Running from June through August, the festival features vibrant dance performances from over 50 international dance companies.

MA-028.9 The Cairn

Here at the summit of Jacob's Ladder, at the corner of Fred Snow Rd., is a pile of rocks, the Jacob's Ladder memorial cairn (GPS: 42.25860, -73.08640), which has stood for over 100 years to commemorate the 1910 opening of the road which was then perceived as a great accomplishment, opening transportation from central to western Massachusetts.

MA-031.2 Bonny Rigg Four Corners

Jacobs Ladder Scenic Byway alt. 1265. (GPS: 42.25870, -73.08595).

Here is the foot of Jacob's Ladder; the climbing highway opens up many vistas of beautiful mountain country. WPA-MA

On a small plateau lies Bonny Rigg Four Corners, a famous old stagecoach crossroads from which State 8 runs right. WPA-MA

Jacob's Well is a wayside spring dating from ox-cart days. Near the top of the Ladder new forests of white pine are slowly restoring the richness of the woodland, damaged by an ice storm in 1920. WPA-MA

Bonny Rigg Four Corners, Jacob's Ladder at Becket in the Berkshires

Jacob's Ladder is the name of the road between Lee (MA-018.4) and Russell (MA-046.4) which served to connect Springfield with the more western part of the state and on to Albany, New York. The 1910 road replaced an earlier carving through the forest and hills which contained a horrific, (to newly minted auto drivers) steep, bumpy way. On the east side, the grade was 17 percent, on the west it was 22 percent. It had strips of sand laid across the road to slow water runoff. As a result, drivers got stuck in the quagmire behind the "steps" and had to pay a farmer to get pulled out. The original, fearful section has since been reclaimed by forest.

By September of 1910 the road got straightened and the worst of the steepness was reduced to 7 percent or was bypassed and Jacob's Ladder was opened for business. On that September day a large crowd gathered at the summit of the road at Morey Hill to celebrate the linking of the east with the west in the broader sense, and central Massachusetts with the vacationland of the Berkshires in a more narrow

sense. A rock cairn was built to mark the occasion of a victory over skeptics and victory over geography. In 1925 a 50-foot high wooden observation tower with

a telescope was built which afforded a fine view of the hills. Soon a small inn, store, restaurant, and gas station appeared. Jacob's Well, a watering hole for both

Jacob's Well

driver's and their cars appeared. Nearby hamlets appreciated the income from the tourists.

Today it is a beautiful, quiet, forested ride, the Massachusetts Turnpike having siphoned off many trucks and impatient drivers. Today's Yellowstone Trail traveler will enjoy it. Jacob's Ladder turned 100 in 2010 and a very informative booklet was issued at that time, supervised by present Yellowstone Trail Association friend Steve Hamlin who also supplied much of the above information in his April 2011 article for the *Arrow*, the Association's newsletter. ✿

Whip City --Westfield, 360 Elm St. **Westfield Whip Manufacturing Company**. This whip manufacturing company, founded in 1884, still manufactures whips today in the same location. Now, Westfield Museum is in the process of preserving the building into a "living museum."

330 Elm St. **Sanford Whip Factory**. The company made whips there, on and off, from 1883 to 2000. It has been converted into affordable housing space.

24 Main St. **United States Whip Company Complex**. There are actually two buildings at this site. The oldest building in the complex was built sometime before 1884. These buildings were used from at least 1888 until 1928 for the manufacture of whips, but then the building fronting on Elm Street was modified to accommodate retail stores and a theater.

42 Arnold St. **H. M. Van Deusen Whip Company.** Henry Martin Van Deusen began making whips in 1872 in Southfield, and moved to Westfield in 1880. In 1925, with the decline in demand for whips occasioned by the success

of the automobile, the factory was acquired by Stanley Home Products which used it as its corporate headquarters into the 1960s. In the 1980s it was converted to apartments. ✿

Van Deusen Whip Co. apartments

WAYSIDE

Keystone Arches near Chester. Along the length of the west branch of the Westfield River sit the first keystone arch railroad bridges built in America. They range in height to 70 feet and made possible the longest railroad in the world, the Western Railroad, in 1840. Most impressive of these edifices were ten keystone arch bridges.

The construction of the arches took place during the late 1830s, and the line opened in 1841. "The stated purpose was to reach the Erie Canal in Albany and get in on the orgy of trade with the interior," said David L. Pierce of Friends of the Keystone Arches Inc. "The canal traffic never amounted to much, due to the fact that The Western Railroad (later Penn Central, CONRAIL and CSX) ended up bringing about an end to the canal era and launching the railroad revolution in earnest."

From Chester take Middlefield St. At about 2.5 miles north, an information sign for the arches is easily found.

Middlefield-Becket Stone Arch Railroad Bridge District is on the National Register of Historic Places. Middlefield vicinity. (GPS: 42.31222, -73.01944).

MA-035.6 Chester

(town, alt. 601, pop. 1363, sett. 1760, incorp. 1765), was incorporated as Murrayfield, in honor of John Murray, treasurer of the proprietors. Ten years later the citizens voted to change the name, apparently as a result of his Tory sympathies. When Murray left the country in 1778, he was forbidden to return. WPA-MA

Agriculture, including the production of maple sugar from 1800 trees, and the mining of mica, emery, and corundum have been the chief occupations of the people. The granite quarries are less important than formerly. The advent of the railroad here drew the population away from Chester Center. WPA-MA

US 20 drops gradually down into a marshy valley where lies Shaw Pond (camping); along its western bank, off State 8, is a thriving cottage colony. WPA-MA

15 Middlefield St. (MA 20 & Yellowstone Trail). **Chester Historical Society** at The Old Jail, built in 1840. The Society's mission is to preserve Chester's heritage and historical buildings. The society maintains resources for local history or genealogical research, as well as a large collection of items from Chester's industrial past.

10 Prospect St. **Chester Railway Museum**. Their website says:

The Western R.R. was completed and it was also the largest and most difficult railroad project ever attempted. When complete, it was the highest (1458 ft.) and longest (150 miles) railroad ever built (1841) and included the longest bridge in the world, across the Connecticut River at West Springfield, Massachusetts.

MA-035.8 to MA-036.4 and MA-038.7 to MA-042.7 are interesting sections of the old YT with some poor gravel and mostly nicely paved.

MA-042.5 Huntington

72 Worthington Rd. **Norwich Bridge School**. Huntington Historical Society manages this 1800s school which was so used until 1919. Since then it has been used for a variety of purposes. About 1971 it was restored to its original purpose and may be seen now as an old one-room school.

Huntington Village Historic District is on the Register of Historic Places. Roughly along E Main, Main, Russell, Upper Russell, and Basket.

MA-046.4 Russell

This is the last town on the east end of Jacob's Ladder.

RUSSELL (town, alt. 266, pop. 1283, sett. 1782, incorp. 1792). Here in 1858 the Chapin and Gould Paper Mills were established. These paper mills, with those in Woronoco and Westfield, are the chief support of the area. WPA-MA

The old highway followed Woronoco Rd. from MA-048.5 to MA-049.5.

MA-048.9 Woronoco

(alt. 255), is best known as the home of the Strathmore Paper Company Plant across the river. The village is at the junction with State 17. WPA-MA

MA-054.7 Westfield

Westfield claims to produce 95 per cent of the world's whips, and has the largest bicycle manufacturing plant. "Crane's Linen" paper is also produced here. BB1921-2

The Westfield Athenaeum (open weekdays, 9-9; Sun. 2-6), corner of Elm and Court Sts., overlooking the Green, is an attractive brick building with limestone trim, housing the library. On the upper floor is the Edwin Smith Historical Museum. WPA-MA

87 S Maple St. **Joseph Dewey House**. The Joseph Dewey House is a Georgian colonial built in about 1735 for Joseph Dewey, whose family had been living in the Westfield area since the mid-17th century. It stayed in Dewey hands for about 100 years, then went through a succession of owners. In the 1970s, under threat of demolition, it was carefully restored to its early colonial state.

171 Main St. (US 20/Yellowstone Trail). **Landlord Fowler Tavern**. According to Mass.historicbuildings.com, it was built around 1761 (perhaps as early as 1755). Daniel Fowler was granted a tavern license in 1761 and the building continued to function as an inn until the 1830s. At the start of the American Revolution, Daniel Fowler served on the Committee of Correspondence, which met at the tavern. It is said that General Burgoyne, when he passed through this town as a prisoner from the field of Saratoga, spent the night at this tavern.

More recently, the former tavern has been restored and converted into apartments. The Fowler Tavern's original Connecticut River Valley broken scroll pediment doorway was removed in 1920 and placed in the Metropolitan Museum of Art in New York.

Westfield was home to several whip-making businesses, which gave it the name of "Whip City." See Whip City History Bit. All of them are on the National Register of Historic Places, three are on the Yellowstone Trail, and all are in the expanded Westfield Center Historic District.

1259 Western Ave. **Sackett Tavern**, a National Underground Railroad Site, one of 14 such recognized in Massachusetts by The Network to Freedom, a program administered by the National Park Service to recognize and tell the story of resistance against slavery in the United States through escape and flight. This tavern was built around 1776 for Stephen Sackett, who ran the tavern. It changed owners several times until William Fuller restored it in 1962 with painstaking care to stay faithful to Georgian colonial construction and detail. It was sold again in the 1990s as a private residence.

MA-061.8 West Springfield

70 Park St. **Josiah Day House** is the oldest known brick saltbox style home in the United States. By 1754 the house had been built and was handed down to family until 1902 when it came to the Ramapogue Historical Society. An addition was added in 1812. It was preserved in its original state and contains an enormous fireplace in each room plus many items and furniture of the Day family. It is on the National Register of Historic Places.

Springfield Northend Bridge, built in 1924, carried the YT, was rebuilt 1984, and is still in service. "In 1923, the previous 1877 bridge's tar-sealed wooden decking caught fire, which was made worse by the gas mains the bridge carried." *Wikipedia article for West Springfield, Mass.*

Landlord Fowler Tavern, Westfield

Josiah Day House, West Springfield

Crossman Bridge, West Warren

At MA-058.3, about halfway between Westfield and Springfield is Old Westfield Rd. which was the old route. It crossed the railroad at each end of that short section at the curve. Shown in the *Goodrich Route Book for New England South*, 1915, 1916.

MA-062.4 Springfield

(pop. 129,556, alt. 204 ft.) is preeminently a manufacturing city. Among its products are rifles and revolvers made for the U. S. government, railway and trolley cars and sporting goods of various kinds. Webster's Dictionary has been published here for many years. BB1921-2

Eighty-two properties are on the National Register of Historic Places and several large commercial buildings ("Blocks") on Main St., are on the Yellowstone Trail.

1571 Main St. (Yellowstone Trail). The **Worthy Hotel** is an historic hotel. Built in 1895 and advertised as "Springfield's leading commercial and tourist house," the Worthy Hotel was Springfield's finest hotel until the opening of the Hotel Kimball in 1911. Located only two blocks south of Springfield Union Station and featuring 250 rooms, the Worthy Hotel's period of greatest significance was from 1895 to 1925. It is on the National Register of Historic Places, and is currently an apartment building.

Bridge and Chestnut Sts. **Hotel Kimball** opened in 1911. Built in what was an affluent residential neighborhood, the Kimball was elegant, offering 309 rooms, and a large dining room and banquet hall. In 1912, room rates were from $1.50 to $3.50 per day. In 1985 the building was converted to 132 condominiums. It is still looking good today.

21 Edwards St. **Springfield Museums**: On this five-Museum Campus are the Museum of Fine Arts, Museum of History, Art Museum, Science Museum and the new Dr. Seuss Museum. Need we say more?

One Armory Square, Suite 2. **Springfield Armory National Historic Site**. This National Landmark Site houses the world's largest collection of American military firearms dating from colonial times and offers year-round programs, exhibits, and events.

The armory manufactured arms from 1777 to 1968 for all wars from the Revolution to Vietnam. This advantageous site was scouted by George Washington and General Henry Knox for an arsenal. Thus began a long history of invention and mass production of weaponry.

Note: The entrance to Armory Square is on Federal St. Armory Square is shared by Springfield Armory National Historic Site and Springfield Technical Community College (STCC). (GPS: 42.10731, -72.58131).

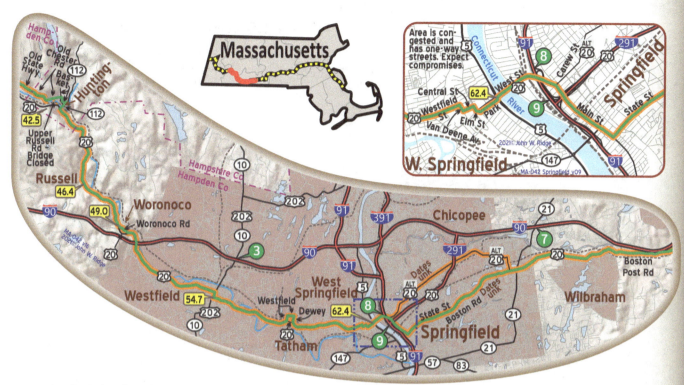

MA-079.0 Palmer

US 20 crosses the Quaboag River. A pile of stones in the middle of the river is the remains of Scott's Bridge, built in Colonial days and used by General Washington on his way to Boston in 1775. WPA-MA

Another quaint, pleasant New England town in a rural forest and hilly setting.

28 Depot St. (US 20/Yellowstone Trail). **19th century Union Station and Steaming Tender Restaurant**. When the station opened in 1884 it was the third largest in Massachusetts, designed with Syrian arches over the windows. The station's train platform has been removed. There is a 1915 Porter Steam Locomotive and its Tender displayed on the grounds along with a 1909 Parlor Car available for parties. The restaurant is in the station. Palmer is known as the "town of seven railroads" which were built through the town 100 years ago.

MA-088.0 West Warren

Crossman Bridge on Gilbert Rd. across the Quaboag River in West Warren. It is one of the few surviving lenticular pony truss bridges in Massachusetts. The 1888 bridge was rehabilitated and reassembled by 2008. The bridge is on the National Register of Historic Places.

 MA-088.1 West Warren: *Goodrich Route Book* suggests Warren Rd. was the YT. (GPS: 42.21522, -72.22807).

MA-090.5 Warren

(pop. 4,200, alt. 600 ft.), is a picturesque little town with the Quaboag river flowing parallel with its main street. The old Keyes house, built in 1740, with a grand old elm tree in front, under which Gen. George Washington halted for a drink of water, is still in possession of the Keyes descendants, as is also the glass from which Washington drank. Marks mountain is another point of interest. BB1921-2

The town has numerous thriving industries. The Warren steam pumps, with which many of the U. S. destroyers were fitted out during the late war, are made here. BB1921-2

Warren is an old industrial town with a few "British" row houses (front doors close to the street), also some pretty Victorian homes and a village green, all placed in a quiet, woodsy, hilly setting.

According to the Warren Historical Commission, the Boston Post Road was the original main thoroughfare through Warren (now MA 67/Yellowstone Trail). "It took its name from its purpose - it was the route of the colonial postal service from New York to Boston established in 1673. About 100 years later, Postmaster Benjamin Franklin ordered mileposts marking the mileage to Boston. Some of these markers still stand." See **Trail Tale: Boston Post Road**, page 417.

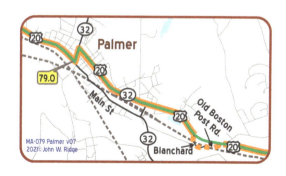 MA-079.0 Palmer: Old West Warren Rd. just NE of Palmer was not YT.

Goodrich Northeast guide says road crossed tracks twice near modern interstate, but modern map shows no way to do it.

MA

Brookfield Inn in Brookfield, 1771

Ye Olde Tavern in West Brookfield, 1760

1921 bridge and pavement at MA-095.7, GPS: 42.218472, -72.114611 which opened the later route of the YT. The older route north of this point along W Bookfield Rd./ Foster Hill Rd. is a pleasant drive.

MA-110.1-MA-111.1: Near Cherry Valley/ Worcester: Another possible route suggested by its name and location is the block long "Great Post Road" between Apricot and Locust St. It needs good local research!

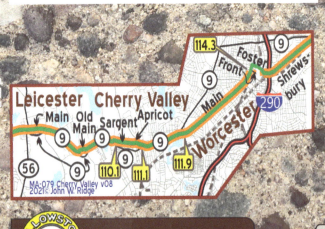

MA-093.6 West Brookfield

(pop. 1.400. alt. 604 ft.), is noted as place of first publication of Webster's Dictionary. "Ye Olde Tavern" is a historic building where General Washington, Jerome Bonaparte and bride, and other notables were entertained. It was built in 1760 by Calvin David Hitchcock, and has been operated continuously since that time; it was known at one time as the Hitchcock tavern. Among interesting points are Indian Rock on Foster Hill Road, where George Whitfield preached. The constitution of the state of Massachusetts was drafted here. BB1921-2

In the two-story Brick Building on Main St., Isaiah Thomas in 1798 edited the first newspaper of the Brookfields. Four years later Ebenezer Merriam & Co. acquired the paper and conducted a general printing business for 60 years. The sons of Ebenezer Merriam opened a printing shop in Springfield and published Noah Webster's dictionary. WPA-MA

Note: "Between West Brookfield and East Brookfield are last remaining mile posts placed by Benjamin Franklin as postmaster," reported a friend. We did not see them. If a reader knows the precise location of a marker, please inform us.

7 E Main St. (MA 9/Yellowstone Trail). **Ye Olde Tavern**. It was known as Hitchcock Tavern in 1760 when it was built by David Hitchcock and became Ye Olde Tavern in 1811. Their website says:

> Built at West Brookfield in 1760, it was a center of colonial life in Massachusetts. Here many men and lovely ladies of olden times were entertained, for the Tavern was located on the Olde Bay Path [Boston Post Road?] over which sped the stages from Boston to Albany.

George Washington, John Adams, Jerome Bonaparte, and others stopped here.

The historic Tavern was extensively modernized in 2014. Reviewers are happy with the modernization. Some reminders of colonial times remain like the big fireplace, plank flooring and period furniture, but recessed lighting in a drop ceiling reminds us that change happens.

West Brookfield Center Historic District on the National Register of Historic Places. Roughly Central and Cottage Sts. from Sherman St. to Lake St. and W, N, and S Main Sts. from Chapman Ave. to Maple St.

27 Front St. (Central and Front). **Quaboag Historical Society Museum** in the old train station. This Museum represents the collected history of several small towns in the Quaboag Plantation area: North, East, West Brookfield, Brookfield, Warren and New Braintree. In this early history-laden part of the country there is certainly much to see.

MA-096.3 Brookfield

(pop. 1,500, alt. 850 ft.). Important point on the old stage route between Boston and Albany; the Brookfield Inn remains as a landmark of those days. Writing desk once owned by Louis XVI now in Merrick Public Library. Shoes and coated paper are the chief local industries. BB1921-2

The Brookfield Inn (open), on State 9, with low ceilings,

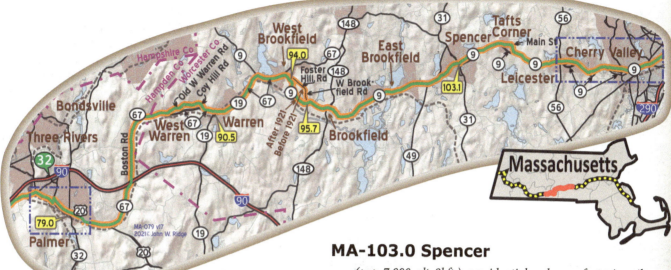

a taproom, and a sign dated '1771,' still has the atmosphere of an ancient hostelry. WPA-MA

8 W Main St. (MA 9/ Yellowstone Trail). **Historic Brookfield Inn**. From the Brookfield Inn website:

The Brookfield Inn was built in 1768, [other sources say 1771] and historically provided a resting place for presidents and aspiring presidents, as well as travelers from all over the world. Since its last heyday in the late 1940s and 1950s, the physical structure deteriorated significantly. Current proprietors, Paul and Melissa Puliafico, purchased the Inn in 1981, and began the process of loving restoration and rehabilitation of the building and property.

In 1789, George Washington traveled through New England, and this has become a basis for all of the 'George Washington slept here' claims.

It seems that Washington's party would have spent the night in Brookfield except for an unfortunate incident.

As the story goes, Washington and his entourage stopped at Brookfield Inn, then owned by a Mrs. Bannister, and wanted to stay the night. Unfortunately, Mrs Bannister was suffering from a migraine headache and turned them away not knowing it was George Washington who wanted to stay the night. Washington moved on to Spencer where the innkeeper there was only too happy to oblige!

MA-099.9 East Brookfield

East Brookfield holds the recognition for the most recently incorporated town in Massachusetts. Although it was first settled in 1664, it wasn't until 1920 that it was incorporated and named for its geographical location from the town from which it seceded, Brookfield.

108 School St. **The Hodgkins School**, first built in 1882, was the oldest operating school in Massachusetts until it was closed in 2002. It now operates as the East Brookfield Historical Museum.

MA-103.0 Spencer

(pop. 7,000, alt. 8l ft.), a residential and manufacturing village, is the birthplace of Elias Howe, inventor of the sewing machine, and of William Howe, original designer of the bridge technically known as the "Howe Truss." Points of interest are the monuments to the two Howes, and one to Capt. Bemis, inventor of a means of taking the spikes out of spiked cannon. BB1921-2

The Richard Sugden Public Library (open daily, 2-8), Pleasant St., is a brick building with brown stone trim, housing the Spencer Museum founded in 1874. This has a collection of Indian relics and historical objects. WPA-MA

Spencer Town Center Historic District is on the National Register of Historic Places. Main St. between High and North Sts. was the original District. It has been substantially expanded over the years to cover almost 300 acres.

MA-113.6 Worcester

(pop. 190,000,. alt. 481 ft.), built upon nearly a score of gently sloping hills is the largest manufacturing city in the United States not on a waterway. It is the county seat of Worcester county. Worcester is one of the greatest machine tool centers in the United States and the center for rolling mill construction. BB1921-2

40 Highland St. (Yellowstone Trail/MA 9). **Salisbury Mansion**. Built in 1772 by Stephen Salisbury, the mansion has been restored to the 1830s period with original furnishings and decor from 1740-1835.

30 Elm St. **Worcester Historical Museum**. Weapons, artwork and the textile industry of Worcester are exhibited along with the city's history.

155 Shrewsbury St. (Yellowstone Trail). **Boulevard Diner**. The Boulevard Diner is an historic diner built by Worcester Lunch Car Company in 1936. It is a well preserved instance of a barrel-roof diner that the company made in significant numbers in the years before the Second World War, and the city's best-preserved 1930s diner. It is listed on the National Register of Historic Places in 2000. Yes, this was built after the Yellowstone Trail era, but diners are Americana.

In Worcester, the YT came from the west on Main St. and turned east on Front St. to meet Shrewsbury St. Most of Front St. does not exist and the detour around on Foster St. is required.

EVER ASSOCIATED WITH

THE CURVE INN

The headquarters for real home cooking served in an atmosphere of pleasure and refinement on the BOSTON POST ROAD, Northboro,—has been sought for years by tourists as well as local parties.

IN JUSTICE

We join the merchants and leading representatives of Marlboro, Northboro, Waltham and other places in bringing to the attention of the State Highway officials the crying need of immediate improvements on BOSTON POST ROAD — Further, we believe these needed repairs and improvements to be of primary import and should precede any other highway improvement project in this vicinity.

The countryside surrounding THE CURVE INN is replete with history-making incidents since the days before the Indian trail leading past the site of the Inn was improved into what is now known as BOSTON POST ROAD.

We Are Now Located On What Is—And What Should Continue To Be—The Main Traffic Artery Between BOSTON and WORCESTER

BOSTON POST ROAD, NORTHBORO   **THE CURVE INN**   RESERVATIONS PHONE NORTHBORO 31-12

1929 was the year in which the state of Massachusetts was going to build a new turnpike (main highway) between Boston and Worcester. Most funds would be diverted in building the new roadway and would neglect improving the Boston Post Road section of US 20/Yellowstone Trail. Many businesses and communities were outraged that their town would be bypassed. In December 1929, the Marlborough Enterprise published many pleas in its paper to bring justice to the Post Road and many businesses joined in with articles such as one from The Curve Inn in Northborough pleading for repairs to the Boston Post Road based on the historicity of the area. *Historic US Route 20 website.* ⚙

WAYSIDE

Old Town Bridge. North of Wayland on MA 27 is an historic stone arch bridge. It is located just north of Old Sudbury Road, and is sited across what was formerly a channel of the Sudbury River, which now flows just west and north of the bridge. The four-arch bridge was built in 1848 by Josiah Russell on a site where it is supposed that the first bridge in Middlesex County was built in the 1640s. It was for many years on the major east-west route (Yellowstone Trail) connecting Boston to points west and south. The bridge was open to vehicular traffic until 1955. *Wayland website and Wikipedia.*

WAYSIDE

About four miles northeast of Longfellow's Wayside Inn is the **Sudbury Historical Society** within the **Sudbury Center Historic District**. The Society has available on the Internet a driving tour of the interesting historical sites in the area, including the Wayside Inn and related sites. It is a good way for the Westerner to explore American history including a house with a space built into the massive chimney stack for homeowners to hide. Native American raids were common in this area until as late as 1714!

WAYSIDE

72 Wayside Inn Rd. (MA-133.6). **Longfellow's Wayside Inn** is one of the country's oldest operating inns, dating from 1716. It was made famous by Henry Wadsworth Longfellow's poems, *Tales of a Wayside Inn*, which he wrote after a brief stay. Refurbished by Henry Ford in the1920s and restored to its original 18th century appearance, the Inn features period artifacts and an 18th century tavern. Watch your head - low beamed ceilings. The fire of 1955 closed the Inn for about three years. The building today does not look exactly like it did in Yellowstone Trail days, but it reopened with its history intact, if not all of the original beams. See **Trail Tale: Wayside Inn**, page 414.

1913 Bancroft Hotel during the Yellowstone Trail days (above), and Bancroft Hotel Apartments today (right)

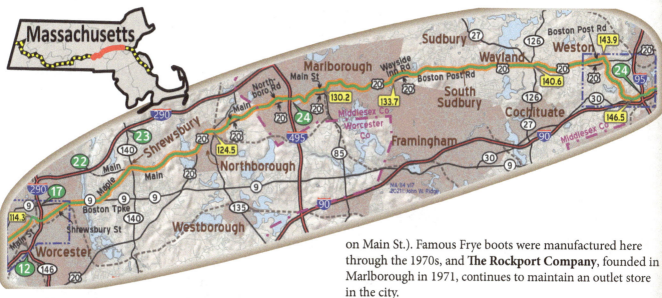

MA-124.3 Northborough

Twenty-three properties and seven districts have been nominated for the National Register of Historic Places. The **Wachusett Aqueduct Linear District**, along Wachusett Aqueduct from Wachusett Reservoir to Sudbury Reservoir has been listed on the Register of Historic Places.

50 Main St. (Yellowstone Trail). **Northborough Historical Society**. The history of the town goes back to 1660, the historical society to 1906. It boasts a fine collection of objects of Northborough art and history, with thousands of documents and pictures detailing the history of the area.

191 Main St. (Yellowstone Trail). **Chet's Diner**. A classic American diner serves classic diner food; regulars give it 5 out of 5 stars. Little has been done to it since the 1950s, it is said. It is included here because "the diner" is an eastern phenomenon and part of the cultural history.

MA-130.4 Marlborough

At 277 Main St. is the **John Brown Bell**, *taken by Marlborough soldiers from the engine house at Harper's Ferry in 1861, and hidden in Williamsport, Md., until 1892, when it was brought to Marlborough.* WPA-MA

On the corner of Maple and Valley Sts. is the **Dennison Factory** which specializes in the manufacture of paper boxes, paper novelties, and office accessories. This is a branch, established in 1925, of the Dennison Manufacturing Company of Framingham.

There are **rock walls** everywhere east of Marlborough. That tells the traveler about the challenge it must have been to farm this New England land.

Shoe manufacturing continued in Marlborough long after the industry had fled from many other New England communities. Rice & Hutchins, Inc. operated several factories in Marlborough from 1875 to 1929 (while the Yellowstone Trail went through town

on Main St.). Famous Frye boots were manufactured here through the 1970s, and **The Rockport Company**, founded in Marlborough in 1971, continues to maintain an outlet store in the city.

A researcher once found several diners in Marlborough: One moved to the Henry Ford Museum in Michigan, one moved to Chattanooga, Tennessee, and the former White City Diner, a Worcester Lunch Car No. 802, is now operated as the **Tropical Cafe** just off Main St. at 22 Rawlins Ave.

377 Elm St. The Peter Rice Homestead, home of the **Marlborough Historical Society and Museum**. House dates from 1688, the society from 1964. A survey conducted in 1994-5 revealed that literally hundreds of houses are historic, dating from the 1600s.

Reportedly, there are 1,767 Milestones between Boston and Springfield along the Old Boston Post Rd.

MA-133.6 Longfellow's Wayside Inn

See Wayside on previous page and **Trail Tale: Wayside Inn**, page 414.

MA-140.6 Wayland

Wayland Center Historic District is an irregular pattern along both sides of US 20 and MA 27. The District and all in it are on the National Register of Historic Places. Concord Road forms its northern border.

Weston Aqueduct Linear District. The area along the Weston Aqueduct from the Sudbury Reservoir to the Weston Reservoir is on the National Register of Historic Places.

MA-143.9 Weston

Weston appears to be a prosperous, quaint town with much greenery and well-maintained historic homes.

241 Wellesley St. **Spellman Museum of Stamps and Postal History** features rare stamps, U.S. and international, and has exhibits describing postal history. The Philatelic Research Library is on site. We include this because it may be missed and would interest history buffs following the Yellowstone Trail.

President Adams Mansion in Quincy, 1732

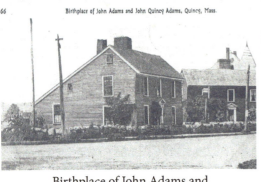
Birthplace of John Adams and
John Quincy Adams in Quincy

Daniel Webster home, Marshfield

WAYSIDE

52 Gore Street, Waltham. About 3.5 miles north of Newton at Waltham is **Gore Place**, the early 1800s estate of Massachusetts Governor Christopher Gore. The home has been called the Monticello of the north and the most significant Federal period mansion in New England. Present events include a sheepshearing festival in April and summer music series in the Carriage House.

MA-146.5 Newton

527 Washington Street. **Jackson Homestead and Museum**. A Federal-style house constructed in 1809, it is a museum containing artifacts of Newton's and New England's history and the role of the Jackson home in the Underground Railway.

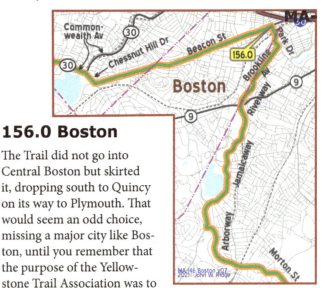

156.0 Boston

The Trail did not go into Central Boston but skirted it, dropping south to Quincy on its way to Plymouth. That would seem an odd choice, missing a major city like Boston, until you remember that the purpose of the Yellowstone Trail Association was to move people in the most direct way "from Plymouth Rock to Puget Sound" and Boston was not exactly on a direct route. One hundred years ago, the Trail's route near Boston would have been somewhat more rural, enabling steady speed with fewer stop signs, despite the electric trolleys and apartment buildings sprouting up in Brookline. Of course, early travelers would probably have gone into Boston for its historic and cultural offerings, but the Association would not compromise in its promise of "the most direct route."

Driving the Trail today near Boston gives one an entirely faulty picture of the experience of early Trail travelers. Urban growth has obliterated the Trail and any sign of it until you get to Quincy.

The Yellowstone Trail Association maps lacked specificity, especially from Boston to the iconic city of Plymouth.

MA-168.3 Quincy

1250 Hancock St. (Yellowstone Trail). **Adams National Historical Park Visitor Center**. Access into the historic homes of John Adams and his son John Quincy Adams is by guided tour only. Buses take visitors to the homes.

20 Muirhead St. **The Josiah Quincy House**. Built in 1770 by Quincy, a prominent lawyer and political leader. The house has period wall paneling and fireplaces surrounded by English tiles in addition to memorabilia from several generations of Quincy descendants.

8 Adams St. (Yellowstone Trail). **Quincy Historical Society Museum**. Displays feature the history of the area related to shipbuilding and granite stonework. There also are displays of the Adams and Hancock families.

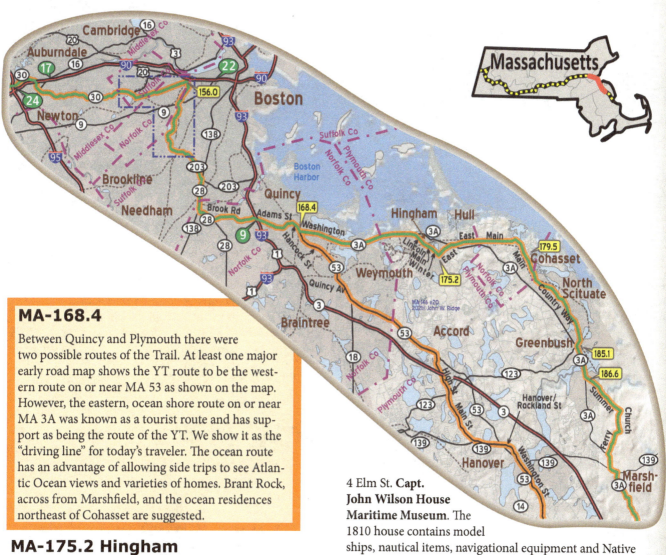

MA-168.4

Between Quincy and Plymouth there were two possible routes of the Trail. At least one major early road map shows the YT route to be the western route on or near MA 53 as shown on the map. However, the eastern, ocean shore route on or near MA 3A was known as a tourist route and has support as being the route of the YT. We show it as the "driving line" for today's traveler. The ocean route has an advantage of allowing side trips to see Atlantic Ocean views and varieties of homes. Brant Rock, across from Marshfield, and the ocean residences northeast of Cohasset are suggested.

MA-175.2 Hingham

The Town of Hingham was founded in 1635 and is located in Plymouth County about 15 miles south of Boston.

21 Lincoln St. **The Old Ordinary**. This 1688 building, enlarged, functioned as a tavern for much of the 18th century. It now serves as a house museum operated by the Hingham Historical Society. There are many touches of life 300 years ago in this former stage stop/tavern. Kitchen utensils, toys, hand-stitched linen bedding, and more are displayed.

90 Main St. (Yellowstone Trail). **The First Parish Old Ship Church** (Unitarian Universalist) is the oldest church structure in the country, having been built in 1681, and, until this day, continues to be used as a place of worship.

MA-179.5 Cohasset

Once a part of Hingham. It is said that Capt. John Smith visited the place as he explored the coast of New England. Elm Street was known as "Ship Cove Lane" as it led to the ship-building yards.

14 Summer St. **Caleb Lothrop House**. Built in 1821, a two story hip-roof wood frame house is a well-preserved example of Federal styling. Caleb Lothrop, its builder, was the grandson of a Revolutionary War militia leader, and was descended from one of the area's first settlers. It is on the National Register of Historic Places.

4 Elm St. **Capt. John Wilson House Maritime Museum**. The 1810 house contains model ships, nautical items, navigational equipment and Native American artifacts and exhibits which document 19th century life in Cohasset.

MA-181.5 North Scituate

100 Lighthouse Rd. **Old Scituate Lighthouse**. Operated on and mostly off 1811-1994. A very scenic site.

301 Driftway. **Scituate Maritime and Irish Mossing Museum**. This small museum in Scituate features an exhibit on Stellwagen Bank National Marine Sanctuary shipwrecks.

MA-185.1 Greenbush

MA-192.8 Marshfield

238 Webster St. **Daniel Webster Estate**. Visit the beautiful Webster Estate and learn about the famous lawyer, senator, orator and statesman Daniel Webster. He used this 16 acres to conduct scientific farming. The original home burned down in 1878, but was rebuilt by his daughter-in-law. Events such as teas and special seasonal programs are carried on.

Careswell St. Jct. of Careswell and Webster Sts. **Winslow House and Cultural Center**. The 1699 residence is of Judge Isaac Winslow, grandson of Mayflower passenger Edward Winslow, governor of Plymouth Colony. On the grounds are the Daniel Webster Law office, also an 18th century carriage shed and a blacksmith shop.

John Alden House in Duxbury

A small Massachusetts road repair crew, 1918

John Howland House in Plymouth, 1667

Court St. in Plymouth.
Most likely the YT.

Plymouth Rock Monumental Canopy, 1920

WAYSIDE

Fifteen miles southeast of Plymouth is the small town of **Sandwich**. Therein is the **Heritage Museums & Gardens** which display 32 antique autos in a round barn, a replica of the famous Shaker barn. "From the earliest 1899 Winton Motor Carriage to a 1962 Corvette, these automobiles are a testimony to American innovation, invention, and aesthetic vision," says their website.

WAYSIDE

Three miles south of Plymouth on MA 3A is **Plimoth Plantation**. Founded in 1947, it is a non-profit living history museum that exhibits the original settlement of the Plymouth Colony established in the 17th century by the English. There are outdoor clay ovens, gravel paths, a grist mill and Wampanoag Homesite. Costumed role players portray actual residents. Explore at your own pace in self-guided tours.

AT THE TOLL-GATE

Toll-Gate Keeper: "Ten Cents." (Cadillac driver pays toll and proceeds).

Driver of Ford: (Coming up a few minutes later): "What's the toll to Alexandria?"

T. G. K.: "Three Fords for a nickle."

Ford Driver: "But there's only one of us."

T. G. K.: "Well, just wait here a minute, and there'll be a couple more."

BUT IT'S A VAIN HOPE

"Have you heard the last Ford story?" someone asked an official of the Ford Motor Co. "I hope so," was the prompt reply.

Funny Stories about the Ford. Presto Publishing Co. 1915

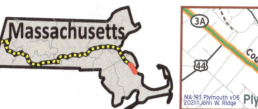

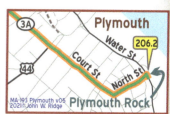

MA-197.0 Duxbury

105 Alden St. **John Alden House Historic Site**. This was the last home of Mayflower Pilgrim John Alden. Purportedly built in the mid-1600s but more probably in the early 1700s, it was occupied by the Alden family until 1920. Interesting features of the expanded home (from two rooms) are the powdered clam-and-oyster shell ceiling in the "great" room and the gunstock posts.

120 King Caesar Rd. **King Caesar House**. Ezra Weston II was called "King Caesar" as he was a shipping magnet. The 1809 house is represented as it appeared in 1820 and displays period furnishings as well as artifacts related to shipbuilding in Duxbury.

Myles Standish Burial Ground is a cemetery and Pilgrim burial site.

MA-201.8 Kingston

MA-200.2

At this point, the two routes of the YT between Quincy and Plymouth meet. See map and note on previous page.

Howlands Ln., Wharf Ln., Braintree Ave. **Rocky Nook Farm**, the farm of John and Elizabeth Howland, passengers on the Mayflower. John was the last living male passenger still in the Plymouth area. He died at age 80 in 1673 and is buried at Burial Hill, Plymouth. The property is owned and managed by the Pilgrim John Howland Society. The farm burned down in 1673. There is a large granite memorial rock on the property.

MA-E206.2 Plymouth

We will not repeat here information readily available about the many famous historical sites one can see in Plymouth. We believe that the Trail ran on Court Street, but the Yellowstone Trail Association maps were sketchy in eastern Massachusetts. If you enter Plymouth from the north on MA 3A and drive south down the main drag, you soon find that that street, MA 3A, has several names. Court St. (Yellowstone Trail) becomes Main St. becomes Sandwich St. becomes Warren Ave. near Plimoth Plantation. This is a carry-over from England. We lived in London for a time and found this idea of multiple names for one road to be frustrating.

75 Court St. (MA 3A/the presumed Yellowstone Trail). **Pilgrim Hall Museum**. Opened in 1824, it houses a collection of Pilgrim furniture, armor, an early American painting collection and a Bible belonging to William Bradford, Plymouth Colony governor. The visitor can even touch a piece of the original Plymouth Rock!

33 Sandwich St. **The Jabez Howland House**. We include it here because it is not listed in some tourist literature and because one of our authors, John Ridge, is a 15th generation descendant of John Howland, Jabez Howland's father. This home is the only one left in Plymouth where Pilgrims actually lived. John Howland and Elizabeth Tilley met as passengers on the Mayflower, married, and had lived on present Leyden St. on the four acres that was granted to John in the 1623 land division. They then moved to Duxbury around 1635 and finally to a farm at Rocky Nook (present Kingston) in 1639. He and Elizabeth were known to visit their son Jabez in this 1667 home in Plymouth. Upon John's death in 1673, Elizabeth lived with son Jabez in this house. "It is fair to presume that its floors have been trodden by those two passengers of the Mayflower, and that its walls have listened to their voices" wrote William T. Davis in *Ancient Landmarks of Plymouth* in 1887.

Burial Hill. At the head of Town Square, just off Main St., is the site of a fort built in 1622-23 and is the burial place of Gov. William Bradford. Today, on August Fridays, citizens dress in Pilgrim garb and walk from Plymouth Rock to Burial Hill to re-enact the church service attended by the 51 survivors of the winter of 1620-21. It can be seen from School St. or Russell St. We include this site because it is often overlooked, even though advertised.

E206.2 Eastern End of the Trail

Plymouth Rock

MA

Longfellow's Wayside Inn

"One Autumn night, in Sudbury town
Across the meadows bare and brown,
The windows of the wayside inn
Gleamed red with fire-light through the leaves ..."
Longfellow's Tales of a Wayside Inn, 1863

Stand anywhere on the lovely 125 acres surrounding the Wayside Inn near Sudbury, Massachusetts, and you might hear its 300 year history passing by. Jangling, horse-drawn carriages still appear occasionally on the grounds, redolent of the Inn's beginnings. Antique cars rattle in for rendezvous, mirroring 100 years ago. Now it is hybrids that quietly glide into the future. The Wayside Inn has seen it all.

The road running in front of the Inn has also evolved. The (Upper) Boston Post Road, one of the first mail routes in the nation, operating since 1673, almost skimmed the front door of the Inn. A 100-yard section is preserved. It was this road and its promise for progress and profit that caused David Howe to build "a haus of entertainment," as an extension of his home, in 1716. And business thrived.

About 60 feet south of that original Boston Post Road is the present Wayside Inn Road, built in 1902, and called the Yellowstone Trail from 1919. Around 1927, when federal road numbers were assigned, it was also named US 20. A new, straighter road was built about 500 feet south and now carries both the US 20 designation and the name Boston Post Road.

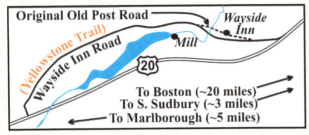

The Wayside Inn is listed as both a Massachusetts Historic Landmark, and a National Register of Historic Places District. The path to that stature has not been smooth. Read Henry Wadsworth Longfellow's second verse of *Tales of a Wayside Inn*. He describes the then-147 year old Inn as in disrepair:

As ancient is this hostelry
As any in the land may be,
Built in the old Colonial day,
When men lived in a grander way,
With ampler hospitality;
A kind of old Hobgoblin Hall,
Now somewhat fallen to decay,
With weather-stains upon the wall,
And stairways worn, and crazy doors,
And creaking and uneven floors,
And chimneys huge, and tiled and tall.

The Inn, about 20 miles west of Boston, was

Wayside Inn front entrance today

called the Red Horse Inn or Howe Tavern when Longfellow visited it in October of 1862. Four generations of Howes had operated the Inn, including Ezekiel who marched off to Concord on April 19, 1775, at the beginning of the Revolutionary War. Lyman Howe, the last of the Howes to manage the Inn, had died in 1861 and his relatives managed the place only as a boarding house. The hostelry had begun to fall into disrepair, possibly due to travelers traveling by railroad rather than by stagecoach. It stood that way for 30 years.

Longfellow had produced a variety of long, narrative poems previous to his visit to the Red Horse, and he thought to place them in a setting as individual tales told by travelers, similar to Geoffrey Chaucer's *Canterbury Tales* or Giovanni Boccaccio's *The Decameron*. The Red Horse Inn, still looking Colonial and quaint, served as that venue. *Tales of a Wayside Inn* is composed of Longfellow's earlier narrative poems set as tales told by six fictitious guests and a landlord who tell individual tales around the fireside. The most memorable, perhaps, was the landlord's tale, "Paul Revere's Ride." Who will ever forget the stirring cadence of:

Listen my children and you shall hear,
Of the midnight ride of Paul Revere ...

The rousingly patriotic "Paul Revere's Ride" had been published in the *Atlantic* magazine three years before. Now it again catapulted Paul Revere to fame, even though there were several "Paul Reveres" who rode off that night, warning of the coming of the British.

The first part of *Tales of a Wayside Inn*, published in 1863 (with two more parts added by 1873), was an immediate hit, selling out the 15,000 copies within two days. *Evangeline, the Courtship of Miles Standish*, and *The Song of Hiawatha*, among many other poems and stories, had already made Longfellow immensely popular, and even called America's beloved poet.

The poem also catapulted the Red Horse Inn to fame. People flocked to the Inn. Tours were given to the few rooms which were presentable. Some say that Longfellow's popular poem saved the place from extinction.

Capitalizing upon the Longfellow connection in 1896, new owner Edward Lemon renamed the Inn "Longfellow's Wayside Inn," a name already commonly used and emblazoned on souvenirs. Lemon had an appreciation of the cultural history of the Inn and operated it as a retreat and a place for literary pilgrims and artists to meet.

Wayside Inn, late 1920s looking west along the Post Road

Henry Ford bought the Inn in 1923. His original plan was to add it to his living history museum at Greenfield Village in Dearborn, Michigan. Fortunately, he saw the ⇒

Wayside Inn parking lot, c.1920s

value of the Inn's historic setting, and left it there. He purchased 3,000 additional acres around the Inn, built a chapel, a grist mill and acquired a 1798 schoolroom for the property.

Old Gristmill at Wayside Inn

Ford was the Inn's last private owner. After 1947 the Inn was governed by a primarily Ford-family-run Board of Trustees. The Inn was then transferred to the National Trust for Historic Preservation, and finally, to Boston-based trustees in 1960. Since that time, the Inn has become successfully self-sustaining due to the careful attentions of its Innkeepers and staff.

This oldest continuously operating Inn in the nation suffered a devastating fire in 1955 which heavily damaged two wings as well as the main building. It reopened in 1958 after extensive professional restoration. During its 300 years of life, the Inn has undergone many changes and expansions, but always it has retained its Colonial style.

When you walk in the front door, you are inclined to look for General George Washington. Today one can sip a drink in the Old Bar Room, the oldest room in the Inn, with pewter mugs hanging from the beamed ceiling. Then move to the Tap Room, added c.1775, or any of the other seven dining areas for a wonderful dinner. One dining room is called Hobgoblin Hall noted in Longfellow's poem (cited above). If you are hosting a small dinner party, ask for the Old Kitchen. It is dark, cozy, and was Henry Ford's

Wayside Inn
Old Bar Room

favorite place to entertain his cronies, Harvey Firestone and Thomas Edison. Celebrities such as Charles Lindbergh, John D. Rockefeller, Jr., and Calvin Coolidge also dined at the Inn.

Should you be staying overnight in one of the ten bedrooms, as we did, you will find a small step stool at the foot of your bed to help you up onto the very high mattress. This Colonial touch we still remember today. The guest also has access to a private lounge. No TV, though.

We dined and breakfasted in a wonderful atmosphere upon wonderful food, some dishes from very old recipes. Somehow we missed the three museum rooms exhibiting Wayside Inn and Howe family memorabilia, including the sword that Ezekiel Howe carried to Concord.

There seems to be something special happening all year long at the Inn. Live fife and drum groups, autumn farmers' markets and Oktoberfest are popular. Re-enactments by Sudbury's Revolutionary War Militia and knowledgeable speakers remind us of Colonial days. In the spring there are wine tastings and family fun days.

Wayside Inn Tap Room
LeBlanc Photo

In 1914, Yellowstone Trail Association officer Michael Dowling traveled east to blaze the eastern part of the Yellowstone Trail along a northern route from Plymouth Rock through Springfield and Pittsfield, Massachusetts to Albany, New York, and Lake Erie. His efforts were thwarted by objections to adding another trail color to those already marked telephone poles –in one case 11 colors on one pole. A more southerly route was chosen from Boston through Connecticut. By 1919, however, the fame of the Yellowstone Trail was such that it gained a place in the preferred northern route, right past the Wayside Inn. A mission of the Yellowstone Trail Association was to promote the Trail in the East. And promote they did! Records from their travel bureaus show easterners were eager to see the wonders of the West and that thousands from the East traveled the Trail past the Inn.

The Howes, Longfellow, and the nation can be proud of the preservation and promotion efforts still taking place at this beautiful, historic site on the old Yellowstone Trail. ✿

We passed beneath the stately trees bordering the old post-road which leads to the door of the "Wayside Inn." The old inn is rich in historic associations. The road which leads to the very door of the inn is the old post-road; the finely macadamized State road which passes a little farther away and is of recent dedication, and is located so as to leave the ancient hostelry a little retired from ordinary travel.

1902 Two Thousand Miles on an Automobile by Arthur Eddy (publisher unknown, 1902).

1916 Race: Plymouth Rock to Seattle

Without a doubt, the main event of 1916 for the Yellowstone Trail Association was the September relay race from Plymouth Rock to Seattle. In February, the Association convention had approved the extension of the Trail from Chicago to Plymouth Rock and a route had been tentatively selected. "Desirous of demonstrating further the superiority of the Yellowstone Trail, the Association challenged the Lincoln Highway Association to an ocean-to-ocean race. The disability [disadvantage] of the Yellowstone Trail was more than 300 miles. The challenge was not accepted," reported Joe Parmley in a 1917 speech. The Lincoln Highway Association had already made a coast-to-coast run in 138.5 hours over 3,384 miles, averaging 24.4 miles per hour from New York to San Francisco. Anxious to beat that record and to test the route even without the Lincoln Highway people competing, Parmley promised a run of 3,673 miles in 120 hours at an average speed of 31 miles per hour.

The run also had the potential of cementing interest in the Trail as a unit, and to advertise its possible use in civil defense. World War I had been raging in Europe for two years and in about seven months the United States would enter it; transcontinental roads were now seen as a military necessity. The War Department was interested in the experiment of running a message from Plymouth to Seattle and readily agreed to dispatch a message over the Trail, making it an official test of road and civilian organization. The organizational machinery of the Association geared up again as it had the previous year.

Bill Binz advertised the race proudly on his Marmon 34 race car
Lance Sorenson

This race followed the Trail as marked in the East before 1919 when they moved it north closer to Lake Ontario through New York and thence to Massachusetts. Thus, this race led drivers from Plymouth Rock through Hartford, Connecticut, Poughkeepsie, Binghamton, and Olean, New York, Meadville, Pennsylvania, and Akron, Fremont, and Defiance, Ohio. Then it joined the already established Trail at Fort Wayne, Indiana, and on west.

The run was planned in fourteen relays with a manager for each relay of 100-400 mile segments. As a result, 64 autos carried the army message. Add 126 "trailer" cars for emergency, and a total of 190 cars participated. The race began under the panoply covering the historic rock at Plymouth at noon September 11 when Colonel W. E. Craighill delivered a sealed message to Robert Harlow who was waiting in a big Packard Twin Six with engine throbbing. The town clock began to strike twelve when

Racers had "trailer cars" as backup

the Packard was off. And they made the run in 121 hours and 12 minutes - 72 minutes more than their announced 120 hours. Jim Parsons in a Stutz dashed into Fort Lawton, Seattle, and handed the letter to Captain H. W. Bunn at 10:12 a.m. September 16. They might have made it early if not for 600 miles and 24 hours of continuous rain and hail across Wisconsin and Minnesota and a cloudburst in South Dakota. They also lost time in the Cascade Mountains of Washington. The official time was published as 30.3 miles per hour for the approximately 3,670 miles.

As unorganized as they were in the East, Trail boosters managed to find relay managers, drivers and "trailer car" drivers to participate. Another shower of hyperbole appeared in newspapers as it had for the 1915 race. Local papers described the daring-do of local drivers, using such phrases as "reckless abandon," and "better than 40 miles an hour" and describing one car as "stripped of its windshield, top and fenders and with the body of the car strapped down to the axles." "Leaving but a streak of dust" was a favorite of reporters, and, once, a viewer was quoted as saying the driver was driving "like a bat out of h--l."

There were no accidents, but break adjustments and flat tires seemed to be common. A close call occurred near Superior, Montana: "... on a downgrade he had to run the car into a gravel bank to avoid a collision with an elderly woman who was driving by team up the road. She had come in from a side road and was not seen by the road patrollers" [men who kept the road clear for the relay]. Careful time was kept by the locals, recording down to the second when one car stopped and the next began. Like last year's race, there was much crowing about being ahead of schedule. Montana was rightfully proud because the message arrived in Montana one hour late and left the Treasure State two hours ahead of time. A remarkable 34 miles per hour was maintained.

At the end, headlines vied for superlatives, two coming up with, "All Records Smashed" and "Relay Ends Brilliantly,"

Newspapers heralded the Yellowstone Trail as the great Northwest route, the best route to the playground of the three National Parks [Yellowstone, Glacier, and Mt. Rainier], and a scenic route with no deserts. The Association bragged that, "we made the fastest time ever made by automobile across the continent and demonstrated the superiority of the Yellowstone Trail over every ⇨

John Berkin in his Reo drove from Butte to Missoula in 3 hours and 43 minutes

Some drivers were humorous

other highway as to its organization, the road itself, and the sportsmanlike spirit of its sponsors."

One of the best things to come out of this huge effort was the acceptance of the new trail by the American Blue Book Company, the pre-eminent auto guide publishing company at the time. They were the folks who published in their many volumes directions like "turn left at the red barn" because there were no, or few, road numbers. Representatives of the company followed the route of the relays at a more leisurely pace to record the exact mileage from point to point for their guide.

Why did the Trail Association do it? They claimed several reasons, but the main one was to prove that the Yellowstone Trail was worthy of serious attention as a major factor in the development of the Northwest. Here, at last, was a way for tourists, businessmen, the military, and Uncle George to get clear across the country on their own time, not dependent on the railroad's time. There was also the economic value the Association expected to accrue for the member towns along their prized route.

Another result of this massive effort was that the Yellowstone Trail was one of four highways named as a military necessity. Trucks ultimately used the Trail as a supply route to the east and to ships bound for France and World War I.

But to the relay drivers, it may just have been the fun of the challenge. ✿

TRAIL DASHERS SMASHING TIME RECORDS ON RUN
WAR MESSAGE CARS 1 HOUR., 10 MIN. AHEAD OF SCHEDULE - DELAYS IN MOUNTAINS CUT 3 HOUR GAIN
CROWDS GREET SPEEDY DRIVERS
September 12, 1916 Aberdeen (SD) Daily News

TRANSCONTINENTAL AUTO RACE ENDS BRILLIANTLY
September 16, 1916 Seattle (WA) Daily News

Boston Post Road   Text begins on next page.

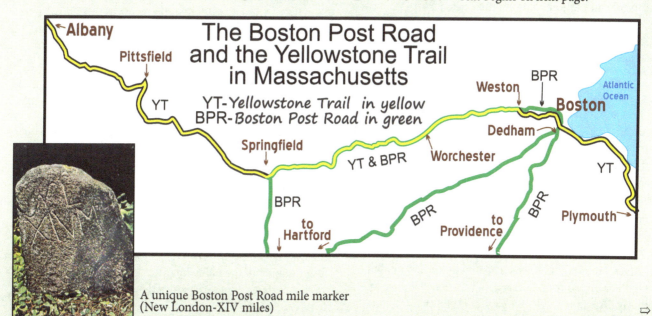

The Boston Post Road and the Yellowstone Trail in Massachusetts
YT-Yellowstone Trail in yellow
BPR-Boston Post Road in green

Albany
Pittsfield
YT
Springfield
BPR
to Hartford
YT & BPR
Worcester
Weston   BPR
Boston
Dedham
BPR   to Providence   BPR
Plymouth
YT
Atlantic Ocean

A unique Boston Post Road mile marker (New London-XIV miles)

Boston Post Road map on previous page

The Yellowstone Trail – A Good Road from Plymouth Rock to Puget Sound. Well, in 1912 that was a great slogan. It was not reality. In the West along the planned route of the Trail, there weren't even usable wagon roads over the Bitterroots or the Cascades to get to Seattle.

Elsewhere along the route, roads were being improved or even rebuilt to be usable by autos. States were beginning to assume responsibility for inter-county roads. One of those state roads had a long and especially interesting history. It was part of the northern route of the Boston Post Road, used, starting in 1673, by post riders carrying letters over the 250 miles from New York City to Boston.

In 1919, when the Yellowstone Trail was formally re-routed along its preferred northern route through Pennsylvania, New York, and Massachusetts, it followed the Boston Post Road between Springfield and Weston (Boston), Massachusetts. The little acknowledged route of the Yellowstone Trail used for the 1916 Relay Race through Rhode Island, Connecticut, and Pennsylvania was abandoned.

The Boston Post Road

Three hundred and fifty years ago the Boston Post Road was part of the King's Best Highway in reference to King Charles II (1660-1685), who, contrary to King Charles I, encouraged a postal system as a means of consolidating the colonies against the Dutch. The Yellowstone Trail followed part of the Upper Route of the Boston Post Road. There were also the Middle and Lower routes of the Boston Post Road, each with branches, each existing at nearly the same time, all of which merged at New Haven, Connecticut. The Boston Post Road and the King's Best Highway were not clearly defined routes.

Most stories of the Boston Post Road begin with 1673 when the first, unnamed, "postman" struggled for four weeks and 250 miles to get from New York to Boston and back. He was instructed to take a route north to New Haven, Connecticut (founded 1660), then to Hartford (founded 1635), then to Springfield, Massachusetts (founded 1636). It was called the "ordinary way," presuming regular traffic between established towns.

Colonial Americans, whether adventurer or farmer or land grant holder, looked to the west and to the fertile Connecticut River valley where towns had already sprung up. But the path eastward from Springfield was not a well-worn highway. Eric Jaffe in *The King's Best Highway* (Scribner,

Quincy market in Boston in 1914.
The horse was still king!
National Archives RG 30-N

2010) described the territory as "trackless, dangerous wilderness." Jaffe also reasoned that, although the route was not described, it was reasonable to assume that the postman would have been instructed to go east from Springfield to Brookfield and Worcester, where friends of the New York Governor, Francis Lovelace, would help him. That northern route from Springfield to Boston, called the Upper Boston Post Road, became part of the Yellowstone Trail 246 years later.

It is well for the Trail traveler to note that the Boston Post Road was very important for our infant nation. The road represented a pipeline for trade, for cultural exchanges, for fluidity of ideas. It was especially important during the American Revolution for groups such as the Committees of Correspondence to use to communicate.

And 250 Years Later

A little more than two centuries later the auto arrived on the scene and it became apparent that named trails and their colors had to be replaced by government road systems. In 1925 when the American Association of State Highway Officials (AASHO) and the federal government met to form the federal highway system, the Upper and Lower Boston Post Roads were selected as major routes. The Upper Road (Yellowstone Trail) became US 20 to the west and the Lower Road became US 1 to the south. The Yellowstone Trail continued to follow the Upper Boston Post Road even after US 20 turned south near Northboro. The Trail was routed closely to the Boston Post Road from Springfield to Weston for approximately 82 miles. It is humbling to know that the green driving line provided on the maps in this book lies on parts of that ancient, rare piece of U.S. transportation history.

The towns along the Trail in Massachusetts have maintained their unique historical aura for almost 400 years even though the Upper Boston Post Road may be on a very busy thoroughfare lined with gas stations and shops. In some areas the fact that you are on the Post Road is very evident. Restaurants, tea shops, real estate offices, gas stations and many other businesses include "On the Boston Post Road" in their name. Although the road may claw through a large city with many distractions, it is still acknowledged and the traveler should pause and doff his hat to it.

As you read the Mile-By-Mile portion of this book for the towns of Springfield to Weston, we hope that you will observe some of the many historic sites we suggest. They reflect a different kind of history than seen from the Trail in the West. ✿

Epilogue

Throughout history, long-distance travel was not easily undertaken by the common man. And then during the mid-to-late 1800's the railroad arrived and by 1900 there were traveling salesmen, relocations to western homesteads, and tours to the national parks. But the "common man" usually had no easy way to "visit mom" back on the farm or to visit Yellowstone National Park.

Then, as part of the Industrial Revolution, there was the explosion of bicycles and autos. The United States was a nation of immigrants and the great westward migration added a desire to see more of the country. By around 1912 the time had come for long-distance auto routes. Along came the "named trails", the Lincoln Highway, the National Old Trails Highway, The Yellowstone Trail, the Dixie Highway and the Jefferson Highway and a plethora of shorter routes along the still relatively primitive roads. Fairly quickly, good roads became desirable for those new flivvers.

Named trails succeeded in their own way and all faded when governments, with much political furor, assumed the responsibility of both road construction and route numbering. And then with the Depression of the 1930s, all named trails pretty much faded away.

What was the legacy of the Yellowstone Trail Association, you ask? The Association once said that if it did nothing more than provide the machinery for public thought to be expressed about national highways, it more than justified itself. The Yellowstone Trail can be said to have been a part of that national thought by making a long-distance highway a national asset.

The modern Yellowstone Trail Association, re-instituted a century later, revived the goal of providing an historic route for a new era of tourism. Travel agencies have reported that travel to historic sites or travel for genealogical reasons has topped the list for the last several years. Better roads, better vehicles and better vacation time have conspired to allow more freedom to drive an open road and to explore.

Today Yellowstone Trail related activities are promoted in several towns along the Trail. For instance, central South Dakota, western Minnesota, central Indiana, and western Wisconsin groups host annual "Trail Days" with appropriate historical attractions and antique car runs on the Trail. More and more highway signs grace the Trail, put there by history-minded citizens.

Visit www.yellowstonetrail.org to learn more about the Trail and to keep up on Yellowstone Trail related activities. Learn of recent discussions and discoveries about its historic alignment and find out more about the modern Yellowstone Trail Association and communicate with the authors.

Remember, much of the Yellowstone Trail remains an open road, but to fully discover it, appreciate it and enjoy it, requires slow travel. Pick a manageable part and really experience it and discover its surroundings and history. It is really compelling when it is not flashing by.

Settled in for a couple of days
Eastern Washington University Archives